World Literature

Shoreview, MN

World Literature Consultants

Jack Cassidy, Ph.D., Associate Dean, College of Education and Professor of Curriculum and Instruction, Texas A & M University-Corpus Christi, Corpus Christi, Texas

Bridget Murphy, English Instructor, North Hennepin Community College, Brooklyn Park, Minnesota

Acknowledgments appear on pages 650–652, which constitutes an extension of this copyright page.

The publisher wishes to thank the following educators for their helpful comments during the review process for *World Literature*. Their assistance has been invaluable.

Linda Benner, Special Education teacher, Muncie Central High School, Muncie, Indiana; **Lynda Callo,** Bulkeley High School, Hartford, Connecticut; **Bonita Lowrance,** Instructional/Inclusion Resource Teacher, Wooddale High School, Memphis, Tennessee; **Chuck Saxton,** Teacher, Centennial High School, Circle Pines, Minnesota; **Beth E. Waltman,** Special Education Teacher, Southwest High School, Houston, Texas; **Barney Woodward,** Teacher, Buena Vista High School, Corona, California

Publisher's Project Staff

Vice President of Curriculum and Publisher: Sari Follansbee, Ed.D.; Director of Curriculum Development: Teri Mathews; Managing Editor: Patrick Keithahn; Senior Editor: Susan Weinlick; Development Assistant: Bev Johnson; Director of Creative Services: Nancy Condon; Senior Project Coordinator/Designer: Laura Henrichsen; Senior Buyer: Mary Kaye Kuzma; Product Manager-Curriculum: Brian Holl

Copyright © 2007 by Pearson Education, Inc., publishing as Pearson AGS Globe, Shoreview, Minnesota 55126.
All rights reserved. Printed in the United States of America. This publication is protected by copyright, and permission should be obtained from the publisher prior to any prohibited reproduction, storage in a retrieval system, or transmission in any form or by any means, electronic, mechanical, photocopying, recording, or likewise. For information regarding permission(s), visit www.agsglobe.com.

Pearson AGS Globe™ is a trademark of Pearson Education, Inc.
Pearson® is a registered trademark of Pearson plc.

ISBN 0-7854-4060-7

4 5 6 V051 13 12 11

1-800-328-2560
www.agsglobe.com

Contents

- How to Use This Book x

Unit 1 Fiction 1
- About Fiction 2

Detective Stories 4
- *The Adventure of the Speckled Band,* by Sir Arthur Conan Doyle (Great Britain) 5
- After Reading the Selection 18
- *Death Arrives on Schedule,* by Hansjörg Martin (Germany) 21
- After Reading the Selection 32

Science Fiction 35
- *The Feeling of Power,* by Isaac Asimov (United States) 36
- After Reading the Selection 50
- *The Expedition,* by Rudolf Lorenzen (Germany) 53
- After Reading the Selection 70

Adventure 73
- *The Cegua,* by Robert D. San Souci (United States) 76
- After Reading the Selection 81
- *Master and Man,* by Leo Tolstoy (Russia) 83
- After Reading the Selection 90
- *Just Lather, That's All,* by Hernando Téllez (Colombia) 92
- After Reading the Selection 100

Turning Points 102
- *Marriage Is a Private Affair,* by Chinua Achebe (Nigeria) 103
- After Reading the Selection 114
- *Cranes,* by Hwang Sun-won (Korea) 115
- After Reading the Selection 123
- *In the Time of the Butterflies,* by Julia Alvarez (Dominican Republic) 125
- After Reading the Selection 131

Folktales..........133
- *A Polite Idiosyncrasy* (China) 136
- After Reading the Selection.......... 138
- *Bye-bye* (Haiti) and *The Story of the Bat* (United States).......... 140
- After Reading the Selections 146
- Skills Lesson: Plot.......... 148
- Unit 1 Summary 149
- Unit 1 Review 150

Unit 2 Nonfiction 152
- About Nonfiction.......... 154

Diaries, Journals, and Letters 156
- *Anne Frank: The Diary of a Young Girl,* by Anne Frank (Netherlands).......... 157
- After Reading the Selection.......... 164
- *Letter to Indira Tagore,* by Rabindranath Tagore (India).......... 166
- After Reading the Selection.......... 170
- *Letter to the Reverend J. H. Twichell,* by Mark Twain (United States).......... 172
- After Reading the Selection.......... 176
- *Writing with Intent,* by Margaret Atwood (Canada).......... 178
- After Reading the Selection.......... 180

Autobiographies 185
- *When Heaven and Earth Changed Places,* by Le Ly Hayslip (Vietnam).......... 186
- After Reading the Selection.......... 194
- *By Any Other Name,* by Santha Rama Rau (India).......... 196
- After Reading the Selection.......... 206
- *Kaffir Boy,* by Mark Mathabane (South Africa).......... 209
- After Reading the Selection.......... 228
- *Reading Lolita in Tehran,* by Azar Nafisi (Iran).......... 231
- After Reading the Selection.......... 236

Biographies 238
- *China Men,* by Maxine Hong Kingston (United States) 239
- After Reading the Selection 244
- *The Last Seven Months of Anne Frank,* by Willy Lindwer (Netherlands) 246
- After Reading the Selection 253

Journalism 255
- *Account Evened With India, Says PM* by M. Ziauddin from *Dawn* (Pakistan) 256
- After Reading the Selection 261
- *Tests Are Nowhere Near India's: Fernandes* from the *Times of India* (India) 263
- After Reading the Selection 270
- *Pakistan Nuclear Moratorium Welcomed* from *BBC Online Network* (Great Britain) 272
- After Reading the Selection 276
- *The Frightening Joy* from *de Volkskrant* (Netherlands) 278
- *Building Atomic Security* by Tomasz Wroblewski from *Zycie Warszawy* (Poland) 281
- After Reading the Selections 282
- Skills Lesson: Point of View 284
- Unit 2 Summary 285
- Unit 2 Review 286

Unit 3 Drama 288
- About Drama 290

Classical Drama 292
- *Macbeth,* by William Shakespeare (England) 293
- After Reading the Selection 308

Realistic Drama 311
- *"Master Harold"... and the Boys,* by Athol Fugard (South Africa) 312
- After Reading the Selection 325

Expressionistic Drama ... 328
- *The Stronger,* by August Strindberg (Sweden) ... 329
- After Reading the Selection ... 339
- Skills Lesson: Characterization ... 342
- Unit 3 Summary ... 343
- Unit 3 Review ... 344

Unit 4 Poetry ... 346
- About Poetry ... 348
- *The Diameter of the Bomb,* by Yehuda Amichai (Israel) ... 350
- After Reading the Selection ... 353
- *Taking Leave of a Friend,* by Li Po (China) ... 355
- After Reading the Selection ... 358
- *Thoughts of Hanoi,* by Nguyen Thi Vinh (Vietnam) ... 360
- *Mindoro,* by Ramón Sunico (Philippines) ... 364
- After Reading the Selections ... 368
- *Ode to a Pair of Socks,* by Pablo Neruda (Chile) ... 370
- After Reading the Selection ... 374
- *Three Haiku* (Japan) ... 376
- After Reading the Selection ... 379
- *Do Not Go Gentle Into That Good Night,* by Dylan Thomas (Wales) ... 381
- After Reading the Selection ... 385
- *The Bird's Last Flight,* by Saadi Youssef (Iraq) ... 387
- After Reading the Selection ... 391
- *Mawu of the Waters,* by Abena Busia (Ghana) ... 393
- After Reading the Selection ... 396
- *Some Advice to Those Who Will Serve Time in Prison,* by Nazim Hikmet (Turkey) ... 398
- After Reading the Selection ... 402
- Skills Lesson: Style ... 404
- Unit 4 Summary ... 405
- Unit 4 Review ... 406

Unit 5 Persuasive Literature 408
- About Persuasive Literature. 410

Speeches. 412
- *Letter to the English,* by Joan of Arc (France) 413
- After Reading the Selection. 417
- *Nobel Lecture,* by Alexander Solzhenitsyn (Russia). 419
- After Reading the Selection. 435
- *The Gettysburg Address,* by Abraham Lincoln (United States) 438
- After Reading the Selection. 442
- *Inaugural Address,* by John F. Kennedy (United States) 444
- After Reading the Selection. 451

Essays 453
- *Of Repentance,* by Michel de Montaigne (France) 454
- After Reading the Selection. 456
- *A Small Place,* by Jamaica Kincaid (Antigua) 460
- After Reading the Selection. 475
- Skills Lesson: Setting. 478
- Unit 5 Summary 479
- Unit 5 Review 480

Unit 6 Humorous Literature 482
- About Humorous Literature. 484

Satire. 486
- *A Modest Proposal,* by Jonathan Swift (Ireland) 487
- After Reading the Selection. 494
- *Cup Inanity and Patriotic Profanity,* by Andrew Graham-Youll, from the *Buenos Aires Herald* (Argentina) 496
- After Reading the Selection. 501
- *The Happy Man,* by Naguib Mahfouz (Egypt) 503
- After Reading the Selection. 516

Columns 519
- *Staying at a Japanese Inn: Peace, Tranquillity, Insects,* by Dave Barry (United States) 520
- After Reading the Selection 527
- *Why Can't We Have Our Own Apartment?* by Erma Bombeck (United States) 529
- After Reading the Selection 533

Stories 535
- *Lohengrin,* by Leo Slezak (Austria) 536
- After Reading the Selection 545
- *A Wedding Without Musicians,* by Sholom Aleichem (Ukraine) 547
- After Reading the Selection 556
- Skills Lesson: Dialogue 558
- Unit 6 Summary 559
- Unit 6 Review 560

Appendixes
- Appendix A—Graphic Organizers 562
- Appendix B—Grammar 566
- Appendix C—Writing 573
- Appendix D—Research 581
- Appendix E—Speaking 583
- Appendix F—Listening 587
- Appendix G—Viewing 589
- Appendix H—Media and Technology 590
- Appendix I—World Atlas 591
- Appendix J—Student Passport to World Cultures 598

Handbook of Literary Terms 612

Glossary 616

Indexes
- Index of Authors and Titles 636
- Index of Selections by Country 638
- Index of Fine Art 640
- Index 641

Acknowledgments 650

Photo Credits 652

How to Use This Book: A Study Guide

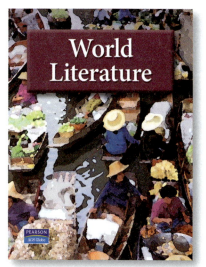

This book is an anthology of world literature. An anthology is a collection of literature written by different authors. The literature can be poems, plays, short stories, essays, parts of novels, folktales, legends, or myths. Sometimes an anthology contains selections from a certain country or continent. For example, you might have an anthology with great literature from around the world. Sometimes anthologies are organized around different genres, or types of literature. Then, you might have sections on poems, short stories, plays, essays, or folktales.

Reading a Literature Anthology

This anthology contains much enjoyable literature. An anthology helps you understand yourself and other people. Sometimes you will read about people from other countries. Sometimes you will read about people who lived in the past. Try to relate what the author is saying to your own life. Ask yourself: Have I ever felt this way? Have I known anyone like this person? Have I seen anything like this?

A literature anthology can also help you appreciate the beauty of language. As you read, find phrases or sentences that you particularly like. You may want to start a notebook of these phrases and sentences. You may also want to include words that are difficult.

This anthology is also important because it introduces you to great works of literature. Many times, you will find references to these works in everyday life. Sometimes you will hear a quotation on TV or read it in the newspaper. Great literature can come in many forms. On the next page are definitions of some kinds of literature genres in an anthology.

Genre Definitions

autobiography a person's life story, written by that person

biography a person's life story told by someone else

diary a daily record of personal events, thoughts, or private feelings

drama a story told through the words and actions of characters, written to be performed as well as read; a play

essay a written work that shows a writer's opinion on some basic or current issue

fable a short story or poem with a moral (lesson about life), often with animals who act like humans

fiction writing that is imaginative and designed to entertain
- In fiction, the author creates the events and characters.
- Short stories, novels, folktales, myths, legends, and most plays are works of fiction.

folktale a story that has been handed down from one generation to another
- The characters are usually either good or bad.
- Sometimes they are called tall tales, particularly if they are humorous and exaggerated.
- Folktales are also called folklore.

journal writing that expresses an author's feelings or first impressions about a subject
- Students may keep journals that record thoughts about what they have read.
- People also keep travel journals to remind themselves of interesting places they have seen.

legend a traditional story that at one time was told orally and was handed down from one generation to another
- Legends are like myths, but they do not have as many supernatural forces.
- Legends usually feature characters who actually lived, or real places or events.

myth an important story, often part of a culture's religion, that explains how the world came to be or why natural events happen
- A myth usually includes gods, goddesses, or unusually powerful human beings.
- Myths were first oral stories, and most early cultures have myths.

nonfiction writing about real people and events
- Essays, speeches, diaries, journals, autobiographies, and biographies are all usually nonfiction.

novel fiction that is book-length and has more plot and character details than a short story

poem a short piece of literature that often has a pattern of rhythm and rhyme; a poet uses imagination to paint powerful or beautiful ideas with words

prose all writing that is not poetry
- Short stories, novels, autobiographies, biographies, diaries, journals, and essays are examples of prose.

science fiction Literature that imagines the effects of science and technology on life in the future

short story a brief work of prose fiction that includes plot, setting, characters, point of view, and theme

How To Use This Book: A Study Guide

How to Read This Book

Different works of literature should be read in different ways. However, there are some basic methods you should use to read all works of literature.

Before Beginning a Unit

- Read the unit title and selection titles.
- Read the paragraphs that introduce the unit.
- Look at the pictures and other artwork in the unit.
- Think about what you already know about the unit.
- Think about what you might want to learn.
- Develop questions in your mind that you think will be answered in this unit.

Before Reading a Selection

- Read the selection's title.
- Look at the pictures and other artwork.
- Read the background material included in About the Author and About the Selection.
- Read the Objectives and think about what you will learn by reading the selection.
- Read the Literary Terms and their definitions.
- Complete the Before Reading the Selection activities. These activities will help you read the selection, understand vocabulary, and prepare for the reading.

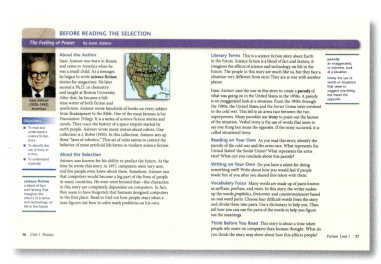

xii *How to Use This Book: A Study Guide*

As You Read a Selection

- Read the notes in the side margins. These will help you understand and think about the main ideas.

- Think of people or events in your own life that are similar to those described.

- Reread sentences or paragraphs that you do not understand.

- Predict what you think will happen next.

- Read the definitions at the bottom of the page for words that you do not know.

- Record words that you do not know. Also, write questions or comments you have about the text.

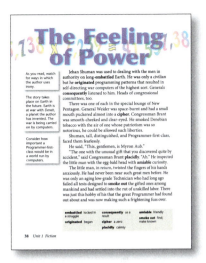

After Reading a Selection

- Reread interesting or difficult parts of the selection.

- Reflect on what you have learned by reading the selection.

- Complete the After Reading the Selection review questions and activities. The activities will help you develop your grammar, writing, speaking, listening, viewing, technology, media, and research skills.

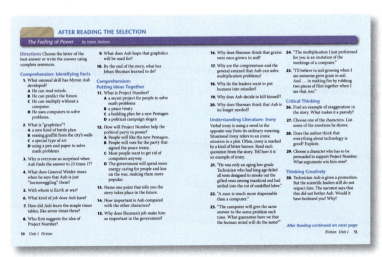

How To Use This Book: A Study Guide **xiii**

Reading Certain Types of Literature

The methods already described will help you understand all kinds of literature. You may need to use additional methods for specific types of literature.

Reading Poetry

- Read the poem aloud.
- Listen to the sounds of the words.
- Picture the images the author is describing.
- Reread poems over and over again to appreciate the author's use of language.

Reading Essays

- Review the questions in the After Reading the Selection before you begin reading.
- Use the questions to think about what you are reading.
- Remember that essays usually express an author's opinions. Try to understand why the author may have formed these opinions.

Reading Plays

- Picture the setting of the play. Since there usually is not much description given, try to relate the setting to something you have seen before.
- Pay attention to what the characters say. How does this give clues about the character's personality? Have you ever known anyone like this? Are you like this?

Tips for Better Reading

Literary Terms

Literary Terms are words or phrases that we use to study and discuss works of literature. These terms describe the ways an author helps to make us enjoy and understand what we are reading. Some of the terms also describe a genre, or specific type of literature. In this anthology, you will see white boxes on the side of the Before Reading the Selection pages. In these boxes are Literary Terms and their definitions. These terms are important in understanding and discussing the selection being read. By understanding these Literary Terms, readers can appreciate the author's craft. You can find the definitions for all of the Literary Terms used in this book in the Handbook of Literary Terms on page 612.

setting the place and time in a story

plot the series of events in a story

theme the main idea of a literary work

Using a Graphic Organizer

A graphic organizer is visual representation of information. It can help you see how ideas are related to each other. A graphic organizer can help you study for a test, organize information before writing an essay, or organize details in a literature selection. You will use graphic organizers for different activities throughout this textbook. There are 14 different graphic organizers listed below. You can read a description and see an example of each graphic organizer in Appendix A in the back of this textbook.

- Character Analysis Guide
- Story Map
- Main Idea Graphic (Umbrella)
- Main Idea Graphic (Table)
- Main Idea Graphic (Details)
- Venn Diagram
- Sequence Chain
- Concept Map
- Plot Mountain
- Structured Overview
- Semantic Table
- Prediction Guide
- Semantic Line
- KWL Chart

How To Use This Book: A Study Guide

Taking Notes

You will read many selections in this literature anthology. As you read, you may want to take notes to help remember what you have read. You can use these notes to keep track of events and characters in a story. Your notes may also be helpful for recognizing common ideas among the selections in a unit. You can review your notes as you prepare to take a test. Here are some tips for taking notes:

- Write down only the most important information.
- Do not try to write every detail or every word.
- Write notes in your own words.
- Do not be concerned about writing in complete sentences. Use short phrases.

Using the Three-Column Chart

One good way to take notes is to use a three-column chart. Make your own three-column chart by dividing a sheet of notebook paper into three equal parts. In Column 1, write the topic you are reading about or studying. In Column 2, write what you learned about this topic as you read or listened to your teacher. In Column 3, write questions, observations, or opinions about the topic, or write a detail that will help you remember the topic. Here are some examples of different ways to take notes using the three-column chart.

The topic I am studying	What I learned from reading the text or class discussion	Questions, observations, or ideas I have about the topic
Fiction	• one genre of literature • many different types of fiction—science fiction, adventure, detective stories, romance, suspense	• The book I am reading right now is fiction. It is an adventure story. • I wonder if poetry is part of the fiction genre.

Vocabulary Word	Definition	Sentence with Vocabulary Word
Premises	a building or part of a building	Students are not allowed on the school **premises** during the weekend.

Literary Term	Definition	Example from Selection
Exaggeration	a use of words to make something seem more than it is; stretching the truth to a great extent	He was exactly five feet six inches in height, and six feet five inches in circumference. His head was a perfect sphere . . . . (Wouter Van Twiller)

Character	Character Traits Found in the Selection	Page Number
John Krakauer	Conflict, person against self—Krakauer wonders if he will run out of oxygen before returning to camp.	p. 355
	Determined—Krakauer is determined to make it back to camp even though his oxygen has run out and it is snowing on the mountain.	p. 358
	Thankful—After reaching camp, Krakauer is thankful that he is safe.	p. 360

Stage of Plot	Example from Text	Questions, Observations, and Ideas
Rising Action	"And how easy it would be to kill him. And he deserves it. Does he? No! What the devil!... I could cut his throat—*zip, zip!* I wouldn't give him time to resist. . . ." (p. 104)	This is a good example of rising action because it introduces the conflict of the story.

How To Use This Book: A Study Guide

What to Do About Words You Do Not Know

- If the word is in **bold type,** look for the definition of the word at the bottom of the page.
- If the word is not in bold type, read to the end of the sentence and maybe the next sentence. Can you determine the meaning now?
- Look at the beginning sound of the unknown word. Ask yourself, "What word begins with this sound and would make sense here?"
- Sound out the syllables of the word.
- If you still cannot determine the meaning, see if you know any parts of the word: prefixes, suffixes, or roots.
- If this does not work, write the word on a note card or in a vocabulary notebook. Then look up the word in a dictionary after you have finished reading the selection. Reread the passage containing the unknown word after you have looked up its definition.
- If the word is necessary to understand the passage, look it up in a dictionary or glossary immediately.

Word Study Tips

- Start a vocabulary file with note cards to use for review.
- Write one word on the front of each card. Write the unit number, selection title, and the definition on the back.
- You can use these cards as flash cards by yourself or with a study partner to test your knowledge.

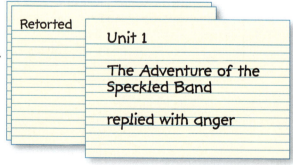

Before the Test Day

- Make sure you have read all of the selections assigned.
- Review the Literary Terms and definitions for each selection.
- Review your answers to the After Reading the Selection questions.
- Reread the Unit Summary and review your answers to the Unit Review.
- Review any notes that you have taken or graphic organizers you have developed.
- Ask your teacher what kinds of questions will be on the test.
- Try to predict what questions will be asked. Think of and write answers to those questions.
- Review the Test-Taking Tip at the bottom of each Unit Review page.

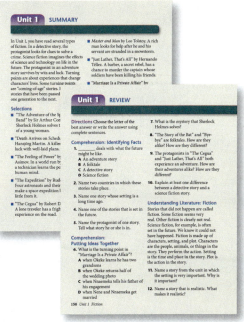

During the Test

- Come to the test with a positive attitude.
- Write your name on the paper.
- Preview the test and read the directions carefully.
- Plan your time.
- Answer the questions that you know first.
- Then go back and answer the more difficult questions.
- Allow time to reread all of the questions and your answers.

How To Use This Book: A Study Guide **xix**

Face With Snake, by Stéphan Daigle.

Unit 1 Fiction

How long have people told stories? Probably as long as they have been able to talk. People made up stories to explain things like why the sky is blue or why ducks have webbed feet. They created stories to entertain themselves. Some stories are scary. Some are funny. Some are short. Others are very long. No matter where in the world you go, people tell stories and have always told stories. In this unit, you will enjoy stories from the countries shown on the map on page 3.

Unit 1 Selections	Page
DETECTIVE STORIES	4
■ GREAT BRITAIN from "The Adventure of the Speckled Band" by Sir Arthur Conan Doyle	5
■ GERMANY "Death Arrives on Schedule" by Hansjörg Martin	21
SCIENCE FICTION	35
■ UNITED STATES "The Feeling of Power" by Isaac Asimov	36
■ GERMANY "The Expedition" by Rudolf Lorenzen	53
ADVENTURE STORIES	73
■ UNITED STATES "The *Cegua*" by Robert D. San Souci	74
■ RUSSIA from *Master and Man* by Leo Tolstoy	83
■ COLOMBIA "Just Lather, That's All" by Hernando Téllez	92
TURNING POINTS	102
■ NIGERIA "Marriage Is a Private Affair" by Chinua Achebe	103
■ KOREA "Cranes" by Hwang Sun-won	115
■ DOMINICAN REPUBLIC from *In the Time of the Butterflies* by Julia Alvarez	125
FOLKTALES	133
■ CHINA "A Polite Idiosyncrasy"	134
■ HAITI "Bye-bye"	142
■ UNITED STATES "The Story of the Bat"	144

"Fiction is not a dream. Nor is it guesswork. It is imagining based on facts, and the facts must be accurate or the work of imagining will not stand up."

—Margaret Culkin Banning, author

"To read a book for the first time is to make an acquaintance with a new friend; to read it for a second time is to meet an old one."

—Chinese Saying

Unit 1

About Fiction

Fiction is writing that is imaginative and entertaining. In fiction, the author creates the events and characters. Some fiction is realistic and may seem like it is from a newspaper. Other fictional stories describe far-off planets, alien life forms, or the future.

All works of fiction share three elements: character, plot, and setting. Characters perform the action. They are usually people, but they can be animals or even objects. Some examples of nonhuman characters are the magic mirror in *Snow White and the Seven Dwarfs* and the rabbits Hazel and Fiver in *Watership Down*.

Plot is the action in a story. As characters act and react, they move the plot along. Plot changes the characters and reveals their true nature and hidden feelings. The plot of *A Christmas Carol,* for instance, is about Ebenezer Scrooge and his experiences on the night before Christmas. He meets three ghosts and ends up becoming a generous and caring person.

Setting is the place and time in which a story happens. For example, the setting of *Star Wars* is "a long time ago in a galaxy far, far away."

Fiction can be grouped by the length of the work. Short stories are short enough to read in one sitting. They usually center on one character or situation. Novels are longer works. They can explore more than one character or situation over a longer period.

Fiction can also be grouped by setting or by where the authors come from. Gabriela Mistral, Pablo Neruda, and Gabriel García Márquez are authors from different Latin American countries. But their works can be grouped together as Latin American fiction.

The fiction in Unit 1 is arranged by genre, or type of story. The authors use character, plot, and setting, to create many kinds of stories. Libraries often place the stories they have in special sections so you can find them easily. Look for sections of detective stories, science fiction, folktales, or other genres. You may also find the complete work from which a selection in this unit was taken.

The following countries are represented in this unit: China, Columbia, the Dominican Republic, Germany, Great Britain, Haiti, Nigeria, Russia, South Korea, and the United States.

Detective Stories

Detective stories are sometimes called mysteries or "whodunits." They present a crime and a main character. The protagonist, or main character, is usually a detective. He or she watches and questions the other characters. The detective finds clues and reveals the criminal.

Detectives originally observed and commented without being part of the plot. Today, they are often right in the middle of the action. V. I. Warshawski, with her hard Chicago attitude, or the English busybody Miss Marple are detectives with strong personalities. Over a cup of tea or a glass of something stronger, they reveal the "bad guy."

Detective stories often contain many twists and turns as the plot builds. Sometimes we don't know who to trust. Detectives dodge bullets, plunge into fights, and take the place of the law. They may protect the innocent or punish the guilty. Modern detectives are not always people to be admired. Characters like Easy Rawlins of Los Angeles are much like the crooks they track. Only their sense of decency and justice separates them from the criminals. Much of the fun in reading a detective story is in spotting the criminal before the detective explains everything.

In "The Adventure of the Speckled Band," we watch the action and follow the clues along with Sherlock Holmes. But it's not until the end of the story that Holmes puts everything together for us. He explains how the crime was done and how he solved the mystery.

In "Death Arrives on Schedule," we know who the criminal is. The suspense lies in waiting to learn how—or if—the criminal will be caught.

DETECTIVE STORIES

Mysteries • Clues • Suspense

BEFORE READING THE SELECTION

from *The Adventure of the Speckled Band* by Sir Arthur Conan Doyle

About the Author

Sir Arthur Conan Doyle was trained as a doctor. He quit medicine to write. His first Sherlock Holmes story was "A Study in Scarlet," which came out in 1887. From 1891 on, Doyle wrote many more Holmes stories. The Sherlock Holmes stories have been made into films and television shows. You can even find fan clubs such as the "Baker Street Irregulars," named for Holmes's London address, 221-B Baker Street. "The Hounds of the Internet" are on the World Wide Web. Doyle wrote other books, too. In fact, he grew very tired of Holmes. He killed off the detective in an 1893 story. People were so upset that Doyle had to bring him back to life. A final book of Holmes stories came out in 1927.

Sir Arthur Conan Doyle
(1859–1930)
British

About the Selection

Sherlock Holmes is one of the greatest detectives in **fiction**. He lived and worked in the city of London in the late 1800s. When many people think of detectives, they think of Holmes. He is usually shown with a deerstalker cap, a pipe, and a magnifying glass. Sherlock Holmes's assistant is Dr. Watson. In this story, Holmes looks into a mysterious death. Notice his attention to details.

Objectives

- To read and understand the plot of a classic detective story
- To describe the role of the narrator in the first-person point of view in stories
- To identify the characters in a story

fiction writing that is imaginative and designed to entertain; the author creates the events and characters

Before Reading **continued on next page**

Fiction Unit 1   5

BEFORE READING THE SELECTION (continued)

from The Adventure of the Speckled Band by Sir Arthur Conan Doyle

mystery a story about a crime that is solved

plot the series of events in a story; an element in all fiction

exposition the beginning of the story, or introduction

rising action the buildup of excitement in a story

climax the high point of interest or suspense in a story or play

falling action the action in a story or play during which the excitement dies down

resolution/ denouement the final outcome of the main event in a story, as when a mystery is solved

character a person or animal in a story, poem, or play

narrator the teller of a story

first person written as if someone is telling the story from his or her point of view

Literary Terms "The Adventure of the Speckled Band" is a classic **mystery**. The **plot** has Sherlock Holmes finding out who killed a young woman. All the parts of a plot are there: **exposition, rising action, climax, falling action, and resolution,** or **denouement**. Look for these places in the story. The **characters** of Sherlock Holmes and his friend Dr. John Watson have become familiar to readers all over the world. A character is a person or animal in a story, poem, or play. Dr. Watson is the **narrator** for most of the adventures. He writes in the **first person**. This means he tells the story as though he is watching the action. In first-person point of view, the narrator is the "I" in the story.

Reading on Your Own Do you know something about Sherlock Holmes, perhaps from a movie or television show? Meet with a partner and list everything you know about him. If you have not heard of Sherlock Holmes before, list instead what you know about detectives in general.

Writing on Your Own Think of any mystery stories you have read. Then write a paragraph about what you think makes for a good mystery.

Vocabulary Focus This selection contains British spellings of some American words, such as *neighbour* instead of *neighbor*. As you read, look for other British spellings in the story. This story was written more than 100 years ago. The English language has changed since then. Some words and terms may sound old-fashioned and unfamiliar; for example, *dog-cart, old family seat, fain*. What do these words tell you about the setting of the story?

Think Before You Read Think about the different meanings for the word *band*. What could the "speckled band" be?

from The Adventure of the Speckled Band

It was early in April in the year '83 that I woke one morning to find Sherlock Holmes standing, fully dressed, by the side of my bed. He was a late riser, as a rule, and as the clock on the mantelpiece showed me that it was only a quarter-past seven, I blinked up at him in some surprise, and perhaps just a little resentment, for I was myself regular in my habits.

"Very sorry to knock you up, Watson," he said, "but it's the common lot this morning. Mrs. Hudson has been knocked up, she **retorted** upon me, and I on you."

"What is it, then—a fire?"

"No; a **client**. It seems that a young lady has arrived in a considerable state of excitement, who insists upon seeing me. She is waiting now in the sitting-room. Now, when young ladies wander about the **metropolis** at this hour of the morning, and knock sleepy people up out of their beds, I presume that it is something very pressing which they have to communicate. Should it prove to be an interesting case, you would, I am sure, wish to follow it from the **outset**. I thought, at any rate, that I should call you and give you the chance."

"My dear fellow, I would not miss it for anything."

I had no keener pleasure than in following Holmes in his professional investigations, and in admiring the rapid **deductions**, as swift as **intuitions**, and yet always founded on a **logical** basis, with which he unravelled the problems which were submitted to him. I rapidly threw on my clothes and was ready in a few minutes to accompany my friend down to the sitting-room. A lady dressed in black and heavily veiled, who had been sitting in the window, rose as we entered.

> As you read, watch for clues that lead to a solution.

> Notice how the narrator uses "I." This shows the story is written in the first person.

> To *knock up* is British slang for to wake by knocking at the door.

> Mrs. Hudson is the landlady and housekeeper for Holmes and Watson.

> The narrator is Dr. Watson. What sentence helps you figure this out?

---

retorted replied with anger

client a customer; a person for whom one does a professional service

metropolis a city

outset the beginning

deductions answers found by reasoning

intuitions ways of knowing without proof

logical reasonable

Fiction Unit 1

"Good-morning, madam," said Holmes cheerily. "My name is Sherlock Holmes. This is my intimate friend and associate, Dr. Watson, before whom you can speak as freely as before myself. Ha! I am glad to see that Mrs. Hudson has had the good sense to light the fire. Pray draw up to it, and I shall order you a cup of hot coffee, for I observe that you are shivering."

"It is not cold which makes me shiver," said the woman in a low voice, changing her seat as requested.

"What, then?"

"It is fear, Mr. Holmes. It is terror." She raised her veil as she spoke, and we could see that she was indeed in a **pitiable** state of **agitation,** her face all drawn and gray, with restless, frightened eyes, like those of some hunted animal. Her features and figure were those of a woman of thirty, but her hair was shot with **premature** gray, and her expression was weary and **haggard**. Sherlock Holmes ran her over with one of his quick, all-**comprehensive** glances.

"You must not fear," said he soothingly, bending forward and patting her forearm. "We shall soon set matters right, I have no doubt. You have come in by train this morning, I see."

"You know me, then?"

"No, but I observe the second half of a return ticket in the palm of your left glove. You must have started early, and yet you had a good drive in a dog-cart, along heavy roads, before you reached the station."

The lady gave a violent start and stared in bewilderment at my companion.

"There is no mystery, my dear madam," said he, smiling. "The left arm of your jacket is **spattered** with mud in no less than seven places. The marks are perfectly fresh. There is no vehicle save a dog-cart which throws up mud in that way, and then only when you sit on the left-hand side of the driver."

"Whatever your reasons may be, you are perfectly correct," said she. "I started from home before six, reached Leatherhead

---

A *dog-cart* is a small, horse-drawn wagon.

This is an example of Holmes's amazing deductions.

Leatherhead is a town south of London.

---

pitiable causing a feeling of pity

agitation strong emotion; disturbance

premature earlier than expected

haggard looking worn because of worry

comprehensive knowing

spattered splashed

at twenty past, and came in by the first train to Waterloo. Sir, I can stand this strain no longer; I shall go mad if it continues. I have no one to turn to—none, save only one, who cares for me, and he, poor fellow, can be of little aid. I have heard of you, Mr. Holmes; I have heard of you from Mrs. Farintosh, whom you helped in the hour of her sore need. It was from her that I had your address. Oh, sir, do you not think that you could help me, too, and at least throw a little light through the dense darkness which surrounds me? At present it is out of my power to reward you for your services, but in a month or six weeks I shall be married, with the control of my own income, and then at least you shall not find me ungrateful."

> *Waterloo* is a train station in London.

Holmes turned to his desk and, unlocking it, drew out a small case-book, which he consulted.

"Farintosh," said he. "Ah yes, I recall the case; it was concerned with an opal **tiara**. I think it was before your time, Watson. I can only say, madam, that I shall be happy to devote the same care to your case as I did to that of your friend. As to reward, my profession is its own reward; but you are at liberty to **defray** whatever expenses I may be put to, at the time which suits you best. And now I beg that you will lay before us everything that may help us in forming an opinion upon the matter."

> Who are the characters in the story so far?

"Alas!" replied our visitor, "the very horror of my situation lies in the fact that my fears are so vague, and my suspicions depend so entirely upon small points, which might seem **trivial** to another, that even he to whom of all others I have a right to look for help and advice looks upon all that I tell him about it as the fancies of a nervous woman. He does not say so, but I can read it from his soothing answers and **averted** eyes. But I have heard, Mr. Holmes, that you can see deeply into the **manifold** wickedness of the human heart. You may advise me how to walk amid the dangers which encompass me."

"I am all attention, madam."

> The visitor is speaking of her fiancé here.

---

tiara a small crown
defray pay the costs
trivial not important
averted looking away
manifold of many kinds

Fiction Unit 1

> About 1,500 years ago, Germanic people from Europe conquered and settled parts of England. They were *Angles* and *Saxons*.

> In English history, the *Regency* lasted from 1811 to 1820. In this period, King George III had a mental illness. His son ruled as regent in his place.

> *Calcutta* is a large city in India. India was a colony of Britain when this story was written.

> The unit of money in Great Britain is the *pound*. Its symbol is £.

"My name is Helen Stoner, and I am living with my stepfather, who is the last survivor of one of the oldest Saxon families in England, the Roylotts of Stoke Moran, on the western border of Surrey."

Holmes nodded his head. "The name is familiar to me," said he.

"The family was at one time among the richest in England, and the estates extended over the borders into Berkshire in the north, and Hampshire in the west. In the last century, however, four **successive** heirs were of a **dissolute** and wasteful disposition, and the family ruin was eventually completed by a gambler in the days of the Regency. Nothing was left save a few acres of ground, and the two-hundred-year-old house, which is itself crushed under a heavy mortgage. The last squire dragged out his existence there, living the horrible life of an **aristocratic** pauper; but his only son, my stepfather, seeing that he must adapt himself to the new conditions, obtained an advance from a relative, which enabled him to take a medical degree and went out to Calcutta, where, by his professional skill and his force of character, he established a large practice. In a fit of anger, however, caused by some robberies which had been **perpetrated** in the house, he beat his native butler to death and narrowly escaped a capital sentence. As it was, he suffered a long term of imprisonment and afterwards returned to England a **morose** and disappointed man.

"When Dr. Roylott was in India he married my mother, Mrs. Stoner, the young widow of Major-General Stoner, of the Bengal **Artillery**. My sister Julia and I were twins, and we were only two years old at the time of my mother's re-marriage. She had a considerable sum of money—not less than £1000 a year—and this she **bequeathed** to Dr. Roylott entirely while we resided with him, with a provision that a certain annual sum should be allowed to each of us in the

---

successive following

dissolute wicked; of bad character

aristocratic of high social class

perpetrated carried out

morose gloomy

Artillery branch of the military armed with large guns

bequeathed gave to, as in a will

10 Unit 1 Fiction

event of our marriage. Shortly after our return to England my mother died—she was killed eight years ago in a railway accident near Crewe. Dr. Roylott then abandoned his attempts to establish himself in practice in London and took us to live with him in the old ancestral house at Stoke Moran. The money which my mother had left was enough for all our wants, and there seemed to be no obstacle to our happiness.

"But a terrible change came over our stepfather about this time. Instead of making friends and exchanging visits with our neighbours, who had at first been overjoyed to see a Roylott of Stoke Moran back in the old family seat, he shut himself up in his house and seldom came out save to indulge in ferocious quarrels with whoever might cross his path. Violence of temper approaching to **mania** has been hereditary in the men of the family, and in my stepfather's case it had, I believe, been **intensified** by his long residence in the tropics. A series of disgraceful brawls took place, two of which ended in the police-court, until at last he became the terror of the village, and the folks would fly at his approach, for he is a man of immense strength, and absolutely uncontrollable in his anger.

Neighbour is a British spelling of the American word neighbor.

"Last week he hurled the local blacksmith over a **parapet** into a stream, and it was only by paying over all the money which I could gather together that I was able to avert another public exposure. He had no friends at all save the wandering gypsies, and he would give these **vagabonds** leave to **encamp** upon the few acres of bramble-covered land which represent the family estate, and would accept in return the **hospitality** of their tents, wandering away with them sometimes for weeks on end. He has a passion also for Indian animals, which are sent over to him by a correspondent, and he has at this moment a cheetah and a baboon, which wander freely over

---

mania an intense, almost insane, excitement

intensified became stronger

parapet a railing along the edge of a roof or wall

vagabonds homeless people who wander from place to place

encamp set up camp

hospitality the friendly treatment of guests

> Why would the villagers be afraid of a cheetah and a baboon?

> Why do you think the hair of the two women turned white so early?

his grounds and are feared by the villagers almost as much as their master.

"You can imagine from what I say that my poor sister Julia and I had no great pleasure in our lives. No servant would stay with us, and for a long time we did all the work of the house. She was but thirty at the time of her death, and yet her hair had already begun to whiten, even as mine has."

"Your sister is dead, then?"

"She died just two years ago, and it is of her death that I wish to speak to you. You can understand that, living the life which I have described, we were little likely to see anyone of our own age and position. We had, however, an aunt, my mother's maiden sister, Miss Honoria Westphail, who lives near Harrow, and we were occasionally allowed to pay short visits at this lady's house. Julia went there at Christmas two years ago, and met there a half-pay major of marines, to whom she became engaged. My stepfather learned of the engagement when my sister returned and offered no objection to the marriage; but within a **fortnight** of the day which had been fixed for the wedding, the terrible event occurred which has deprived me of my only companion."

Sherlock Holmes had been leaning back in his chair with his eyes closed and his head sunk in a cushion, but he half opened his lids now and glanced across at his visitor.

"Pray be precise as to details," said he.

"It is easy for me to be so, for every event of that dreadful time is **seared** into my memory. The **manor**-house is, as I have already said, very old, and only one wing is now inhabited. The bedrooms in this wing are on the ground floor, the sitting-rooms being in the central block of the buildings. Of these bedrooms the first is Dr. Roylott's, the second my sister's, and the third my own. There is no communication

---

fortnight a period of two weeks   **seared** burned   **manor** the main house on an estate

between them, but they all open out into the same corridor. Do I make myself plain?"

"Perfectly so."

"The windows of the three rooms open out upon the lawn. That fatal night Dr. Roylott had gone to his room early, though we knew that he had not retired to rest, for my sister was troubled by the smell of the strong Indian cigars which it was his custom to smoke. She left her room, therefore, and came into mine, where she sat for some time, chatting about her approaching wedding. At eleven o'clock she rose to leave me, but she paused at the door and looked back.

"'Tell me, Helen,' said she, 'have you ever heard anyone whistle in the dead of the night?'

"'Never,' said I.

"'I suppose that you could not possibly whistle, yourself, in your sleep?'

"'Certainly not. But why?'

"'Because during the last few nights I have always, about three in the morning, heard a low, clear whistle. I am a light sleeper, and it has awakened me. I cannot tell where it came from—perhaps from the next room, perhaps from the lawn. I thought that I would just ask you whether you had heard it.'

"'No, I have not. It must be those **wretched** gypsies in the plantation.'

"'Very likely. And yet if it were on the lawn, I wonder that you did not hear it also.'

"'Ah, but I sleep more heavily than you.'

"'Well, it is of no great **consequence,** at any rate.' She smiled back at me, closed my door, and a few moments later I heard her key turn in the lock."

"Indeed," said Holmes. "Was it your custom always to lock yourselves in at night?"

"Always."

"And why?"

---

wretched worthless; seen with scorn

consequence importance

"I think that I mentioned to you that the doctor kept a cheetah and a baboon. We had no feeling of **security** unless our doors were locked."

"Quite so. Pray proceed with your statement."

"I could not sleep that night. A vague feeling of **impending** misfortune **impressed** me. My sister and I, you will recollect, were twins, and you know how subtle are the links which bind two souls which are so closely allied. It was a wild night. The wind was howling outside, and the rain was beating and splashing against the windows. Suddenly, amid all the hubbub of the gale, there burst forth the wild scream of a terrified woman. I knew that it was my sister's voice. I sprang from my bed, wrapped a shawl round me, and rushed into the corridor. As I opened my door I seemed to hear a low whistle, such as my sister described, and a few moments later a clanging sound, as if a mass of metal had fallen. As I ran down the passage, my sister's door was unlocked, and revolved slowly upon its hinges. I stared at it horror-**stricken,** not knowing what was about to issue from it. By the light of the corridor-lamp I saw my sister appear at the opening, her face **blanched** with terror, her hands groping for help, her whole figure swaying to and fro like that of a drunkard. I ran to her and threw my arms around her, but at that moment her knees seemed to give way and she fell to the ground. She **writhed** as one who is in terrible pain, and her limbs were dreadfully **convulsed**. At first I thought that she had not recognized me, but as I bent over her she suddenly shrieked out in a voice which I shall never forget, 'Oh, my God! Helen! It was the band! The speckled band!' There was something else which she would fain have said, and she stabbed with her finger into the air in the direction of the doctor's room, but a fresh convulsion seized her and choked her words. I rushed out, calling loudly for my stepfather, and I met him hastening from his room in his dressing-gown. When he reached my sister's

> What do you think happened to Julia?

> *Fain* means "willingly."

security safety
impending about to happen
impressed affected deeply
stricken struck; strongly affected
blanched turned pale
writhed twisted as in pain
convulsed shaken or pulled jerkily

side she was unconscious, and though he poured brandy down her throat and sent for medical aid from the village, all efforts were in vain, for she slowly sank and died without having recovered her consciousness. Such was the dreadful end of my beloved sister."...

[Holmes takes the case. Holmes and Watson travel to the house and examine the bedrooms. At night, they are waiting in the room where Julia Stoner had died. (Because of some repairs to her own room, Helen Stoner was forced to move into the room that had been her sister's.) Holmes has not told Watson why they are there. Suddenly they see a small light and hear a very gentle sound. Holmes jumps up and yells.]

"You see it, Watson?" he yelled. "You see it?"

But I saw nothing. At the moment when Holmes struck the light I heard a low, clear whistle, but the sudden glare flashing into my weary eyes made it impossible for me to tell what it was at which my friend lashed so savagely. I could, however, see that his face was deadly pale and filled with horror and **loathing**.

He had ceased to strike and was gazing up at the **ventilator** when suddenly there broke from the silence of the night the most horrible cry to which I have ever listened. It swelled up louder and louder, a hoarse yell of pain and fear and anger all mingled in the one dreadful shriek. They say that away down in the village, and even in the distant **parsonage,** that cry raised the sleepers from their beds. It struck cold to our hearts, and I stood gazing at Holmes, and he at me, until the last echoes of it had died away into the silence from which it rose.

"What can it mean?" I gasped.

"It means that it is all over," Holmes answered. "And perhaps, after all, it is for the best. Take your pistol, and we will enter Dr. Roylott's room."...

On the wooden chair, sat Dr. Grimesby Roylott, clad in a long gray dressing-gown, his bare ankles **protruding** beneath,

---

loathing intense dislike

ventilator a passage in a house that air is blown through

parsonage a house where a church minister lives

protruding sticking out

and his feet thrust into red heelless Turkish slippers. Across his lap lay the short stock with the long lash which we had noticed during the day. His chin was cocked upward and his eyes were fixed in a dreadful, rigid stare at the corner of the ceiling. Round his brow he had a peculiar yellow band, with brownish speckles, which seemed to be bound tightly round his head. As we entered he made neither sound nor motion.

"The band! the speckled band!" whispered Holmes.

I took a step forward. In an instant his strange headgear began to move, and there reared itself from among his hair the squat diamond-shaped head and puffed neck of a **loathsome** serpent.

"It is a swamp *adder!*" cried Holmes; "the deadliest snake in India. He has died within ten seconds of being bitten."

[Later Holmes explained,] "It became clear to me that whatever danger threatened an **occupant** of the room could not come either from the window or the door. My attention was **speedily** drawn, as I have already remarked to you, to this ventilator, and to the bell-rope which hung down to the bed. The discovery that this was a dummy, and that the bed was clamped to the floor, instantly gave rise to the suspicion that the rope was there as a bridge for something passing through the hole and coming to the bed. The idea of a snake instantly occurred to me, and when I coupled it with my knowledge that the doctor was furnished with a supply of creatures from India, I felt that I was probably on the right track. The idea of using a form of poison which could not possibly be discovered by any chemical test was just such a one as would occur

> *Adders* are highly poisonous snakes in the viper family.

> Here Holmes explains how he put the clues together and solved the mystery.

---

loathsome disgusting   **occupant** a person who lives or stays in a certain place   **speedily** quickly

to a clever and **ruthless** man who had had an Eastern training. The **rapidity** with which such a poison would take effect would also, from his point of view, be an advantage. It would be a sharp-eyed **coroner,** indeed, who could distinguish the two little dark **punctures** which would show where the poison fangs had done their work. Then I thought of the whistle. Of course he must **recall** the snake before the morning light **revealed** it to the victim. He had trained it, probably by the use of the milk which we saw, to return to him when summoned. He would put it through this ventilator at the hour that he thought best, with the certainty that it would crawl down the rope and land on the bed. It might or might not bite the occupant, perhaps she might escape every night for a week, but sooner or later she must fall a victim.

"I had come to these conclusions before ever I had entered his room. An inspection of his chair showed me that he had been in the habit of standing on it, which of course would be necessary in order that he should reach the ventilator. The sight of the safe, the saucer of milk, and the loop of whipcord were enough to finally **dispel** any doubts which may have remained. The metallic clang heard by Miss Stoner was obviously caused by her stepfather hastily closing the door of his safe upon its terrible occupant. Having once made up my mind, you know the steps which I took in order to put the matter to the proof. I heard the creature hiss as I have no doubt that you did also, and I instantly lit the light and attacked it."

"With the result of driving it through the ventilator."

"And also with the result of causing it to turn upon its master at the other side. Some of the blows of my cane came home and roused its snakish temper, so that it flew upon the first person it saw. In this way I am no doubt indirectly responsible for Dr. Grimesby Roylott's death, and I cannot say that it is likely to weigh very heavily upon my conscience."

---

ruthless cruel

rapidity speed

coroner the official who decides the cause of death

punctures small holes caused by a sharp object

recall call back; remember

revealed showed

dispel make disappear

AFTER READING THE SELECTION

from The Adventure of the Speckled Band by Sir Arthur Conan Doyle

Directions Choose the letter of the best answer or write the answer using complete sentences.

Comprehension: Identifying Facts

1. What does Holmes call Dr. Watson when he introduces him?
   A his intimate friend
   B his employee
   C his brother
   D his neighbor

2. Why is Helen Stoner shivering?
   A She is cold.   C She is scared.
   B She is sick.   D She is angry.

3. How does Helen Stoner travel to London?

4. What helps Holmes remember details of the opal tiara case?

5. How do members of Dr. Roylott's family lose the family fortune?

6. What does Dr. Roylott do that forces him to return to England?

7. What has Julia Stoner heard during the night?

8. How does the speckled band get into Julia's room?

9. Who is the speckled band's final victim?

10. What is the speckled band?

Comprehension: Putting Ideas Together

11. Which of these facts about Helen Stoner does Holmes learn just by observing her?
    A She has a sister named Julia.
    B She rode in a dog-cart.
    C Her mother is dead.
    D Her stepfather was once in prison.

12. Why will Helen Stoner be unable to pay Holmes right away?
    A She will not have control of her money for six more weeks.
    B Her husband will not let her.
    C She has to borrow the money from a friend.
    D The bank is closed.

13. Why do you think Sherlock Holmes agrees to take the case?

14. Why is Holmes's attention drawn to the ventilator?

15. Why do the Stoner sisters always lock their doors at night?

16. Why do the Stoner sisters seldom have company?

17. What words do you think Julia Stoner wanted to say just before she died?

18. Why does Holmes not tell Watson the reason for their visit to the room where Julia Stoner died?

19. What clues does Holmes say helped him solve the mystery?

20. How does Holmes feel about Dr. Roylott's death?

Understanding Literature: First Person

A story told in the first person uses pronouns such as *I, me, my,* and *we*. It is told from the narrator's point of view. The narrator is a character in the story. In the Sherlock Holmes stories, the narrator is his friend Watson. Watson reports events as they are happening, drawing the reader into the story. The reader knows only what Watson knows. The reader cannot know what Sherlock Holmes is thinking.

21. Watson tells us a little bit about himself. Describe one thing about Watson.

22. Why is it important that Watson be in the room with Holmes and the woman? *(Hint: Watson is telling the story from the first-person point of view.)*

23. How would the story be different if Holmes were the narrator?

24. A third-person narrator knows the thoughts and acts of all the characters. Suppose this story were told in the third person. What role would Watson have? Explain.

25. Think of other stories you have read. Do you prefer first-person stories or third-person stories? Why?

Critical Thinking

26. What do you think life was like for Helen Stoner after Dr. Roylott's death?

27. Do you think you could be a detective like Sherlock Holmes? Explain your answer.

28. Could the events in this story possibly have happened? Explain.

29. Is "The Adventure of the Speckled Band" a good title for this story? Why or why not?

Thinking Creatively

30. Why do you think Sherlock Holmes stories are so popular?

After Reading **continued on next page**

AFTER READING THE SELECTION (continued)

from The Adventure of the Speckled Band   by Sir Arthur Conan Doyle

 ### Grammar Check

A fragment is a phrase that is punctuated like a sentence. Sometimes a writer uses fragments because they sound more like natural speech. For example, on page 13, Doyle writes, "Because during the last few nights I have always, about three in the morning, heard a low, clear whistle." Other times fragments are really mistakes in the writing. Identify another fragment in this selection. Rewrite it as a complete sentence. Which format sounds better to you? Explain.

 ### Writing on Your Own

Imagine Sherlock Holmes is arrested for the murder of Dr. Roylott. Write an essay defending Sherlock Holmes. Make sure to use logical arguments based on the facts in the story.

 ### Speaking

The development of character is an important element of fiction. Choose one character from the story to role-play. Have a partner interview you. Your partner will ask you questions about yourself and what has happened to you. Answer as if you are that character. When your interview is finished, have your partner choose a character. Then you interview your partner.

 ### Listening

Reread the end of the story. Pay close attention to Holmes's explanation of how he solves the case. With a partner, take turns reading aloud parts of this explanation. Try to speak as if you are Sherlock Holmes. Listen to your partner carefully. Then help your partner to read it aloud more like Holmes would have said it. Think about Holmes's tone of voice. Also think about whom he is speaking to.

 ### Viewing

Graphic organizers help us to organize or picture our thoughts. Look back carefully at the story. Think about what happened on the night Julia was killed. Use a Sequence Chain to show the order of events as they happened that night. This graphic organizer is described in Appendix A.

 ### Media

More than 200 films have been made of Sherlock Holmes stories. Check your media center to see which films are available. Or ask your teacher to rent one from a video store. View the film as a class. Then read the story that the film was based on. How is watching the film different from reading the story? Which do you prefer? Why?

BEFORE READING THE SELECTION

Death Arrives on Schedule   by Hansjörg Martin (trans. by Charles E. Pederson)

About the Author

Hansjörg Martin was born in 1920 in Leipzig, Germany. He served in the German army during World War II. After the war, he held many jobs. He was an artist, clown, decorator, stage set builder, editor, and teacher. In 1962, he became a full-time writer.

Martin was called the "founder of the modern German detective story." He wrote more than 70 novels and books of short stories. His books have been translated into at least 14 languages, with millions of copies sold. Besides detective stories, he also wrote scripts for television movies. His writing won many awards. Martin used everyday language in his writing.

About the Selection

"Death Arrives on Schedule" was first published in 1974. The story uses short sentences and everyday language. This story is different from other detective stories because it follows the criminal. It shows how the murderer plans and commits the crime. But the luck of this bad guy is about to run out.

Objectives

- To read and understand a detective story
- To identify the protagonist in the story

Before Reading continued on next page

BEFORE READING THE SELECTION (continued)

Death Arrives on Schedule by Hansjörg Martin (trans. by Charles E. Pederson)

detective story story in which the protagonist, or main character, usually solves a crime

protagonist the main character of the story

novel fiction that is book-length and has more plot and character details than a short story

Literary Terms Most **detective stories** have a main character who solves a crime. In this story, the **protagonist** is the criminal instead. The main character is the person that the story is about. Detective stories can be in the form of short stories or **novels**. A novel is much longer than a short story. It gives more details about the characters. It has a more involved plot. The plot is the series of events in a story. The parts of a plot are the exposition, rising action, climax, falling action, and resolution, or denouement.

Reading on Your Own In this story, the murderer is the protagonist. You will read about what he is thinking before he even commits the crime. Brainstorm with a partner. What do you think the mystery will be in the story? What do you want to find out from this story? Write a sentence stating what you hope to learn.

Writing on Your Own Do you remember a time when someone did something mean to you? Write a paragraph about what happened. Make sure that the person who was mean to you is the protagonist.

Vocabulary Focus The title of this story is "Death Arrives on Schedule." The word *schedule* has several meanings. List some different meanings for the word. Which of these meanings makes sense in the title? For each meaning of *schedule* that you have listed, write a sentence using the word. Decide which meaning the author had in mind when he wrote the title.

Think Before You Read Preview the notes in the margins of the story. What do you think the story will be about?

Death Arrives on Schedule

At a time in his life when he possessed almost everything a man could want, Alfred Algernissen's eyes fell on Loni Leisegang. And his heart beat as it never had before. His wealth, his luxury limousine, his **exclusive bungalow** home, everything became unimportant—everything but Loni Leisegang, whose looks (and this must be said both to explain and to defend Alfred Algernissen's behavior) had already caused many other men to lose their heads in the same way. Besides, it's understandable why men might lose their heads over Loni. After all, chestnut-red hair and green eyes like Loni's are the best guarantee of masculine head loss. And when such hair and eyes crown a **regally** curvy shape, men might even become **aggressive**. Alfred Algernissen became aggressive.

It was not Loni Leisegang's fault (or **merit**, if you prefer) that she met Alfred Algernissen at a party. It's not her fault that she led him to understand that she certainly was not against aggressiveness, or at least not against certain *kinds* of aggressiveness—and especially not against rich **aggressors** such as Alfred Algernissen obviously was. In any case, it cannot be proven whether Loni's **inclination** toward violence included at this point the idea of her becoming a widow.

> As you read, think about why the characters act as they do.

> Notice the exposition of the plot here.

> This story is all about Alfred Algernissen. He is the protagonist.

---

exclusive having a lot of style; in fashion

bungalow a low, one-story house

regally in a royal way

aggressive ready to do combat

merit a positive quality

aggressors aggressive people

inclination a way of thinking

Fiction Unit 1

> Do you think Loni wants her husband to be killed?

> *Herr* is German for *Mr.*

> This detective story is about a murder. As you read what happens, look for the mystery.

> Do you think Algernissen will get away with his plan?

Financial broker Helfried Leisegang, Loni's husband, was far too healthy for thoughts of widowhood, anyway.

Herr Leisegang's only real **passion** was whiskey. Because of this passion, he had lost his driver's license several months before. That his passion had put him on the quickest path to losing his wife, too, had not yet become clear to him. And that shortly, he would lose his life—well, he could hardly **foresee** that.

Fourteen days after that first party, however, the fate of the whiskey lover Herr Leisegang was sealed. In those two weeks Alfred Algernissen had found three opportunities to test whether he and Loni were suited to each other. They found themselves so well suited, in fact, that Algernissen decided to win his lover completely. It was certain that Leisegang would never freely release his Loni. So Algernissen began to forge a plan that would help him sweep away, risk free, the only **barrier** to Loni's release: Helfried Leisegang himself. And because Algernissen was a self-confident and clear-thinking man, and because he had no taste for a years-long visit to jail, the plan grew slowly, was altered, rethought, and improved. Finally, it was so good that it led to an almost-perfect **murder**. And this is what happened:

Alfred Algernissen knew that Leisegang's company (Leisegang & Co., Building Contractors) provided Helfried Leisegang enough profits that he wanted to **invest** in property.

---

financial broker one who helps others invest money

passion an object of deep interest

foresee know in advance

barrier something that blocks

murder a killing of another

invest use money for later profit

So one beautiful evening, Algernissen called up the **hale** and healthy husband and said he had available 12,000 square meters of land to sell. Prime land for **development**. **Favorable** location in the country. Cheap. Inside tip.

Leisegang was extremely interested.

Algernissen gave him a few other tempting **tidbits**. The very healthy candidate for death promptly took the bait.

They agreed to take a look at the property the day after tomorrow. Algernissen told Leisegang that it lay near Nienburg, about a hundred kilometers, or an hour's drive, outside the city. Naturally, Leisegang swore himself to **absolute secrecy**—if only in his own interest. Algernissen offered to pick him up by car—yes, early in the morning, how did seven-thirty sound? That's okay with you? Great, thank you!

The evening before the meeting, Algernissen called again: "Sorry, Leisegang, slight problem. This afternoon I went out to the property and . . ."

"What has happened?" Leisegang interrupted, shocked. "Has the property been sold?"

"No, no, of course not. It's just that—well, my car went on strike! Something with the **ignition**. I don't know anything about cars. I just dropped it off at the repair shop. They said they'll drive it over to the Nienburg train station by tomorrow morning. I have a second key. We'll have to—if you're still interested, as I assume you are?—we'll have to take the train

Here is the rising action of the plot.

12,000 square meters of land is about three acres.

Why is Leisegang called "a very healthy candidate for death"?

100 kilometers is about 60 miles.

Do you think Algernissen's car is really at the repair shop?

---

hale full of life
development an area prepared for commercial use
favorable promoting success
tidbits small bits of knowledge
absolute complete
secrecy the condition of being hidden
ignition a car's starter

Fiction Unit 1

Hamburg is a large seaport in northern Germany.

over, and then drive back to Hamburg in my car. Sorry about the **inconvenience** . . ."

"Don't worry about it," said Leisegang, "it's no trouble at all. Maybe taking a **rental** car to pick up your car would be best . . . ?"

"I can't drive two cars at once," Algernissen patiently explained. "And you have no driver's license, if I remember correctly."

"That's right," Leisegang said with a curse. "Then we'll take the train. Have you already looked into connections, or should I?"

Algernissen had already done so. In fact, he had found a fine connection. He had sat for almost two hours studying the timetables until he had found exactly the right train—or rather, the right trains. He told Leisegang that a train left the central Hamburg train **terminal**, track 11, at 8:24 the next morning, arriving in Nienburg at 9:58. They could meet on the track 11 platform.

inconvenience trouble or annoyance	**rental** available to be rented	**terminal** station

Leisegang had three more whiskeys—the last ones in this life—and went to sleep next to Loni about eleven. He fell asleep right away while she read. It can be assumed that she knew nothing, though perhaps she had a feeling something was going to happen.

Algernissen, meanwhile, had packed a small suitcase and laid out and rechecked his train tickets and schedule. He loaded his small pistol, set the safety, and pocketed it in his loose, double-sided jacket. He had bought the gun a week earlier from a dealer in Frankfurt. In the morning, shortly before eight, Algernissen boarded the express train for Munich, which **originated** in Hamburg, and which—as he had found out by asking careful questions—was always ready a half hour before departure.

He walked down the corridor of the still-empty train, said a few friendly words to the conductor, and finally found a second-class **compartment** in which an elderly couple sat. They were full of travel fever.

Algernissen lifted his suitcase into the luggage rack above the vacant third seat and chatted with the **elderly** couple. He made fun of himself for always being too early, always too excited at the prospect of traveling, and now they had a half hour before departure—but better thirty minutes too early than thirty minutes too late, right? Ha ha!

He asked the elderly pair to watch his suitcase, saying he was just going to slip out for a quick smoke and a magazine, then head over to the dining car for a bit of breakfast. "At the latest, I'm sure I'll be back by the time we reach Hannover, full and contented," he said after hearing that they were going only as far as Würzburg.

At 8:13, twenty minutes before the express was to depart, he stepped off the train. He crossed to track 11, putting on sunglasses as he went—although even outside there was no sun to speak of, and certainly none inside the train terminal.

> Do you think Loni really "knew nothing"?

> *Frankfurt* is a large city in central Germany. *Munich* is far to the south.

> Algernissen is "proving" he will be on the train.

> On its way to Munich, the train will stop in *Hannover. Nienburg* is about 20 miles away. *Würzburg* is farther south.

---

originated started   **compartment** an enclosed space   **elderly** old

Fiction Unit 1

> Why does Algernissen turn his jacket inside out and put on sunglasses?

> Algernissen rented this car. His own car is parked in Hamburg, as you will see.

> Algernissen wants to reach Hannover before the Hamburg-to-Munich train arrives.

He greeted Leisegang, who was already nervously waiting for him. They climbed aboard this train, which was bound for Nienburg. That train left the terminal three minutes later, with him and Leisegang on board. Crossing from the express train to the Nienburg train, Algernissen had turned his jacket inside out—now the light-colored side faced in and the dark side faced out. And he was still wearing the same dark jacket and sunglasses as he got off the train again with Leisegang at the end of the line.

Five minutes later they sat in a car.

Ten minutes later they were leaving the village of Nienburg.

Fourteen minutes later Algernissen turned the car off the highway into a small woods, drove a couple hundred meters along a small forest path among the beech trees, birches, and firs, and stopped the car.

"Here?" Leisegang sounded **irritated**. "But this is certainly not 'prime land for development,' Herr Algernissen, is it?"

"Of course it is," said Algernissen. "Get out. I'll show you."

Leisegang hesitated—maybe it was an instinct that warned him of danger, or maybe he felt a sudden distrust of Algernissen. But finally he got out.

Algernissen had also left the car. He now approached Leisegang and smoothly drew his pistol, shooting Leisegang twice. He was surprised that it was not louder. He had feared it would be much worse. In the basement of his lovely home, where he had practiced for so many hours, it had seemed almost to roar.

Leisegang had no time for any other doubts. He died immediately.

Algernissen pulled him beneath a bushy blue spruce tree, hurriedly brushing over the tracks they had made as he dragged the body. He got back in the car and quickly drove back to the highway, which was empty—and from the highway to the freeway, where he got from the car everything its motor was capable of. He reached the Hannover train

irritated annoyed

station at the same time a voice on the loudspeaker announced, "Attention on track 3. The express train for Munich will arrive in several minutes. Stand back on the platform, please."

Algernissen grinned. He stood behind a pillar on the platform until the train had arrived. Then he stepped up into the dining car, took off the jacket—which he had reversed again so that the light side was facing out—and sat down at an empty table.

He must have returned the rental car.

He took a deep breath, ordered an egg, coffee, and cold cuts with double butter on the bread—and with a start saw a fir needle stuck to the leg of his pants. He discovered it as he bent to **retrieve** his lighter, which had fallen from his pocket. He quickly picked the needle from his pants.

After a good, relatively hasty breakfast, he strolled back to the compartment where he had left his suitcase in the care of the elderly married couple.

The fir needle comes from the spot where he killed Leisegang. Why might he be startled?

retrieve pick up

> A novel would describe the elderly couple in much greater detail.

> Why can't Algernissen sleep?

The woman slept. The man gave a **curt** nod to his greeting and to his "Thanks very much for watching my things" and then went on reading the thick book he held in his hands.

Algernissen carefully hung up his double-sided jacket and settled himself comfortably in his corner. He would have liked to sleep too, but he couldn't. After ten minutes, he stood, went to the toilet, and then remained standing in the corridor to smoke a cigarette.

The married couple left the train in Würzburg with friendly good-byes. In Munich, Alfred Algernissen climbed from the train. There he experienced a severe shock: his pistol had disappeared. He could have sworn that after using it on Leisegang, he had stuck it back in his jacket pocket. But it was not there now.

He forced himself to calm down. It was probably in his car, which stood in the parking lot at the Hamburg train terminal. He would find it when he went back tomorrow.

The next afternoon in Hamburg, as Algernissen unlocked his car, he was arrested.

The following police **deposition** had led to his arrest:

> I happened to follow the man, since I wanted a newspaper before our express for Munich left. I was surprised that he put on sunglasses and took off the light-colored jacket to put it on again with the dark side out. It also surprised me that he did not go to the newsstand, as he had said he was going to, but instead ran over to a different platform. There he greeted another man and to my astonishment climbed with him into another train, which left immediately. As our train pulled in to Hannover, the man was standing on the platform. He wore the

curt short

deposition a statement

jacket with the light side facing out again and no sunglasses, although the sun was brightly shining there. He got into the dining car and half an hour after that returned to our compartment. He acted as though he had been in the train the entire time. The man was not calm. When he left for the toilet, I searched his jacket. I found his car's **registration** papers, including its license number and, in the left-hand inside pocket a 7.65 caliber Smith and Wesson revolver. I was able to **ascertain** that it had been fired shortly before then. Along with that I found a train ticket for Nienburg.

> Can you identify the climax, falling action, and resolution of the story?

The deposition, dated at Würzburg on May 26, 19____, was given into the criminal records, signed by the elderly man from the train: Heinrich Hafermass, Criminal Inspector (retired).

Leisegang's body was found and shown to Alfred Algernissen. In light of the pistol, the train ticket, and the statement of the retired criminal inspector, Algernissen confessed to the killing. He was convicted and sentenced to life in prison.

> Hafermass is the elderly man. It is bad luck for Algernissen to meet a retired policeman.

Nothing could be proven against the attractive Loni L., and a short time later she married a film producer who promised to make her a movie star. Instead, he wasted her fortune before dying of a heart attack.

---

registration an official document

ascertain find out

AFTER READING THE SELECTION

Death Arrives on Schedule by Hansjörg Martin (trans. by Charles E. Pederson)

Directions Choose the letter of the best answer or write the answer using complete sentences.

Comprehension: Identifying Facts

1. What does Loni Leisegang look like?
   A She has blue eyes and brown hair.
   B She is very tall.
   C She has green eyes and red hair.
   D She is very short.

2. What is Herr Leisegang's only real passion?
   A women
   B whiskey
   C driving
   D real estate

3. Why does Leisegang have no driver's license?

4. There are two trains. Which cities are they bound for?

5. Why does Helfried Leisegang agree to meet Algernissen in the country?

6. What is Algernissen wearing when he goes to track 11?

7. Why doesn't Leisegang get out of the car right away?

8. What surprise does Algernissen find in the dining car?

9. What does the elderly man find in Algernissen's jacket pocket?

10. What was Heinrich Hafermass's profession before retiring?

Comprehension: Putting Ideas Together

11. How does Algernissen get Leisegang to take the train?
    A He says his car broke down.
    B He says he cannot find the property.
    C He says the property has already been sold.
    D He says he does not like rental cars.

12. There are two trains. How does Algernissen use them?
    A He makes sure to ride the train with his luggage both ways.
    B He rides the first train halfway. Then he and Leisegang change to the other train.
    C He does not know there are two trains.
    D He puts his luggage on one train. Then he meets Leisegang on the other train.

13. Why does Algernissen ask the elderly couple to watch his suitcase?

14. Why does Algernissen wear a double-sided jacket?

15. What is Algernissen doing when he is arrested?

16. Why does he confess when shown Leisegang's body?

17. Why does Hafermass follow Algernissen?

18. Name the three things that surprise Hafermass.

19. Do you think Algernissen could have done anything differently to avoid getting caught?

20. Things don't turn out well for Loni Leisegang. Do you think she deserves this fate?

Understanding Literature: Detective Story

A detective story is sometimes called a mystery. This is because a detective story usually has a mystery—like a puzzle that the reader tries to solve. A good writer does not give the answer away until the end. But the solution to the mystery must make sense when you look back at the clues the author used.

21. What is the mystery in this story?

22. What are some early clues about Algernissen's plan?

23. What are the elderly man's reasons for having the police arrest Algernissen?

24. How well did you do at figuring out the mystery as you read? Are there any clues that you should have paid better attention to? How can this help you as you read other detective stories?

25. Were you surprised by the ending? Why or why not?

Critical Thinking

26. How does the title of the story apply to the story's action?

27. Suppose that you were on the first train. Would you have gotten involved the way that Hafermass did? Why or why not?

28. How do you think Hafermass felt about solving the crime?

29. Do you think Loni Leisegang was involved in planning the murder? Explain your answer.

Thinking Creatively

30. At the beginning of the story, the narrator describes Loni's appearance. He says that her looks can "explain and . . . defend Algernissen's behavior." Do you think that this is a good defense of murder? Why?

After Reading continued on next page

AFTER READING THE SELECTION (continued)

Death Arrives on Schedule   by Hansjörg Martin (trans. by Charles E. Pederson)

Grammar Check

A colon can be used to introduce a statement that is an explanation of what came before it. On page 24, the author uses the colon to introduce the events leading up to the murder. On page 30, he uses it to introduce the police deposition. Writers should use the colon sparingly.

Writing on Your Own

Write a personal narrative as if you are Loni Leisegang. Tell what has happened to the different men in your life. Be sure to explain how you feel about it all.

Speaking

In this story, the crime is solved by a man who gets involved in someone else's business. What are your ideas about community involvement? Should people worry about their own problems and leave everyone else alone? Should people help others, even strangers in need? When is it too dangerous to get involved? Give a speech telling your ideas. Try to persuade your listeners to see things your way.

Media

Write a newspaper article about the murder of Herr Leisegang. Be sure to include the types of details you would find in a newspaper article—what you know about who, what, when, where, and why it happened. Also remember that a newspaper article is factual. It should not include your opinions or personal thoughts.

Research

Criminal investigators often use fingerprints as evidence. Write a list of questions you have about fingerprinting. Then do some research online to find the answers to your questions. Organize what you learned in a question-and-answer format.

Science Fiction

Science fiction imagines the effects of science and technology on life in the future. It is often divided into "sci-fi" and fantasy. Sci-fi may try to predict what the world will be like in the future. It may take place on another planet, or even in different dimensions of time. Fantasy includes tales with objects that can talk or characters who save the day with unusual powers.

In science fiction, the writer describes a world with certain rules. The characters in these stories help us understand our world more clearly. That is because good, evil, power, love, stupidity, and fear affect these imaginary beings and places. Often these things affect us here and now in the same way.

Since the world of sci-fi is different from ours, setting is a very important element. Readers who enjoy sci-fi are fascinated by the strange worlds created by their favorite authors. Writers, in turn, view their imaginary settings in many ways. Some science fiction is hopeful. Arthur C. Clarke (the *Space Odyssey* books) and Isaac Asimov believe that humanity will improve. The future will be a better place. Work will be less boring. There will be more excitement and challenge. Other writers, though, predict a loss of personal freedom. George Orwell's *1984* shows such a grim world. C. J. Cherryh in her *Alien* series and Frank Herbert in *Dune* see the future as a mixture of challenge and danger. They raise thoughtful and entertaining questions. Their writing is often a serious comment on present-day reality. These writers write about good and evil and excite our imaginations.

As you sample science fiction, you may find authors who share your view of the future. Many libraries and bookstores have special science fiction sections. Look there to find more stories like these.

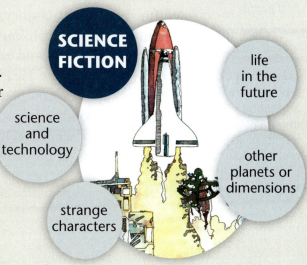

BEFORE READING THE SELECTION

The Feeling of Power   by Isaac Asimov

Isaac Asimov
(1920–1992)
American

Objectives

- To read and understand a science fiction story
- To identify the use of irony in a story
- To understand a parody

science fiction
a blend of fact and fantasy that imagines the effects of science and technology on life in the future

About the Author

Isaac Asimov was born in Russia and came to America when he was a small child. As a teenager, he began to write **science fiction** stories for magazines. He later earned a Ph.D. in chemistry and taught at Boston University. After that, he became a full-time writer of both fiction and nonfiction. Asimov wrote hundreds of books on every subject from Shakespeare to the Bible. One of the most famous is his *Foundation Trilogy*. It is a series of science fiction stories and novels. They trace the history of a space empire started by earth people. Asimov wrote many stories about robots. One collection is *I, Robot* (1950). In this collection, Asimov sets up three "laws of robotics." This set of rules seems to control the behavior of most artificial life forms in modern science fiction.

About the Selection

Asimov was known for his ability to predict the future. At the time he wrote this story, in 1957, computers were very new, and few people even knew about them. Somehow, Asimov saw that computers would become a big part of the lives of people in many countries. He even went beyond that—the characters in this story are completely dependent on computers. In fact, they seem to have forgotten that humans designed computers in the first place. Read to find out how people react when a man figures out how to solve math problems on his own.

36   Unit 1 Fiction

Literary Terms This is a science fiction story about Earth in the future. Science fiction is a blend of fact and fantasy. It imagines the effects of science and technology on life in the future. The people in this story are much like us, but they face a difficult situation: They are at war with another planet.

Isaac Asimov uses the war in this story to create a **parody** of what was going on in the United States in the 1950s. A parody is an exaggerated look at a situation. From the 1950s through the 1980s, the United States and the Soviet Union were involved in the cold war. This led to an arms race between the two superpowers. Many parodies use **irony** to point out the humor of the situation. Verbal irony is the use of words that seem to say one thing but mean the opposite. If the irony occurred, it is called situational irony.

Reading on Your Own As you read this story, identify the parody of the cold war and the arms race. What represents the United States? the Soviet Union? What represents the arms race? What can you conclude about this parody?

Writing on Your Own Do you have a talent for doing something well? Write about how you would feel if people made fun of you after you shared this talent with them.

Vocabulary Focus Many words are made up of parts known as suffixes, prefixes, and roots. In this story, the writer makes up the words *graphitics, firstcomer,* and *countermaneuver* based on real word parts. Choose four difficult words from the story and divide them into parts. Use a dictionary to help you. Then tell how you can use the parts of the words to help you figure out the meanings.

Think Before You Read This story is about a time when people rely more on computers than human thought. What do you think the story may show about how this affects people?

> **parody** an exaggerated, or extreme, look at a situation
>
> **irony** the use of words or situations that seem to suggest one thing but mean the opposite

The Feeling of Power

As you read, watch for ways in which the author uses irony.

The story takes place on Earth in the future. Earth is at war with Deneb, *a planet the author has invented. The war is being carried on by computers.*

Consider how important a Programmer-first-class would be in a world run by computers.

Jehan Shuman was used to dealing with the men in authority on long-**embattled** Earth. He was only a civilian but he **originated** programming patterns that resulted in self-directing war computers of the highest sort. Generals **consequently** listened to him. Heads of congressional committees, too.

There was one of each in the special lounge of New Pentagon. General Weider was space-burnt and had a small mouth puckered almost into a **cipher**. Congressman Brant was smooth-cheeked and clear-eyed. He smoked Denebian tobacco with the air of one whose patriotism was so notorious, he could be allowed such liberties.

Shuman, tall, distinguished, and Programmer-first-class, faced them fearlessly.

He said, "This, gentlemen, is Myron Aub."

"The one with the unusual gift that you discovered quite by accident," said Congressman Brant **placidly**. "Ah." He inspected the little man with the egg-bald head with **amiable** curiosity.

The little man, in return, twisted the fingers of his hands anxiously. He had never been near such great men before. He was only an aging low-grade Technician who had long ago failed all tests designed to **smoke out** the gifted ones among mankind and had settled into the rut of unskilled labor. There was just this hobby of his that the great Programmer had found out about and was now making such a frightening fuss over.

embattled locked in a struggle	**consequently** as a result	**amiable** friendly
originated began	**cipher** a zero	**smoke out** find; make known
	placidly calmly	

General Weider said, "I find this atmosphere of mystery childish."

"You won't in a moment," said Shuman. "This is not something we can leak to the firstcomer. —Aub!" There was something **imperative** about his manner of biting off that one-syllable name, but then he was a great Programmer speaking to a mere Technician. "Aub! How much is nine times seven?"

Aub hesitated a moment. His pale eyes **glimmered** with a feeble anxiety. "Sixty-three," he said.

Congressman Brant lifted his eyebrows. "Is that right?"

"Check it for yourself, Congressman."

The congressman took out his pocket computer, nudged the milled edges twice, looked at its face as it lay there in the palm of his hand, and put it back. He said, "Is this the gift you brought us here to demonstrate. An **illusionist**?"

"More than that, sir. Aub has memorized a few operations and with them he **computes** on paper."

"A paper computer?" said the general. He looked pained.

"No, sir," said Shuman patiently. "Not a paper computer. Simply a sheet of paper. General, would you be so kind as to suggest a number?"

"Seventeen," said the general.

"And you, Congressman?"

"Twenty-three."

"Good! Aub, multiply those numbers and please show the gentlemen your manner of doing it."

"Yes, Programmer," said Aub, ducking his head. He fished a small pad out of one shirt pocket and an artist's hairline **stylus** out of the other. His forehead **corrugated** as he made **painstaking** marks on the paper.

General Weider interrupted him sharply. "Let's see that."

> When scientists cannot multiply nine times seven in their heads, you know you have entered the world of science fiction.

> Why do you think these people need a computer to do simple multiplication?

9 × 7 = 63

imperative commanding

glimmered gave off a dim light

illusionist a magician

computes finds a number; works mathematical problems

stylus a sharp, pointed tool

corrugated wrinkled

painstaking very careful

Fiction Unit 1

> Do you think people used computers for all writing as well as all mathematics?

Aub passed him the paper, and Weider said, "Well, it looks like the figure seventeen."

Congressman Brant nodded and said, "So it does, but I suppose anyone can copy figures off a computer. I think I could make a passable seventeen myself, even without practice."

"If you will let Aub continue, gentlemen," said Shuman without heat.

Aub continued, his hand trembling a little. Finally he said in a low voice, "The answer is three hundred and ninety-one."

Congressman Brant took out his computer a second time and flicked it, "By Godfrey, so it is. How did he guess?"

"No guess, Congressman," said Shuman. "He computed that result. He did it on this sheet of paper."

"Humbug," said the general impatiently. "A computer is one thing and marks on paper are another."

"Explain, Aub," said Shuman.

"Yes, Programmer. —Well, gentlemen, I write down seventeen and just underneath it, I write twenty-three. Next, I say to myself: seven times three—"

The congressman interrupted smoothly, "Now, Aub, the problem is seventeen times twenty-three."

"Yes, I know," said the little Technician earnestly, "but I start by saying seven times three because that's the way it works. Now seven times three is twenty-one."

"And how do you know that?" asked the congressman.

"I just remember it. It's always twenty-one on the computer. I've checked it any number of times."

"That doesn't mean it always will be, though, does it?" said the congressman.

"Maybe not," stammered Aub. "I'm not a mathematician. But I always get the right answers, you see."

"Go on."

"Seven times three is twenty-one, so I write down twenty-one. Then one times three is three, so I write down a three under the two of the twenty-one."

40 Unit 1 Fiction

"Why under the two?" asked Congressman Brant at once.

"Because—" Aub looked helplessly at his superior for support. "It's difficult to explain."

Shuman said, "If you will accept his work for the moment, we can leave the details for the mathematicians."

Brant **subsided**.

Aub said, "Three plus two makes five, you see, so the twenty-one becomes a fifty-one. Now you let that go for a while and start fresh. You multiply seven and two, that's fourteen, and one and two, that's two. Put them down like this and it adds up to thirty-four. Now if you put the thirty-four under the fifty-one this way and add them, you get three hundred and ninety-one and that's the answer."

There was an instant's silence and then General Weider said, "I don't believe it. He goes through this **rigmarole** and makes up numbers and multiplies and adds them this way and that, but I don't believe it. It's too **complicated** to be anything but **hornswoggling**."

"Oh no, sir," said Aub in a sweat. "It only seems complicated because you're not used to it. Actually, the rules are quite simple and will work for any numbers."

"Any numbers, eh?" said the general. "Come then." He took out his own computer (a severely styled GI model) and struck it at **random**. "Make a five seven three eight on the paper. That's five thousand seven hundred and thirty-eight."

"Yes, sir," said Aub, taking a new sheet of paper.

"Now," (more punching of his computer), "seven two three nine. Seven thousand two hundred and thirty-nine."

"Yes, sir."

"And now multiply those two."

"It will take some time," **quavered** Aub.

"Take the time," said the general.

"Go ahead, Aub," said Shuman crisply.

> Why do you think the author makes a parody of the process of multiplying?

> *GI* stands for "Government Issue." It refers to a soldier or to equipment issued by the military.

subsided became quiet	**complicated** difficult; hard	**random** by chance; without purpose
rigmarole nonsense	**hornswoggling** tricking someone	**quavered** spoke in a trembling voice

Fiction Unit 1

Aub set to work, bending low. He took another sheet of paper and another. The general took out his watch finally and stared at it. "Are you through with your magic-making, Technician?"

"I'm almost done, sir. —Here it is, sir. Forty-one million, five hundred and thirty-seven thousand, three hundred and eighty-two." He showed the scrawled figures of the result.

General Weider smiled bitterly. He pushed the multiplication contact on his computer and let the numbers whirl to a halt. And then he stared and said in a surprised squeak, "Great Galaxy, the fella's right."

$$5{,}738 \times 7{,}239 = 41{,}537{,}382$$

Terrestrial Federation refers to a group of people on Earth.

The President of the Terrestrial Federation had grown **haggard** in office and, in private, he allowed a look of settled **melancholy** to appear on his sensitive features. The Denebian war, after its early start of vast movement and great popularity, had trickled down into a **sordid** matter of maneuver and countermaneuver, with discontent rising steadily on Earth. Possibly, it was rising on Deneb, too.

And now Congressman Brant, head of the important Committee on Military **Appropriations** was cheerfully and smoothly spending his half-hour appointment spouting nonsense.

"Computing without a computer," said the president impatiently, "is a **contradiction** in terms."

"Computing," said the congressman, "is only a system for handling **data**. A machine might do it, or the human brain might. Let me give you an example." And, using the new skills he had learned, he worked out sums and products until the president, despite himself, grew interested.

"Does this always work?"

haggard looking thin and tired

melancholy sadness

sordid dirty; selfish

appropriations public money to be spent on certain things

contradiction something that means its opposite

data information

"Every time, Mr. President. It is foolproof."

"Is it hard to learn?"

"It took me a week to get the real hang of it. I think you would do better."

"Well," said the president, considering, "it's an interesting parlor game, but what is the use of it?"

"What is the use of a newborn baby, Mr. President? At the moment there is no use, but don't you see that this points the way toward liberation from the machine. Consider, Mr. President," the congressman rose and his deep voice automatically took on some of the **cadences** he used in public debate, "that the Denebian war is a war of computer against computer. Their computers forge an **impenetrable** shield of counter-missiles against our missiles, and ours forge one against theirs. If we advance the efficiency of our computers, so do they theirs, and for five years a **precarious** and profitless balance has existed.

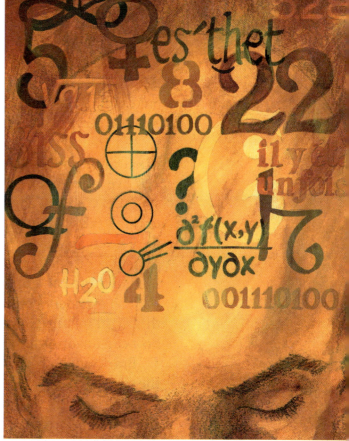

Forehead with Phrases and Numbers, by Lisa Zador.

"Now we have in our hands a method for going beyond the computer, leapfrogging it, passing through it. We will combine the mechanics of computation with human thought; we will have the **equivalent** of intelligent computers; billions of them. I can't predict what the consequences will be in detail but they will be **incalculable**. And if Deneb beats us to the punch, they may be unimaginably **catastrophic**."

The president said, troubled, "What would you have me do?"

> What is the irony here? Did some people once think that using computers was just for entertainment, whereas using pencil and paper was more useful?

cadences rhythms of speech	**precarious** dangerous	**incalculable** not possible to measure in advance
impenetrable not able to be pierced or broken	**equivalent** something that is equal	**catastrophic** terrible

Fiction Unit 1

"Put the power of the administration behind the establishment of a secret project on human computation. Call it Project Number, if you like. I can vouch for my committee, but I will need the administration behind me."

"But how far can human computation go?"

"There is no limit. According to Programmer Shuman, who first introduced me to this discovery—"

"I've heard of Shuman, of course."

"Yes. Well, Dr. Shuman tells me that in theory there is nothing the computer can do that the human mind cannot do. The computer merely takes a **finite** amount of data and performs a finite number of operations upon them. The human mind can duplicate the process."

The president considered that. He said, "If Shuman says this, I am inclined to believe him—in theory. But, in practice, how can anyone know how a computer works?"

Brant laughed genially. "Well, Mr. President, I asked the same question. It seems that at one time computers were designed directly by human beings. Those were simple computers, of course, this being before the time of the **rational** use of computers to design more advanced computers had been established."

"Yes, yes. Go on."

"Technician Aub apparently had, as his hobby, the **reconstruction** of some of these ancient devices and in so doing he studied the details of their workings and found he could imitate them. The multiplication I just performed for you is an imitation of the workings of a computer."

"Amazing!"

The congressman coughed gently, "If I may make another point, Mr. President— The further we can develop this thing, the more we can **divert** our Federal effort from computer production and computer maintenance. As the human brain takes over, more of our energy can be directed into peacetime

---

finite limited
rational based on reason

reconstruction the rebuilding of something

divert turn aside

pursuits and the **impingement** of war on the ordinary man will be less. This will be most advantageous for the party in power, of course."

"Ah," said the president, "I see your point. Well, sit down, Congressman, sit down. I want some time to think about this. —But meanwhile, show me that multiplication trick again. Let's see if I can't catch the point of it."

Programmer Shuman did not try to hurry matters. Loesser was **conservative**, very conservative, and liked to deal with computers as his father and grandfather had. Still, he controlled the West European computer combine, and if he could be persuaded to join Project Number in full enthusiasm, a great deal would be accomplished.

But Loesser was holding back. He said, "I'm not sure I like the idea of relaxing our hold on computers. The human mind is a **capricious** thing. The computer will give the same answer to the same problem each time. What guarantee have we that the human mind will do the same?"

"The human mind, Computer Loesser, only **manipulates** facts. It doesn't matter whether the human mind or a machine does it. They are just tools."

"Yes, yes. I've gone over your **ingenious** demonstration that the mind can duplicate the computer but it seems to me a little in the air. I'll grant the theory but what reason have we for thinking that theory can be converted to practice?"

"I think we have reason, sir. After all, computers have not always existed. The cave men with their triremes, stone axes, and railroads had no computers."

"And possibly they did not compute."

"You know better than that. Even the building of a railroad or a ziggurat called for some computing, and that must have been without computers as we know them."

Triremes are ancient Greek or Roman warships. A *ziggurat* is an ancient tower built something like a pyramid.

---

impingement the act of intruding or disturbing

conservative not liking change

capricious acting on impulse; hard to predict

manipulates handles or manages

ingenious clever

Fiction Unit 1   45

> What other words can you think of that are also based on the root *graph-*?

> What does this tell you about life on Earth during the time of this story?

> What do you think *mass-transference* could mean here?

> *Transcendental function* refers to a function that cannot be expressed by a limited number of operations.

"Do you suggest they computed in the fashion you demonstrate?"

"Probably not. After all, this method—we call it 'graphitics,' by the way, from the old European word 'grapho' meaning 'to write'—is developed from the computers themselves so it cannot have **antedated** them. Still, the cave men must have had some method, eh?"

"Lost arts! If you're going to talk about lost arts—"

"No, no. I'm not a lost art enthusiast, though I don't say there may not be some. After all, man was eating grain before **hydroponics**, and if the primitives ate grain, they must have grown it in soil. What else could they have done?"

"I don't know, but I'll believe in soil-growing when I see someone grow grain in soil. And I'll believe in making fire by rubbing two pieces of flint together when I see that, too."

Shuman grew **placative**. "Well, let's stick to graphitics. It's just part of the process of **etherealization**. Transportation by means of bulky **contrivances** is giving way to direct mass-transference. Communications devices become less massive and more efficient constantly. For that matter, compare your pocket computer with the massive jobs of a thousand years ago. Why not, then, the last step of doing away with computers altogether? Come, sir, Project Number is a going concern; progress is already headlong. But we want your help. If patriotism doesn't move you, consider the **intellectual** adventure involved."

Loesser said **skeptically**, "What progress? What can you do beyond multiplication? Can you integrate a transcendental function?"

"In time, sir. In time. In the last month I have learned to handle division. I can determine, and correctly, integral quotients and decimal quotients."

---

antedated came before

hydroponics a method of growing plants in water

placative calming; ready to ease another person's mind

etherealization making things lighter

contrivances mechanical devices

intellectual having to do with the mind

skeptically with doubt

"Decimal quotients? To how many places?"

Programmer Shuman tried to keep his tone casual. "Any number!"

Loesser's jaw dropped. "Without a computer?"

"Set me a problem."

"Divide twenty-seven by thirteen. Take it to six places."

Five minutes later, Shuman said, "Two point oh seven six nine two three."

Loesser checked it. "Well, now, that's amazing. Multiplication didn't impress me too much because it involved **integers** after all, and I thought trick manipulation might do it. But decimals—"

"And that is not all. There is a new development that is, so far, top secret and which, strictly speaking, I ought not to mention. Still— We may have made a **breakthrough** on the square root front."

"Square roots?"

"It involves some tricky points and we haven't licked the bugs yet, but Technician Aub, the man who invented the science and who has an amazing **intuition** in connection with it, maintains he has the problem almost solved. And he is only a Technician. A man like yourself, a trained and talented mathematician, ought to have no difficulty."

"Square roots," muttered Loesser, attracted.

"Cube roots, too. Are you with us?"

Loesser's hand thrust out suddenly, "Count me in."

General Weider stumped his way back and forth at the head of the room and addressed his listeners after the fashion of a savage teacher facing a group of **recalcitrant** students. It made no difference to the general that they were the civilian scientists heading Project Number. The general was the over-all head, and he so considered himself at every waking moment.

He said, "Now square roots are all fine. I can't do them myself and I don't understand the methods, but they're fine.

> This conversation is about various kinds of mathematical processes. A *quotient* is the answer in a division problem. It can be a whole number *(integral)* or a *decimal*.

integers whole numbers such as 1, 2, 3	**intuition** a way of knowing without proof	**recalcitrant** stubborn; resisting authority
breakthrough a major accomplishment		

Fiction Unit 1 47

Still, the Project will not be sidetracked into what some of you call the **fundamentals**. You can play with graphitics any way you want to after the war is over, but right now we have **specific** and very practical problems to solve."

In a far corner, Technician Aub listened with painful attention. He was no longer a Technician, of course, having been relieved of his duties and assigned to the project, with a fine-sounding title and good pay. But, of course, the social distinction remained and the highly placed scientific leaders could never bring themselves to admit him to their ranks on a footing of **equality**. Nor, to do Aub justice, did he, himself, wish it. He was as uncomfortable with them as they with him.

The general was saying, "Our goal is a simple one, gentlemen; the replacement of the computer. A ship that can navigate space without a computer on board can be constructed in one fifth the time and at one tenth the expense of a computer-**laden** ship. We could build fleets five times, ten times, as great as Deneb could if we could but **eliminate** the computer.

"And I see something even beyond this. It may be fantastic now; a mere dream; but in the future I see the manned missile!"

There was an instant murmur from the audience.

The general drove on. "At the present time, our chief bottleneck is the fact that missiles are limited in intelligence. The computer controlling them can only be so large, and for that reason they can meet the changing nature of anti-missile defenses in an unsatisfactory way. Few missiles, if any, accomplish their goal and missile warfare is coming to a dead end; for the enemy, fortunately, as well as for ourselves.

"On the other hand, a missile with a man or two within, controlling flight by graphitics, would be lighter, more mobile, more intelligent. It would give us a lead that might well mean the margin of victory. Besides which, gentlemen, the **exigencies** of war **compel** us to remember one thing. A man

---

fundamentals the basics

specific particular

equality state of being equal

laden loaded with; heavy

eliminate get rid of

exigencies things that demand immediate attention

compel force

is much more **dispensable** than a computer. Manned missiles could be launched in numbers and under **circumstances** that no good general would care to undertake as far as computer-directed missiles are concerned—"

He said much more but Technician Aub did not wait.

> What is the irony of saying that it is easier to lose a human than a computer?

Technician Aub, in the **privacy** of his quarters, labored long over the note he was leaving behind. It read finally as follows:

"When I began the study of what is now called graphitics, it was no more than a hobby. I saw no more in it than an interesting **amusement**, an exercise of mind.

"When Project Number began, I thought that others were wiser than I; that graphitics might be put to practical use as a benefit to mankind, to aid in the production of really practical mass-transference devices perhaps. But now I see it is to be used only for death and destruction.

"I cannot face the responsibility involved in having invented graphitics."

He then deliberately turned the focus of a protein-depolarizer on himself and fell instantly and painlessly dead.

> The *protein-depolarizer* is a weapon of science fiction.

They stood over the grave of the little Technician while tribute was paid to the greatness of his discovery.

Programmer Shuman bowed his head along with the rest of them, but remained unmoved. The Technician had done his share and was no longer needed, after all. He might have started graphitics, but now that it had started, it would carry on by itself **overwhelmingly**, triumphantly, until manned missiles were possible with who knew what else.

Nine times seven, thought Shuman with deep satisfaction, is sixty-three, and I don't need a computer to tell me so. The computer is in my own head.

And it was amazing the feeling of power that gave him.

---

dispensable not necessary

circumstances conditions

privacy state of being alone, away from others

amusement entertainment

overwhelmingly with strength impossible to resist

Fiction Unit 1 49

AFTER READING THE SELECTION

The Feeling of Power   by Isaac Asimov

Directions Choose the letter of the best answer or write the answer using complete sentences.

Comprehension: Identifying Facts

1. What unusual skill has Myron Aub developed?
    A He can read minds.
    B He can predict the future.
    C He can multiply without a computer.
    D He uses computers to solve problems.

2. What is "graphitics"?
    A a new kind of battle plan
    B erasing graffiti from the city's walls
    C a special type of art
    D using a pen and paper to solve math problems

3. Why is everyone so surprised when Aub finds the answer to 23 times 17?

4. What does General Weider mean when he says that Aub is just "hornswoggling" them?

5. With whom is Earth at war?

6. What kind of job does Aub have?

7. How did Aub learn the simple times tables, like seven times three?

8. Who first suggests the idea of Project Number?

9. What does Aub hope that graphitics will be used for?

10. By the end of the story, what has Jehan Shuman learned to do?

Comprehension: Putting Ideas Together

11. What is Project Number?
    A a secret project for people to solve math problems
    B a peace treaty
    C a building plan for a new Pentagon
    D a political campaign slogan

12. How will Project Number help the political party in power?
    A People will like the new Pentagon.
    B People will vote for the party that signed the peace treaty.
    C Most people want to get rid of computers anyway.
    D The government will spend more energy caring for people and less on the war, making them more popular.

13. Name one point that tells you the story takes place in the future.

14. How important is Aub compared with the other characters?

15. Why does Shuman's job make him so important in the government?

16. Why does Shuman think that grains were once grown in soil?

17. Why are the congressman and the general amazed that Aub can solve multiplication problems?

18. Why do the leaders want to put humans into missiles?

19. Why does Aub decide to kill himself?

20. Why does Shuman think that Aub is no longer needed?

Understanding Literature: Irony

Verbal irony is using a word in the opposite way from its ordinary meaning. Situational irony refers to an ironic situation in a plot. Often, irony is marked by a kind of bitter humor. Read each quotation from the story. Tell how it is an example of irony.

21. "He was only an aging low-grade Technician who had long ago failed all tests designed to smoke out the gifted ones among mankind and had settled into the rut of unskilled labor."

22. "A man is much more dispensable than a computer."

23. "The computer will give the same answer to the same problem each time. What guarantee have we that the human mind will do the same?"

24. "The multiplication I just performed for you is an imitation of the workings of a computer."

25. "I'll believe in soil-growing when I see someone grow grain in soil. And . . . in making fire by rubbing two pieces of flint together when I see that, too."

Critical Thinking

26. Find an example of exaggeration in the story. What makes it a parody?

27. Choose one of the characters. List some of the emotions he shows.

28. Does the author think that everything about technology is good? Explain.

29. Choose a character who has to be persuaded to support Project Number. What arguments win him over?

Thinking Creatively

30. Technician Aub is given a promotion. But the scientific leaders still do not respect him. The narrator says that this did not bother Aub. Would it have bothered you? Why?

After Reading **continued on next page**

AFTER READING THE SELECTION (continued)

The Feeling of Power   by Isaac Asimov

 Grammar Check

In some stories, the characters speak for several sentences or even paragraphs. When this happens, the writer does not always tell who is talking. This can make it more difficult to remember who is speaking. Look back at the story. Find a quotation that does not identify the speaker. Figure out who is speaking. Then rewrite the dialogue. This time include a phrase that tells who is talking. Make sure to use the proper punctuation. (Use quotation marks only around the words the speaker says.)

 Writing on Your Own

It seems clear toward the end of the story that Aub does not want to continue to help Project Number. What reasons did he give for feeling this way? Write a list of the reasons. Which reason do you think is most important?

 Speaking and Listening

In the past, people debated whether or not to allow high school students to use calculators. Have a class debate on this topic. Use the ideas in this story to support your views. Make sure to listen to your opponents' ideas. Do not interrupt each other. Be sure to present your own ideas clearly.

 Research

This story is about space travel to another planet. Choose a real planet in our solar system. In the library, research how far that planet is from the earth. Then research how fast the typical spaceship can travel. Figure out how long it would take a spaceship to travel from the earth to that planet.

BEFORE READING THE SELECTION

The Expedition   by Rudolf Lorenzen (trans. by Charles E. Pederson)

About the Author

Rudolf Lorenzen was born in 1922 in Lübeck, a seaport in northern Germany. His first jobs were in the shipping industry. He wrote many short stories and newspaper articles before publishing his best-known work, *Anything but a Hero*, in 1959. This book has been translated into English. It has also been made into a movie. Lorenzen has written novels, short stories, screenplays and television plays, and documentary movie scripts. He lives in Berlin, Germany.

Rudolf Lorenzen
(1922–)
German

About the Selection

"The Expedition" was published in 1974. It tells the story of four astronauts on a space journey to Cerberus, an imaginary planet. The voyage will take about 80 years. The travelers expect to have children and die before their spaceship can return to Earth. They plan for their children and grandchildren to take over. The children of the original four travelers will be born, live their lives, and die on the spaceship. They will never see the planet that their parents left and their children will return to. The story has been translated into English and Japanese.

Objectives

- To understand the conflicts the characters in the story face
- To explain ambiguity in a story
- To identify the denouement in a story

Before Reading continued on next page

Fiction Unit 1   53

BEFORE READING THE SELECTION (continued)

The Expedition   by Rudolf Lorenzen (trans. by Charles E. Pederson)

conflict the struggle of the main character against himself or herself, another character, or nature

ambiguity being difficult to understand; able to be understood in more than one way

denouement/ resolution the final outcome of the main event in a story

Literary Terms This story takes place over a very long time, so there are new characters throughout the story. Some characters die and new characters are born. In fact, the protagonist, or main character, changes during the story. Each protagonist has **conflicts** with the other characters and the situation on the spaceship. A conflict is the struggle that the main character has against himself or herself, other characters, or nature.

This story is different from other stories in an important way. The ending of Lorenzen's story is an example of **ambiguity.** We don't know what happens to the characters once they leave the spaceship. The **denouement,** or **resolution,** is the final outcome of the main event. In this story, the main event is the trip to Cerberus and back. Most readers end up having more questions than answers about how things worked out in the end.

Reading on Your Own This story has more than one protagonist. However, there is only one protagonist at a time. Why might the protagonist in a story change? Take notes as you read. Work with a small group to write down your ideas.

Writing on Your Own Sometimes parents and grandparents expect children to do certain things. Are there things that you feel you cannot live up to? Write about one of these expectations and how you feel about it.

Vocabulary Focus A compound word is made up of two other words. Most of the time you can figure out the meaning of the compound word from the meanings of the two words. List five compound words from the story. Write the meanings of the two word parts and then the meaning of the compound word.

Think Before You Read What are some conflicts you think the characters may face in living on a spaceship?

The Expedition

Part I

They came together for the experiment. Strictly speaking, visiting Cerberus, the outermost of the known planets, was no longer an experiment. The result of an exact **calculation** had already assured success. Both men and the two women who had come together were good calculators.

They met at the space station *Halifax*. One of the men was an engineer, the other, a chemist. They had known each other since they were schoolboys. Cerberus was thirteen light hours, eight minutes distant from earth. Nothing was known about its volume, density, or **rotation**. Leichrieder had discovered the planet two years ago. He expected to find methane and ammoniac gas on it. The two women came from Springfield. They were medical students in their eighth semester. They had become acquainted with their fellow travelers at a ball. They had danced well together. Now they wanted to go to Cerberus with the men.

All four **participants** were healthy. Knowing this fact was important, because the distance of Cerberus to earth was so great that there was almost no chance any of them would reach their goal. The trip depended on children, and those children depended on their children to bring back to earth the results of the expedition.

They went into the station bar before departing from Halifax. They were jolly. It made no difference to them that this was to be their last departure ever. To them, such expressions as

> As you read, watch for conflicts among the people on the spaceship.

> *Cerberus* is not a real planet. The most distant known planet in the solar system today is Pluto. Many other stars and planets mentioned in the story are real, however.

> Frozen gases surround the biggest planets in the solar system—Jupiter, Saturn, Neptune. They are mainly helium, hydrogen, *methane,* and *ammonia.*

> How does the trip depend on children?

calculation a mathematical process or answer

rotation the motion of a planet spinning on its axis

participants people who take part in something

Fiction Unit 1 55

"homesickness" and "Mother Earth" were foreign. They laughed at their parents, who were not **indifferent** where they died. "My father," said the engineer, "wants to die on the terrace of his summer home, with the sight of the Alps before his eyes." They all laughed. Even the barkeeper laughed. "Have you packed enough toothbrushes for eighty-six years?" he asked, but no one answered him. They had heard similar jokes ever since they had begun preparing for the trip. They had thought of everything. They even had plenty of diapers for the grandchildren. These had been placed in **sterile** packing, entered as Item 53 in the **inventory** list. Melanie, who was responsible for **administering** the supplies, knew the items by heart.

> In this part of the story, who is the protagonist?

Their spaceship was named *Galaxis*. Bruno, the engineer, was commander. At the moment, he was being interviewed by two reporters who had entered the bar to report on the start of the *Galaxis* for Cerberus. Bruno was annoyed that it was only two reporters. In the old days, such events had received huge **coverage**.

"You are counting on dying before reaching Cerberus," said one reporter, the one who wrote for a news agency. Bruno answered, "That seems certain. Under such conditions, who could live longer than seventy?"

"Aren't you afraid of being bored until the day you die?" the reporter went on.

Bruno answered, "We won't be any more bored than we would be on earth. Aren't you a little bit bored?"

"Sometimes, yes," said the reporter. Then he turned to questions about technical **data** and amount of supplies.

Olaf, the chemist, was just dancing with Vera on the small dance floor. "As I left early this morning," said Vera, "my mother asked when I was coming back. I said, 'Read about it in tomorrow's paper.' Then she asked where she could write me."

"I would definitely never make such a trip," said the other reporter to Bruno. "Just thinking that I could never again lie

---

indifferent not caring

sterile free from germs

inventory the stock of supplies

administering managing

coverage the way something is reported in newspapers or on television

data information

on the beach in the sun makes me uncomfortable."

"Has lying in the sun on the beach ever made you happy?" asked Bruno.

The reporter considered. "Sometimes, yes," he said. "Sometimes, no."

"There you are then," said Bruno, adding that the time had come, and he paid their bar tab.

They went down Corridor C to the starting pad. The two reporters followed them. They noted that besides the technical inspector, the inspector general of space station *Halifax* accompanied them to take leave of the four adventurers as they started this journey, which after all was still uncommon. The inspector general shook the hand of each. As the rocket left the base, the reporters went to the radio station to file their reports with their home office.

The ship was large and comfortable. It had come from last year's production at the Clavenna Works. All difficulties with handling had been reduced to a minimum. Heat, air pressure, and **humidity** were **self-regulating**. It was hardly necessary to touch the instruments. Still, Bruno never neglected to make his **rounds** every eight hours, as recommended in the training course. During his rounds, he also checked for meteor damage. But meteor damage was rare.

Mostly, the company sat in the main room of the ship, played cards, and listened to music from earth's radio stations. They looked through the portholes only now and again. They had all seen the pictures of a space trip in countless films—the ever-shrinking earth, the **waning** earth, the half earth, the crescent earth, the orange of Mars, the green spots on its surface. There was nothing new to it. First-grade children made trips to Mars all the time during school film period.

Meteors are small pieces of rock in space. Because the spacecraft is moving very fast, even a small object could cause damage.

Do the people seem excited about traveling in space?

humidity the amount of moisture in the air

self-regulating making adjustments without outside help

rounds a pattern of assigned duties

waning growing smaller, as the visible part of the moon

Fiction Unit 1   57

Asteroids are pieces of rock, smaller than a planet, that orbit the sun. Most are found in the asteroid belt, between the orbits of Mars and Jupiter.

Are the crew members completely on their own now?

A *primer* is a small book used to teach children how to read.

At the far edge of the asteroid belt, Vera had a child. It was a girl, and the company named her Astraea, after the asteroid that was closest to them in the belt. Bruno entered the event in the logbook, along with the exact time and their universal position.

After four years, radio reception with earth was weakening, three-quarters of a year later it faded out altogether. The last news reports that they could hear, Melanie recorded in **calligraphy** on a piece of tinted cardboard. In Nepal, there was a temporary truce. The post office had raised its rates. An heir to the Bourbons had married an Ostrowski in San Sebastian. The couple had ridden in a coach drawn by horses, a spy was executed in the electric chair, European beer **consumption** continued to rise. Melanie framed the reports and hung them next to the ship's rules and regulations. She had good taste in such artistic matters.

As they crossed Neptune's orbit, Astraea had already passed astronautical mathematics. She had learned to make entries in the logbook and to read the instruments. For the past year, she had been responsible for the care of the test plants. Her mother had trained her, urging her to take **conscientious** care of the continued **pollination**. In the following year, her medical training would begin.

Astraea's brother, Japetus, born in the vicinity of Saturn, had begun being able to read in his primer at this time. "The planet is beautiful. The moons are beautiful too. Our rocket is fast. I like to live on a rocket."

Melanie and Bruno's son, named for Uranus's moon Umbriel, still lay next to the map cabinet in the bunk that had been **designated** for newborns. A fourth child, Melanie's daughter, was due to be born. But there was no doubt that it would come on time. There also was no doubt that it would be a girl. Birth control and the **predetermination** of **gender** were

calligraphy artistic handwriting

consumption the process of eating or drinking

conscientious careful to do things right

pollination transfer of pollen to make plants fertile

designated selected for a role or purpose

predetermination arranging in advance

gender sex; male or female

reliable. One used Ryders-Schelde's tables, which were the most dependable, being based on hundreds of experiments.

Six years after exiting the angle of the **ecliptic** of Pluto, Olaf died. The ship was shortly to cross the orbit of Monokeros, a small, **eccentrically** orbiting planet. Monokeros, like Cerberus, had been little researched. Its brightness varied. Melanie and Vera agreed about time and cause of death. Bruno had Astraea enter the death in the logbook. Astraea wrote, "At kilometer position 7,862,447,350, on 30 October 2145, at 0:43:15, Olaf Tyde died at the age of fifty-nine years. Cause of death: **dystrophy** of the liver. Nothing else to report. No meteor damage. He was a good husband, friend, and father to us all." Bruno judged that the last sentence did not belong in the logbook.

Olaf's body was released into space through the airlock in Opening D.

After five years of elementary school, eight years of technical schooling, and six years of **internship**, Japetus was **certified** as an engineer. Bruno presented his diploma, which Japetus hung at the head of his bunk. The education of all the children on the trip was one-sided, but thorough in the specialties. They learned from their parents, and then from books in the various fields. At the end of their education, they knew somewhat more than their parents. They knew nothing of geography, history, or foreign languages. They had no experience of art, literature, or music. Even their parents had forgotten what they had known of literature, art, and music. But they did not miss it.

When Cometa was born, they had only ten years until arrival at Cerberus. Umbriel and Astraea had been engaged for a year. They wanted to marry within the next year. Astraea was the oldest of the second-generation children. Bruno had looked forward to the day when he could hand over command

> *Neptune, Saturn, Uranus,* and *Pluto* are the outer planets in the solar system. *Monokeros* is imaginary.

> What conflict is developing among the characters here?

> Do you think the children's education was better or worse than their parents' education?

---

reliable trusted
ecliptic circle formed where the plane of Earth's orbit and another object cross
eccentrically oddly, in an unexpected way
dystrophy illness caused by poor nutrition
internship a time of supervised training
certified confirmed that standards have been met

> How is Astraea different from the others on the ship?

of the ship to her. But Astraea seemed to lack the **aptitude** for the position. She was more inclined to dream. When she dreamed, she neglected her duty. One day, some of the test plants in her care died, and the cause was pinpointed as **negligence**. Bruno removed the duty from Astraea. The remaining plants came under Umbriel's care. In place of the plants, Astraea administered the wash, **disbursed** the dry soap, and distributed the vitamins. Only a pot of moss with boat-shaped leaves was left to her.

Cometa learned to recognize the sun as a tiny spot among the other stars. The sun lay in the constellation Great Dog (Canis Major) and was outshone by Sirius. Earth could no longer be seen with the ship's telescope. When Cometa asked what was happening on earth, her mother answered, "What does it matter? Everything is the same there as it is here on board, only larger. Be happy that we will be on Cerberus in a couple of years."

> *Sirius* is also called the *Dog Star*. It is about the same size as our sun but gives off about 30 times as much light.

One day Bruno began to suffer from panic attacks, although they were not based in his **psychic** nature. He imagined he could not get his breath. Many times a day, he staggered to the instruments, stared at them. He pounded his fists against the glass of the air pressure monitor and screamed, "Air! I can't get any air. The instrument is broken." The instruments were **functioning** perfectly. It was guessed that Bruno had a mild heart condition; but the medicine that Vera gave him did not help. The fear of **suffocation** constantly grew in Bruno, until one day he dashed into the air lock and also into the lockless Exit A, to get some air. He had to be overpowered by Japetus and Umbriel.

When Bruno's condition did not improve and he threatened to become a general **hazard**, the company decided he had to be killed. Vera gave him an injection. Japetus oversaw removal of the body through Opening D. While entering the death

---

aptitude natural ability or talent

negligence carelessness

disbursed paid out or handed out

psychic having to do with mind and spirit

functioning working properly

suffocation suffering from not having enough air

hazard something dangerous

into the logbook, Astraea was watched by her mother, so that no **extraneous** remarks would find their way into the official record. Astraea did not write that Bruno was a good husband, father, and friend, but only entered the position, time, and kilometer position. She wrote, "Bruno Perneder died at the age of seventy-one years. Cause of death: complications of **psychoneurotic** disturbances. No evidence of organic disease. Since early today, Cerberus clearly visible at 2° 12' to starboard. Nothing else to report."

When Melanie died eleven months later, Vera overtook sole command of the ship. She handed over complete technical supervision to her son, Japetus.

Four years before arrival at Cerberus, Japetus and Umbriel had begun daily preparations for the landing. They practiced the **maneuvers**, learned the regulations by heart. "Power units on. Approaching **tangential**. Rotate the machine. Stern forward. Check pressure suits before exiting ship." Every three days they held a general exercise to practice emergency **procedures**. Vera and little Cometa had to take part in these exercises too. Only Astraea was left in peace, with her logbook and her pot of moss. She was expecting a child.

The child that Astraea had was a boy. She called him Boötes. He lay in the bunk next to the map cabinet. Every twenty-four hours Astraea prayed with him, "Deliver us from meteors. And protect our equipment. Let us not suffer lack of oxygen, moisture, and vitamins. Lead us not into false calculations. And turn your eyes to us when we land."

As *Galaxis* reached Cerberus, Boötes was three years old. As the stay on the planet was to last two years and the child couldn't be denied a chance to go outside the ship and play a little, his mother made a little protective suit for him. With a small oxygen tank on his back, he sat in it at the foot of a

> As you read, notice a change in the protagonist.

> Are you surprised at how easily the group decides to kill Bruno?

> *Boötes* is the name of a constellation.

extraneous not necessary

psychoneurotic having mental problems

maneuvers changes in course or position

tangential change of course

procedures ways of doing something

> Does the work on Cerberus seem interesting or valuable?

pumice hill, building little **pyramids** of stones. Now and then his mother called him when it was time to eat his pills or his oxygen should be topped up. She said, "Be careful of your spacesuit! If you tear it, poison gas will come in and make you very sick!" At the same time, the two men undertook **excursions** over a wide area. They made measurements and tested the rocks and atmosphere. Leichrieder had been correct about methane and ammoniac gas on the planet. The period of rotation was one and a half days, the angle of the elliptic was nineteen degrees. These results had no practical value, as their distance from the sun was so great that day and night, summer and winter were unnoticeable. The test plants that were exposed to Cerberus died.

Only in the afternoons would Cometa watch the measurements. In the mornings she had school. She solved simple astronautical problems, studied scientific laws, and wrote compositions. Astraea gave her the topic "A Beautiful Day in My Life." Cometa wrote:

> "A beautiful day in my life was when we landed on Cerberus. My father and mother gave me a holiday from school on this day, and I did not have to study. When our ship stood firmly on the ground, I was allowed to put on my new protective suit and breathe oxygen from a bottle. That was very fun. Then I was allowed to jump outside through Exit D. I held little Boötes's hand. I played outside all day long, until Mother called and I had to go to bed. That was a beautiful day. When I get big, I will tell my children about it."

pumice a light rock from a volcano

pyramids figures with four triangles for sides

excursions trips

Part II

Almost two years later, the time that Bruno had calculated arrived. It was the best time to leave Cerberus and begin the return trip. Japetus followed Uncle Bruno's instructions to the letter, laid out in many carefully **compiled** notebooks. On the day before liftoff, little Boötes celebrated his fifth birthday. His parents gave him building blocks and puzzles. From Grandma Vera he received a picture book, "Hansi and Möpsi in the Milky Way." For the evening meal, Boötes got $C_6H_{12}O_6$ tablets—as many as he wanted. He was allowed to stay up two hours past his bedtime.

Ten years later, at his fifteenth birthday, Boötes's father gave him a do-it-yourself electric motor and a biography of explorers, called *Look Forward!* But Boötes did not like to read, and he also disliked building things, and was definitely not a stay-at-home type. His favorite thing was to play ball in the forward cabin of the ship with Lyride, his little sister, who had been born eight years earlier, and little Cassiopeia, Cometa's daughter.

Sometimes, when the children were too loud, Japetus came to the forward cabin and scolded them, "Pay a little more attention to your lessons. What will you do when we are all gone? Boötes, you don't even know how to regulate the heat and measure the air pressure!" But the children did not listen, they had no technical interests, they preferred to play ball. "What would your grandmother say if she saw you," said Cometa. But Grandmother Vera did not see them. She had been dead seven years. She had died shortly before the start of the return trip. No one was left alive of the first generation that had planned the expedition fifty-four years ago back on earth.

The company's worries about the children grew. Little Cassiopeia could not even understand the multiplication table, and Lyride refused even the simplest task her parents set her. She messed the supply rooms and mixed up their **vital**

> The writer gives the chemical formula for fructose, a sugar. Why do you suppose he doesn't just say "sugar"?

compiled put together information into a record

vital very important; necessary

pills. At fourteen she still chewed her fingernails. Her brother Boötes was not expected ever to pass the engineering tests.

So all hopes came to rest on Capricornus, the youngest, born to Cometa sixteen years after leaving Cerberus. Capricornus was a strong baby, and his father, Japetus, often sat for hours at the infant's bunk next to the map cabinet, speaking to the newborn. "Your parents," he said, "live only for you. They have never seen earth, and never will. When our ship arrives there, we will all be dead. Only you will be alive, and your sister, and Boötes and Lyride. But they are all ungrateful and can't see that we live only for all of you, they don't understand the sacrifice that we have made for you. We take on ourselves the gloomy, disgusting life of this miserable steel casing, the **monotonous** days on this pointless trip, the uselessness of our daily **manipulations**, so that all of you can one day land on earth. Boötes, Lyride, and your sister Cassiopeia do not understand that. So we live only for you, Capricornus."

Six years later, Japetus was still saying the same things to Capricornus. He sat at his son's bunk and said, "Our daily activities are useless, our life is disgusting, and this trip makes no sense." But Capricornus did not understand his father. He understood nothing, took in nothing that happened around him, did not speak, only made little gurgling sounds. His look was numb. If he did move around the ship, he crawled on all fours. Capricornus was one spoon short of a silverware drawer.

When there clearly was no hope of improvement for his son, Japetus killed himself. He injected himself with a poison **serum**. He felt no pain. Umbriel dispatched the body through the air lock. Boötes **sullenly** helped him with this procedure.

Astraea entered her brother's death in the logbook. Making entries in the logbook was one of the few duties that had been left to her. She was the oldest on board, but the company was **reluctant** to give her other assignments. Her **tendency** to

> *What conflicts do Japetus's words show?*

> *What does this phrase tell you about Capricornus?*

---

monotonous dull; boring

manipulations actions of control or operation

serum a liquid containing medicine

sullenly in a gloomy way

reluctant not willing

tendency a pattern of doing things a certain way

dream, which she had shown early in life, became stronger with every passing year. She was now sixty-four years old. In her youth, there had still been light outside the porthole, the sun was a small, glowing ball, one could see earth through the telescope. Astraea remembered hearing the radio when she was four years old. The programs from earth had sometimes come weakly and unclearly, often accompanied by static. On other days, clear and pure, came music. Sometimes someone spoke on the radio and reported happenings on earth. The last reports, which had been received sixty years ago on the outward voyage, Aunt Melanie had **transcribed** in calligraphy, framed, and hung next to the house rules and regulations. The document still hung there. A Bourbon had married an Ostrowski. That was in San Sebastian, and the couple had ridden in a coach pulled by horses. Truce in Nepal, higher rates at the post office. In Europe, beer consumption continued to rise, and a spy was sent to the electric chair.

    Astraea sat at her place near the porthole, looking into the darkness and the stars. She dreamed that the sun was a small glowing ball, and outside, everything shone with brightness. She dreamed of stepping up to the telescope and seeing the earth as a big, round disk, half dark, half lighted by the sun. She dreamed that music came from the radio, and that a voice on the radio said postage rates had gone down again and that the spy had been pardoned. She sat at the porthole, looking into the darkness. The moss with the boat-shaped leaves, which her Uncle Bruno had given her as a present, had died thirty years ago. The empty pot still stood next to her bunk.

    One day Astraea surprised the company with the news that **precisely** at this point on the outward trip, her father had died and been **dispatched** into space. Umbriel and Cometa were not able to convince Astraea that their Uncle Olaf had not died on this spot. "We have taken a completely different return path," said Umbriel, and Cometa added, "Dear Astraea, you're wrong,

> Are Astraea's feelings about life different from the others' feelings?

---

transcribed made a copy of   **precisely** exactly   **dispatched** sent out

your father died six years beyond Pluto. And we are now a year and a half inside Pluto's orbit." Astraea would not listen to reason. She sat at the porthole, looked out, and waited to meet her father's body. But she saw nothing.

Between the orbits of Pluto and Neptune, Cometa contracted a lung infection. She had chills, fever, and chest pains. Her **sputum** left no doubt about the diagnosis, and everyone wondered where such germs had come from. In twelve days, Cometa was dead. Umbriel took care of **disinfection**, and in the logbook, Astraea wrote, "Cometa died at age thirty-nine. She always had weak health. She was a good mother, sister, sister-in-law, and aunt to us all." When, only a few years later, Astraea's husband, Umbriel, followed his sister in death, she added a similar line in the logbook. No one stopped her from such personal entries anymore. Her children, Boötes and Lyride, and her niece, Cassiopeia, did not care what she did. Making entries in the logbook seemed **superfluous** to the young people. They left such games to Astraea, who had reached the age of seventy-one.

With the third generation, a new era came to *Galaxis*. The youngsters did not possess the strict outlook that their parents had, nor the sporting spirit of their grandparents. They lived only for the moment, expecting nothing of the future. Mostly the three of them sat in the main room of the ship and played cards. Astraea, watching them, was surprised at how **primitive** their card-playing was. The players constantly chose several random cards from the pile, threw them down on the table, and laughed. It was nothing compared to the **complicated** games with which their grandparents had occupied themselves, back in the days of the outward trip. But Astraea said nothing, stayed out of it, was happy that her children and nieces left her in peace.

She sat at the porthole, watching the stars. Capricornus chewed at her feet. He still could not speak, could not run.

---

sputum spit
disinfection getting rid of germs that can cause disease
superfluous extra; unnecessary
primitive simple or crude
complicated not easy to understand

This year he turned fourteen. Slowly over years, the sun emerged from the constellation Hydra. It became larger, gave light, soon was the size of a screw head, DIN M 8. "Day by day, I feel it getting warmer," Astraea said, but her children laughed. "The inside temperature is always the same," they said. "You're imagining things." But Astraea was not to be talked out of what she felt. "For seventy years, I've frozen," she said. "Finally, I feel better."

A couple of years later, it was possible to receive radio signals from earth. But the company made no use of the privilege. The music hurt their ears, the news was meaningless to them. Only Astraea would have liked to listen now and then, but her hearing was failing. Soon she would be eighty. She was also unable to see earth's disk through the telescope, her eyes were too weak. She sat at the porthole again, watching the sun through the protective glass and imagining that she could feel the warmth on her skin.

At Jupiter's orbit, the company gradually considered it might become necessary to learn how to land the ship. Lyride looked in her grandfather's papers and found a notebook that precisely described the landing maneuvers and all possible dangers that came with it. It is true that the notes were for landing on Cerberus; but Boötes thought that the difference of landing on earth couldn't be that much. They practiced the necessary manipulations and also **improvised** a way to use the radio. When they believed they had mastered everything, they went back to playing cards until they reached earth's vicinity.

The *Galaxis* landed, following radioed commands, at space station *Wellington*. At touchdown, there was some slight damage, but the company did not bother about it. They left the ship and followed the directions of the ground crew, who sent them down Corridor C to register. Boötes carried his cousin Capricornus on his shoulders, Lyride and Cassiopeia carried the crates of rock samples from Cerberus and the test tube samples of its atmosphere. They carried all the papers

> *Hydra* is a constellation of stars in the southern sky of Earth.

> *DIN M 8* is an industrial measurement.

> Why do they realize they are nearing the earth?

> Would the company have gone back to playing cards if Bruno or Japetus were in command?

improvised invented or put together on the spur of the moment

Fiction Unit 1

that had been issued almost ninety years ago: permission to depart, Bruno's commission, their grandparents' health certificates, and the logbook kept by Astraea. They were uncertain what might be asked of them. They had no experience with the **formalities** of a space station on earth.

Astraea remained behind in the ship. She had no wish to climb out and make acquaintance with the ground that her parents had left. A few years ago she had often thought, while sitting in her place at the porthole, what a space station might be like, or even how earth itself might look. She had looked at the sun and dreamed that she walked down corridor after endless corridor.

But the dream had ceased, and with the dream, her last wishes had disappeared. Astraea was eighty-four years old. As her children **debarked**, she said, "Leave me at my place. From here I've seen everything. I've seen all the stars, and I've seen the sun as it disappeared and came back again. As a child I saw the earth as a tiny point, and now as a great round disk. What else is there? What else don't I know about?"

So the children went without mother and aunt. At the end of Corridor C they found the registration office. They heard that their papers were no longer valid and if they wished to renew them, a certain fee was required. From registration they were sent for a technical inspection, and from the technical inspection to a physical inspection. The doctor gave them trouble about Capricornus. "How could you make a space journey with a mentally retarded boy?" the doctor scolded them, and Boötes had to describe in detail that the *Galaxis* had just finished a long journey and that his cousin had been born underway.

With the formalities taken care of, the four of them went to Counter G, where they could buy shuttle tickets for earth. Counter G was busy, a tour group had just arrived from the moon. The people stood in a long line before the counter. They had been underway for several days and were in a hurry because after the Easter holiday, they had to be at

> Think of how Astraea is the protagonist. Why does she stay on the ship?

> The doctor does not understand how long the *Galaxis* has been gone. Does anyone on Earth seem to understand this expedition?

formalities official rules; customs

debarked got off, as from a ship

their workplaces promptly the next day. Joining the line, the crew of the *Galaxis* briefly attracted the attention of these Easter vacationers. The tourists poked each other and laughed. They joked about Lyride and Cassiopeia, about their hairstyles and clothes. The tour group also joked about Capricornus, who sat drooling on the floor.

Meanwhile, a mechanic entered the *Galaxis*. He had been sent to inspect the damage done at landing. He met Astraea in the main room. "Well, Grandma, did you have a nice trip?" But Astraea did not understand him. The mechanic repeated his question. "Yes, yes," said Astraea. "The sun is getting warmer. I've frozen for eighty years." The mechanic laughed, tapping his forehead behind Astraea's back as he left.

Not long afterward, an inspector arrived at the *Galaxis*'s landing place. The mechanic reported the damage he had found. "An old grandma is sitting inside," he added. "She must be older than eighty. I always wonder what use these old people have with flying around in space."

"Yeah," answered the inspector. "I always think the same thing. We live in crazy times."

The mechanic said, "You're right about that, sir. Crazy times." Then he took a pencil and the pad of forms to write down the damage he had found.

> Why don't the inspector and the mechanic know that Astraea was born in space?

> This story ends without showing how the characters solve their conflicts. How would this story be different if it had a denouement that was clear?

AFTER READING THE SELECTION

The Expedition by Rudolf Lorenzen (trans. by Charles E. Pederson)

Directions Choose the letter of the best answer or write the answer using complete sentences.

Comprehension: Identifying Facts

1. About how long will the expedition to Cerberus and back take?
   A 80 weeks   C 80 years
   B 80 months D 800 years

2. What does Melanie do with the last news reports they hear from Earth?
   A erases them from the ship's log
   B frames them on the wall
   C publishes them in a newspaper
   D pretends she never heard them

3. Who gives birth to the first child?

4. Who is the first person to die on board?

5. Who takes over control of the ship after Melanie dies?

6. Who is Bruno and Melanie's son?

7. Who are Boötes's grandparents?

8. What does Bruno suffer from?

9. On the return trip, who is the only one who wants to hear the radio signals from Earth?

10. Why do the grandchildren have to pay a fee when they get back to Earth?

Comprehension: Putting Ideas Together

11. Who are the first women to travel on *Galaxis*?
    A Astraea and Cometa
    B Vera and Melanie
    C Sirius and Cerberus
    D Lyride and Cassiopeia

12. Why doesn't the first crew look out the window a lot?
    A It is too dark.
    B They are too afraid.
    C They have already seen many pictures of space trips.
    D They will be sad to see Earth fading away in the distance.

13. What is one way in which Boötes is different from his uncle, Japetus?

14. Why does Japetus kill himself?

15. How are the grandchildren born on the trip different from their grandparents?

16. Why do the grandchildren finally learn how to make a landing?

17. Why does Astraea put personal information about Cometa in the logbook?

18. Why does the company have to kill Bruno?

70   Unit 1 Fiction

19. What are two examples of Astraea's daydreaming?

20. What is strange about Cometa's death?

Understanding Literature: Conflict

Conflict is what makes stories interesting. If everything were perfect all the time, how boring that would be! Conflict is the struggle that the main character in the story has. (In this story, different people become the main character at different points in the story.) The conflict may force the character to grow or change. The conflict may be with something outside the character. It may also take place in the character's head or heart.

21. Think about the four people who started the expedition. Do they seem to have conflicts with each other? Give an example to support your answer.

22. What conflict arises over what should be put in the logbook?

23. What is the conflict between what Bruno wants for Astraea and Astraea's ways?

24. What is the conflict between Japetus and Boötes?

25. Give an example of conflict between Astraea and the younger people.

Critical Thinking

26. Why do Vera and Melanie make the expedition? Do you think this is a good reason?

27. Is it wise for the parents not to teach their children about art, literature, and music? Why or why not?

28. Was the trip worth it for anyone? Explain your answer.

29. The end of this story is ambiguous. We are not told the outcome, or denouement. Why do you think the author did this?

Thinking Creatively

30. Which group would you rather travel with: the parents, children, or grandchildren? Explain your reasons.

After Reading continued on next page

AFTER READING THE SELECTION (continued)

The Expedition   by Rudolf Lorenzen (trans. by Charles E. Pederson)

 Grammar Check

A gerund is a verb that acts as a noun in a sentence. Gerunds always end in *–ing*. A gerund can be used as the subject or object of the sentence. Consider these sentences from the story.

- *Making* entries in the logbook seemed superfluous to the young people.
- Astraea remembered *hearing* the radio when she was four years old.

In the first sentence, the gerund is the subject (making entries). In the second sentence, the gerund is the object (hearing the radio).

Write two of your own sentences with gerunds. In one sentence, use the gerund as the subject. In the other sentence, use the gerund as the object.

 Writing on Your Own

Think about the last travelers on *Galaxis*. How have things changed since their grandparents left Earth years ago? How do you think they will adjust to life on Earth? Write your own ending for this story, telling what happens to these space travelers.

 Speaking

What things would you need to bring with you on a trip that would last 80 years? Work with a group to make a list. When it is your turn to name items for the list, make sure to tell why those items would be important.

 Listening

Review a part of the story with a partner. Have your partner tell you what happened in that part. Make sure that you listen carefully to your partner's summary. Then give your own summary of a different part of the story while your partner listens.

 Media

Work with a small group to create a magazine article about the crew that is leaving on *Galaxis*. Use a word processor to type the article. Make sure to illustrate your article. You can draw pictures, or use a digital camera to take pictures of classmates posing as the characters. Use real magazines as a model to make your article as realistic as possible.

Adventure Stories

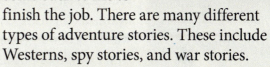

Adventure stories are like those you have read so far, but their appeal comes from their exciting plots. Certain authors are known for their writing about fast-paced, dangerous events. For instance, the bestselling American author John Grisham makes sure someone tries to kill his main characters at least once in every book. Adventure stories may be based on events that really happened or people who really lived. But they are still fiction because the author has imagined what it would be like to live through such events, and what people might have said or done.

The action in adventures rarely changes the characters. They may go broke, fall in love, or betray friends. Danger brings out the basic strengths and values of the protagonist. This is why adventures often make great TV or film series—or even computer games. You can always count on Captain Picard and the trusty crew of the starship *Enterprise* or *Tomb Raider's* Lara Croft to save the day. The protagonist might even have to die and come back to life to finish the job. There are many different types of adventure stories. These include Westerns, spy stories, and war stories.

These stories attract those who enjoy lots of action, suspense, and thrills. Adventure stories can take you to faraway places, where you do exciting things. You may never actually travel to those places or have such adventures yourself. By reading the stories, you can almost feel as if you have been there. Some adventure stories put the characters in dangerous settings and have them carry out dangerous actions. When the adventurer is in peril, you might be glad you are not in the same situation!

The stories in this section all have adventure. They also have brave and clever protagonists who use their wits and strength to survive.

Adventure Stories

action

danger

bravery

thrills

suspense

Fiction Unit 1 73

BEFORE READING THE SELECTION

The Cegua   by Robert D. San Souci

Robert D. San Souci
(1946–)
American

Objectives

- To read and understand an adventure story
- To understand how regionalisms add to the setting of a story
- To explain mood and action in a story

About the Author

Robert D. San Souci was born in San Francisco, California. He grew up in a family that loved books and reading. San Souci began writing books as a young child. When he was in second grade, he sent his first book to a publisher. This book was not published, but San Souci continued writing books. His first real book was not published until he was in college. Since then, San Souci has written more than 60 books and has won many awards. *The Talking Eggs* won both a Caldecott Honor and a Coretta Scott King Honor. He also won an award from the Smithsonian Institution. San Souci lives in the San Francisco Bay Area of California.

About the Selection

The story was published in 1987. It takes place in the rural countryside near San José, the capital city of Costa Rica. A young man is traveling alone on horseback. He is warned about a terrible monster known as the *Cegua*. It tricks careless travelers into giving it a ride. Then the Cegua kills the rider or drives him mad. The traveler decides to travel alone and take his chances. Find out if he meets the Cegua and what happens on the journey.

74   Unit 1 Fiction

Literary Terms Robert D. San Souci uses many **regionalisms** in this story. Regionalisms are words, phrases, habits, or customs that come from a particular area. The regionalisms in this story help create a **mood** for the **action**. Mood is the feeling created by the story. The action is what happens in the story. Regionalisms also help make the **setting** seem real. This story is set in the countryside near the capital of Costa Rica. The characters use words and phrases that real people from that area would use. As you read, notice how the setting adds to the mood of the story. What regionalisms help increase the story's suspense?

Reading on Your Own Around the world people have stories about local monsters or creatures. The *Cegua* is one of those types of creatures. Have you read other stories like this? With those stories in mind, predict what you will learn about the *Cegua*.

Writing on Your Own This story uses many regionalisms. These are words or phrases that are typical in Costa Rica. Suppose you were going to write a story set in your community. What are some regionalisms you would want to include? List these regionalisms and tell why you chose them.

Vocabulary Focus This story uses many Spanish words. Look for these words, which are in italics, as you read. Write the sentences that use the words. Then rewrite the sentence using only English words. Do you think that using Spanish words improved this story? Why or why not?

Think Before You Read Do you expect this story to be full of suspense? Why or why not?

---

regionalism a word, phrase, habit, or custom that comes from a particular area

mood the feeling created by a piece of writing

action what goes on in a story

setting the time and place in a story

Fiction Unit 1 75

The Cegua

> As you read, picture the settings in your mind.

> The word *cantina* is Spanish for a tavern.

> A *peso* is a unit of money.

> The name of the *Cegua* is an example of a regionalism. The term—and the legend—are found only in certain places.

> *Señor* means "mister" in Spanish.

One evening, a young man from San José, the capital of Costa Rica, rode into a small town north of the city. He was on his way to visit the ranch of a friend situated in a lonely area, but he wasn't sure which road to take out of the town.

He decided to stop in the local *cantina* to **quench** his thirst and ask directions.

When the **proprietor** brought him a mug of beer, he told the traveler he still had a fair distance to cover. "But," the proprietor warned, "no one travels these roads after dark. Stay here: I have a room I will let for a few *pesos*—then you can finish your journey in the morning."

The young man shook his head. "I have to reach my friend's ranch tonight."

The older man shook his head. "Only a fool would risk meeting the *Cegua*."

"The *Cegua!*" the traveler exclaimed. "What kind of creature is *that?*"

The *cantina* owner smiled, as if he was unable to believe such ignorance existed. "*Señor*," he said, "don't folks in San José know what the *Cegua* is? She is a demon—and heaven keep you from meeting her on the road!"

"I've never heard of such a thing," said the young man. "Bring me another mug of beer, and please explain what you know about this *Cegua*."

When the older man returned with the beer the traveler had ordered, he brought a second mug for himself. He sat down across the **rude** wooden table and said, "No one who sees the *Cegua* is left with a sound mind. Strong men, in the peak of health, have gone mad from the sight. Some have even died of fright." He began to rattle off the names of locals who had lost

---

quench to satisfy; to put out   **proprietor** the owner of a business   **rude** rough; crudely made

their minds or lives because of this monster.

But the younger man interrupted him, saying, "If she is such a terrible devil, why haven't I heard of her before?"

"She prefers certain parts of our country; we have the misfortune to be one such place," explained the proprietor patiently. "For that reason, no one here rides alone after dark. If someone must travel after nightfall, he always goes with a companion."

"Why? Doesn't she like crowds?" laughed the young man, who was beginning to feel the effects of his long ride and the beer.

"The *Cegua* only appears to someone who travels alone," said the older man gravely, finishing his own beer and starting to rise. "She appears as a beautiful *señorita*, smiling sadly and fluttering her eyes, pleading for a ride—but **woe** to the traveler who stops to help her! If the **unsuspecting** rider sits her in front, she turns her head. If he has placed her behind him, she will make him turn to look at her. In either case, his doom is sealed."

"How so?" traveler asked.

"When he looks, the beautiful *señorita* is gone. The creature riding with him has a huge horse's head, with monstrous fangs. Her eyes burn fiery red, like hot coals, and her breath stinks like *sulfur*. With a hiss, she will bury her claws in the shoulders of the rider and hang on like a wild animal. A horse, sensing that he is being ridden by a demon, will bolt in such a **frenzy** that no one can stop him."

A *señorita* is a young unmarried woman.

What is the setting at this point in the story?

Sulfur is often associated with the devil. It has a smell like rotten eggs.

| **woe** misfortune; great sorrow | **unsuspecting** trusting; not suspicious | **frenzy** a wild excitement |

> How does the mood of the story change here?

"What then?" asked the younger man, no longer smiling quite so broadly.

"Those who are found the next day, if they are still alive, will have gone mad from the sight of her."

"Nonsense," said the traveler, suddenly standing up and tossing down a few *pesos* to pay for the beer. "I must be on my way, if I'm to reach my friend's ranch tonight."

The older man shrugged, gathered up the coins, and turned away. Clearly, he thought to himself, there is no arguing with a fool.

The little town square was deserted. The traveler untied his horse from the hitching post and set out along the road the *cantina's* proprietor had pointed out to him earlier.

It was a warm night. Not a breath of wind stirred the leaves in the trees on either side of the road. Nothing disturbed the silence, except the *clop-clop* of his horse's hoofs on stones in the roadway.

> As you read, note the action.

Suddenly, around the bend, when the town was out of sight behind him and no other building was visible, he saw a slender figure standing in the thick shadows where the trees overhung the road.

Slowing his horse, the young man discovered a beautiful girl, with a pale face framed by the black-lace *mantilla* that covered her head, and which she held under her chin with her left hand. In the moonlight he could see she had curly black hair, huge dark eyes, and deep red lips.

> A *mantilla* is a scarf worn over the head.

"*Señor*," she began. Her voice was sweet, but so weak and weary that he feared she must be near fainting. "I am so tired, but I must go to see my mother, who is ill. Would you take me to Bagaces?"

"Of course," he said, bringing his horse to a stop and climbing down. Bowing slightly and removing his hat, he said, "My friend's ranch is just south of that town. You can spend the night there. In the morning I will escort you the rest of the way."

"You are very kind, *señor*," she said, in such a faint whisper that he had to lean close to make out her words. Then he helped her onto the horse—which had grown

restive during their halt—behind his saddle. He mounted himself, and they took off at a good trot.

A breeze had arisen to freshen the still air and flutter the leaves on the nearby trees. The moon and stars tinted the **landscape** pale silver. Several times the traveler tried to make conversation with the woman, but she didn't answer. She only leaned her head against his back and clung to his shoulders with her hands, as if she were afraid of fainting and tumbling from his horse.

Abruptly his horse, without any prodding, broke into a gallop. The woman dug her fingers into his shoulder, clearly afraid of falling. The young man was too polite to tell her that her nails were digging into his skin.

The horse gave a cry and charged down the dark road as though something terrible were pursuing them. The traveler pulled back on the reins and shouted, but it did no good. His horse only galloped faster.

Suddenly he felt **razor**-sharp teeth lock onto his neck so that only the collar of his coat saved his skin. An instant later, he heard a cry that came from no human throat as the awful teeth suddenly pulled away a mouthful of his coat collar.

He wrapped the ends of the reins around the fingers of one hand, and with his free hand he struggled to pry loose the fingers that were clamped on his shoulder. As shadow, then moonlight, then shadow

---

restive hard to handle

landscape a stretch of land forming a single scene

abruptly suddenly

razor an instrument used for shaving

again, washed over the horse and its two riders, the young man saw that the fingers clutching him were too pale—they were the white of bone, rather than fair skin.

He heard another screech and smelled the creature's foul breath. He felt his strength giving out, while the bony fingers pulling at him seemed to grow stronger. The jaws snapped at the back of his neck, this time drawing blood.

Then, ahead, he could see his friend's ranch. He thought he could hear dogs barking, to signal his arrival. Lights were burning in the *hacienda*. There were figures running up the road toward him, carrying torches.

> A *hacienda* is a ranch house.

There was a final, ear-splitting scream from the demon behind him. He felt his whole body jerked backward. The hand that was tangled in the reins pulled backward suddenly, causing his horse to rear up, then fall sideways. Both riders fell with the animal.

The traveler was knocked senseless for a moment. When he came to, his friend, holding a torch, was staring at him, asking if he was all right. He nodded, still shaking from his near-brush with death. When he touched his hand to the stinging at the back of his neck, his fingers came away bloody. He looked around **hastily**, but all he saw was a crowd of friendly-looking *campesinos*, countrymen, watching him. One was calming his horse, which was on its feet again.

"Where is it—the creature?" he asked his friend.

"What creature?"

"The *Cegua*."

"My friend," laughed the other man, "you stayed too long at some *cantina*, I think. The *Cegua* is a story to frighten children, nothing more. Still, next time you ride at night, be sure you travel with a companion. These lonely roads can be dangerous in the dark."

> What do you think really happened?

The young man said nothing, but he shivered just a little when the night breeze brought the **lingering** odor of sulfur to his nostrils.

---

hastily quickly

lingering lasting a long time; staying on

AFTER READING THE SELECTION

The Cegua   by Robert D. San Souci

Directions Choose the letter of the best answer or write the answer using complete sentences.

Comprehension: Identifying Facts

1. Where is the young man from?
   A Cantina   C Cegua
   B San José   D the countryside

2. Where is the young man traveling to?

3. Why does the young man stop?

Comprehension: Putting Ideas Together

4. How does the *Cegua* trick people into giving it a ride?
   A The *Cegua* threatens to kill the travelers.
   B The *Cegua* offers travelers money.
   C The *Cegua* holds a lamp to light the night sky.
   D The *Cegua* disguises itself as a beautiful woman.

5. What happens when the young man tries to talk to the woman?

6. What is the traveler's experience on the road?

Understanding Literature: Regionalism

A regionalism is something that comes from a particular area. It can be a word or a phrase. It can be a custom or a folktale. People in another region do not use that word or phrase. They do not practice that custom or tell that folktale. This is why regionalisms help give a story a local flavor. They help us understand the setting and the characters.

7. How does the writer give us an idea of the language of the region?

8. How is the *Cegua* an example of regionalism?

Critical Thinking

9. Do you think the traveler actually met the *Cegua*? Why or why not?

Thinking Creatively

10. The proprietor and the traveler's friend both agree that it is not safe to travel alone at night. They have different reasons for saying this. Who do you think has a better reason? Why?

After Reading continued on next page

Fiction Unit 1

AFTER READING THE SELECTION (continued)

The Cegua   by Robert D. San Souci

 Grammar Check

This story has many "If . . . then . . ." sentences. However, the author often leaves out the word *then*. For example, "If she is such a terrible devil, why haven't I heard of her before?" The second phrase could easily have the word *then* as part of it ("*then* why haven't I heard of her before?").

The *if* clause is a subordinate clause. This means it cannot stand alone as a sentence. It is not a complete thought. The *then* clause is an independent clause. It can be a sentence all by itself.

Find two "If . . . then. . ." sentences from the story. Identify the subordinate and independent clause in each sentence.

 Writing on Your Own

Think of a time in your life when you were afraid of something. Was it really something scary or did it turn out to be nothing to fear? Write a paragraph about that event.

 Speaking

Use your own words to retell this story. Give an oral presentation to the class telling what happened in the story.

 Listening

The proprietor of the *cantina* makes a persuasive speech to the traveler. Have a classmate read the speech that starts on page 76 aloud to you. Close your eyes and listen to the speech. Think about what makes the speech convincing. Then switch roles and let your partner listen as you read the speech aloud.

 Technology

Work with a small group to create an interview between the author and a TV host. Everyone in the group should brainstorm a list of questions that a TV host could ask the author. Then choose a student to act as the TV host. This person asks the questions and acts as the interviewer. Another student will act as the author. This person answers the questions as if he or she really were Robert D. San Souci. Another person will film the interview using a video camera.

BEFORE READING THE SELECTION

from *Master and Man*   by Leo Tolstoy (trans. by Paul Foote)

About the Author

Count Leo Tolstoy was born at Yasnaya Polyana. This was the name of his wealthy family's estate. The estate was south of Moscow. Tolstoy's parents died when he was nine years old. Then he lived with relatives. Tolstoy attended college but did not finish. Tolstoy later became a soldier and took part in the Crimean War. After the war, he began to write stories. Tolstoy married in 1862 and had a large family. While managing his estates, he wrote two of the greatest modern novels. *War and Peace* was written in 1865–1868; *Anna Karenina* was written about eight years later. Tolstoy worked to make life better for the peasants on his land. In later life, he wrote about morals and religion.

Leo Tolstoy
(1828–1910)
Russian

Objectives

- To read and understand part of a novel
- To understand the use of naturalism in a story

About the Selection

Master and Man takes place in the 1870s in Russia. The selection that follows is taken from this novel. This story is about Vasilii Andreich, a rich businessman, who gets lost in a snowstorm. Since Vasilii Andreich is very wealthy, he has servants. This makes him a "master." But, during the story, he experiences the troubles that face all people. This shows how he is still just a "man."

Before Reading continued on next page

Fiction Unit 1   83

BEFORE READING THE SELECTION (continued)

from Master and Man   by Leo Tolstoy (trans. by Paul Foote)

naturalism
writing that presents the world in a natural, or realistic, way; often shows characters and their environment in conflict

Literary Terms Tolstoy uses **naturalism** to describe a snowstorm in the woods. He presents the snowstorm and the woods in a natural, or realistic, way. Naturalistic writing is careful and avoids value judgments. It often shows characters and their environment in conflict. Conflict is the struggle of the main character against himself or herself, another person, or nature. In this story, Vasilii Andreich is in conflict with nature in the form of a snowstorm. He is lost and has no control over the weather and his surroundings.

Reading on Your Own This story is about a wealthy man, Vasilii Andreich, who is lost in a snowstorm. Notice how Tolstoy describes the man's experiences. Notice how Andreich's attitudes change in the story. Identify the sequence of events that cause him to change. How has he changed by the end of the story?

Writing on Your Own Think of a time when you have been lost. How did you feel? How did you try to find your way? Write about your experience.

Vocabulary Focus This story was written in the late 1800s. At that time, writers wrote in a more formal style. This affected their word choices, too. Write out three sentences from a paragraph in the story. Circle at least five words that you would like to replace. Then replace the words with easier words. Make sure that your new words have the same meanings as the original words.

Think Before You Read Look at the picture on page 88. Describe the picture in your own words. Think about your description as you read Tolstoy's description of the snowy woods.

from Master and Man

Meanwhile Vasilii Andreich was driving the horse on with feet and reins towards where for some reason he supposed the forest and the keeper's hut to be. He was blinded by the snow, the wind seemed anxious to hold him back, but **relentlessly** he drove the horse on, crouching forward and continually drawing his coat across him and tucking it between himself and the small cold saddle which stopped him sitting properly. Though with difficulty, the horse obediently went at an **ambling** pace along the way he was made to go.

For some five minutes Vasilii Andreich rode as he thought in a straight line, seeing nothing but the horse's head and the white wilderness, hearing nothing but the wind whistling past the horse's ears and the collar of his fur top-coat.

There was suddenly something dark ahead. His heart thumped with joy and he headed towards this dark something, already seeing it as the walls of houses in the village. But the dark shape did not keep still, it kept moving, and it was not the village but a tall patch of wormwood that had grown up along the edge of a field and stood up clear of the snow, frantically tossing in the wind, which bent it over and whistled through it. For some reason the sight of this wormwood tormented by the **merciless** wind made Vasilii Andreich shudder and he hastily urged the horse on, not noticing that in going towards the wormwood he had completely changed course and was now pointing the horse in a quite different direction, though he still supposed he was heading for where the keeper's hut should

> As you read, watch how Vasilii Andreich struggles against nature.

> *Wormwood* is a tall, weedy plant that has a bitter flavor.

relentlessly without stopping
ambling slow-moving
merciless cruel; without mercy

> Which do you think knows the way, the man or the horse?

be. But the horse kept pulling to the right and Vasilii Andreich continually had to make him go left.

Once more there was something dark ahead. He was **overjoyed**, certain that this really must now be the village. But again it was a field-boundary with wormwood growing along it. The tall dry weeds tossed and swayed as frantically as ever and **unaccountably** terrified Vasilii Andreich. But it was not only that the weeds were the same—alongside ran hoof-prints partly covered with blown snow. Vasilii Andreich stopped and bent to take a closer look: it was the lightly covered tracks of a horse and it could be no one else's but his own. He had evidently been going in a circle and in quite a small **compass**. This way I'm done for! he thought, but so as not to give way to his fear he drove the horse on more urgently than before, peering ahead into the snowy white gloom in which shining dots seemed to appear, only to vanish the moment he tried to focus on them. Once he thought he heard the bark of a dog or the howl of a wolf, but the sound was so faint and **indistinct** that he could not tell if he had actually heard it or if it was just his **fancy**, so he stopped to listen.

> What do the hoof-prints tell Vasilii Andreich?

All at once there was a terrible deafening cry right in his ears and everything shuddered and shook beneath him. Vasilii Andreich grabbed the horse's neck, but that too was shuddering and the terrible cry was more terrifying than before. For some seconds Vasilii Andreich could not collect himself and realize what it was. In fact all that had happened was that Dapple—for good cheer or as a cry for help—had let out a loud, well-tuned neigh. 'Cursed horse! Proper put the wind up me!' said Vasilii Andreich to himself. But even though he now knew what had caused his fear he could not shake it off.

> To *put the wind up* is to be startled or alarmed.

---

overjoyed delighted; very happy

unaccountably mysteriously; without explanation

compass limited area

indistinct not clear

fancy imagination

I've got to come to and get a grip on myself, he thought, but still he could not help himself and pressed the horse on, without noticing that he now had the wind behind him and not in his face. His body, especially in the crutch, where it was exposed and touched the saddle, was chilled through and aching, his arms and legs trembled, his breath came in gasps. He could see that he would perish in this awful waste of snow and saw no way of escape.

> Tolstoy uses naturalism when he describes Vasilii Andreich in the grip of fear.

Suddenly the horse collapsed under him. It was deep in a drift and began to struggle, falling over on its side. Vasilii Andreich sprang off. In doing so he pulled over the **breeching** which supported his foot and twisted **askew** the saddle to which he held while jumping off. No sooner had Vasilii Andreich sprung clear than the horse found its feet again and plunged ahead. It gave a couple of leaps, let out another neigh and disappeared from sight, trailing the **sackcloth** and breeching behind and leaving Vasilii Andreich alone in the snowdrift. Vasilii Andreich dashed after it, but the snow was so deep and his fur coats so heavy that with every step he sank in over his knees and after running some twenty yards he was out of breath and stopped. What will become of it all? he thought. The **coppice**, the **wethers**, the **leasehold**, my shop and taverns, my metal-roofed house and barn, my son and heir? What's going on? It just can't be true! And for some reason he remembered the wormwood tossing in the wind which he had twice passed and experienced such a feeling of terror that he did not believe that this was actually happening to him. He thought it must all be a dream and tried to wake up, but there was no other, waking world. It was real snow which lashed his face and settled on him and numbed his right hand

> Vasilii Andreich is thinking of his wealth and property.

---

breeching strap of harness behind a horse's rear legs

askew to one side

sackcloth rough, coarse cloth

coppice a dense growth of bushes; a small wood

wethers male sheep or goats

leasehold property held by lease

Woodland Trail in Winter, by Boris Walentinowitsch Scherkow.

Icons are religious paintings, usually of Jesus or saints. They are considered holy images in Eastern Orthodox churches.

whose glove he had lost; and this was a real wilderness, this place where he was now alone, like the wormwood, waiting for death, **inevitable**, swift and pointless.

Mother of Heaven, Holy Father Nicholas, thou who teachest the way of **abstinence** . . . he recalled the prayers said the day before, and the icon with the black face framed in the golden riza [robe], and the candles he sold for lighting to this icon which were then promptly returned to him and stored away in a bin, scarcely used. And he begged this same Nicholas the miracle-worker to save him, and promised to offer prayers and candles to him. But at the same time he realized clearly and certainly that the face on the icon, the frame, the candles, the priest and the prayers were all very important and necessary *there,* in church, but that where

inevitable sure to happen

abstinence stopping oneself from doing something; self-denial

he was they could do nothing for him, and that there was not and could not be any possible connection between these candles and prayers and his present desperate **plight**. I must not despair, he thought. And he had an idea. I must follow the tracks of the horse before they get covered. The horse will lead me **aright**. I might even catch him. The great thing is not to hurry or I'll get tired out and be worse off still. But despite his **intention** to go slowly, he hurried on and ran, continually falling and getting up and falling again. The horse tracks were already hard to see where there was no depth of snow. I'm done for, thought Vasilii Andreich. I can't follow the tracks and I'll never catch up with the horse. But at that very moment as he looked ahead he saw something black. It was Dapple—and not only Dapple, but also the sledge and the upright shafts with his kerchief. With the breeching and sackcloth pulled over to one side Dapple now stood where he had been before, only nearer the shafts; he was shaking his head, which was held down by the reins caught up in his leg. It turned out that Vasilii Andreich had got stuck in the same gully where he and Nikita had got stuck earlier; the horse was taking him back to the sledge and where he had jumped off was no more than fifty yards away from it.

A *sledge* is a heavy sled.

Kerchief is another form of handkerchief.

Nikita is Vasilii Andreich's servant.

plight a serious problem or condition

aright correctly

intention aim; plan

AFTER READING THE SELECTION

from Master and Man   by Leo Tolstoy (trans. by Paul Foote)

Directions Choose the letter of the best answer or write the answer using complete sentences.

Comprehension: Identifying Facts

1. What is Vasilii Andreich trying to reach?
   - **A** his estate
   - **B** his servant's home
   - **C** a horse farm
   - **D** a village

2. What is the loud cry that he hears?

3. Whom does Andreich beg to save him?

Comprehension: Putting Ideas Together

4. Why does Andreich get off his horse?
   - **A** The horse collapses in the snow.
   - **B** The horse has broken its leg.
   - **C** The horse throws him off.
   - **D** He wants to walk.

5. Where does Andreich finally find himself?

6. What does Andreich think is going to happen?

Understanding Literature: Naturalism

Naturalism was a popular writing style at the end of the 19th century. It presents the world in a natural, or realistic, way. The author describes settings objectively, not romantically. The characters are realistic and have to deal with real-life problems. A common theme in naturalism is how people struggle against nature or the environment. The characters do not have any special powers. No outside forces help them solve their problems. Instead, the characters must face their conflicts with the limitations set by real life.

7. What are some details that make the snowstorm seem realistic?

8. How is Andreich a realistic character?

Critical Thinking

9. How does this story make you feel about the power of nature?

Thinking Creatively

10. Tolstoy uses a snowstorm to show how a wealthy *master* is also just a *man*. Do you think that Andreich learned something about himself as a man by the end of the story? Why or why not?

Grammar Check

When Tolstoy was writing this story, most writers used very long sentences. These sentences included several clauses. Remember that clauses can be independent or subordinate. An independent clause can be a sentence on its own. A subordinate clause cannot be a sentence on its own. For example, look at this sentence on page 87: "It was deep in a drift and began to struggle, falling over on its side." The clause "falling over on its side" is subordinate because it cannot be a sentence by itself. You could make this clause a separate sentence by saying "It was falling over on its side." Choose a different sentence from the story. Notice the different clauses. Rewrite each clause as a separate sentence. You will need to change the subordinate clause a little so that it is a complete sentence.

 ### Writing on Your Own

Think of a real natural disaster you know about or have been through. (It might be a flood, storm, or hurricane.) Write a paragraph about the power of the event.

 ### Speaking and Listening

Pretend you are Vasilii Andreich. You have been asked to speak to a group of schoolchildren about your experience in the woods. Tell the children what happened. Remember to keep your audience in mind as you speak. Will you give the children advice about what to do if they get lost? Will you tell them how frightened you were? Will you tell them what you learned from your experience?

Listen carefully to your classmates as they give their presentations about their experience in the woods. Take notes as you listen to them speak. Use an outline to organize your notes.

 ### Technology

Create your own set of Internet searches for Tolstoy and his works. Begin by doing some online research about Tolstoy and this story. Write down your favorite sites. Add a sentence that tells what is on each site. Then write one or two paragraphs about Tolstoy. Include the topics that are covered by these sites. Underline the words that would link to those sites. Make a key at the bottom of your paper showing which words lead to which sites.

BEFORE READING THE SELECTION

Just Lather, That's All by Hernando Téllez (trans. by Donald A. Yates)

Hernando Téllez
(1908–1966)
Colombian

About the Author

Hernando Téllez was born in Bogotá, Colombia, in 1908. He worked for several magazines and newspapers. Téllez also was active in Colombian politics. He served as a diplomat and a senator. As a writer, Téllez is best known for a book of short stories, *Ashes for the Wind and Other Tales*, published in 1950. Téllez also wrote essays. "Just Lather, That's All" was made into a movie with the name *Just Lather, Please*.

Objectives

- To read and understand a short story
- To read and understand the exposition, rising action, climax, falling action, and resolution or denouement in a story

About the Selection

The following story is told by a barber. The barber is secretly a rebel during a civil war. In the story, he is shaving a captain in the army. Captain Torres hunts down rebels and puts them to death in public. As the barber works, he thinks about killing Captain Torres. The action builds with every stroke of his razor against the captain's unprotected neck. The suspense builds. Will the barber let the captain go? Will he kill him?

Literary Terms This story really takes place in the narrator's mind. He describes what is happening around him, or the **plot**. The plot is the series of events in a story. The plot begins with the **exposition**. This is the introduction of the story. As the plot unfolds, the narrator describes the **rising action**, or the buildup of excitement in a story. The buildup leads to a **climax,** or high point of **suspense**. After that high point, the excitement dies down. This is called the **falling action**. Finally, the story is brought to a close. This is known as the **resolution, or denouement**. As you read the story, look for these stages in the plot.

Reading on Your Own As you read, notice how the first-person point of view lets us follow the barber's thoughts: should he or should he not take action? Predict what he will decide. Does your prediction change as you read the story?

Writing on Your Own The narrator of this story writes about his thoughts as he is thinking of doing something. What have you been thinking about doing? Write a paragraph telling the advantages and disadvantages of taking this action.

Vocabulary Focus A good writer chooses words carefully. A word has a denotation, or dictionary definition. It can also have a connotation, or emotional meaning. For example, *shake* and *tremble* have the same denotation, but their connotations are different. People can *shake* for different reasons, people *tremble* when they are afraid. Look for these words in the first two paragraphs of the story: *conceal, tested, dangled, loosening.* Write a synonym for each word's denotation. Does the connotation affect the meaning in the story?

Think Before You Read You know that the climax of a story is the highest point of suspense. Predict what will happen in the climax of this story.

plot the series of events in a story; an element of all fiction

exposition the beginning of the story, or introduction

rising action the buildup of excitement in a story

climax the high point of interest or suspense in a story or play

suspense a feeling of uncertainty about what will happen next

falling action the action in a story or play during which the excitement dies down

resolution/ denouement the final outcome of the main event in a story, as when a mystery is solved

Just Lather, That's All

> Notice how the plot begins. This is the exposition.

He said nothing when he entered. I was passing the best of my razors back and forth on a **strop**. When I recognized him I started to tremble. But he didn't notice. Hoping to conceal my emotion, I continued sharpening the razor. I tested it on the meat of my thumb, and then held it up to the light.

At that moment he took off the bullet-studded belt that his gun **holster** dangled from. He hung it up on a wall hook and placed his military cap over it. Then he turned to me, loosening the knot of his tie, and said, "It's hot as hell. Give me a shave." He sat in the chair.

> Is this story being told in first person or in third person?

I estimated he had a four-day beard—the four days taken up by the latest expedition in search of our troops. His face seemed reddened, burned by the sun. Carefully, I began to prepare the soap. I cut off a few slices, dropped them into the cup, mixed in a bit of warm water, and began to stir with the brush. Immediately the foam began to rise. "The other boys in the group should have this much beard, too," he remarked. I continued stirring the lather.

"But we did all right, you know. We got the main ones. We brought back some dead, and we got some others still alive. But pretty soon they'll all be dead."

"How many did you catch?" I asked.

"Fourteen. We had to go pretty deep into the woods to find them. But we'll get even. Not one of them comes out of this alive, not one."

He leaned back on the chair when he saw me with the lather-covered brush in my hand. I still had to put the sheet

---

strop a strip of leather used for sharpening razors

holster a case for a pistol

on him. No doubt about it, I was upset. I took a sheet out of a drawer and knotted it around his neck. He wouldn't stop talking. He probably thought I was in sympathy with his party.

"The town must have learned a lesson from what we did," he said.

"Yes," I replied, securing the knot at the base of his dark, sweaty neck.

"That was a fine show, eh?"

"Very good," I answered, turning back for the brush.

The man closed his eyes with a gesture of **fatigue** and sat waiting for the cool **caress** of the soap. I had never had him so close to me. The day he ordered the whole town to file into the patio of the school to see the four rebels hanging there, I came face to face with him for an instant. But the sight of the **mutilated** bodies kept me from noticing the face of the man who had directed it all, the face I was now about to take into my hands.

It was not an unpleasant face, and the beard, which made him look a bit older than he was, didn't suit him badly at all. His name was Torres—Captain Torres. A man of imagination, because who else would have thought of hanging the naked rebels and then holding target practice on their bodies?

> Why was the barber upset? Who were the people the other man had been hunting?

In the Barbershop, by Ilya Bolotowsky, 1934. Estate of Ilya Bolowtowsky/Licensed by VAGA, New York, NY.

> What does this detail tell you about Captain Torres?

---

fatigue a tired feeling   **caress** a gentle touch   **mutilated** cut up; badly damaged

Fiction Unit 1   95

> What problem is the barber facing?

I began to apply the first layer of soap. With his eyes closed, he continued. "Without any effort I could go straight to sleep," he said, "but there's plenty to do this afternoon."

I stopped the lathering and asked with a **feigned** lack of interest, "A firing squad?"

"Something like that, but a little slower."

I got on with the job of lathering his beard. My hands started trembling again. The man could not possibly realize it, and this was in my favor. But I would have preferred that he hadn't come. It was likely that many of our **faction** had seen him enter. And an enemy under one's roof imposes certain conditions.

> Notice how the suspense builds. That is the rising action.

I would be obliged to shave that beard like any other one, carefully, gently, like that of any customer, taking pains to see that no single pore **emitted** a drop of blood. Being careful to see that the little tufts of hair did not lead the blade astray. Seeing that his skin ended up clean, soft, and healthy, so that passing the back of my hand over it I couldn't feel a hair. Yes, I was secretly a rebel, but I was also a **conscientious** barber, and proud of the **precision** required of my profession.

I took the razor, opened up the two protective arms, exposed the blade, and began the job—from one of the sideburns downward. The razor responded beautifully. His beard was **inflexible** and hard, not too long, but thick. Bit by bit the skin emerged. The razor **rasped** along, making its customary sound as fluffs of lather, mixed with bits of hair, gathered along the blade.

I paused a moment to clean it, then took up the strop again to sharpen the razor, because I'm a barber who does things properly. The man, who had kept his eyes closed, opened them now, removed one of his hands from under the sheet, felt the spot on his face where the soap had been cleared off, and said, "Come to the school today at six o'clock."

---

feigned pretended

faction a group; often one that disagrees with others

emitted sent out

conscientious careful to do things right

precision exactness

inflexible stiff; rigid

rasped scraped with a harsh sound

"The same thing as the other day?" I asked, horrified.

"It could be even better," he said.

"What do you plan to do?"

"I don't know yet. But we'll amuse ourselves." Once more he leaned back and closed his eyes. I approached with the razor **poised**.

"Do you plan to punish them all?" I **ventured** timidly.

"All."

The soap was drying on his face. I had to hurry. In the mirror I looked towards the street. It was the same as ever—the grocery store with two or three customers in it. Then I glanced at the clock—2:20 in the afternoon.

The razor continued on its downward stroke. Now from the other sideburn down. A thick, blue beard. He should have let it grow like some poets or priests do. It would suit him well. A lot of people wouldn't recognize him. Much to his benefit, I thought, as I attempted to cover the neck areas smoothly.

> Why might Torres not want to be recognized?

There, surely, the razor had to be handled masterfully, since the hair, although softer, grew into little swirls. A curly beard. One of the tiny pores could open up and issue forth its pearl of blood, but a good barber prides himself on never allowing this to happen to a customer.

How many of us had he ordered shot? How many of us had he ordered mutilated? It was better not to think about it. Torres did not know that I was his enemy. He did not know it nor did the rest. It was a secret shared by very few, precisely so that I could inform the revolutionaries of what Torres was doing in the town and of what he was planning each time he undertook a rebel-hunting **excursion**.

So it was going to be very difficult to explain that I had him right in my hands and let him go peacefully—alive and shaved.

The beard was now almost completely gone. He seemed younger, less burdened by years than when he had arrived. I suppose this always happens with men who visit barber shops.

---

poised held up; balanced   **ventured** dared to say   **excursion** a trip; an expedition

Rural Landscape, by Susana Gonzales Pagliere.

Under the stroke of my razor Torres was being **rejuvenated**—rejuvenated because I am a good barber, the best in the town, if I may say so.

How hot it is getting! Torres must be sweating as much as I. But he is a calm man, who is not even thinking about what he is going to do with the prisoners this afternoon. On the other hand I, with this razor in my hands—I stroking and restroking this skin, can't even think clearly.

Damn him for coming! I'm a revolutionary, not a **murderer**. And how easy it would be to kill him. And he deserves it. Does he? No! What the devil! No one deserves to have someone else make the sacrifice of becoming a murderer. What do you gain by it? Nothing. Others come along and still others, and the first ones kill the second ones, and they the next ones—and it goes on like this until everything is a sea of blood.

I could cut this throat just so—*zip, zip!* I wouldn't give him time to resist and since he has his eyes closed he wouldn't see the glistening blade or my glistening eyes. But I'm trembling like a real murderer. Out of his neck a gush of blood would sprout onto the sheet, on the chair, on my hands, on the floor. I would have to close the door. And the blood would keep inching along the floor, warm, **ineradicable**, uncontainable, until it reached the street, like a little scarlet stream.

rejuvenated restored to youthfulness	**murderer** someone who kills another person	**ineradicable** impossible to erase or remove

I'm sure that one solid stroke, one deep **incision**, would prevent any pain. He wouldn't suffer. But what would I do with the body? Where would I hide it? I would have to flee, leaving all I have behind, and take refuge far away. But they would follow until they found me. "Captain Torres' murderer. He slit his throat while he was shaving him—a coward."

And then on the other side. "The **avenger** of us all. A name to remember. He was the town barber. No one knew he was defending our cause."

Murderer or hero? My **destiny** depends on the edge of this blade. I can turn my hand a bit more, press a little harder on the razor, and sink it in. The skin would give way like silk, like rubber. There is nothing more tender than human skin and the blood is always there, ready to pour forth.

But I don't want to be a murderer. You came to me for a shave. And I perform my work honorably . . . I don't want blood on my hands. Just lather, that's all. You are an executioner and I am only a barber. Each person has his own place in the scheme of things.

Now his chin had been stroked clean and smooth. The man sat up and looked into the mirror. He rubbed his hands over his skin and felt it fresh, like new.

"Thanks," he said. He went to the hanger for his belt, pistol, and cap. I must have been very pale; my shirt felt soaked. Torres finished adjusting the buckle, straightened his pistol in the holster, and after automatically smoothing down his hair, he put on the cap. From his pants pocket he took out several coins to pay me for my services and then headed for the door.

In the doorway he paused for a moment and said, "They told me that you'd kill me. I came to find out. But killing isn't easy. You can take my word for it." And he turned and walked away.

> What is the climax of the story?

> Why does the barber decide not to kill the captain?

> Notice how the excitement begins to die down. This is the falling action. The resolution often follows quickly as the action slows.

> Does the ending surprise you?

---

incision a thin cut   **avenger** someone who does harm in return for a wrong   **destiny** fate

Fiction Unit 1

AFTER READING THE SELECTION

Just Lather, That's All   by Hernando Téllez (trans. by Donald A. Yates)

Directions Choose the letter of the best answer or write the answer using complete sentences.

Comprehension: Identifying Facts

1. Why does the barber think Captain Torres comes into the barbershop?
   A to arrest the barber
   B to question the barber
   C for a shave
   D for directions

2. What has Captain Torres done to the barber's political friends?

3. Where has Captain Torres been for four days?

Comprehension: Putting Ideas Together

4. The barber has to decide whether or not he will
   A kill the captain.
   B run away.
   C call his rebel friends.
   D give the captain a shave.

5. What will happen at the school at six o'clock?

6. How does the barber explain his decision?

Understanding Literature: Rising Action

Rising action is the buildup of excitement in the story. The author first introduces the conflict in the plot. The conflict is the struggle of the main character against himself or herself, another person, or nature. This is the beginning of the rising action. As the conflict continues, the excitement builds. The rising action is not one single event or moment. It is all the events that create suspense. The rising action builds to a climax or turning point. Then the conflict is resolved. Think about the excitement that builds after the conflict is introduced in this story.

7. What is the conflict in this story?

8. Describe the events that take place during the rising action.

Critical Thinking

9. What does Captain Torres say as he leaves? What do you think he means?

Thinking Creatively

10. Do you think the barber did the right thing? Why or why not?

Grammar Check

Your writing will be more clear if you use parallel structure, or parallelism. Sentences are parallel when their structure is balanced, or equal. Items in a list are parallel when they follow the same structure. Repeating words can create a parallel structure. Look at this sentence from the story: "Out of his neck a gush of blood would sprout onto the sheet, on the chair, on my hands, on the floor." Carefully break down the sentence. Notice that each item in the list begins with *on*. Now write your own sentence using parallel structure.

 Writing on Your Own

What if the barber had killed Torres? Write a paragraph telling what might have happened. Make sure that your paragraph has a topic sentence with supporting details.

 Speaking

Talk with a group about how you felt about this story. Did you like the way the author presented the barber? How did you feel about reading the barber's thoughts instead of just his actions? What did you like best about the style of the writing?

 Listening

Take turns reading parts of the story aloud with a partner. Listen as your partner reads. Help your partner to use a voice and tone that reflect the mood of the text.

 Viewing

A Plot Mountain is a graphic organizer that shows the different stages of a story's plot. Use a Plot Mountain to describe each of these stages in this story: the exposition, rising action, climax, falling action, and resolution, or denouement. This graphic organizer is described in Appendix A.

Turning Points

The experiences of a character often move the plot toward an exciting ending. Sometimes an experience may show an important part of the character's personality. When an experience changes a character's life, the story belongs to a genre called turning points.

Perhaps turning points is such a popular genre of fiction because it reflects real life. Think of biographies of famous people you have read or seen on television or in the movies. They often deal with turning points in the famous person's life. Take Martin Luther King Jr. as an example. Taking part in the Montgomery, Alabama, bus boycott in 1955 was a turning point in his life. Turning points are not limited to the lives of famous people, however. Many people can look back to times when they chose one path over another, and that choice changed their lives.

Turning points in fiction are often events that, at the time, seem frightening or confusing. The protagonist may not understand the importance of the event right away. It is not until later that he or she understands. For this reason, the narrator's point of view is important in these stories. The point of view is the position from which the author or storyteller tells the story. If the events happen to the narrator, the first-person point of view is used. This point of view has limits. The reader will only know what the narrator knows. Sometimes a story is told by an outsider. This is known as the third-person point of view.

Characters can face all different types of turning points. They can also face them at different times of their lives. When a young person faces a turning point, the story is called a "coming-of-age" story. Usually, in a coming-of-age story, the characters do not fully understand what the childhood experiences meant until they are adults. Often, they can then understand and explain how the change happened.

All the stories in this section are about turning points. Read to see what types of situations the characters deal with and how their lives are changed as a result.

TURNING POINTS

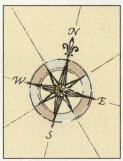

- change
- real life
- confusing or frightening
- coming-of-age story

BEFORE READING THE SELECTION

Marriage Is a Private Affair   by Chinua Achebe

About the Author

Chinua Achebe is one of Nigeria's most popular writers. He was born in Ogidi, Nigeria, on November 16, 1930. He graduated from the University College at Ibadan in 1953. He has been a teacher and has worked in radio. Achebe often writes about the conflict between traditional African culture and new ideas. His first novel, published in 1958, was *Things Fall Apart*. Others are *No Longer at Ease* and *A Man of the People*. Achebe has also written poems and short stories. Since Nigeria is an English-speaking country, Achebe writes in English. His books have been translated into many other languages.

Chinua Achebe
(1930–)
Nigerian

About the Selection

Achebe looks at conflicts between customs in this story, published in 1991. A young Nigerian, Nnaemeka, plans to marry Nene. She is city-bred and from another tribe. Back in his home town, Nnaemeka's father Okeke has already chosen a wife for Nnaemeka. Nnaemeka still marries Nene. Okeke believes in tradition and is angry when his son defies his wishes. He will have nothing to do with the new wife. The son and father in this story are Ibos, which is one of Nigeria's many large tribal groups. (The author is also Ibo.) The story reveals how old customs continue. It is told in third person. Find out which character has a turning point and what changes everything.

Objectives

- To read and understand a short story
- To understand and identify the turning point in a story
- To describe how the third-person point of view helps the story

Before Reading continued on next page

Fiction Unit 1   **103**

BEFORE READING THE SELECTION (continued)

Marriage Is a Private Affair by Chinua Achebe

coming-of-age story a story that tells how a young person matures

turning point an experience that changes the life of a literary character

third person a point of view that refers to characters as "he" or "she" and expresses the thoughts of some characters

Literary Terms A **coming-of-age story** is one that tells how a young person matures. In a typical coming-of-age story, the protagonist, or main character, will have a life-changing experience. This is a **turning point**.

Another idea, or theme, running through this story, is how new ideas challenge customs and traditions. The old customs in this story are arranged marriages and the belief that people should marry only within their tribe. Another theme is the power of love and patience in family relationships.

This story is told by an all-knowing narrator. It is written in the **third person**, so that the characters are referred to as "he" or "she." It means that the narrator describes some characters' thoughts. The narrator knows what all the characters are thinking.

Reading on Your Own Think about the ways stories can be told. Discuss the difference between first-person and third-person points of view. Preread the story to find information that can be given only by an all-knowing narrator.

Writing on Your Own Think about customs that are important in your family. Are there any traditions that you find old-fashioned? How can you respect your parents while choosing new traditions? Write your ideas in a paragraph.

Vocabulary Focus The *–tion* suffix is used to change a verb into a noun. For example, look at the words *negotiation* and *qualification*. What verbs did these words come from? Think of at least two other words ending in *–tion*. Write them down and tell the verb they came from.

Think Before You Read Predict which character will have an experience that changes him or her. What might that change be?

Marriage Is a Private Affair

"Have you written to your dad yet?" asked Nene one afternoon as she sat with Nnaemeka in her room at 16 Kasanga Street, Lagos.

"No. I've been thinking about it. I think it's better to tell him when I get home on **leave**!"

"But why? Your leave is such a long way off yet—six whole weeks. He should be let into our happiness now."

Nnaemeka was silent for a while, and then began very slowly as if he groped for his words: "I wish I were sure it would be happiness to him."

"Of course it must," replied Nene, a little surprised. "Why shouldn't it?"

"You have lived in Lagos all your life, and you know very little about people in remote parts of the country."

"That's what you always say. But I don't believe anybody will be so unlike other people that they will be unhappy when their sons are engaged to marry."

"Yes. They are most unhappy if the engagement is not arranged by them. In our case it's worse—you are not even an Ibo."

This was said so seriously and so bluntly that Nene could not find speech immediately. In the **cosmopolitan** atmosphere

Lagos is the largest city in Nigeria.

As you read, notice when the author seems to know the thoughts of a character.

Nigeria has many different ethnic groups, each with its own customs and language. The Ibo are one of the largest. As you will see, tribal differences are still important, especially in rural areas.

leave a vacation; permission to be away from work

cosmopolitan including people from many places

Fiction Unit 1 105

> In Nnaemeka's tribe, parents choose marriage partners for their children. This is called an arranged marriage.

of the city it had always seemed to her something of a joke that a person's tribe could determine whom he married.

At last she said, "You don't really mean that he will object to your marrying me simply on that account? I had always thought you Ibos were kindly disposed to other people."

"So we are. But when it comes to marriage, well, it's not quite so simple. And this," he added, "is not peculiar to the Ibos. If your father were alive and lived in the heart of Ibibio-land he would be exactly like my father."

"I don't know. But anyway, as your father is so fond of you, I'm sure he will forgive you soon enough. Come on then, be a good boy and send him a nice lovely letter. . . ."

"It would not be wise to break the news to him by writing. A letter will bring it upon him with a shock. I'm quite sure about that."

"All right, honey, suit yourself. You know your father."

As Nnaemeka walked home that evening he turned over in his mind the different ways of overcoming his father's opposition, especially now that he had gone and found a girl for him. He had thought of showing his letter to Nene but decided on second thoughts not to, at least for the moment. He read it again when he got home and couldn't help smiling to himself. He remembered Ugoye quite well, an Amazon of a girl who used to beat up all the boys, himself included, on the way to the stream, a complete **dunce** at school.

> In Greek mythology, an *Amazon* was a woman warrior.

*I have found a girl who will suit you admirably—Ugoye Nweke, the eldest daughter of our neighbour, Jacob Nweke. She has a proper Christian upbringing. When she stopped schooling some years ago her father (a man of sound judgment) sent her to live in the house of a **pastor** where she has received all the training a wife could need. Her Sunday School teacher has told me that she reads her Bible very **fluently**. I hope we shall begin **negotiations** when you come home in December.*

On the second evening of his return from Lagos Nnaemeka sat with his father under a cassia tree. This was

> *Cassia trees* are found in warm climates. They are related to peas and have fruit that can be eaten.

dunce a stupid person
pastor a Christian minister
fluently using language easily
negotiations discussions leading to an agreement

the old man's retreat where he went to read his Bible when the **parching** December sun had set and a fresh, reviving wind blew on the leaves.

"Father," began Nnaemeka suddenly, "I have come to ask forgiveness."

"Forgiveness? For what, my son?" he asked in amazement.

"It's about this marriage question."

"Which marriage question?"

"I can't—we must—I mean it is impossible for me to marry Nweke's daughter."

> For Nnaemeka's father, love is not important in choosing a marriage partner.

"Impossible? Why?" asked his father.

"I don't love her."

"Nobody said you did. Why should you?" he asked.

"Marriage today is different...."

"Look here, my son," interrupted his father, "nothing is different. What one looks for in a wife are a good character and a Christian background."

Nnaemeka saw there was no hope along the present line of argument.

"Moreover," he said, "I am engaged to marry another girl who has all of Ugoye's good qualities, and who...."

His father did not believe his ears. "What did you say?" he asked slowly and **disconcertingly**.

"She is a good Christian," his son went on, "and a teacher in a Girls' School in Lagos."

> St. Paul wrote letters to the church at Corinth. These letters called Corinthians, make up two books of the New Testament of the Christian Bible.

"Teacher, did you say? If you consider that a **qualification** for a good wife I should like to point out to you, Emeka, that no Christian woman should teach. St. Paul in his letter to the Corinthians says that women should keep silence." He rose slowly from his seat and paced forwards and backwards. This was his pet subject, and he condemned **vehemently** those church leaders who encouraged women to teach in their schools. After he had spent his emotion on a long **homily** he at last came back to his son's engagement, in a seemingly milder tone.

---

parching causing to become dry

disconcertingly in an upsetting way

qualification suitable ability

vehemently with strong emotion

homily a sermon

"Whose daughter is she, anyway?"

"She is Nene Atang."

"What!" All the mildness was gone again. "Did you say Neneataga, what does that mean?"

"Nene Atang from Calabar. She is the only girl I can marry." This was a very **rash** reply and Nnaemeka expected the storm to burst. But it did not. His father merely walked away into his room. This was most unexpected and perplexed Nnaemeka.

His father's silence was **infinitely** more menacing than a flood of threatening speech. That night the old man did not eat.

When he sent for Nnaemeka a day later he applied all possible ways of **dissuasion**. But the young man's heart was hardened, and his father eventually gave him up as lost.

"I owe it to you, my son, as a duty to show you what is right and what is wrong. Whoever put this idea into your head might as well have cut your throat. It is Satan's work." He waved his son away.

"You will change your mind, Father, when you know Nene."

"I shall never see her," was the reply. From that night the father scarcely spoke to his son. He did not, however, cease hoping that he would realize how serious was the danger he was heading for. Day and night he put him in his prayers.

Nnaemeka, for his own part, was very deeply affected by his father's grief. But he kept hoping that it would pass away. If it had occurred to him that never in the history of his people had a man married a woman who spoke a different tongue, he might have been less optimistic.

"It has never been heard," was the verdict of an old man speaking a few weeks later. In that short sentence he spoke for all of his people. This man had come with others to **commiserate** with Okeke when news went round about his son's behaviour. By that time the son had gone back to Lagos.

"It has never been heard," said the old man again with a sad shake of his head.

"What did Our Lord say?" asked another gentleman. "Sons shall rise against their Fathers; it is there in the Holy Book."

> Note that the father is not interested in the woman herself. He only wants to know about her family.

> Notice how the narrator describes Nnaemeka's feelings. This is possible when the author uses the third-person point of view.

rash bold; hasty
infinitely without any limits
dissuasion discouraging someone from an action
commiserate to express sorrow and sympathy

"It is the beginning of the end," said another.

The discussion thus tending to become **theological**, Madubogwu, a highly practical man, brought it down once more to the ordinary level.

"Have you thought of consulting a native doctor about your son?" he asked Nnaemeka's father.

"He isn't sick," was the reply.

"What is he then? The boy's mind is diseased and only a good **herbalist** can bring him back to his right senses. The medicine he requires is *Amalile,* the same that women apply with success to recapture their husbands' straying affection."

"Madubogwu is right," said another gentleman. "This thing calls for medicine."

"I shall not call in a native doctor." Nnaemeka's father was known to be **obstinately** ahead of his more superstitious neighbours in these matters. "I will not be another Mrs. Ochuba. If my son wants to kill himself let him do it with his own hands. It is not for me to help him."

"But it was her fault," said Madubogwu. "She ought to have gone to an honest herbalist. She was a clever woman, **nevertheless**."

"She was a wicked **murderess**," said Jonathan who rarely argued with his neighbours because, he often said, they were **incapable** of reasoning. "The medicine was prepared for her husband, it was his name they called in its preparation and I am sure it would have been perfectly **beneficial** to him. It was wicked to put it into the herbalist's food, and say you were only trying it out."

Six months later, Nnaemeka was showing his young wife a short letter from his father:

It amazes me that you could be so unfeeling as to send me your wedding picture. I would have sent it back. But on further thought I decided just to cut off your wife and

---

The title of the story is "Marriage Is a Private Affair." Yet in this society there seems to be little that is private about marriage. Notice how private actions can affect an entire community.

Nnaemeka's father does not hold with every tradition among the Ibo.

---

theological related to the study of religion

herbalist a person who makes medicines from herbs

obstinately stubbornly

nevertheless all the same

murderess a woman who kills someone

incapable without the ability

beneficial doing good; helpful

send it back to you because I have nothing to do with her. How I wish that I had nothing to do with you either.

When Nene read through this letter and looked at the mutilated picture her eyes filled with tears, and she began to sob.

"Don't cry, my darling," said her husband. "He is essentially good-natured and will one day look more kindly on our marriage." But years passed and that one day did not come.

For eight years, Okeke would have nothing to do with his son, Nnaemeka. Only three times (when Nnaemeka asked to come home and spend his leave) did he write to him.

"I can't have you in my house," he replied on one occasion. "It can be of no interest to me where or how you spend your leave—or your life, for that matter."

The prejudice against Nnaemeka's marriage was not confined to his little village. In Lagos, especially among his people who worked there, it showed itself in a different way. Their women, when they met at their village meeting were not **hostile** to Nene. Rather, they paid her such **excessive deference** as to make her feel she was not one of them. But as time went on, Nene gradually broke through some of this prejudice and even began to make friends among them. Slowly and **grudgingly** they began to admit that she kept her home much better than most of them.

The story eventually got to the little village in the heart of the Ibo country that Nnaemeka and his young wife were a most happy couple. But his father was one of the few people who knew nothing about this. He always displayed so much temper whenever his son's name was mentioned that everyone avoided it in his presence. By a tremendous effort of will he had succeeded in pushing his son to the back of his mind. The strain had nearly killed him but he had **persevered**, and won.

Then one day he received a letter from Nene, and in spite of himself he began to glance through it **perfunctorily** until

> Do you think that Nnaemeka and Nene are strong people? Why or why not?

hostile angrily opposed to

excessive too much

deference respect

grudgingly unwillingly

persevered carried on in spite of difficulties

perfunctorily without thought or care

all of a sudden the expression on his face changed and he began to read more carefully.

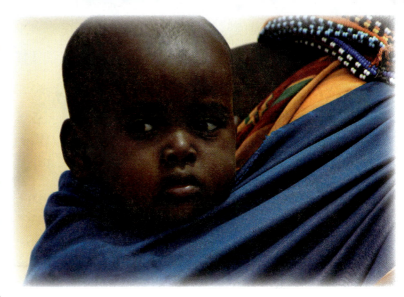

*Our two sons, from the day they learnt that they have a grandfather, have insisted on being taken to him. I find it impossible to tell them that you will not see them. I **implore** you to allow Nnaemeka to bring them home for a short time during his leave next month. I shall remain here in Lagos. . . .*

The old man at once felt the resolution he had built up over so many years falling in. He was telling himself that he must not give in. He tried to steel his heart against all emotional appeals. It was a **re-enactment** of that other struggle. He leaned against a window and looked out. The sky was overcast with heavy black clouds and a high wind began to blow filling the air with dust and dry leaves. It was one of those rare occasions when even Nature takes a hand in a human fight. Very soon it began to rain, the first rain in the year. It came down in large sharp drops and was accompanied by the lightning and thunder which mark a change of season. Okeke was trying hard not to think of his two grandsons. But he knew he was now fighting a losing battle. He tried to hum a favourite hymn but the pattering of large rain drops on the roof broke up the tune. His mind immediately returned to the children. How could he shut his door against them? By a curious mental process he imagined them standing, sad and **forsaken**, under the harsh angry weather—shut out from his house.

That night he hardly slept, from **remorse**—and a vague fear that he might die without making it up to them.

> Where is the turning point for Okeke?

> How is the stormy weather like what is going on in Okeke's heart?

implore beg
re-enactment acting out something that happened once before
forsaken abandoned; left alone
remorse regret for having done something harmful

AFTER READING THE SELECTION

Marriage Is a Private Affair   by Chinua Achebe

Directions Choose the letter of the best answer or write the answer using complete sentences.

Comprehension: Identifying Facts

1. Where do Nnaemeka and Nene live?
   A the countryside
   B Lagos, Nigeria
   C Ibo of Nigeria
   D Ibibio

2. Who is Ugoye?
   A the girl that Okeke wants his son to marry
   B an Ibibio girl
   C Nene's mother
   D Nnaemeka's cousin

3. Why does Nnaemeka want to tell his father about their engagement in person?

4. What two things does the father say are important in a wife?

5. How do the other men in the village feel about Nnaemeka's marriage?

6. What does Okeke, the father, do with the wedding picture?

7. What story gets back to the village about Nene and Nnaemeka?

8. Why has Okeke not heard the story?

9. Why does Nene write to Okeke?

10. What does Okeke worry about that night?

Comprehension: Putting Ideas Together

11. What does Nene want Nnaemeka to write about in a letter to his dad?
    A their engagement
    B his new job
    C his new house in the country
    D their first child

12. Why does Nene think the tribal difference will not matter?
    A She is really an Ibo, too.
    B Love is all that matters in marriage.
    C She grew up in the city, where tribal differences did not seem as important.
    D Most Ibo people do not worry about these differences.

13. How does Okeke expect his son to get a wife?

14. Why does Nnaemeka ask for his father's forgiveness?

15. Why does Okeke object to women being teachers?

16. How does Nnaemeka react to his father's grief?

17. What happened to Mrs. Ochuba?

112   Unit 1 Fiction

18. In what way is Okeke less traditional than other men in the village?

19. How does Nene get along with the Ibo women in Lagos?

20. What changes Okeke's mind about the marriage?

Understanding Literature: Third Person

This is a story told in the third-person omniscient, or all-knowing, point of view. The writer speaks of all the characters as "he" or "she." The reader knows the thoughts and actions of the major characters. A third-person story can show what is going on in Lagos with Nene and Nnaemeka. It can also show what is going on in the village with Okeke and his friends.

21. Whose thoughts does the reader know about?

22. Who is the first person whose thoughts the reader knows? Who is the last?

23. How does the reader know what the villagers think?

24. If the story were told in the first person, who would the narrator probably be? Explain.

25. Who writes the letters in the story?

Critical Thinking

26. How was Nnaemeka's childhood different from Nene's?

27. How does Nnaemeka feel about the letter from his father?

28. In what way is Nnaemeka surprised by his father's reaction to the news of his marriage?

29. What happened when the village woman consulted the herbalist?

Thinking Creatively

30. Are you surprised by the change in Okeke after he learned of his grandchildren? Explain. What do you think he will do about his grandchildren?

After Reading continued on next page

AFTER READING THE SELECTION (continued)

Marriage Is a Private Affair   by Chinua Achebe

 Grammar Check

Ellipses are used to show that words from a passage have been left out or that dialogue is interrupted. Look at this section from the story.

> "Moreover," he said, "I am engaged to marry another girl who has all of Ugoye's good qualities, and who . . ."
>
> His father did not believe his ears. "What did you say?" he asked slowly and disconcertingly.

The narrator wants the reader to know that Nnaemeka wanted to tell his father more about the girl he plans to marry. Because the father interrupted Nnaemeka, he never finished what he planned to say. Finish the statement for Nnaemeka. Explain how Nene would be a good wife.

 Writing on Your Own

Write the beginning of a story. Use the third person. In your beginning, show that there will be several characters and situations. Share your story beginning with a partner.

 Speaking and Listening

Work with a group to make up a skit about an old tradition that is no longer followed. Try to make your skit funny, but without showing disrespect for the tradition. Perform your skit for the class. Watch and listen to the skits by the other groups in your class. Did you and your classmates all think the same parts were funny? Were there any jokes that you did not understand? Were there any parts that amused only you?

 Technology

Think about the types of pictures you would use to illustrate this story. What would the pictures show? Look in the library and on the Internet to find several pictures. Use a word processor to print out any information about each picture. Explain how each picture relates to the story.

BEFORE READING THE SELECTION

Cranes by Hwang Sun-won (trans. by J. Martin Holman)

Hwang Sun-won
(1915–)
Korean

About the Author

Hwang Sun-won was born near Pyongyang, Korea. After World War II, Korea was divided. In 1946, his family moved from the Soviet-occupied North Korea to South Korea. Hwang Sun-won lived through the Korean War in the 1950s. These wartime experiences affected his writing. Hwang Sun-won is a major figure in modern Korean literature. From 1957 to 1993, he taught Korean literature at Kyung Hee University in Seoul, South Korea. He is known as a master of the short story. He has also written novels and poems. His novel *Trees on the Cliff* won a major award in Korea. It has been published in English. Hwang Sun-won lives in Seoul, South Korea.

About the Selection

"Cranes" is the story of friends divided by war. Its setting is divided Korea. One man, Tok-jae, is a North Korean Communist. He has been taken prisoner by the South Korean army. The other is a South Korean soldier, Song-sam. Song-sam is to take Tok-jae for questioning. But they recognize each other as old childhood friends. The two grew up together, but the war separated them. Find out which is more powerful— their friendship or their loyalties to their governments.

Objectives

- To read and understand a short story
- To understand an author's style of writing
- To explain the symbols in a story
- To describe the purpose of a flashback

Before Reading continued on next page

Fiction Unit 1 **115**

BEFORE READING THE SELECTION (continued)

Cranes   by Hwang Sun-won (trans. by J. Martin Holman)

---

style an author's way of writing

symbol a person, place, or thing that represents something else

flashback a look into the past at some point in a story

Literary Terms Pay attention to Hwang Sun-won's **style**, his way of writing. It is simple, but he is saying much more than just words. Carefully read the story, looking to see what the author is trying to say. One way that Hwang Sun-won gets his ideas across is by using **symbols**. A symbol is a person, place, or thing that represents something else. As you read this story, think about the ideas of freedom, war, and death. Look for symbols of these ideas. Another way the author gets ideas across is through the use of **flashbacks**. A flashback is a look into the past at some point in the story.

Reading on Your Own As you read, look for the flashbacks in the story. Think about why the author includes them. What do they have to do with what is happening to the characters right now? How does this add to the author's style and purpose?

Writing on Your Own Do you have a friend whom you have not seen in several years? Imagine that he or she is now your enemy. Write about how you would feel if you saw that person.

Vocabulary Focus Homophones are words that sound the same but are spelled differently and have different meanings. Look at the list of homophones below. The italicized words are in the story. Write a sentence for each of the words. Work with a partner to think of three other sets of homophones.

    there, their, they're   *been*, bin
    son, sun   *due*, do

Think Before You Read How do you think the old friends will react when they first see each other?

116   Unit 1   *Fiction*

Cranes

The village just north of the thirty-eighth parallel was quiet beneath the clear, **lofty** autumn sky.

A white **gourd** lay where it had tumbled, leaning against another on the dirt-floored space between the rooms of an **abandoned** house.

An old man Song-sam happened to meet put his long tobacco pipe behind his back. The children, as children would, had already fled from the street to keep their distance. Everyone's face was masked with fear.

Overall, the village showed few signs of the **conflict** that had just ended. Still, it did not seem to Song-sam to be the same village where he had grown up.

He stopped walking at a grove of **chestnut** trees on the hill behind the village. He climbed one of the trees. In his mind, from far away, he could hear the shouts of the old man with a wen. Are you kids climbing my chestnut tree again?

Had that old man died during Song-sam's absence? He had not seen him among the men he had met so far in the village. Hanging onto the tree, Song-sam looked up at the clear autumn

> The *thirty-eighth parallel*, or line of latitude, is the dividing line between North Korea and South Korea.

> As you read, notice the author's style, or way of writing.

> A *wen* is an unusual growth on the skin.

lofty high
gourd a kind of vegetable that grows on a vine
abandoned no longer lived in
conflict a battle; the fighting
chestnut a type of tree that has nuts enclosed in a prickly casing

Fiction Unit 1   117

> Read on to see why Song-sam has been away from the village.

sky. Though he did not shake the branch, some of the remaining chestnut **burrs** burst open, and the nuts fell to the ground.

When he reached the house that was being used temporarily as the Public Peace Office, he found someone there bound tightly with rope. This was the first young man he had seen in the village. As Song-sam drew closer and examined his face, he was **taken aback**. It was none other than his boyhood friend Tok-jae.

Song-sam asked one of the security guards from his **detachment** who had accompanied him from Ch'ont'ae what the situation was. The guard answered that the prisoner had been vice-chairman of the Communist Farmers' Alliance and that he had just been captured while hiding in his own house here in the village.

Song-sam squatted by the house and lit a cigarette. Tok-jae was to be escorted to Ch'ongdan by one of the young security guards.

After a while Song-sam lit a cigarette from the one he had been smoking, then stood up.

"I'll take the guy myself."

Tok-jae kept his face turned away; he did not even glance at Song-sam.

They left the village.

Song-sam kept smoking, but he could not taste the tobacco. He just sucked and puffed. He suddenly realized that Tok-jae might like a smoke. He **recalled** when they were boys how they had shared a smoke of dried pumpkin leaves, hiding from the adults in the corner of the wall around the house. But how could he offer a guy like this a cigarette?

> Why does Song-sam think of Tok-jae as a *"guy like this"*?

Once, when they were boys, he had gone with Tok-jae to steal chestnuts from the old man with the wen. Song-sam was taking his turn climbing the tree when suddenly they heard the old man shouting. Song-sam slid down the tree and got chestnut burrs stuck in his rear end. Yet he **dashed** off without doing anything about them. Once they had run far enough

---

burrs rough or prickly coverings around nuts

taken aback startled

detachment a small military unit of soldiers

recalled remembered

dashed ran quickly

118 Unit 1 Fiction

that the old man could not catch them, he turned his backside toward Tok-jae. It hurt even more to have the prickly chestnut **spines** pulled out. Tears ran freely down Song-sam's face. Tok-jae held out a fistful of his own chestnuts, then thrust them into Song-sam's pocket.

Song-sam had just lit a cigarette from the last one he had smoked, but he tossed it away. He made up his mind not to smoke anymore while he was escorting . . . Tok-jae.

They reached the mountain ridge road. He had often come to the ridge with Tok-jae to cut **fodder** before Song-sam moved to the area around Ch'ont'ae, south of the thirty-eighth parallel, two years before the Liberation in 1945.

Song-sam felt an **inexplicable** urge. He burst out shouting. ". . . How many people have you killed?"

Tok-jae glanced toward Song-sam, then looked away again.

"How many people have you killed?"

Tok-jae turned his face toward Song-sam and glared. The light in his eyes grew fierce and his mouth, which was surrounded by a **stubble** beard, twitched.

"So, is that what you've been doing? Killing people?"

. . . Still, Song-sam felt a clearing in the center of his chest, as if something caught there had been released. But then he said, "Why wouldn't someone like the vice-chairman of the Farmers' Alliance try to escape? You must have been hiding out because you had been given some assignment."

Tok-jae did not respond.

"Well? Answer me. What kind of **mission** were you hiding out to do?"

Silent, Tok-jae just kept walking. The guy certainly seems **cowed**. At a time like this, it would be good to get a look at his face. But Tok-jae did not turn toward Song-sam again.

Song-sam took hold of the pistol in his belt.

"It's no use trying to explain your way out of it. You'll have to be shot anyway, so go ahead and tell the truth."

> The 1945 *Liberation* freed Korea from Japanese rule. Japan had been defeated in World War II. American troops occupied the South, below the thirty-eighth parallel. Soviet troops occupied the North.

---

spines thorns
fodder dry food for farm animals
inexplicable not possible to explain
stubble short, stiff growth
mission a task; an assignment
cowed frightened by threats

> Do you think Song-sam believes Tok-jae?

> What does this paragraph tell you about Shorty's personality?

Tok-jae began to speak. "I'm not trying to get out of anything. First and last, I'm the son of a dirt farmer. I was made vice-chairman of the Farmers' Alliance because they said I was a hard worker. If that's a crime worthy of death, there is nothing I can do. The only skill I've got is **tilling** the ground." After a moment he continued. "My father is sick in bed at home. It's been six months now."

Tok-jae's father was a **widower**, a poor farmer who had grown old with only his son by his side. Seven years ago his back had already been bent, and his face had dark age spots.

"Are you married?"

"Yes," Tok-jae answered after a moment.

"Who to?"

"To Shorty."

Not Shorty! Now that's interesting. Shorty, a fat little girl who knew the **breadth** of the earth but not the height of the sky. Always such a **prig**. Song-sam and Tok-jae had hated that about her. They were always teasing and laughing at her. So that's who Tok-jae had married.

"And how many kids do you have?"

"Our first is due this fall."

Song-sam tried to **stifle** a smile that rose to his lips in spite of himself. Asking how many children Tok-jae had and having him answer that the first was due in autumn was so funny he could not stand it. Shorty—holding up her armload of a belly on that little body. But Song-sam realized that this was not the place to laugh or joke about such things.

"Anyway, don't you think it looks **suspicious** that you stayed behind and didn't flee?"

"I tried to go. They said if there was an **invasion** from the south, every last man who was a man would be captured and killed, so all the men between seventeen and forty

---

tilling making land ready for growing crops

widower a man whose wife has died

breadth width; extent

prig a person who is easily offended

stifle to hold back

suspicious causing distrust

invasion an entering by force

were forced to head north. I really didn't have any choice. I thought I would carry my father on my back and go. But he wouldn't stand for it. He said if a farmer leaves the fields he has already tilled and planted, where can he go? My father has always depended on me alone. He's grown old farming all these years, and I have to be the one to close his eyes when the end comes. The truth is, people like us who just till the ground wouldn't be any better off even if we *did* flee...."

Song-sam himself had fled the past June. One night he secretly spoke to his father about escaping, but his father had said the same thing as Tok-jae's. How could a farmer flee and leave his work behind? Song-sam fled alone. As he wandered along the strange roads through strange towns in the south, he never stopped thinking of the farm work he had left to his old parents and his wife and children. Fortunately, then as now, his family was healthy.

They crossed the ridge. Now, somehow, Song-sam was the one who kept his eyes **averted**. The autumn sun was hot on his forehead. What a perfect day this would be for harvesting, he thought.

After they had gone down the far side of the ridge, Song-sam **hesitated**.

It looked like a group of people wearing white clothes were stooped over working in the middle of the field. It was actually a flock of cranes, here in the so-called Demilitarized Zone at the thirty-eighth parallel. Even though people were no longer living here, the cranes remained as before.

Once when Song-sam and Tok-jae were about twelve years old, they had secretly set a **snare** and caught a crane. They even bound its wings with a straw rope. The two boys came out to the place they kept the crane almost every day; they would hold the crane around the neck and raise a **ruckus** trying to ride on its back. Then one day they heard

> Does Song-sam wonder whether he should have stayed with his family like Tok-jae did?

> The *Demilitarized Zone* was a no-fighting zone on either side of the boundary dividing the two sides.

> Look for the flashback on this page.

averted turned away **snare** a trap **ruckus** a noisy disturbance
hesitated stopped

Fiction Unit 1 **121**

> Korea was under Japanese rule until 1945.

the adults in the village talking in whispers. Some people had come from Seoul to hunt cranes. They had special permission from the Japanese governor-general to collect **specimens** of some kind. When they heard this, the two boys raced off to the field. They were not worried about being caught by the adults and scolded. Now they had only one thought: their crane must not die. Without stopping to catch their breath, they scrambled through the weeds. They took the snare off the crane's leg and loosened the straw rope from its wings. But the crane could hardly walk, probably because it had been tied up for so long. The boys held the crane up between them and tossed it into the air. They heard a gunshot. The bird flapped its wings two, three, four times, but fell back to the ground. It was hit! But in the next instant, another crane in the grass nearby spread its wings. Their own crane, which had been lying on the ground, stretched out its long neck, gave a cry, and rose into the sky, too. They circled over the boys' heads, then flew off into the distance. The boys could not take their eyes off the spot in the blue sky where the cranes had disappeared.

"Let's go catch a crane," Song-sam said **abruptly**.

Tok-jae was bewildered. He did not know what was going on.

"I'll make a snare out of this, and you drive the cranes this way." Song-sam untied Tok-jae's bonds and took the cord. Before Tok-jae knew it, Song-sam was crawling through the grass.

At once, Tok-jae's face went white. The words "you'll have to be shot" flashed through his mind. At any moment a bullet would come from wherever Song-sam had crawled.

Some distance away, Song-sam rose and turned toward Tok-jae. "What do you mean standing there like an idiot! Go drive some cranes this way!"

Only then did Tok-jae realize what was happening. He started crawling through the weeds.

> What are the cranes a symbol of?

Above, two cranes were soaring, their vast wings spread against the high, blue autumn sky.

---

specimens examples of different groups of things

abruptly all of a sudden

AFTER READING THE SELECTION

Cranes by Hwang Sun-won (trans. by J. Martin Holman)

Directions Choose the letter of the best answer or write the answer using complete sentences.

Comprehension: Identifying Facts

1. Why is Song-sam so surprised when he sees the man who is tied up?
   A It is his father.
   B It is the old man who used to yell at him as a child.
   C It is his old childhood friend.
   D It is his brother.

2. Why didn't Tok-jae run away with the others?

3. What is supposed to happen to Tok-jae in Ch'ongdan?

Comprehension: Putting Ideas Together

4. How are the fathers of the two men alike?
   A Both are farmers who would not leave their land.
   B Both are soldiers.
   C They are brothers.
   D Both are Communists.

5. What does Song-sam remember about Tok-jae?

6. As boys, what did they do with the crane they had captured?

Understanding Literature: Style

Style is how the author combines ideas with expression. An author's style is as unique as his or her signature or fingerprints.

Style is a combination of several things. It is the way the author uses dialogue and the attitude the author has toward the subject. The style may be humorous, solemn, or tense. "Cranes" is written in a simple style, but it tells a powerful story. The style is matter-of-fact. The author does not describe the characters' feelings. He just states the actions and the words. He also draws on the power of visual symbols.

7. When in the story does the author tell about Song-sam crying? Describe the event.

8. The author gives strong, simple pictures of the village. Point one out.

Critical Thinking

9. In what ways are Song-sam and Tok-jae alike?

Thinking Creatively

10. Why do you think Song-sam releases Tok-jae?

After Reading continued on next page

AFTER READING THE SELECTION (continued)

Cranes   by Hwang Sun-won (trans. by J. Martin Holman)

 Grammar Check

An adjective is a word that describes a noun, pronoun, or another adjective. In the sentence below, the adjective is *perfect*. It describes *day*.

> What a perfect day this would be for harvesting, he thought.

Choose a paragraph from the story. Rewrite it by replacing the adjectives with your own adjectives. Notice how the story can be changed by using different adjectives.

 Writing on Your Own

What do you think happens after Song-sam lets Tok-jae go? Write your own ending to this story. Make sure that your ending follows what you have already read in the story.

 Speaking and Listening

Pretend that you are Tok-jae. Persuade Song-sam to free you. Remind him of your childhood friendship. Use what you learned from the story to think of what you will say.

Pretend that you are Song-sam. Listen to Tok-jae ask for his freedom. What questions do you have for him? How can he persuade you to let him go?

 Research

The Korean War was the first large conflict in which the United Nations was involved. The United Nations sent troops from different countries to support South Korea. Several Communist countries sent troops to North Korea. Use the Internet and the library to find out what countries were involved. Make a world map showing the different countries that sent troops to fight in the war. Use one color to show which countries fought for North Korea. Use a different color to show which countries fought for South Korea.

BEFORE READING THE SELECTION

from In the Time of the Butterflies   by Julia Alvarez

About the Author

Julia Alvarez was born in New York City to Dominican parents. She spent her early childhood years in the Dominican Republic with her extended family. The Dominican Republic was ruled by a brutal dictator, Rafael Trujillo. His government killed many people. In 1960, Alvarez and her family fled back to the United States. She found herself homesick and lonely there, so she turned to reading books and writing. In 1987, she published her first book, *How the Garcia Girls Lost Their Accents.* She has since written more books, including *In the Time of the Butterflies,* from which this excerpt is taken. Alvarez has also won many awards for her writing.

Julia Alvarez
(1950–)
Dominican

Objectives

- To read and understand a work of historical fiction
- To explain idioms in a story
- To identify a paradox in a story

About the Selection

This novel, published in 1995, is about a time when the Dominican Republic had a dictatorship. This means the government was run by one man. Rafael Trujillo did not allow people to speak out against him in any way. The story is based on the true story of the Mirabal sisters, who grew up in the 1940s. Three of the four sisters had secretly worked to overthrow the government. They ended up in jail. Finally, in 1960, they were killed. At the point when this excerpt begins, the women have been let out of jail.

Read to find out about the experiences of one sister returning home after serving time in jail. The title of the novel refers to the Spanish word for butterfly, *mariposa.* The Mirabal sisters were called "Las Mariposas."

Before Reading **continued on next page**

Fiction Unit 1 125

BEFORE READING THE SELECTION (continued)

from In the Time of the Butterflies   by Julia Alvarez

historical fiction fictional writing that draws on factual events in history

idioms phrases that cannot be understood by knowing the meanings of the words in them

paradox a statement that seems to mean two opposite things

Literary Terms This story is a piece of **historical fiction**, fictional writing that draws on factual events in history. *In the Time of the Butterflies* is a novel based on a true story. However, it is a mix of fiction and events that really happened. The author skillfully blends in imagined details about the sisters.

This story contains several **idioms**. An idiom is a phrase that cannot be understood just by knowing the meanings of the words in it. Different cultures often have different idioms.

The story is written from the first-person point of view. However, in this book, the narrator is not always the same person. Each of the four sisters tells part of the story. This selection is told by Minerva. Just released from prison, Minerva describes the wonders of everyday life. She ends her account with a **paradox**. On the surface, she appears calm and confident; inside, she is fearful.

Reading on Your Own In historical fiction, the author writes about real people. But because the author was not present, he or she must imagine what a character might have said. Think of an event that you have read about. Write two or three sentences that a person living through that event might think.

Writing on Your Own Think about a time when you had mixed feelings about something. Identify the feelings; then write a paragraph explaining your experience.

Vocabulary Focus Look at the words the writer uses to describe her children and the pinto beans. Think of synonyms (words that have the same meaning) for some of these words. How does the writer's word choice make the story come alive?

Think Before You Read What do you expect to learn about Minerva in this story?

from

In the Time of the Butterflies

"House Arrest"

All my life, I had been trying to get out of the house. Papá always complained that, of his four girls, I should have been the boy, born to cut loose. First, I wanted to go to boarding school, then university. When Manolo and I started the underground, I traveled back and forth from Monte Cristi to Salcedo, connecting cell with cell. I couldn't stand the idea of being locked up in any one life.

So when we were released in August and put under house arrest, you'd have thought I was getting just the punishment for me. But to tell the truth, it was as if I'd been served my sentence on a silver platter. By then, I couldn't think of anything I wanted more than to stay home with my sisters at Mamá's, raising our children.

Those first few weeks at home took some getting used to. After seven months in prison, a lot of that time in **solitary**, the **overload** was too much. The phone ringing; a visitor

> Manolo is Minerva's husband. They began a secret effort to overthrow the government. This is known as an *underground*. The different groups in the underground are called *cells*.

> *House arrest* means being made to stay in the house.

> Why is staying home no longer a punishment for Minerva?

solitary being made to stay in a jail cell all alone

overload constant activity

> This excerpt contains several idioms. Can you identify them?

dropping by (with permission from Peña, of course); Peña himself dropping by to see about the visitor; Don Bernardo with **guavas** from his tree; rooms to go in and out of; children wanting their shoelaces tied; the phone ringing again; what to do with the **curdled** milk.

In the middle of the day when I should have been out soaking up sun and getting good country air in my **infected** lungs, I would seek the quiet of the bedroom, slip out of my dress and lie under the sheets watching the sun speckling the leaves through the barely opened **jalousies**.

But as I lay there, the same overload would start happening in my head. Bits and pieces of the past would bob up in the watery soup of my thoughts those days—Lió explaining how to hit the volleyball so there was a curve in its fall; the rain falling on our way to Papá's funeral; my hand coming down on Trujillo's face; the doctor slapping her first breath into my newborn baby girl.

> This historical fiction includes real facts about the Dominican Republic. *Trujillo* was the dictator of the Dominican Republic.

I'd sit up, shocked at what I was letting happen to me. I had been so much stronger and braver in prison. Now at home I was falling apart.

Or, I thought, lying back down, I'm ready for a new life, and this is how it starts.

I grew stronger gradually and began taking part in the life of the household.

None of us had any money, and the **dwindling** income from the farm was being stretched mighty thin across five families. So we started up a specialty business of children's christening gowns. I did the simple stitching and seam **binding**.

> Christening gowns are special outfits that babies wear when they are baptized or christened in the Catholic church.

The **pneumonia** in my lungs cleared up. I got my appetite back and began to regain the weight I'd lost in prison. I could wear again my old clothes Doña Fefita had brought down from Monte Cristi.

---

guavas a kind of tropical fruit

curdled spoiled

infected sick; diseased

jalousies window shutters or blinds

dwindling getting smaller

binding sewing the edges together

pneumonia an infection in the lungs

And, of course, my children were a wonder. I'd swoop down on them, showering them with kisses. "Mami!" they'd shriek. How lovely to be called mother again; to have their little arms around my neck; their **sane**, sweet breath in my face.

Mami is the Spanish spelling for Mommy.

And pinto beans—were they always so colorful? "Wait, wait, wait," I'd cry out to Fela before she dunked them in the water. I'd scoop up handfuls just to hear the soft rattle of their downpour back in the pot. Everything I had to touch. Everything I had to taste. I wanted everything back in my life again.

But sometimes a certain slant of light would send me back. The light used to fall just so at this time of day on the floor below my top bunk.

And once, Minou got hold of a piece of pipe and was rattling it against the *galería* rail. It was a sound exactly **recalling** the guards in prison running their nightsticks against the bars. I ran out and yanked the pipe from her hand, screaming, "No!" My poor little girl burst out crying, frightened by the terror in my voice.

A galería is an inside balcony.

But those memories, too, began to fade. They became stories. Everyone wanted to hear them. Mate and I could keep the house entertained for hours, telling and retelling the horrors until the sting was out of them.

We were allowed two outings a week: Thursdays to La Victoria to visit the men, and Sundays to church. But for all that I was free to travel, I dreaded going out of the house. The minute we turned onto the road, my heart started pounding and my breathing got shallow.

---

sane healthy; well   **recalling** remembering

Viva la Mariposa means *Life to the Mariposas*. The sisters' underground code name is *Las Mariposas*.

Here, Minerva behaves one way but feels a different way. How is this a paradox?

The open **vistas** distressed me, the sense of being adrift in a crowd of people pressing in on all sides, wanting to touch me, greet me, wish me well. Even in church during the privacy of Holy Communion, Father Gabriel bent down and whispered *"¡Viva la Mariposa!"*

My months in prison had **elevated** me to superhuman status. It would hardly have been **seemly** for someone who had challenged our **dictator** to suddenly **succumb** to a nervous attack at the communion rail.

I hid my **anxieties** and gave everyone a bright smile. If they had only known how frail was their iron-will heroine. How much it took to put on that hardest of all performances, being my old self again.

vistas large areas of land	**seemly** in good taste; proper	**succumb** give in
elevated raised up	**dictator** the ruler in a government with only one person in charge	**anxieties** fears

AFTER READING THE SELECTION

from In the Time of the Butterflies by Julia Alvarez

Directions Choose the letter of the best answer or write the answer using complete sentences.

Comprehension: Identifying Facts

1. Why did Papá think Minerva should have been the boy?
   A She was very tall.
   B She wanted to be out on her own.
   C She was very athletic.
   D She had a boy's name.

2. How does Minerva's family try to earn money?

3. Where is Minerva allowed to go when she's under house arrest?

Comprehension: Putting Ideas Together

4. Why is Minerva happy to be under house arrest?
   A She prefers to stay out of the sun.
   B She thinks she deserves to be in jail.
   C She hated boarding school.
   D She wants to be home with her family.

5. In what way does Minerva feel that being back home again is a burden?

6. Why does Minerva try to act like she is her old self?

Understanding Literature: Idiom

This excerpt from *In the Time of the Butterflies* contains several idioms. An idiom is a phrase that cannot be understood just by knowing the meanings of the words that make up the phrase. You might think of it as "a figure of speech." For example, when Minerva says she would "swoop down on them, showering them with kisses," she is using an idiom. She is not really pouring water on her children to wash them.

7. Why would an author use idioms?

8. Can you think of an idiom you use frequently in your own conversations? How could it be misunderstood?

Critical Thinking

9. The priest, Father Gabriel, whispers something to Minerva. What does this comment reveal about him?

Thinking Creatively

10. Minerva wants to enjoy everything about her life now that she is home. She even wants to see, touch, hear, and taste the pinto beans in the pot. Before she was sent to jail, she took these simple things for granted. What are some simple things that you sometimes take for granted?

After Reading continued on next page

AFTER READING THE SELECTION (continued)

from In the Time of the Butterflies   by Julia Alvarez

 ### Grammar Check

The writer uses long sentences, with phrases strung together with semicolons. In one instance, Minerva is listing experiences and events at home that were too much for her to take in. Do you think this is a good way to list several things in one sentence? Explain your answer.

 ### Writing on Your Own

Pretend that you are living in the United States during the time that this story takes place. You have learned about Minerva and her sisters. Write a letter to the editor of your local newspaper, telling how you feel about the government of the Dominican Republic.

 ### Speaking and Listening

Did you like this excerpt? Why or why not? Tell your class how you felt about it. Give examples from the excerpt to support your ideas.

Listen carefully as your classmates tell what they thought of the excerpt. Make sure to take notes as you listen. Which classmates felt the same way about the excerpt? Did they have the same reasons for their opinions?

 ### Research

This is a fictional story based on facts from history. One way to learn about history is to look at primary and secondary sources. A primary source is something created by a person who lived during that time. Examples of primary sources are photographs, personal letters, newspaper articles, or diaries. A secondary source is something that is created by an outsider but is factual. Examples of secondary sources are textbooks and encyclopedias. Go to the library or look online to find one primary and one secondary source about Rafael Trujillo and his rule of the Dominican Republic. Write a paragraph summarizing what you have read.

Folktales

Folktales are one of the oldest forms of literature. We imagine that even people in the Stone Age told stories to each other. These stories existed long before people had developed written forms of language.

Folktales are stories that have been handed down from one generation to another. Many of them were first passed down orally. People told them to their children and grandchildren. They, in turn, told *their* children and grandchildren. This oral literature led to many versions of the same folktales. In time, the stories were written down. You may have read different versions of "The Pied Piper of Hamlin," for example.

Folktales are popular among cultures all over the world. They deal with a people's way of life or beliefs. They may try to explain something about nature. The West African folktale "Ananzi's Hat-Shaking Dance" explains why spiders are bald and live in tall grass. Other folktales deal with people's everyday problems. In the Jewish folktale "It Could Always Be Worse," a man complains about his home being too crowded.

Some folktale characters may be well known to you. They include Sinbad the Sailor, Paul Bunyan, and Pecos Bill.

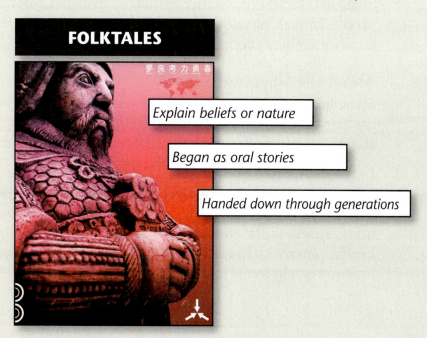

FOLKTALES
- Explain beliefs or nature
- Began as oral stories
- Handed down through generations

BEFORE READING THE SELECTION

A Polite Idiosyncrasy A Chinese Folktale

Objectives
- To read and understand a folktale
- To identify the dialogue spoken by the characters
- To recognize and understand how irony is used in the story

About the Authors
China is one of the oldest countries in the world. It was first joined as one country more than 3,000 years ago. It has had many different forms of government over the years.

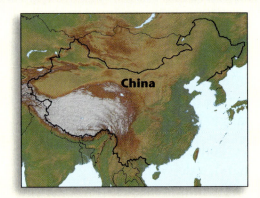

China is also one of the largest countries in the world. Its population is over one billion people. In China, there are many different ethnic groups.

Manners are rules for polite behavior. They are often unspoken rules. Some manners deal with everyday activities, such as eating. Other rules are about dealing with strangers, family members, and even leaders or other important people. Some of the rules deal with conflict, or struggles among people. In the Chinese folktale that follows, you will see how family members choose to deal with conflict.

About the Selection
Some folktales deal with people's fears. This tale deals with the fear of embarrassment or bad feelings. The story is also about how people deal with conflicts among family members.

In the story, three women are talking. At one point, the lights go out. The daughter of one of the women leaves, and two of the women are left alone. One woman begins to talk to the other. However, the woman talking thinks she is talking to her daughter who has left the room. As you read, think about how you might feel if you were in that position.

134 Unit 1 Fiction

Literary Terms **Folktales** have been handed down from one generation to another. Some folktales explain things in nature. Some are riddles. Some are told to warn people what will happen if they do something wrong. "A Polite Idiosyncrasy" is told by an all-knowing narrator. This helps the reader know more about what is happening than if one character told the story. Even though a narrator tells the story, the characters also speak to each other. Quotation marks show what the characters say. The words spoken by the characters are the **dialogue**.

"A Polite Idiosyncrasy" does not state a **moral,** and it doesn't explain something in nature. The story does, however, offer a lesson. It uses irony to help make its point. When a writer uses verbal irony, he or she says one thing but means the opposite.

Reading on Your Own As you read the story, predict what might happen next. Which situation is the opposite of what you expect? This is called situational irony.

Writing on Your Own This story is about a mother and a mother-in-law. The mother does not like the way the mother-in-law treats her guests. Think about how this might make the daughter feel. Write a letter to the mother as if you are the daughter. In the letter, ask your mother to treat your mother-in-law with respect. Be sure to tell why this is important to you.

Vocabulary Focus An *idiosyncrasy* is a habit or odd response that a person has. The title of the story is "A Polite Idiosyncrasy." As you read, try to figure out why the strange behaviors are described as "polite."

Think Before You Read Sometimes people assume that a mother and a mother-in-law cannot get along together. What do you think may happen between these two women?

> **folktale** a story that has been handed down from one generation to another
>
> **dialogue** the conversation among characters in a story
>
> **moral** a lesson or message told in a story

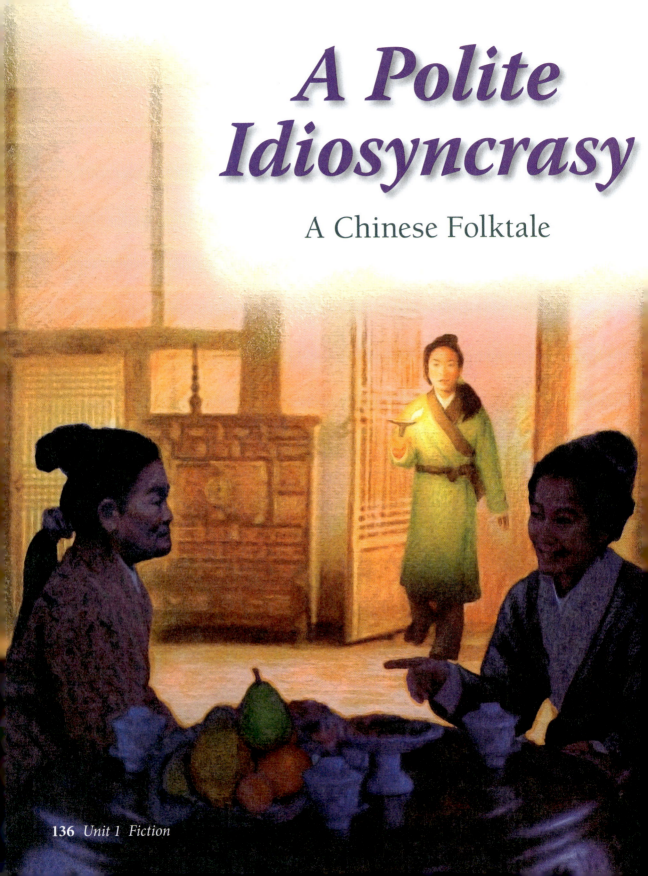

An old woman went to visit a married daughter who lived with her husband's mother. She found all the family absent, except her daughter, and her daughter's mother-in-law. The mother was invited to stay and take supper with the other two women, and just after nightfall, the three sat down to take their evening meal together. They were barely seated at the table, when a gust of wind blew out the lamp and they were left in darkness. The mother-in-law said: "Sit still, both of you, and I will go and light the lamp." But while she was speaking the daughter took the lamp and went away to light it.

The mother, supposing that the mother-in-law had gone, and that her daughter sat beside her in the dark, **hastened** to say that, during meals, a guest should be served with the choicest of the **viands**. That side of the platter holding the tenderest portions of the meat, and that side of the dish on which lay the ripest of the fruit, should be turned toward the guest, so that the best might be taken, without an appearance of greediness. If the guest were one's own mother, then **filial piety**, as well as **hospitality**, required that these attentions should be **scrupulously bestowed**. She had scarcely given these instructions when the light reappeared, and she discovered that she had been talking, not to her daughter, but to her son-in-law's mother! Horrified by her mistake, she at once cast about in her own mind for a way of recovering the mother-in-law's respect, and then said: "I have a curious peculiarity which has **afflicted** me all my life. If, at any time, the light suddenly goes out, and I am left in the dark, my mind wanders and I talk without purpose till the light reappears." "Ah," responded the mother-in-law, "I wholly understand a peculiarity of that sort, for I myself have a somewhat similar one. Whenever the lamp goes out in the evening, I at once become stone-deaf, and only recover my hearing after the lamp is again lighted!"

This story takes place long before people used electricity as a source of light. The women are using an oil lamp. The daughter leaves to relight the lamp.

Notice that the writer uses quotation marks to identify only spoken dialogue. In other places, the narrator reports what is being said. The writer does not use quotation marks for this.

This is an example of something that an all-knowing narrator would say.

Curious has more than one meaning. In this sentence, it means "strange or unusual."

---

hastened hurried
viands foods or drinks
filial piety respect for family members
hospitality the practice of going out of one's way to treat guests well
scrupulously with great care and in good conscience
bestowed given
afflicted troubled or harmed

Fiction Unit 1 137

AFTER READING THE SELECTION

A Polite Idiosyncrasy — A Chinese Folktale

Directions Choose the letter of the best answer or write the answer using complete sentences.

Comprehension: Identifying Facts

1. Why were the women in the dark?
   A It was their custom to eat in the dark.
   B The daughter did not pay her electric bill.
   C They ran out of oil for their lamp.
   D The wind blew out the lamp.

2. Why did the daughter leave the room?

3. What did the mother-in-law say happened to her in the dark?

Comprehension: Putting Ideas Together

4. Why did the mother think she was talking to her daughter?
   A The daughter was still talking.
   B The mother-in-law had offered to light the lamp.
   C The mother-in-law was deaf.
   D The mother-in-law had fallen asleep.

5. How do you know that the mother-in-law is willing to forgive the mother?

6. Think about what the mother said in the dark. What do you think happened earlier when the women sat down to eat?

Understanding Literature: Folktales

Folktales are part of the traditions and customs of a culture. They help form the folklore of that culture. Even though folktales don't usually have morals the way that fables do, they can still teach lessons. The stories passed down from parents to children help the children learn about themselves and their society.

7. Think back to the title of the folktale. What are the "polite idiosyncrasies" in this story?

8. Many folktales began as oral stories told by older people to their children and grandchildren. Why might someone tell this story to his or her child?

Critical Thinking

9. This story is about how people deal with uncomfortable situations. What do you think the author's purpose is?

Thinking Creatively

10. Suppose you were the mother-in-law in this story. How would you respond to the mother's explanation? Explain your answer.

Grammar Check

Parts of this story are written in the passive voice. In the passive voice, the subject-verb-object word order is reversed. Look at the sentences below. Notice that in the active sentences the subject comes before the verb. In the passive sentences, the subject is either left out or is the object of a preposition.

Active Voice	Passive Voice
Anne ate the apple.	The apple was eaten by Anne.
You should give me the book.	The book should be given to me.

Read the narrator's description of what the mother said to the mother-in-law. Rewrite this section of text using the active voice. The first phrase is done for you below.

Passive Voice: . . . a guest should be served with the choicest of the viands.

Active Voice: You should serve your guest the choicest of the viands.

 Writing on Your Own

Write a paragraph telling people how to treat each other. Use the ideas in this story to help you. Use correct subject-verb agreement in your sentences. Make sure that your paragraph has a topic sentence and supporting details.

 Speaking and Listening

Think about how the folktale might have ended differently. What if the daughter had gotten involved in the situation? What if one of the characters had become very angry? Work in pairs or small groups. Discuss some possible endings and choose the one you find most interesting. Present your alternate ending to the class.

Listen carefully as the other groups describe possible endings to the folktale. As a class, choose the ending that shows the most imagination. What would be the lesson of the story if it had this ending?

 Research

Use the folktale and fable section of the library and the Internet to find other Chinese folktales. Read at least two other Chinese folktales. Give a summary of your favorite Chinese folktale to the class.

Fiction Unit 1 139

BEFORE READING THE SELECTIONS

Bye-bye and The Story of the Bat — Folktales from Haiti and the United States

Objectives
- To read and understand folktales
- To explain symbolism in a story

About the Authors

"Bye-bye" is a folktale from Haiti. Haiti is located on part of an island in the Caribbean Sea. The Dominican Republic is on the other side of the island. Haiti was once a French colony with many slaves. The slaves overthrew French rule in 1803. In 1804, it became the second country in this hemisphere to declare independence. Today, Haiti is the poorest country in the Western Hemisphere.

"The Story of the Bat" comes from the Creek Indians of the United States. The Creek Indians, also known as the Muskogee Indians, were made up of many different tribes. They lived in the area that is now Georgia, Alabama, and Florida. In the 1600s, Europeans began to take over parts of North America. Other American Indians moved south and also forced the Creeks off of their land. The Creeks moved west, to Oklahoma.

About the Selections

Both of these folktales use animals to tell a story. "Bye-bye" is about a pigeon who travels from Haiti to New York City. It describes a turtle who also wants to go to New York.

"The Story of the Bat" describes an imaginary ball game. This folktale was first written down in the 1880s. It was told to Creek children for many generations before that.

In some ways, these stories are like myths, explaining why certain things are as they are today. "Bye-bye" tells why there are few turtles in New York. "The Story of the Bat" might explain why bats are classified as mammals, not as birds. These stories are part of the folklore of people in Haiti and the native culture of the Creeks.

Literary Terms Both of these selections are folktales. Children heard these stories from their parents and grandparents. Then they grew up and told them to their children. In these folktales, the characters are animals.

The stories also use **symbolism**. Symbolism is the use of a person, place, or thing to represent something larger than itself. For example, the pigeon and the bat in the folktales could represent different types of people.

> **symbolism** the use of a person, place, or thing to represent something larger than itself

Reading on Your Own As you read the tales, try to think about someone telling you these stories aloud. How would you feel as you listened? What would make you want to hear one of the stories again and again?

Writing on Your Own Have you ever forgotten to do something important, such as returning a library book? Write a paragraph telling what you forgot and what happened as a result.

Vocabulary Focus Many vocabulary words in "The Story of the Bat" are verbs in the past tense. For example, *challenged* is the past tense of the verb *challenge*. This expresses an action that was completed in the past. Sometimes verbs in the past tense take helping verbs. For example, the past perfect tense of *challenge* is *had challenged*. Write the past perfect tense of these words: *gather, began,* and *fall*.

Think Before You Read Who do you think will be the hero of each folktale?

BYE-BYE

> What do you think the turtle and the pigeon symbolize?

All the birds were flying from Haiti to New York. But Turtle could not go, for he had no wings.

Pigeon felt sorry for Turtle and said, "Turtle, I'll take you with me. This is what we'll do. I'll hold in my mouth one end of a piece of wood and you hold on to the other end. But you must not let go. No matter what happens, do not let go or you'll fall into the water."

Pigeon took one end of a piece of wood and Turtle the other end. Up into the air Pigeon flew and Turtle with him, across the land and toward the sea.

As they came near the ocean, Turtle and Pigeon saw on the shore a group of animals who had gathered together to wave goodbye to the birds who were leaving. They were waving steadily until they noticed Turtle and Pigeon. Turtle? They stopped waving and a great **hubbub** broke out.

"Look!" they cried to each other. "Turtle is going to New York. Even Turtle is going to New York!"

And Turtle was so pleased to hear everyone talking about him that he called out the one English word he knew:

"Bye-bye!"

Oh-oh. Turtle had opened his mouth, and in opening his mouth to speak, he let go of the piece of wood and fell into the sea.

For that reason there are many Pigeons in New York, but Turtle is still in Haiti.

hubbub noise; sound of people all talking at once

The Story

Who are the characters in this story?

The birds **challenged** the four-footed animals to play them in a ball game. Each group agreed that all creatures that had teeth should play on the side of the animals, and all those that had feathers should play on the side of the birds.

They chose a **suitable** day, cleared a playing field, **erected** poles, and **obtained** balls from the medicine men.

When the players gathered, all that had teeth went on one side and those that had feathers went on the other. When the Bat came, he joined the animals that had teeth.

"No," the animals said to Bat. "You have wings. You must play with the birds."

Why do you think this story would have been told to children?

Bat went over to the side of the birds, but they said: "No, you have teeth. You must play with the animals." They drove him away, saying: "You are so small, you could do us no good anyway."

And so Bat went back to the animals, begging them to let him play with them. At last they agreed: "You are too small to help us, but as you have teeth we will let you remain on our side."

The game began, and the birds quickly took the lead because they could catch the ball in the air where the four-footed animals could not reach it. The Crane was the best player, and he caught the ball so often that it looked as if the birds were going to win the game. As none of the animals could fly, they were in **despair.**

---

challenged dared; invited to do something difficult

suitable fitting; proper for the purpose

erected put upright; built

obtained got

despair a heavy feeling of hopelessness

144   Unit 1 Fiction

of the Bat

The little bat now entered the game, flying into the air and catching the ball while the Crane was flapping slowly along. Again and again Bat caught the ball, and he won the game for the four-footed animals.

They agreed that even though Bat was very small and had wings he should always be **classed** with the animals having teeth.

"Bat Design on Mola," by Kevin Schafer, ca. 1994. From Cuna Indians in Panama's San Blas Archipelago.

classed grouped

AFTER READING THE SELECTIONS

Bye-bye and The Story of the Bat — folktales from Haiti and the United States

Directions Choose the letter of the best answer or write the answer using complete sentences.

Comprehension: Identifying Facts

1. Turtle cannot go to New York on his own. Why?
   - **A** He cannot swim.
   - **B** He has no wings.
   - **C** He is too small.
   - **D** He is too slow.

2. Who agrees to help Turtle?

3. Why do the birds tell Bat he cannot be with them?

Comprehension: Putting Ideas Together

4. Why does Turtle let go of the piece of wood?
   - **A** He wants to say good-bye.
   - **B** He does not want to go to New York.
   - **C** He does not want to stay in Haiti.
   - **D** He really should be classified with the animals having teeth.

5. How does flying help the birds take the lead in the ballgame with the four-footed animals?

6. Why do the animals with teeth finally accept Bat?

Understanding Literature: Symbolism

Symbolism is the use of a person, place, or thing to represent something larger than itself. In the folklore of some North American Indian tribes, the bat symbolizes, or stands for, people who don't fit in. Because bats have both teeth like the animals and wings like the birds, they don't really belong in either category. Bats symbolize different things in different cultures. For example, bats are thought of as messengers or guardians in some cultures. In Chinese folklore, they symbolize good luck.

7. Think of some animals you are familiar with. What could they symbolize?

8. Why do you think so many cultures use animal symbolism in their folktales?

Critical Thinking

9. What types of people do you think Pigeon and Bat symbolize? Explain your reasoning.

Thinking Creatively

10. "Bye-bye" is a folktale, not a fable. It does not end with a stated moral. Write a moral that could be added to the end of this story.

Grammar Check

There are simple rules to help you know when to use *who* or *whom* in a sentence. *Who* is only used when it is the subject. *Whom* is only used when it is the object. Rewrite this sentence from "Bye-bye":

> As they come near the ocean, Turtle and Pigeon saw on the shore a group of animals *who* had gathered together to wave goodbye to the birds *who* were leaving.

Notice that the first *who* describes *a group of animals* that *had gathered*. *A group of animals* is the subject and *had gathered* is the verb. The second *who* describes *the birds* that *were leaving*. Again, *the birds* is the subject and *were leaving* is the verb.

 Writing on Your Own

Which folktale did you like better? Write a paragraph explaining why you liked that one.

 Speaking

Both of these stories were told orally long before they were written down. Think of a story that has been told again and again in your family. It can be a true story or one that is fictional. Make sure it is OK with your family to share the story. Tell your story to the class.

 Listening

Often people use jargon and slang in their casual speech. Jargon is a language of words that are related to a certain job or area of study. People who do not work in those jobs or areas of study may not know what the words mean. Slang is a language of words that are usually made up by a group of people. Outsiders often do not know what the words mean. Listen carefully as your classmates tell their family stories. Try to notice if they use any jargon or slang. Write down these words. Ask your classmates to explain any words you do not understand.

 Viewing

Show how Bat fits with both the birds and the four-footed animals. You can write words in a Venn Diagram, or you can use a chart and draw pictures in each section of the chart. See Appendix A for descriptions of graphic organizers.

Fiction Unit 1   147

Unit 1 SKILLS LESSON
Plot

Plot is the action or the main events in a story. Each plot has a beginning, middle, and end. It might begin with a puzzle. Action starts when the characters learn about the puzzle. The middle tells the events as the characters try to solve the puzzle. The end solves the puzzle. For example:

Beginning
- Introduce the puzzle.

Middle
- Try to solve the puzzle by working through conflict.

End
- Solve the puzzle.

Below is a list of events in "The Adventure of the Speckled Band." They are divided into parts of the plot:

Beginning
- Helen Stoner calls on Sherlock Holmes. She asks him to solve the mystery of her sister's death.
- Holmes takes the case.

Middle
- Holmes and Watson visit the manor house. They wait in the dark.
- Holmes hears something. He hits at it with his cane.
- The stepfather screams. He is found dead. The "speckled band" around his head is a deadly snake.

End
- Holmes shows how the stepfather caused the snake to bite the sister. Holmes had scared the snake and sent it back through the air vent. Then the snake bit the stepfather.
- Holmes also explains why the stepfather wanted Julia Stoner dead.

Review

1. What is a plot?
2. Which part of a plot gives the puzzle to be solved?
3. In which part of the plot does Holmes figure out about the snake?
4. In which part of the plot does Holmes explain what he has learned?
5. Did Doyle use a plot that kept you interested? Why or why not?

Writing on Your Own

Make up your own story. Think about the plot. What will be the beginning, middle, and end? Write two sentences for each part of the plot.

Unit 1 SUMMARY

In Unit 1, you have read several types of fiction. In a detective story, the protagonist looks for clues to solve a crime. Science fiction imagines the effects of science and technology on life in the future. The protagonist in an adventure story survives by wits and luck. Turning points are about experiences that change characters' lives. Some turning points are "coming-of-age" stories. Folktales are stories that have been passed down from one generation to the next.

Selections

- "The Adventure of the Speckled Band" by Sir Arthur Conan Doyle. Sherlock Holmes solves the murder of a young woman.

- "Death Arrives on Schedule" by Hansjörg Martin. A killer has bad luck with well-laid plans.

- "The Feeling of Power" by Isaac Asimov. In a world run by computers, a technician learns the power of the human mind.

- "The Expedition" by Rudolf Lorenzen. Four astronauts and their descendants make a space expedition but learn little from it.

- "The Cegua" by Robert D. San Souci. A lone traveler has a frightening experience on the road.

- *Master and Man* by Leo Tolstoy. A rich man looks for help after he and his servant are stranded in a snowstorm.

- "Just Lather, That's All" by Hernando Téllez. A barber, a secret rebel, has a chance to murder the captain whose soldiers have been killing his friends.

- "Marriage Is a Private Affair" by Chinua Achebe. A Nigerian family is split when a man marries a woman who is not of his tribe.

- "Cranes" by Hwang Sun-won. A South Korean soldier meets a boyhood friend who has been taken prisoner.

- *In the Time of the Butterflies* by Julia Alvarez. A woman tells what it is like to live at home after spending time in prison.

- "A Polite Idiosyncrasy," a Chinese folktale. Two women handle conflict by pretending that nothing happened.

- "Bye-bye," a Haitian folktale. A turtle and a pigeon leave Haiti for New York, but only the pigeon makes it.

- "The Story of the Bat," a Creek Indian folktale. Bat helps the four-footed animals win a ball game against the birds.

Unit 1 REVIEW

Directions Choose the letter of the best answer or write the answer using complete sentences.

Comprehension: Identifying Facts

1. _____ deals with what the future might be like.
   A An adventure story
   B A folktale
   C A detective story
   D Science fiction

2. Name two countries in which these stories take place.

3. Name one story whose setting is a long time ago.

4. Name one of the stories that is set in the future.

5. Name the protagonist of one story. Tell what story he or she is in.

Comprehension: Putting Ideas Together

6. What is the turning point in "Marriage Is a Private Affair"?
   A when Okeke learns he has two grandsons
   B when Okeke returns half of the wedding photo
   C when Nnaemeka tells his father of his engagement
   D when Nene and Nnaemeka get married

7. What is the mystery that Sherlock Holmes solves?

8. "The Story of the Bat" and "Bye-bye" are folktales. How are they alike? How are they different?

9. The protagonists in "The Cegua" and "Just Lather, That's All" both experience an adventure. How are their adventures alike? How are they different?

10. Explain at least one difference between a detective story and a science fiction story.

Understanding Literature: Fiction

Stories that did not happen are called fiction. Some fiction seems very real. Other fiction is clearly not real. Science fiction, for example, is often set in the future. We know it could not have happened. Fiction is made up of characters, setting, and plot. Characters are the people, animals, or things in the story. They perform the action. Setting is the time and place in the story. Plot is the action in the story.

11. Name a story from the unit in which the setting is very important. Why is it important?

12. Name a story that is realistic. What makes it realistic?

13. Name a story that is not realistic. How do you know it is not realistic?

14. Some of these stories show a change in the main character's feelings. Name one of these stories. What was the change?

15. Choose one story. Briefly, what happens in the plot?

Critical Thinking

16. Which genre would you most enjoy watching as a movie? Why?

17. Which story did you like best? Why?

18. Name a story that had a moral, or lesson. What is the moral?

19. Choose a character from this unit that you do not like. Tell why.

Thinking Creatively

20. Which genre of fiction do you like best? Why?

Speak and Listen

Choose a story that has dialogue, or characters talking to each other. Work with a partner. Each of you will choose one of the characters. Practice reading each character's words aloud. Think about how that person would speak. Try to make your words sound like a real conversation. Read the dialogue for the class.

Writing on Your Own

Endings can be very important to stories. Write an essay about why the ending of a story is often the most important part. Begin your essay with a general statement about endings. Add statements to support your idea. Use stories from this unit as examples.

Beyond Words

Choose one of these fiction stories you think would make a good movie. Think of an exciting scene from the story. What is the setting and action? What characters are in it? Draw a poster of that scene to advertise the movie. Remember that your poster should make people want to see the movie.

Test-Taking Tip

Be sure you understand what a test question is asking. Read it twice if necessary.

"Old Photographs in the International House Museum"
Saint Kitts and Nevis. Photograph by Bob Krist.

BIOGRAPHY

Unit 2: Nonfiction

Nonfiction by authors all over the world gives us new ways to look at people and places. Their letters, autobiographies, biographies, and articles are a valuable resource for learning about our world.

Unit 2 Selections	Page
DIARIES, JOURNALS, AND LETTERS	156
■ NETHERLANDS from *Anne Frank: The Diary of a Young Girl* by Anne Frank	157
■ INDIA "Letter to Indira Tagore" by Rabindranath Tagore	166
■ UNITED STATES "Letter to the Reverend J. H. Twichell" by Mark Twain	172
■ CANADA from *Writing with Intent: Essays, Reviews, Personal Prose 1983–2005* by Margaret Atwood	178
AUTOBIOGRAPHIES	185
■ VIETNAM from *When Heaven and Earth Changed Places* by Le Ly Hayslip	186
■ INDIA "By Any Other Name" by Santha Rama Rau	196
■ SOUTH AFRICA from *Kaffir Boy* by Mark Mathabane	209
■ IRAN from *Reading Lolita in Tehran* by Azar Nafisi	231
BIOGRAPHIES	238
■ UNITED STATES from *China Men* by Maxine Hong Kingston	239
■ NETHERLANDS from *The Last Seven Months of Anne Frank* by Willy Lindwer	246
JOURNALISM	255
■ PAKISTAN *Account Evened With India, Says PM* by M. Ziauddin from *Dawn*	256
■ INDIA *Tests Are Nowhere Near India's: Fernandes* from the *Times of India*	263
■ GREAT BRITAIN *Pakistan Nuclear Moratorium Welcomed* from the *BBC Online Network*	272
■ NETHERLANDS *The Frightening Joy* from *De Volkskrant*	278
■ POLAND *Building Atomic Security* by Tomasz Wroblewski from *Zycie Warszawy*	278

"Everybody has a story and all stories are interesting if they are told in the right tone."
—Isabelle Allende, author

"Writing has been a way of explaining to myself the things I do not understand."
—Rosario Castellanos, poet

Unit 2

About Nonfiction

Nonfiction literature is about real people, settings, and events. It can be divided into several genres, or types of stories. The most personal kinds of nonfiction are diaries, journals, and letters. In diaries and journals, writers express feelings. Journals often contain a writer's first impressions and reactions about places and events as well as emotions. Letters are written to a specific person. This means the writer might leave out certain kinds of information. The writer might also include information of interest to the specific person.

Nonfiction that describes a person's life can be an autobiography or a biography. Both genres describe events, people, places, and feelings from the person's life. They can also give a colorful picture of the person. When people tell their own stories, the books are called autobiographies. In an autobiography, the author usually tells how he or she personally felt about what happened. When a different person tells the story, it is called a biography. Biographies don't focus on feelings as much as autobiographies.

Journalism is another type of nonfiction. It answers the "who," "what," "where," "when," "why," and "how" of an event clearly and quickly. The first reports of journalists are news stories. These are the stories you see on the front page of a newspaper or on the cover of a magazine. Feature stories come after the first reports. They examine, explain, and judge the importance of the news. Sometimes, feature stories grow into books as their authors collect information. The Internet is having an enormous effect on journalism. Many newspapers are putting their stories online. Two of the journalism selections in this unit were first published on the Internet.

The following countries are represented in this unit: Canada, Great Britain, India, Iran, Netherlands, Pakistan, Poland, South Africa, United States, and Vietnam.

Nonfiction Unit 2

Diaries, Journals, and Letters

The most personal form of writing is the diary or journal. A writer often thinks of a diary as an imaginary friend. Keeping a diary gives a writer a chance to express anger, fear, or jealousy that he or she may be embarrassed to tell anyone. A writer might also explore more positive thoughts and feelings, including love and spirituality.

Diaries and journals are helpful to people trying to sort out problems in their lives, especially when they are going through times of growth and change. A person may also keep a journal to remind himself or herself of interesting events, sights, or ideas. For example, many people keep journals as they travel. This record of places they visit and people they meet can help them remember their travel experiences.

A letter also can discuss opinions or events, but it communicates with a real person. A writer keeps that person in mind while writing, which helps the letter "speak" effectively.

A writer of a diary, journal, or letter may use that source in later writing. Sometimes the events and people change. This is because the writer has thought about how to use the experiences effectively. These peeks into a writer's life can sometimes help a reader better understand the writer.

Today, handwritten communication is less popular than it once was, especially among young people. Most people use telephones or computers to reach others. They like being able to contact people and get information instantly. Perhaps you have read a book of letters that historical figures sent to each other. You will agree that the written word holds a special charm that you cannot find in electronic writing.

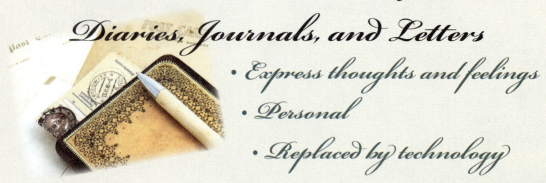

Diaries, Journals, and Letters
- *Express thoughts and feelings*
- *Personal*
- *Replaced by technology*

BEFORE READING THE SELECTION

from Anne Frank: The Diary of a Young Girl   by Anne Frank (trans. B. M. Mooyaart)

Anne Frank
(1929–1945)
Dutch

About the Author

Anne Frank was the younger of two daughters in a wealthy Jewish family. She was born in Germany in 1929. A few years later, the Frank family moved to Holland (also called the Netherlands). In 1940, Germany invaded Holland. Adolf Hitler, leader of Nazi Germany, wanted to destroy all the Jews in Europe. Within one year, Dutch Jews were being sent to concentration camps. Many Jewish people went into hiding in an effort to escape the Nazis. In 1942, Anne and her family went into hiding in a space above her father's office that Anne called the "secret annex." An annex is an added part of a building.

The group lived in this secret annex for two years. In 1944 the Nazis discovered them and sent them to concentration camps. In 1945, shortly before the end of World War II, Anne died of typhus in the Bergen-Belsen camp. She was 15 years old.

Objectives

- To read and understand a diary excerpt
- To identify where parts of a selection are left out

About the Selection

Anne received a diary for her 13th birthday. She thought of it as a secret friend. (She even called it "Kitty.") Her diary records the boredom of daytime silence, quarrels with her family, and dreams of a romance with Peter, a 16-year-old boy hiding with them.

After World War II, Anne's father returned to Holland. There he found his daughter's diary. He decided to share it with the world in a book. The book, *Anne Frank: The Diary of a Young Girl*, was later made into a play and a film.

Before Reading continued on next page

BEFORE READING THE SELECTION (continued)

from Anne Frank: The Diary of a Young Girl by Anne Frank (trans. B. M. Mooyaart)

diary a daily record of personal events, thoughts, or private feelings

nonfiction writing about real people and events

excerpt a short passage from a longer piece of writing

Literary Terms The following passages come from Anne Frank's **diary**. A diary is a daily record of personal events, thoughts, or private feelings. Frank's diary is a record of two years in hiding. It is a work of **nonfiction,** writing about real people and events.

In this selection, there are three **excerpts** from the entire diary. An excerpt is a short passage from a longer piece of writing. Parts of each short passage have been left out as well. You can tell when there are missing parts of the text by the ellipses. Ellipses are three or four periods that are put in place of text that has been left out.

Reading on Your Own Look for the ellipses as you read. What do you think might have been left out of each excerpt?

Writing on Your Own Do you think that writing in a diary would be helpful to you? Why or why not? Write a paragraph explaining your answer.

Vocabulary Focus Sometimes people use the same adjectives over and over again. It might get boring if you always described things as "good" or "bad." This selection uses some different adjectives in place of those words. Write the words "good" and "bad" at opposite ends of a Semantic Line. Then look through the story to find the words that Frank uses instead of these. Write each word on the Semantic Line. Finally, work with a partner to write sentences of your own, using the words from your Semantic Line. See Appendix A for a description of this graphic organizer.

Think Before You Read Think of a time you have been crowded together with your family for a long time. Examples are a long trip by car, or being kept inside your house by a storm. What difficulties did people in your family experience from being too close together over too long a time?

from Anne Frank: The Diary of a Young Girl

Thursday, 16 March 1944

Dear Kitty,

The weather is lovely, **superb**, I can't describe it; I'm going up to the attic in a minute.

Now I know why I'm so much more **restless** than Peter. He has his own room where he can work, dream, think, and sleep. I am shoved about from one corner to another. I hardly spend any time in my "double" room and yet it's something I long for so much. That is the reason too why I so frequently escape to the attic. There, and with you, I can be myself for a while, just a little while. Still, I don't want to moan about myself, on the contrary, I want to be brave. Thank goodness the others can't tell what my inward feelings are, except that I'm growing cooler towards Mummy daily, I'm not so **affectionate** to Daddy and don't tell Margot a single thing. I'm completely closed up. Above all, I must maintain my outward reserve, no one must know that war still **reigns incessantly** within. War between desire and common sense. The **latter** has won up till now; yet will the former prove to be the stronger of the two? Sometimes I fear that it will and sometimes I long for it to be!

> As you read, remember that Anne Frank is writing in the small hiding place she shares with her family and several other people.

---

superb of unusually high quality

restless never still or quiet

affectionate showing loving, fond feelings for someone

reigns rules or controls

incessantly without stopping

latter the second of two things mentioned

Oh, it is so terribly difficult never to say anything to Peter, but I know that the first to begin must be he; there's so much I want to say and do, I've lived it all in my dreams, it is so hard to find that yet another day has gone by, and none of it comes true! Yes, Kitty, Anne is a crazy child, but I do live in crazy times and under still crazier **circumstances**.

But, still, the brightest spot of all is that at least I can write down my thoughts and feelings, otherwise I would be absolutely **stifled**! . . .

Yours, Anne

> How does writing in her diary help Anne Frank?

Friday, 17 March 1944

Dear Kitty, . . .

Margot and I are getting a bit tired of our parents. Don't **misunderstand** me, I can't get on well with Mummy at the moment, as you know. I still love Daddy just as much, and Margot loves Daddy and Mummy, but when you are as old as we are, you do want to decide just a few things for yourself, you want to be independent sometimes.

> *Kitty* is Anne's name for her diary. How does this show that she thinks of the diary as a friend?

If I go upstairs, then I'm asked what I'm going to do, I'm not allowed salt with my food, every evening regularly at a quarter past eight Mummy asks whether I ought not to start undressing, every book I read must be inspected. I must admit that they are not at all strict, and I'm allowed to read nearly everything, and yet we are both sick of all the remarks plus all the questioning that go on the whole day long.

> Why do you think Anne is not allowed salt with her food?

Something else, especially about me, that doesn't please them: I don't feel like giving lots of kisses any more and I think fancy nicknames are terribly **affected**. In short, I'd really like to be rid of them for a while. Margot said last evening, "I think it's awfully annoying, the way they ask if

> Who is Margot?

circumstances the way someone lives

stifled choked or smothered

misunderstand take in a wrong way

affected false; used to impress others

The building that Anne Frank and her family lived in is now a museum.

you've got a headache, or whether you don't feel well, if you happen to give a sigh and put your hand to your head!"

It is a great blow to us both, suddenly to realize how little remains of the confidence and **harmony** that we used to have at home. And it's largely due to the fact that we're all "skew-wiff" here. By this I mean that we are treated as children over outward things, and we are much older than most girls of our age inwardly.

Although I'm only fourteen, I know quite well what I want, I know who is right and who is wrong, I have my opinions, my own ideas and principles, and although it may sound pretty mad from an **adolescent**, I feel more of a person than a child, I feel quite independent of anyone.

harmony agreement **adolescent** a teenager or young person

I know that I can discuss things and argue better than Mummy, I know I'm not so **prejudiced**, I don't **exaggerate** so much, I am more **precise** and **adroit** and because of this—you may laugh—I feel superior to her over a great many things. If I love anyone, above all I must have admiration for them, admiration and respect. Everything would be all right if only I had Peter, for I do admire him in many ways. He is such a nice, good-looking boy!

Yours, Anne

Saturday, 15 July 1944

Dear Kitty,

> Notice the ellipses at the beginning of this entry. What do they tell you about this excerpt?

... "For in its **innermost** depths youth is lonelier than old age." I read this saying in some book and I've always remembered it, and found it to be true. Is it true then that grownups have a more difficult time here than we do? No. I know it isn't. Older people have formed their opinions about everything, and don't **waver** before they act. It's twice as hard for us young ones to hold our ground, and maintain our opinions, in a time when all ideals are being shattered and destroyed, when people are showing their worst side, and do not know whether to believe in truth and right and God.

Anyone who claims that the older ones have a more difficult time here certainly doesn't realize to what extent our problems weigh down on us, problems for which we are probably much too young, but which thrust themselves upon us continually, until, after a long time, we think we've found a solution, but the solution doesn't seem able to resist the facts which reduce it to nothing again. That's the difficulty in these times: ideals, dreams, and **cherished** hopes rise within us, only to meet the horrible truth and be shattered.

> As a Jew during World War II, what might Anne mean about "the horrible truth"?

prejudiced having an unfair opinion

exaggerate make something greater or more serious than it really is

precise exact

adroit skillful

innermost most personal; deepest

waver be unsure

cherished kept fondly in mind

It's really a wonder that I haven't dropped all my ideals, because they seem so absurd and impossible to carry out. Yet I keep them, because in spite of everything I still believe that people are really good at heart. I simply can't build up my hopes on a foundation consisting of confusion, **misery**, and death. I see the world gradually being turned into a wilderness, I hear the ever approaching thunder, which will destroy us too, I can feel the suffering of millions and yet, if I look up into the heavens, I think that it will all come right, that this **cruelty** too will end, and that peace and **tranquillity** will return again.

In the meantime, I must **uphold** my ideals, for perhaps the time will come when I shall be able to carry them out.

Yours, Anne

> What ideals is Anne holding on to?

The actual pages from Anne Frank's diary are on view at the Anne Frank museum in Amsterdam.

misery great pain

cruelty something that causes pain or suffering

tranquillity calmness; peace

uphold maintain; keep

AFTER READING THE SELECTION

from Anne Frank: The Diary of a Young Girl   by Anne Frank (trans. B. M. Mooyaart)

Directions Choose the letter of the best answer or write the answer using complete sentences.

Comprehension: Identifying Facts

1. Besides Anne, who else is getting tired of parents?
   A Peter C Margot
   B Mummy D Kitty

2. What does Anne think about Peter?

3. Why doesn't Anne tell Peter how she feels?

Comprehension: Putting Ideas Together

4. Why do her parents' questions bother Anne?
   A Her parents are secretly working with the Nazis.
   B She thinks she is too old for these kinds of questions.
   C She doesn't love her parents anymore.
   D She thinks her parents love her sister more than they love her.

5. Why does Anne "escape" to the attic?

6. How has hiding changed Anne?

Understanding Literature: Diary

A diary entry is often written in the form of a letter. In fact, many people begin each entry with "Dear Diary." People then write their most private thoughts and feelings in those letters. It is as if the diary were a very close friend. Anne seemed to think of her diary as a close friend, too. She even named her diary. She began each entry with "Dear Kitty."

7. List one advantage of thinking of a diary as a person rather than as a book.

8. How would the "letters" be different if they were written to a real person? Explain your answer.

Critical Thinking

9. On July 15, 1944, Anne asked, "Is it true then that grownups have a more difficult time here than we do?" Do you agree with her answer? Explain.

Thinking Creatively

10. List the most important problems Anne faced. How would you deal with those problems if they were yours?

Grammar Check

Sometimes a writer uses an unusual word order in a sentence. The writer does this to make the language more poetic. Here are a few examples of this style from this selection.

"the first to begin must be he"

"I hear the ever approaching thunder"

"this cruelty too will end"

Rewrite each of these phrases using a more typical word order. Then decide whose sentences you like better—yours or Anne Frank's.

 Writing on Your Own

The last two paragraphs of Anne's July 15 entry explain her beliefs. They also predict what will happen in the future. Think about what really happened. Write a paragraph explaining which ideas you agree with and which ideas you disagree with.

 Speaking

For more than two years, Anne lived in a small, hidden apartment. Everyone had to be very quiet, especially during the day, when people worked in the office below them. Many of them did not know that the Franks and other people were hiding above them. Discuss with a partner how living in a crowded, secret place changed things in Anne's family.

 Listening

Have your teacher or a classmate read one entry aloud. Listen as the person reads, thinking about how Anne must have felt as she wrote. Take the time to reflect on what you have heard. Write a short paragraph telling how you felt as you listened to Anne's diary entry.

 Media

The mass killing of Jews by the Nazis during World War II is called the Holocaust. Borrow a documentary about World War II and the Holocaust from your library. Watch part of the documentary with your class. Then write a paragraph comparing a diary to a documentary.

 Research

There are many Holocaust memorials, traveling exhibits, and museums throughout the United States and other parts of the world. Research some of them. Write and ask for brochures and other information. Make a booklet, poster, or "museum wall" from the information that you receive.

BEFORE READING THE SELECTION

Letter to Indira Tagore by Rabindranath Tagore (trans. by Krishna Dutta & Andrew Robinson)

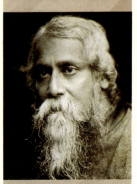

Rabindranath Tagore
(1861–1941)
Indian

Objectives

- To read and understand a letter
- To understand the importance of the audience for a letter
- To identify and explain personification in a piece of writing

About the Author

Rabindranath Tagore was born in Calcutta, India. Many people in his family were artists, musicians, and social reformers. A social reformer is someone who tries to change laws in order to help people. Tagore was brought up among books and other literature. He began writing poems in the Bengali language when he was young. Tagore greatly admired the English poets Shelley and Keats.

Tagore received the Nobel Prize for Literature in 1913. The prize was for an English translation of *Gitanjali,* a collection of his poetry. King George V of England knighted him in 1914. (Tagore later gave back his knighthood. He was angry about Britain's treatment of Indians.) Tagore also wrote essays, novels, and short stories. Many of his poems were set to music.

Tagore had other interests, too. In 1901 he started a "world university" near Calcutta. This school was called Shantiniketan. This means "The House of Peace." At this school, Tagore gave Indian boys a retreat from the modern world. He taught them ideals of their culture. In Tagore's later years he became a well-known painter.

About the Selection

Tagore often wrote to his favorite niece, Indira Tagore. She was a young woman in her 20s. His gentleness and love of nature come through in his writing. The following selection shows how Tagore reacts to the natural beauty of moonlight. Notice how he describes the lamp he is using and the book he is reading. Then look at how he describes the moon and the night.

166 Unit 2 Nonfiction

Literary Terms In this **letter**, Tagore describes his impressions and feelings. The audience for this letter, the person he wrote to, is Tagore's niece. It is important to think about the audience when you read a letter. Imagine how different the letter would be if it were written to a different person.

In this letter, Tagore uses **personification** to describe what he sees. He gives human characteristics to nonhuman objects. For example, Tagore writes, "The glare from a satanic little lamp had been mocking an infinite radiance." He is describing the lamp as mocking something else, or making fun of it. Lamps are not people. They do not make fun of things. Writers use personification to create vivid images.

Reading on Your Own Think of where Tagore lived and the things he loved. What examples of personification might Tagore use in his letter? Write down your ideas. After reading, compare and contrast your ideas to the images Tagore used.

Writing on Your Own Imagine that you're traveling around the world. You want to write a letter to your favorite relative about your trip. What might the relative want to know about your travels? Write a short letter to this relative about the new people and places you have seen.

Vocabulary Focus This letter has many words that may be new to you. One way to remember a word's meaning is to think about its origin. Use a dictionary to find out more about the origins of these words: *mirage, mortal,* and *protest.* Note that word origins tell which language the word came from. They also tell how the word changed to have its present meaning.

Think Before You Read The audience for this letter is Tagore's niece. Think about your aunts and uncles, or other older relatives, and how they would write to you. What kinds of things do you think Tagore will write?

> **letter** a document of impressions and feelings written to a particular person
>
> **personification** giving human characteristics to a nonhuman object

Nonfiction Unit 2 **167**

Letter to Indira Tagore

Shelidah, East Bengal

12 December 1895

[Bibi]

The other evening an **insignificant** incident startled me. As I mentioned before, of late I have taken to lighting a lamp in the boat and sitting and reading till I feel sleepy . . . That evening I was reading a book of critical essays in English full of

contorted disputation about poetry, art, beauty and so forth. As I plodded through these artificial discussions, my weary mind seemed to have strayed into a **mirage**, a land where things were constructed out of words. A **deadening** spirit seemed to dance before me like a **mocking** demon. The night was far advanced, so I shut the book with a snap and flung it on the table, intending to head for bed after blowing out the lamp. But the moment I **extinguished** the flame, moonlight burst through the open window and flooded the boat. It was like a shock to an infatuated man. The glare from a satanic little lamp had been mocking an infinite radiance. What on earth had I been hoping to find in the empty wordiness of that book? The heavens had been waiting for me soundlessly outside all the time. Had I chanced to miss them and gone off to bed in darkness, they would not have made the slightest protest. Had I never given them a glance during my mortal existence and remained unenlightened even on my death-bed, that lamp would have triumphed. But the moon would always have been there, silent and sweetly smiling, neither concealing nor advertising her presence.

Since then I have begun doing without the lamp in the evenings.

[Uncle Rabi]

Literary and art critics judge what others have written or drawn. Their opinions appear in critical essays.

How does the author use personification in describing the moon?

Tagore describes the lamp as satanic, or cruel. What do you think he means by that?

---

insignificant small; not important

contorted twisted; hard to follow

disputation a discussion or debate

mirage an optical illusion; something you see that is not really there

deadening making less intense or lively

mocking laughing in disgust and anger

extinguished put out

Nonfiction Unit 2

AFTER READING THE SELECTION

Letter to Indira Tagore by Rabindranath Tagore (trans. by Krishna Dutta & Andrew Robinson)

Directions Choose the letter of the best answer or write the answer using complete sentences.

Comprehension: Identifying Facts

1. Where is Tagore when the events are taking place?
   - A in a boat
   - B in his bedroom
   - C at an art museum
   - D at the library

2. At what time of day do the events in the letter happen?

3. How does Tagore react at first to the moonlight?

Comprehension: Putting Ideas Together

4. What had Tagore been doing at the time he is describing?
   - A sleeping
   - B swimming
   - C reading
   - D writing

5. How does the light from the lamp compare with the moonlight?

6. Tagore says this was "an insignificant incident." However, it clearly means a lot to him. In your own words, describe what it means to him.

Understanding Literature: Personification

When a writer gives human qualities to objects, animals, or ideas, it is called *personification*. Tagore uses personification several times in this letter. For example, he writes, "that lamp would have triumphed." The human quality given to the lamp is the ability to triumph, or win. Personification is a kind of figurative language. The writer goes against the usual way to express something. Figurative language gives strength and freshness of expression to one's writing.

7. Explain how Tagore uses personification to describe the moon.

8. How does Tagore use personification to describe the heavens?

Critical Thinking

9. What discovery does Tagore make?

Thinking Creatively

10. What do you think Tagore wants his niece to do?

Grammar Check

An adverb is a word that describes a verb. It tells how something was done. Adverbs end in *-ly*. Look at these sentences from Tagore's letter. The adverbs are in italics.

"The heavens had been waiting for me *soundlessly*. . . ."

"The moon would always have been there, silent and *sweetly* smiling. . . ."

In the first sentence, *soundlessly* tells how the heavens were waiting. In the second sentence, *sweetly* tells how the moon was smiling. Now, write two sentences of your own. Use adverbs to describe the verbs in your sentences.

 Writing on Your Own

Think about something in nature that surprises or delights you. Use personification to describe its qualities. For example, you might write about a flower that nods and dances in the breeze, or a winter storm that cries and howls outside your window.

 Speaking

Use figurative language to describe something to your class. You can describe your bedroom, a favorite sport, a hobby, or even something in the classroom.

 Listening

Have a partner read the letter aloud to you. Be sure to listen carefully as your partner reads. Why do you think Tagore wrote this letter? Write a short paragraph answering this question.

 Viewing

In Tagore's later years, he became known as a painter. Try to find some of his work in art books or on the Internet. Does his art show the same ideas about nature as his letter? Explain.

BEFORE READING THE SELECTION

Letter to the Reverend J. H. Twichell   by Mark Twain

About the Author

Mark Twain
(1835–1910)
American

Samuel L. Clemens was born in a small Missouri town. As a young man, he was a Mississippi riverboat pilot. Later he was a gold miner in Nevada and a printer. For his writing, he chose to be known as "Mark Twain." Twain's humorous stories about American life quickly made him popular. His traveling experiences helped his writing.

He is best known for the novels *The Adventures of Tom Sawyer* and *Adventures of Huckleberry Finn*. Twain wrote many other pieces of literature as well. Some were fiction and others were nonfiction. He is regarded as one of the first truly American writers.

Late in life, Twain lost most of his wealth due to poor investments. In 1895, he started a long lecture tour to earn money to repay debts. During the tour, one of his daughters died. Shortly after he returned home, his wife and another daughter also died. These losses affected the way he wrote. His later works had a different mood. They were more powerful and serious than his earlier works. *The Mysterious Stranger* is one example.

About the Selection

After his writing became popular, Twain married and moved to Connecticut. There he began a friendship with a local minister, the Reverend Joseph H. Twichell. Twain wrote this letter to Twichell while he was in Munich, Germany. It is the kind you might enjoy getting from a friend who happens to be a writer. It contains many funny images. Try to picture the situation that Twain is describing. Enjoy the humor.

Objectives

- To read and understand satire
- To explain the difference between a pen name and the author's name
- To identify a pun in a piece of writing

Literary Terms When he wrote, Samuel L. Clemens used the **pen name** of Mark Twain. A pen name is a false name a writer might use. Clemens was such a famous writer that people seldom think of the name Samuel L. Clemens at all. Instead, they think about Mark Twain.

Mark Twain is known for his use of **puns** and **satire**. A pun is a humorous use of words or phrases. Puns are often based on words with multiple meanings. Other times, a pun is a joke that uses words that almost sound the same. This type of pun can be found in knock-knock jokes that children tell.

Satire is humorous writing that makes fun of foolishness or evil. It looks at something bad in a different way. A writer can use satire to show how foolish something really is.

pen name a false name used for writing

pun humorous use of words or phrases

satire humorous writing that makes fun of foolishness or evil

Reading on Your Own As you read this letter, think about Mark Twain's actions. How does Twain use satire to point out his foolish behavior? If you have trouble understanding the selection, reread the parts that you didn't understand.

Writing on Your Own Have you ever tried to do something without bothering the people around you? Maybe you have tried to open a hard candy in a quiet room. Write about what happens when everyone ends up noticing you anyway.

Vocabulary Focus Make a list of words with multiple meanings from the letter. Write each word and at least two of its meanings. Then try to write your own pun using one of these words.

Think Before You Read Mark Twain is writing a letter to a friend. He calls the friend "Old Joe." What kind of relationship do you think the two men have? How do you think the letter will show this?

Nonfiction Unit 2

Letter to the Reverend J. H. Twichell

To the Reverend J. H. Twichell

Munich, January 26, 1879

Dear Old Joe:

> As you read, watch for clues to help you figure out who *Livy* is.

Sunday. Your **delicious** letter arrived exactly at the right time. It was laid by my plate as I was finishing breakfast at 12 noon. Livy and Clara [Spaulding] arrived from church 5 minutes later. I took a pipe and spread myself out on the sofa and Livy sat by and read, and I warmed to that butcher the moment he began to swear. There is more than one way of praying and I like the butcher's way because the **petitioner** is so apt to be **in earnest**. I was peculiarly alive to his performance just at this time for another reason, **to wit**: Last night I awoke at 3 this morning and after raging to myself for 2 **interminable** hours, I gave it up. I rose, assumed a catlike **stealthiness,** to keep from waking Livy, and proceeded to dress in the **pitch** dark. Slowly but surely I got on garment after garment—all down to one sock; I had one slipper on and the other in my hand. Well, on my hands and knees I crept softly around, pawing and feeling and scooping along the carpet and among chair-legs for that missing sock; I kept

> Twain is referring to a story he read in a letter from Twichell.

> The word *swear* has multiple meanings. Twain makes a pun with it. Think of the two meanings that Twain has in mind.

---

delicious delightful

petitioner one who asks for help

in earnest sincere; honest

to wit an expression meaning "that is to say"

interminable endless

stealthiness quietness

pitch complete

that up;—and still kept it up and *kept* it up. At first I only said to myself "Blame that sock," but that soon ceased to answer; my **expletives** grew steadily stronger and stronger and at last, when I found I was *lost*, I had to sit flat down on the floor and take hold of something to keep from lifting the roof off with the **profane** explosion that was trying to get out of me. I could see the dim blur of the window, but of course it was in the wrong place and could give me no information as to where I was. But I had one comfort, I had not waked Livy; I believed I could find that sock in silence if the night lasted long enough. So I started again and softly pawed all over the place, and sure enough at the end of half an hour I laid my hand on the missing article. I rose joyfully up and butted the wash-bowl and pitcher off the stand and simply raised - - - - so to speak. Livy screamed, then said, "Who is that? what *is* the matter?" I said, "There ain't anything the matter—I'm hunting for my sock." She said, "Are you hunting for it with a club?" . . .

> The phrase "ceased to answer" means stopped helping.

> In the late 1800s, hotel rooms did not have bathrooms or running water. Guests were given a pitcher of water and a bowl to pour it in. The pitcher and bowl sat on a washstand.

> How does Twain use satire to poke fun at his own actions?

> *Mark Twain* is a pen name. Do you think he uses his pen name to sign this letter?

expletives curse words
profane not holy or sacred

AFTER READING THE SELECTION

Letter to the Reverend J. H. Twichell   by Mark Twain

Directions Choose the letter of the best answer or write the answer using complete sentences.

Comprehension: Identifying Facts

1. Who is Livy?
   A the hotel housemaid
   B the person to whom Mark Twain writes the letter
   C Reverend Twichell's wife
   D Mark Twain's wife

2. What time does Twain wake up?

3. Why is Twain trying to dress in the dark?

Comprehension: Putting Ideas Together

4. Which of these events happens first?
   A Twain bumps his head.
   B Livy wakes up.
   C Twain cannot sleep.
   D Twain loses his temper.

5. Twain writes that he used bad language during the night. Why do you think Twain does not use any bad language in the letter?

6. Why did Twain take time to sit down on the floor?

Understanding Literature: Letters

We can learn a lot about history by reading old letters. In the past, people from all walks of life wrote letters to family members and friends. They wrote business letters too. Today, people use the phone or e-mail more than they write letters. When people write e-mail, they are not as careful to use correct grammar or just the right words. Think about how this will affect what historians of the future can learn about us.

7. Think about the e-mails that people send to their friends today. How are they different from the letter that Twain wrote to his friend?

8. Imagine that Twain had telephoned his friend instead of writing to him. We would not have his letter to read today. What would we have lost by not having that letter?

Critical Thinking

9. Do you think Twain should have just turned on the light from the beginning? Why or why not?

Thinking Creatively

10. Think about the purpose of Rabindranath Tagore's letter. Contrast this with the purpose of Twain's letter.

Grammar Check

In this letter, Mark Twain describes something that happened the day before. He uses the past tense in the entire letter. There are only a few sentences that are not in the past tense. These are the quotations of what Livy said. Explain why these are not in the past tense.

 Writing on Your Own

Pretend that you are the Reverend J. H. Twitchell. Write a letter back to Twain. You can tell him a funny story, or just reply to his letter to you.

 Speaking and Listening

Think of something funny that has happened to you. Maybe, like Twain, you were on vacation at the time. Maybe you were home. Tell your class about what happened. Make sure that you plan how you will tell the story ahead of time. You want your classmates to find the story as funny as you do.

Listen carefully as your classmates tell their funny stories. Pay attention as you listen for details. Try to predict the funny event that will happen next.

 Technology

Work with a small group to create a videotape of Mark Twain and Livy. Plan who will play the roles of Twain and Livy. Choose a student to videotape them as they tell the story of what happened that night. Then have another student edit the tape, cutting out parts that are not needed. Have your group decide what Twain and Livy will talk about. You can videotape them talking together or separately.

 Research

Puns and satire have been used for many years—you can even find many examples in the plays of William Shakespeare. Do computer research to identify a novel or short story by Mark Twain that sounds interesting to you. Find the book in your library and look for the use of puns or satire. On a sheet of paper, copy an example of one of these literary forms. Be sure to note the bibliographic information for your source. Then write two or three sentences explaining why your example is funny or uses humor to make a point.

BEFORE READING THE SELECTION

from Writing with Intent   by Margaret Atwood

Margaret Atwood
(1939–)
Canadian

Objectives

- To read and understand an essay
- To explain the author's purpose for writing
- To describe the writer's tone

About the Author

Margaret Atwood was born in Ottawa, Ontario, Canada. One of Canada's best-known authors, she writes both poetry and novels. She began writing poetry in her senior year of high school. In her last year of college, she decided to self-publish a book of poems. She sold them for 50 cents each. Today, just one of those books would cost you more than $1,800! A few years later, Atwood moved to British Columbia where she taught English grammar. During that one year of teaching, Atwood wrote a great deal. She wrote a novel, a book of poetry, several short stories, and began two other novels. Her book of poetry, *The Circle Game,* won an award in Canada.

About the Selection

This selection is from "Nine Beginnings," one of the essays from Atwood's book *Writing with Intent: Essays, Reviews, Personal Prose 1983–2005.* The book is a collection of writings by Atwood covering many topics, and it has some characteristics of both an autobiography and a diary. She discusses her experiences in writing, gives us a look into her own life, and reviews the work of other writers. In "Nine Beginnings," she gives nine different answers to the question, "Why do you write?" Two of her answers are provided here.

178   Unit 2 Nonfiction

Literary Terms "Nine Beginnings" is an **essay**. An essay is a written work that shows a writer's opinion on some issue. In "Nine Beginnings," Margaret Atwood gives her thoughts about being a writer. The essay's **tone** shows that Atwood likes being a writer, and that being a writer is difficult. The tone is the attitude an author takes toward a subject.

In this essay, Atwood answers the question, "Why do you write?" Answering that question is the **author's purpose**, or reason for writing. Atwood does not state this reason directly but suggests it through the essay.

Reading on Your Own As you read this selection, think about Atwood's purpose. What different points does Atwood make? What is the main idea of the essay?

Writing on Your Own Think of something that you are very good at doing. It can be a sport or a hobby. It can be writing or helping other people. Why do you do this thing? Write a paragraph explaining why.

Vocabulary Focus A writer often chooses a word because of its connotation. Connotation is the images or emotions that are connected to a word. Denotation is the dictionary meaning of a word. Look at the first paragraph under the second answer. Several words in this paragraph have a negative connotation. Make a list of these words. Replace at least three of these words with other words that have a similar dictionary meaning but a more positive connotation. How does this change the meaning of the paragraph?

Think Before You Read You are going to read about some of the reasons why Atwood writes. What do you think some of these reasons will be?

---

essay a written work that shows a writer's opinion on some basic or current issue

tone the attitude an author takes toward a subject

author's purpose the reason the author writes: to entertain, to inform, to express opinions, or to persuade

from Writing

As you read the essay, look for the writer's opinions about writing, herself, and the setting in which she writes.

Why do you write?

Not long ago, in the course of clearing some of the **excess** paper out of my workroom, I opened a filing cabinet drawer I hadn't looked into for years. In it was a bundle of loose sheets, folded, creased, and grubby, tied up with leftover string. It consisted of things I'd written in the late fifties, in high school and the early years of university. There were scrawled, inky poems, about snow, despair, and the Hungarian Revolution. There were short stories dealing with girls who'd had to get married, and **dispirited,** mousy-haired high-school English teachers—to end up as either was at that time my vision of Hell—typed finger-by-finger on an ancient machine that made all the letters half red.

There I am, then, back in grade twelve, going through the writers' magazines after I'd finished my French composition homework, typing out my **lugubrious** poems and my grit-filled stories. (I was big on grit. I had an eye for lawn litter and dog turds on sidewalks. In these stories it was usually snowing damply, or raining; at the very least there was slush. If it was summer, the heat and humidity were always wiltingly high and my characters had sweat marks under their arms; if it was spring, wet clay stuck to their feet. Though some would say all this was just normal Toronto weather.)

In the top right-hand corners of some of these, my hopeful seventeen-year-old self had typed, "First North American Rights Only." I was not sure what "First North American Rights" were; I put it in because the writing magazines said you

Notice how Atwood sets the tone here.

---

excess more than is needed; too much

dispirited discouraged; depressed

lugubrious extremely sad; mournful

with Intent

should. I was at that time an **aficionado** of writing magazines, having no one else to turn to for professional advice.

If I were an archaeologist, digging through the layers of old paper that mark the eras in my life as a writer, I'd have found, at the lowest or Stone Age level—say, around ages five to seven—a few poems and stories, unremarkable **precursors** of all my **frenetic** later scribbling. (Many children write at that age, just as many children draw. The strange thing is that so few of them go on to become writers or painters.) After that there's a great blank. For eight years I simply didn't write. Then, suddenly, and with no missing links in between, there's a wad of manuscripts. One week I wasn't a writer, the next I was.

Before computers, people could use typewriters to write. Sometimes the typewriter ribbon was both red and black, so a writer could type a letter in either color. But the letters sometimes came out part black and part red.

aficionado a fan; someone who knows about and admires someone or something, following it closely

precursors things that announce something else is coming

frenetic very excited; active

> How do the questions help the reader figure out the purpose of the essay?

Who did I think I was, to be able to get away with this? What did I think I was doing? How did I get that way? To these questions I still have no answers.

Why do you write?

There's the blank page, and the thing that **obsesses** you. There's the story that wants to take you over and there's your resistance to it. There's your longing to get out of this, this **servitude,** to play hooky, to do anything else: wash the laundry, see a movie. There are words and their **inertias,** their **biases,** their **insufficiencies,** their glories. There are the risks you take and your loss of nerve, and the help that comes when you're least expecting it. There's the **laborious** revision, the scrawled-over, crumpled-up pages that drift across the floor like spilled litter. There's the one sentence you know you will save.

> What tone does Atwood take at the end of the essay?

Next day there's the blank page. You give yourself up to it like a sleepwalker. Something goes on that you can't remember afterward. You look at what you've done. It's hopeless.

You begin again. It never gets any easier.

obsesses takes up all of one's thoughts

servitude lack of freedom; slavery

inertias desires not to move or change; stillness

biases ideas that have already been formed and are not based on new experiences; prejudices

insufficiencies lack of enough of some things

laborious requiring hard work

AFTER READING THE SELECTION

from Writing with Intent by Margaret Atwood

Directions Choose the letter of the best answer or write the answer using complete sentences.

Comprehension: Identifying Facts

1. What does Margaret Atwood *not* want to be when she grows up?
   A a magazine editor
   B an artist
   C a high school English teacher
   D a writer

2. Why does Atwood write "First North American Rights Only" on her papers?

3. What does Atwood call the earliest era of her life as a writer?

Comprehension: Putting Ideas Together

4. Atwood points out that most five- to seven-year-old children draw and write. What surprises her about this?
   A Most of them actually hate drawing and writing.
   B Most of them do not grow up to be artists or writers.
   C Most of them are quite good.
   D No one asks them to draw or write.

5. Atwood describes her early childhood poems and stories as "unremarkable precursors of all my frenetic later scribbling." What does she mean?

6. Atwood says that she sometimes wants to get away from her writing. What does she think of doing instead?

Understanding Literature: Tone

The tone of a work is the writer's attitude toward the subject. Look at the language the writer uses. Does the writer take the topic seriously? Are there examples of humor, satire, or sarcasm? Consider everything together and then decide how the writer really feels about the subject.

7. Look at Atwood's first answer. What is the tone of this answer? How do the last questions in this response help show the writer's attitude?

8. How do you think Atwood feels about the question that is asked of her? Give examples from the selection to support your answer.

Critical Thinking

9. What does Atwood mean by "grit"? Why do you think she included it in her early work?

Thinking Creatively

10. Atwood says that writing "never gets any easier." Why does she keep on doing it?

After Reading continued on next page

AFTER READING THE SELECTION (continued)

from Writing with Intent   by Margaret Atwood

 Grammar Check

In her first answer, Atwood remembers something about her past. She uses the past tense in the entire section. In her second answer, she uses the present tense. Choose one paragraph from either section. Change all of the verbs from past tense to present tense or present tense to past tense. How does changing the verb tense change the meaning of the paragraph?

 Writing on Your Own

Pretend you are an English teacher who has just given a writing assignment to students. The students need suggestions about how to get started with this task. Write a paragraph suggesting ways for them to get started on their writing.

 Speaking

What is the reason that Atwood writes? Give a speech to your class telling the reason or reasons. Use Atwood's statements from the selection as evidence.

 Listening

Many of Atwood's works are recorded. Borrow one of these from your school or public library. Listen to a part of the book as it is read aloud. Then read that same section silently to yourself. Did you prefer reading the book or having it read to you? Why?

 Research

Write a research report about Atwood or one of her books. Go to the library and find several of her books. Also look for critiques of her work in books, literary magazines, newspapers, or on the Internet. You can begin by looking for an answer to a question you already have about Atwood or her writing. Or you can think of a question to answer as you do your research. Either way, make sure that your research paper tries to answer a question. Create a bibliography of the sources you used for your paper. Refer to Appendixes C and D for tips on writing a research paper.

Autobiographies

A person's life story written by that person is known as an autobiography. Many people who write autobiographies are famous. You can read autobiographies by past presidents of the United States, movie stars, or sports legends. People are interested in finding out how these people became successful.

Other authors of autobiographies may not be famous. Some grew up in difficult situations and became successful in spite of these conditions. They hope that their stories will inspire others who have some of the same problems. Readers are very interested in these true stories that show how strong the human spirit can be.

If talented enough, the person may write the story alone. Or the person may choose to write the book "as told to" someone. A ghost writer may be paid to write the book and let its subject take credit.

In any case, the author shapes and arranges the life experiences. Some events will be pointed out; others ignored. This helps the reader share the author's view of his or her life.

Some authors of autobiographies try to be honest and write about all parts of their lives, good and bad. Others may tell only what they think is most important. Whatever the choice, these authors must leave out some personal experiences. They can talk about their lives only from their own points of view.

An author's personal knowledge and viewpoint limit an autobiography. A good autobiography offers a glimpse at the author's mistakes and the decisions that shaped his or her life. In this section you will learn how people react to something in their lives. As you read, think about how these people are the same as or different from you.

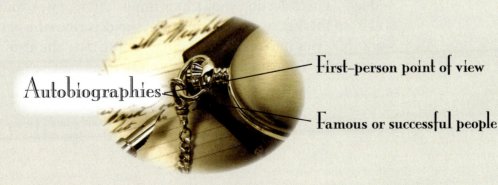

Autobiographies
- First-person point of view
- Famous or successful people

Nonfiction Unit 2 185

BEFORE READING THE SELECTION

from When Heaven and Earth Changed Places   by Le Ly Hayslip

Le Ly Hayslip
(1949–)
Vietnamese

Objectives

- To read and understand an autobiography
- To describe the sequence of events in a story
- To explain the meaning of a legend

About the Author

Le Ly Hayslip was born in central Vietnam, in the village of Ky La. She was the youngest girl in a peasant family. The country was a French colony, but some Vietnamese were fighting for independence. The fighters were led by Communists in the North. America became involved in this area of Southeast Asia in the 1950s, providing weapons and economic aid to South Vietnam. In 1964, American involvement increased. Villages like Ky La were caught between the armies during the Vietnam War.

In 1969, Hayslip married an older American who worked in Vietnam. They moved to the United States and she became a citizen. In 1973, her husband died and Hayslip was left to make her own way. In 1987, she founded the East Meets West Foundation, which helps people in Vietnam. The organization builds schools and homes, provides health care, and more.

About the Selection

When Heaven and Earth Changed Places is Hayslip's story of her life in Vietnam. Her wartime life was full of love and hate and fear. This selection shows how important rice was, and still is, to the Vietnamese people. Hayslip describes the hard work that goes into planting and harvesting rice. She also shares some Vietnamese stories about rice.

Literary Terms In this story, Hayslip describes the work involved in growing rice. She tells the steps involved in that **sequence**. A sequence is the order of events.

This story tells much more than just how rice is grown. Hayslip also tells a Vietnamese **legend** about rice. A legend is a story handed down from one generation to the next, usually about real people, places, or events in history. People often have legends about things that are important to them. Read to find out why growing rice is such an important part of Vietnamese life. Notice how the legend adds interest and humor to the story.

Reading on Your Own Carefully read the legend in the story. Why do you think people would have told this story to their children and grandchildren?

Writing on Your Own Try to think of a food or foods that your family would have trouble living without. Write a paragraph telling why this food is important to your family.

Vocabulary Focus Context clues can help you figure out the meanings of unfamiliar words or phrases. When you read a word you do not understand, think about what the sentences around it are about. That is the context of the word. Then try to figure out what the word means. In this story, there are many Vietnamese words and phrases. Write down each of these words and phrases. Use the context clues to figure out what they mean.

Think Before You Read What are some questions you have about the planting, growing, and harvesting of rice? Use a K-W-L Chart to write down your questions. As you read, add information to the different parts of the chart: *What I Know, What I Want to Know, What I Have Learned*. See Appendix A for a description of the K-W-L Chart.

---

sequence the order of events

legend a story handed down from one generation to the next, usually about real people, places, or events in history

FROM WHEN HEAVEN AND EARTH CHANGED PLACES

> As you read, notice that the author is telling about simple, everyday events. Even in wartime, they are essential to life in the village.

Twice a year, in May and October, we villagers prepared the land for planting. Because these months followed the winter and summer **monsoons,** it meant we had a variety of natural (as well as war-made) disasters to repair: from floods and high winds to **plagues** of grasshoppers and the wearing out of the soil itself.

Although we grew many crops around Ky La—sweet potatoes, peanuts, cinnamon, and **taro**—the most important by far was rice. Yet for all its long history as the staff of life in our country, rice was a **fickle** provider. First, the spot of ground on which the rice was thrown had to be just right for the seed to sprout. Then, it had to be protected from birds and animals who needed food as much as we did. As a child, I spent many hours with the other kids in Ky La acting like human scarecrows—making noise and waving our arms—just to keep the raven-like *se-se* birds away from our future supper.

> About 200 to 400 pounds of rice per person is eaten per year in Asia, compared with 6 pounds per person in North America.

According to legend, god did not mean for us to work so hard for our rice. My father told me the story of *ong trang bu hung*, the spirit messenger who had been **entrusted** by god to bring rice—the heavenly food—to earth for humans to enjoy. God gave the messenger two magic sacks. "The seeds in the first," god said, "will grow when they touch the ground and give a plentiful harvest, anywhere, with no effort. The seeds

> The author uses words from the Vietnamese language throughout her story to remind you of the setting.

---

monsoons seasonal winds that bring rain to southern Asia

plagues destructive things that come suddenly; nuisances

taro a plant grown for its edible, starchy root

fickle not faithful; not reliable

entrusted to hand over for care

A family travels by boat with their sacks of rice.

in the second sack, however, must be **nurtured;** but, if tended properly, will give the earth great beauty."

Of course, god meant for the first seeds to be rice, which would feed millions with little effort; and the second to be grass, which humans couldn't eat but would enjoy as a cover for bare ground. Unfortunately, the heavenly messenger got the sacks mixed up, and humans immediately paid for his error: finding that rice was hard to grow whereas grass grew easily everywhere, especially where it wasn't wanted.

When god learned of this mistake, he booted the messenger out of heaven and sent him to earth as a hard-shelled beetle, to crawl on the ground forever lost in the grass to dodge the feet of the people he had so carelessly injured. This harsh **karma,** however, did nothing to make life easier for farmers.

> Notice the sequence of events in this legend.

nurtured cared for   **karma** fate; destiny

> A *rice paddy* is a field, usually small, surrounded by banks of dirt that serve as dams to hold the water when the field is flooded.

When the seeds had grown into stalks, we would pull them up—*nho ma*—and replant them in the paddies—the place where the rice matured and our crop eventually would be harvested.

After the hard crust had been turned and the clods broken up with **mallets** to the size of gravel, we had to wet it down with water **conveyed** from nearby ponds or rivers. Once the field had been flooded, it was left to soak for several days, after which our buffalo-powered plows could finish the job. In order to accept the seedling rice, however, the ground had to be *bua ruong*—even softer than the richest soil we used to grow vegetables. We knew the texture was right when a handful of watery mud would ooze through our fingers like soup.

Transplanting the rice stalks from their "nursery" to the field was primarily women's work. Although we labored as fast as we could, this chore involved bending over for hours in knee-deep, muddy water. No matter how practiced we were, the constant search for a foothold in the sucking mud made the **tedious** work exhausting. Still, there was no other way to transplant the seedlings properly; and that **sensual** contact between our hands and feet, the baby rice, and the wet, **receptive** earth, is one of the things that preserved and **heightened** our connection with the land. While we worked, we sometimes sang to break the **monotony** and raise our spirits. One song my mother taught me went:

> We love the *hoa binh*;
> *Hoa binh* means peace—first *hoa*, then *binh*:
> *Hoa* means "together" and *binh* means "all the same."
> When we're all together, no one is parted.
> When we're the same, no one's at war.

> Why do you think the author included this song in her story?

mallets short-handled, heavy hammers

conveyed brought from one place to another; carried

tedious boring

sensual pleasing to the senses

receptive ready to accept

heightened made stronger

monotony sameness

Peace means no more suffering,
Hoa binh means no more war.

When the planting was done, the ground had to be watered every other day and, because each **parcel** had supported our village for centuries, fertilized as well. Unless a family was very wealthy, it could not buy chemicals for this purpose, so we had to shovel **manure** from the animal pens and carry it in baskets to the fields where we would cast it evenly onto the growing plants. When animals became scarce later in the war, we sometimes had to add human waste collected from the **latrines** outside the village. And of course, wet, fertile ground breeds weeds and pulling them was the special task of the women and children. The first big weeding was called *lam co lua di,* followed a month later by a second "weeding party" called *lam co lua lai.* The standing water was also home for mosquitoes, leeches, snakes, and freshwater crabs and you were never too sure just what you would come up with in the next handful of weeds. It was backbreaking, unpleasant labor that ran fourteen hours a day for many days . . . .

But planting was only part of village life. Like daylight and darkness, wakefulness and sleep, the labors and **rituals** of harvest defined the other half of our existence.

According to legend, human problems with rice didn't end with the forgetful beetle. When god saw that the mix-up in magic sacks had caused so much trouble on earth, he commanded the rice to "present itself for cooking" by rolling up to each home in a ball. Of course, the rice obeyed god and rolled into the first house it was supposed to serve. But the housewife, unprepared for such a sight, became frightened and hit it with a broom, scattering the rice ball into a thousand pieces. This so angered the rice that it went back outside and shouted, "See if I come back to let you cook me! Now you'll have to come out to the fields and bring me in if you want your supper!"

> The author refers back to the legend telling the story of how rice came to Earth.

---

parcel an area of land
manure animal waste used as fertilizer
latrines toilets
rituals series of acts done in a traditional order

That was the closest any Vietnamese ever came to a free bowl of rice.

Beginning in March, and again in August, we would bring the mature rice in from the fields and process it for use during the rest of the year. In March, when the ground was dry, we cut the rice very close to the soil—*cat lua*—to keep the plant alive. In August, when the ground was wet, we cut the plant halfway up—*cat gat*—which made the job much easier.

The separation of stalk and rice was done outside in a special smooth area beside our house. Because the rice was freshly cut, it had to dry in the sun for several days. At this stage, we called it *phoi lua*—not-yet rice. The actual separation was done by our water buffalo, which walked in lazy circles over a heap of cuttings until the rice fell easily from the stalks.

These women are working in a rice paddy. The process of growing and harvesting rice requires long, hard work.

We gathered the stalks, tied them in bundles, and used them to fix roofs or to kindle our fires. The good, light-colored rice, called *lua chet*, was separated from the bad, dark-colored rice—*lua lep*—and taken home for further processing. The very best rice, of course, we gave back to Mother Earth. This seed rice was called *lua giong* and we put it into great jars which we filled with water. The wet rice was then packed under a haystack to keep warm. The **nutrients,** moisture, and heat helped the rice seeds to sprout, and after three days (during which we watered and fertilized the seedbed like a garden), we recovered the jars and cast the fertile *geo ma* seeds onto the ground we had prepared. But this was rice we would enjoy another day . . .

We always blamed crop failures on ourselves—we had not worked hard enough or, if there was no other explanation, we had failed to **adequately** honor our ancestors. Our solution was to pray more and sacrifice more and eventually things always got better. Crops ruined by soldiers were another matter. We knew prayer was useless because soldiers were human beings, too, and the god of nature meant for them to work out their own karma just like us.

In any event, the journey from seedling to rice bowl was long and **laborious** and because each grain was a symbol of life, we never wasted any of it. Good rice was considered god's **gemstone**—*hot ngoc troi*—and was cared for accordingly on pain of **divine** punishment. Even today a peasant seeing lightning will crouch under the table and look for lost grains in order to escape the next bolt. And parents must never strike children, no matter how naughty they've been, while the child is eating rice, for that would interrupt the sacred **communion** between rice-eater and rice-maker. Like my brothers and sisters, I learned quickly the advantages of chewing my dinner slowly.

> The villagers made use of everything they grew and harvested. The stalks were used to patch roofs, the best rice as seeds for replanting, and the rest of the rice for food.

nutrients food needed for growth
adequately well enough
laborious requiring long, hard work
gemstone a jewel
divine coming from a god
communion a sharing of feelings

AFTER READING THE SELECTION

from When Heaven and Earth Changed Places   by Le Ly Hayslip

Directions Choose the letter of the best answer or write the answer using complete sentences.

Comprehension: Identifying Facts

1. According to the legend, what is in the two magic sacks that god sent to earth?
   A grass and rice
   B rice and beans
   C peanuts and rice
   D grass and beans

2. Whose job is it to transplant the rice stalks?

3. What is the rice called just after it is cut?

Comprehension: Putting Ideas Together

4. How many crops of rice do the villagers harvest in one year?
   A one   C three
   B two   D four

5. Why do the villagers need to fertilize the rice paddies?

6. Why do they use water buffalo instead of tractors to plow the paddies?

Understanding Literature: Legend

Hayslip retells the legend of how rice came to Earth. A legend is a story the older generation tells to the younger generation. Many legends talk about important people or events in the history of a society. This legend is about growing rice, which is a very important part of Vietnamese culture.

7. What happens after the heavenly messenger mixes up the sacks? What does this part of the legend try to explain?

8. What happens to the messenger? Do you think his punishment fit his crime?

Critical Thinking

9. Planting, caring for, and harvesting a rice crop is hard work. Everyone in the village had to help out. Hayslip writes that it defined their existence. What does she mean by this?

Thinking Creatively

10. Think about the different kinds of foods that Americans find important in their everyday lives. Identify one and explain how it is just as important to Americans as rice is to the Vietnamese.

Grammar Check

A declarative sentence makes a statement. It ends in a period. An interrogative sentence asks a question. It ends with a question mark. Write three declarative sentences from the story. Change them into interrogative sentences. Make sure to punctuate the questions properly.

 Writing on Your Own

What do you think life was like for a child in Hayslip's village? Write a paragraph describing this topic. Take notes from the reading to help develop your thoughts. Make sure that your paragraph has a topic sentence and supporting details. The paragraph should also have a concluding sentence.

 Speaking

When a person asks a rhetorical question, he or she does not expect anyone to answer it. For example, when someone asks "How are you?" it may be more of a greeting than a question. Think about what you liked or did not like about this story. Give a short speech to your class telling them why you feel this way. Try to include at least one rhetorical question.

Here are some rhetorical questions to help you get started.

Why would somebody do that?

What makes me like this story so much?

 Listening

All legends began as oral stories. Retell the legend from this story to a partner. Do not read it from the book. Use your memory alone. Then have your partner tell the legend to you. Do not interrupt your partner or correct any "mistakes." Notice how the story can change from speaker to speaker.

 Media and Technology

Work with a group to write a song that tells the legend from this selection. If possible, use music as you sing the song. Use a tape recorder or video camera to record your song.

Nonfiction Unit 2 195

BEFORE READING THE SELECTION

By Any Other Name   by Santha Rama Rau

Santha Rama Rau
(1923–)
Indian

Objectives

- To read and understand the first-person point of view in an autobiography
- To read and understand a sketch
- To identify an allusion and explain its meaning in a story

About the Author

Santha Rama Rau was born in Madras, India, in 1923. Her father held an important job in the British colonial government. The job took him many different places, and his family moved with him. As a child, Rau lived in many parts of India. She also lived in England and South Africa. Rau went to college in the United States. She attended Wellesley College in Massachusetts. In her early 20s, she wrote about her childhood and growing-up years. The book was called *Home to India*. Rau went on to write several more books about her life. She also wrote fiction and articles about her travels.

About the Selection

In 1961, Rau published a book titled *Gifts of Passage*. It is a collection of brief writings about her life. They all deal with different topics and different times in her life. Each writing has its own title. Some of them are funny and others are more serious. "By Any Other Name" is from that book. In this writing, Rau tells about her first school experience. She is living in India but goes to a British school. What problems might an Indian girl have in a British school? Read to find out.

196 Unit 2 Nonfiction

Literary Terms This excerpt comes from Santha Rama Rau's **autobiography**. An autobiography is a person's life story written by that person. An autobiography is written from the **first-person point of view**. The "I" in the story is the author.

This excerpt of Rau's autobiography is called a **sketch**. A sketch is a brief work that often runs from subject to subject. Many sketches are humorous. This excerpt is about Rau's first school experience. The title makes an **allusion** to a line from William Shakespeare's play *Romeo and Juliet*. An allusion is a statement that refers to a literary or historic figure, event, or object. *Romeo and Juliet* is about two young people who are in love. Their families are fighting each other, so Romeo and Juliet are not free to marry. Juliet describes the problem. She says, "What's in a name? That which we call a rose by any other word [name] would smell as sweet." Read to find out what Rau means by this allusion.

Reading on Your Own As you read the selection, what clues show that it is written from the first-person point of view?

Writing on Your Own Think of a memorable school experience you have had. It can be a good or a bad experience. Write a paragraph describing it.

Vocabulary Focus Rau uses the adjectives *Indian* and *British* to show how she saw the difference between people and things. To better understand Rau's viewpoint, make a two-column chart. Title one column "Indian" and the other "British." Then write the information in the correct column. For example, under "Indian," you could write *Premila and Santha*. On the same line, under "British," you would write *Pamela and Cynthia*.

Think Before You Read What kinds of things do you think Rau will describe about her first school experience?

---

autobiography a person's life story written by that person

first person written as if the author is telling the story

point of view the position from which the author or storyteller tells the story

sketch a brief written work that often runs from subject to subject and is often humorous

allusion a statement that refers to a literary or historic figure, event, or object

By Any Other Name

Think about the allusion that the title makes to the line from Romeo and Juliet. *Look for ways that the story relates to the ideas in that play.*

The term Anglo-Indian *usually meant a person from Britain living in India. It could also mean a person of English and Indian descent. This school is run by the British.*

At the Anglo-Indian day school in Zorinabad to which my sister and I were sent when she was eight and I was five and a half, they changed our names. On the first day of school, a hot, windless morning of a north Indian September, we stood in the **headmistress**'s study and she said, "Now you're the *new* girls. What are your names?"

My sister answered for us. "I am Premila, and she"—nodding in my direction—"is Santha."

The headmistress had been in India, I suppose, fifteen years or so, but she still smiled her helpless **inability** to **cope** with Indian names. Her rimless half-glasses glittered, and the **precarious** bun on the top of her head trembled as she shook her head. "Oh, my dears, those are much too hard for me. Suppose we give you pretty English names. Wouldn't that be more jolly? Let's see, now—Pamela for you, I think." She shrugged in a baffled way at my sister. "That's as close as I can get. And for *you*," she said to me, "how about Cynthia? Isn't that nice?"

---

headmistress female principal of a school
inability lack of ability
cope manage successfully
precarious not secure

My sister was always less easily **intimidated** than I was, and while she kept a stubborn silence, I said, "Thank you," in a very tiny voice.

We had been sent to that school because my father, among his responsibilities as an officer of the **civil service,** had a tour of duty to perform in the villages around that steamy little **provincial** town, where he had his headquarters at that time. He used to make his shorter inspection tours on horseback, and a week before, in the stale heat of a typically **postmonsoon** day, we had waved good-by to him and a little procession—an assistant, a secretary, two bearers, and the man to look after the bedding rolls and luggage: They rode away through our large garden, still bright green from the rains, and we turned back into the twilight of the house and the sound of fans whispering in every room.

Up to then, my mother had refused to send Premila to school in the British-run establishments of that time, because, she used to say, "you can bury a dog's tail for seven years and it still comes out curly, and you can take a Britisher away from his home for a lifetime and he still remains **insular**." The examinations and degrees from entirely Indian schools were not, in those days, considered **valid**. In my case, the question had never come up, and probably never would have come up if Mother's **extraordinary** good health had not broken down. For the first time in my life, she was not able to continue the lessons she had been giving us every morning. So our **Hindi** books were put away, the stories of the Lord Krishna as a little boy were left in mid-air, and we were sent to the Anglo-Indian school.

That first day at school is still, when I think of it, a remarkable one. At that age, if one's name is changed, one develops a curious form of dual personality. I remember having a certain detached and disbelieving concern in

> The writer uses *I* and *my*. She is writing from the first-person point of view.

> The girls' mother believes that the British always act as if they were still in England although they are really living and working in India.

> *Lord Krishna* is a Hindu deity, or god. His triumph over a demon god is celebrated each year in a festival of lights.

intimidated frightened

civil service jobs that nongovernment workers do for the government, such as post office workers

provincial small; limited in attitude

postmonsoon after the rainy season

insular limited in outlook and experience

valid completely acceptable; genuine

extraordinary remarkable

Hindi a language widely spoken in India

the actions of "Cynthia," but certainly no responsibility. Accordingly, I followed the thin, erect back of the headmistress down the **veranda** to my classroom feeling, at most, a passing interest in what was going to happen to me in this strange, new atmosphere of School.

The building was Indian in design, with wide verandas opening onto a central courtyard, but Indian verandas are usually whitewashed, with stone floors. These, in the tradition of British schools, were painted dark brown and had matting on the floors. It gave a feeling of extra **intensity** to the heat.

I suppose there were about a dozen Indian children in the school—which contained perhaps forty children in all—and four of them were in my class. They were all sitting at the back of the room, and I went to join them. I sat next to a small, solemn girl who didn't smile at me. She had long, glossy-black braids and wore a cotton dress, but she still kept on her Indian jewelry—a gold chain around her neck, thin gold bracelets, and tiny ruby studs in her ears. Like most Indian children, she had a rim of black **kohl** around her eyes. The cotton dress should have looked strange, but all I could think of was that I should ask my mother if I couldn't wear a dress to school, too, instead of my Indian clothes.

I can't remember too much about the **proceedings** in class that day, except for the beginning. The teacher pointed to me and asked me to stand up. "Now, dear, tell the class your name."

I said nothing.

"Come along," she said, frowning slightly. "What's your name, dear?"

"I don't know," I said, finally.

The English children in the front of the class—there were about eight or ten of them—giggled and twisted around in their chairs to look at me. I sat down quickly and opened my eyes very wide, hoping in that way to dry them off. The little

> The dark paint and mats absorbed the heat from the sun. The whitewashed floors reflected it and were therefore cooler.

---

veranda a roofed porch running along the outside of a building

intensity strength

kohl dark powder used as eye makeup

proceedings series of events

girl with the braids put out her hand and very lightly touched my arm. She still didn't smile.

Most of that morning I was rather bored. I looked briefly at the children's drawings pinned to the wall, and then concentrated on a lizard clinging to the ledge of the high, barred window behind the teacher's head. Occasionally it would shoot out its long yellow tongue for a fly, and then it would rest, with its eyes closed and its belly **palpitating,** as though it were swallowing several times quickly. The lessons were mostly concerned with reading and writing and simple numbers—things that my mother had already taught me— and I paid very little attention. The teacher wrote on the easel blackboard words like "bat" and "cat," which seemed babyish to me; only "apple" was new and **incomprehensible**.

When it was time for the lunch recess, I followed the girl with braids out onto the veranda. There the children from the other classes were assembled. I saw Premila at once and ran over to her, as she had charge of our lunchbox. The children were all opening packages and sitting down to eat sandwiches. Premila and I were the only ones who had Indian food—thin wheat chapatties, some vegetable **curry,** and a bottle of buttermilk. Premila thrust half of it into my hand and whispered fiercely that I should go and sit with my class, because that was what the others seemed to be doing.

The enormous black eyes of the little Indian girl from my class looked at my food longingly, so I offered her some. But she only shook her head and plowed her way solemnly through her sandwiches.

I was very sleepy after lunch, because at home we always took a **siesta**. It was usually a pleasant time of day, with the bedroom darkened against the harsh afternoon sun, the drifting off into sleep with the sound of Mother's voice reading

> Why didn't Santha know what an apple was? Why did the teacher present it as a word to learn?

> *Chapatties* are delicate flatbreads served with almost every meal in northern India. They may be used in place of a fork or spoon to scoop up bites of food.

palpitating rapidly beating

incomprehensible not capable of being understood

curry a food dish seasoned with a spicy powder

siesta a nap, usually taken after the noonday meal

Nonfiction Unit 2 201

> An *ayah* in India is a person who cares for young children. In America, the person would be called a nanny.

a story in one's mind, and, finally, the shrill, fussy voice of the ayah waking one for tea.

At school, we rested for a short time on low, folding cots on the veranda, and then we were expected to play games. During the hot part of the afternoon we played indoors, and after the shadows had begun to lengthen and the slight breeze of the evening had come up we moved outside to the wide courtyard.

I had never really grasped the system of **competitive** games. At home, whenever we played tag or guessing games, I was always allowed to "win"—"because," Mother used to tell Premila, "she is the youngest, and we have to allow for that." I had often heard her say it, and it seemed quite reasonable to me, but the result was that I had no clear idea of what "winning" meant.

When we played twos-and-threes that afternoon at school, in **accordance** with my training, I let one of the small English boys catch me, but was naturally rather puzzled when the other children did not return the **courtesy**. I ran about for what seemed like hours without ever catching anyone, until it was time for school to close. Much later I learned that my attitude was called "not being a good sport," and I stopped allowing myself to be caught, but it was not for years that I really learned the spirit of the thing.

When I saw our car come up to the school gate, I broke away from my classmates and rushed toward it yelling, "Ayah! Ayah!" It seemed like an eternity since I had seen her that morning—a **wizened**, affectionate figure in her white cotton **sari** giving me dozens of urgent and useless instructions on how to be a good girl at school. Premila followed more **sedately**, and she told me on the way home never to do that again in front of the other children.

> Why did Premila criticize Santha's behavior?

When we got home we went straight to Mother's high, white room to have tea with her, and I immediately climbed

competitive involving the effort to win

accordance agreement

courtesy an act of politeness

wizened dried up; wrinkled

sari a draped outer garment of lightweight cloth traditionally worn by Indian women

sedately calmly; with dignity

onto the bed and bounced gently up and down on the springs. Mother asked how we had liked our first day in school. I was so pleased to be home and to have left that peculiar Cynthia behind that I had nothing whatever to say about school, except to ask what "apple" meant. But Premila told Mother about the classes, and added that in her class they had weekly tests to see if they had learned their lessons well.

I asked, "What's a test?"

Premila said, "You're too small to have them. You won't have them in your class for donkey's years." She had learned the expression that day and was using it for the first time. We all laughed enormously at her wit. She also told Mother, in an aside, that we should take sandwiches to school the next day. Not, she said, that *she* minded. But they would be simpler for me to handle.

That whole lovely evening I didn't think about school at all. I **sprinted** barefoot across the lawns with my favorite playmate, the cook's son, to the stream at the end of the garden. We quarreled in our usual way, waded in the **tepid** water under the lime trees, and waited for the night to bring out the smell of the **jasmine**. I listened with fascination to his stories of ghosts and demons, until I was too frightened to cross the garden alone in the semidarkness. The ayah found me, shouted at the cook's son, scolded me, hurried me in to supper—it was an entirely usual, wonderful evening.

It was a week later, the day of Premila's first test, that our lives changed rather **abruptly.** I was sitting at the back of my class, in my usual **inattentive** way, only half listening to the teacher. I had started a rather guarded friendship with the girl with the braids, whose name turned out to be Nalini (Nancy, in school). The three other Indian children were already fast friends. Even at that age it was **apparent** to all of us that friendship with the English or Anglo-Indian children was out of

> In Santha Rama Rau's autobiography, she tells about her family. How would an autobiography by Premila be different from this story?

> What do you think is the real reason that Premila wants to take sandwiches?

> Notice that Nalini has also been given an English name to use in school.

sprinted ran a short distance at top speed
tepid slightly warm
jasmine a vine or bush with sweet-smelling flowers
abruptly suddenly
inattentive not paying attention
apparent easily understood

the question. Occasionally, during the class, my new friend and I would draw pictures and show them to each other secretly.

The door opened sharply and Premila marched in. At first, the teacher smiled at her in a kindly and encouraging way and said, "Now, you're little Cynthia's sister?"

Premila didn't even look at her. She stood with her feet planted firmly apart and her shoulders **rigid,** and addressed herself directly to me. "Get up," she said. "We're going home."

I didn't know what had happened, but I was aware that it was a crisis of some sort. I rose obediently and started to walk toward my sister.

"Bring your pencils and your notebook," she said.

I went back for them, and together we left the room. The teacher started to say something just as Premila closed the door, but we didn't wait to hear what it was.

In complete silence we left the school grounds and started to walk home. Then I asked Premila what the matter was. All she would say was "We're going home for good."

It was a very tiring walk for a child of five and a half, and I dragged along behind Premila with my pencils growing sticky in my hand. I can still remember looking at the dusty hedges, and the tangles of thorns in the ditches by the side of the road, smelling the faint **fragrance** from the **eucalyptus** trees and

rigid stiff
fragrance sweetness of smell
eucalyptus a tall tree with strong-smelling leaves

wondering whether we would ever reach home. Occasionally a horse-drawn tonga passed us, and the women, in their pink or green silks, stared at Premila and me trudging along on the side of the road. A few **coolies** and a line of women carrying baskets of vegetables on their heads smiled at us. But it was nearing the hottest time of day, and the road was almost **deserted**. I walked more and more slowly, and shouted to Premila, from time to time, "Wait for me!" with increasing **peevishness**. She spoke to me only once, and that was to tell me to carry my notebook on my head, because of the sun.

> A *tonga* is a wagon.

When we got to our house the ayah was just taking a tray of lunch into Mother's room. She immediately started a long, worried questioning about what are you children doing back here at this hour of the day.

Mother looked very startled and very concerned, and asked Premila what had happened.

Premila said, "We had our test today, and She made me and the other Indians sit at the back of the room, with a desk between each one."

Mother said, "Why was that, darling?"

"She said it was because Indians cheat," Premila added. "So I don't think we should go back to that school."

Mother looked very distant, and was silent a long time. At last she said, "Of course not, darling." She sounded displeased.

We all shared the curry she was having for lunch, and afterward I was sent off to the beautifully familiar bedroom for my siesta. I could hear Mother and Premila talking through the open door.

> What was Mother thinking? Remember what she said about the British earlier in the story.

Mother said, "Do you suppose she understood all that?"

Premila said, "I shouldn't think so. She's a baby."

Mother said, "Well, I hope it won't bother her."

Of course, they were both wrong. I understood it perfectly, and I remember it all very clearly. But I put it happily away, because it had all happened to a girl called Cynthia, and I never was really particularly interested in her.

> Notice how this sketch comments on relations between the British and the Indians at the same time that it describes Santha's experiences.

---

coolies unskilled workers who do odd jobs

deserted empty

peevishness annoyance; bad temper

Nonfiction Unit 2 **205**

AFTER READING THE SELECTION

By Any Other Name   by Santha Rama Rau

Directions Choose the letter of the best answer or write the answer using complete sentences.

Comprehension: Identifying Facts

1. Why do Santha Rama Rau and her sister get English names?
   A The girls ask for English names.
   B It is a school rule.
   C Their parents wanted it.
   D The teacher cannot pronounce their Indian names.

2. Why does their mother stop teaching the girls at home?
   A She believes an English education is better.
   B She gets sick.
   C She does not know English.
   D She can pay for the school after the girls get scholarships.

3. How are the Indian and English children separated in the classrooms?

4. How many of the children in the school are Indian?

5. What kind of clothes does Santha wear to school?

6. How is the girls' lunch different from the other children's lunches?

7. Who picks up the girls from school?

8. Why does Santha not make friends with the English children?

9. Why do the girls walk home on their last day of school?

10. Why does Premila tell her sister to carry her notebook on her head?

Comprehension: Putting Ideas Together

11. Why did the girls' mother want to teach them at home instead of sending them to school?
    A She does not think the English people will treat her children well.
    B She wants to keep the girls with her as long as she can.
    C She wants to save money.
    D She went to college to be a teacher.

12. What makes the school look like a British school?
    A It has wide verandas with a central courtyard.
    B It has an English name.
    C It has a dark floor with matting.
    D It has British pictures on the walls.

13. Why is Santha bored on her first day of school?

14. What does Santha say happens if a young child's name is changed?

15. How does Santha show that she does not understand competitive games?

16. After her first day, Santha is happy to be home and "to have left that peculiar Cynthia behind." What does she mean when she says that?

17. What is the real reason that Premila asks to take sandwiches for lunch?

18. Why does Premila leave school?

19. How long do the girls go to this school?

20. Why does Santha's mother hope Santha will not understand what happened?

Understanding Literature: Autobiography and First-Person Point of View

"By Any Other Name" is an excerpt from an autobiography. Santha Rama Rau writes this story from the first-person point of view. She uses the pronouns *I, me,* and *my.* This lets the reader know that she was there.

21. Look at this sentence from the selection: "Most of that morning I was rather bored." How do you know that the story is told from the first-person point of view?

22. Choose a person that Santha meets in the sketch. How does she feel about this person? How do you know?

23. List three examples from the story where Santha tells how she feels.

24. How would the story be different if it was written from the third-person point of view?

25. Do you think the story is more effective because it is told in the first person? Why or why not?

Critical Thinking

In this school, the Indian students are given new "school" names and made to sit in the back of the classroom.

26. At first, how does Santha feel about being called by an English name? How does her sister feel about it?

27. How does Premila try to fit in?

28. What does the teacher's behavior show about her attitude toward Indians?

29. How does their mother react to the news of the teacher's order?

Thinking Creatively

30. Think about the allusion to *Romeo and Juliet.* ("What's in a name? That which we call a rose by any other word [name] would smell as sweet.") Why do you think Rau named her story "By Any Other Name"?

After Reading continued on next page

AFTER READING THE SELECTION (continued)

By Any Other Name by Santha Rama Rau

 ### Grammar Check

There are many rules for capitalization. Here are three:

Capitalize the first word in a sentence.

Capitalize a person's name.

Capitalize the names of languages.

Look in this story to find an example for each of these capitalization rules.

 ### Writing on Your Own

Think of a time when you were the new person. This could be when you moved to a new town, joined a new team, or went to a new club. Write a sketch about what happened and how you felt.

 ### Speaking

Santha's mother had this expression: "You can bury a dog's tail for seven years and it still comes out curly, and you can take a Britisher away from his home for a lifetime and he still remains insular." Use your own words to tell the class what you think she meant by this. Tell whether or not you agree with Santha's mother.

 ### Listening

Suppose that you were Premila. Would you have left the school? Why or why not? Take turns answering this question with a partner. Listen carefully to your partner's answers. Try to paraphrase your partner's answer back to him or her. In this way, you can check to see if you really understood what your partner said.

 ### Research

The title of this selection is based on a famous line from Shakespeare's *Romeo and Juliet*. Do some research to learn more about this play. Read *Romeo and Juliet* or watch it on video. Pay close attention to the scene in which Juliet talks about "a rose by any other name." Think about the title of Rau's work. Did she make a good choice when she chose the title?

BEFORE READING THE SELECTION

from Kaffir Boy   by Mark Mathabane

Mark Mathabane
(1960–)
South African

About the Author

For many years, the government of South Africa had a policy, or system of laws, known as *apartheid*. This policy kept the different races apart. Black South Africans had very few rights and almost no freedoms. For example, black South Africans were not allowed to live in certain areas. In fact, all black South Africans were kept out of certain areas. This meant that almost all black South Africans ended up living in slums. Most also lived in poverty.

Mark Mathabane grew up in Alexandra, which was one of Johannesburg's worst slums. Mathabane's early life was full of gangs, police raids, and death. Then he found out he had a talent for tennis. He began to hope for a life outside Alexandra. Finally, he was allowed to play in tournaments that usually allowed only white people to play. Later, he received a tennis scholarship to an American college where he continued to play tennis. He also found the freedom to write about his life under apartheid. *Kaffir Boy* was first published in 1986. Years later, in 1994, apartheid was finally stopped.

Objectives

- To read an autobiography that has a narrator
- To describe the turning point in a nonfiction story
- To understand how the setting is important to a story

About the Selection

Kaffir Boy is a remarkable story of courage. It tells how Mathabane survived 18 years in Alexandra. He got his start with a good head on his shoulders. His mother and grandmother lent him their strength and they made him go to school. This selection tells about what happened when they first brought him to school. At first, Mathabane refuses to go to school. Read to learn why he changed his mind.

Before Reading continued on next page

Nonfiction Unit 2   209

BEFORE READING THE SELECTION (continued)

from Kaffir Boy   by Mark Mathabane

narrator the teller of a story

setting the time and place of a story

turning point a type of story where an experience changes the life of a literary character

Literary Terms This selection is part of Mark Mathabane's autobiography. Mathabane is the **narrator,** or the person who tells the story. In this selection, Mathabane tells what happened after he was first enrolled in school. Mathabane was seven and a half years old at the time.

The **setting,** or time and place of the story, is a South African slum in the 1960s. South Africa was under the system of apartheid at that time. Most black South Africans lived in extreme poverty. There was much unemployment and many gangs. At this young age, Mathabane had already decided he wanted to be in a gang. He did not want to go to school. Then something happened to change his mind. This was a **turning point** for Mathabane. Turning point stories tell about an experience that changes the life of a literary character.

Reading on Your Own As you read, use Mathabane's descriptions to visualize the setting of the story. Why is the setting so important in this story?

Writing on Your Own What is something that your family thinks is important for you to do? Do you agree with them about this? Why or why not? Write a paragraph describing it.

Vocabulary Focus *Kaffir* is a cruel word that white South Africans sometimes called black South Africans. It showed a lack of respect for them. Notice how people in Mathabane's town feel about themselves. As you read the story, look for ways that some characters show that they have no respect for black South Africans.

Think Before You Read Think back to how you felt about school when you were seven years old. What do you think will be some reasons that Mathabane does not want to go to school?

from KAFFIR BOY

"Education will open doors where none seem to exist."

When my mother began dropping hints that I would soon be going to school, I vowed never to go because school was a waste of time. She laughed and said, "We'll see. You don't know what you're talking about." My **philosophy** on school was that of a gang of ten-, eleven- and twelve-year-olds whom I so **revered** that their every word seemed that of an **oracle**.

These boys had long left their homes and were now living in various neighbourhood junkyards, making it their own. They slept in abandoned cars, smoked glue and **benzene,** ate pilchards and brown bread, sneaked into the white world to caddy and, if unsuccessful, came back to the township to steal beer and soda bottles from shebeens, or goods from the Indian traders on First Avenue. Their life-style was exciting, adventurous and full of surprises; and I was attracted to it. My mother told me that they were no-gooders, that they would amount to nothing, that I should not associate with them, but I paid no heed. What does she know? I used to tell myself. One thing she did not know was that the gang's way of life had **captivated** me wholly, particularly their philosophy on school: they hated it and considered an education a waste of time.

They, like myself, had grown up in an environment where the value of an education was never emphasized, where the first thing a child learned was not how to read and write and spell, but how to fight and steal and rebel; where the money to send children to school was **grossly** lacking, for survival was first **priority**. I kept my membership in the gang, knowing that for as long as I was under its influence, I would never go to school.

> As you read, think about the quotation at the beginning of the story. Mathabane has placed it there to tell you that it's what his story will be about.

> A *pilchard* is a small fish related to the herring.

> *Shebeens* were illegal drinking places. People made their own liquor and beer. That was illegal because it took business away from government-run beer halls.

philosophy a basic theory; a viewpoint
revered honored; respected
oracle a person who gives wise advice
benzene a colorless, flammable liquid
captivated fascinated; deeply interested
grossly totally
priority order of importance

Mathabane's family and others like them lived in fear of the police. The police often treated black South Africans harshly while enforcing apartheid laws.

One day my mother woke me up at four in the morning.

"Are they here? I didn't hear any noises," I asked in the usual way.

"No," my mother said. "I want you to get into that washtub over there."

"What!" I **balked**, upon hearing the word *washtub*. I feared taking baths like one feared the plague. Throughout seven years of **hectic** living the number of baths I had taken could be counted on one hand with several fingers missing. I simply had no natural **inclination** for water; cleanliness was a **trait** I still had to acquire. Besides, we had only one bathtub in the house, and it constantly sprung a leak.

"I said get into that tub!" My mother shook a finger in my face.

Granny holds a great-grandchild.

Reluctantly, I obeyed, yet wondered why all of a sudden I had to take a bath. My mother, armed with a **scropbrush** and a piece of Lifebuoy soap, **purged** me of years and years of grime till I ached and bled. As I howled, feeling pain shoot through my limbs as the thistles of the brush encountered stubborn callouses, there was a loud knock at the door.

Instantly my mother leaped away from the tub and headed, on tiptoe, toward the bedroom. Fear seized me as I, too, thought of the police. I sat frozen in the bathtub, not knowing what to do.

balked stopped and refused to go

hectic confused; full of fast activity

inclination a liking

trait a quality of character

reluctantly unwillingly

scropbrush a brush to scrub with

purged cleaned; washed away

"Open up, Mujaji [my mother's maiden name]," Granny's voice came shrilling through the door. "It's me."

My mother heaved a sigh of relief; her tense limbs relaxed. She turned and headed to the kitchen door, unlatched it and in came Granny and Aunt Bushy.

"You scared me half to death," my mother said to Granny. "I had forgotten all about your coming."

"Are you ready?" Granny asked my mother.

"Yes—just about," my mother said, **beckoning** me to get out of the washtub.

She handed me a piece of cloth to dry myself. As I dried myself, questions raced through my mind: What's going on? What's Granny doing at our house this **ungodly** hour of the morning? And why did she ask my mother, "Are you ready?" While I stood debating, my mother went into the bedroom and came out with a stained white shirt and a pair of faded black shorts.

"Here," she said, handing me the **togs**, "put these on."

"Why?" I asked.

"Put them on I said!"

I put the shirt on; it was grossly loose-fitting. It reached all the way down to my ankles. Then I saw the reason why: it was my father's shirt!

"But this is Papa's shirt," I complained. "It don't fit me."

"Put it on," my mother insisted. "I'll make it fit."

"The pants don't fit me either," I said. "Whose are they anyway?"

"Put them on," my mother said. "I'll make them fit."

Moments later I had the garments on; I looked ridiculous. My mother started working on the pants and shirt to make them fit. She folded the shirt in so many **intricate** ways and stashed it inside the pants, they too having been folded several times at the waist. She then choked the pants at the waist with

> How do you know that Mathabane is the narrator of the story?

beckoning signaling with a motion of the hand	**ungodly** wicked; awful	**intricate** complex; difficult to arrange
	togs clothes	

Nonfiction Unit 2 213

Centre is the British spelling for the word *center*. Look for other British spellings in this story.

a piece of **sisal** rope to hold them up. She then **lavishly** smeared my face, arms and legs with a mixture of pig's fat and Vaseline. "This will insulate you from the cold," she said. My skin gleamed like the morning star and I felt as hot as the centre of the sun and I smelled God knows like what. After **embalming** me, she headed to the bedroom.

"Where are we going, Gran'ma?" I said, hoping that she would tell me what my mother refused to tell me. I still had no idea I was about to be taken to school.

"Didn't your mother tell you?" Granny said with a smile. "You're going to start school."

"What!" I gasped, leaping from the chair where I was sitting as if it were made of hot lead. "I am not going to school!" I **blurted** out and raced toward the kitchen door.

My mother had just reappeared from the bedroom and guessing what I was up to, she yelled, "Someone get the door!"

Aunt Bushy immediately barred the door. I turned and headed for the window. As I leaped for the windowsill, my mother lunged at me and brought me down. I **tussled**, "Let go of me! I don't want to go to school! Let me go!" but my mother held fast onto me.

"It's no use now," she said, grinning triumphantly as she pinned me down. Turning her head in Granny's direction, she shouted, "Granny! Get a rope quickly!"

Granny grabbed a piece of rope nearby and came to my mother's aid. I bit and clawed every hand that grabbed me, and howled **protestations** against going to school; however, I was no match for the two determined **matriarchs**. In a jiffy they had me bound, hands and feet.

"What's the matter with him?" Granny, bewildered, asked my mother. "Why did he suddenly turn into an imp when I told him you're taking him to school?"

---

sisal a long, strong white fiber used to make rope and twine

lavishly generously; using more than is necessary

embalming preserving; making something smell good

blurted said suddenly and without thinking

tussled struggled; wrestled

protestations strong objections

matriarchs women who rule their families

"You shouldn't have told him that he's being taken to school," my mother said. "He doesn't want to go there. That's why I requested you come today, to help me take him there. Those boys in the streets have been a bad influence on him."

As the two matriarchs hauled me through the door, they told Aunt Bushy not to go to school but stay behind and mind the house and the children.

The sun was beginning to rise from beyond the **veld** when Granny and my mother dragged me to school. The streets were beginning to fill with their everyday traffic: old men and women, **wizened**, bent and ragged, were beginning to assemble in their usual **coteries** and head for shebeens in the backyards where they discussed how they escaped the morning pass raids and **contemplated** the conditions of life amidst intense beer drinking and vacant, uneasy laughter; young boys and girls, some as young as myself, were beginning their aimless wanderings along the narrow, dusty streets in search of food, carrying **bawling** infants piggyback.

As we went along some of the streets, boys and girls who shared the same fears about school as I were making their feelings known in a variety of ways. They were howling their protests and trying to escape. A few managed to break loose and make a mad dash for freedom, only to be recaptured in no time, **admonished** or whipped, or both, and ordered to march again.

As we made a turn into Sixteenth Avenue, the street leading to the tribal school I was being taken to, a short, chubby black woman came along from the opposite direction. She had a

Mathabane learned to play tennis on a court like this in Alexandra.

Under apartheid, black South Africans had to carry government papers, or passes, that told where they were assigned to live and work. The police often conducted *pass raids* during the night to look for people who were not where they were supposed to be.

veld the South African grassland	**coteries** groups of people who meet often	**bawling** crying loudly
wizened dried up; wrinkled	**contemplated** looked at thoughtfully	**admonished** warned; scolded with a warning

scuttle overflowing with coal on her *doek*-covered (cloth-covered) head. An infant, bawling deafeningly, was loosely **swathed** with a piece of sheepskin onto her back. Following closely behind the woman, and picking up pieces of coal as they fell from the scuttle and placing them in a small plastic bag, was a half-naked, potbellied and thumb-sucking boy of about four. The woman stopped **abreast**. For some reason we stopped too.

"I wish I had done the same to my oldest son," the strange woman said in a **regretful** voice, gazing at me. I was **confounded** by her stopping and offering her **unsolicited** opinion.

"I wish I had done that to my oldest son," she repeated, and suddenly burst into tears; amidst sobs, she continued, "before . . . the street claimed him . . . and . . . turned him into a *tsotsi*."

> A *tsotsi* is a gang member.

Granny and my mother offered **consolatory** remarks to the strange woman.

"But it's too late now," the strange woman continued, tears now streaming freely down her puffy cheeks. She made no attempt to dry them. "It's too late now," she said for the second time, "he's beyond any help. I can't help him even if I wanted to. *Uswile* [He is dead]."

"How did he die?" my mother asked in a sympathetic voice.

"He shunned school and, instead, grew up to live by the knife. And the same knife he lived by ended his life. That's why whenever I see a boy-child refuse to go to school, I stop and tell the story of my dear little *mbitsini* [heartbreak]."

> How did the strange woman's son die?

Having said that, the strange woman left as mysteriously as she had arrived.

"Did you hear what that woman said!" my mother screamed into my ears. "Do you want the same to happen to you?"

I dropped my eyes. I was confused.

"Poor woman," Granny said **ruefully**. "She must have truly loved her son."

---

swathed wrapped with a band of material

abreast side by side; in an even line

regretful remembering with sorrow or grief

confounded confused; puzzled

unsolicited not requested

consolatory comforting

ruefully expressing regret or pity

Finally, we reached the school and I was **ushered** into the principal's office, a tiny **cubicle** facing a row of **privies** and a patch of yellowed grass.

"So this is the rascal we'd been talking about," the principal, a tall, wiry man, **foppishly** dressed in a black pin-striped suit, said to my mother as we entered. His **austere**, shiny face, **inscrutable** and imposing, reminded me of my father. He was sitting behind a brown table upon which stood piles of dust and cobweb-covered books and papers. In one upper pocket of his jacket was arrayed a variety of pens and pencils; in the other nestled a lily-white handkerchief whose presence was more decorative than utilitarian. Alongside him stood a disproportionately portly black woman, fashionably dressed in a black skirt and a white blouse. She had but one pen, and this she held in her hand. The room was hot and stuffy and buzzing with flies.

Disproportionately portly means the woman was very heavy.

"Yes, Principal," my mother answered, "this is he."

"I see he's living up to his **notoriety**," remarked the principal, noticing that I had been bound. "Did he give you too much trouble?"

"Trouble, Principal," my mother sighed. "He was like an imp."

"He's just like the rest of them, Principal," Granny sighed. "Once they get out into the streets, they become wild. They take to the many vices of the streets like an infant takes to its mother's milk. They begin to think that there's no other life but the one shown them by the *tsotsis*. They come to hate school and forget about the future."

"Well," the principal said. "We'll soon remedy all that. Untie him."

"He'll run away," my mother cried.

"I don't think he's that foolish to attempt that with all of us here."

---

ushered escorted
cubicle a small room
privies outhouses
foppishly vainly; overly proud of one's looks
austere stern and serious
inscrutable not easily understood
notoriety bad name; reputation

Nonfiction Unit 2

"He *is* that foolish, Principal," my mother said as she and Granny began untying me. "He's tried it before. Getting him here was an **ordeal** in itself."

The principal rose from his seat, took two steps to the door and closed it. As the door swung closed, I spotted a row of canes of different lengths and thicknesses hanging behind it. The principal, seeing me staring at the canes, grinned and said, in a manner suggesting that he had wanted me to see them, "As long as you behave, I won't have to use any of those on you."

Use those canes on me? I gasped. I stared at my mother—she smiled; at Granny—she smiled too. That made me abandon any **inkling** of escaping.

"So they finally gave you the birth certificate and the papers," the principal addressed my mother as he returned to his chair.

"Yes, Principal," my mother said, "they finally did. But what a battle it was. It took me nearly a year to get all them papers together." She took out of her handbag a neatly wrapped package and handed it to the principal. "They've been running us around for so long that there were times when I thought he would never attend school, Principal," she said.

"That's pretty much standard procedure, Mrs. Mathabane," the principal said, unwrapping the package. "But you now have the papers and that's what's important.

> Do you think Mathabane likes the principal? Why or why not?

> How would this school be different if its setting were in 2007 in the United States?

Mathabane attended Bovet Community School.

ordeal a severe test   **inkling** a hint or idea

"As long as we have the papers," he continued, **minutely perusing** the contents of the package, "we won't be breaking the law in admitting your son to this school, for we'll be in full **compliance** with the requirements set by the authorities in Pretoria."

"Sometimes I don't understand the laws from Pitori," Granny said. "They did the same to me with my Piet and Bushy. Why, Principal, should our children not be allowed to learn because of some piece of paper?"

"The piece of paper you're referring to, Mrs. Mabaso," the principal said to Granny, "is as important to our children as a pass is to us adults. We all hate passes; therefore, it's only natural we should hate the regulations our children are subjected to. But as we have to live with passes, so our children have to live with the regulations, Mrs. Mabaso. I hope you understand, that is the law of the country. We would have admitted your grandson a long time ago, as you well know, had it not been for the papers. I hope you understand."

"I understand, Principal," Granny said, "but I don't understand," she added **paradoxically**.

One of the papers caught the principal's eye and he turned to my mother and asked, "Is your husband a Shangaan, Mrs. Mathabane?"

"No, he's not, Principal," my mother said. "Is there anything wrong? He's Venda and I'm Shangaan."

The principal reflected for a moment or so and then said, concernedly, "No, there's nothing seriously wrong. Nothing that we can't take care of. You see, Mrs. Mathabane, technically, the fact that your child's father is a Venda makes him **ineligible** to attend this tribal school because it is only for children whose parents are of the Shangaan tribe. May I ask what language the children speak at home?"

South Africa has three capital cities. *Pretoria* is the administrative capital; *Cape Town* the legislative capital; and *Bloemfontein* the judicial capital.

Granny mispronounces the name *Pretoria*.

The people of South Africa belong to many tribes and ethnic groups, which speak different languages.

---

minutely paying attention to small details

perusing reading carefully

compliance agreeing to a demand

paradoxically in a way that seems to mean two opposite things

ineligible not qualified

"Both languages," my mother said worriedly, "Venda and Shangaan. Is there anything wrong?"

The principal coughed, clearing his throat, then said, "I mean which language do they speak more?"

"It depends, Principal," my mother said, swallowing hard. "When their father is around, he wants them to speak only Venda. And when he's not, they speak Shangaan. And when they are out at play, they speak Zulu and Sisotho."

"Well," the principal said, heaving a sigh of relief. "In that case, I think an exception can be made. The reason for such an exception is that there's currently no school for Vendas in Alexandra. And should the authorities come asking why we took in your son, we can tell them that. Anyway, your child is half-half."

Everyone broke into a nervous laugh, except me. I was bewildered by the whole thing. I looked at my mother, and she seemed greatly relieved as she watched the principal register me; a broad smile broke across her face. It was as if some enormously heavy burden had finally been lifted from her shoulders and her conscience.

"Bring him back two weeks from today," the principal said as he saw us to the door. "There're so many children registering today that classes won't begin until two weeks **hence**. Also, the school needs repair and cleaning up after the holidays. If he refuses to come, simply notify us, and we'll send a couple of big boys to come fetch him, and he'll be very sorry if it ever comes to that."

As we left the principal's office and headed home, my mind was still against going to school. I was thinking of running away from home and joining my friends in the junkyard.

I didn't want to go to school for three reasons: I was reluctant to surrender my freedom and independence over to what I heard every school-going child call "**tyrannous discipline**." I had heard many bad things about life in tribal school—from daily beatings by teachers and mistresses who

> What are Mathabane's three reasons against going to school?

| **hence** from this time | **tyrannous** unfairly cruel | **discipline** punishment given as a correction |

worked you like a mule to long school hours—and the sight of those canes in the principal's office gave **ample credence** to rumors that school was nothing but a torture chamber. And there was my allegiance to the gang.

But the thought of the strange woman's **lamentations** over her dead son presented a somewhat strong case for going to school: I didn't want to end up dead in the streets. A more **compelling** argument for going to school, however, was the vivid recollection of all that **humiliation** and pain my mother had gone through to get me the papers and the birth certificate so I could enroll in school. What should I do? I was torn between two worlds.

> What are two reasons Mathabane lists for going to school?

But later that evening something happened to force me to go to school.

I was returning home from playing soccer when a neighbour **accosted** me by the gate and told me that there had been a bloody fight at my home.

"Your mother and father have been at it again," the neighbour, a woman, said.

"And your mother left."

I was stunned.

"Was she hurt badly?"

"A little bit," the woman said. "But she'll be all right. We took her to your grandma's place."

I became hot with anger.

"Is anyone in the house?" I stammered, trying to control my rage.

"Yes, your father is. But I don't think you should go near the house. He's raving mad. He's armed with a meat cleaver. He's chased out your brother and sisters, also. And some of the neighbours who tried to **intervene** he's threatened to carve them to pieces. I have never seen him this mad before."

---

ample enough to satisfy
credence belief; proof
lamentations cries of grief or sorrow
compelling forceful
humiliation the state of being disgraced or shamed
accosted approached and spoke to in a challenging way
intervene come in between

These boys are playing in a typical slum in Johannesburg, South Africa, in 1955.

I brushed aside the woman's warnings and went. Shattered windows convinced me that there had indeed been a **skirmish** of some sort. Several pieces of broken bricks, evidently broken after being thrown at the door, were lying about the door. I tried opening the door; it was locked from the inside. I knocked. No one answered. I knocked again. Still no one answered, until, as I turned to leave:

"Who's out there?" my father's voice came growling from inside.

"It's me, Johannes," I said . . .

I went to the broken window and screamed **obscenities** at my father, daring him to come out, hoping that if he as much as ever stuck his black face out, I would pelt him with the half-a-loaf brick in my hand. He didn't come out. He continued launching a **tirade** of obscenities at my mother and her mother . . . He was drunk, but I wondered where he had gotten the money to buy beer because it was still the middle of the week and he was dead broke. He had lost his entire wage for the past week in dice and had had to borrow bus fare.

---

skirmish a conflict; dispute   **obscenities** curses   **tirade** a long, violent, scolding speech

"I'll kill you someday for all you're doing to my mother," I threatened him, overwhelmed with rage. Several nosey neighbours were beginning to **congregate** by open windows and doors. Not wanting to make a spectacle of myself, which was something many of our neighbors seemed to always expect from our family, I **backtracked** away from the door and vanished into the dark street. I ran, without stopping, all the way to the other end of the township where Granny lived. There I found my mother, her face swollen and bruised and her eyes puffed up to the point where she could scarcely see.

"What happened, Mama?" I asked, fighting to hold back the tears at the sight of her **disfigured** face.

"Nothing, child, nothing," she mumbled, almost **apologetically**, between swollen lips. "Your papa simply lost his temper, that's all."

"But why did he beat you up like this, Mama?" Tears came down my face. "He's never beaten you like this before."

My mother appeared reluctant to answer me. She looked searchingly at Granny, who was pounding **millet** with pestle and mortar and mixing it with **sorghum** and nuts for an African **delicacy**. Granny said, "Tell him, child, tell him. He's got a right to know. Anyway, he's the cause of it all."

"Your father and I fought because I took you to school this morning," my mother began. "He had told me not to, and when I told him that I had, he became very upset. He was drunk. We started arguing, and one thing led to another."

"Why doesn't he want me to go to school?"

"He says he doesn't have money to waste paying for you to get what he calls a useless white man's education," my mother replied. "But I told him that if he won't pay for your schooling, I would try and look for a job and pay, but he didn't want to hear that, also. 'There are better things for you to work for,' he

> There had been other disagreements in Mathabane's house. The neighbors had seen other spectacles.

> Why does Mathabane's mother hesitate to tell him why she was beaten? Why does she finally tell him?

---

congregate collect or gather

backtracked went back the way one came

disfigured damaged or spoiled

apologetically in a way that shows regret

millet a cereal grain whose small seeds are used for food

sorghum cereal grain ground into fine meal or made into a sweet syrup

delicacy a special, enjoyable food

said. 'Besides, I don't want you to work. How would I look to other men if you, a woman I owned, were to start working?' When I asked him why shouldn't I take you to school, seeing that you were now of age, he replied that he doesn't believe in schools. I told him that school would keep you off the streets and out of trouble, but still he was **belligerent**."

"Is that why he beat you up?"

"Yes, he said I disobeyed his orders."

"He's right, child," Granny **interjected**. "He paid *lobola* [bride price] for you. And your father ate it all up before he left me."

To which my mother replied, "But I desperately want to leave this beast of a man. But with his *lobola* gone I can't do it. That worthless thing you call your husband shouldn't have sold Jackson's scrawny cattle and left you penniless."

"Don't talk like that about your father, child," Granny said. "Despite all, he's still your father, you know. Anyway, he asked for *lobola* only because he had to get back what he spent raising you. And you know it would have been **taboo** for him to let you or any of your sisters go without asking for *lobola*."

"You and Papa seemed to forget that my sisters and I have minds of our own," my mother said. "We didn't need you to tell us whom to marry, and why, and how. If it hadn't been for your interference, I could have married that schoolteacher."

Granny did not reply; she knew well not to. When it came to the act of "selling" women as marriage partners, my mother was **vehemently** opposed to it. Not only was she opposed to this one aspect of tribal culture, but to others as well, particularly those involving relations between men and women and the upbringing of children. But my mother's sharply differing opinion was an exception rather than the rule among tribal women. Most times, many tribal women questioned her **sanity** in daring to question well-established **mores**. But my mother did not seem to care;

> Mother wishes that they had enough money to return the *bride price* to her husband. She wants to buy her freedom back.

> An exception rather than the rule means that it is unusual.

belligerent hostile; warlike
interjected inserted a remark
taboo forbidden by social customs
vehemently forcefully; violently
sanity soundness of mind
mores traditional customs

she would always **scoff** at her **opponents** and call them fools in letting their husbands enslave them completely.

Though I disliked school, largely because I knew nothing about what actually went on there, and the little I knew had painted a dreadful picture, the fact that a father would not want his son to go to school, especially a father who didn't go to school, seemed hard to understand.

"Why do you want me to go to school, Mama?" I asked, hoping that she might, somehow, clear up some of the confusion that was building in my mind.

"I want you to have a future, child," my mother said. "And, contrary to what your father says, school is the only means to a future. I don't want you growing up to be like your father."

The latter statement hit me like a bolt of lightning. It just about shattered every defense mechanism and every **pretext** I had against going to school.

"Your father didn't go to school," she continued, dabbing her puffed eyes to reduce the swelling with a piece of cloth dipped in warm water, "that's why he's doing some of the bad things he's doing. Things like drinking, gambling and neglecting his family. He didn't learn how to read and write; therefore, he can't find a decent job. Lack of any education has narrowly focused his life. He sees nothing beyond himself. He still thinks in the old, tribal way, and still believes that things should be as they were back in the old days when he was growing up as a tribal boy in Louis Trichardt. Though he's my husband, and your father, he doesn't see any of that."

"Why didn't he go to school, Mama?"

"He refused to go to school because his father led him to believe that an education was a tool through which white people were going to take things away from him, like they did black people in the old days. And that a white man's education was worthless insofar as black people were concerned because it prepared them for jobs they can't have. But I know it isn't totally so, child, because times have changed somewhat.

Louis Trichardt is the name of the township where the author's father grew up.

| **scoff** show disrespect | **opponents** those on the other side of a fight or discussion | **pretext** an excuse for not doing something |

> How does Mathabane's mother think an education will help him?

Though our **lot** isn't any better today, an education will get you a decent job. If you can read or write you'll be better off than those of us who can't. Take my situation: I can't find a job because I don't have papers, and I can't get papers because white people mainly want to register people who can read and write. But I want things to be different for you, child. For you and your brother and sisters. I want you to go to school, because I believe that an education is the key you need to open up a new world and a new life for yourself, a world and life different from that of either your father's or mine. It is the only key that can do that, and only those who seek it earnestly and **perseveringly** will get anywhere in the white man's world. Education will open doors where none seem to exist. It'll make people talk to you, listen to you and help you; people who otherwise wouldn't bother. It will make you soar, like a bird lifting up into the endless blue sky, and leave poverty, hunger and suffering behind. It'll teach you to learn to **embrace** what's good and **shun** what's bad and evil. Above all, it'll make you a somebody in this world. It'll make you grow up to be a good and proud person. That's why I want you to go to school, child, so that education can do all that, and more, for you."

A long, awkward silence followed, during which I reflected upon the **significance** of my mother's lengthy speech. I looked at my mother; she looked at me.

> Think about the setting in this story. How does the time and place of the story affect Mathabane?

Finally, I asked, "How come you know so much about school, Mama? You didn't go to school, did you?"

"No, child," my mother replied. "Just like your father, I never went to school." For the second time that evening, a mere statement of fact had a thunderous impact on me. All the confusion I had about school seemed to leave my mind, like darkness giving way to light. And what had previously been a dark, yawning **void** in my mind was suddenly transformed into a beacon of light that began to grow larger and larger, until it

---

lot fate; state in life
perseveringly keeping at something in spite of difficulties
embrace adopt; welcome
shun avoid
significance meaning
void a feeling of emptiness

had swallowed up, blotted out, all the blackness. That beacon of light seemed to reveal things and facts, which, though they must have always existed in me, I hadn't been aware of up until now.

"But unlike your father," my mother went on, "I've always wanted to go to school, but couldn't because my father, under the **sway** of tribal traditions, thought it unnecessary to educate females. That's why I so much want you to go, child, for if you do, I know that someday I too would come to go, old as I would be then. Promise me, therefore, that no matter what, you'll go back to school. And I, in turn, promise that I'll do everything in my power to keep you there."

With tears streaming down my cheeks and falling upon my mother's **bosom**, I promised her that I would go to school "forever." That night, at seven and a half years of my life, the battlelines in the family were drawn. My mother on one side, **illiterate** but determined to have me drink, for better or worse, from the well of knowledge. On the other side, my father, he too illiterate, yet determined to have me drink from the well of **ignorance**. Scarcely aware of the **magnitude** of the decision I was making, or, rather, the decision which was being emotionally thrust upon me, I chose to fight on my mother's side, and thus my **destiny** was forever altered.

sway influence
bosom the breast of a human
illiterate not knowing how to read or write
ignorance lack of knowledge or understanding
magnitude greatness; importance
destiny a person's fate or future

What words show that Mathabane thinks his decision was a turning point in his life?

AFTER READING THE SELECTION

from Kaffir Boy   by Mark Mathabane

Directions Choose the letter of the best answer or write the answer using complete sentences.

Comprehension: Identifying Facts

1. What does Mathabane want to do instead of going to school?
   A He wants to hang out with his friends in the gang.
   B He wants to be a mechanic.
   C He wants to be a robber.
   D He wants to stay home and help his mother and father on the farm.

2. Why does Mathabane's mother wake him up so early?
   A He needs to milk the cows.
   B He has to take his brother to school.
   C He has to catch an early bus.
   D He needs to take a bath before going to school.

3. Who comes to help Mathabane's mother take him to school?

4. What is wrong with the clothes his mother finds for him?

5. Whom does Mathabane meet on his way to school? What does she say?

6. What is a *tsotsi*?

7. Why is Mathabane tied up when he first gets to the school?

8. Why does Mathabane give up any idea of escaping from the principal's office?

9. What languages does Mathabane speak?

10. What happens to Mathabane's mother when his father returns home?

Comprehension: Putting Ideas Together

11. Why was it so hard to enroll Mathabane in school?
    A Mathabane did not behave well enough.
    B His mother had to find the money first.
    C His mother had to get papers from the government.
    D Mathabane needed a uniform.

12. The school is for people of the Shangaan tribe. How does Mathabane, whose father is a Venda, qualify to attend the school?
    A He has friends who are Shangaans.
    B There is no school for Vendas in Alexandra.
    C He is not allowed to attend the school for Vendas.
    D His mother says he speaks only Venda.

13. Mathabane is finally registered for school. He still does not want to go to school. Why?

14. Why does Mathabane's father lose his temper? List two reasons.

15. Why doesn't Mathabane's mother leave her husband?

16. How is Mathabane's mother different from other women in her tribe?

17. How does Mathabane's mother know so much about school?

18. Why can't Mathabane's mother get a job?

19. How could Mathabane's mother finally get an education?

20. What does Mathabane finally decide to do?

Understanding Literature: Turning Points

A turning point story is about an experience that changes a person's life. Mathabane's decision to go to school truly is a turning point in his life. Getting an education changed his life forever. This selection tells why Mathabane did not want to go to school at first. It also helps the reader understand what finally changed his mind.

21. How would Mathabane's life in the neighborhood be different if he was educated?

22. How would his life in his family be different?

23. Does his mother agree with his choice? Why or why not?

24. Does his father agree with his choice? Why or why not?

25. Do you agree that this is a turning point story? Explain your answer.

Critical Thinking

26. Why did his father not attend school as a boy?

27. Why does his mother think it will be different for her sons?

28. She says, "It'll make people talk to you, listen to you and help you. . . ." Do you agree with her? Why or why not?

29. She says education is "like a bird lifting up into the endless blue sky. . . ." What does she mean?

Thinking Creatively

30. Why is the setting so important to this story?

After Reading **continued on next page**

AFTER READING THE SELECTION (continued)

from Kaffir Boy   by Mark Mathabane

 Grammar Check

Pronouns are words that replace nouns. Possessive pronouns can be used as adjectives to tell who or what something belongs to. They can also be used as nouns. Look at the following charts. Find several of these possessive pronouns in the story. Then write your own sentences using all of these pronouns.

Possessive pronouns used as adjectives (This is _____ book.)	
my	our
your	your
his/her/its	their

Possessive pronouns used as nouns (That is _____.)	
mine	ours
yours	yours
his/hers/its	theirs

 Writing on Your Own

Reread the quotation at the beginning of the story. Find it again in Mathabane's mother's speech near the end of the story. Think about how it applies to your life, too. Write a paragraph about what you hope education will do for you. How will it make your life different?

 Speaking

Pretend you have been asked to speak to a group of young children about why school is important. What would you say to these children? Write a speech and then present it to your class. Be sure to develop and support your argument. Refer to Appendix E for suggestions on preparing a speech.

 Listening

Have a partner read pages 213 to 214, from "I put the shirt on" to "to hold them up." aloud. As you listen to your partner, try to picture the scene. Can you get a sense of how Mathabane looked wearing his father's shirt?

 Media

Apartheid lasted for hundreds of years in South Africa. However, in the 1950s it became an official government policy. The world learned about what was happening through the media: newspapers, radio, and television news. Think about the way that information is presented in each of these types of media. How do you think people might react differently to each of them?

 Research

What are two questions you have about Mathabane or the period of apartheid in South Africa? Write down your questions. Then do some research on the Internet or at the library to find the answers to your questions.

BEFORE READING THE SELECTION
from Reading Lolita in Tehran   by Azar Nafisi

Azar Nafisi
(1955–)
Iranian

About the Author
Azar Nafisi was born in Iran. During her early years, her parents both worked for the Iranian government. But this did not last. In 1963, Nafisi's father was arrested for his political views. Nafisi went to school in several different countries. She even went to college in the United States. In 1979, Nafisi took a job teaching literature at the University of Tehran. Tehran is the capital of Iran. That same year, a revolution began in Iran. Its new government enforced strict Islamic rules. Many of these rules were unfair to women. In time, Nafisi left her teaching job at the university. She and her family moved to the United States in 1997. She now teaches in the United States at the university level.

Objectives
- To read and understand a memoir
- To identify an author's style
- To explain a writer's use of description

About the Selection
After the revolution in Iran, women were forced to wear a veil. They had to cover their faces and their bodies. Eventually, Nafisi stopped teaching at the university. She secretly taught literature to a group of female students at her home. Together, they read books that the government did not allow them to read. The complete title of Nafisi's book is *Reading Lolita in Tehran, A Memoir in Books*. Published in 2003, it is the story of these women and their adventure. This selection tells about the first day that the women met in Nafisi's home.

Before Reading continued on next page

BEFORE READING THE SELECTION (continued)

from Reading Lolita in Tehran   by Azar Nafisi

memoir writing based on personal experience

style an author's way of writing

description a written picture of the characters, events, and settings in a story

Literary Terms *Reading Lolita in Tehran* is not exactly an autobiography. It is a **memoir**, writing based on personal experience. In a memoir, the writer tells about the people around him or her. In an autobiography, the main focus is the writer. In a memoir, the main focus is on the people the writer met and spent time with.

In this selection, you will notice Azar Nafisi's **style**, or her way of writing. For one thing, Nafisi does not follow the basic rules for punctuating dialogue. She does not start a new paragraph when she changes to a new speaker. Instead, the reader has to pay close attention to figure out who is speaking. Another feature of Nafisi's style is her use of **description**. Description is a written picture of the characters, events, and settings in a story. Nafisi creates many pictures with her descriptions.

Reading on Your Own As you read this selection, what details do you learn about people other than Nafisi? This will help you recognize the writing as a memoir.

Writing on Your Own How has a book or author changed your view of life? Write a paragraph about the way your life was changed.

Vocabulary Focus Nafisi takes an expression from famous Russian writer Vladimir Nabokov. She writes, "We were, to borrow from Nabokov, to experience how the ordinary pebble of ordinary life could be transformed into a jewel through the magic eye of fiction." Use a Venn Diagram to show the way a pebble and a jewel are alike and how they are different. Appendix A has a description of this graphic organizer.

Think Before You Read What details do you think Nafisi will remember about the first day the women met?

232   Unit 2 Nonfiction

from Reading Lolita in Tehran

And so it happened that one Thursday in early September we gathered in my living room for our first meeting... First I hear the bell, a pause, and the closing of the street door. Then I hear footsteps coming up the winding staircase and past my mother's apartment. As I move towards the front door, I register a piece of sky through the side window. Each girl, as soon as she reaches the door, takes off her robe and scarf, sometimes shaking her head from side to side. She pauses before entering the room. Only there is no room, just the teasing **void** of memory.

More than any other place in our home, the living room was symbolic of my **nomadic** and borrowed life. **Vagrant** pieces of furniture from different times and places were thrown together, partly out of financial necessity, and partly because of my **eclectic** taste. Oddly, these **incongruous** ingredients created

> Look for personal experiences as you read this memoir.

> Look for places where Nafisi refers to things that are *symbolic* (representing something else).

void empty space
nomadic marked by traveling and having no home
vagrant random; wandering from place to place
eclectic made up of things from all different places
incongruous not in agreement with each other; not belonging together

a **symmetry** that the other, more deliberately furnished rooms in the apartment lacked.

My mother would go crazy each time she saw the paintings leaning against the wall and the vases of flowers on the floor and the curtainless windows, which I refused to dress until I was finally reminded that this was an Islamic country and windows needed to be dressed. I don't know if you really belong to me, she would **lament**. Didn't I raise you to be orderly and organized? Her tone was serious, but she had repeated the same complaint for so many years that by now it was an almost tender **ritual**. Azi—that was my nickname—Azi, she would say, you are a grown-up lady now; act like one. Yet there was something in her tone that kept me young and fragile and **obstinate**, and still, when in memory I hear her voice, I know I never lived up to her expectations. I never did become the lady she tried to will me into being.

That room, which I never paid much attention to at that time, has gained a different **status** in my mind's eye now that it has become the precious object of memory. It was a spacious room, **sparsely** furnished and decorated. At one corner was the fireplace, a fanciful creation of my husband, Bijan. There was a love seat against one wall, over which I had thrown a lace cover, my mother's gift from long ago. A pale peach couch faced the window, accompanied by two matching chairs and a big square glass-topped iron table.

My place was always in the chair with its back to the window, which opened into a wide **cul-de-sac** called Azar. Opposite the window was the former American Hospital, once small and **exclusive**, now a noisy, overcrowded medical facility for wounded and disabled veterans of the war. On "weekends"—Thursdays and Fridays in Iran—the small street was crowded with hospital visitors who came as if for a picnic,

> Try to picture the living room as you read Nafisi's description of it.

> This story takes place during the Iran-Iraq war, which was fought from 1980 to 1988. The wounded and disabled veterans are Iranian soldiers who fought against Iraq.

symmetry balanced; even; being the same on both sides

lament regret; express concern about

ritual routine; something done regularly

obstinate stubborn

status standing or position

sparsely thinly scattered; very spread out

cul-de-sac a dead-end street with houses all around it

exclusive keeping most people out; reserved for a small, select group

with sandwiches and children. The neighbor's front yard, his pride and joy, was the main victim of their assaults, especially in summer, when they helped themselves to his beloved roses. We could hear the sound of children shouting, crying and laughing, and, mingled in, their mothers' voices, also shouting, calling out their children's names and threatening them with punishments. Sometimes a child or two would ring our doorbell and run away, repeating their **perilous** exercise at intervals.

From our second-story apartment—my mother occupied the first floor, and my brother's apartment, on the third floor, was often empty, since he had left for England—we could see the upper branches of a generous tree and, in the distance, over the buildings, the Elburz Mountains. The street, the hospital and its visitors were **censored** out of sight. We felt their presence only through the **disembodied** noises **emanating** from below.

I could not see my favorite mountains from where I sat, but opposite my chair, on the far wall of the dining room, was an antique oval mirror, a gift from my father, and in its reflection, I could see the mountains capped with snow, even in summer, and watch the trees change color. That censored view **intensified** my impression that the noise came not from the street below but from some far-off place, a place whose **persistent** hum was our only link to the world we refused, for those few hours, to acknowledge.

That room, for all of us, became a place of **transgression**. What a wonderland it was! Sitting around the large coffee table covered with bouquets of flowers, we moved in and out of the novels we read. Looking back, I am amazed at how much we learned without even noticing it. We were, to borrow from Nabokov, to experience how the ordinary pebble of ordinary life could be **transformed** into a jewel through the magic eye of fiction.

> An *oxymoron* is a pair of words or ideas that have the opposite meaning but are used together. Why do you think Nafisi calls her place of transgression a *wonderland*? How is this an oxymoron?

> Vladimir Nabokov was the author of the novel *Lolita*, referred to in the title of Nafisi's book.

perilous dangerous
censored kept away from people's view
disembodied existing apart from a body
emanating coming out
intensified made stronger or deeper
persistent not giving up
transgression act of disobeying the law; sin
transformed changed

AFTER READING THE SELECTION

from Reading Lolita in Tehran   by Azar Nafisi

Directions Choose the letter of the best answer or write the answer using complete sentences.

Comprehension: Identifying Facts

1. What do the women do when they first enter Nafisi's home?
   A tell what book they have just read
   B take off their robes and scarves
   C pour a cup of tea
   D close all the curtains

2. What does Nafisi's mother think of her home?

3. Where in the living room does Nafisi sit?

Comprehension: Putting Ideas Together

4. Why is it so loud outside the apartment when the women meet?
   A People are visiting wounded soldiers at the hospital.
   B News reporters are following the women.
   C Nafisi has a playground outside her house.
   D There is a school nearby.

5. Why does the noise seem to come from far away?

6. What do the women do when they meet each week?

Understanding Literature: Style

A writer's style is the way that she or he writes. A writer's style can be marked by many different things. Some writers use a certain type of sentence structure again and again. Other writers use a lot of description. Still other writers ignore certain rules of punctuation or grammar. Think about this selection. Try to notice any common features of the writing. These may help you determine Nafisi's style.

7. Look at the way that Nafisi uses commas in her sentences. Find three sentences that use the comma to set off further explanations.

8. Nafisi does not follow the rules for punctuating dialogue. Give an example of this. Explain how this can be an example of a writer's style. What effect does this have?

Critical Thinking

9. How do you think the women felt as they discussed books that Iranians were not supposed to read?

Thinking Creatively

10. Nafisi describes the room as being filled with furniture of different styles. How could this be symbolic of the women who meet there?

Grammar Check

Use this rule to help you figure out when to use *which* and when to use *that*. Use the word *that* when the phrase or clause is important to the meaning of the sentence. Ask yourself, "If I delete the phrase or clause, can the sentence have a different meaning?" If the answer is *yes*, then use the word *that*. If the answer is *no*, use the word *which*. *Which* often follows a comma. The sentences below show how this works.

Cars that are broken down should be towed away. (This sentence says that only broken-down cars should be towed away.)

Cars, which are broken down, should be towed away. (This sentence says that all cars are broken down and should be towed away.)

From the selection, choose one example of a sentence that uses *which*. Rewrite the sentence using *that*. Tell how the meaning of the sentence changes.

 Writing on Your Own

Reading Lolita in Tehran is about the response of a group of women to the practice of forbidding, or banning, certain books. Rulers in Iran thought that some books, such as Nabokov's *Lolita*, would change the way women felt about themselves. They were afraid that the women would demand more freedom if they learned about other countries through these books.

What do you think about banning books? Write two paragraphs expressing your opinion.

 Speaking and Listening

Pretend that you are Azar Nafisi. Give a persuasive speech, telling Americans to protect and value their freedoms. Tell about how you have to meet secretly just to talk about certain books.

Listen to your classmates' speeches about freedom. Choose one speech to analyze. Did the speaker tell you what actions he or she wanted you to take? Did the speaker support his or her argument with reasons and examples?

 Viewing

Nafisi uses vivid descriptions in this selection. Carefully read the excerpt again. Make a diagram or a drawing of her street or the inside of her home. Check your work against Nafisi's descriptions.

Nonfiction Unit 2 237

Biographies

In some ways, a biography is like an autobiography. It tells all or part of a person's life. But biographies are not written by the people themselves. They are told from the third-person point of view, not the first person. They are written by authors who are interested in certain people. They can't know the person's thoughts. These writers must rely on conversations with the person, or those who knew him or her. The writer usually uses information from several places and tries to judge how the person's actions affect others. An authorized, or approved, biography is likely to show the person in a positive way. That is because most of the information in it comes from the person, or from people speaking for the person.

Until recently, many biographers wrote about their chosen person by selecting facts, quotations, and anecdotes that supported the biographer's opinion. Carl Sandburg wrote a three-part biography of Abraham Lincoln. In it, Sandburg makes Abraham Lincoln into an almost godlike figure. Sandburg obviously admired Lincoln. He wanted his readers to admire him too. Modern Lincoln biographers write about Lincoln's mistakes and weaknesses as well as his greatness. Readers of this more balanced viewpoint often find the story of the person's life to be more truthful. They can more easily feel a connection to a person who has both strengths and weaknesses.

But the goal of the biographer is to give an accurate account of the person: his or her life, personality, and character.

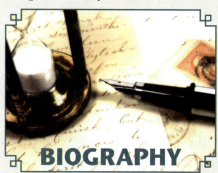

BIOGRAPHY
—written from a third-person point of view
—contains balance of facts and opinions
—can have many sources

BEFORE READING THE SELECTION

from China Men   by Maxine Hong Kingston

About the Author

Maxine Hong Kingston was born in California. Her parents were Chinese immigrants. Kingston felt the conflict between her Asian heritage and the American culture around her. Her family had a strong tradition of storytelling. She also wanted to talk about her family's experiences. For those reasons, she began a writing career. Besides *China Men,* she also wrote *The Woman Warrior.* It focuses on Chinese American women.

Maxine Hong Kingston
(1940–)
American

About the Selection

Kingston writes about things that happened long before she was born. *China Men,* published in 1980, tells the story of how the men in her family came to America. It also tells how they tried to succeed in the "Land of the Gold Mountain." At the same time, they tried to keep their Chinese identity. They kept many old attitudes and ideas. Kingston describes how these ideas made it hard for them to fit in.

Kingston's father, Ed, left China without his wife. He started a laundry in New York City with three other men. Then he brought his wife (Kingston's mother) here. The following selection tells about what happened after she arrived. Ed takes his wife around New York City. As they explore the city, he explains different ideas about his new country and the people here. You can learn a lot about his ideas from the things that he tells his wife.

Objectives

- To read and summarize a biography
- To explain how the setting affects a story
- To understand how a writer uses dialogue to show a character's feelings and thoughts

Before Reading **continued on next page**

Nonfiction Unit 2   239

BEFORE READING THE SELECTION (continued)

from China Men   by Maxine Hong Kingston

biography
a person's life story told by someone else

dialogue
the conversation among characters in a story

Literary Terms This selection is a **biography**, or story of a person's life told by someone else. Kingston has not been born at the time that this story takes place. Still, she uses **dialogue** to help make the characters come alive. Dialogue is the conversation among characters. In some ways, the dialogue comes from the writer's imagination. However, the dialogue is also based on Kingston's knowledge of her parents. Kingston's parents may have told her this story many times as a child.

The setting of this story is the early 1930s in New York City. A story's setting is its time and place. At that time, people dressed up when they went out. This is not always the case today.

Reading on Your Own Discuss with a partner how the setting affects a story. As you read the story, think about the setting. What helps the reader identify the setting? Draw some conclusions about the time period by paying attention to the setting.

Writing on Your Own Think of some places that you have visited or that you want to go. Choose one that is very different from where you live now. Write a paragraph describing the place you choose.

Vocabulary Focus You can use the meanings of a word's parts to help you figure out its meaning. *Telescope* is made up of *tele* + *scope*. *Tele* means "from far away." *Scope* means "to see." So *telescope* is an instrument that allows you "to see" objects "from far away." Think of other words beginning with *tele-*. Make a second list of words ending with *-scope*. Define the parts of the word, and then write a definition of the whole word.

Think Before You Read What ideas do you think Kingston's father will have about this new country?

from

They strolled in their **finery** along Fifth Avenue. "I washed all these windows," he told her. "When I first came here, I borrowed a **squeegee** and rags and a bucket, and walked up and down this street. I went inside each store and asked if they wanted the windows washed. The white foreigners aren't so hard to get along with; they nod to mean Yes and shake their heads to mean No, the same as anybody." New York glittered and shined with glass. He had liked pulling the water off the panes and leaving brief rainbows. While working, he had looked over the displays of all the wonderful clothes to own and wear. He had made the money to **pool** for starting the laundry. "In the spring," he promised her, "we'll buy you white cotton gloves." . . .

"You ought to put your earrings in the safe deposit box at the bank. Pierced ears look a little **primitive** in this country." He also told her to buy makeup at a drugstore. "American people don't like oily faces. So you ought to use some powder. It's the custom. Also buy some **rouge**. These foreigners dislike yellow skin."

> As you read, think about how the setting affects the story.

> Notice Ed's mixed feelings about his new country. For instance, he still calls white Americans *foreigners*.

> In the 1930s and 1940s, few American women had pierced ears.

> What can you learn about Ed and his wife from their dialogue?

finery elegant, dressy clothing

squeegee a tool used to scrape water from a flat surface

pool combine one's money with others in a group project

primitive too simple or crude

rouge reddish powder used to add color to the face

Nonfiction Unit 2 **241**

> Some women's hairstyles in the 1930s and early 1940s used false hairpieces, called *rats*. Another hairstyle, the *marcel*, had tight curls.

> The *Empire State Building* was built in 1931 and was the tallest building in the world until 1972. Today, it is the tallest building in New York City.

> The *Gold Mountain* is what many Chinese immigrants called America.

> Chinese immigrants called white Americans "ghosts" or "demons." A *demoness* is a female demon.

She also bought a long black rat of hair to roll her own hair over for an upswept hairdo. At a beauty parlor, she had her wavy hair cut and curled tighter with a marcel. She washed, ironed, and wrapped her silk pants and dresses and never wore them again.

He took her to see the Statue of Liberty. They climbed the ladder, she in high heels, up the arm to the torch, then the stairs to the crown. "Now we're inside her chin. This part must be the nose." From the windows of the crown, he showed her his city.

They also went to the top of the Empire State Building, took the second elevator to the very top, the top of the world. Ed loved the way he could look up at the **uncluttered** sky. They put money in the telescopes and looked for the laundry and their apartment. "So I have been on the tallest building in the world," she said. "I have seen everything. Wonderful. Wonderful. Amazing. Amazing."

"Yes," he said. "Everything's possible on the Gold Mountain. I've danced with blondes." "No, really?" she said. "You didn't. You're making that up, aren't you? You danced with demonesses? I don't believe it."

Her favorite place to go was the free aquarium, "the fish house," where all **manner** of creatures swam. Walking between the lighted tanks, she asked, "When do you think we'll go back to China? Do you think we'll go back to China?" "Shh," he said. "Shh." The **electric eels** glowed in their dark tank, and the talking fish made noises. "There are bigger fish in China," she said.

---

uncluttered empty; not filled with things

manner kinds

electric eels long, thin fish that can produce an electric current

New York City streets were filled with people and automobiles in the early 1930s.

They went to the movies and saw *Young Tom Edison* with Mickey Rooney. They both liked the scene where the mother took Eh-Da-Son into the barn, but only pretended to **thrash** him; she faked the slaps and crying and scolding to fool the strict father, the father "the severe parent," according to Confucius, and the mother "the kind parent." . . . After the movie, Ed explained to his wife that this cunning, **resourceful**, successful inventor, Edison, was who he had named himself after. "I see," she said. "Eh-Da-Son. Son as in **sage** or **immortal** or *saint*."

Confucius (551?–479 B.C.) was an important Chinese philosopher. His teachings are called Confucianism. They state that people's behavior should be based on duty and virtue.

thrash beat or strike

resourceful able to find ways to get things done

sage a wise person

immortal one who lives forever

AFTER READING THE SELECTION

from China Men   by Maxine Hong Kingston

Directions Choose the letter of the best answer or write the answer using complete sentences.

Comprehension: Identifying Facts

1. How did Ed earn money to start the laundry?
   A He asked his wife's family for the money.
   B He worked in a restaurant.
   C He sold white cotton gloves.
   D He washed windows.

2. List two things Ed and his wife see in New York City.

3. What does his wife keep asking at the aquarium?

Comprehension: Putting Ideas Together

4. Why does Ed want his wife to put her earrings away and wear makeup?
   A He thinks she is ugly without makeup.
   B He wants to sell her jewelry to help pay for the laundry.
   C He wants her to fit in.
   D He does not want her to get robbed.

5. Why do Ed and his wife go up in the Statue of Liberty and the Empire State Building?

6. Why do you think Ed's wife is so surprised that he danced with a blonde woman?

Understanding Literature: Dialogue

Dialogue is the conversation between characters in a story. It is often a clue to a character's personality. It can also reflect feelings and attitudes. Kingston did not know exactly what her parents said long ago. She does know about her parents' ideas and attitudes. She uses what she knows to write dialogue for this biography.

7. Choose two of Ed's quotations. What attitudes is Kingston trying to show with these quotations?

8. Kingston uses dialogue to show the individual personalities of Ed and his wife. Give an example.

Critical Thinking

9. Why do you think that Chinese immigrants called America "the Gold Mountain"?

Thinking Creatively

10. Think about the reasons that Kingston's father named himself after Thomas Edison. What does he want to be like? What does he value in a person?

Grammar Check

Many writers have trouble knowing when to use *who* or *whom*. This is the rule: Use *who* when it is the subject of the sentence. (*Who* is sitting here?) Use *whom* when it is the object of the sentence or the object of a preposition. (For *whom* are you waiting?)

Write one sentence using *who*. Write another sentence using *whom*. Trade sentences with a partner. Do you agree with your partner's use of *who* and *whom*?

 Writing on Your Own

Write a brief summary of this selection. A summary tells the main points in a story but does not have a lot of detail.

 Speaking

Pretend that you are Ed or his wife. Describe for your class what you saw in New York City. Be careful to use *I* and *me* as you speak.

 Listening

Kingston must have been a good listener. This story is partly based on how her parents described what happened when they first came to America. Ask a parent or another adult to tell you something about their younger days. Then write a brief description of what they told you. Try to include statements that show how the person felt.

 Research

Immigrants have been coming to the shores of America for hundreds of years. They often carried with them things from their homeland that were important to their culture. Research one of these, such as sports, foods, or customs, and prepare a report. Refer to Appendixes C and D for suggestions on writing your report.

BEFORE READING THE SELECTION

from The Last Seven Months of Anne Frank   by Willy Lindwer

Willy Lindwer
(1946–)
Dutch

Objectives

- To read and understand excerpts from an interview
- To explain what is included in an excerpt

About the Author

Willy Lindwer is a Dutch filmmaker. He was born in Amsterdam, Holland, just after World War II. His Jewish parents survived the war by hiding. His grandmother, though, was killed by the Nazis in Poland. As an adult, Lindwer has concentrated on making documentary films. A documentary is a nonfiction movie. It tells the true stories of real people.

About the Selection

Earlier in this unit, you read a part of Anne Frank's diary. In August 1944, four days after the last diary entry, the Nazis arrested the family. *The Last Seven Months of Anne Frank* picks up Frank's story where her diaries end.

Lindwer found six women who had known Anne Frank and her family. Some were childhood friends. Others knew the Franks only in the Nazi concentration camps. All of them spent some time in the camps. Lindwer interviewed these women and made a documentary film about the last months of Frank's life. The film was first shown on television in 1988.

Lindwer could use only short pieces of the interviews in the film. He decided to publish the full interviews in a book. The women in Lindwer's book, published in 1991, tell their memories of the Frank family. They also tell their own stories and how they feel today about their past suffering. In this selection, we hear from four of those women.

Literary Term Lindwer interviewed women who knew Anne Frank. All of them had spent time with her during her final months. Their stories are important because they are eyewitness accounts. They report what the women saw and what they heard.

> **excerpt** a short passage from a longer piece of writing

The following selection has **excerpts** of four of those interviews. An excerpt is a short passage from a longer work. An interview is usually written with the questions and answers. This selection does not tell what question or questions the women were answering. It only includes parts of what the women said. As you read, keep in mind that the women were answering questions.

Reading on Your Own As you read, think about what questions Willy Lindwer might have asked the women. Look at what each woman says. What question might she be answering? List out possible questions as you read.

Writing on Your Own Think about someone who has been important in your life. The person can be a relative or a friend. It can even be someone that you have known for a short time. Write a paragraph about this person.

Vocabulary Focus This selection has some unfamiliar words. One of them is *Kalverstraat*, which is the name of a street in Amsterdam. The Dutch word for street is *Straat*, so in America we would call it Kalver Street.

Think Before You Read What do you hope to learn about Anne Frank from this selection?

from *The Last Seven Months of Anne Frank*

As you read, remember what you have already learned about Anne Frank and her family from reading her diary.

This is an excerpt from Hannah Elisabeth Pick-Goslar's interview. What else could she have talked about?

Hannah Elisabeth Pick-Goslar (Pick-Goslar was Frank's childhood friend. In Frank's published diary, she is called "Lies Goosens."):

Anne was given a diary on her thirteenth birthday. There was a party in the afternoon and we saw that she had gotten a very beautiful diary from her parents. I don't know if it was the first or second one that she had, because I remember that Anne was always writing in her diary, **shielding** it with her hand, even at school during the break. Everybody could see that she was writing. But no one was allowed to see what she had written. And I thought that she was writing entire books. I was always very curious to know what was in the diary, but she never showed it to anyone.

I never could find out what was in it, but I have thought that there must have been much more than there was in the published diary. Maybe they never found all that she wrote before she went into hiding—she had already been writing for a couple of years—I remember that very well.

shielding hiding

Hannah Elisabeth Pick-Goslar

She did write in the diary that if she had a choice after the war, she wanted to become a writer in the Netherlands.

As I remember it, she was a bit spoiled, particularly by her father. Anne was her Daddy's girl; Margot was more like her mother. It's a good thing there were only two children. Mrs. Frank was a little religious, and Margot went in that direction too. Margot always said that after the war, if she could choose, she wanted to be a nurse in Israel.

> Janny Brandes-Brilleslijper (Brandes-Brilleslijper met the Frank family in the Amsterdam central train station. They all were waiting to be sent away to Auschwitz.):

In those days, I also went immediately to the Red Cross to look at the lists that showed who had survived and who had died. And I put a cross next to the names of those who I knew had actually died.

I also put a cross next to the names of Anne and Margot. Much later, in the summer of 1945, a tall, thin, **distinguished** man stood on the sidewalk. He looked through our window and Bob (my husband) opened the door, because he often protected me. In the beginning, I had to deal so much with family members whom I had to tell that their sons, daughters, and husbands would not be coming back. That was often **unbearable**. And it was especially difficult to deal with because I had **survived** and had come back.

And there stood Otto Frank. He asked if I knew what had happened to his two daughters. I knew, but it was hard to get the words out of my mouth. He had already heard from the Red Cross, but he wanted to have it **confirmed**. . . . I had to tell him that . . . that his children were no more.

Many European Jews moved to Israel in the 1920s and 1930s. It was a place where Jews could live in safety. Israel became a nation in 1948.

Auschwitz was a Nazi concentration camp in Poland.

This woman has been in a concentration camp herself. Why would that make it harder for her to meet the family members of people who died?

---

distinguished appearing important or famous

unbearable painful; hard to endure

survived made it out alive

confirmed made sure by having someone else agree

Nonfiction Unit 2

He took it very hard. He was a man who didn't show his feelings **openly**, he had tremendous self-control. He was a tall, thin, **aristocratic** man. Later, we saw him frequently. By a remarkable chance, Anne's manuscript (her diary) was found at Annie Romijn's. And Annie Romijn was in our circle of friends. That's really amazing. And later he came often. He always stayed at the Hotel Suisse on Kalverstraat, where my relatives from Brussels always stayed. I always found that so nice.

Kalverstraat is a street in Amsterdam. Brussels is a city in Belgium, a country next to the Netherlands.

> **Rachel van Amerongen-Frankfoorder (van Amerongen-Frankfoorder first knew the Frank family while they were in a detention camp near Amsterdam.):**

In Israel, where we live, Anne Frank is a legend, and at the same time, a living girl. People are very interested in her. I believe that there is an Anne Frank Street in practically every town. Her diary has been translated into Modern Hebrew.

Modern Hebrew is the national language of Israel.

People think that she is very special. Once, when my daughter was in the Netherlands with her twin daughters, one of the first things they wanted me to show them was the Anne Frank House. I didn't feel up to it; actually, I didn't want to go at all. For more than forty years, I had pushed that aside because I really wanted to live normally, and I didn't want to talk about it anymore.

Many tourists in Amsterdam visit the house where Anne and her family hid.

Nonetheless, I went to the Anne Frank House, and I had a very special feeling there. I had seen her, after all, from the time that she came to Westerbork. People took pictures there of every corner, every plank, everything; especially the Japanese, who you would suppose wouldn't be as **emotionally touched** as the Europeans. My daughter panicked, because she knew that I had known Anne. She looked around and she said, "Mama, shouldn't you tell these people that you knew her? Shouldn't you do something? Tell them, tell them."

Westerbork was a Nazi detention camp near Amsterdam. It was the first stop for people being taken to the concentration camps.

I couldn't do it; I absolutely couldn't. I wouldn't have known how to tell it.

openly publicly; in front of others

aristocratic noble or superior in appearance

emotionally with strong feelings

touched affected

Bloeme Evers-Emden (Evers-Emden got to know Anne and Margot Frank at a Jewish school in Amsterdam.):

I especially remember the last time I saw the Frank family [in Auschwitz]. Another selection had taken place. I spoke to Mrs. Frank, who was with Margot. Anne was somewhere else; she had *Krätze* (scabies). She had a rash of some kind or other. The Germans, **unhindered** by medical knowledge—at least the Germans who had the **say-so** over our lives—were terribly afraid because it might be **infectious** and she had to be **isolated**. As a result, Anne couldn't go with our group. Mrs. Frank, echoed by Margot, said, "We are, of course, going with her." I remember that I nodded, that I understood that.

That was the last time I saw them.

Before that, we naturally saw each other regularly, and I talked with them. They were always together—mother and daughters. Whatever **discord** you might **infer** from the diary was swept away now by **existential** need. They were always together. It is certain that they gave each other a great deal of support.

What interview questions do you think Willy Lindwer asked Bloeme Evers-Emden?

In the camps, a *selection* divided people into groups. Some were moved to other places; some were killed.

Scabies is an itchy skin disease.

Rachel van Amerongen-Frankfoorder

unhindered not prevented or stopped
say-so the right to decide
infectious easily spread from person to person
isolated kept apart from others
discord arguments; disagreements
infer conclude
existential based on real experience

Nonfiction Unit 2 251

All the things that a teenager might think of her mother were no longer of any **significance**.

What I mean is that there are people who talk about the war, whose bike was **requisitioned**, how terrible that was, and then they stop. For them, that was the very worst that happened. If you say, "Yes, but there are people who went into hiding, and, much worse, there were also people in the camps."

"Oh yes, that was too bad, but I had to give up my bike."

I think it was that way with Anne. When she was in hiding, which was a very unhealthy situation, her mother was someone against whom she **rebelled**. But in the camp, all of that actually completely fell away. By giving each other **mutual** support, they were able to keep each other alive—although no one can fight typhus.

Typhus is a serious illness, from which Anne Frank died. It is carried by fleas and other tiny insects. Typhus is common in places such as the camps, where living conditions are crowded and dirty.

Bloeme Evers-Emden

significance	requisitioned	rebelled went against
importance	demanded; taken	rules or authority
		mutual shared

AFTER READING THE SELECTION

from The Last Seven Months of Anne Frank   by Willy Lindwer

Directions Choose the letter of the best answer or write the answer using complete sentences.

Comprehension: Identifying Facts

1. Which of the women was a close childhood friend of Anne Frank?
   A Hannah Elisabeth Pick-Goslar
   B Janny Brandes-Brilleslijper
   C Rachel van Amerongen-Frankfoorder
   D Bloeme Evers-Emden

2. Where do the other women meet Anne Frank and her family?

3. Why was Anne isolated at Auschwitz?

Comprehension: Putting Ideas Together

4. Why does Hannah Elisabeth Pick-Goslar think that Anne Frank wrote more than what was in the published diary?
   A Anne wanted to be a writer when she grew up.
   B Anne had been writing for a couple of years before she went into hiding.
   C Anne told her that she had written much more than this.
   D Anne showed Hannah her diary.

5. How do people in Israel today think about Anne Frank?

6. How did Anne's relationship with her mother change in the camps?

Understanding Literature: Excerpts

This selection includes only a few short excerpts of several interviews. An excerpt is a short passage from a longer piece of writing. As you know, a movie was made from those interviews, too. The movie had excerpts of the interviews. When a writer or editor uses excerpts, he or she must choose which parts to include—and which parts to cut, or leave out.

7. How do you think that Willy Lindwer decided which excerpts to include in the movie?

8. Which of these excerpts did you find the most powerful? Why?

Critical Thinking

9. Rachel van Amerongen-Frankfoorder is surprised by the way the Japanese people respond to the Anne Frank House. What might this tell you about her?

Thinking Creatively

10. Why do you think it was so important to Otto Frank to ask a second person about his daughters' deaths?

After Reading **continued on next page**

AFTER READING THE SELECTION (continued)

from The Last Seven Months of Anne Frank   by Willy Lindwer

 Grammar Check

An infinitive is *to* + the base form of the verb. Here are examples of infinitives: *to run, to play, to write, to sing*. Infinitive phrases have objects or subjects, just like other phrases. Find three examples of infinitive phrases from the selection.

 Writing on Your Own

You have now seen Anne Frank from two different points of view. Earlier, you read parts of her diary. In this selection, you have heard from others who knew her. Now it's your turn. Write a paragraph explaining what you think about Anne Frank. Why do you think her story is so important to so many people?

 Speaking

This selection gives the thoughts and ideas of four different women. Willy Lindwer does not write about his own ideas or thoughts. Think of what he could have said in conclusion. Give a short speech presenting this conclusion.

 Listening

The interviews in this selection were spoken aloud. Have a classmate read one of the interviews aloud. As you listen, think about the speaker's purpose and point of view. Write a summary of this purpose and point of view.

 Research

Sometimes a writer does not state the main idea directly. You can use Main Idea Graphic (Details) to help figure out the main idea. Choose one of the women from this selection. Use the graphic organizer to list supporting details about her or her story. Then write the main idea in the bottom box. See Appendix A for a description of this graphic organizer.

Journalism

The purpose of journalism is to gather and present news to the public. The Constitution guarantees freedom of the press to American journalists. This gives them the right to speak freely and write their opinions without government control. However, along with this freedom comes the responsibility to report in a fair and accurate way. Imagine there is a fight between two public officials. A reporter covering the story should talk to both sides before writing the story. He or she might also need to talk to witnesses. The story should use all these different points of view.

Some journalists report immediate news. Such "breaking news" is in newspapers and on TV as an event happens. Feature stories look at the importance of an event. Sidebars are short articles running next to the main story. They may provide more background. This is called "in-depth" reporting. Stories that tell one person's point of view are called human interest stories.

The public expects journalists to report the facts of an event. Journalists often do this and more. A journalist may provide a certain point of view on an event by including some information and leaving out other information. A journalist may also interpret an event by discussing its possible long-term effects.

One of the most immediate news sources is the Internet, a worldwide network of computers. Anyone connected to the Internet can get information from all over the world at any time. Many newspapers, big and small, have Web sites. These can be updated whenever there is something new to report. This shortens the news cycle. The news cycle starts when a news item is printed and ends when an update or a reaction to it is printed.

The following articles represent news stories and editorials about a world event. Notice how much of each article reports facts and how much is analysis, or the reporter's thoughts about the event. Identifying what is fact and what is opinion will help you understand the articles. Several of the selections were taken from the Internet edition of a newspaper.

Journalism

- freedom and responsibility
- immediate news
- in-depth reporting
- news stories
- feature and human interest stories
- news cycle

BEFORE READING THE SELECTION

Account Evened With India, Says PM   from Dawn (29 May 1998)

Dawn
(established 1947)
Pakistani

Objectives

- To read and understand a news story
- To recognize bias, or a particular viewpoint

About the Newspaper

Dawn is an English-language morning paper. It is published in Karachi and Lahore, Pakistan, and is one of the leading papers in Pakistan. Karachi and Lahore are Pakistan's largest cities. Karachi has more than 10 million people. Pakistan has many newspapers written in English. Pakistanis also speak many other languages. Many papers are published in those languages, especially Urdu and Sindhi.

You will find articles from *Dawn* on its Web site. Other foreign newspapers also have Web sites.

About the Selection

In 1947 India and Pakistan gained their independence from Great Britain. India and Pakistan have been enemies ever since. Most Pakistanis are Muslim. India's people are more varied, and Hindu is the main religious group.

Early in May 1998, India held tests of nuclear weapons. They were the first in this part of the world to do this. A few weeks later, Pakistan held its own tests. Other nations with nuclear weapons had already agreed to stop testing them. The Indian and Pakistani tests frightened many people.

This selection is a news story from Pakistan. It tells about what the prime minister (PM) had to say about his country's actions. The prime minister predicted that other nations would punish Pakistan. Read to learn why Pakistan chose to do the tests anyway.

Literary Term In May 1998, Pakistan held nuclear tests. The prime minister of Pakistan explained why they did this. He also talked about how his country would handle any problems that might come as a result of this action. One of the leading Pakistani newspapers printed a report about what the prime minister had to say. It does not quote the prime minister's speech. Instead the writer tells about what was said.

This selection is that **news story**. A news story is the first report of an event. It covers the basic facts. As you read this section, try to decide if the writer might want to entertain, to inform, to express and opinion, or to persuade.

> **news story** the first report of an event; mainly covers the basic facts

Reading on Your Own Think about the things that can affect what a news reporter writes. For example, the article that apprears in a Pakistani newspaper will most likely support the actions of leaders in Pakistan. Do you think there will be any bias in the story?

Writing on Your Own Think of a time when you felt you were not treated fairly. Write a paragraph to tell your side of the story. What happened and how did it make you feel?

Vocabulary Focus You can use context clues to help you figure out the meanings of new words. Sometimes, the context clues, or the other words in the sentence, are enough. Other times, you will need to read a few paragraphs. Read this news story and look for the word *austerity*. Use the whole story to help you figure out the meaning of the word. Write your own definition. Then check a dictionary.

Think Before You Read Carefully read the title of this selection. What do you think the prime minister of Pakistan is going to say about India?

Nonfiction Unit 2

Account Evened With India, Says PM

> As you read, look for the facts in this news story.

> *Islamabad* is the capital of Pakistan.

> The prime minister expects other countries to impose sanctions because they oppose the nuclear tests.

ISLAMABAD: Pakistan on Thursday joined the exclusive club of nuclear nations by conducting five nuclear tests of varying **intensity** in Chagai hills, a remote region of Balochistan desert near the border with Iran and Afghanistan. Announcing the successful completion of a series of tests in response to those conducted by India on May 11–13, Prime Minister Nawaz Sharif told the nation on radio and television that he took the decision in the interest of national **security** and **integrity**.

He, however, warned the nation to be prepared to pay the price for taking this decision in the face of immense world pressure. The prime minister said in a few days time he would present to the nation a complete national **agenda** for meeting the **anticipated** hardships. He announced a number of official austerity measures to meet the challenges of the expected **sanctions** and asked the nation to **reciprocate** by trying to live within its means.

Pakistani citizens demonstrated in the streets to show their support of the nuclear tests.

---

intensity strength
security safety
integrity honesty
agenda a list of things to be done
anticipated expected
sanctions actions to stop or cut down trade and aid
reciprocate to give something in return

The prime minister also served final notice on the country's tax **evaders** and **corrupt** tax collectors, cautioning them to mend their ways; otherwise he warned that the government would not spare them. He assured the nation that the government would stop **forthwith** all of its demonstrative and wasteful **expenditures** and said all **palatial** official buildings would be pressed into the service of the nation. Some of these buildings would be turned into schools, some into hospitals and some others into women's universities. And some would be sold to retire debts. The prime minister announced that he would not use the Prime Minister's Secretariat and said the government has decided to observe complete austerity at the official level.

> The *Secretariat* is a large government building in Islamabad.

He said the president was in complete agreement with these decisions and all provincial governors, chief ministers, federal ministers, chiefs of navy, army, and air-force and high civil and military officials will join the nation in its sacrifices and austerity efforts. He asked those who had borrowed billions of rupees from the banks to return the national wealth and warned tax evaders to give up their anti-national habits. Describing the nuclear tests as a **defensive** step, the prime minister said these tests were conducted solely in the interest of national security and integrity.

> Pakistan is divided into four provinces. Each has a provincial governor.
>
> The *rupee* is the unit of money in both India and Pakistan.

Prime Minister Nawaz Sharif said every time Pakistan brought to the world attention India's massive arms build-up, New Delhi attributed it to Chinese threat to India's security. But he said despite its tremendous superiority in defensive capability, China was against **expansionism** while India had proven on more than one occasion that it harboured strong expansionist ambitions. Under the circumstances it was natural for Pakistan, Mr. Nawaz Sharif said, to feel concerned and in order to ward off the threat to national security, the

> *New Delhi* is the capital of India.

---

evaders people who avoid doing something
corrupt dishonest
forthwith immediately
expenditures spending
palatial elaborate; like a palace
defensive done to defend oneself
expansionism a country's practice of spreading out to gain land

country had even proposed that America, Russia and China should **mediate** and save Asia from arms race.

He said if Pakistan had wanted it would have conducted nuclear tests 15–20 years ago but the **abject** poverty of the people of the region **dissuaded** Pakistan from doing so. But the world, he said, instead of putting pressure on India not to take the destructive road imposed all kinds of sanctions on Pakistan for no fault of her [own]. He said after the Indian tests, Pakistan had expected the world to impose a total economic blockade on India but unfortunately no such action was taken.

Prime Minister Nawaz Sharif praised China for its support during "this hour of crisis" and said Pakistan was proud of its great neighbour. Stating that Japan's position on the nuclear issue was based on the highest human principles, he, however, thought if Japan had had its own nuclear capability Hiroshima and Nagasaki would not have suffered destruction. He thanked President Clinton for his five telephone calls to express his sympathies following Indian explosions but said he expected the American president to appreciate Pakistan's **compulsions** for carrying out its own tests despite American advice against it.

The prime minister said Pakistan has taken the extreme step without bothering about the expected sanctions and **spurning** promises of all kinds of gifts and goodies. He said the world should not believe India when it says that it would use the 'big bomb' only if attacked because both in 1965 and 1971 India went to war against Pakistan accusing it of committing **aggression** and even today New Delhi was accusing Pakistan of keeping Azad Kashmir under its occupation. He asked the world to see Pakistan's nuclear tests in the context of India's aggressive and **hegemonic** designs but said if even then the world decided to impose sanctions on the country then Pakistan would accept these as the will of God.

> Near the end of World War II, the United States dropped atomic bombs on *Hiroshima* and *Nagasaki*, Japan. Japan today opposes nuclear weapons.

> The *big bomb* refers to a nuclear weapon. *Kashmir* is a disputed region on the Indian border.

> Look at the kinds of information the writer gives. How can these help you figure out the purpose of this news story?

---

mediate to help settle a disagreement

abject miserable

dissuaded persuaded someone not to take a certain action

compulsions the forces or reasons behind an action

spurning refusing

aggression a move to attack

hegemonic having influence over others

AFTER READING THE SELECTION

Account Evened With India, Says PM   from Dawn (29 May 1998)

Directions Choose the letter of the best answer or write the answer using complete sentences.

Comprehension: Identifying Facts

1. When did India conduct its nuclear tests?
   A May 11–13, 1998
   B May 28, 1998
   C May 29, 1998
   D June 5, 1998

2. How does the prime minister expect other countries to react to Pakistan's tests?

3. What specific actions will the Pakistani government take to cut down spending?

Comprehension: Putting Ideas Together

4. What can the people of Pakistan do to help their country?
   A stop traveling to India
   B buy products made in China
   C pay their taxes
   D send money to help Japan build nuclear weapons

5. What other country seems to have supported Pakistan's actions?

6. What are Pakistan's reasons for conducting nuclear tests?

Understanding Literature: News Story

A news story presents the basic facts about an event. It answers the questions "who, what, when, where, why, and how." The first sentence of this story answers some of those questions. This is called the "lead." In the rest of the news story, the prime minister explains more of the "why" of the story.

7. Reread the first sentence of the news story. What *W-* questions does it answer?

8. Several paragraphs of the story are meant for a world audience, not just Pakistan. Which paragraphs are they?

Critical Thinking

9. What can you tell about Pakistan's relations with India from the tone of this article?

Thinking Creatively

10. Think about the reasons that Pakistan tested nuclear weapons. Do you think these are good reasons? Explain your answer.

After Reading continued on next page

AFTER READING THE SELECTION (continued)

Account Evened With India, Says PM   from Dawn (29 May 1998)

 Grammar Check

In Pakistan, people speak British English. They use phrases that we do not use in American English. For example, the journalist uses the phrase "took the decision" in the news story. What is the correct wording in American English? Rewrite the sentence using the matching American English phrase.

 Writing on Your Own

Think of a recent event that happened in your city or in the world. Write one or two sentences that would be the "lead" of a news story about that event. Your sentences should answer the basic questions: who, what, when, where, why, and how.

 Speaking and Listening

Pretend you are the prime minister of Pakistan. Write your own version of his speech. Base your speech on the details that are included in this news story. Give your speech to the class. Refer to Appendix E for tips on writing a speech.

Make a checklist of details from the prime minister's speech. Use this checklist as you listen to your classmates give their speeches. Did each speaker include all the information from the selection? If a speaker left something out, was it an important detail?

 Viewing

On a map of this region of the world, find Pakistan, Iran, Afghanistan, and India. Locate the Balochistan desert in Pakistan. About how far is this from each of the other countries? Now use a map of your area of the country. What are some places that are about the same distance from where you live?

BEFORE READING THE SELECTION

Tests Are Nowhere Near India's: Fernandes *from the* Times of India *(1 June 1998)*

The *Times of India* (established 1838) Indian

About the Newspaper

This newspaper first appeared in Bombay, India, in 1838. It was originally called the *Bombay Times and Journal of Commerce*. It was a paper mainly by and for the British residents who ran India's colonial government. Today the *Times of India* is published in New Delhi. It is the most widely circulated English-language daily newspaper in India. It is part of a large Indian publishing group that also prints newspapers in Indian languages. Every day, more than a million copies are sold from its printing plants in Mumbai, Delhi, Bangalore, Ahmadabad, Lucknow, and Patna. The *Times of India* is published every day including Sunday. It is a well-established newspaper with a good reputation for objective reporting, or reporting that is true to the facts.

The *Times of India Online* is the Internet version of the *Times of India*.

Objectives

- To read a news story and understand the point of view
- To describe the different aspects of journalism

About the Selection

People who work in journalism have the job of finding, collecting, and communicating news. The news reported in this story adds more information about India and Pakistan's nuclear tests. It is based on a TV interview. In that interview, an Indian government official compared his country's tests to Pakistan's tests. The official, George Fernandes, also talks about India's future nuclear plans.

Before Reading **continued on next page**

Nonfiction Unit 2   263

BEFORE READING THE SELECTION (continued)

Tests Are Nowhere Near India's: Fernandes from the Times of India (1 June 1998)

journalism
the gathering and presenting of news to the public

point of view
the position from which the author tells the story

Literary Terms **Journalism** is the gathering and presenting of news to the public. This includes television news reports, newspaper articles, radio news, and more. The people who gather and report the news are called journalists or reporters. Good reporters do more than gather the basic facts. They will look for background information and expert opinions. As you read this news article, look for background information and opinions.

Also think about the article's **point of view**, or the position from which the author tells the story. This news article is written from the point of view of an Indian newspaper. The facts are the same as those available to reporters from Pakistan, but the reporter chooses experts and background information that support India and not Pakistan.

Reading on Your Own As you read, remember that this news story is written from India's point of view. You have already read Pakistan's point of view. Write a sentence summarizing each country's point of view.

Writing on Your Own How do you feel about people who try to show off their skills or strength? Why?

Vocabulary Focus A suffix is an ending that is added to a word or its root. Some suffixes change a word from one part of speech to another. Look at the words in the chart below. Write the suffix at the top of each column. Think of other words that can be changed with either one or both of these endings. Write the words in a chart like this one.

Base Word:	Suffix:	Suffix:
explode	explosion	explosive

Think Before You Read What do you think an Indian newspaper will have to say about Pakistan's nuclear tests?

Tests Are Nowhere Near India's: Fernandes

NEW DELHI: Defence minister George Fernandes has asserted that Pakistan's nuclear blasts were "nowhere near" the Indian tests and said New Delhi exercised its nuclear **option** without holding **strategic** defence review because "scientists did not feel that the tests were needed." In an interview to a private TV channel, Mr Fernandes said, "Everything that we have learnt about their [Pakistani] nuclear tests show that they are nowhere near where we are. In terms of our tests we [also] went in for low-intensity sub-kiloton tests. They are the most important tests in any kind of nuclear testing."

Asked if Islamabad's claim that it conducted tests similar to those by India was "mistaken and **deliberately** wrong," he said, "that's the general understanding that we have." Noting that New Delhi's concerns were much bigger and it had acted on those bigger concerns, he said there had been no testing since 1974 despite a lot of **development** in the nuclear science area and its **application** and "the scientists wanted to test it."

> This story is from *New Delhi,* India's capital city. What do you expect the writer's point of view to be?

> India was a British colony for many years. Indian newspapers use British spellings such as *defence* for *defense.*

> Nuclear weapons are measured in *kilotons,* a force equal to the explosion of 1,000 tons of TNT. TNT is an explosive compound.

---

option a choice
strategic related to military planning
deliberately on purpose
development growth; progress
application use of something

These are different types and sizes of nuclear devices.

The Central Intelligence Agency (CIA) is an American government agency. It gathers information about foreign governments.

Fernandes is talking about whether India will now build nuclear weapons. To weaponise is to adapt something for use as a weapon.

Here, across the border means Pakistan.

India had tested a 45 kiloton (KT) hydrogen bomb, a 15 KT fission bomb and a low-yield device on May 11 and two sub-kiloton devices on May 13. Pakistan conducted its tests on May 28 and 30.

Maintaining that Pakistan had carried out only one test on May 28, he said, "We got a bit of information that in fact there may not have [been] five tests. The US agency, the CIA, has put out a piece of information that the number five is only to match India's five. The general feeling is that there was only one."

Admitting that India carried out the Pokhran tests without holding a strategic defence review, he said, "There has been a lot of development in the nuclear science area. There has been **militarisation** of nuclear **weaponry**. We have to show not only to ourselves, but tell the world we [too] are there."

Asked whether India would conduct more tests, Mr Fernandes said, "We do not need to go for any more testing, whatever we needed to know we got it," but also added "in terms of a country's security concerns one does not say the last word at any point of time."

To a question if India would go in for weaponisation, the minister noted "What I have said is that any nuclear tests without weaponising do not make sense.

"Whether one needs to weaponise in the **context** of what has happened across the border is a matter on which in Parliament the Prime Minister had made a public offer to Pakistan that we should sit together, we should talk and we should not get into any kind of a nuclear weapon race. Therefore, it is going to be a two-way traffic and I hope Pakistan responds to the Prime Minister's appeal," he said.

maintaining insisting

militarisation (American *militarization*) the process of being taken over or used by the military

weaponry different types of weapons seen as a group

context the setting or situation

Asked about control and command structure Mr Fernandes said "there will be the same kind of control which exist in those countries which have nuclear weaponry. They cannot be any different." Observing that the Prime Minister will be the only person to have his finger on the nuclear button, he said, "In India the Prime Minister is the **executive** head of government . . . And it shall be the Prime Minister."

On nuclear **deterrent**, he said, "The Army is happy that it has it and the Army believes that no one can push us around."

Mr Fernandes refused to give details on the size of deterrent that India required or the cost of creating it saying "these are matters which I do not believe can be **aired** in public." He said that the cost of developing a deterrent and an appropriate delivery system would not be "**backbreaking**" and added "a delivery system is something that we always had. Your aircraft are there. Your missiles are there. India is producing missiles."

Meanwhile, in Washington, the **global** network that tracks earthquakes and underground atomic blasts found only a faint echo from Saturday's Pakistan nuclear test that could mean the test was successful, but small or that the test was a failure and produced relatively few shock waves, says the *New York Times* quoting US experts. "It's a small event," said Terry Wallace, a **seismologist** at the University of Arizona, who works with the incorporated research institutions for seismology, a scientific group in Washington.

Mr Wallace said the blast had a preliminary magnitude of 4.3 equal to about 1,000 tons of high explosive; by contrast, the atomic bomb dropped on Hiroshima in 1945 had an explosive force of 15,000 tons.

Control and command structure means the government and military officials who are in charge of nuclear weapons.

In military language, a *delivery system* is the device, such as a missile, that carries a weapon to its target.

The shock waves from nuclear tests are measured with the Richter scale. This is the same scale used to measure the magnitude, or size, of earthquakes.

---

executive relating to the branch of government that carries out the laws

deterrent something that prevents or discourages an action

aired openly discussed

backbreaking very difficult

global worldwide

seismologist a person who studies earthquakes

> *Tonnes* is a British spelling for *tons*.

> The New Delhi paper has gathered information from an American newspaper and American scientists, as well as from local sources.

> *Nawaz Sharif* was prime minister of Pakistan at the time this article was written.

The main Pakistani blast on Thursday was **monitored** as having magnitude of 4.8, equal to 8,000 to 15,000 tonnes. Such bombs are considered relatively small by the standards of world **arsenals**, where the explosive power of **warheads** can exceed millions of tonnes. Saturday's explosion was too small to show up on the government's main network for monitoring earthquakes around the world. "We've searched everything we have and we don't see anything," said Waverly Person, a spokesman at the national earthquake informations centre, in Golden, Colo. "We didn't record anything at all."

The daily quoted arms-control experts as saying that the truly **alarming** thing that prime minister Nawaz Sharif's government announced on Thursday was not that Pakistan had successfully conducted its own tests. Rather it was the declaration that Pakistan was already fitting nuclear warheads on top of a missile.

Michael Krepon, president of the Henry L. Stimson Centre, an independent research institute, said, "A **crucial threshold** has been crossed, if it's true and that means we have only two thresholds left. **Deployment** and use."

---

monitored measured with an instrument or a device

arsenals storehouses for weapons

warheads the front parts of missiles or bombs that contain the explosive

alarming frightening

crucial very important

threshold the beginning point

deployment the spreading of troops or weapons in a larger area

The daily says India is said to have enough fissile material for perhaps 50 nuclear devices, maybe more. Pakistan has enough for perhaps 12. There is almost no evidence that either country has mastered the ability to make warheads small enough to fit on missiles, though not for lack of trying. It says senior administration officials cast doubt on Pakistan's claims to have already fitted its longest range missile with nuclear warheads. "That would be a fateful and foolish [decision]," one official said on condition of **anonymity**.

Fissile means the material could release large amounts of energy.

Indian Prime Minister Vajpayee (center) pays a visit to the site of the Indian blast.

anonymity
being unknown

AFTER READING THE SELECTION

Tests Are Nowhere Near India's: Fernandes *from the* Times of India *(1 June 1998)*

Directions Choose the letter of the best answer or write the answer using complete sentences.

Comprehension: Identifying Facts

1. Who is George Fernandes?
   A the prime minister of Pakistan
   B the defence minister of India
   C the reporter who wrote the news story
   D the editor of the *Times of India*

2. When, before 1998, was the last time that India tested nuclear weapons?

3. How many tests does Fernandes think Pakistan carried out?

Comprehension: Putting Ideas Together

4. How did scientists in the United States monitor Pakistan's tests?
   A They sent government officials to watch the tests.
   B They watched it on cable TV.
   C They measured it with equipment they use to measure earthquakes.
   D They took pictures from a weather balloon.

5. Arms control experts are upset with Pakistan. What are they most upset about?

6. What is the main point of the Indian official's interview?

Understanding Literature: Journalism

The article from the *Times of India* is a good example of journalism. The story gives facts about an interview with a government official. It then adds background material. It brings in facts and figures from experts. Another part of journalism is informing people. This story, for example, was published on the Internet. Of course, journalism also appears in newspapers or is aired on the radio or television.

7. What are some facts that you learned from this article?

8. Who is Michael Krepon? Why is it important that he is from an independent research institute?

Critical Thinking

9. Why do you think this Indian newspaper quotes American scientists?

Thinking Creatively

10. The official says that only the prime minister will "have his finger on the nuclear button." What does he mean?

Grammar Check

Most abbreviations have a period after them. Abbreviations for people's titles all need periods. This news story does not use a period for the abbreviation of *mister*. This is British style. It would not be correct in American English. Write the abbreviations for the following titles: *doctor, missus, mister, junior,* and *reverend.* Use American style for the abbreviations.

 ### Writing on Your Own

Make a list of each journalistic source you use. (Remember that journalism includes radio, TV, newspapers, and magazines.) Then write a sentence about each source. Tell what kind of news or information you get from it. For example, where do you get sports news?

 ### Speaking and Listening

Pretend to be one of the experts quoted in the article. Read aloud the section that tells about your expert opinions.

Listen as different classmates read parts of the article aloud. Do you agree with the logic of the experts' arguments? Why or why not?

 ### Media

Work with a small group. Think about how this story would be different if it were in a different medium. Choose a format that could be videotaped, such as a news report, television interview, or a documentary. Write a short script and plan what you will show. Choose different students to act out the scenes.

BEFORE READING THE SELECTION

Pakistan Nuclear Moratorium Welcomed from BBC Online Network *(12 June 1998)*

BBC Online Network
(BBC established 1927)
British

Objectives

- To read and understand a feature story
- To explain what a news cycle is

About the News Source

Radio listeners around the world know the voice of the BBC. Those letters stand for British Broadcasting Corporation. It was set up by the British government in 1927. It operates independently from the government, though. In the 1930s the BBC began to send short-wave radio programs to all the countries in the British Empire. In 1967, it started the first regular color TV service in Europe. Today, the BBC sends radio and TV programs to audiences all over the United Kingdom. Local programs include music, sports, plays, and news. BBC radio news and other programs are heard all over the world. The network has reporters in many foreign countries. It broadcasts in English and 35 other languages.

Like other world news sources, the BBC posts articles and information on its Web site. You may also be able to hear the BBC on your local public radio station.

About the Selection

In 1998, India and Pakistan held nuclear tests. You have already read news stories from India and Pakistan. Of course, other countries around the world had a lot to say about what had happened. Some countries praised India and Pakistan for the tests. Others punished the countries. They cut down trade and financial help. This news story appeared online about two weeks after Pakistan's tests. It followed another new event in the continuing story.

Literary Terms On May 11 and May 13 in 1998, India held nuclear tests. About two weeks later, on May 28, Pakistan also held nuclear tests. News stories were written all during this two-week period. The **news cycle** was not over yet. The news cycle is the length of time between the publishing of a news item and an update or a reaction to the item.

Countries around the world reacted to both India's and Pakistan's actions. Some of the countries pressured India and Pakistan to promise they would not hold any more nuclear tests. This **feature story** tells how Pakistan responded to this pressure. A feature story analyzes, or carefully examines, the effect and importance of an event.

news cycle
the length of time between the publishing of a news item and an update or a reaction to the item

feature story
a news story that examines the effect and importance of an event

Reading on Your Own Identify statements that analyze the importance of Pakistan's actions. What is so important about Pakistan's statement? Draw a conclusion about how this could change things in the region.

Writing on Your Own Sometimes it is difficult for people to solve their differences. What are three different ways that they can try to do this? Write your list on a piece of paper.

Vocabulary Focus You can sometimes learn the meaning of a word by breaking it into parts. The first paragraph in this selection contains the word *non-proliferation*. The word *proliferation* means "a growth in number." If you know that *non-* means "no," you can figure out that *non-proliferation* must mean to "stop growing." Try this out with the words *nonliving* and *nonfattening*.

Think Before You Read What do you hope to learn about the reaction to Pakistan's actions?

Nonfiction Unit 2

Pakistan Nuclear Moratorium Welcomed

> As you read, keep in mind the rivalry between India and Pakistan.

> Look at words such as *welcomed* and *hailed*. Think about the tone of these words. What does this feature story seem to say about the effect of this event?

Pakistan's announcement of a **unilateral moratorium** on nuclear testing has been welcomed by the United States and the United Nations. UN Secretary General Kofi Annan hailed the move as an "important step in joining the international **norm** of nuclear testing and non-proliferation." A White House spokesman said the decision would help to limit **tensions** in the area.

A statement issued by Pakistan's foreign ministry said the country was ready to arrive at a "no-nuclear test agreement with India, as an important confidence-building measure at the regional level." "We are ready to engage **constructively** with India and other members of the international community to **formalise** this arrangement," the statement said. Pakistan hopes India will reciprocate and contribute towards a 'durable peace' in South Asia. Pakistan's Prime Minister, Nawaz Sharif, and his Indian **counterpart**, Atal Bihari Vajpayee, are due to meet at a regional summit in Sri Lanka.

> India and Pakistan are part of the larger area, or region, of Asia. A *regional summit* is a meeting among the heads of government of the countries in a region.

India and Pakistan provoked world condemnation last month by carrying out nuclear tests, which triggered economic sanctions against them by the US, Japan and other states.

Austerity measures

In response to the sanctions, Mr Sharif has unveiled a series of economic austerity measures. The measures, announced in a television address, include the transfer of

> *Austerity* refers to very strict, simple living.

---

unilateral involving only one side in an issue

moratorium a temporary pause or delay in an action

norm the usual pattern

tensions uneasy or angry relationships

constructively helpfully

formalise (American *formalize*) to make official; to sign an agreement

counterpart equal

274 *Unit 2 Nonfiction*

more than one million acres of land from rich farmers to poorer farmers, and help for small businesses. Mr Sharif also said it was an honour for Pakistan to have joined the world's nuclear powers.

On May 21, India announced its own moratorium on nuclear testing, marking the end of its series of five nuclear tests, and also invited world powers to hold talks on formalising new agreements on **arms** testing. Pakistan's nuclear **detonations**, set off to counteract the Indian explosions, were followed by statements of the country's **intention** to build nuclear missiles.

> When did India agree to end nuclear testing? How is this part of the same news cycle?

Arms race can be stabilised

Thursday's announcement came ahead of a meeting of foreign ministers from the G8 countries who will discuss Pakistan and India's nuclear tests when they gather in London on Friday. Mr Sharif is hoping that the G8 leaders will not impose further measures.

A BBC correspondent said that the announcement of the unilateral moratorium seemed to be designed to show that the arms race in South Asia could be **stabilised** and that Islamabad was now showing the **restraint** that the international community has been calling for.

> The *G8*, or Group of Eight, includes the world's major industrial countries. Officials from those countries often meet to discuss issues.

The prime ministers of India and Pakistan shake hands as they meet to discuss nuclear issues.

arms weapons
detonations explosions
intention a plan to do something
stabilised (American *stabilized*) stopped making changes; made steady
restraint control over actions or feelings

Nonfiction Unit 2 275

AFTER READING THE SELECTION

Pakistan Nuclear Moratorium Welcomed from BBC Online Network (12 June 1998)

Directions Choose the letter of the best answer or write the answer using complete sentences.

Comprehension: Identifying Facts

1. What is the main point of the announcement made by Pakistan's prime minister?
   A to announce Pakistan's power
   B to declare war on India
   C to condemn the G8
   D to announce that Pakistan will stop nuclear testing

2. What is a moratorium?

3. Why will the prime ministers of India and Pakistan meet in Sri Lanka?

Comprehension: Putting Ideas Together

4. Why will rich farmers have to give land to poorer farmers?
   A to punish rich farmers
   B to help the country survive during the sanctions
   C to help poorer farmers get richer
   D to stop rich farmers from owning too much land

5. Which country announced the moratorium on nuclear testing first?

6. What other steps toward peace are India and Pakistan taking?

Understanding Literature: News Cycle

This news cycle began with India's nuclear tests early in May. Newspapers around the world printed the news story and they offered opinions in editorials. A few weeks later, Pakistan also held nuclear tests. People reacted again. About two weeks later, Pakistan declared it would halt testing. This online report was on the BBC the next day.

7. Do you think the Internet and other electronic media make the news cycle shorter? Why or why not?

8. Write a timeline showing some of the events in this news cycle. Start with India's first nuclear test.

Critical Thinking

9. Reread the Pakistani prime minister's announcement on pages 274 and 275. Do you think Pakistan would have halted tests if India had not done so first? Why?

Thinking Creatively

10. The prime minister said it was "an honour for Pakistan to have joined the world's nuclear powers." Do you think these other countries think of Pakistan as part of their group? Why or why not?

Grammar Check

There are many words in this news story that use British spellings. Find these words and write their correct American spellings. You may use a dictionary.

 ### Writing on Your Own

An expository paragraph explains how something happened. Write an expository paragraph explaining what had been happening in Pakistan during May and June 1998.

 ### Speaking and Listening

This story came from the Internet. The BBC is well known around the world as a radio service. Rewrite the first section of this story as a radio announcement. Try to use shorter sentences that will be easier for listeners to follow. Read your radio announcement to a partner. Use the tone and voice of a radio news reporter.

Listen as your partner reads his or her radio announcement. Do you find it easier to listen to the news or read it? Why?

 ### Research

Nuclear weapons and nuclear testing are still important issues. Work with a group to research information about nuclear testing. As a group, decide what type of information you will look for. Have each member of the group choose a different news story to summarize. Remember to use your own words in your summary. Also make sure that your summary tells the main ideas of the news story.

BEFORE READING THE SELECTIONS

The Frightening Joy from de Volkskrant (29 May 1998)

de Volkskrant
(established 1919)
Dutch

Zycie Warszawy
(established 1944)
Polish

Objectives

- To read and understand an editorial
- To understand the purpose of a byline in a news article
- To understand an allusion in a piece of writing

About the Newspapers

De Volkskrant is published in Amsterdam, the capital of the Netherlands. (In Dutch, its name means "people's newspaper.") It is the second-largest paper in the city. It comes out in the mornings every day except Sunday.

More than 20 newspapers are published in Warsaw, the capital of Poland. Many of them belong to various political parties. They give the opinions of those parties. *Zycie Warszawy*, however, is an independent newspaper. Its name means "Warsaw life." It is one of the city's largest papers. More than 200,000 people read it on weekdays. About 330,000 read the Saturday edition.

About the Selections

India held nuclear tests early in May 1998. Pakistan answered with its own tests later in the month. At home, many Indians and Pakistanis were happy. The tests gave an image of national strength and pride. Others thought that the money should be spent to help the poor.

World reactions differed greatly. In general, there were two different types of reactions. Some countries were shocked and afraid. They wanted India and Pakistan to end the testing right away. Other countries were proud of India and Pakistan. Read the selections to find an example of each type of reaction.

Building Atomic Security from *Zycie Warszawy (2 June 1998)*

Literary Terms Newspapers around the world reported on the nuclear tests in India and Pakistan in 1998. In some newspapers, the editors commented on these tests. They did this by writing an **editorial,** a news writer's opinion about an event or a topic. These selections are editorials from newspapers in the Netherlands and Poland. The editorial from Poland includes a **byline**. A byline is a line in a news article that tells who wrote it.

The editorial from *de Volkskrant* does not have a byline. As you read this editorial, look for the **allusion** to the end of the world. An allusion is a reference to a historical event, a person, a place, or a work of literature. The writer of this editorial mentions *Armageddon*. This is a great battle that is described in the Christian Bible. It is supposed to occur at the end of the world.

editorial a news writer's opinion about an event or a topic

byline a line in a news article that tells who wrote it

allusion a statement that refers to a historical event, a person, a place, or a work of literature

Reading on Your Own As you read these two editorials, think about their different reactions to nuclear testing. Compare and contrast the editorials to see how they are alike and how they are different.

Writing on Your Own There are always people who disagree with a country's actions or political ideas. Why do you think it is important that these people express their opinions?

Vocabulary Focus Sometimes a writer hyphenates two words that describe something. The hyphen makes the two words into one adjective. Look for the word *still-vivid* in "The Frightening Joy." The writer is saying that the memory is *very real in people's minds,* even today. How does a hyphen used this way help you understand what you read?

Think Before You Read These selections will give different ideas about nuclear tests. Which editorial do you think will be against the testing? Why?

THE FRIGHTENING JOY

Indian Muslims shout slogans in favor of their prime minister's decision on nuclear testing.

Look for the writer's point of view as you read this editorial.

Why do you think the writer makes an allusion to *Armageddon*? How does this help the writer make his or her point?

    Despite the still-vivid memory of A-bombs falling on Japan, the world has been **perilously** close to the edge of nuclear war several times. Most frightening is the great joy in India and Pakistan over these shows of national power, because it clearly demonstrates that the people do not understand the **gravity** of the danger. . . . This is cheering on the way to Armageddon.

perilously dangerously

gravity seriousness

Building Atomic Security

BY TOMASZ WROBLEWSKI

There is a tired **slogan** that we all would be better off without nuclear warheads. The truth is that it is nuclear **potential**, not the lack of it, that is the **guarantor** of peace. It is the **escalation** of **armaments** and fear of atomic doom, not common sense or **disarmament**, that have **shielded** us from World War III. . . . Indians and Pakistanis in reality are doing nothing less than what Americans and Russians did for the past half century—they are building an atomic security zone.

---

slogan a saying or motto used by a group

potential the ability for action or growth in the future

guarantor a person or thing that promises a certain result

escalation an increase; rapid growth

armaments weapons

disarmament the decrease of weapons

shielded protected

AFTER READING THE SELECTIONS

The Frightening Joy from de Volkskrant (29 May 1998)

Directions Choose the letter of the best answer or write the answer using complete sentences.

Comprehension: Identifying Facts

1. How soon after Pakistan's tests did these editorials appear?
   A one day
   B two days
   C one week
   D one month

2. What does the Dutch paper say that people in India do not understand?

3. What idea does the Polish paper call a "tired slogan"?

Comprehension: Putting Ideas Together

4. According to the Polish editorial, what has saved us from World War III?
   A disarmament
   B common sense
   C treaties
   D nuclear weapons and potential

5. Why is it important to remember the A-bombs falling on Japan?

6. How are the Indians and Pakistanis doing the same thing that Americans and Russians did?

Understanding Literature: Editorials

Almost every newspaper has an editorial page. This page usually contains editorials and letters from readers. An editorial is a kind of essay. The editor of the paper gives his or her opinion about a current issue or event—local or global. Many editorials are about political events. The writer expresses a political viewpoint. A writer might use background information to support his or her opinions.

7. These newspapers are published far from India and Pakistan. Why was this event important enough for an editorial?

8. What does the title of the Dutch editorial mean?

Critical Thinking

9. Imagine a debate between the writers of these two pieces. What do you think they would say to each other?

Thinking Creatively

10. These editorials were written before the attacks on America on September 11, 2001. Do you think the writers would feel different today? Why or why not?

Building Atomic Security from Zycie Warszawy (2 June 1998)

 Grammar Check

Parallel structure occurs when a writer repeats the same sentence pattern or other grammatical pattern. Writers use parallel structure to give their writing a rhythm and a better flow. Parallel structure is especially powerful in editorials and speeches. Read "Building Atomic Security" and look for this sentence structure: *It is _____, not the _____, that is the _____.* You will find this repeated twice. Read this article aloud. Now read "The Frightening Joy" aloud. How can parallelism help an editorial or a speech?

 Writing on Your Own

Write a letter to the editor of one of these newspapers. Tell why you agree or disagree with the point of view in the editorial.

A good letter to the editor of a newspaper should be clear and exact. Put your main points within the first paragraph or two. A short, well-written letter is more likely to be published than a letter that rambles, or one that needs many corrections. Be sure to proofread your letter carefully.

 Speaking and Listening

Should the rest of the world allow India and Pakistan to hold nuclear tests? Have a class debate. One group of students will defend the ideas in the first editorial. Another group will defend the ideas in the second editorial.

Remember these rules as you debate your classmates. In a debate you cannot interrupt the other team. Listen to what the person is saying. Take notes as he or she speaks. This will help you remember any comments you have about something that was said.

 Technology

Gather several of the letters to the editor that your classmates wrote. Use a page layout program to create an editorial page for your own newspaper. You may want to look at an editorial page from your local newspaper for ideas about layout.

Unit 2 SKILLS LESSON
Point of View

Did you ever tell friends about something you did? You described people and places the way you saw them. You told the story from your point of view. In this unit, many of the authors told their stories as they remembered and lived them. They used a first-person point of view: *I*.

Journals, diaries, and letters are almost always written from a first-person point of view. So are autobiographies. A biography is more complicated. Biographies are usually written from a third-person point of view. The writer speaks of everyone as "he" or "she." At the same time, a biography often tries to show the point of view of the person who is its subject. Many biographies give a good picture of the person. Some, though, attack or criticize that person.

Margaret Atwood gives her point of view about being a writer:

> "One week I wasn't a writer, the next I was."

The reader sees Mark Mathabane's school and family through his eyes, too:

> "I ran, without stopping, all the way to the other end of the township where Granny lived. There I found my mother, her face swollen and bruised."

In *The Last Seven Months of Anne Frank*, the reader learns more about Anne Frank. At the same time, the women tell their own stories. Those take a first-person point of view:

> "He [Otto Frank] asked if I knew what had happened to his two daughters. I knew, but it was hard to get the words out of my mouth."

Review

1. What is point of view?
2. If a story refers to all the characters as "he" or "she," what is its point of view?
3. What is the usual point of view in a journal?
4. What is the point of view in Mark Mathabane's *Kaffir Boy*?
5. Is *The Last Seven Months of Anne Frank* a biography or an autobiography? How do you know?

Writing on Your Own

Write a short paragraph about something you have done. Use the first-person point of view. Underline the words in the paragraph that show your point of view.

Unit 2   SUMMARY

Unit 2 contains several types of nonfiction writing. All are about real life and real people. But they are also different. Diaries and journals are private and personal. Other nonfiction is written to be read by others. People write letters to each other. Biographies and autobiographies are about people's lives. People write their own autobiographies. Someone else writes a person's biography. Journalism is an account of real events.

Selections

- *Anne Frank: The Diary of a Young Girl* by Anne Frank. A Dutch Jewish girl's diary shows her thoughts during World War II.

- "Letter to Indira Tagore" by Rabindranath Tagore. The Indian Nobel Prize winner writes a letter to his niece about a moonlit night.

- "Letter to the Reverend J. H. Twichell" by Mark Twain. Twain writes about looking for a lost sock in the dark.

- *Writing with Intent: Essays, Reviews, Personal Prose 1983–2005* by Margaret Atwood. A writer talks about why she writes.

- *When Heaven and Earth Changed Places* by Le Ly Hayslip. A Vietnamese villager tells the importance of rice.

- "By Any Other Name" by Santha Rama Rau. Two Indian girls do not fit in at the British colonial school.

- *Kaffir Boy* by Mark Mathabane. A young black South African describes his life in a Johannesburg slum.

- *Reading Lolita in Tehran* by Azar Nafisi. Iranian women meet to secretly read banned books.

- *China Men* by Maxine Hong Kingston. Kingston's father, a Chinese immigrant, shows his wife New York City.

- *The Last Seven Months of Anne Frank* by Willy Lindwer. Interviews with women who knew the Frank family.

These journalism selections report reactions to nuclear tests:

- "Account Evened With India, Says PM" from *Dawn* (Pakistan)

- "Tests Are Nowhere Near India's: Fernandes" from the *Times of India*

- "Pakistan Nuclear Moratorium Welcomed" from the *BBC Online Network* (Great Britain)

- "The Frightening Joy" from *de Volkskrant* (Netherlands)

- "Building Atomic Security" from *Zycie Warszawy* (Poland)

Unit 2 REVIEW

Directions Choose the letter of the best answer or write the answer using complete sentences.

Comprehension: Identifying Facts

1. What is the term for a person's life story written by that person?
   A biography   C letter
   B editorial   D autobiography

2. In what country did Mark Mathabane grow up?

3. When did Margaret Atwood first become a writer?

4. About whom did Maxine Hong Kingston write the biography, *China Men*?

5. The newspaper articles and editorials in this unit all focus on one subject. What is that subject?

Comprehension: Putting Ideas Together

6. Why is Anne Frank's diary so important to her?
   A She is mean and has no friends.
   B She is hiding in an attic with her family.
   C She wants to become a doctor someday.
   D She is afraid someone will read it.

7. How is school a turning point in *Kaffir Boy* and "By Any Other Name"?

8. Why was growing rice important in a Vietnamese village?

9. Compare the tone of the letters from Twain and Tagore. What makes these letters personal?

10. How did India react to Pakistan's nuclear tests? What did it show about the relationship between the countries?

Understanding Literature: Setting

The time and place of a story is its setting. The places in Unit 2 range from steamy rice paddies in Vietnam to the skyscrapers of New York. Setting includes time, too. *When* events take place is sometimes as important as *where*. The setting of Anne Frank's diary, for instance, is the crowded "secret annex" in 1944, when she wrote down her thoughts.

11. Think about what happens in *Reading Lolita in Tehran*. How would this story be different if it took place somewhere else?

12. The couple in *China Men* visit sights in New York City. What do they see? How do they react?

13. What is the setting of Mark Twain's letter?

14. What is the setting of *Kaffir Boy*? How does it affect the story?

15. In which of this unit's selections is setting most important? Explain your choice.

Critical Thinking

16. In "By Any Other Name," what did the teacher think of Indians? Give two examples.

17. Why do you think people still care about Anne Frank's story?

18. In *China Men,* Ed and his wife are both newcomers. Who do you think will be happier in the United States? Why?

19. Both Mark Mathabane and Azar Nafisi lived under harsh, unfair governments. Which person do you think had a more difficult time? Why?

Thinking Creatively

20. Which of the authors in this unit would you like to meet? Explain your choice.

Speak and Listen

Many selections in this unit are written in the first person. Choose part of one of these selections. Then practice reading it aloud. As you practice, think about who wrote it. What gestures or expressions would he or she use? Read your selection to the class.

Writing on Your Own

Write a section of your own autobiography. Describe an important event from your life. It can be a turning point. It can be a family or religious ritual. Or it can be a very special memory. Use the first-person point of view in your writing.

Beyond Words

Think back to a setting from this unit that you remember well. Draw a picture to illustrate the story and its setting. Add details from what you read. If you need to, research other details. For example, you might want to find out what kind of hats and clothes Vietnamese villagers wore in the 1960s. Write a caption to explain your picture. Be sure your caption includes the time and place.

Test-Taking Tip

When a test item asks you to write a paragraph, make a plan first. Jot down the main idea of your paragraph. List supporting details to include. Then write your paragraph.

Performers, by Freshman Brown.

"When I read great literature, great drama, speeches, or sermons, I feel that the human mind has not achieved anything greater than the ability to share feelings and thoughts through language."
—James Earl Jones, actor

"There is no better indication of what the people of any period are like than the plays they go to see."
—Edith Hamilton, author

Unit 3: Drama

The writer of a play is called a playwright. Playwrights draw on many different sources for ideas about what to write. They may write a play based on a historical event. They may take a story from their own experience. Or they may totally invent the story. No matter where it comes from, a story told in the form of a play is enjoyable because we can see it, hear it, smell it, and feel it. A play shows us how someone else interprets a story. Watching a play brings an added way to experience it.

There are many forms of drama. This unit covers three of those forms: classical, realistic, and expressionistic.

Unit 3 Selections	Page
CLASSICAL DRAMA	292
■ ENGLAND from *Macbeth* by William Shakespeare	293
REALISTIC DRAMA	311
■ SOUTH AFRICA from *"Master Harold" . . . and the Boys* by Athol Fugard	312
EXPRESSIONISTIC DRAMA	328
■ SWEDEN *The Stronger* by August Strindberg	329

Unit 3

About Drama

A drama is a play that tells a story through dialogue and action performed by actors. Drama is an old form of literature. Dramatic plays started long ago as religious ceremonies in Greece. Over time, they developed into two distinct forms of drama: the tragedy and the comedy.

The protagonist is the main character in any drama. The antagonist is the opponent. In a tragedy, the antagonist destroys the protagonist. The antagonist could be the protagonist's own weaknesses. It could be another character's actions. The antagonist could also be a "bad guy," social injustice, or fate. A well-written tragedy offers its audience emotional release. It also reveals the workings of human nature. Shakespeare's Othello, for instance, is one of drama's greatest protagonists. The antagonist is an evil friend named Iago. Iago takes advantage of Othello's jealousy and violent temper. Finally Othello destroys his wife, his career, and himself. The audience experiences Othello's grief as they identify with what he says and does.

A comedy is a play with a "happy ending." The conflict does not destroy the protagonist. The audience enjoys seeing the protagonist beat the antagonist. *Harvey*, for example, tells the story of Elwood P. Dowd. His best friend is Harvey, an invisible rabbit who is six feet tall. By the end of the play, Dowd has triumphed. He has avoided being sent to a hospital for the mentally ill. He has also convinced several other characters of Harvey's charms.

Tragic or comic, early drama followed a strict form. Greek dramas included a chorus. This was a group of actors who commented on and explained the action. Actors wore masks. Dialogue was spoken in verse. Verse is made up of word patterns that follow a definite, repeating rhythm and sometimes rhyme.

As you read, remember that you are not experiencing the complete play. Much of the power of drama comes from the voices and movements of the cast. Scenery and costumes add to the effect. Reading the following selections aloud may help you get more of the feeling of a real play.

The following countries are covered in this unit: England, South Africa, and Sweden.

Classical Drama

Ancient dramas in the Western world were written in the Greek and Latin languages. These are called "classical languages." After the fall of the Roman Empire late in the 5th century, classical plays were no longer produced. Hundreds of years passed. Then, in the 15th century, the Renaissance brought in a renewed interest in the classics. People began to perform Greek and Roman drama again.

In England, playwrights started writing their own plays in the English language. By the time Shakespeare wrote during the 16th century, English-language drama had become what is now called classical drama. These plays were usually stories about royalty or other wealthy, important people.

Classical drama has five acts. Each act consists of one or more scenes. These are similar to chapters in a book. Acts are separate sections that often involve changes in setting. Time may pass between acts. The first and second acts introduce and develop the action or conflict. The third act features the climax. This is an event that triggers the comic or tragic ending. Acts four and five tie together the loose plot strands to create a neat ending.

In classical drama, the dialogue, or the words the characters speak, is often in a form called blank verse. Blank verse is written in iambic pentameter and does not rhyme. This form of writing developed in England during the Renaissance and was improved by Shakespeare. Iambic pentameter is one of the best ways to write dramatic verse in English.

Shakespeare's plays are considered some of the best examples of classical drama ever written. Many people who wrote plays at this time also wrote in this style. Plays of later times that follow the classical form are called *neoclassical*. (*Neo-* means "new.")

Classical Drama

—began in 16th century

—usually royal or wealthy characters

—had five acts

—written in blank verse and iambic pentameter

BEFORE READING THE SELECTION

from Macbeth   by William Shakespeare

About the Author

William Shakespeare was born in the small English town of Stratford-upon-Avon. He most likely read the classic plays of ancient Greece and Italy at school. He was well known as an actor and a writer of plays, many based on familiar stories. In 1582, he married Anne Hathaway, and they had three children.

William Shakespeare
(1564–1616)
English

Many of his plays are set in far-off places or ancient times. *Julius Caesar* is set in ancient Rome. *A Midsummer Night's Dream* takes place in a fantasyland with fairies and magic. Still other plays are set in European cities, such as Verona and Venice in Italy. Many are set around the time that Shakespeare lived.

About the Selection

The selection is act 3, scene 4, of *Macbeth*. Macbeth is a Scottish lord who wants to be king. His wife convinces him to kill the rightful king so that Macbeth himself can become king. Macbeth fears that Banquo, his best friend, will find out that he murdered the king. Macbeth then has Banquo killed. Macbeth also believes a prediction that Banquo will have children who will want to take the throne. When Banquo is killed, his son, Fleance, escapes. Having had his friend killed, Macbeth is overcome by guilt. In the following scene, Macbeth and Lady Macbeth host a dinner party. During the party, Macbeth sees Banquo's Ghost. The guests see Macbeth speaking, but they do not see the ghost. They wonder if he has gone mad. Is this the beginning of the end for Macbeth? Read to find out.

Objectives

- To identify the playwright of a play
- To read and understand a tragedy
- To understand classical drama
- To identify iambic pentameter, blank verse, and dialogue

Before Reading **continued on next page**

BEFORE READING THE SELECTION (continued)

from Macbeth by William Shakespeare

playwright
the author of a play

classical drama
plays, usually written in blank verse, that are often about wealthy or important people; they follow the style of ancient Greek and Latin drama

comedy a play with a happy ending, intended to amuse its audience

tragedy a play that ends with the suffering or death of one or more of the main characters

dialogue
the words that characters in a play speak

blank verse
unrhymed iambic pentameter

iambic pentameter
five two-beat sounds in a line of poetry where the second syllable is stressed in each pattern

Literary Terms Shakespeare was a great author of plays, or **playwright**. He wrote **classical drama**, both **comedies** and **tragedies**. He wrote them in the style of ancient Greek and Latin drama. A comedy ends happily. A tragedy is a play that ends with the suffering or death of one or more of the main characters. In Shakespeare's plays, the **dialogue** of the characters has a special rhythm. Dialogue is the words that characters in a play speak. This rhythm is called **blank verse**, or unrhymed **iambic pentameter**. In iambic pentameter, each line has 10 syllables. The second, fourth, sixth, eighth, and last syllables are accented. The other syllables are not accented. Look at the first line from the selection for an example of iambic pentameter:

You knów your ówn degreés, sit dówn at fírst

Macbeth is one of Shakespeare's best-known tragedies. Macbeth is the main character of this play. He is killed at the end of the play.

Reading on Your Own Shakespeare is a well-known and much-loved playwright. Today, some people find his work hard to understand. Try reading this play aloud. It will help make the words come alive.

Each left-hand page shows the play as Shakespeare wrote it. The facing page shows the same scene written in modern English. It uses words more familiar to you to help you understand the play.

Writing on Your Own Think about what can happen if a person gets away with a crime. The person might not think another thing about it. Or the person might be troubled by his or her own guilt. Write about one of these types of people. What do you think of this kind of person? Why?

Vocabulary Focus Macbeth tells the first murderer that he is sick. He describes himself as *closed in*, *cramped*, *confined*, and a *prisoner*. Macbeth also says that if he were not sick, he would be *sound*, *flawless*, *solid*, *free*, and *liberated*. Write the words *ill* and *healthy* at opposite ends of a Semantic Line. Then write Shakespeare's synonyms near the correct words. Add one or two of your own words to each part of the Semantic Line. See Appendix A for a description of this graphic organizer.

Think Before You Read What do you think the dinner guests will do when they see how strange Macbeth is behaving? What would you do?

Macbeth has stood the test of time. Above, *The Weird Sisters* take the stage in this modern adaptation of the play, by the Royal Shakespeare Company. These three witches, or "weird sisters," can see into the future. They have an evil effect on Macbeth. At the start of the play, which is not included in this excerpt, they tell Macbeth that he will become king. Although they do not appear often, they set the feeling of gloom for the entire play.

from Macbeth
Shakespeare's Original

> This version of *Macbeth* appears as Shakespeare wrote it. It uses words that were common in England at the time. It is written in blank verse. As you read, compare it with the modern English version on the facing page.

Act 3, scene 4: *The hall of the palace.*

A banquet prepared. Enter Macbeth, Lady Macbeth, Ross, Lennox, Lords, and Attendant.

Macbeth You know your own degrees, sit down at first
And last, the hearty welcome.

Lords Thanks to your majesty.

Macbeth Ourself will mingle with society,
And play the humble host:
Our hostess keeps her state, but in best time
We will require her welcome.

Lady Macbeth Pronounce it for me, sir, to all our friends,
For my heart speaks they are welcome.

First Murderer appears at the door

Macbeth See, they encounter thee with their hearts' thanks.
Both sides are even: here I'll sit i'th' midst.
Be large in mirth, anon we'll drink a measure
The table round. [*turns to the door*]
There's blood upon thy face.

Murderer 'Tis Banquo's then.

Macbeth 'Tis better thee without than he within.
Is he dispatched?

Murderer My lord, his throat is cut, that I did for him.

Macbeth Thou art the best o'th' cut-throats! Yet he's good
That did the like for Fleance: if thou didst it,
thou art the nonpareil.

> Notes called *stage directions* describe where each scene is set. They tell the actors where and how to move.

> The words following each character's name tell the character what to say. These speeches are called lines of *dialogue*.

from MACBETH
Modern English

Act 3, scene 4: The hall of the palace.

A banquet has been prepared. Macbeth, Lady Macbeth, Ross, Lennox, Lords, and Attendants enter.

Macbeth You know your **ranks**. Sit down accordingly. From the top table downward, I give you **hearty** welcome!

Lords Thanks to Your Majesty!

Macbeth I'll **mingle** with the guests and play the humble host. Our hostess will stay seated. She'll welcome you at the proper time.

Lady Macbeth Do so on my **behalf**, sir, to all our friends, for they are welcome with all my heart.

The Lords rise and bow. The First Murderer enters

Macbeth *[To Lady Macbeth]* See—their heartfelt thanks are yours. *[He looks for a vacant seat]* Both sides are even. I'll sit here in the middle. *[He spots the Murderer]* Enjoy yourselves! We'll pass around the drinking cup just now! *[To the Murderer]* There's blood on your face.

First Murderer It's Banquo's then.

Macbeth It's better outside you than inside him. Is he killed?

First Murderer My lord, his throat is cut. That I did for him.

Macbeth You are the best of cutthroats! Yet he's as good who did the same for Fleance. If you did it, you have no equal!

This version of *Macbeth* is written in modern English, the language we use today. Read it aloud to follow the action more easily. As you read, compare this version with the original. Find words and phrases that you know.

As Macbeth is walking among his seated guests, he sees the First Murderer at the doorway. The stage direction [*To the Murderer*] means they are speaking to each other in private. Only the audience—not the guests—can hear their conversation.

Macbeth has ordered the murders of Banquo and his son, Fleance. He is pleased to know Banquo has been killed.

| **ranks** official positions | **hearty** sincere | **behalf** interest |
| | **mingle** mix | |

Drama Unit 3

	Murderer	Most royal sir, Fleance is 'scaped.
Macbeth is upset that Fleance has escaped unhurt.	Macbeth	Then comes my fit again: I had else been perfect; Whole as the marble, founded as the rock, As broad and general as the casing air: But now I am cabined, cribbed, confined, bound in To saucy doubts and fears. But Banquo's safe?
	Murderer	Ay, my good lord: safe in a ditch he bides, With twenty trenchéd gashes on his head; The least a death to nature.
What does the dialogue between Macbeth and the Murderer reveal?	Macbeth	Thanks for that: There the grown serpent lies; the worm that's fled Hath nature that in time will venom breed, No teeth for th' present. Get thee gone; to-morrow We'll hear ourselves again.

Murderer goes

Sometimes, a character's first line is indented. This shows that the line is part of the blank verse of the line before it. The line before it has fewer than 10 syllables. Together, the two lines have 10 syllables with the accents in the right places.

Lady Macbeth My royal lord,
You do not give the cheer. The feast is sold
That is not often vouched, while 'tis a-making,
'Tis given with welcome: to feed were best at home;
From thence the sauce to meat is ceremony;
Meeting were bare without it.

First Murderer Most royal sir—
Fleance escaped.

Macbeth My illness comes back. I'd otherwise be **sound**. **Flawless** as marble. Solid as rock. As free and **liberated** as the air around us. Now I'm closed in, cramped, confined—the prisoner of nagging doubts and fears. But Banquo's fixed?

First Murderer Yes, my good lord. Safe in a ditch he **dwells**, with twenty trench-like **gashes** in his head, the least of them fatal.

> Macbeth wants to be sure that Banquo is dead. He asks the question again.

Macbeth Thanks for that. The adult serpent's dead. The youngster that escaped has the makings of trouble, but he's harmless now. Go. Tomorrow we'll talk together again.

The First Murderer leaves

Lady Macbeth My royal lord, you do not play the host! A tavern meal lacks welcoming **toasts**. Mere food alone is best consumed at home. What gives a feast its flavor is the ceremony. It's a poor feast without it.

> Lady Macbeth gently scolds Macbeth for deserting the banquet guests. She asks him to make a toast to start the banquet.

---

sound healthy
flawless perfect; without any marks
liberated free from outside control
dwells lives; makes a home
gashes long, deep cuts
toasts speeches made along with drinks to honor someone

The Ghost of Banquo appears, and sits in Macbeth's place

Macbeth	Sweet remembrancer! Now good digestion wait on appetite, And health on both!
Lennox	May't please your highness sit?
Macbeth	Here had we now our country's honour roofed, Were the graced person of our Banquo present; Who may I rather challenge for unkindness Then pity for mischance!
Ross	His absence, sir, Lays blame upon his promise. Please't your highness To grace us with your royal company?
Macbeth	The table's full.
Lennox	Here is a place reserved, sir.
Macbeth	Where?
Lennox	Here, my good lord . . . What is't that moves your highness?
Macbeth	Which of you have done this?
Lords	What, my good lord?
Macbeth	Thou canst not say I did it: never shake Thy gory locks at me.
Ross	Gentlemen, rise, his highness is not well.
Lady Macbeth	Sit, worthy friends: my lord is often thus, And hath been from his youth: pray you, keep seat, The fit is momentary, upon a thought He will again be well: if much you note him, You shall offend him and extend his passion: Feed, and regard him not. [*aside*] Are you a man?
Macbeth	Ay, and a bold one, that dare look on that Which might appal the devil.

> Remember who the playwright is and when he lived. How do you think a modern playwright would write the play differently?

The ghost of Banquo enters and sits in Macbeth's place

Macbeth	*[affectionately]* I'm glad you reminded me! *[To the company]* To appetites and good digestion! And health to both!
Lennox	Do please sit, sir.
Macbeth	We'd have here under one roof the noblest in the land if our friend Banquo were present. I hope it's a case of thoughtlessness, not **mischance**.
Ross	His absence, sir, is a **breach** of his promise. *[Indicating a seat]* Would Your Highness grace us with your royal company?
Macbeth	The table's full.
Lennox	Here's a place reserved, sir.
Macbeth	Where?
Lennox	Here, my good lord. What is upsetting Your Highness?
Macbeth	*[pointing to the Ghost]* Which of you has done this?
Lords	What, my good lord? *[The Ghost makes signals]*
Macbeth	You cannot say I did it! Don't shake your **gory locks** at me!
Ross	Gentlemen, rise. His Highness is not well.
Lady Macbeth	Sit, good friends. My lord is often like this and has been since his youth. Please, stay in your seats. The **fit** will soon pass. He'll be well again in a moment. If you take too much notice, you'll offend him and extend his fit. Eat up, and ignore him. *[To Macbeth, angrily]* Are you a man?
Macbeth	Yes, and a bold one, that dares to look at what might scare the devil.

> Why do you think Macbeth calls attention to Banquo's absence from the banquet?

> Lennox offers an empty chair to Macbeth. Only Macbeth can see the Ghost sitting in the chair. Macbeth's outburst upsets his guests.

> Remember, only Macbeth (and the audience) can see the Ghost.

> Lady Macbeth tries to turn attention away from Macbeth. She says that he often has this kind of fit. In fact, she knows what he has done. She is afraid others may guess his crimes by watching his behavior.

---

affectionately with love and tenderness
mischance bad luck
breach failure
gory stained with blood
locks the hair of the head
fit sudden outburst

Lady Macbeth	O proper stuff!
	This is the very painting of your fear:
	This is the air-drawn dagger which, you said,
	Led you to Duncan. O, these flaws and starts
	(Imposter to true fear) would well become
	A woman's story at a winter's fire,
	Authorized by her grandam. Shame itself!
	Why do you make such faces? When all's done,
	You look but on a stool.
Macbeth	Prithee, see there! behold! look! lo! how say you?
	Why what care I? If thou canst nod, speak too.
	If charnel-houses and our graves must send
	Those that we bury back, our monuments
	Shall be the maws of kites.

The Ghost vanishes

Lady Macbeth	What! quite unmanned in folly?
Macbeth	If I stand here, I saw him.
Lady Macbeth	Fie, for shame!
Macbeth	Blood hath been shed ere now, i'th' olden time,
	Ere humane statute purged the gentle weal;
	Ay, and since too, murders have been performed
	Too terrible for the ear: the time has been,
	That, when the brains were out, the man would die,
	And there an end: but now they rise again,
	With twenty mortal murders on their crowns,
	And push us from our stools. This is more strange
	Than such a murder is.
Lady Macbeth	My worthy lord,
	Your noble friends do lack you.
Macbeth	I do forget.
	Do not muse at me, my most worthy friends;
	I have a strange infirmity, which is nothing
	To those that know me. Come, love and health to all;
	Then I'll sit down. Give me some wine, fill full.

Lady Macbeth Oh, really!
This is a fear of your imagination.
This is that air-borne dagger which you said
led you to Duncan! Oh, these fits and **starts**—
these fake fears—would better suit an old
wife's tale told at a winter fireside. Shame on
you! Why are you making such faces? When
all is said and done, you are only looking at a stool!

Macbeth See there—look! There! Now what do I say?
[To the Ghost] Why, what do I care? If you can
nod, speak too! If graves and tombs will send back
those we bury, we'd better feed our corpses to
the vultures!

The Ghost disappears

Lady Macbeth Is your foolishness taking away your **manhood**?

Macbeth As sure as I stand here, I saw him!

Lady Macbeth What nonsense!

Macbeth *[To himself]* Blood has been shed before now, in
the old days before just laws reformed society.
Yes, and since then, too, murders have been
committed, too terrible to hear about. There
was a time when smashed brains meant the
man would die, and that was that. But now men rise
again, with twenty fatal gashes in their heads, and
steal our seats. This is stranger than murder.

Lady Macbeth My worthy lord. Your noble friends are missing you.

Macbeth *[Recovering]* I'm forgetting. *[To the guests]* Don't
brood over me, my most worthy friends. I have a
strange **disability**, which is nothing to those who
know me. Come! *[Raising his glass]* Love and health
to all! Then I'll sit down. Give me some wine. Fill it up!

> Earlier in the play, Macbeth describes a vision in which he sees a dagger covered in blood. It is hanging in midair and pointing toward Duncan's room. He says it was a sign telling him to kill the king.

> Lady Macbeth finally succeeds in getting Macbeth's attention. He realizes he needs to explain his odd behavior.

starts quick, jerking movements
manhood courage
committed done or performed
brood think about something in a moody way
disability a weakened physical or mental condition

Drama Unit 3

The Ghost reappears

	I drink to th' general joy o'th' whole table,
	And to our dear friend Banquo, whom we miss;
	Would he were here! to all, and him we thirst,
	And all to all!
Lords	Our duties, and the pledge.
Macbeth	Avaunt! and quit my sight! let the earth hide thee!
	Thy bones are marrowless, thy blood is cold;
	Thou hast no speculation in those eyes
	Which thou dost glare with!
Lady Macbeth	Think of this, good peers,
	But as a thing of custom: 'tis no other;
	Only it spoils the pleasure of the time.
Macbeth	What man dare, I dare:
	Approach thou like the ruggèd Russian bear,
	The armed rhinoceros, or th'Hyrcan tiger,
	Take any shape but that, and my firm nerves
	Shall never tremble: or be alive again,
	And dare me to the desert with thy sword;
	If trembling I inhabit then, protest me
	The baby of a girl. Hence, horrible shadow!
	Unreal mock'ry, hence! *[The Ghost vanishes]*
	Why, so; being gone,
	I am a man again. Pray you, sit still.
Lady Macbeth	You have displaced the mirth, broke the good meeting,
	With most admired disorder.
Macbeth	Can such things be,
	And overcome us like a summer's cloud,
	Without our special wonder? You make me strange
	Even to the disposition that I owe,
	When now I think you can behold such sights,
	And keep the natural ruby of your cheeks,
	When mine is blanched with fear.

The Ghost returns

	I drink to the general joy of the whole table, and to our dear friend Banquo, who is not present. Would he were here! *[Proposing a toast]* To all, and to him we lack, and health to everyone!
Lords	Our duties, and the toast!
Macbeth	*[Seeing the Ghost]* Go away! **Quit** my sight! Back to your grave! Your bones are marrowless, your blood is cold. You have no power of seeing in those glaring eyes!
Lady Macbeth	Think of this, good noblemen, as a **chronic ailment**. That's what it is. Unfortunately, it upsets things.
Macbeth	*[To the Ghost]* Whatever man dares, I dare! Approach me like a rugged Russian bear, an armor-plated rhinoceros, or a wild tiger! Take any shape but your own, and my firm nerves will never tremble. Or come alive again, and dare me to the desert with your sword! If I fall to trembling then, call me a baby girl! **Begone**, horrible shadow! Unreal mockery, begone! *[The Ghost goes]* Why, then. Once it is gone, I am a man again. *[To the guests]* Please—keep your seats.
Lady Macbeth	*[**Reproaching** him]* You've spoiled the enjoyment—destroyed the atmosphere—with your ridiculous behavior!
Macbeth	Can such things happen—like a cloud spoiling a summer's day—without astonishing us? You make me doubt myself. You can behold such sights and keep the natural color of your cheeks. Mine turn white with fear.

> Why does Macbeth propose a toast to Banquo?

> When Macbeth begins to rave again, Lady Macbeth makes an excuse for it.

> The tragedy is not revealed until the end of the play. As Macbeth becomes more and more ill, the audience can see it coming.

---

quit leave
chronic continuing for a long time
ailment sickness
begone a command meaning "go away"
reproaching scolding; blaming

Ross	What sights, my lord?
Lady Macbeth	I pray you, speak not; he grows worse and worse;
	Question enrages him: at once, good night.
	Stand not upon the order of your going,
	But go at once.
Lennox	Good night, and better health
	Attend his majesty!
Lady Macbeth	A kind good night to all! *[They leave]*
Macbeth	It will have blood; they say, blood will have blood:
	Stones have been known to move and trees to speak;
	Augures and understood relations have
	By maggot-pies and choughs and rooks brought forth
	The secret'st man of blood. . . . What is the night?
Lady Macbeth	Almost at odds with morning, which is which.
Macbeth	How say'st thou, that Macduff denies his person
	At our great bidding?
Lady Macbeth	Did you send to him, sir?
Macbeth	I hear it by the way; but I will send:
	There's not a one of them but in his house
	I keep a servant fee'd. I will to-morrow
	(And betimes I will) to the Weïrd Sisters:
	More shall they speak; for now I am bent to know,
	By the worst means, and worst. For mine own good
	All causes shall give way: I am in blood
	Stepped in so far that, should I wade no more,
	Returning were as tedious as go o'er:
	Strange things I have in head that will to hand,
	Which must be acted ere they may be scanned.
Lady Macbeth	You lack the season of all natures, sleep.
Macbeth	Come, we'll to sleep. My strange and self-abuse
	Is the initiate fear that wants hard use:
	We are yet but young in deed.

They go

Ross	What sights, my lord?	
Lady Macbeth	Please don't say anything. He gets worse and worse. Questions enrage him. Now, goodnight! No ceremonial leave-taking. Go at once.	Ross asks Macbeth what he saw. Why does Lady Macbeth interrupt?
Lennox	Good night, and may His Majesty enjoy better health.	
Lady Macbeth	A kind goodnight to all! *[She hustles them out]*	
Macbeth	It will have blood. They say, "Blood will have blood." Gravestones have been known to move, and trees to speak. Magpies, crows and ravens have spotted the most secretive of murderers. What time of night is it?	Macduff is a nobleman who opposed the choice of Macbeth as king. He also discovered the body of murdered King Duncan. He is suspicious about who really murdered him.
Lady Macbeth	Almost morning. It's hard to tell the difference.	
Macbeth	What do you make of Macduff ignoring our invitation?	
Lady Macbeth	Did you **summon** him, sir?	
Macbeth	I hear rumors. But I'll summon him all right. I keep a spy in all their houses. Early tomorrow, I'll go to the Weird Sisters. They must tell me more. I must know the worst, by whatever means. Nothing shall stand in the way of my interests. My path has been so bloody, stopping now and going back would be no easier than going forward. I have some projects in my head that need action first and thought later. They must be done before they are thought of.	The *Weird Sisters* are witches who appeared at the beginning of the play. They predicted that Macbeth would be king. Macbeth wants to see them now to learn what will happen in his future.
Lady Macbeth	You lack what all creatures need—sleep.	
Macbeth	Come, we'll go to sleep. My **delusions** are beginner's fear. I need experience. We've only just started.	Macbeth believes that he is afraid because he's new to crime and violence. He says that, as he carries out more bloody deeds, he'll become used to it.

They go

---

summon call; tell to come

delusions false or imaginary visions; things a person hears or sees that are not real

AFTER READING THE SELECTION

from Macbeth   by William Shakespeare

Directions Choose the letter of the best answer or write the answer using complete sentences.

Comprehension: Identifying Facts

1. How do the guests know where to sit at the table?
   A There are name cards near each seat.
   B The guests sit by their rank or level of honor.
   C They come for dinner every week.
   D Lady Macbeth tells each guest where to sit.

2. Who interrupts Macbeth as he is greeting his guests?
   A Banquo   C the Lords
   B Lady Macbeth   D the First Murderer

3. Whom has the Murderer killed?

4. Why does Macbeth call the Murderer a *cutthroat*?

5. Macbeth finds out that Fleance got away. How does Macbeth react to this news?

6. Why does Lady Macbeth want Macbeth to give a toast?

7. Where does the Ghost sit?

8. What does Ross say about Banquo not being there?

9. How does Lady Macbeth explain Macbeth's odd behavior?

10. Whom does Macbeth want to ask for advice? Why?

Comprehension: Putting Ideas Together

11. Macbeth knows that Banquo is dead. Still, he talks about him as if he were alive. Why?
    A He wants people to think he knows nothing of Banquo's death.
    B He thinks Banquo may not really be dead.
    C He thinks of the ghost as the real Banquo.
    D He is afraid of Banquo's son.

12. Why does Lady Macbeth ask Macbeth, "Are you a man?"
    A He is dressed like a boy.
    B He is sitting under the table.
    C He is talking to someone who is not there.
    D He did not pull the chair out for her like a proper gentleman.

13. Why do you think Macbeth is the only character who sees the Ghost?

14. What other vision does Macbeth tell Lady Macbeth about? Why does she not believe him?

15. Macbeth says to Lady Macbeth, "You can behold such sights and keep the natural color of your cheeks. Mine turn white with fear." What does he mean?

16. How does Lady Macbeth get the guests to leave quickly?

17. Macduff is not at the banquet. Why does this worry Macbeth?

18. Macbeth is seeing things—a dagger in midair and the Ghost at the table. What else does he do that might mean he is mentally unstable?

19. Macbeth says he has projects in mind that "need action first and thought later." What does he mean?

20. What does Macbeth think will make the Ghost go away?

Understanding Literature: Drama

In a drama, the story is told by actors performing for an audience. The playwright writes dialogue to tell the actors what to say. Stage directions describe the setting and tell the actors what to do.

21. Which stage direction, in the modern English version of this scene from *Macbeth*, tells us that only the Murderer can hear Macbeth?

22. Which stage direction shows that Macbeth is about to propose a toast?

23. Which stage direction tells Lady Macbeth to speak as if she is annoyed with Macbeth?

24. When Lennox says, "Good night, and may His Majesty enjoy better health," to whom is he speaking?

25. Lady Macbeth says, "A kind goodnight to all!" Whom does she mean?

Critical Thinking

26. Do you think Lady Macbeth's first line in the scene is fitting for a queen? Why or why not?

27. How does Lady Macbeth try to reassure the guests?

28. Later she says, "Shame on you! Why are you making such faces?" Why has her tone changed?

29. Look at her last line. How do you think she feels about Macbeth?

Thinking Creatively

30. At the end of the scene, Macbeth says, "We've only just started." What do you think he is predicting?

After Reading continued on next page

AFTER READING THE SELECTION (continued)

from Macbeth   by William Shakespeare

 Grammar Check

Many playwrights use brackets [ ] or parentheses () to show stage directions. These are not lines to be read. They tell the actor what to do. Sometimes, they tell the actor what tone of voice to use. They may direct the actor to say his or her lines to another person on stage. Find four different stage directions that are in the middle of a character's lines. Tell what the stage directions mean.

 Writing on Your Own

The Ghost in this scene from *Macbeth* does not have any lines. If he did, what do you think he would say? Write two lines of dialogue for his first appearance. Write another two lines of dialogue for his second appearance.

 Speaking and Listening

Read this scene aloud with a small group. Decide whether you will read the original or the modern English version. Each student should read the lines for one or two characters. Try to read with feeling.

Listen to another group of students as they read the scene aloud. How does hearing the dialogue help you better understand what is happening?

 Media

Go to the library and borrow a videotape of a production of *Macbeth*. Watch it with your class. Did you find that viewing it is easier to follow than reading it? Explain your answer.

 Technology

Pretend that Macbeth and Lady Macbeth are on a television talk show. The topic of the show is "My husband ruined our dinner party." Have one student act as Macbeth. Another student can take the part of Lady Macbeth. A third student can act as the television host. A fourth student can videotape the talk show. Have the rest of the class act as the television audience.

Realistic Drama

As drama developed, many rules about writing plays changed or disappeared. Students and audiences still study and enjoy classical drama. But other kinds of plays speak just as strongly to audiences.

Realistic drama gets its name from "real life." It aims to reflect what life is really like. In realistic drama, average people are shown with heroic traits. Realistic drama may also try to show the problems of society. In this sense, it points out the need for social change.

A pioneer of realistic drama in the late 1800s was Henrik Ibsen of Norway. His plays created a revolution in modern theater. He wrote such plays as *A Doll's House* and *An Enemy of the People*. Realistic drama was a strong force in the theater in the 1950s. A realistic drama tells a story just as it might happen in real life. It looks at life more honestly and in greater detail. The characters speak in everyday language, not in verse. They are ordinary people rather than royalty or the wealthy. Their problems center on job and family. The play is set in an average home and neighborhood.

Many television dramas would be considered realistic. Modern American writers in the realistic style include Arthur Miller and William Inge. Miller wrote many plays, including *Death of a Salesman* and *The Crucible*. Inge is known for his plays *Picnic* and *The Dark at the Top of the Stairs*, among others. Both were strongly influenced by earlier realistic playwrights such as Ibsen.

Even Shakespeare's dramas have moments that might be called realistic. These moments usually concern the poor or minor characters. They do not speak in verse but in normal language. They face everyday problems and events.

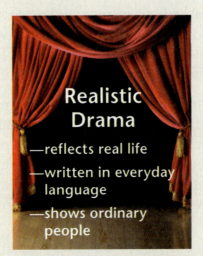

Realistic Drama
—reflects real life
—written in everyday language
—shows ordinary people

BEFORE READING THE SELECTION

from "Master Harold" . . . and the Boys   by Athol Fugard

Athol Fugard
(1932–)
South African

Objectives

- To read and understand a realistic drama
- To describe a character's feelings based on the character development in a play
- To predict how characters will resolve a conflict between them

About the Author

Athol Fugard was born in Middleburg, South Africa. His plays focus on the politics of South Africa. He often writes about apartheid, a government policy in South Africa for many years. It kept blacks and whites strictly separated and denied black South Africans many rights. Fugard's works show the destruction apartheid caused. But Fugard also shows how the human spirit can win over hatred. Fugard has acted in, written, and directed many plays.

South Africa

About the Selection

Fugard wrote *"Master Harold" . . . and the Boys* in 1982. The play is based on actual events in Fugard's life. This drama shows people affected by apartheid. It is a realistic drama about South Africans. It tells a story about everyday life. Hally (short for Harold) is the teenage son of a white, middle-class family. They own a restaurant. He goes to a private school where he is an average student. Sam and Willie are black waiters in the restaurant. They have known Hally since he was a child. Sam has become a sort of foster father to Hally. Hally's own father is an alcoholic and an embarrassment to him.

The following selection is in two parts. In the first part of the selection, Hally and Sam talk about a special memory from Hally's childhood. In the second part, Hally and Sam fight. Find out if Sam and Hally are able to learn from each other. Will their friendship die? Or will their relationship grow even stronger? Is there hope for a future, even under apartheid?

Literary Terms This selection is part of a **realistic drama**. It tells a story just as it might happen in real life. **Character development** is important in a realistic drama. The writer can make a character realistic by showing personality traits that an ordinary person might have.

In this play, three characters—two black waiters and one white teenager—are in a restaurant owned by the teenager's family. They live in South Africa under apartheid. Fugard uses dialogue and action to show what these characters are like. There is no narrator, so the reader learns about the characters from their words and actions. Fugard also uses **conflict** to develop his characters. Conflict is the struggle of the main character against himself or herself, another person, or nature. Read to find out about the conflict between the young white man and his older black friend.

Reading on Your Own Before reading this selection, think about your purpose for reading. Is it to understand apartheid better? Is it to enjoy a good drama? After reading, see if the purpose was fulfilled. What else did you experience?

Writing on Your Own Write about a time when you were angry with one person and took it out on someone else. Write about how you felt.

Vocabulary Focus Under apartheid, many South African whites called black men "boys." They did this to try to make the men feel that they were not as good as white people. In this story, one black man calls a white man a "boy." He says that the young man is really acting like a child. As you read, think about how Fugard uses this common word to make a point.

Think Before You Read Think about the good times and bad times that you have had with your own friends. What do you hope to learn about friendship from this story?

---

realistic drama a play that tells a story just as it might happen in real life

character development the way a writer develops characters by revealing personality traits

conflict the struggle of the main character against himself or herself, another person, or nature

Drama Unit 3 313

from "Master Harold" . . . and the Boys

This scene is from a one-act play. All the action takes place in one act. There are no breaks or scene changes. As you read, look for the events and speeches that make this play realistic.

Hally is a 17-year-old boy dressed in a school uniform. Sam and Willie are black men in their 30s. They are wearing white waiters' coats.

Earlier, we learned that, as a young boy, Hally often visited Sam and Willie at home in the Jubilee Boardinghouse. During these visits, Sam and Hally talked about his schoolwork. They learned a lot from each other.

Time: 1950

Place: The St. George's Park Tea Room on a wet and windy afternoon in Port Elizabeth, South Africa.

Hally   Come on, guess. If your memory is so good, you must remember it as well.

Sam   We got up to a lot of tricks in there, Hally.

Hally   This one was special, Sam.

Sam   I'm listening.

Hally   It started off looking like another of those useless nothing-to-do afternoons. I'd already been down to Main Street looking for adventure, but nothing had happened. I didn't feel like climbing trees in the Donkin Park or pretending I was a private eye and following a stranger . . . so as usual: See what's cooking in Sam's room. This time it was you on the floor. You had two thin pieces of wood and you were smoothing them down with a knife. It didn't look particularly interesting, but when I asked you what you were doing, you just said, "Wait and see, Hally. Wait . . . and see" . . . in that secret sort of way of yours, so I knew there was a surprise coming. You teased me, you bugger, by being **deliberately** slow and not answering my questions!

deliberately carefully considered; on purpose

(Sam laughs)

And whistling while you worked away! God, it was **infuriating**! I could have brained you! It was only when you tied them together in a cross and put that down on the brown paper that I realized what you were doing. "Sam is making a kite?" And when I asked you and you said "Yes" . . . ! *(Shaking his head with **disbelief**)* The **sheer audacity** of it took my breath away. I mean, seriously, what . . . does a black man know about flying a kite? I'll be honest with you, Sam, I had no hopes for it. If you think I was excited and happy, you got another guess coming. In fact, I was . . . scared that we were going to make fools of ourselves. When we left the **boarding house** to go up onto the hill, I was praying quietly that there wouldn't be any other kids around to laugh at us.

> The word *brained* means "hit on the head."

> What does Hally's remark about Sam making a kite show you about South Africa at this time?

Sam *(Enjoying the memory as much as Hally)* Ja, I could see that.

> *Ja* means "yes."

Hally I made it obvious, did I?

Sam Ja. You refused to carry it.

Hally Do you blame me? Can you remember what the poor thing looked like? Tomato-box wood and brown paper! Flour and water for glue! Two of my mother's old stockings for a tail, and then all those bits and pieces of string you made me tie together so that we could fly it! . . . No, that was now only asking for a miracle to happen.

> Why did Sam have to use old, used materials to build the kite?

Sam Then the big argument when I told you to hold the string and run with it when I let go.

---

infuriating causing great anger

disbelief a refusal to believe

sheer pure; not mixed with anything

audacity boldness

boarding house a place to live where one pays for a room and meals

Drama Unit 3

Read the dialogue between Sam and Hally. What do you learn about each of the characters from what they say? How is this an example of character development?

Hally	I was prepared to run, all right, but straight back to the boarding house.
Sam	*(Knowing what's coming)* So what happened?
Hally	Come on, Sam, you remember it as well as I do.
Sam	I want to hear it from you.

(Hally pauses. He wants to be as accurate as possible)

Hally	You went up a little distance from me down the hill, you held it up ready to let it go. . . . "This is it," I thought. "Like everything else in my life, here comes another **fiasco**." Then you shouted, "Go, Hally!" and I started to run. *(Another pause)* I don't know how to describe it, Sam. Ja! The miracle happened! I was running, waiting for it to crash to the ground, but instead suddenly there was something alive behind me at the end of the string, tugging at it as if it wanted to be free. I looked back . . . *(Shakes his head)* . . . I still can't believe my eyes. It was flying! Looping around and trying to climb even higher into the sky. You shouted to me to let it have more string. I did, until there was none left and I was just holding that piece of wood we had tied it to. You came up and joined me. You were laughing.
Sam	So were you. And shouting, "It works, Sam! We've done it!"
Hally	And we had! I was so proud of us! It was the most **splendid** thing I had ever seen. I wished there were hundreds of kids around to watch us. The part that scared me, though, was when you showed me how to make it dive down to the ground and then just when it was on the point of crashing, swoop up again!
Sam	You didn't want to try it yourself.

fiasco a complete failure

splendid glorious; excellent

Hally Of course not! I would have been **suicidal** if anything had happened to it. Watching you do it made me nervous enough. I was quite happy just to see it up there with its tail fluttering behind it. You left me after that, didn't you? You explained how to get it down, we tied it to the bench so that I could sit and watch it, and you went away. I wanted you to stay, you know. I was a little scared of having to look after it by myself.

Sam *(Quietly)* I had work to do, Hally.

Hally It was sort of sad bringing it down, Sam. And it looked sad again when it was lying there on the ground. Like something that had lost its soul. Just tomato-box wood, brown paper and two of my mother's old stockings! But, . . . I'll never forget that first moment when I saw it up there. I had a stiff neck the next day from looking up so much.

Notice the stage directions in this play. They often tell the actors exactly how to look or move.

(Sam laughs. Hally turns to him with a question he never thought of asking before)

Why did you make that kite, Sam?

Sam *(Evenly)* I can't remember.

Hally Truly?

Sam Too long ago, Hally.

Hally Ja, I suppose it was. It's time for another one, you know.

Sam Why do you say that?

suicidal deeply unhappy; wanting to kill oneself

evenly without a change in tone

> Remember that this selection is an excerpt. Part of the play has been left out. The information in the brackets summarizes the part that has been left out.

Hally Because it feels like that. Wouldn't be a good day to fly it, though.

Sam No. You can't fly kites on rainy days.

*[Later, Sam and Hally are arguing about Hally's father. Hally seems to both hate and love his father, who is **addicted** to alcohol.]*

Sam *(Almost shouting)* Stop now!

Hally *(Suddenly **appalled** by how far he has gone)* Why?

Sam Hally? It's your father you're talking about.

Hally So?

Sam Do you know what you've been saying?

*(Hally can't answer. He is **rigid** with **shame**. Sam speaks to him sternly)*

No, Hally, you mustn't do it. Take back those words and ask for forgiveness! It's a terrible sin for a son to **mock** his father with jokes like that. You'll be punished if you carry on. Your father is your father, even if he is a . . . cripple man.

Willie Yes, Master Hally. Is true what Sam say.

Sam I understand how you are feeling, Hally, but even so . . .

Hally No, you don't!

Sam I think I do.

Hally And I'm telling you you don't. Nobody does.

(Speaking carefully as his shame turns to rage at Sam)

It's your turn to be careful, Sam. Very careful! You're **treading** on dangerous ground. Leave me and my father alone.

Sam I'm not the one who's been saying things about him.

> Why is Willie's manner of speaking different from Sam's and Hally's?

---

addicted controlled by a bad habit

appalled filled with horror or dismay

rigid stiff

shame a painful feeling caused by having done something wrong

mock make fun of

treading walking

Hally   What goes on between me and my Dad is none of your business!

Sam   Then don't tell me about it. If that's all you've got to say about him, I don't want to hear.

(For a moment Hally is at a loss for a response)

Hally   Just get on with your bloody work and shut up.

Sam   Swearing at me won't help you.

Hally   Yes, it does! Mind your own . . . business and shut up!

Sam   Okay. If that's the way you want it, I'll stop trying.

(He turns away. This infuriates Hally even more)

Hally   Good. Because what you've been trying to do is **meddle** in something you know nothing about. All that concerns you in here, Sam, is to try and do what you get paid for—keep the place clean and serve the customers. In plain words, just get on with your job. My mother is right. She's always warning me about allowing you to get too familiar. Well, this time you've gone too far. It's going to stop right now.

(No response from Sam)

You're only a servant in here, and don't forget it.

(Still no response. Hally is trying hard to get one)

And as far as my father is concerned, all you need to remember is that he is your boss.

Sam   **(Needled** at last) No, he isn't. I get paid by your mother.

Hally   Don't argue with me, Sam!

Sam   Then don't say he's my boss.

Hally   He's a white man and that's good enough for you.

Sam   I'll try to forget you said that.

> Think about what Hally's parents have been telling him about Sam all along. What inner conflict does Hally seem to be facing? How does this lead to a struggle between Sam and Hally?

meddle interfere   **needled** made angry

	Hally	Don't! Because you won't be doing me a favor if you do. I'm telling you to remember it.
		(A pause. Sam pulls himself together and makes one last effort)
Remember that Sam is older than Hally. Why is Sam warning Hally? What is he afraid will happen?	**Sam**	Hally, Hally . . . ! Come on now. Let's stop before it's too late. You're right. We *are* on dangerous ground. If we're not careful, somebody is going to get hurt.
	Hally	It won't be me.
	Sam	Don't be so sure.
	Hally	I don't know what you're talking about, Sam.
	Sam	Yes, you do.
	Hally	*(Furious)* . . . I wish you would stop trying to tell me what I do and what I don't know.
		(Sam gives up. He turns to Willie)
	Sam	Let's finish up.
	Hally	Don't turn your back on me! I haven't finished talking.
This stage direction tells Sam to act very angry when Hally grabs him.		*(He grabs Sam by the arm and tries to make him turn around. Sam **reacts** with a flash of anger)*
	Sam	Don't do that, Hally! *(Facing the boy)* All right, I'm listening. Well? What do you want to say to me?
	Hally	*(Pause as Hally looks for something to say)* To begin with, why don't you also start calling me Master Harold, like Willie.
	Sam	Do you mean that?
	Hally	Why . . . do you think I said it?
	Sam	And if I don't?
	Hally	You might just lose your job.
	Sam	*(Quietly and very carefully)* If you make me say it once, I'll never call you anything else again.

reacts acts in response to something

Hally So? *(The boy confronts the man)* Is that meant to be a threat?

Sam Just telling you what will happen if you make me do that. You must decide what it means to you.

Hally Well, I have. It's good news. Because that is exactly what Master Harold wants from now on. Think of it as a little lesson in respect, Sam, that's long **overdue**, and I hope you remember it as well as you do your geography. I can tell you now that somebody who will be glad to hear I've finally given it to you will be my Dad. Yes! He agrees with my Mom. He's always going on about it as well. "You must teach the boys to show you more respect, my son."

Sam So now you can stop complaining about going home. Everybody is going to be happy tonight.

Hally That's perfectly correct. You see, you mustn't get the wrong idea about me and my Dad, Sam. We also have our good times together. . . .

Sam . . . Come, Willie, let's finish up and go.

(Sam and Willie start to tidy up the tea room. Hally doesn't move. He waits for a moment when Sam passes him)

Hally *(Quietly)* Sam . . .

*(Sam stops and looks **expectantly** at the boy. Hally spits in his face. A long and **heartfelt** groan from Willie. For a few seconds Sam doesn't move)*

Sam *(Taking out a handkerchief and wiping his face)* It's all right, Willie.

(To Hally)

Ja, well, you've done it . . . Master Harold. Yes, I'll start calling you that from now on. It won't be difficult anymore. You've hurt yourself, Master Harold. I saw it coming, I warned you, but you

> Why does Hally's father call Sam and Willie "the boys"?

overdue past due; late

expectantly eagerly waiting to hear or see something

heartfelt deeply felt; sincere

> What just happened here? What does Sam mean? How does Hally's white skin protect him?

wouldn't listen. You've just hurt yourself *bad*. And you're a coward, Master Harold. The face you should be spitting in is your father's . . . but you used mine, because you think you're safe inside your fair skin . . .

*(Pause, then moving **violently** toward Hally)* Should I hit him, Willie?

> *Boet* is an expression meaning "brother" or "close friend."

Willie   *(Stopping Sam)* No, Boet Sam.

Sam   *(Violently)* Why not?

Willie   It won't help, Boet Sam.

Sam   I don't want to help! I want to hurt him.

Willie   You also hurt yourself.

Sam   And if he had done it to you, Willie?

Willie   Me? Spit at me like I was a dog? *(A thought that had not occurred to him before. He looks at Hally)* Ja. Then I want to hit him. I want to hit him hard!

(A dangerous few seconds as the men stand staring at the boy. Willie turns away, shaking his head)

But maybe all I do is go cry at the back. He's little boy, Boet Sam. Little *white* boy. Long trousers now, but he's still little boy.

Sam   *(His violence **ebbing** away into defeat as quickly as it flooded)* You're right. So go on, then: groan again, Willie. You do it better than me. *(To Hally)* You don't know all of what you've just done . . . Master Harold. It's not just that you've made me feel dirtier than I've ever been in my life . . . I mean, how do I wash off yours and your father's **filth**? . . . I've also failed. A long time ago I promised myself I was going to try and do something, but you've just shown me . . . Master Harold . . . that I've failed. . . .

Hally   *(Great pain)* I love him, Sam.

---

violently with strong physical force or rough action

ebbing fading away; becoming less

filth foul matter; dirt

Sam I know you do. That's why I tried to stop you from saying these things about him. It would have been so simple if you could have just **despised** him for being a weak man. But he's your father. You love him and you're ashamed of him. You're ashamed of so much! . . . And now that's going to include yourself. That was the promise I made to myself: to try and stop that happening. *(Pause)* After we got him to bed you came back with me to my room and sat in a corner and carried on just looking down at the ground. And for days after that! You hadn't done anything wrong, but you went around as if you owed the world an **apology** for being alive. I didn't like seeing that! That's not the way a boy grows up to be a man! . . . But the one person who should have been teaching you what that means was the cause of your shame. If you really want to know, that's why I made you that kite. I wanted you to look up, be proud of something, of yourself . . . *(Bitter smile at the memory)* . . . And you certainly were that when I left you with it up there on the hill. Oh, ja . . . something else! . . . If you ever do write it as a short story, there *was* a twist in our ending. I couldn't sit down there and stay with you. It was a "Whites Only" bench. You were too young, too excited to notice then. But not anymore. If you're not careful . . . Master Harold . . . you're going

During apartheid, signs like this were posted throughout South Africa.

> Now we know why Sam built the kite for Hally. He wanted to give him a reason to look up. He didn't want Hally to feel that he had to look down because he was ashamed of his father.

despised looked down upon

apology an expression of regret for something one has done

to be sitting up there by yourself for a long time to come, and there won't be a kite in the sky. *(Sam has got nothing more to say. He exits into the kitchen, taking off his waiter's jacket)*

(Hally goes behind the counter and collects the few coins in the cash register. As he starts to leave . . .)

Sam Don't forget the comic books.

(Hally returns to the counter and puts them in his case. He starts to leave again)

Sam *(To the retreating back of the boy)* Stop . . . Hally . . .

(Hally stops, but doesn't turn to face him)

Hally . . . I've got no right to tell you what being a man means if I don't behave like one myself, and I'm not doing so well at that this afternoon. Should we try again, Hally?

Hally Try what?

Sam Fly another kite, I suppose. It worked once, and this time I need it as much as you do.

Hally It's still raining, Sam. You can't fly kites on rainy days, remember.

Sam So what do we do? Hope for better weather tomorrow?

Hally *(Hopeless gesture)* I don't know. I don't know anything anymore.

Sam You sure of that, Hally? Because it would be pretty hopeless if that was true. It would mean nothing has been learnt in here this afternoon, and there was a . . . a lot of teaching going on . . . one way or the other. But anyway, I don't believe you. I reckon there's one thing you know. You don't *have* to sit up there by yourself. You know what that bench means now, and you can leave it any time you choose. All you've got to do is stand up and walk away from it.

> Why is Sam willing to take the first step to heal the damage done to their relationship?

> Sam says he's hoping for better weather tomorrow. What else is he hoping tomorrow will bring?

AFTER READING THE SELECTION

from "Master Harold" . . . and the Boys by Athol Fugard

Directions Choose the letter of the best answer or write the answer using complete sentences.

Comprehension: Identifying Facts

1. Where are Sam and Hally?
   A at a bookstore C at Sam's house
   B at a tea room   D at a park

2. How did Hally feel when he first saw the kite?
   A happy   C tired
   B sad   D embarrassed

3. What did Sam use to make the kite? Why did he use these materials?

4. What reason does Sam give for leaving Hally and the kite?

5. How does Hally feel about his father?

6. Why does Hally get mad at Sam?

7. Hally tells Sam to "just get on with your job." What is Sam's job?

8. According to Hally, who is Sam's boss? According to Sam, who is his boss?

9. What does Willie call Hally?

10. Who else will be glad that Hally is demanding respect from Sam?

Comprehension: Putting Ideas Together

11. Why does Sam tell Hally to stop making fun of his father?
    A Sam thinks Hally's father is a great person.
    B Sam is afraid that Hally's father will hear them talking.
    C Sam thinks that people should respect their parents no matter what they do.
    D Sam thinks Hally is making things up.

12. Sam tells Hally, "If we're not careful, somebody is going to get hurt." What does he mean?
    A Sam will quit his job, and Hally's family will lose the restaurant.
    B Sam is going to hit Hally.
    C Sam is going to start saying mean things about Willie.
    D Sam and Hally will not be friends anymore.

13. Hally tells Sam to call him Master Harold. Why is this so important?

14. Hally spits on Sam. What does Sam think is the real reason he does this?

15. Why does Sam start to move violently toward Hally?

After Reading continued on next page

AFTER READING THE SELECTION (continued)

from "Master Harold" . . . and the Boys   by Athol Fugard

16. Willie describes Hally by saying, "Long trousers now, but he's still little boy." What does he mean?

17. Sam says that he's failed. How does he fail?

18. Why is Hally ashamed of his father?

19. What is the real reason that Sam left Hally alone with the kite?

20. What does Sam apologize for?

Understanding Literature: Realistic Drama

"Master Harold". . . and the Boys is a realistic drama. It's a play that tells a story that could have happened in real life. A realistic drama must be set in a believable time and place. It must have characters who speak and act like real people. When an audience is watching a realistic drama, they should believe that they are watching a "slice of life."

21. What is the setting of this play? How is it realistic?

22. Look back at what the characters say to each other. Is there anything that reminds you of the way that you and your friends speak to each other? If so, give an example.

23. Think about how Sam acts when Hally spits on him. Is this a realistic reaction? Explain your answer.

24. Hally is troubled by real problems. What are they?

25. This selection does not have a nice, neat ending. How does this make the play more realistic?

Critical Thinking

26. Why did Sam really make the kite for Hally?

27. What role does Sam play in Hally's life?

28. Why does Sam call Hally a coward?

29. How has apartheid affected the relationship between Sam and Hally?

Thinking Creatively

30. Reread Sam's final words. What does Sam believe that Hally will decide to do? Do you agree with Sam? Why or why not?

Grammar Check

Choose one character from this play. Think about the things that he says and does. Write a paragraph about him. First, write a topic sentence. Then, write supporting details. Be sure to use active, not passive, voice. Each detail should support the main idea. Refer to Appendix C for writing tips.

 Writing on Your Own

Think about what might happen next between Sam and Hally. Write the rest of the play. Use dialogue and stage directions.

 Speaking

Pretend that you are Willie. You are speaking to a group of high school students. Tell them a little bit about what your life was like under apartheid. Use what happened in this play to help you.

 Listening

Drama is meant to be heard and seen, not read silently. Do you agree or disagree? Use your experiences with this play to explain your reasoning.

 **Viewing**

Complete a Character Analysis Guide for Hally or Sam. See Appendix A for a description of this graphic organizer. Write the character's name at the center of your graphic organizer. In the "event" boxes, you can write things the character does or says. Then write the trait that is revealed through those actions or words. After you finish your Character Analysis Guide, find a classmate who chose to analyze the same character. Compare and contrast your Character Analysis Guides. How are they the same? How are they different? Do you agree on the character traits?

 Research

In the United States, there were many "whites only" parks, schools, and restaurants. Those who took part in the civil rights movement of the 1950s and 1960s worked hard to end this. Do some research to find an organization that was important during that time period. Write an essay telling about who led the group and what its actions were. Refer to Appendix C for tips on writing an essay.

Expressionistic Drama

The expressionistic style of drama began in Europe and became popular after 1900. Expressionist playwrights did not like the realistic style of drama. They thought it did not look deeply into human experience. They wanted to write about hidden thoughts and feelings. At the same time, the new field of psychology was growing. Psychology deals with the actions and emotions, or strong feelings, of people. Expressionistic playwrights tried to find ways to show these emotions on stage. They wanted the audience to feel involved with the characters. Some writers exaggerated their characters' inner feelings, or made them greater than usual.

Sometimes, the playwrights did not give names to their characters. This was another way they made the play seem less realistic. For example, the characters might be called just the "Father" or the "Bank Clerk." These labels describe the characters' purposes in the play, or to suggest their place in society. In *The Stronger*, the characters have no names. They are identified only by whether they are married (Mme. X is a married woman; Mlle. Y is a single woman).

Expressionistic writers used lighting, staging, and directing in new ways. For example, Thornton Wilder's *Our Town* uses a narrator, as a realistic play might. Very little scenery is used to move the action. In Eugene O'Neill's *Strange Interlude*, the protagonist, or main character, is split into two characters. The split shows the conflict between the character's public nature, or personality, and his private nature. In *The Stronger*, one of the main characters never speaks, and there is no change of scenery.

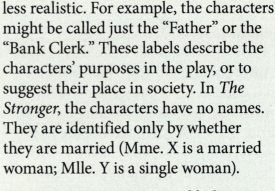

Expressionistic Drama
— is not realistic
— shows deep feelings
— has unusual staging

BEFORE READING THE SELECTION

The Stronger by August Strindberg (trans. by Ants Oras)

About the Author

August Strindberg was one of 11 children in a poor Swedish family. After an unhappy childhood, he went to college in Uppsala, Sweden. He was so poor that he had to drop out after just one semester. He tried teaching and acting. He also began writing. One of his plays helped him win a stipend, or scholarship. Strindberg went back to college. He continued writing. Strindberg later got a job at the Royal Library. While working for the library, he wrote many short stories, novels, and plays. Strindberg's plays often show conflicts between men and women. He is remembered for leading the way in the field of expressionist drama. He is also known for his unusual paintings.

August Strindberg (1849–1912) Swedish

Objectives

- To read and identify an expressionistic drama
- To identify examples of simile and irony in a play
- To understand the purpose of a monologue in a play

About the Selection

The Stronger is different from most other plays. There are only two main characters, and one of them does not speak at all. She seems to be present only so the other woman is not speaking to herself. The two characters are women who used to be friends. One woman is married, and the other is single. The married woman talks about why she thinks her friend should have gotten married. She also talks a lot about her own marriage. As the woman talks, she comes to some conclusions about her husband and her friend. Read to find out what she thinks happened and what she decides to do about it.

Before Reading continued on next page

Drama Unit 3 329

BEFORE READING THE SELECTION (continued)

The Stronger by August Strindberg (trans. by Ants Oras)

expressionistic drama a form of drama that is not realistic; the characters' inner feelings are more important than their actions

monologue a longer story or speech told by one person

simile a figure of speech that compares two unlike objects using the word *like* or *as*

verbal irony the use of words that seem to say one thing but mean the opposite

Literary Terms This play is an example of **expressionistic drama**. It may seem realistic at first, but you will find some elements that are not. One difference in this play is that only one of the characters speaks. This character is Mme. X. Her lines are a sort of **monologue,** a story or speech told by one person.

Mme. X is talking about her husband and Mlle. Y. As she talks, Mme. X uses many **similes** to describe Mlle. Y. A simile is a figure of speech that compares two unlike objects using the word *like* or *as*. Another feature of Mme. X's monologue is **verbal irony**. Verbal irony is the use of words that seem to say one thing but mean the opposite. She seems to understand things in one way, but the reader can see a different side of things.

Reading on Your Own Expressionistic drama is not completely realistic. As you read this play, think about what is unrealistic. Think about the main ideas of the situation. How would real people act differently from these two characters?

Writing on Your Own Think of a time when you felt betrayed by your friends, or a time when you felt like you were all alone with life's problems. Write about how you felt.

Vocabulary Focus The English language has many words that are "borrowed" from other languages. This story has a few words that came from the French language. One way to identify these words is to look for the accent (é) at the end of the word. Another way is to look for words that start with the letters *ch-* but have the *sh-* sound. Look for these words in the story: *café, fiancé, chiffonier*. Write each one in a sentence of your own.

Think Before You Read You know that only one character will speak in this play. What do you think the other character will be doing as this happens?

The Stronger

PERSONS

Mme. X, *actress, married*

Mlle. Y, *actress, single*

A Waitress

A corner in a ladies' café; two small iron tables, a red velvet sofa and some chairs. Mme. X enters in winter clothing, wearing a hat and a cloak and carrying a fine Japanese basket on her arm. Mlle. Y sits with a half-empty beer bottle in front of her, reading an illustrated paper, then changing it for another.

> Mme. X is the abbreviation for Madame X. This is similar to Mrs. X in English. *Mlle. Y* is the abbreviation for Mademoiselle Y. This is similar to Miss Y in English.

Mme. X: How are you, little Amelie?—You're sitting alone here on Christmas Eve like a **disconsolate** old bachelor.

(Mlle. Y looks up from the paper, nods, goes on reading)

Mme. X: You know, I am **heartily** sorry to see you like this, alone, all alone in a café on Christmas Eve. I feel quite as sorry as that evening in a Paris restaurant when I saw a bridal party, with the bride sitting and reading a comic paper and the groom playing **billiards** with the witnesses. Goodness, I thought, with such a beginning how is this to continue and to end!

He played billiards on his wedding evening!—Yes, and she read a comic paper! Well, but that is hardly the same situation as here.

> As you read, think about why the author did not give specific names to his characters. How might this be a feature of expressionistic drama?

> The witnesses were the wedding guests. They sign, or witness, a paper that makes the wedding legal.

---

disconsolate very sad

heartily with enthusiasm

billiards a game similar to pool, played with a cue and solid balls on a large oblong table with raised edges

Drama Unit 3

(The Waitress enters, places a cup of hot chocolate before Mme. X and goes out)

Mme. X: I tell you what, Amelie! Now I really believe you would have done better to have kept him. Remember, I was the first to urge you "Forgive him!" Don't you recall it?—You could have been married to him, with a home of your own. Don't you remember last Christmas, how happy you felt out in the country with your **fiancé**'s parents; How you praised the happiness of a home and how you **longed** to get away from the theater?—Yes, darling Amelie, a home is the best of all things—next to the theater—a home and some brats too—but that you wouldn't understand.

*(Mlle. Y looks **contemptuous**)*

Mme. X: *(drinks a few spoonfuls from her cup, opens her basket and shows her Christmas presents):* Now you'll see what I've bought for my piglets. *(Shows a doll)* Look at this. This is for Lisa. Look how it rolls its eyes and turns its neck. There! And here is Maja's pop gun. *(Loads it and shoots at Mlle. Y)*

(Mlle. Y makes a scared gesture)

Mme. X: Did this startle you? Did you fear I'd shoot you? What?—Good heavens, I don't believe you could possibly have thought that. I'd be less surprised if you were shooting me, since I got in your way—I know you can't forget that—although I was completely innocent. You still believe I eased you out of the theater with my **intrigues**, but I didn't! I didn't, even though you think I did!—But what is the use of telling you, for you still believe I did it. *(Takes out a pair of embroidered slippers)*

---

fiancé the man a woman is engaged to marry

longed greatly wished for

contemptuous showing dislike

intrigues secrets or underhanded plans

What seems to have happened in Mlle. Y's personal life?

Whom is Mme. X referring to as her piglets?

Notice that only Mme. X is speaking. This makes the play a dramatic monologue.

And these are for my old man. With tulips embroidered, by myself—I **abhor** tulips, you understand, but he wants tulips on everything.

(*Mlle. Y looks up from her paper ironically and with some curiosity*)

Mme. X: (*puts a hand in each slipper*) Look how small Bob's feet are. Well? And you ought to see how daintily he walks. You've never seen him in his slippers.

(*Mlle. Y laughs aloud*)

Mme. X: Look, I'll show you. (*Makes the slippers walk along the table*)

(*Mlle. Y laughs aloud*)

Mme. X: Now look, and when he is out of sorts he stamps with his foot like this. "What! . . . Those servants, they'll never learn how to make coffee! Goodness! Now those **morons** haven't clipped the lamp wick properly." And then there's a **draught** from the floor and his feet freeze: "Blast it, how cold it is, and these **unspeakable** idiots can't keep the fire going." (*Rubs one slipper's sole against the other's upper*)

(*Mlle. Y bursts out laughing*)

Mme. X: And then he comes home and has to search for his slippers, which Marie has put under the chiffonier . . . Oh, but it is sinful to sit thus and

This play was written before people used electricity for lights. Every day, someone had to trim the wicks in the oil-burning lamps. The wicks were tightly woven fibers that drew the fuel to the flame. A neatly trimmed wick gave better light.

A *chiffonier* is a high chest of drawers, often with a mirror.

abhor to dislike intensely; to find disgusting

morons very stupid people

draught (American *draft*) a current of air

unspeakable too bad to be described

Drama Unit 3 333

make a fool of one's old man. Whatever he is, he is nice, a decent little fellow—you ought to've had such a husband, Amelie.—Why are you laughing! Why? Why?—And look here, I know he is faithful to me; yes, I do know that, for he told me himself . . . What are you grinning at? . . .When I was on my Norway tour, that nasty Frédérique came and tried to seduce him—Could you imagine such an **infamy**? *(Pause)* But I'd have scratched out her eyes if she'd come near me after my return! *(Pause)* What a good thing Bob told me about it himself rather than let me hear it through gossip! *(Pause)* But Frédérique was not the only one, believe me! I don't know why, but the women are positively crazy about my husband—perhaps they think he has some say about theater engagements because he is in the government department!— Who knows but you yourself may have been chasing him!—I never trusted you more than just so much—but now I do know he doesn't care for you, and I always thought you were bearing him some grudge.

(Pause. They view each other, both embarrassed)

Mme. X: Come to see us in the evening, Amelie, and show you aren't cross with us, at least not with me! I don't know why, but it is so uncomfortable to be at loggerheads with you, of all people. Possibly because I got in your way that time—*(rallentando)* or—I just don't know why in particular!

(Pause. Mlle. Y gazes curiously at Mme. X)

Mme. X: *(pensively)* Our acquaintance was such an odd one—when I first saw you I was afraid of you, so afraid that I couldn't risk letting you out of my sight; whenever I came or went I was always near

---

At loggerheads is an expression that means at odds or in conflict.

Rallentando is an Italian musical term. It means the tempo or speed is gradually slowing. It is used here as a stage direction. It tells the character to speak the rest of the line more slowly. Why does the author give this direction?

---

infamy disgrace

pensively in a sadly thoughtful way

you—I couldn't afford to have you for an enemy, so I became your friend. But there was always something **discordant** in the air when you came to our home, for I saw my husband couldn't stand you—it all felt somehow awkward, like ill-fitting clothes—and I did what I could to make him take to you but to no purpose—until you got yourself engaged to be married! Then a **violent** friendship flared up so that for a moment it looked as though the two of you had only now ventured to show your real feelings because you were safe—and so what?—What happened?—I wasn't jealous—how queer!—And I recall the **christening** when you stood godmother to our baby—I made Bob kiss you—and he did, but you were so confused—that is to say, I didn't notice at the time—haven't thought about it since—not once until—this moment. *(Gets up furiously)*

Why are you silent? You haven't said a word all this time, you've only let me sit and talk. You've been sitting and staring and making me unwind all these thoughts which lay like raw silk in their cocoon—thoughts—maybe suspicious ones—let me see.—Why did you break off your engagement? Why haven't you been to our house since that happened? Why aren't you coming to see us tonight?

(Mlle. Y seems on the point of speaking)

Mme. X: Be quiet! You needn't say a word, for now I grasp it all myself. It was because—because—because!—Yes indeed!—Every bit of it falls into its place! That's it!—Shame! Shame! I won't sit at the same table with you. *(Moves her things to the other table)*

> Silkworms spin raw silk threads into a *cocoon* about their bodies. Unraveling a cocoon is a difficult, time-consuming task. Mme. X is finding it difficult to unravel her thoughts.

---

discordant unpleasant; disturbing

violent caused by a strong feeling

christening a ceremony for naming and baptizing a child

Lake Mälar is near Stockholm, Sweden. It is a popular resort area.

A *rind* is the outer skin or peel of something.

When the moon is *waxing*, it is growing gradually larger. When the moon is *waning*, it is becoming gradually smaller.

So that was why I had to embroider tulips on his slippers although I hate tulips—because you like them! That was why—*(throws the slippers on the floor)*—that was why we had to spend the summer on Lake Mälar—because you couldn't bear the sea at Saltsiö; that was why my son had to be christened Eskil—because such was the name of your father; that was why I had to wear your colors, read your authors, eat your favorite dishes, drink your drinks—your chocolate, for example; that was why—Oh, my God—this is frightful to think of, frightful!—Everything came from you to me, even your **passions** and **addictions**!—Your soul **slithered** into mine like a worm into an apple, eating and eating, digging and digging, until all that was left was a rind with some black, messy substance inside! I wanted to escape from you but couldn't; you lay like a snake **bewitching** me with your black eyes—I felt how my wings rose only to drag me down; I lay with tied feet in the water, and the harder my hands struck out, the more I worked myself down, down right to the bottom where you lay like an enormous crab in order to grip me with your claws—and this is where I now am.

Shame, shame! How I hate you, how I hate you, how I hate you! Yet you only sit, silent, calm, uncaring; not caring whether the moon is waxing or waning, whether it is Christmas or New Year's, whether people are happy or unhappy; incapable of love or hatred; **rigid** like a stork over a mousehole—unable to grab your quarry, unable to chase it, yet well able to wait until it comes into your clutches. Here you sit in your

passions strong feelings for or about something

addictions harmful habits

slithered moved along by gliding, as a snake

bewitching fascinating

rigid stiff

corner—do you know that it is because of you that it's called the Rat-trap?—Here you scan your paper to find out whether anybody has got into trouble or is **wretched** or must give up the theater; here you sit, watching out for victims, **calculating** your chances like a pilot planning a shipwreck, and collecting your tribute!

Poor Amelie, do you know that I pity you because you are unhappy, unhappy like a hurt beast and full of **malice** because you are hurt?—I can't feel angry with you although I would like to—you are the cornered one after all—well yes, that affair with Bob, why should I bother about it?—In what way does it harm me?— And whether it was you or somebody else who taught me to drink chocolate, what of it? *(Drinks a spoonful from her cup; knowingly)* After all, chocolate is good for one's health. And if I learned from you how to dress—*tant mieux*—that only strengthened my husband's affection for me—and so you lost what I won—Yes, there are **indications** that you really have lost him. Yet of course, you intended me to fade out of the picture—as you have done, sitting here as you do and regretting

Girls Seated at the Table, by Jules Pascin.

> Look for the similes on this page. What is Mme. X saying about Mlle. Y?

> *Tant mieux* is a French expression meaning "so much the better."

wretched miserable; very unhappy
calculating deciding; figuring out
indications signs
malice ill will

what you did—but look here, I just won't do it!—We **shan't** be **petty**, don't you agree? And why should I take only what no one else wants!

Perhaps, all things considered, I may indeed be the stronger—for you never got anything out of me, you only gave—and now I am like that thief—as you woke up you found I had all the things you missed.

How else could it come about that everything turned worthless and barren in your hand? With all your tulips and fine **affections** you never managed to keep a man's love—as I have done; you never learned the art of living from your writers, as I did; nor did you ever get any little Eskil of your own, even though Eskil is the name of your father!

And why are you always silent, silent, silent? Yes, I mistook this for strength; but perhaps all it meant was that you hadn't anything to say—that you never were able to think a thought. *(Gets up and takes the slippers from the floor)* Now I'm going home—with the tulips—*your* tulips! You were unable to learn anything from people—unable to bend—and so you snapped like a dry stalk—but I won't snap.

Thanks ever so much, Amelie, for all your kind lessons; thanks for teaching my husband how to love! Now I'm going home to love him. *(Goes)*

What is ironic about Mme. X thanking Mlle. Y?

---

shan't a short form of *shall not*

petty mean

affections emotions or feelings

AFTER READING THE SELECTION

The Stronger   by August Strindberg (trans. by Ants Oras)

Directions Choose the letter of the best answer or write the answer using complete sentences.

Comprehension: Identifying Facts

1. Which of the characters does all the talking?
   A waitress
   B Mme. X
   C Mlle. Y
   D Bob

2. When Mme. X talks about "brats," to whom is she referring?
   A a bridal party in a Paris restaurant
   B her husband and his friends
   C her children
   D the waitresses in the café

3. Where did Mlle. Y spend last Christmas?

4. What gifts does Mme. X have in her basket? Whom are they for?

5. How has Mme. X decorated her husband's slippers? Why?

6. What happened when Mme. X was away in Norway?

7. Who is Bob?

8. Who is Frédérique?

9. How did Mme. X feel about Mlle. Y when they first met?

10. Who is godmother to Mme. X's son?

Comprehension: Putting Ideas Together

11. What has happened to Mlle. Y's plans to marry?
    A She broke the engagement.
    B Her fiancé died.
    C Her fiancé broke the engagement.
    D She had to delay the wedding.

12. When was the last time Mlle. Y was at Mme. X's home?
    A last Christmas
    B yesterday
    C the day she got engaged
    D just before she broke off her engagement

13. A stage direction tells Mme. X to move to the other table. Why does she move?

14. Mme. X has done many things to please her husband. Why does he really want her to do them?

15. Mme. X compares Mlle. Y to several living creatures. List them.

16. How do these comparisons help the reader understand Mme. X's feelings about Mlle. Y?

17. Why does Mme. X say that she pities Mlle. Y? Do you think she is being honest with herself?

After Reading continued on next page

Drama Unit 3   339

AFTER READING THE SELECTION (continued)

The Stronger by August Strindberg (trans. by Ants Oras)

18. What does Mme. X say that she gained from Mlle. Y and her affair?

19. How is Mme. X like a thief?

20. What does Mme. X decide to do at the end of the play?

Understanding Literature: Expressionistic Drama

The Stronger is an example of expressionistic drama. Strindberg, the author of this play, was one of the first playwrights to write in this style. An expressionistic drama seems realistic in many ways. But some elements are changed for dramatic effect. For example, the play might happen in a strange place, or events may not happen in logical order. Think about the features of *The Stronger* that make it expressionistic rather than realistic.

21. What is unusual about the characters' names? Why is this an important element of the play?

22. Think about how much action takes place in this play. How is this different from other plays?

23. How do you think most real women would react in this situation? Is the play realistic about the women? Or is this another feature of its expressionism?

24. What is unrealistic about the setting? *(Hint: Where would you expect a woman like Mme. X to be on a night like this?)*

25. Think about the title. Who do you think is the stronger of the two women? Why?

Critical Thinking

26. What do you think about Mme. X's husband and their marriage?

27. At one point in the play, Mlle. Y almost says something. Why do you think she decides not to? What could she be thinking?

28. What do you think happened between Mlle. Y and Mme. X's husband? Has Mme. X's imagination run wild?

29. Mme. X says that she is sorry to see Mlle. Y alone in a café on Christmas Eve. Where is Mme. X when she says this? How is this ironic?

Thinking Creatively

30. Mme. X tells Mlle. Y, "I couldn't afford to have you for an enemy, so I became your friend." Think about this reason for starting a friendship. Do you think Mme. X was ever a true friend to Mlle. Y? Why or why not?

Grammar Check

This play uses dashes to show when the character pauses or stutters during her lines. You may have seen ellipses showing when a person pauses. Ellipses are periods within the text that show that the person is pausing, or to show that part of the text has been left out. Look at the use of dashes in this play. Mme. X is not pausing to think. Why is she stopping as she speaks? What do the dashes show?

 ### Writing on Your Own

Many people write letters to advice columnists in the newspaper. You may know of "Dear Abby" and "Tell Me About It." Write your own letter to an advice columnist. Pretend that you are Mme. X or Mlle. Y. If you are writing as Mme. X, ask for advice about how to deal with your husband Bob and your friend. If you are writing as Mlle. Y, ask for advice about how to deal with Bob and his wife.

 ### Speaking

Write your own monologue as if talking to someone you disagree with who is forced to listen to you. Try to make the person understand your point of view. Then read it aloud to yourself.

 ### Listening

Exposition, narration, persuasion, and description are forms of speech. Listen as a classmate reads Mme. X's speech. Make a note of any of the forms you hear. For example, if you hear an example of persuasion, write a short note to yourself about what this was. Overall, what form does Mme. X use the most?

 ### Media

When Strindberg was alive, many people were not happy about the topics he wrote about. For example, they did not want to see plays about married people who were unfaithful. He even had to defend himself in court. In the United States, the Bill of Rights grants citizens freedom of speech. Of course, Strindberg was not an American playwright. Use the Bill of Rights to defend Strindberg and *The Stronger*.

 ### Technology

This play was written when theaters had little, if any, technology. Today's theaters can use lighting and sound effects in many different ways. Research the types of equipment that are used in theaters today. Which technology do you think is most important?

Drama Unit 3

Unit 3 SKILLS LESSON
Characterization

Characterization is the way a writer develops characters by revealing their personality traits. In a play, physical descriptions help reveal characters. What characters say and do shows still more about them. What others say about them adds to the characterization. How others react to them reveals still more.

When we first see a character, we develop an idea about him or her. This is based simply on how the actor looks and moves. We learn more about the character as we listen to the dialogue. Now we begin to form an opinion about the character's personality. We are using external clues, or things we can see and hear. Playwrights use external clues to show what the internal person is really like.

In *Macbeth*, Shakespeare shows that Macbeth is going mad. Shakespeare uses actions and dialogue to show this. When Macbeth plans to murder King Duncan, he sees a vision of a blood-stained dagger. The dagger hangs in midair and points toward Duncan's sleeping chamber. Later, Macbeth orders the murder of Banquo. After this, Macbeth sees and talks to Banquo's ghost. At the end of this scene, Macbeth says that he has spies in the homes of noblemen. He's now afraid to trust anyone. He wants the advice of the Weird Sisters. He believes they can foretell the future. Shakespeare uses Macbeth's words and actions to show how Macbeth is gradually losing his mind.

Review

1. Why do you think most plays begin with physical descriptions of the characters?

2. In *"Master Harold" . . . and the Boys*, what does Willie's manner of speech reveal about him?

3. In *The Stronger*, what does Mlle. Y's behavior reveal about her?

4. What does Mme. X's dialogue reveal about her?

5. Who is the least likable character in the plays in this unit? Why?

Writing on Your Own

Choose one of the characters from the plays in this unit. Write one paragraph describing the character. Be sure to answer these questions: How does the person look, move, and speak? How does the person behave toward others? How do others react to this person?

Unit 3 SUMMARY

In Unit 3, you read three types of plays. Shakespeare's *Macbeth* is called a classical drama. Fugard's *"Master Harold"... and the Boys* is a realistic drama. Strindberg's *The Stronger* is an expressionistic drama.

These different types of plays have much in common with each other. For instance, each of the playwrights describes a setting. They tell us when and where a play takes place. All plays have stage directions. Actors follow these directions to know when and how to speak and move. Characters, the people in a story, are very important in a play. So is dialogue, the conversations among the characters. Playwrights use more than just words to tell a story. They skillfully bring together setting, stage directions, characters, and dialogue.

Playwrights use these elements differently depending on the type of play they are writing. Some plays may even have elements of more than one type of play. For example, the dialogue in classical drama is written in blank verse. The dialogue in a realistic play or expressionistic drama is written in everyday language. The settings of classical dramas are sometimes places where you would find royalty and other people of high position in society. They may be imaginary places from myths and legends. In contrast, the settings for realistic plays are ordinary, real places. In expressionistic drama, one of these elements may be changed or exaggerated for a special effect. In realistic drama, each element is carefully used to create a story just as it might happen in real life.

Selections

- *Macbeth* by William Shakespeare. In one of Shakespeare's best-known plays, Macbeth commits murder to become king. He then has to deal with both his own guilt and his enemies.

- *"Master Harold"... and the Boys* by Athol Fugard. The attitudes of apartheid threaten the friendship between a white boy and the black man who is like a father to him.

- *The Stronger* by August Strindberg. In a play in which only one character speaks, the audience learns about the inner thoughts of Mme. X as she realizes something about her marriage.

Unit 3 REVIEW

Directions Choose the letter of the best answer or write the answer using complete sentences.

Comprehension: Identifying Facts

1. What is the term for the words the characters in a play speak?
   A excerpt
   B irony
   C dialogue
   D stage direction

2. What country is the setting for "Master Harold" . . . and the Boys?

3. Who is murdered in one of the plays? In which play?

4. Who does all the talking in The Stronger?

5. How long ago did Shakespeare write Macbeth?

Comprehension: Putting Ideas Together

6. What type of play usually shows the inner feelings of the characters?
   A realistic drama
   B expressionistic drama
   C humorous drama
   D classical drama

7. What play shows some effects of apartheid?

8. Macbeth sees two visions. What are they?

9. Why is Sam so fond of Hally?

10. When Mme. X says that "a home is the best of all things," Mlle. Y looks "contemptuous." Why?

Understanding Literature: Setting

The setting—the time and place—in a play is very different from the setting in a story. In a story, the setting can be anything a writer can imagine and describe with words. In a play, the setting is much more limited. The setting has to be shown or represented on a stage. The stage sets in Shakespeare's day were small and quite simple. The audience had to imagine events such as battles. Today, stage sets can be much more detailed and creative. Still, a playwright must tell the story within the limits of a stage.

11. The objects on stage in a play are called "properties," or "props." What props are needed for the stage setting in the scene from Macbeth? Remember to include costumes, too.

12. Two of the plays have similar settings—a café or a restaurant. Why does a café make a good setting?

13. Two of the plays are set in certain periods of time. Which ones? Why?

14. Strindberg sets his play on Christmas Eve. However, he doesn't name a year. Is the play timeless? Why?

15. Which playwright provides the most details about the setting? How does this contribute to your understanding and enjoyment of the play?

Critical Thinking

16. What does *"Master Harold" . . . and the Boys* seem to say about apartheid?

17. Although you read these plays, they were written to be performed. How would your experience be different if you were in a theater audience?

18. Why do you think Shakespeare is still popular with audiences?

19. What do realistic drama and expressionistic drama have in common?

Thinking Creatively

20. Choose the play in the unit you liked best. Explain the reasons for your choice.

Speak and Listen

Choose a short part of dialogue between two characters from Shakespeare's original *Macbeth*. Work with a partner. Read the dialogue aloud, putting emphasis on certain words to convey meaning. Refer to the Modern English version to help you understand the passage. Present the scene to the class.

Writing on Your Own

Newspapers and magazines publish reviews of play performances written by theater critics who have seen the play. The reviews are their opinions about the play's dialogue, the actors' work, and the stage sets. Imagine that you have just seen a production of one of the plays in this unit. Write your opinion in a review.

Beyond Words

Plays are often advertised on playbills, or small posters. Suppose that your school's drama club is going to perform one of the plays from this unit. Design and produce a playbill for them. Use a drawing or graphic to draw attention. Include the names of the actors or characters in the play and the names of the play and the playwright. Don't forget to tell the time and place of the performance.

Test-Taking Tip

If you know you will have to define certain terms on a test, write each term on one side of an index card. Write its definition on the other side. Use the cards to test yourself or to study with a partner.

Illustration with Moon and Birds, by Ron Rovtar.

Unit 4 Poetry

People who love poetry find it exciting and vivid. They like the images and feelings that are packed into a few lines. Others may find it hard to understand the meaning of a poem. They may never read it aloud to hear the rhyme and rhythm. They may not realize that songs they love are also poetry. This unit has a variety of poems. Some will be easy to understand, others will not. It is OK for people to disagree about what a poem means. Each person might have his or her own idea of the meaning of a poem. To enjoy a poem, relax. Slow down. Do not try to understand all the ideas at once. Read it aloud more than once. Think about the images. Enjoy.

Unit 4 Selections	Page
■ ISRAEL "The Diameter of the Bomb" by Yehuda Amichai	350
■ CHINA "Taking Leave of a Friend" by Li Po	355
■ VIETNAM "Thoughts of Hanoi" by Nguyen Thi Vinh	360
■ PHILIPPINES "Mindoro" by Ramón Sunico	364
■ CHILE "Ode to a Pair of Socks" by Pablo Neruda	370
■ JAPAN Three Haiku	376
■ WALES "Do Not Go Gentle Into That Good Night" by Dylan Thomas	381
■ IRAQ "The Bird's Last Flight" by Saadi Youssef	387
■ GHANA "Mawu of the Waters" by Abena Busia	393
■ TURKEY "Some Advice to Those Who Will Serve Time in Prison" by Nazim Hikmet	398

"I often think of a poem as a door that opens . . . into a room where I want to go."

—Minnie Bruce Pratt, author

"To read a poem is to hear it with our eyes; to hear it is to see it with our ears."

—Octavio Paz, author

Unit 4

About Poetry

Poems can be divided into many different genres, or types. Early poems were usually songs to a god. Others were epics, long stories written in verse. They were sung or chanted aloud. Over time, other forms developed. A popular genre in English was the sonnet, a 14-line poem in blank verse. It has any one of several rhyme schemes (patterns of rhyming words). Haiku is a traditional Japanese poetic form. A haiku has 17 unrhymed syllables. Free verse often does not rhyme. A villanelle is a 19-line poem with several repeating rhymes.

The writer of a poem is called a poet. A poet usually expresses ideas within the limits of a particular poetic form. Classical poets developed many different combinations of rhyme, rhythm, and length. Rhyme is the use of words with the same vowel and ending sounds. Rhythm is the beat. It is a pattern created by the stressed and unstressed syllables in a line of poetry.

Poets often use carefully chosen symbols. A symbol is a person, place, thing, or event that represents something else. By using a familiar symbol, the poet shows the feelings connected with it. A flying bird, for instance, may stand for freedom in one poem. In another poem, a bird may stand for death or disaster. Word choice is important in poetry. This is because the words must fit a certain rhythm or rhyme. At the same time, the words must create an image. The poet "paints" a picture with words.

Poems can also be grouped by purpose or literary approach. An elegy, for example, is a poem that mourns someone's death. In a dramatic monologue, a character talks to the reader. Many of today's poets use simpler forms. Some may combine several genres in new ways.

All poems use some kind of rhythmic pattern. They express ideas and feelings. In this unit, notice the wide range of forms. Remember that enjoying a good poem may take time and effort. Sometimes, reading a poem aloud adds to your appreciation. The more you think about a poem, the better it becomes.

The following countries are represented in this unit: Chile, China, Ghana, Iraq, Israel, Japan, Philippines, Turkey, Vietnam, and Wales.

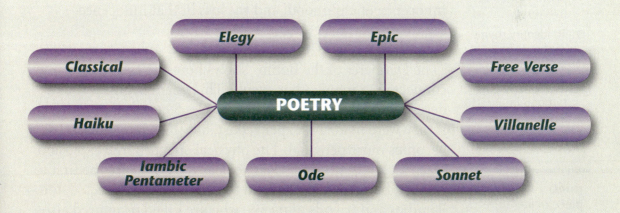

BEFORE READING THE SELECTION

The Diameter of the Bomb   by Yehuda Amichai (trans. by Chana Bloch)

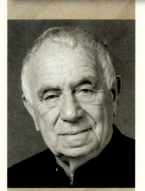

Yehuda Amichai
(1924–2000)
Israeli

Objectives

- To read and understand a poem written in free verse
- To identify rhyme and rhythm in a poem
- To explain the symbols in a poem

poetry a short piece of literature that often has a pattern of rhythm and rhyme and paints powerful or beautiful ideas with words

About the Author

Yehuda Amichai was one of Israel's most important writers. He was born in Würzburg, Germany. His family was Jewish. They left Germany in 1936, after Adolf Hitler came to power, and moved to Jerusalem. Amichai began to publish **poetry** in magazines in the 1940s. He addresses many of his poems to Jerusalem. He also wrote novels, short stories, and plays. He won many awards, including, in 1982, the Israel Prize for poetry. This prize is his country's highest honor. Amichai's works have been translated into more than 20 languages. Much of his poetry is about modern life and the concerns that we face every day. He often writes about the innocence of childhood, and the loss of that innocence.

About the Selection

"The Diameter of the Bomb" shows how one event is connected to many other events. This poem begins by describing the facts about a bomb. The facts are written as if they were in a newspaper report, but the poem quickly becomes more personal. The physical effects of the explosion reach a certain distance. People near the bomb are the first to be hurt, but people far beyond this circle can be affected, too. Families and friends of people who are killed or injured also suffer. In this poem, Amichai takes us along into a widening circle of pain.

Literary Terms This poem is written in **free verse**. That means that it does not **rhyme** or have a regular line length. The poet uses real speech patterns for the **rhythms** of sound. The sentences in this poem are written as if someone were telling a story.

In "The Diameter of the Bomb," the poet uses **symbols** to help the reader feel connected to the subject. A symbol is a person, place, thing, or event that stands for something else. One of the symbols in this poem is the circle. As you read, think about what a circle represents. Look for other symbols, too.

Reading on Your Own As you read the poem, identify and describe the details that help you figure out the poet's point of view. Do you agree with the poet? Why or why not?

Writing on Your Own When something happens to our friends or family, it affects us too. It can be something good, such as winning a trophy or celebrating a birthday. It can also be something bad, such as getting sick or losing a game. Think about a time when you were affected by something that happened to someone you care about. Write a paragraph describing the event and your feelings.

Vocabulary Focus Word choice is especially important in a poem. Poems have fewer words than short stories or novels. Think about the many meanings for the word *circle*. Write a synonym (a word that has the same meaning as another word) for each meaning that is used in this poem. Do you think that the poem would be as powerful if the writer chose one of those synonyms instead? Talk with a partner about your ideas.

Think Before You Read The diameter of a circle is the distance across its center, from one side to the other. What do you predict the poem will be about: facts and figures about bombs, or how bombs affect people? Explain your answer.

---

free verse poetry that does not have a set rhyming pattern or line length; it uses real speech patterns for the rhythms of sound

rhyme words with the same vowel and ending sounds

rhythm a pattern created by the stressed and unstressed syllables in a line of poetry

symbol a person, place, thing, or event that stands for something else

The Diameter of the Bomb

> As you read, look for symbols used by the poet.

The diameter of the bomb was thirty centimeters
and the diameter of its **effective** range about seven meters,
with four dead and eleven wounded.

And around these, in a larger circle
5 of pain and time, two hospitals are scattered
and one **graveyard**. But the young woman
who was buried in the city she came from,
at a distance of more than a hundred
   kilometers,
enlarges the circle considerably,
10 and the **solitary** man mourning her death

at the distant shores of a country far across the sea
includes the entire world in the circle.
And I won't even mention the howl of orphans
that reaches up to the throne of God and
15 beyond, making
a circle with no end and no God.

> The poet uses metric measurements.
> - 30 centimeters = about 1 foot
> - 7 meters = about 23 feet
> - 100 kilometers = about 62 miles

> Why is the man now alone?

> Notice that the lines do not rhyme. This is one feature of free verse.

---

effective true; actual
graveyard a place where people are buried
kilometers distances of 1,000 meters; each equals about .62 mile
enlarges makes bigger
solitary alone

AFTER READING THE SELECTION

The Diameter of the Bomb   by Yehuda Amichai (trans. by Chana Bloch)

Directions Choose the letter of the best answer or write the answer using complete sentences.

Comprehension: Identifying Facts

1. What is the diameter of the bomb?
   A 30 inches   C 7 meters
   B 30 centimeters D 100 kilometers

2. How many people are killed and wounded?

3. Where is one woman buried? Why is she buried there?

Comprehension: Putting Ideas Together

4. Amichai says that the hospitals and graveyard make "a larger circle of pain and time." What does he mean?
   A You can draw a circle from the graveyard to the bomb site.
   B The hospital is farther away from the bomb site than the graveyard.
   C Many more people were in pain at the hospital than just the ones harmed by the bomb.
   D The people hurt and killed make the bomb's effect wider than its blast.

5. How is the entire world brought into the circle?

6. How do you know that some of those killed were parents? Explain.

Understanding Literature: Free Verse

"The Diameter of the Bomb" is written in free verse. Some of the lines may rhyme, but they do not have to. Poems written in free verse do not have set line lengths. The poet uses the wording and sentence patterns of everyday speech. Poets use free verse to "free" themselves from the typical rules of poetry.

7. This poem is written in everyday language, just the way that people talk. What is an example of this?

8. Do you think that the last part of the poem uses more "poetic" language than the first part? Why or why not?

Critical Thinking

9. What do you think is the main idea of "The Diameter of the Bomb"?

Thinking Creatively

10. The poet gives some facts about one bombing. How could this poem describe feelings about other bombings, too?

After Reading continued on next page

AFTER READING THE SELECTION (continued)

The Diameter of the Bomb by Yehuda Amichai (trans. by Chana Bloch)

Grammar Check

Poetry does not always follow the rules of standard grammar. This poem has a run-on sentence. A run-on sentence is two sentences that are punctuated as one. Read the sentence that begins on line 6 and ends on line 12. Rewrite this run-on sentence as two or more sentences. Whose form do you find more poetic, yours or Amichai's?

Writing on Your Own

Think of an event that happened at your school, in your country, or in the world. Write a paragraph telling how that event could have led to other events. For example, you could write about your school's sports team winning a championship. As a result, a student far away from you might be inspired to join her school's team. You could write about a natural disaster in another part of the world. That event could set off other events. For example, a person seeing pictures of the disaster on TV vows to help more in his hometown.

Speaking

Amichai says the bomb affects people around the world. Is the same thing true for acts of kindness? Write a speech about this topic. Decide what kind of speech you want to write. Organize your speech with a beginning, middle, and end. You should clearly state your point of view. Give your speech to your class. Look in Appendix E for suggestions about writing a speech.

Listening

Listen as a partner reads the poem aloud. Why do you think that people say that poetry is meant to be heard, not just read? Talk with your partner about this idea.

Media

This poem begins as if it were a news report. This makes sense because people would expect to read about a bombing in a newspaper. A reporter is one person who works in the media. Who are some other people who work to put together a news report? What do these men and women do? Research some of these careers. Write a report to describe your three favorite jobs in the field of journalism.

BEFORE READING THE SELECTION

Taking Leave of a Friend   by Li Po (trans. by Ezra Pound)

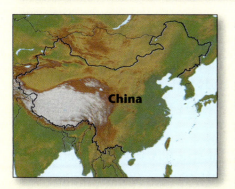

About the Author

Li Po lived more than 1,200 years ago. He is still remembered as one of China's greatest poets. (His name is sometimes spelled Li Bo.) He was a popular poet in his lifetime, too. He was born in what is now Szechwan, in western China. Li Po spent much of his life traveling across China. In about 742, he worked as a poet at the court of the Chinese emperor. Then he went traveling again. He became a poet for one of the emperor's sons, Prince Lin. Later, he got into political trouble. He spent some time in prison but then was freed. Li Po probably wrote about a thousand poems. The poems followed traditional Chinese forms.

Ezra Pound was a well-known American poet. He had a strong influence on English and American poetry in the early 1900s. While living in Paris in the 1920s, Pound translated from Italian, Chinese, and Japanese literature. "Taking Leave of a Friend" is one of the poems he translated. Pound published it in 1909 in his collection titled *Personae*.

Li Po
(701–762)
Chinese

Objectives

- To read and understand a poem
- To identify similes in a poem
- To describe the theme of a poem

About the Selection

This poem is about friends who are traveling together on horseback. The poet describes the beautiful scenery around them. There are mountains nearby with a river flowing around them. Li Po writes about how the friends split up and go separate ways. The poem does not actually tell who the people are. Read to find out how Li Po shows the feelings of the friends without having them speak.

Before Reading continued on next page

BEFORE READING THE SELECTION (continued)

Taking Leave of a Friend   by Li Po (trans. by Ezra Pound)

simile a figure of speech that makes a comparison between two unlike objects using the word *like* or *as*

theme the main idea of a literary work

Literary Terms Many of Li Po's poems are about nature, friendship, and the passing of time. This poem is about two friends who are traveling together in the mountains. Li Po uses **similes** to describe how the friends feel. A simile is a figure of speech that makes a comparison between two unlike objects using the word *like* or *as*.

Even though the poem is short, it still has a strong **theme**. The theme is the main idea of a literary work. Look for clues about the theme as you read. Think about how the friends feel as they say good-bye.

Reading on Your Own As you read, try to picture in your mind what you are reading about. Does this poem make you think of any place that you have ever been? Where was it?

Writing on Your Own Think of a time when you have had to say good-bye to a close friend or relative. Write a letter to that person telling how you felt. As you look back, you may identify feelings you did not know you had at the time.

Vocabulary Focus The word *as* can be used in two very different ways. Sometimes, it means *while* or *during*. It is used differently in a simile. Then, it is used to mean *like* or *similar to*. Find the word *as* in this poem. Is it used for a comparison or to mean *while* or *during*?

Think Before You Read Think of a time when you have said good-bye to a close friend. How did you show your feelings without using words?

356   Unit 4 Poetry

Taking Leave of a Friend

Blue mountains to the north of the walls,
White river winding about them:
Here we must make **separation**
And go out through a thousand miles
    of dead grass.
5   Mind like a floating wide cloud,
Sunset like the parting of old acquaintances
Who bow over their clasped hands at a distance.
Our horses **neigh** to each other
    as we are **departing**.

> Find two similes in the poem.

> As you read, notice how the poet pictures nature.

> Even a short poem has a theme. What is the theme here?

separation the act of leaving one another
neigh the cry of a horse
departing leaving; going away

AFTER READING THE SELECTION

Taking Leave of a Friend by Li Po (trans. by Ezra Pound)

Directions Choose the letter of the best answer or write the answer using complete sentences.

Comprehension: Identifying Facts

1. What color do the mountains seem to be?
   A red
   B white
   C blue
   D green

2. Describe the rest of the scene.

3. To whom do the horses belong?

Comprehension: Putting Ideas Together

4. At what time of day do the friends say good-bye?
   A early morning
   B noon
   C afternoon
   D early evening

5. Do you think the friends will see each other again soon? Use evidence from the poem to explain your answer.

6. Why do the horses neigh to each other?

Understanding Literature: Simile

A simile is a figure of speech that compares two things. Similes use the word *like* or *as* in their comparisons. The two things are unlike in general. But they resemble each other in this one aspect of comparison. For example, the poet Robert Burns compares his love to a flower in this line: "O, my luve's like a red, red rose." By using similes, a poet gives the reader a new way of seeing things.

7. Look for the simile that describes the person's mind. Use your own words to explain the meaning of this simile.

8. What does the poet say is like a sunset?

Critical Thinking

9. Is this a truly sad poem? Explain your answer.

Thinking Creatively

10. Is the place where the friends part a pleasant one? Explain your answer.

Grammar Check

A participle is a verb that is used as an adjective in a sentence. Participles end in -*ing*. Look for the -*ing* words in this poem. Which one is used like an adjective in its sentence? This is a participle.

 Writing on Your Own

Imagine you are one of the two friends in this poem. Write a short poem telling how you feel about leaving your friend. You might include details about where you are going and what your trip will be like.

 Speaking and Listening

Plan to do a group report about this poem. Imagine that these friends have known each other for a very long time. Ask: Who are they? What is their friendship based on? Why must they part? Make sure that each person in your group has something to talk about. Give your report to the class.

Listen to the different group presentations. Take notes for each group. Write down the speakers' names. Describe each person's role in the report. What is that person's point of view?

 Viewing

This poem paints a picture with words. Paint your own picture to represent an image from this poem, or look through art books to find a picture that could go with it. Tell a partner why you chose your picture, or explain why you included certain details in your painting.

BEFORE READING THE SELECTION

Thoughts of Hanoi   by Nguyen Thi Vinh

Objectives

- To read and understand a lyric poem
- To describe an elegy
- To describe the role of the narrator in a poem

About the Author

Nguyen Thi Vinh was born in 1924 in Ha dong Province in North Vietnam. She was one of a group of writers in South Vietnam who became known in the early 1960s. She is best known for her short stories and books of poetry. These works reflect her experiences of the many years of war in Vietnam. She was also very active in Saigon as a publishing executive. She remained in Vietnam during the Communist takeover of South Vietnam in 1975. In 1983, she was able to immigrate to Norway, where several of her family members had settled.

About the Selection

After the end of World War II, Vietnam suffered years of civil war. Its capital city was Hanoi. In 1954, the country was split in two. Communists ruled the North. Hanoi was part of North Vietnam. South Vietnam became a republic and had its own capital, Saigon.

In "Thoughts of Hanoi," Nguyen Thi Vinh looks back to the time before the country was divided. The poem describes everyday events that took place in Hanoi. It also describes how friends became enemies, fighting on opposite sides in the war.

360 Unit 4 Poetry

(trans. by Nguyen Ngoc Bich with Burton Raffel and W. S. Merwin)

Literary Terms "Thoughts of Hanoi" is a **lyric poem**. It has rhythm and expresses one strong emotion, or feeling: grief. The poem describes what Vietnam was like before the war. There is a sadness about what war has taken from the country. This makes the poem a sort of **elegy**. A true elegy is a poem that mourns someone's death. This poem does not mourn a person's death, but the loss of a peaceful city, Hanoi.

A poem can have a **narrator** who is not the poet. The narrator is the teller of the story. In this poem, the narrator talks to a brother who is now fighting on the other side in the war. He asks him about life in Hanoi, Vietnam. Before the war, this city was the capital of the entire country. After the war began, Hanoi became part of North Vietnam. The speaker in this poem is in South Vietnam. Hanoi is no longer his city. The speaker also asks the brother if he is now his friend or his enemy.

Reading on Your Own Before you read this poem, think about how rhythm is important in a poem. Rhythm is a pattern created by the stressed and unstressed syllables in a poem. How would the poem be different if it had little rhythm? Read the poem aloud at least twice to hear its rhythm.

Writing on Your Own Imagine you are grown and have not seen one of your childhood friends for many years. Write a letter to this friend. Remind your friend of some of the things that you used to do together.

Vocabulary Focus This poem gives an image of the gap between the past and the present. It says they are separated by a "frontier of hatred." What is a *frontier*? If you are not sure, use a dictionary to find out. Then explain this image.

Think Before You Read The narrator is remembering happier times before the war. What do you think is the poet's purpose in writing the poem?

---

lyric poem a poem that has rhythm and expresses one strong emotion

elegy a poem that mourns someone's death

narrator the teller of a story

Thoughts of Hanoi

> As you read, notice what the poet is remembering.

The night is deep and chill
as in early autumn. Pitchblack,
it thickens after each lightning flash.
I dream of Hanoi:
5   Co-ngu Road
ten years of separation
the way back sliced by a frontier of hatred.

> Read lines 8–13 aloud. Notice how the poet uses rhythm in this lyric poem.

I want to bury the past
to burn the future
10 still I **yearn**
still I fear
those endless nights
waiting for dawn.
Brother,
15 how is Hang Dao now?
How is Ngoc Son temple?
Do the trains still run
each day from Hanoi
to the neighboring towns?

> *Ngoc Son* ("Jade Mountain") temple is on an island in a lake in the center of Hanoi.

20 To Bac-ninh, Cam-giang, Yen-bai,
the small villages, islands
of brown thatch in a **lush** green sea?

> The poet names some of the towns near Hanoi.

The girls
    bright eyes
25   **ruddy** cheeks
    four-piece dresses
        raven-bill scarves
    sowing harvesting
        spinning weaving
30   all year round,
the boys

> *Ploughing* is another spelling of the word *plowing*.

    ploughing
        transplanting
    in the fields
35   in their shops
    running across
        the meadow at evening
    to fly kites
        and sing alternating songs.

---

yearn wish for deeply   **lush** having lots of plants   **ruddy** having a healthy, reddish color

40 Stainless blue sky,
   jubilant voices of children
stumbling through the alphabet,
   village **graybeards** strolling to the temple,
grandmothers basking in twilight sun,
45   chewing **betel** leaves
while the children run—

Brother,
how is all that now?
Or is it **obsolete**?
50 Are you like me,
   reliving the past,
imagining the future?
Do you count me as a friend
or am I the enemy in your eyes?
55 Brother, I am afraid
that one day I'll be with the March-North Army
meeting you on your way to the South.
I might be the one to shoot you then
or you me
60 but please
not with hatred.

For don't you remember how it was,
you and I in school together,
plotting our lives together?
65 Those roots go deep!

Brother, we are men,
conscious of more
than material needs.
How can this
   happen to us
70 my friend
   my foe?

> What is this elegy mourning more—the loss of a friend or of a city?

> What clues make you think the narrator is a man?

> Why does the narrator in the poem call the person both his friend and his foe?

jubilant happily excited

graybeards old men

betel an Asian plant whose leaves are chewed

obsolete out of date

reliving living over again; remembering

BEFORE READING THE SELECTION

Mindoro by Ramón Sunico

Ramón C. Sunico
(1955–)
Filipino

Objectives

- To read and understand a poem about nature
- To identify the imagery in a poem
- To describe how the setting is important

About the Author

Ramón Sunico was born in 1955 in the Philippines. (He is also called "RayVi.") He is a teacher at a university in the Philippines. Sunico also manages Cacho Publishing House in Manila, Philippines. His company has published fiction and books on medicine and law. He is now especially interested in books for children. He has translated stories from English, German, and Filipino. Sunico wants books to tackle present-day issues. His company publishes stories with themes such as relationships, the environment, and dealing with handicaps. Sunico has won awards for his poetry and for his work in children's literature.

About the Selection

In the poem "Mindoro," some people are riding on a boat. It is late in the day, and the sun begins to set. This poem describes the amazing scenery the people see. Mindoro is the name of a Philippine island. It is a peaceful island full of life. The boaters are returning to Mindoro. As you read this poem, think about how different this island is from the city of Hanoi that Nguyen Thi Vinh wrote about in her poem.

364 Unit 4 Poetry

Literary Terms This poem uses **imagery** to describe a special place. Imagery is the use of word pictures that appeal to the five senses. These senses are sight, sound, touch, smell, and taste.

> **imagery** the use of word pictures that appeal to the five senses
>
> **setting** the time and place in a story

The special place is the Philippine island of Mindoro. In some ways this poem is like "Thoughts of Hanoi." Both poems describe a special place. This makes the **setting** an important part of these poems. The setting is the time and place in a story.

The theme of each poem is different. "Thoughts of Hanoi" is about a city that no longer exists. "Mindoro" celebrates a living island. It uses images of nature, such as mayflies, mountains, and the sea. Look for images that tell you about the life of people living on Mindoro. Is that life hard or easy?

Reading on Your Own Accuracy is an important reading skill. When you are using this skill, you are making sure to read exactly what is written in the poem. You are also taking your time to understand every detail. Use this skill as you read "Mindoro." How can this skill help a reader better understand poetry?

Writing on Your Own Think of a time when you were with friends and did not want to leave to go home. Write about how you felt. What made you want to stay where you were?

Vocabulary Focus Compound words are words made of two separate words. Look for these compound words in the poem: *last-light, oarsman, mayflies, fishhook,* and *afternoon.* Tell how the separate word parts help you figure out the meaning of the compound word.

Think Before You Read What do you hope to learn about the island of Mindoro?

Poetry Unit 4 365

MINDORO

As you read, notice how the imagery makes the poem seem real.

The sun dissolves:
some pieces float
on the green sea
which hurries to darkness.

5   The blood light flickers
while **sporadically**
a wave
slaps against the side of our slippery boat.

The red threads
10 of last-light
dance
on the shoulders of our **oarsman**.

Last-light is a poetic term for the last rays of the sun. What color is the light?

sporadically now and then   **oarsman** the one rowing a boat

No one notices
the stars
15 begin
to cluster like **mayflies**.

The call
of land
to us
20 is sharper than a fishhook:
the rented
home
and dinner steaming.

We are
25 all **mutes**
riding along on this boat.

To the left
the sea
slices the afternoon in two.

30 To the right
the mountains of Mindoro ripen.

> Describe the setting of the poem.

> Why do you think everyone in the boat is quiet?

mayflies insects that hatch in the water and live only a few days

mutes people who cannot talk

AFTER READING THE SELECTIONS

Thoughts of Hanoi by Nguyen Thi Vinh   **Mindoro** by Ramón Sunico

Directions Choose the letter of the best answer or write the answer using complete sentences.

Comprehension: Identifying Facts

1. Where does the narrator live when he writes "Thoughts of Hanoi"?
   A South Vietnam
   B Hanoi
   C North Vietnam
   D Mindoro

2. What time of day is it in the poem "Mindoro"?

3. In "Mindoro," how are the poet and his friends traveling?

Comprehension: Putting Ideas Together

4. Think about the two men in "Thoughts of Hanoi." What did they used to do together?
   A plant trees
   B chew betel leaves
   C dream of the future
   D plan for war

5. In "Mindoro," what are the people thinking about?

6. How are the themes of these two poems different?

Understanding Literature: Imagery

Poets use imagery to create a picture with words. Images usually appeal to the five senses—sight, smell, sound, taste, and touch. This helps the reader better imagine the scene. After all, in real life people use all of their senses. They hear the sounds, taste the foods, feel the breeze, and smell the air all around them. Imagery can touch the reader's feelings. It can also help the reader share what the poet is imagining.

7. Look at "Thoughts of Hanoi." What are some of the sights the poet remembers from before the war?

8. Reread lines 5–8 of "Mindoro." How do these lines help you hear the sounds on the boat?

Critical Thinking

9. Do you think the person in "Thoughts of Hanoi" is really the brother of the person to whom he writes? Why or why not?

Thinking Creatively

10. What would be another good title for "Mindoro"? Explain your answer.

Grammar Check

The poets use colons to separate two main phrases. The phrase after the colon adds detail to the first phrase. Look for the colons in the poems. In each case, tell what the second phrase is explaining.

 Writing on Your Own

Name a place that means a lot to you. Write the words *Sight, Sound, Smell, Taste,* and *Touch.* Now, write a few words telling how each sense is affected when you are in that place. Look at the example below for help. Then use your notes to write a poem or a paragraph about the place.

> Place: park
> Sight: people all around, strollers and bicycles
> Sound: children laughing
> Smell: freshly cut grass
> Taste: cool water from the fountain
> Touch: the feel of sand inside my shoe

 Speaking and Listening

Practice reading "Thoughts of Hanoi" or "Mindoro." Recite the poem for your class. Be sure to say the lines with feeling. Listen to a classmate recite one of the poems. Answer the questions below to rate your listening skills.

- Did you understand the meaning of the poem as your classmate recited it?
- Did you watch your classmate as he or she spoke?
- Did you concentrate on his or her words?

 Technology

Work with a small group to make a video of one of the poems. Decide which poem to act out and record. Be creative as you build props and scenery for your video. You can even have a narrator read the lines of the poem for each scene as it is shown on the video.

 Viewing

Use a Venn Diagram to compare "Thoughts of Hanoi" to "Mindoro." Label one circle "Thoughts of Hanoi." Label the other circle "Mindoro." Write what is different in each poem's space. Write what is the same in the area where the circles overlap. See Appendix A for an example of this graphic organizer.

BEFORE READING THE SELECTION

Ode to a Pair of Socks by Pablo Neruda (trans. by Ken Krabbenhoft)

Pablo Neruda
(1904–1973)
Chilean

Objectives

- To read and understand an ode
- To explain the figurative language in a poem
- To identify surrealism and realism in poetry

About the Author

Pablo Neruda was born in Parral, in the rainy southern part of Chile. (His real name was Neftalí Ricardo Reyes y Basoalto.) During his career, he became Latin America's best-known poet. A book of poems, published in 1924, made him famous. It was called *Twenty Love Poems and a Song of Despair.* At the same time, Neruda worked as a diplomat. A diplomat travels to many countries to work with people and businesses. Over the years, he wrote many books of poetry. One major work is *Canto General,* published in 1950. In 1971, he received the Nobel Prize for Literature. Neruda was active in Chilean politics and the government of Salvador Allende. He was ambassador to France from 1970 to 1972. He died in 1973 in Santiago, Chile.

About the Selection

This poem comes from *Odes to Common Things* (a translation published in 1994). In the poem, Neruda describes a pair of socks. He writes about how special they are. He also tells how they make his feet seem ugly in comparison. He wonders if he should even put these special socks on his feet. Read to see how Neruda makes a poem from such a simple topic as a pair of socks.

Literary Terms One critic calls Neruda "many poets in one." His poetry changed during his lifetime. He began as a symbolist poet, using many symbols to represent his thoughts. He moved from there to **surrealism**. This is a writing style that has a dreamlike quality and odd, unexpected images.

In the 1950s, Neruda changed his writing style and moved toward **realism** in his poetry. He looked at everyday objects and saw wonder in them. He wrote several books of **odes** to ordinary things. An ode is a poem that praises someone or something. Neruda described the objects using **figurative language**. His comparisons were not meant to be understood exactly as they are written. Similes and metaphors are examples of figurative language.

Reading on Your Own Sometimes, when you read something, it does not make sense. You may have read a word incorrectly, or maybe you missed a punctuation mark. If anything in this poem does not make sense, stop reading. Reread that section again. Did you make any mistakes as you read this poem the first time? What were they? How could you make fewer mistakes next time you read a poem?

Writing on Your Own Have you ever had a favorite shirt or pair of pants? Write about how hard it was to finally give up that piece of clothing, or tell why you refuse to give it up.

Vocabulary Focus Write down the words *outrageous* and *incandescent*. Use a dictionary to find the meaning of each word. Write a synonym for the word or a short phrase that explains it. Then find the words in the poem. Rewrite these lines of the poem using your synonyms or phrases.

Think Before You Read This poem praises an ordinary pair of socks. As you read, think about the poet's purpose. Does he make you see the socks as something wonderful?

---

surrealism a writing style that has a dreamlike quality and odd, unexpected images

realism a writing style that looks at ordinary people and objects

ode a poem in praise of someone or something

figurative language writing or speech not meant to be understood exactly as it is written; writers use figurative language to express ideas in imaginative ways

Ode to a Pair of Socks

Look for figurative language as you read.

Maru Mori brought me
a pair
of socks
that she knit with her
5 shepherd's hands.

Here is a realistic image.

Two socks as soft
as rabbit fur.
I thrust my feet
inside them
10 as if they were
two
little boxes
knit
from threads

This is an example of a surreal image.

15 of sunset
and sheepskin.

My feet were
two woolen
fish
20 in those **outrageous** socks,
two **gangly**,
navy-blue sharks
impaled
on a golden thread,
25 two giant blackbirds,
two cannons:

What does the poet first think about doing with the new socks? What does he do instead?

thus
were my feet
honored
30 by
those
heavenly
socks.
They were
35 so beautiful
I found my feet
unlovable
for the very first time,
like two **crusty** old
40 firemen, firemen
unworthy
of that embroidered
fire,
those **incandescent**
45 socks.

Nevertheless
I fought
the sharp temptation
to put them away
50 the way schoolboys
put
fireflies in a bottle,

---

outrageous extreme
gangly tall, thin, and ungraceful
impaled speared; stuck on a sharp stick

unlovable difficult to love
crusty gruff; stern in manner
unworthy not deserving

incandescent glowing; very bright
nevertheless however

372 Unit 4 Poetry

the way scholars
hoard
55 **holy writ**.
I fought
the mad urge
to lock them
in a golden
60 cage
and feed them birdseed
and **morsels** of pink melon
every day.
Like jungle
65 explorers
who deliver a young deer
of the rarest species
to the roasting **spit**
then **wolf** it down
70 in shame,
I stretched
my feet forward
and pulled on
those
75 gorgeous
socks,
and over them
my shoes.
So this is
80 the moral of my ode:
beauty is beauty
twice over
and good things are doubly
good
85 when you're talking about a
pair of wool
socks
in the dead of winter.

> Why might socks be doubly good in winter?

> How does this ode praise socks? Is the poet serious or is he trying to be funny?

hoard save for the future

holy writ a piece of religious writing such as the Bible

morsels small bits of food

spit a narrow rod that holds meat to be cooked over a fire

wolf eat hungrily, like an animal

AFTER READING THE SELECTION

Ode to a Pair of Socks by Pablo Neruda (trans. by Ken Krabbenhoft)

Directions Choose the letter of the best answer or write the answer using complete sentences.

Comprehension: Identifying Facts

1. How does Neruda get the socks?
   A He buys them in a store.
   B He knits them.
   C Someone else buys them in a store.
   D Someone else knits them for him.

2. What are the socks made of?

3. What does the poet finally do with the socks?

Comprehension: Putting Ideas Together

4. Why do the poet's feet suddenly seem "unlovable"?
   A His feet smell like fish.
   B His feet look ugly next to the socks.
   C He has fallen in love with Maru Mori's feet.
   D The socks do not fit his feet.

5. Why does the poet think about putting the socks away?

6. What does the poet say about beauty in his moral?

Understanding Literature: Figurative Language

Poets often use figurative language. This is language that makes a comparison but is not meant to be taken literally, or exactly as it is written. It is also called a "figure of speech." Two kinds of figurative language are similes and metaphors. Both make comparisons. A simile uses *like* or *as*. A metaphor says one thing *is* another. For example, Neruda says, "My feet were two woolen fish . . ." Clearly, this is not a literal comparison. His feet are not fish. But the words make a picture so that you see the object differently.

7. When the poet first gets the socks, he compares them to something. Write the words he uses about the socks themselves.

8. Besides fish, Neruda compares his feet to other things. Name two of them.

Critical Thinking

9. How do you think the knitter would feel about this poem? Explain your answer.

Thinking Creatively

10. What kind of person do you think Pablo Neruda was? Base your answer on what you read in this poem.

Grammar Check

A fragment is a phrase that is written as a complete sentence but does not make a complete thought. A fragment can be used in poetry in one of two ways. First, the fragment may flow naturally in the text of the poem. The reader may not even notice that it is a fragment. Second, the fragment can cause a reader to stop and reread it. A poet might do this to get a reader to pay close attention to something. Read lines 6 and 7. Which way does this fragment work in the poem?

 Writing on Your Own

Think of something ordinary that you like. Why do you like it so much? Write a short poem or paragraph about it. Tell what it is and how it makes you feel.

 Speaking

Pretend that you won a contest for the piece you wrote for the writing activity. Imagine you are going to be reading your poem or paragraph at an awards banquet. Rehearse how you will read this aloud by reading it to a friend or family member. Practice how you will walk on and off the stage. Practice making eye contact with your audience. Practice reading slowly and clearly.

 Listening

Listen as your teacher reads this poem aloud to the class. Write a review of the poem. Do not look back at the poem. Base your review only on what you heard.

 Research

You know that Pablo Neruda wrote many odes to everyday items. Go to the library and find an English translation of *Odes to Common Things*. Read at least three of Neruda's odes. Which ode do you like best? Write a report about this ode and tell why you chose it.

BEFORE READING THE SELECTIONS

Three Haiku   by Basho (trans. by Olivia Gray);

About the Authors

Basho made **haiku** a respected poetry form in Japan. He was born in 1644 into a samurai, or warrior, family. Until his early 20s he served as a samurai warrior. Among samurai, writing poetry was an admired skill. Later, Basho turned entirely to writing and teaching. He used different pen names. His pen name Basho comes from a kind of banana tree that grew near where he lived.

Basho
(1644–1694)
Japanese

Japan

Takarai Kikaku was born in 1661. He became one of Basho's students. Some of Kikaku's works have been put to music. Writing poetry was so important in Japanese society that poets competed. Basho and Kikaku often wrote verses on the same themes. Often they answered each other's verses. One story says that they were sitting in a garden together when Basho wrote the haiku that appears on page 378.

We do not know who wrote the third haiku. The word *anonymous* means "not known."

About the Selections

These poems are about different animals. The poems tell what the animals are doing. Since the poems are short, you will need to read them very carefully. Think about what the poet could mean by each description.

Objectives

- To read and understand some of the first haiku ever written
- To explain the features of a haiku
- To understand why a translated haiku might not follow the rules
- To understand the meaning of onomatopoeia

haiku a form of Japanese poetry having three lines with five syllables in the first, seven in the second, and five in the third

by Kikaku (trans. by Harry Behn); by Anonymous (trans. by Harry Behn)

Literary Terms These poems are traditional Japanese haiku. This is a form of Japanese poetry having three lines with five syllables in the first, seven in the second, and five in the third. When a poem is translated from Japanese into English, it may not always follow this rule. The English words may not have the same number of syllables as the Japanese words.

onomatopoeia the use of words that sound like their meaning

One of the poems also uses **onomatopoeia**. This is a word that sounds like its meaning, such as *buzz* or *hiss*. Look for the use of onomatopoeia in the haiku. Notice the number of syllables it has in English. How many syllables would its Japanese word have?

Reading on Your Own Compare and contrast the three haiku as you read them. How are they alike? How are they different?

Writing on Your Own In Basho's time, poetry writing was an honored skill among samurai soldiers. Do you think that writing poetry should be an important skill for American soldiers today? Why or why not? Write a letter to the U.S. Army. Tell why soldiers should (or should not) write poetry.

Vocabulary Focus Find the onomatopoeia in the haiku. What sounds would you hear if you could listen to the animals in the other haiku? Write a word or phrase using onomatopoeia for each of these sounds.

Think Before You Read Think about the animals described in these poems—a frog, a rooster, and a bird. What do you think the poets will say about these animals?

Poetry Unit 4

Three Haiku

> The first poem does not have five syllables in the first and third lines. How can it be a haiku?

Ancient pool. Sound
of a frog's leap—
Splissssshhhhh. . . .

—Basho

> Where is the onomatopoeia in the haiku?

A **bantam** rooster
spreading his **ruff** of feathers
thinks he's a lion!

—Kikaku

> What is the mood of this poem?

Small bird, forgive me.
I'll hear the end of your song
in some other world.

—Anonymous

bantam a small barnyard fowl

ruff a collar that stands out from the neck

AFTER READING THE SELECTIONS

Three Haiku   by Basho, Kikaku, Anonymous

Directions Choose the letter of the best answer or write the answer using complete sentences.

Comprehension: Identifying Facts

1. What does the rooster think he is?
   - **A** a bantam
   - **B** a frog
   - **C** a bird
   - **D** a lion

2. Name the three animals in the three poems.

3. What is the setting of the haiku by Basho?

Comprehension: Putting Ideas Together

4. Why does Kikaku say the rooster thinks he is a lion?
   - **A** The rooster likes to cool off in a pool.
   - **B** The rooster fans his feathers as if they were a mane.
   - **C** The rooster roars like a lion.
   - **D** The rooster lives with lions.

5. What does the poet ask the small bird to do?

6. Why do you think the bird has stopped singing?

Understanding Literature: Haiku

Haiku is a Japanese poetry form. It has a strict style. A haiku is three lines long. The first line has five syllables. The middle line has seven syllables. The last line has five syllables. (When a haiku is translated from Japanese, the syllable count may not be the same.) A haiku uses images and the power of suggestion to create emotion. Usually it draws images from nature. It may give a "snapshot" of a single image. A snapshot is a quick view of something that lasts a short time.

7. Choose two of these poems. Compare the "snapshots" in them. Do you think the poets have similar feelings about nature? Why or why not?

8. Describe the emotion of the poem you did *not* use for number 7 above.

Critical Thinking

9. How does the poet make the rooster seem funny?

Thinking Creatively

10. Which haiku do you like best? Explain your answer.

After Reading continued on next page

AFTER READING THE SELECTIONS (continued)

Three Haiku   by Basho, Kikaku, Anonymous

 Grammar Check

Some haiku are written in sentence form. Many are not. The first haiku on page 378 has no verbs. Write your own sentences to tell what happens in this haiku.

 Writing on Your Own

Think of some beautiful images from nature. Some of the most beautiful haiku are about very small things in nature. Write a haiku to show them. Do not try to crowd too many images into your haiku. Use at least two images, but no more than three. Try to create a certain mood in your poem.

 Speaking and Listening

Describe to a partner your experiences trying to write a haiku. Tell why it was easy or hard, giving examples from your experience.

Read your partner's haiku from the Speaking activity silently to yourself. Then listen as your partner reads the haiku aloud. How did the poet read the poem differently than you?

 Media

Imagine your class is going to have a poetry reading. You need music for the event. What kind of music will you use while people are arriving? What kind of music will you play while you read the haiku? First, decide on the type of music. Then, pick several songs. Practice for your reading. Play the background music. Record yourself reading the poem. Do you like the music you chose? If not, choose something else and record it again.

BEFORE READING THE SELECTION

Do Not Go Gentle Into That Good Night by Dylan Thomas

About the Author

Dylan Thomas was born in 1914 in Swansea, in southwest Wales. Wales, like England, is part of the United Kingdom. Thomas left school when he was 16 and worked as a newspaper reporter. He began writing poetry as a young man. His first book of poems was published when he was 20. His poetry shows an intense energy and love of life. He used language and rhythm musically. Thomas's short stories and plays also show a love of words. The radio play *Under Milk Wood* describes a day in a Welsh village. Audiences loved to hear Thomas read his own works aloud. He made several tours in the United States in the early 1950s.

Dylan Thomas
(1914–1953)
Welsh

About the Selection

In this poem, Thomas describes his feelings about death. He calls death "that good night." The poet gives advice about how to deal with this final stage of life. He is writing this poem to older people. He does not want them to just give in and accept death quietly. Read to find out how Thomas does want people to act in the face of death.

Objectives

- To read and understand a villanelle
- To identify the parts of a poem, such as rhyme scheme and stanza
- To explain iambic pentameter

Before Reading continued on next page

Poetry Unit 4 **381**

BEFORE READING THE SELECTION (continued)

Do Not Go Gentle Into That Good Night   by Dylan Thomas

villanelle a 19-line poem with several repeating rhymes

rhyme scheme a pattern of end rhymes in a poem

stanza a group of lines that form a unit in a poem and often have the same rhythm and rhyme

iambic pentameter five two-beat sounds in a line of poetry where the second syllable is stressed in each pattern

Literary Terms "Do Not Go Gentle Into That Good Night" is a fine example of a **villanelle**. A villanelle is a form of poetry first used in France in the 1500s. It has 19 rhymed lines. They follow a pattern of repeating rhymes. This pattern is called the **rhyme scheme**. A villanelle has five **stanzas** of three lines and one stanza of four lines. A stanza is a group of lines that form a unit in a poem.

The rhythm of "Do Not Go Gentle Into That Good Night" is called **iambic pentameter**. This means that there are five two-beat sounds in each line. The second syllable is stressed in each pattern. Two of the lines in this poem are repeated four times each. As you read, watch for these lines.

Reading on Your Own Use the stress marks to help you read the first two lines of the poem.

> Do nót go géntle ínto thát good níght,
> Old áge should búrn and ráve at clóse of dáy;

Read the whole poem aloud. Remember to follow the same rhythm that you used for the first two lines. Did reading the poem this way make it easier to understand? Why or why not?

Writing on Your Own What is something that you think all people should fight against? Write a short paragraph about it.

Vocabulary Focus The connotation of a word is the way it makes the reader feel. This gives a word an emotional meaning. A word also has a denotation. This is its dictionary definition. Look for the words *burn* and *rage* in the poem. What are the connotations of these words? Choose a synonym for each word. Rewrite those lines of the poem using the synonyms. Does this change the meaning of the poem?

Think Before You Read Read the title of the poem. What do you think this poem will say about dealing with death?

Do Not Go Gentle Into That Good Night

Do not go gentle into that good night,
Old age should burn and **rave** at close of day;
Rage, rage against the dying of the light.

Though wise men at their end know dark is right,
5   Because their words had forked no lightning they
Do not go gentle into that good night.

Good men, the last wave by, crying how bright
Their frail deeds might have danced in a green bay,
Rage, rage against the dying of the light.

10 Wild men who caught and sang the sun in flight,
And learn, too late, they **grieved** it on its way,
Do not go gentle into that good night.

Grave men, near death, who see with blinding sight
Blind eyes could blaze like meteors and be gay,
15 Rage, rage against the dying of the light.

> As you read, remember that the poem is written in iambic pentameter.

> "Forked no lightning" means that their words had not lit up the world, like a lightning flash.

> How do the rhyme scheme and stanzas make this poem a villanelle?

rave speak wildly
rage speak furiously
grieved caused harm or sadness
grave serious

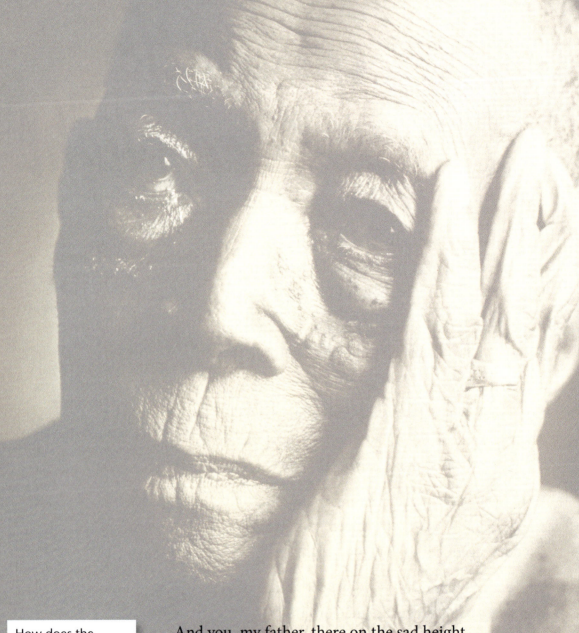

> How does the poet want his father to feel about dying?

And you, my father, there on the sad height,
Curse, bless, me now with your fierce tears, I pray.
Do not go gentle into that good night.
Rage, rage against the dying of the light.

AFTER READING THE SELECTION

Do Not Go Gentle Into That Good Night by Dylan Thomas

Directions Choose the letter of the best answer or write the answer using complete sentences.

Comprehension: Identifying Facts

1. How does the poet say that people should behave when death is near?
   A fight death and hold onto life
   B breathe their last in silence
   C accept death as natural
   D act as if they do not care

2. Why do wise men hold onto life so strongly?

3. To whom is Thomas writing this poem?

Comprehension: Putting Ideas Together

4. What do the words "dark is right" mean?
   A Only old people die.
   B Death will only come during the night.
   C Death will come gently.
   D Death is a natural part of life.

5. What four kinds of men does the poet name?

6. What is the theme, or main idea, of the poem?

Understanding Literature: Rhyme Scheme

The rhyme scheme is the pattern of rhymes in a poem. This poem is a villanelle. Its first five stanzas have three lines. The first and third lines rhyme. This rhyme scheme, or pattern, is *a b a*. The letter *a* stands for the lines whose last words rhyme with night. In the last stanza, the first, third, and fourth lines rhyme. The rhyme scheme for the last stanza is *a b a a*.

7. Look at the third stanza. What two words rhyme?

8. Look at the second line of each stanza. What rhyming words do you find at the ends of the lines?

Critical Thinking

9. What regrets keep both wise men and good men from dying quietly?

Thinking Creatively

10. Thomas wrote this poem for his father, who was dying. How do you think the poet feels about his father? Explain your answer.

After Reading **continued on next page**

AFTER READING THE SELECTION (continued)

Do Not Go Gentle Into that Good Night — by Dylan Thomas

 Grammar Check

An adverb is a word that tells how or when something is done. It describes the verb. Many adverbs end in *-ly*. In this poem, gentle acts as an adverb. *Gentle* is really an adjective, and the correct form should be *gently*. Would you like the poem as much if it were "Do Not Go Gently Into That Good Night"?

 Writing on Your Own

Do you agree with the poet about what a dying person should do? Why or why not? Write a paragraph telling your own outlook.

 Speaking and Listening

Read the paragraph you wrote for Writing on Your Own to a group of students. Let the group ask you questions about your paragraph and your ideas. Answer their questions and explain your thinking.

Listen to other students as they read their paragraphs. Take notes to help you understand their ideas. Jot down notes about any questions you have while they are speaking. When they are done speaking, see if you still have the same questions. (Sometimes a speaker answers the questions later in the speech.) Ask your questions politely. Make sure you understand the answers.

 Viewing

Use a Concept Map to show the ideas from this poem. Write *death* or *that good night* in the center hexagon. In the areas outside the hexagon, write the different things that Thomas wrote about dealing with death. Use your own words to explain each of the poet's ideas. Look at the Concept Map in Appendix A to see an example of this graphic organizer.

BEFORE READING THE SELECTION

The Bird's Last Flight   by Saadi Youssef (trans. from Arabic by Khaled Mattawa)

About the Author

Saadi Youssef was born in 1934 in Iraq. Many consider him the most important poet in the Arab world. He has been writing for more than 50 years. His works include short stories, essays, a novel, and more than 30 books of poetry. Youssef has also translated many great works of literature from other languages into Arabic. He has spent time in jail for his political views and his writing. He has worked as a teacher, journalist, and publisher. He left Iraq in 1979 and now lives in London, England.

About the Selection

This poem comes from a collection called *Seven Poems*. Youssef wrote "The Bird's Last Flight" in 1995. In this poem, we hear a bird thinking about how it will feel when it dies. The bird thinks it will not be sad. It asks others not to be sad, either. As you read the poem, pay attention to how you feel about what the bird is thinking and saying. Also think about any larger ideas the poet might be trying to express.

Saadi Youssef
(1934–)
Iraqi

Objectives

- To read and understand personification in a poem
- To identify the metaphors in a poem
- To explain the symbols in a poem

Before Reading continued on next page

BEFORE READING THE SELECTION (continued)

The Bird's Last Flight by Saadi Youssef (trans. from Arabic by Khaled Mattawa)

personification giving human characteristics to a nonhuman object

symbolism the use of a person, place, or thing to represent something larger than itself

metaphor a figure of speech that says one thing is another; it makes a comparison, but no words of comparison (*like* or *as*) are used

Literary Terms Saadi Youssef uses **personification** in this poem. He gives human characteristics to a nonhuman object. In this case, that nonhuman object is a bird. The bird is the narrator of this poem. Read what the bird has to say about its death. Think about whether or not its thoughts are the kinds of things people expect birds to have.

Saadi Youssef also uses **symbolism** in this poem. Symbolism is the use of a person, place, or thing to represent something larger than itself. Some of the symbols are explained. Others are not. The poem uses **metaphors**, or figures of speech that say one thing is something else. They do not use words of comparison (*like* or *as*).

Reading on Your Own This poem is about the serious topic of death. As you read the poem, think of how you would identify it. Is it a poem about nature or a poem about life and death? How else could you identify this poem?

Writing on Your Own Imagine that you have to write a poem about yourself. The only rule is that you have to use an animal to represent you. Which animal would you choose? Write your answer in your journal. Tell why you chose that animal.

Vocabulary Focus In this poem, the bird is going to "the earth's nest." What do you usually think of when you think of a bird's nest? Describe it in a paragraph. Are these the ideas that you would use if you were describing a grave site? Why do you think the poet chose these words?

Think Before You Read Before you read the poem, think about some of the birds you see every day. What do you think you will find out about the bird in this poem?

THE BIRD'S LAST FLIGHT

When I enter the earth's nest
contented
and glad,
my wings resting,
5 I will free my eyelids so not to see
the trees swaying nearer.
Do not cry over me.
I said do not cry.
If you wish, remember that my wings
10 are water
and there is no water without waves
and no waves without a shore where they crash.

> What does the earth's nest symbolize?

> What metaphor does the bird use to describe its wings?

> What is one human trait the poet gives to the bird?

I rest here
contented
15 and glad
to have reached the last shore.
Do not cry.
Even the sound of my breathing cannot reach me . . .

AFTER READING THE SELECTION

The Bird's Last Flight by Saadi Youssef (trans. from Arabic by Khaled Mattawa)

Directions Choose the letter of the best answer or write the answer using complete sentences.

Comprehension: Identifying Facts

1. How does the bird feel about its death?
   A scared   C happy
   B sad   D regretful

2. Why can the bird not see what is happening around it?

3. What does the bird say that the reader should not do?

Comprehension: Putting Ideas Together

4. Where is the bird going?
   A to its nest in the tree
   B to its burial ground
   C to the beach
   D to the bottom of the ocean

5. What is "the last shore"?

6. Why can the bird not hear its breathing?

Understanding Literature: Symbolism

Symbolism is the use of a person, place, or thing to represent something larger than itself. For example, the Statue of Liberty represents the United States. It is a symbol of the United States. It is also a symbol of immigration and freedom. Sometimes, poets use objects and places to symbolize, or stand for, ideas and emotions. A poet can describe the object or place with the symbolism in mind. The features of the object can help the reader figure out what it symbolizes.

7. What do the water and the waves symbolize in this poem?

8. Why do you think the poet uses a bird, and not a person, to tell this poem?

Critical Thinking

9. Why do you think the bird does not want anyone to cry?

Thinking Creatively

10. What do you think "free my eyelids" means? Read lines 5–6. What do you think of the poet's choice of the word *free* in these lines? Why do you think he wrote it this way?

After Reading **continued on next page**

Poetry Unit 4

AFTER READING THE SELECTION (continued)

The Bird's Last Flight   by Saadi Youssef (trans. from Arabic by Khaled Mattawa)

Grammar Check

Sentences can have dependent and independent clauses. An independent clause can be a sentence all by itself. A dependent clause cannot. Many dependent clauses begin with the words *after, if, since, when,* or *where.* The poem begins with a dependent clause. Can you identify it? What is the independent clause that it is connected to?

Writing on Your Own

Choose one image from this poem that you really like. Write a paragraph about your thoughts.

Speaking

Pretend that the Board of Education has to narrow down a long list of poems to teach. They are deciding whether to teach this one in your school. What is your opinion? Write a speech giving three reasons for your opinion. Give your speech to the class as if they were the Board of Education.

Listening

Work with your class to prepare a form to use when judging a speech. The form will list all of the things that make a successful speech. You will use this form as you listen to each other give your presentations. Listen to your classmates speak. Fill in the form. Give your classmates helpful hints for next time. Do not say, "You never looked at me." Instead, say, "Try to make better eye contact next time."

Research

Many poets write about the approach of death. Do research to find four other poems about this subject. Compare and contrast the poems. Look for common images in the poems. Then find ways that the poems are different from each other. Do they express great fear? Do the poets welcome death? Do some poets take a humorous approach? Write a paragraph about what you found in your research.

BEFORE READING THE SELECTION

Mawu of the Waters by Abena Busia

About the Author

Abena Busia was born in Accra, Ghana, in Africa. She has lived in Ghana, Holland, and Mexico. Then, Busia's family moved to England. Today, Busia writes poetry and is an English professor in the United States.

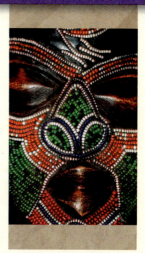

She co-directed a project called "Women Writing Africa." This project collected songs and other oral stories from all over Africa. Many of these songs and stories were put in a book. One song tells the story of what happened when the British came to take slaves from Ghana. The facts are so clear that Busia has been able to date the exact year the song was first sung. Busia is very interested in women's issues, especially in Africa. She teaches African and English literature at Rutgers University in New Jersey.

Objectives

- To read and understand a myth told in the form of a poem
- To describe imagery and symbols in a poem

About the Selection

Abena Busia wrote "Mawu of the Waters" to tell about Mawu. Mawu is an African goddess of the Fon people of West Africa. She represents the moon, while her partner Liza represents the sun. Some believe Mawu and Liza created the universe. This poem describes how Mawu made the oceans. Busia says that this poem is not really about creation but shows the power that women have to create things. Keep this in mind as you read the poem.

Before Reading continued on next page

BEFORE READING THE SELECTION (continued)

Mawu of the Waters by Abena Busia

myth a story that explains how some things in the natural world came to be

Literary Terms This poem is based on a **myth** from the Fon people. A myth is a story that explains how some things in the natural world came to be. This poem tells how lakes, rivers, and oceans were created. Mawu is the creator and goddess. This poem's imagery helps the reader see Mawu as she works. Imagery is the use of word pictures that appeal to the five senses.

Mawu is more than just a mythical goddess. In this poem she is a symbol of women. A symbol is something that stands for something else. Mawu represents women and their creative power.

Reading on Your Own Think of other symbols you know about. If Mawu is a symbol of women, what qualities of women do you think the poet will write about?

Writing on Your Own Think of a symbol in your own life. It can be political, religious, or social. In your journal, name the symbol. Tell what it represents to you.

Vocabulary Focus Some words can be used both as nouns and as verbs. Look for these examples from the poem: *curls, cup, fling, springs,* and *surge.* Which of these words are used as nouns? Which are used as verbs?

Think Before You Read Busia says that her poem is more about the power of women to create than it is about the creation of the world. Do you think "Mawu of the Waters" is a creation myth? Explain your answer.

Mawu of the Waters

Abstract Face, **by Polyakov.**

I am Mawu of the Waters.
With mountains as my footstool
and stars in my curls
I reach down to **reap** the waters with my fingers
5   and look! I cup lakes in my palms.
I fling oceans around me like a shawl
and I am **transformed**
into a waterfall.
Springs flow through me
10   and spill rivers at my feet
as fresh streams **surge**
to make seas.

> Notice how Mawu symbolizes women and their creative power.

> Read carefully to find out what this myth explains.

> How does this poem appeal to the reader's sense of touch?

reap get a reward; gather something in
transformed changed
surge rise up from the ground

AFTER READING THE SELECTION

Mawu of the Waters by Abena Busia

Directions Choose the letter of the best answer or write the answer using complete sentences.

Comprehension: Identifying Facts

1. How does Mawu make lakes?
   A She flings the oceans around her shoulders.
   B She speaks them into being.
   C She cries big tears.
   D She cups the water in her hands.

2. Describe what Mawu looks like.

3. What changes Mawu into a waterfall?

Comprehension: Putting Ideas Together

4. How are the seas made, according to the myth?
   A They are knit like a shawl.
   B Springs flow through Mawu.
   C They come from the mountains.
   D Lakes change into seas.

5. Where is Mawu sitting?

6. From where do the fresh streams come?

Understanding Literature: Myth

A myth is a story or poem that explains how some things in the natural world came to be. At their most meaningful, myths try to explain creation and death. Some myths also retell the adventures of heroes. The literature of groups of people around the world is rooted in myth. A myth differs from a legend in that it has less background in history. It is not like a fable, which usually teaches a lesson.

7. What part of creation does this myth try to explain? How does this show the power of Mawu, and the power of women?

8. A myth explains how things in the natural world came to be. A fable is a short story or poem with a moral. A legend is a traditional story handed down through generations; it features real events or places. How can you tell that this poem is a myth and not a fable or a legend?

Critical Thinking

9. Did you like this poem? Why or why not?

Thinking Creatively

10. Abena Busia wanted to show women's power to create. Why do you think she chose an African goddess?

Grammar Check

Punctuation marks can help a reader understand the meaning of a poem. An exclamation point at the end of a sentence shows excitement or strong feelings. The poet uses an exclamation point in line 5. The next few lines seem to show why Busia is so excited. She could have used a colon instead of an exclamation point. (Remember that a colon can be used to tell the reader that a list or details are coming.) How would this have changed the meaning of the poem?

Writing on Your Own

People are different from animals in many ways. We can think about the future, and we can make things. What amazes you most about people? Write a poem or short story about it.

Speaking

Meet with a partner. Read "Mawu of the Waters" as if you lived thousands of years ago and were telling the children of the Fon people the story of creation.

Listening

Listen to your partner read the poem in the Speaking activity. Did he or she give a sense of the wonder and greatness of Mawu? Tell your partner your response to the reading. Give feedback in a positive way.

Research and Technology

Abena Busia does more than write poetry about African myths. She also teaches people about the slave trade in Ghana and Benin. She even took high school teachers on a trip to these two countries. The teachers learned with Busia all about the slave routes. Do some research to learn more about this trip by visiting the Web site for the Center for African Studies at Rutgers University. Use a desktop publishing program to make a brochure about the trip. Include pictures and details in your brochure.

BEFORE READING THE SELECTION

Some Advice to Those Who Will Serve Time in Prison

Objectives

- To read and understand a poem that is a dramatic monologue
- To identify concrete and abstract images

About the Author

Nazim Hikmet was born in 1902 in Salonika, in what is now Greece. At that time, this city was part of the Ottoman Empire. In 1919, at the end of World War I, the Ottoman Empire was split up. Salonika then became part of Turkey. During this time, Hikmet began writing poetry. His poetry has been translated into many different languages. In the 1920s, Hikmet went to the University of Moscow. He also joined the Turkish Communist Party.

In 1938, Hikmet was sent to jail for his political views. He was actually sentenced to more than 28 years in prison. People around the world were upset about what happened to Hikmet. They spoke out against the Turkish government. This public pressure helped Hikmet. The government let him out of jail in 1950. Hikmet was still afraid the government might have him killed. He fled the country. Over the next several years, Hikmet lived in different Communist countries. He died in Moscow in 1963.

About the Selection

Hikmet wrote this poem in 1949. By that time, he had spent more than 10 years in jail. He wrote this poem to other political prisoners, people who are jailed for their ideas. Sometimes, these ideas are about overthrowing a government. Sometimes, they are just ideas the government does not like. Many political prisoners write about their ideas. Other political prisoners are people who speak about their beliefs. Either way, Hikmet wants them to be strong in jail. Most of the poem tells about things they should and should not do.

by Nazim Hikmet (trans. by Randy Blasing and Mutlu Konuk)

Literary Terms This poem is a **dramatic monologue**. That means that the poet talks directly to the readers. In this poem, the poet tells prisoners how to live in prison. He gives advice about things the prisoners should do—and try not to do.

Some of Hikmet's advice deals with **concrete images**. Concrete images refer to people and things that can be reached with the five senses. Hikmet also writes about **abstract images**. These are images that describe thoughts or feelings. They cannot be reached by the five senses. Some examples of abstract images are hunger, anger, or love.

Reading on Your Own Look for the author's purpose as you read. Why do you think Hikmet wrote this poem?

Writing on Your Own What is something you have learned about life through your experiences? Write a letter to a friend. Give your friend some advice. Use your experiences to help you write the letter.

Vocabulary Focus Many people confuse the words *hanged* and *hung*. These are both past tense forms of *hang*. They do not mean the same thing. Use *hung* for an object. Use *hanged* for a person being put to death by hanging.

	Present Tense	Past Tense
(object)	Please hang that picture on the wall.	I hung the picture for you.
(person)	When will they hang the murderer?	They hanged the murderer yesterday.

Think Before You Read This poem gives advice to prisoners about how to survive in prison. The poet himself spent time in prison because of his political views. What types of things do you think this poem will talk about?

dramatic monologue
a poem in which a character talks to the reader

concrete image
an image that refers to people and things that can be reached by the five senses

abstract image
an image that refers to something general, a state of being, or a quality that cannot be reached by the five senses

Poetry Unit 4

Some Advice to Those Who Will Serve Time in Prison

> Remember this is a dramatic monologue. Imagine that the poet is speaking to you.

If instead of being hanged by the neck
   you're thrown inside
   for not giving up hope
in the world, your country, your people,
5   if you do ten or fifteen years
   apart from the time you have left,
you won't say,
   "Better I had swung from the end of a rope like a flag"—
You'll put your foot down and live.

> How does the poet explain why he is in jail?

10 It may not be a pleasure exactly,
   but it's your **solemn** duty
      to live one more day
         to **spite** the enemy.
Part of you may live alone inside,
15   like a stone at the bottom of a well.

> Here is an abstract image. What does it mean to "put your foot down and live"?

But the other part
      must be so caught up
      in the **flurry** of the world
      that you shiver there inside
20   when outside, at forty days' distance, a leaf moves.
To wait for letters inside,
to sing sad songs,
or to lie awake all night staring at the ceiling
   is sweet but dangerous.

> Notice how the poet does not tell how far the leaf is in miles. A prisoner will know distance by the time it takes to walk that far. How far is "forty days' distance"?

solemn serious; important in a religious way

spite to show ill will

flurry burst of activity

Prisoner of the State,
by Eastman Johnson.

25 Look at your face from shave to shave,
    forget your age,
    watch out for lice
        and for spring nights,
    and always remember
30   to eat every last piece of bread—
    also, don't forget to laugh **heartily**.
    And who knows,
    the woman you love may stop loving you.
    Don't say it's no big thing:
35 it's like the snapping of a green branch
        to the man inside.
    To think of roses and gardens inside is bad,
    to think of seas and mountains is good.
    Read and write without rest,
40 and I also advise weaving
    and making mirrors.
    I mean, it's not that you can't pass
        ten or fifteen years inside
            and more—
45   you can,
        as long as the jewel
        on the left side of your chest doesn't lose its **luster!**

> The poet tells the prisoner exactly what to do. Which lines deal with concrete images?

> The speaker is talking about more than just passing the time in prison. He is talking about staying sane no matter how many years the prison sentence lasts.

heartily completely; with excitement; with all one's heart

luster shine

AFTER READING THE SELECTION

Some Advice to Those Who Will Serve Time in Prison

Directions Choose the letter of the best answer or write the answer using complete sentences.

Comprehension: Identifying Facts

1. This poem says that something else could have happened to the prisoner. What is it?
   A He could have been sent to another country.
   B He could have been set free.
   C He could never have been arrested.
   D He could have been killed.

2. Why should the prisoner stand firm and be strong?

3. What are some things the prisoner should remember to do?

Comprehension: Putting Ideas Together

4. The poet uses the word *inside* seven times in this poem. What does the word mean in this poem?
   A a jail cell   C the club
   B his home   D a box

5. How is life in prison like "the stone at the bottom of a well"?

6. The poet warns the prisoner that he may lose the woman he loves. Why should the prisoner not pretend it is "no big thing"?

Understanding Literature: Abstract and Concrete Images

Abstract images are thoughts and feelings. They do not have any physical qualities. They cannot be seen, smelled, heard, touched, or tasted. Concrete images are just the opposite. You experience them with your five senses. You can taste and touch a loaf of bread. You can even smell it baking in the oven. This makes some people think of home, family, and love. The smell is concrete. The thoughts and emotions that the smell brings to mind are abstract.

7. Read lines 21–24. What do you think is dangerous about waiting for letters?

8. The poet describes how a man feels when a woman stops loving him. What concrete image does he use?

Critical Thinking

9. Read the last two lines of the poem again. What is "the jewel on the left side of your chest"? How can it "lose its luster"?

Thinking Creatively

10. Hikmet writes that it is good to think of seas and mountains. He also says it is bad to think of roses and gardens. What do you think he means by this?

by Nazim Hikmet (trans. by Randy Blasing and Mutlu Konuk)

 Grammar Check

An infinitive is a verb that starts with the word *to*. Here are some infinitives: *to eat, to play,* and *to run*. An infinitive phrase is a phrase that begins with an infinitive and has an object. Here are some examples: *to eat rice, to play the violin,* and *to run around the track*. Look for infinitive phrases in the poem.

 Writing on Your Own

Take time to listen to the noises outside your classroom or home. These can be the sounds of nature: chirping birds, rustling leaves, and barking dogs. Or they can be the sounds of city life: honking horns, blaring trucks, and people talking. Write a paragraph about how the poet would feel if he could hear these sounds.

 Speaking

Practice reading this poem aloud with a partner. Get comfortable with the phrases. Read it with feeling. Pause when it makes sense to pause. Then read the poem aloud to a family member or friend who is not in your class. Ask them what they think about the poem.

 Listening

Most of the time, political prisoners are not allowed to speak to the outside world. They cannot tell other people what they are thinking or feeling. Think about the power of a person's voice. Have a partner choose a few lines of the poem to read aloud to you. Talk with your partner about why a government would not let its prisoners speak.

 Viewing

Use Main Idea Graphic (Details) to show the main idea and details from this poem. List the details on the lines above the bold line. Think about all the details. Then, write a main idea sentence in the box under the bold line. See Appendix A for an example of this graphic organizer.

Unit 4 SKILLS LESSON
Style

Style is an author's way of writing. It describes what a writer says and how he or she says it. These examples show two different styles:

> The thief lied.
>
> That rascal was never on friendly terms with the truth.

The first sentence is serious and factual. The second is in a humorous style. The author seems amused but not bothered by the other person's lies.

The poems in this unit have many styles. In "The Diameter of the Bomb," Yehuda Amichai begins on a low key. His words could almost come from a police report:

> The diameter of the bomb was
>   thirty centimeters
> and the diameter of its effective
>   range about seven meters,
> with four dead and eleven wounded.

As he continues on, it is clear how upset he really is:

> And I won't even mention the howl
>   of orphans
> that reaches up to the throne of
>   God and
> beyond, making a circle with no end
> and no God.

Pablo Neruda writes about a pair of socks. His style is not ordinary, though. His style is to have fun.

> I fought
> the mad urge
> to lock them
> in a golden
> cage
> and feed them birdseed
> and morsels of pink melon
> every day.

Review

1. What is style?
2. Does style give you a sense of who the writer is? Why or why not?
3. How are the styles of "Do Not Go Gentle Into That Good Night" and "Some Advice to Those Who Would Serve Time in Prison" alike?
4. Choose two poems that have different styles. Which poems did you choose? Why?
5. Which do you prefer, free verse, haiku, or rhymed verses? Explain.

Writing on Your Own

Think about the poems you read, then write your own poem. You can use free verse, haiku, or rhymed lines. Write about something serious or something funny. Try to develop your own style.

Unit 4 SUMMARY

In this unit you read poetry from 10 countries. The poems cover a time span from the 8th century to the 20th century.

Poems belong to many forms. These depend on length and meter, or rhythm. For instance, a sonnet has 14 lines and a certain meter. A haiku has three lines and 17 syllables. Free verse does not rhyme. Blank verse is unrhymed verse with five beats in a line. (Shakespeare's plays are in blank verse.) Some poets combine traditional forms to create new forms.

Poems can also be grouped by their purpose. An ode is a poem of praise. Some odes praise beautiful landscapes. Others honor great athletes. An elegy mourns a death.

You may think that poetry is not as easy to read as prose. Keep in mind that a poem is like the words of a song. It can help to read a poem aloud.

Selections

- "The Diameter of the Bomb" by Yehuda Amichai. An Israeli poet shows how one tragic event has a widespread effect.

- "Taking Leave of a Friend" by Li Po. A Chinese poet of the 8th century looks at two friends parting.

- "Thoughts of Hanoi" by Nguyen Thi Vinh. A poet from Vietnam looks back at the city before war split the country.

- "Mindoro" by Ramón Sunico. A modern Filipino poet describes sunset near an island.

- "Ode to a Pair of Socks" by Pablo Neruda. A winner of the Nobel Prize describes the joy of getting a pair of socks.

- "Three Haiku" by Basho, Kikaku, and Anonymous. Three very short poems are in a traditional Japanese form. They give glimpses of a frog by a pool, a boastful rooster, and a singing bird.

- "Do Not Go Gentle Into That Good Night" by Dylan Thomas. A Welsh poet talks about fighting against death.

- "The Bird's Last Flight" by Saadi Youssef. A bird gives instructions about how to act after it dies.

- "Mawu of the Waters" by Abena Busia. This poem paints a picture of the creation of the oceans.

- "Some Advice to Those Who Will Serve Time in Prison" by Nazim Hikmet. A Turkish poet tells political prisoners how to stay strong.

Unit 4 REVIEW

Directions Choose the letter of the best answer or write the answer using complete sentences.

Comprehension: Identifying Facts

1. What form of poetry is used in "The Diameter of the Bomb"?
   - **A** sonnet
   - **B** villanelle
   - **C** elegy
   - **D** free verse

2. What is the name of the Japanese poetry form in this unit?

3. One of these selections has a traditional rhyming form. Which is it? Who wrote it?

4. Name a poet who wrote odes to everyday things.

5. "Mawu of the Waters" is based on a myth from what country?

Comprehension: Putting Ideas Together

6. What does Pablo Neruda think about the gift he receives?
   - **A** his socks are not warm enough
   - **B** his socks are too beautiful for his ugly feet
   - **C** his socks are too ugly to wear
   - **D** his socks are too big

7. Name one poem that is happy or funny. What is it about the poem that creates this happy or funny mood?

8. Compare and contrast "Thoughts of Hanoi" and "The Diameter of the Bomb." How are they alike and different?

9. Name one poem that is about something serious. What words does the poet use to set the tone of the poem?

10. There is no dialogue in the poem "Taking Leave of a Friend." How does the poet show what the friends are feeling if they don't talk to each other?

Understanding Literature: Mood

Mood is the feeling that a piece of writing creates. Writers can use images to create mood. Neruda describes feet as navy-blue sharks to create a playful mood. Hikmet writes about an execution for an entirely different mood. Word choices are another way to create mood. Words such as *burn* and *rage* help create the mood of "Do Not Go Gentle Into That Good Night."

11. What is mood?

12. Think about "The Diameter of the Bomb." How does the mood change from the beginning to the end of the poem?

13. Choose one of the three haiku. Explain how an image creates the mood.

14. What are some of the images in "Mindoro"? What mood do they create?

15. What is the mood of "Thoughts of Hanoi"? Name three words or phrases that help create this mood.

Critical Thinking

16. What is the most powerful image in "Some Advice to Those Who Will Serve Time in Prison?" What makes this image so strong?

17. The poem "Taking Leave of a Friend" was written more than 1,200 years ago. Why do people like it so much that they still read it?

18. Dylan Thomas's poem has a pattern of rhyme and meter. Do you think this makes the poem more powerful? Why or why not?

19. What is your favorite poem from this unit? Explain your choice.

Thinking Creatively

20. If you could meet one of these poets, whom would it be? Explain your choice.

Speak and Listen

Think of a poem you like. It could be one from this unit. It could be one you find in the library. Read the poem to yourself several times, then practice reading the poem aloud. Read the poem to the class when you can read it well. Explain to the class what the poem means to you.

Writing on Your Own

Think about how a poem and a short story are alike and different. Write an essay comparing poems with short stories. Use examples from this unit in your essay.

Beyond Words

Images are very important in poetry. Choose one image you like from the poems in this unit. Draw a picture to show what that image suggests to you. Your drawing can be realistic. It can also just suggest an image. For example, you might just use color to show the image. Your drawing might barely suggest a tree or boat.

Test-Taking Tip

Before you begin a test, look it over quickly. Try to set aside enough time to complete each section.

"Spirit of labor...begets more love among mankind"
1960s Cuban Poster.

Unit 5: Persuasive Literature

You see or hear persuasive writing every day. Think about advertisements, speeches, editorials, and commercials. Ads are all around us. You may not like this. You may think that people are being led to buy, buy, buy—that the ads persuade us all too well. Or, you may think that ads are fine because they show us choices and help us share ideas. Either way, your life is affected by persuasive writing.

In this unit, you will read two forms of persuasive writing. They are speeches and essays. You will also see that persuasive writing has long been a part of literature.

Unit 5 Selections	Page
SPEECHES	412
■ FRANCE "Letter to the English" by Joan of Arc	413
■ RUSSIA "Nobel Lecture" by Alexander Solzhenitsyn	419
■ UNITED STATES "The Gettysburg Address" by Abraham Lincoln	438
■ UNITED STATES "Inaugural Address" by John F. Kennedy	444
ESSAYS	453
■ FRANCE "Of Repentance" by Michel de Montaigne	454
■ ANTIGUA from *A Small Place* by Jamaica Kincaid	460

"If you would persuade, you must appeal to interest rather than intellect."
—Benjamin Franklin

"If speaking is silver, then listening is gold."
—Turkish Proverb

Unit 5

About Persuasive Literature

Persuasive literary works are written to influence opinion. The purpose of persuasive writing is more important than its form. Because of that, persuasive writing is found in all genres, or types of writing.

In the 1500s, Edmund Spenser wrote his poem "The Faerie Queene." Its purpose was to praise Elizabeth I of England as both a ruler and a woman. In the 1850s, Harriet Beecher Stowe wrote the novel *Uncle Tom's Cabin*. (A novel is a longer work of fiction.) With her book, Stowe tried to turn the American public against slavery. During the 1950s Arthur Miller wrote the play *The Crucible*. It tried to expose the American anti-Communist panic being spread by Senator Joseph McCarthy. The play showed McCarthyism as a destructive force, much like the Salem witch hunts 300 years earlier. The Russian writer Alexander Solzhenitsyn wrote a series of novels, *The Gulag Archipelago*. He meant to show the evils and inhumanity of the Soviet prison system.

Poems, novels, and plays written to persuade are not always great literature. Besides, you have read those genres elsewhere in *World Literature*. For those reasons, the selections in this unit are nonfiction, as is most persuasive writing. The authors of these selections criticize, reassure, threaten, praise, argue with, and inspire their audiences. However, they do use literary techniques. For example, the speeches of Abraham Lincoln and John F. Kennedy use metaphors. A metaphor is a figure of speech that says one thing is another. For example, "My love is a rose" is a metaphor. Jamaica Kincaid uses irony. This form uses words that seem to say one thing but mean the opposite.

As you read, notice the language, imagery, and organization of these selections. Though some were written long ago, they are models that present-day authors still copy.

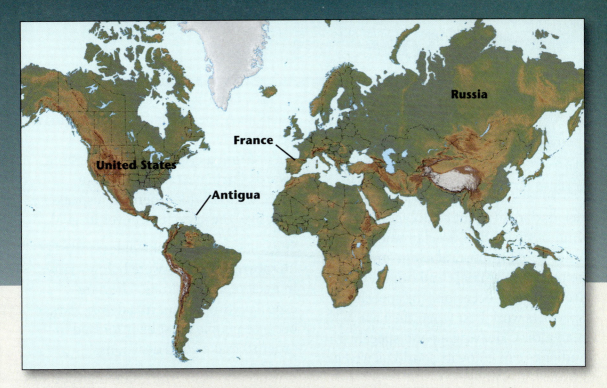

The following countries are represented in this unit: Antigua, France, Russia, and the United States.

Speeches

Speeches are usually written, but they are meant to be spoken to an audience. They respond to an event or occasion. One kind of speech is a proclamation, a letter about important events meant to be read aloud. Trials and other events are also good occasions for speeches. Speeches work best when they are read aloud. Hearing a good speech, an audience can enjoy its sound as well as its ideas and images.

Speeches are written for many reasons. They may inform, persuade, or entertain. A political speech may help people decide whom to vote for in an election. A speech in a courtroom may persuade people that someone did not commit a crime. People receiving awards during ceremonies make speeches to thank others. If a speaker is effective, the speech achieves its goal.

Speeches are one of the oldest forms of literature. Speeches were being written in ancient Greek times. They are especially important in a democracy, because people must be informed in order to make good decisions.

The occasions for the following speeches have passed. Their audiences are gone. Yet the form and content of each still "speaks" to similar events today. Speakers all around the world still quote from these selections.

SPEECHES

inform • persuade • entertain

BEFORE READING THE SELECTION

Letter to the English   by Joan of Arc (trans. by Willard Trask)

About the Speaker

Joan of Arc was the uneducated daughter of a farmer in France. France and England had been at war, on and off, for many years. Now the English held most of France, including Paris. At age 13, Joan claimed that she began to hear voices. She believed they were saints with a message from God. The voices told her to support the young French king, Charles VII, and help him drive the English out of France. Joan convinced the king to let her lead an army to Orléans. The city was under attack by the English. Joan inspired the French troops to drive the English away. After that victory, Charles VII was officially crowned king.

Soon after, French enemies turned Joan over to the English. A church court found her guilty of being a heretic, a questioner of the faith. Joan was burned at the stake in Rouen in May 1431. Joan is a national heroine in France today.

Joan of Arc (1412–1431) French

Objectives

- To read and understand a proclamation
- To explain how a writer creates mood
- To identify the audience for a proclamation

About the Selection

Joan of Arc was also known as the Maid of Orléans. She wrote this letter to the English, telling them to leave France. In the speech, Joan does not use *I*. Instead, she refers to herself as "the Maid."

She explains that she (the Maid) has been sent by God. She thinks this will convince the English to believe her and do what she says. When she wrote the letter, Joan knew that it would be read aloud to both the English and French. The letter was, in fact, read aloud just before the French attacked the English.

Before Reading **continued on next page**

Persuasive Literature Unit 5 413

BEFORE READING THE SELECTION (continued)

Letter to the English — by Joan of Arc (trans. by Willard Trask)

proclamation a letter about important events that is meant to be read aloud

mood the feeling created by a piece of writing

Literary Terms This selection is a kind of letter called a **proclamation**. A proclamation is a letter about important events that is meant to be read aloud. After it is read aloud, it is hung where people can read and study it. Most people in the 1400s could not read. They found out what a proclamation said by listening to it being read aloud. A proclamation is the old version of a news broadcast.

When Joan of Arc wrote this proclamation, she thought about all the people who would hear it. She wanted to create a certain **mood**, or feeling, of fear. She addressed the letter to the King of England and the Duke of Bedford. Of course, Joan knew that many other people would also hear the letter. She wanted them to be more afraid of her than of the king and duke.

Reading on Your Own Proclamations were read aloud by town criers and other "reporters." A town crier walked through the streets and shouted—or cried—important news. Read this proclamation aloud as if you are a town crier. Do you think you would have liked being the town crier? Explain your answer.

Writing on Your Own Think of a time when you believed you were right and someone else was wrong. How would you have felt if everyone believed the other person, and not you? Explain your answer.

Vocabulary Focus A speaker chooses words carefully. In this selection, the meanings of some words are very important to the speech. Find a synonym for each of these four words: *surrender, royal, justice,* and *peace.* Explain how the speech would be less powerful if it did not use these words.

Think Before You Read How do you think Joan will try to convince the English to leave?

414 Unit 5 *Persuasive Literature*

Letter to the English

King of England, and you, Duke of Bedford, who call yourself **Regent** of the Kingdom of France . . . Do justice to the King of Heaven; surrender to the Maid, who is sent here from God, King of Heaven, the keys of all the good towns you have taken and **violated** in France. She is come from God to uphold the blood royal. She is ready to make peace if you will do justice, **relinquishing** France and paying for what you have **withheld**.

The English king, Henry VI, was only a child. The Duke of Bedford was his uncle.

Blood royal refers to the claim that Charles was the true heir to the French throne.

regent one who rules in place of a king

violated ruined by force

relinquishing releasing or letting go

withheld kept

> As you read, remember that most people would have heard this proclamation read aloud.

As to you, you archers and men-at-arms, gentle and others, who are before the town of Orléans, go **hence** into your own country in God's name; and if you do not so, expect to hear news of the Maid, who will shortly come to see you, to your very great damage.

King of England, if you do not do so, I am a commander, and in whatever place in France I come upon your men, I will make them leave it, will they or nill they; and if they will not yield obedience, I will have them all slain. I am sent here from God, King of Heaven, to put you, hand to hand, out of all France. Yet if they will yield obedience, I will grant them mercy.

> *Nill* is an old word meaning "will not."

And think not otherwise: for you shall not hold the Kingdom of France from God, King of Heaven, Saint Mary's son, but King Charles shall hold it, the true heir. For so God, King of Heaven, wills it; and so it has been **revealed** to him by the Maid, and he shall enter Paris with a fair company.

> How does Joan try to create a mood of fear?

If you will not believe this news from God and the Maid, wherever we find you, there we shall strike; and we shall raise such a battle-cry as there has not been in France in a thousand years, if you will not do justice. And know surely that the King of Heaven will send more strength to the Maid than you can bring against her and her good soldiers in any assault. And when the blows begin, it shall be seen whose right is the better before the God of Heaven.

You, Duke of Bedford: The Maid prays and beseeches you not to bring on your own destruction. If you will do her justice, you may yet come in her company there where the French shall do the fairest deed that ever was done for **Christendom**. So answer if you will make peace in the city of Orléans. And if you do not so, consider your great danger speedily.

---

hence from here **revealed** showed **Christendom** all Christians

AFTER READING THE SELECTION

Letter to the English by Joan of Arc (trans. by Willard Trask)

Directions Choose the letter of the best answer or write the answer using complete sentences.

Comprehension: Identifying Facts

1. Whom does Joan address at the beginning of her letter?
   A the King of England and the Duke of Bedford
   B the King of Heaven and the Maid
   C the Mayor of Orléans and the King of France
   D Saint Mary and King Charles

2. Whom does Joan say has sent her to lead this battle?

3. What is Joan's main goal for France?

Comprehension: Putting Ideas Together

4. Why does Joan want the English to give money to France?
   A to pay for the French soldiers' uniforms
   B to pay for what they have taken during the war
   C to pay taxes to King Charles
   D to pay to free the captured soldiers

5. How does Joan plan to force the English out of France?

6. Why does Joan believe she and her troops will win this battle?

Understanding Literature: Proclamation

A proclamation is a letter that is first read aloud. Then it is hung in a public place. People can freely read the proclamation whenever they like. Joan wrote her proclamation more than 500 years ago. Most people could not read at that time. The proclamation was read aloud to them. The best proclamations were clear and had memorable phrases. Today, proclamations are still used. They may be used to celebrate events. The mayor of a town may issue a proclamation to honor a good citizen, for example.

7. Joan threatens the English. How can you tell that she would rather they left on their own?

8. Why does Joan address one part of her proclamation to the English soldiers?

Critical Thinking

9. How do you think the English leaders reacted to this letter? What about ordinary soldiers?

Thinking Creatively

10. Do you think that the French people believed that Joan had heard from God?

After Reading continued on next page

Persuasive Literature Unit 5 417

AFTER READING THE SELECTION (continued)

Letter to the English by Joan of Arc (trans. by Willard Trask)

 Grammar Check

An appositive is a word or phrase that describes a noun. Appositives often give more information about the nouns they describe. An appositive is set off from the rest of the sentence by commas. In this example, the appositive is underlined:

> Mary, <u>my mother's sister</u>, is coming to stay with us.

Find some appositives in Joan of Arc's speech. Write the sentences and underline the appositives. Circle the words or phrases that they describe.

 Writing on Your Own

Think of someone you would like to honor. Write a proclamation to declare a certain day that person's day. You might have a day to honor a teacher or a sports hero. Keep two things in mind as you write the proclamation: 1) you are going to read it aloud and 2) it is going to be printed and hung on a wall. Make sure you tell what day you are choosing. Tell who you are honoring and why.

 Speaking and Listening

Read your proclamation from Writing on Your Own aloud to the class. Use a clear, strong voice. Take your time and pause as you read. You want to help your listeners remember what you are saying. Listen as your classmates read aloud their proclamations from the Speaking activity. Note the main details. Imagine what it would be like if you could not read the proclamation again later.

 Media

Pretend that Joan was dealing with England in today's world. Would she give her speech on a television news show or on the radio? Would she create a Web site? Work with a small group to decide how you would like Joan to tell her story. Choose students to play the roles of Joan, reporters, outsiders, and others. Record Joan as she speaks. If you decide that Joan would use a Web site, then create a mock-up drawing of what it would show. Each person in your group should write e-mail letters to Joan telling her what you think of her ideas.

 Viewing and Research

Predict what will happen after Joan gives her proclamation. Use a Prediction Guide to help you. See Appendix A for an example of this graphic organizer. Write in the time, place, characters, and problem. You will find these in the proclamation and About the Selection. Write your prediction in the circle labeled "Possible Solution." Then research what happened after her proclamation. Did it work?

BEFORE READING THE SELECTION

Nobel Lecture   by Alexander Solzhenitsyn

About the Speaker

Alexander Solzhenitsyn was born in Kislovodsk, Russia. In World War II, he fought in the Soviet army. After the war, Solzhenitsyn was arrested for writing critical remarks about Josef Stalin. (Stalin was the leader of the Soviet Union.) Solzhenitsyn spent eight years in prison. This was the background for his first novel, *One Day in the Life of Ivan Denisovich*. A few years later, though, the government stopped letting him publish his work. In 1969, Solzhenitsyn was forced out of the Soviet Writers Union. The next year, he won the Nobel Prize for Literature.

In 1973, the first part of *The Gulag Archipelago* was published in France. It exposed the Soviet prison system. Solzhenitsyn was arrested and then exiled, or driven out of the country. He lived in the United States for many years. In 1994, after the Soviet Union collapsed, Solzhenitsyn returned to live in Russia.

Alexander Solzhenitsyn
(1918–)
Russian

Objectives

- To read and understand a persuasive speech
- To identify the themes in a speech

About the Selection

This is the speech that Solzhenitsyn wrote when he won the Nobel Prize. He never actually gave the speech. In 1970, he was afraid to go to Sweden and get his prize. He thought Russian officials would not let him return home. The speech was read in his absence. Use vocabulary definitions and context clues to help you understand the meanings of difficult words.

The speech is about the power of artists and writers to expose evil. Solzhenitsyn knows the cost of being an honest writer. His government will not allow him to publish his work. This makes the speech that much more powerful.

Before Reading continued on next page

BEFORE READING THE SELECTION (continued)

Nobel Lecture   by Alexander Solzhenitsyn

speech a written work meant to be read aloud

persuasive meant to influence

theme the main idea of a literary work

Literary Terms Solzhenitsyn begins his **speech** by explaining the differences among cultures. Then he talks about the reasons that people need to be able to agree on some basic values. He says that artists and writers can help people do this. The rest of the speech is **persuasive,** or meant to influence. He is trying to convince other writers to help create this main set of "human" values. That is the **theme** of his speech. The theme is the main idea of a literary work. As you read, think about what other things Solzhenitsyn wants artists and writers to do.

Reading on Your Own As you read, take notes about the main idea of each paragraph. What are the central ideas in this speech?

Writing on Your Own How are writers really artists? Explain your answer in a paragraph.

Vocabulary Focus Two of the words in this speech that have British spellings are *travellers* and *levelling*. When words have more than one syllable and end in *l*, the *l* is doubled before adding *-ing*, *-er*, and *-ed*. American English is different. In American English, the final consonant is doubled in words of more than one syllable *only* when the final syllable is stressed. For example, *be<u>gin</u>* becomes *beginning* (the *n* is doubled), but *<u>of</u>fer* becomes *offering* (the *r* is not doubled). Write the American English *-ing* form for *travel* and *level*.

Think Before You Read What do you think Solzhenitsyn will say to convince other writers to speak boldly for truth?

420   Unit 5 Persuasive Literature

NOBEL LECTURE

Touching Hands, by Todd Davidson.

Persuasive Literature Unit 5 **421**

> As you read this speech, look for persuasive expressions and ideas. Think about what Solzhenitsyn wants to convince people to do.

From time **immemorial** man has been made in such a way that his vision of the world, so long as it has not been instilled under hypnosis, his motivations and scale of values, his actions and intentions are determined by his personal and group experience of life. As the Russian saying goes, "Do not believe your brother, believe your own crooked eye." And that is the most sound basis for an understanding of the world around us and of human conduct in it. And during the long **epochs** when our world lay spread out in mystery and wilderness, before it became **encroached** by common lines of communication, before it was transformed into a single, **convulsively pulsating** lump—men, relying on experience, ruled without mishap within their limited areas, within their communities, within their societies, and finally on their national territories. At that time it was possible for individual human beings to perceive and accept a general scale of values, to distinguish between what is considered normal, what incredible; what is cruel and what lies beyond the boundaries of wickedness; what is honesty, what **deceit**. And although the scattered peoples led extremely different lives and their social values were often strikingly at odds, just as their systems of weights and measures did not agree, still these **discrepancies** surprised only occasional travellers, were reported in journals under the name of wonders, and bore no danger to mankind which was not yet one.

> Solzhenitsyn uses *men* and *mankind* to mean all people, men and women.

But now during the past few decades, imperceptibly, suddenly, mankind has become one—hopefully one and dangerously one—so that the **concussions** and inflammations of one of its parts are almost instantaneously passed on to others, sometimes lacking in any kind of necessary immunity.

---

immemorial beyond the limits of memory

epochs long periods of history

encroached gradually entered or occupied

convulsively shaking violently

pulsating moving in a regular rhythm

deceit a trick

discrepancies differences; conflicts

concussions shocks; injuries

Global Communication, by Jose Ortega.

Mankind has become one, but not steadfastly one as communities or even nations used to be; not united through years of **mutual** experience, neither through possession of a single eye, affectionately called crooked, nor yet through a common native language, but, surpassing all barriers, through international broadcasting and print. An avalanche of events descends upon us—in one minute half the world hears of their splash. But the yardstick by which to measure those events and to **evaluate** them in **accordance** with the laws of unfamiliar parts of the world—this is not and cannot be conveyed via soundwaves and in newspaper columns. For these yardsticks were matured and **assimilated** over too many years of too specific conditions in individual countries and societies; they cannot be exchanged in midair. In the various parts of the

Solzhenitsyn refers back to the Russian saying in the first paragraph.

How does the world hear about international events so fast? Do you think he really means one minute?

mutual shared
evaluate judge the worth of
accordance agreement
assimilated took in

world men apply their own hard-earned values to events, and they judge stubbornly, confidently, only according to their own scales of values and never according to any others.

And if there are not many such different scales of values in the world, there are at least several; one for evaluating events near at hand, another for events far away; aging societies possess one, young societies another; unsuccessful people one, successful people another. The **divergent** scales of values scream in **discordance**, they dazzle and daze us, and in order that it might not be painful we steer clear of all other values, as though from insanity, as though from illusion, and we confidently judge the whole world according to our own home values. Which is why we take for the greater, more painful and less bearable disaster not that which is in fact greater, more painful and less bearable, but that which lies closest to us. Everything which is further away, which does not threaten this very day to invade our threshold—with all its groans, its stifled cries, its destroyed lives, even if it involves millions of victims—this we consider on the whole to be perfectly bearable and of **tolerable** proportions.

In one part of the world, not so long ago, under persecutions not inferior to those of the ancient Romans', hundreds of thousands of silent Christians gave up their lives for their belief in God. In the other hemisphere a certain madman, (and no doubt he is not alone), speeds across the ocean to DELIVER us from religion—with a thrust of steel into the high priest! He has calculated for each and every one of us according to his personal scale of values!

That which from a distance, according to one scale of values, appears as enviable and flourishing freedom, at close quarters, and according to other values, is felt to be infuriating **constraint** calling for buses to be overthrown.

> Which events and disasters attract people's attention most?

> Words in capital letters are more important than others.

---

divergent drawing apart; differing

discordance a harsh, confused sound

tolerable able to be endured

constraint force that limits freedom of thought or action

That which in one part of the world might represent a dream of incredible prosperity, in another has the **exasperating** effect of wild **exploitation** demanding immediate strike. There are different scales of values for natural catastrophes: a flood craving two hundred thousand lives seems less significant than our local accident. There are different scales of values for personal insults: sometimes even an **ironic** smile or a **dismissive** gesture is **humiliating**, while for others cruel beatings are forgiven as an unfortunate joke. There are different scales of values for punishment and wickedness: according to one, a month's arrest, banishment to the country, or an isolation-cell where one is fed on white rolls and milk, shatters the imagination and fills the newspaper columns with rage. While according to another, prison sentences of twenty-five years, isolation-cells where the walls are covered with ice and the prisoners stripped to their underclothes, lunatic asylums for the sane, and countless unreasonable people who for some reason will keep running away, shot on the frontiers—all this is common and accepted. While the mind is especially at peace concerning that exotic part of the world about which we know virtually nothing, from which we do not even receive news of events, but only the trivial, out-of-date guesses of a few correspondents.

Yet we cannot reproach human vision for this duality, for this **dumbfounded incomprehension** of another man's distant grief, man is just made that way. But for the whole of mankind, compressed into a single lump, such mutual incomprehension presents the threat of **imminent** and violent destruction. One world, one mankind cannot exist in the face of six, four or even two scales of values: we shall be torn apart by this disparity of rhythm, this **disparity** of vibrations.

White rolls and milk are used as symbols for "soft" prison treatment.

What different sets of values does the writer contrast? Notice the results he discusses in the next paragraph.

exasperating annoying

exploitation the unfair use of something for selfish reasons

ironic mocking

dismissive in a manner that discards or sends away

humiliating causing shame or loss of dignity

dumbfounded stunned into silence

incomprehension lack of understanding

imminent about to happen

disparity difference

A man with two hearts is not for this world, neither shall we be able to live side by side on one Earth.

But who will co-ordinate these value scales, and how? Who will create for mankind one system of interpretation, **valid** for good and evil deeds, for the unbearable and the bearable, as they are **differentiated** today? Who will make clear to mankind what is really heavy and intolerable and what only grazes the skin locally? Who will direct the anger to that which is most terrible and not to that which is nearer? Who might succeed in transferring such an understanding beyond the limits of his own human experience? Who might succeed in impressing upon a **bigoted**, stubborn human creature the distant joy and grief of others, an understanding of dimensions and deceptions which he himself has never experienced? Propaganda, constraint, scientific proof—all are useless. But fortunately there does exist such a means in our world! That means is art. That means is literature.

They can perform a miracle: they can overcome man's **detrimental** peculiarity of learning only from personal experience so that the experience of other people passes him by in vain. From man to man, as he completes his brief spell on Earth, art transfers the whole weight of an unfamiliar, lifelong experience with all its burdens, its colours, its sap of life; it recreates in the flesh an unknown experience and allows us to possess it as our own.

And even more, much more than that; both countries and whole continents repeat each other's mistakes with time lapses which can amount to

> Notice that the writer restates the question in several ways. He is leading up to an answer.

> How do art and literature help people understand others' values?

Crowd XVI, by Diana Ong.

valid reliable
differentiated shown to be different
bigoted stubbornly holding a belief and disliking those who disagree
detrimental harmful

centuries. Then, one would think, it would all be so obvious! But no; that which some nations have already experienced, considered and rejected, is suddenly discovered by others to be the latest word. And here again, the only substitute for an experience we ourselves have never lived through is art, literature. They possess a wonderful ability: beyond distinctions of language, custom, social structure, they can convey the life experience of one whole nation to another. To an inexperienced nation they can convey a harsh national trial lasting many decades, at best sparing an entire nation from a superfluous, or mistaken, or even disastrous course, thereby **curtailing** the **meanderings** of human history. It is this great and noble property of art that I urgently recall to you today from the Nobel **tribune**.

And literature conveys **irrefutable** condensed experience in yet another **invaluable** direction; namely, from generation to generation. Thus it becomes the living memory of the nation. Thus it preserves and kindles within itself the flame of her spent history, in a form which is safe from deformation and slander. In this way literature, together with language, protects the soul of the nation.

> Solzhenitsyn says that the lessons of art and literature can be passed from country to country. They can also be passed down through history.

(In recent times it has been fashionable to talk of the levelling of nations, of the disappearance of different races in the melting-pot of **contemporary** civilization. I do not agree with this opinion, but its discussion remains another question. Here it is merely fitting to say that the disappearance of nations would have impoverished us no less than if all men had become alike, with one personality and one face. Nations are the wealth of mankind, its **collective** personalities; the very least of them wears its own special colours and bears within itself a special **facet** of divine intention.)

curtailing cutting short
meanderings winding paths
tribune a platform from which to speak to a group
irrefutable impossible to prove wrong
invaluable beyond price
contemporary current; modern
collective grouped together
facet one part or angle

What does Solzhenitsyn say are the effects of censorship?

Anna Achmatova was a Russian poet whose works were attacked by authorities. Yevgeny Zamjatin was another writer whose books were banned.

But woe to that nation whose literature is disturbed by the **intervention** of power. Because that is not just a violation against "freedom of print," it is the closing down of the heart of the nation, a slashing to pieces of its memory. The nation ceases to be mindful of itself, it is deprived of its spiritual unity, and despite a supposedly common language, **compatriots** suddenly cease to understand one another. Silent generations grow old and die without ever having talked about themselves, either to each other or to their descendants. When writers such as Achmatova and Zamjatin—**interred** alive throughout their lives—are condemned to create in silence until they die, never hearing the echo of their written words, then that is not only their personal tragedy, but a sorrow to the whole nation, a danger to the whole nation.

In some cases moreover—when as a result of such a silence the whole of history ceases to be understood in its entirety—it is a danger to the whole of mankind.

At various times and in various countries there have arisen heated, angry and exquisite debates as to whether art and the artist should be free to live for themselves, or whether they should be for ever mindful of their duty towards society and serve it albeit in an unprejudiced way. For me there is no **dilemma**, but I shall refrain from raising once again the train of arguments. One of the most brilliant addresses on this subject was actually Albert Camus' Nobel speech, and I would happily subscribe to his conclusions. Indeed, Russian literature has for several decades **manifested** an **inclination** not to become too lost in contemplation of itself, not to flutter about too **frivolously**. I am not ashamed to continue this tradition to the best of my ability. Russian literature has long been familiar with the notions that a writer can do much within his society, and that it is his duty to do so.

Camus, a French writer, won the 1957 Nobel Prize.

intervention an act of interfering
compatriots people from the same country
interred buried
dilemma a situation that requires a difficult choice
manifested showed
inclination a leaning toward something
frivolously not seriously; playfully

Let us not violate the RIGHT of the artist to express exclusively his own experiences and **introspections**, disregarding everything that happens in the world beyond. Let us not DEMAND of the artist, but—reproach, beg, urge and **entice** him—that we may be allowed to do. After all, only in part does he himself develop his talent; the greater part of it is blown into him at birth as a finished product, and the gift of talent imposes responsibility on his free will. Let us assume that the artist does not OWE anybody anything: nevertheless, it is painful to see how, by retiring into his self-made worlds or the spaces of his subjective whims, he CAN surrender the real world into the hands of men who are **mercenary**, if not worthless, if not insane. . . .

What then is the place and role of the writer in this cruel, **dynamic,** split world on the brink of its ten destructions? After all we have nothing to do with letting off rockets, we do not even push the lowliest of hand-carts, we are quite scorned by those who respect only material power. Is it not natural for us too to step back, to lose faith in the steadfastness of goodness, in the **indivisibility** of truth, and to just impart to the world our bitter, **detached** observations: how mankind has become hopelessly corrupt, how men have **degenerated,** and how difficult it is for the few beautiful and refined souls to live amongst them?

> How is a writer affected by terrible events?

But we have not even **recourse** to this flight. Anyone who has once taken up the WORD can never again evade it; a writer is not the detached judge of his compatriots and contemporaries, he is an accomplice to all the evil committed in his native land or by his countrymen. And if the tanks of his fatherland have flooded the asphalt of a foreign capital with blood, then the brown spots have slapped against the face

> Here, Solzhenitsyn gives an example of how writers have power to do good.

introspections personal thoughts or ideas

entice tempt

mercenary concerned only with making money

dynamic full of energy; changing

indivisibility state of not being able to be divided

detached not connected

degenerated became much worse

recourse something to turn to for help

Persuasive Literature Unit 5

of the writer forever. And if one fatal night they suffocated his sleeping, trusting Friend, then the palms of the writer bear the bruises from that rope. And if his young fellow citizens breezily declare the superiority of **depravity** over honest work, if they give themselves over to drugs or seize hostages, then their stink mingles with the breath of the writer.

Shall we have the **temerity** to declare that we are not responsible for the sores of the present-day world?

Born to Starve, by Susanne Schuenke, 1993.

However, I am cheered by a vital awareness of WORLD LITERATURE as of a single huge heart, beating out the cares and troubles of our world, albeit presented and **perceived** differently in each of its corners.

Apart from age-old national literatures there existed, even in past ages, the **conception** of world literature as an **anthology** skirting the heights of the national literatures, and as the sum total of mutual literary influences. But there occurred a lapse in time: readers and writers became acquainted with writers of other tongues only after a time lapse, sometimes lasting

> What symbol does Solzhenitsyn choose for world literature?

---

depravity a wicked act

temerity foolish boldness

perceived seen; known through the senses

conception an idea; a mental picture

anthology a collection of writings

centuries, so that mutual influences were also delayed and the anthology of national literary heights was revealed only in the eyes of descendants, not of contemporaries.

But today, between the writers of one country and the writers and readers of another, there is a **reciprocity** if not instantaneous then almost so. I experience this with myself. Those of my books which, alas, have not been printed in my own country have soon found a responsive, worldwide audience, despite hurried and often bad translations. Such distinguished western writers as Heinrich Böll have undertaken critical **analysis** of them. All these last years, when my work and freedom have not come crashing down, when contrary to the laws of gravity they have hung suspended as though on air, as though on NOTHING—on the invisible dumb **tension** of a sympathetic public **membrane**; then it was with grateful warmth, and quite unexpectedly for myself, that I learnt of the further support of the international brotherhood of writers. On my fiftieth birthday I was astonished to receive congratulations from well-known western writers. No pressure on me came to pass by unnoticed. During my dangerous weeks of exclusion from the Writers' Union the WALL OF DEFENCE advanced by the world's prominent writers protected me from worse persecutions; and Norwegian writers and artists hospitably prepared a roof for me, in the event of my threatened exile being put into effect. Finally even the advancement of my name for the Nobel Prize was raised not in the country where I live and write, but by François Mauriac and his colleagues. And later still entire national writers' unions have expressed their support for me.

Thus I have understood and felt that world literature is no longer an abstract anthology, nor a generalization invented by literary historians; it is rather a certain common body and a common spirit, a living heartfelt unity reflecting the growing

> Mauriac was a French writer who won the Nobel Prize in 1952. How does this kind of support help prove the writer's point about world literature?

reciprocity an equal exchange

analysis a study of how parts fit together

tension the condition of being stretched

membrane a thin layer of material

unity of mankind. State frontiers still turn crimson, heated by electric wire and bursts of machine fire; and various ministries of internal affairs still think that literature too is an "internal affair" falling under their **jurisdiction**; newspaper headlines still display: "No right to interfere in our internal affairs!" Whereas there are no INTERNAL AFFAIRS left on our crowded Earth! And mankind's sole **salvation** lies in everyone making everything his business; in the people of the East being vitally concerned with what is thought in the West, the people of the West vitally concerned with what goes on in the East. And literature, as one of the most sensitive, responsive instruments possessed by the human creature, has been one of the first to adopt, to assimilate, to catch hold of this feeling of a growing unity of mankind. And so I turn with confidence to the world literature of today—to hundreds of friends whom I have never met in the flesh and whom I may never see.

Friends! Let us try to help if we are worth anything at all! Who from time immemorial has **constituted** the uniting, not the dividing, strength in your countries, **lacerated** by discordant parties, movements, **castes** and groups? There in its **essence** is the position of writers: expressers of their native language—the chief binding force of the nation, of the very earth its people occupy, and at best of its national spirit.

I believe that world literature has it in its power to help mankind, in these its troubled hours, to see itself as it really is, notwithstanding the **indoctrinations** of prejudiced people and parties. World literature has it in its power to convey condensed experience from one land to another so that we might cease to be split and dazzled, that the different scales of values might be made to agree, and one nation learn correctly and **concisely**

> What does Solzhenitsyn say that he believes? How can this help you figure out the theme?

jurisdiction the area where one has authority

salvation rescue from evil or problems

constituted made up

lacerated torn

castes social classes

essence the basic quality of something

indoctrinations teachings from a certain point of view

concisely briefly

the true history of another with such strength of recognition and painful awareness as it had itself experienced the same, and thus might it be spared from repeating the same cruel mistakes. And perhaps under such conditions we artists will be able to cultivate within ourselves a field of vision to embrace the WHOLE WORLD: in the centre observing like any other human being that which lies nearby, at the edges we shall begin to draw in that which is happening in the rest of the world. And we shall **correlate**, and we shall observe world proportions.

Centre is the British spelling of center.

And who, if not writers, are to pass judgment—not only on their unsuccessful governments, (in some states this is the easiest way to earn one's bread, the occupation of any man who is not lazy), but also on the people themselves, in their cowardly humiliation or self-satisfied weakness? Who is to pass judgment on the light-weight sprints of youth, and on the young pirates **brandishing** their knives?

We shall be told: what can literature possibly do against the ruthless **onslaught** of open violence? But let us not forget that violence does not live alone and is not capable of living alone: it is necessarily interwoven with falsehood. Between them lies the most **intimate**, the deepest of natural bonds. Violence finds its only refuge in falsehood, falsehood its only support in violence. Any man who has once **acclaimed** violence as his METHOD must **inexorably** choose falsehood as his PRINCIPLE. At its

How are violence and lies connected?

correlate show a relationship
brandishing waving in a threatening way
onslaught an attack
intimate very close
acclaimed stated strongly
inexorably in a way that will not be stopped

birth violence acts openly and even with pride. But no sooner does it become strong, firmly established, than it senses the **rarefaction** of the air around it and it cannot continue to exist without descending into a fog of lies, clothing them in sweet talk. It does not always, not necessarily, openly throttle the throat, more often it demands from its subjects only an oath of allegiance to falsehood, only **complicity** in falsehood.

And the simple step of a simple courageous man is not to **partake** in falsehood, not to support false actions! Let THAT enter the world, let it even reign in the world—but not with my help. But writers and artists can achieve more: they can CONQUER FALSEHOOD! In the struggle with falsehood art always did win and it always does win! Openly, irrefutably for everyone! Falsehood can hold out against much in this world, but not against art.

> What is Solzhenitsyn trying to persuade his listeners to do?

And no sooner will falsehood be **dispersed** than the nakedness of violence will be revealed in all its ugliness—and violence, **decrepit**, will fall.

That is why, my friends, I believe that we are able to help the world in its white-hot hour. Not by making the excuse of possessing no weapons, and not by giving ourselves over to a frivolous life—but by going to war!

Proverbs about truth are well-loved in Russian. They give steady and sometimes striking expression to the **not inconsiderable** harsh national experience:

ONE WORD OF TRUTH SHALL OUTWEIGH THE WHOLE WORLD.

And it is here, on an imaginary fantasy, a **breach** of the principle of the conservation of mass and energy, that I base both my own activity and my appeal to the writers of the whole world.

> The law of conservation of mass and energy says that matter and energy can neither be created nor destroyed.

---

rarefaction the state of being thin or less dense

complicity state of being involved in a wrong action

partake share; take part

dispersed scattered in different directions

decrepit worn out

not inconsiderable important enough to demand attention

breach a break

AFTER READING THE SELECTION

Nobel Lecture by Alexander Solzhenitsyn

Directions Choose the letter of the best answer or write the answer using complete sentences.

Comprehension: Identifying Facts

1. Which of the following do people use to decide what is good and bad?
   A ideas from the government
   B ideas of one artist
   C personal experiences
   D ideas written in travel magazines

2. In earlier times, why was it OK that groups had different values?
   A The groups hated each other.
   B The groups were all separated from each other.
   C The groups could not read or write.
   D The groups did not want to understand each other.

3. Solzhenitsyn says that different groups of people have different scales of values. Name two of these groups.

4. Which is most upsetting to people, small disasters at home or large disasters that happen far away?

5. How can literature become the "living memory of the nation"?

6. Why does the writer say that censorship is "a danger to the whole nation"?

7. What is the debate over the role of the artist?

8. From where does an artist get his or her talent?

9. Who sent congratulations to Solzhenitsyn on his 50th birthday?

10. Who suggested Solzhenitsyn for a Nobel Prize?

Comprehension: Putting Ideas Together

11. What does Solzhenitsyn believe about his role as a writer?
    A He should write what the government thinks is good.
    B He does not want to be a writer anymore.
    C He thinks he is free to create whatever he wants.
    D He feels he has a duty to society.

12. According to this speech, how is a writer connected to his countrymen?
    A He is guilty of all the evil they do.
    B He is only responsible for his own actions and words.
    C He is only guilty if he writes words that say the actions are OK.
    D He is always innocent until proven guilty.

After Reading continued on next page

AFTER READING THE SELECTION (continued)

Nobel Lecture   by Alexander Solzhenitsyn

13. Today, writers can easily find works written in other languages. How has this changed the way that writers influence each other?

14. How did world writers build a "WALL OF DEFENCE" around Solzhenitsyn?

15. The speaker says that "mankind's sole salvation lies in everyone making everything his business." What does he mean?

16. How can world literature help people understand each other better?

17. What is the relationship between violence and lies?

18. How do writers and artists fight falsehood?

19. Why, according to Solzhenitsyn, will art win in the end?

20. What is Solzhenitsyn asking other writers and artists to do?

Understanding Literature: Persuasive Writing

Solzhenitsyn's speech is a form of persuasive writing. It tries to convince the reader to think a certain way, or to take action. Persuasive writing can be found in drama, poetry, short stories, or novels. Most often, it is found in nonfiction.

21. What ideas does Solzhenitsyn want to convince his readers to believe?

22. What does Solzhenitsyn want to convince his readers to do?

23. Whom do you think the writer is trying to persuade?

24. How is this speech hopeful?

25. Think about the Russian proverb at the end of the speech. How can this proverb help persuade people to speak the truth?

Critical Thinking

26. Imagine you are a writer in a country that controls what writers write. How would you feel about this speech?

27. Solzhenitsyn could not attend the Nobel ceremonies. Why do you think he sent this speech?

28. If you had been Solzhenitsyn, would you have gone back to Russia? Explain.

29. Do you agree that writers can change the world? Why or why not?

Thinking Creatively

30. The writer quotes a Russian saying: "Do not believe your brother, believe your own crooked eye." What do you think he means by this? Do you agree? Explain your answer.

Grammar Check

Solzhenitsyn uses many different types of complex sentences. There are long sentences with many noun phrases. A noun phrase is a group of words that act as a noun in the sentence. Look at the first sentence of the speech. Here are the noun phrases from that sentence:

    vision of the world
    motivations and scale of values
    actions and intentions
    personal and group experience of life

Find another sentence in the speech that uses several noun phrases. Write down all the noun phrases. How can this help you understand what you are reading?

 ### Writing on Your Own

An outline can help you understand a subject. Make an outline of the Nobel lecture. Your outline can list the main idea of each paragraph or section.

 ### Speaking

Work with a small group of students. Take turns reading parts of the speech aloud. Take time to read your section silently and make sure you really understand it before you read it aloud.

 ### Listening

Listen carefully as your teacher reads a section of the speech aloud to the class. Take notes about important ideas. Focus on what your teacher is saying. Was this speech easier to understand when you read it silently or when you listened to someone read it aloud?

 ### Research

The Nobel Prize Foundation has its own Web site. Search for this site using "Nobel Prize Foundation" as keywords. The site gives information about everyone who has won an award. Visit this Web site to learn all about the different people who won awards in literature. Read Albert Camus' speech to find out what he said. Look for the ideas that Solzhenitsyn was referring to in his speech.

BEFORE READING THE SELECTION

The Gettysburg Address   by Abraham Lincoln

Abraham Lincoln
(1809–1865)
American

Objectives

- To read and understand an important speech from United States history
- To describe how the setting affects a speech
- To explain the power of repetition in a speech

About the Speaker

Abraham Lincoln was born in Kentucky and grew up in Indiana. As a young man, he moved to a small town in Illinois. Lincoln educated himself by reading a lot.

Lincoln tried many jobs before his speaking skills led him into politics. His campaign debates put Lincoln in the national spotlight as a spokesman against the spread of slavery into the territories. In 1860, the new Republican Party named him its candidate for president. He won the election.

Soon after the election, the Civil War began. The struggle to save the Union claimed most of Lincoln's attention. Many moving words about democracy and freedom come from his speeches during this time. In 1865, President Lincoln was shot and killed while watching a play.

About the Selection

During the first two years of the Civil War, the Union army lost several major battles. In July 1863, they won their first big victory against the Confederate army of the South. The battle took place near Gettysburg, Pennsylvania. More than 50,000 soldiers were killed or wounded there. In November 1863, the Union decided to keep part of the Gettysburg battlefield as a cemetery. Lincoln was asked to speak. His three-minute speech disappointed some who heard it. Today, it is considered one of the world's great speeches.

Literary Terms Presidents and other government leaders give speeches all the time. A speech is a written work that is meant to be read aloud. In modern times, many U.S. presidents hire writers who write their speeches for them. Abraham Lincoln wrote his own speeches. In this speech, he said some powerful things about the country and the men who were fighting for it.

> **setting** the time and place in a story
>
> **repetition** using a word, phrase, or image more than once to show that it is important

Lincoln gave this speech during the Civil War. He spoke on a battlefield where many soldiers had died. This is the **setting,** or time and place. It is part of what makes this speech so important in U.S. history.

Lincoln used **repetition** to help make his point. Repetition is using a word, phrase, or image more than once to show that it is important. It is especially powerful in a speech.

Reading on Your Own This is a short speech with one main idea. As you read this speech, look for that idea. What is the main idea of the speech? What line or lines best state this idea?

Writing on Your Own How do you think a country should honor soldiers who have died in battle? Write a paragraph telling your ideas.

Vocabulary Focus Many words have both a denotation and a connotation. The denotation is the word's dictionary definition. The connotation is the way a word makes a reader feel. A good speaker will choose the word that exactly expresses the desired meaning. In this speech, Abraham Lincoln talks about the "brave" men. What are the connotations of brave? Talk with a partner about why Lincoln used this word to describe both the "living and dead."

Think Before You Read What do you hope that Lincoln will say about the men who died on the battlefield?

Persuasive Literature Unit 5

A *score* is 20 years. Four score and seven would equal 87 years.

As you read the speech, think about the setting. What was on the minds of the listeners?

Four score and seven years ago our fathers brought forth on this continent, a new nation, **conceived** in liberty, and dedicated to the **proposition** that all men are created equal.

Now we are engaged in a great civil war, testing whether that nation, or any nation so conceived and so dedicated, can long endure. We are met on a great battlefield of that war. We have come to dedicate a portion of that field, as a final resting place for those who here gave their lives that that nation might live. It is altogether fitting and proper that we should do this.

But in a larger sense, we cannot dedicate—we cannot **consecrate**—we cannot **hallow**—this ground. The brave men, living and dead, who struggled here, have consecrated it, far above our poor power to add or **detract**. The world will little note, nor long remember, what we say here, but it can never forget what they did here. It is for us the living, rather, to be

The Gettysburg Address

dedicated here to the unfinished work which they who fought here have thus far so nobly advanced.

It is rather for us to be here dedicated to the great task remaining before us—that from these honored dead we may take increased devotion to that cause for which they gave the last full **measure** of devotion—that we here highly resolve that these dead shall not have died in vain—that this nation, under God, shall have a new birth of freedom—and that government of the people, by the people, for the people, shall not **perish** from the earth.

> Imagine yourself listening to this speech. How would listening to it be different from reading it?

> Look for repetition in this speech.

conceived formed in the mind

proposition an idea or statement

consecrate dedicate to a serious purpose

hallow set apart as holy

detract take away

measure an amount

perish be destroyed; die

Painting of the Battle of Gettysburg, by Edwin Forbes.

AFTER READING THE SELECTION

The Gettysburg Address by Abraham Lincoln

Directions Choose the letter of the best answer or write the answer using complete sentences.

Comprehension: Identifying Facts

1. How long after the United States became a nation did Lincoln give this speech?
   A 4 years   C 20 years
   B 11 years   D 87 years

2. Why does Lincoln say that the future of the United States is being tested?

3. What is special about the field where they are standing?

Comprehension: Putting Ideas Together

4. Why does Lincoln say he cannot "dedicate" the ground?
   A The dead soldiers already made it holy.
   B The United States does not own the land.
   C He is not the president yet.
   D The Confederate soldiers will not let him.

5. How can the people make sure the soldiers did not die in vain?

6. How does Lincoln show that he thinks his speech is less important than the soldiers' deaths?

Understanding Literature: Repetition

Repetition is using a word, phrase, or image more than once to show that it is important. Repetition adds force and clearness to a speech. This is a very powerful tool for a speaker. Repetition can help the speaker make sure everyone hears and remembers the most important ideas. Repetition also is pleasing as a literary device. As a result of repetition, a speech takes on a rhythm that is almost like listening to poetry.

7. In the third paragraph, Lincoln repeats the word *cannot*. What point is he trying to make?

8. Lincoln uses the words *dedicate* and *dedicated* six times in this short speech. What do they mean? Why would Lincoln want people to remember these words?

Critical Thinking

9. How does Lincoln describe the government of the United States? In your own words, tell what he means by this.

Thinking Creatively

10. How has Lincoln's speech helped people remember what happened at Gettysburg?

Grammar Check

An em dash (—) can show an important break in the speaker's thoughts. It is as if the speaker interrupts himself or herself in the middle of a sentence. Here, Lincoln wants to make an important point about what he has just said. Find the sentences that use em dashes in this speech. Do they show what Lincoln felt strongly about? Why or why not?

 ### Writing on Your Own

Pretend that you were there when Lincoln gave this speech. Write a letter to your family telling them what the president said and how it made you feel. Remember that the people listening to Lincoln did not know how the war would end.

 ### Speaking

President Lincoln said that he wanted the country to "have a new birth of freedom." Write a speech explaining what Lincoln meant. Tell whether or not you think this happened. Explain why you think this. Give your speech to your class.

 ### Listening

Watch the news on a public television station or listen to it on a public radio station. Try to listen to a president or other leader give a speech. You may only hear a small part of the speech—that's OK. Think about how the speaker's words compare with the powerful words of Lincoln's speech. Do you think that Lincoln's speech is powerful because of the topic or because of the speaker?

 ### Media

In today's world, presidents giving important speeches know they will have a large audience when the speech is shown on television. This usually affects the way the speech is written. The president may try to include sound bites. These are words that sound good and will be easily remembered. Talk with a small group about how President Lincoln's speech would have been different if he had used sound bites. Do you think this would have made his speech better or worse?

Persuasive Literature Unit 5 443

BEFORE READING THE SELECTION

Inaugural Address   by John F. Kennedy

John F. Kennedy
(1917–1963)
American

Objectives

- To read and understand an inaugural speech
- To identify the speaker's tone
- To explain the images and figurative language in a speech

About the Speaker

John F. Kennedy was born in Massachusetts. He was the second son in a wealthy Irish Catholic family. Kennedy went to private schools as a child and graduated from Harvard University. He served in the navy during World War II and then went into politics. In 1952, he became a United States senator. Kennedy quickly became a recognized leader in the Democratic Party.

Kennedy ran for president in 1960. A Catholic had never been elected president before. This was also the first year that the presidential debates were shown on television. Kennedy did well on national TV. He appeared confident. He convinced the American public that his religion and inexperience with foreign policy were not serious problems. He narrowly defeated Richard Nixon to become the 35th president of the United States. Kennedy was shot and killed in November 1963.

About the Selection

An inaugural address is the speech a president gives when inaugurated, or sworn in. This speech was given in Washington on January 20, 1961.

In 1961, the United States was deeply involved in the cold war. This term describes the bad feelings between the United States and the former Soviet Union after World War II. Both countries had a lot of power. They also both had nuclear weapons aimed straight at each other. Kennedy speaks to the leaders of the Soviet Union in this speech. He also speaks to other people around the world.

444 Unit 5 Persuasive Literature

Literary Terms In this speech, Kennedy talks about many different ideas. He uses his words to create **images,** or pictures, in the listeners' minds. Kennedy also uses **figurative language**. This is writing or speech that is not meant to be understood exactly as it is written.

Some of the ideas that Kennedy talks about are painful. He talks about war, about poverty, and about the struggle between the United States and the Soviet Union. Yet, Kennedy's **tone** is positive. The tone is the attitude an author or speaker takes toward a subject.

Reading on Your Own Use a Structured Overview graphic organizer to help you find the main idea and subtopics in this speech. Refer to Appendix A for an example of this graphic organizer. Fill it in as you read. What is the main idea of the speech?

Writing on Your Own What do you know about John F. Kennedy? Write a paragraph telling what you know or listing some of the questions you have about him.

Vocabulary Focus The suffix -*al* can be used to change a noun to an adjective. There are several examples of this in the speech: *inaugural, global, accidental, colonial, cultural, spiritual,* and *national*. Find these words in the speech. Write their meanings as Kennedy used them. Then write each word's noun form and its meaning.

Think Before You Read What are some ideas you expect to read about in an inaugural address?

---

image a picture in the reader's mind created by words

figurative language writing or speech not meant to be understood exactly as it is written

tone the attitude an author takes toward a subject

Persuasive Literature **Unit 5 445**

Inaugural Address

John F. Kennedy delivers his inaugural speech.

As you read, watch for passages that show Kennedy means his words for the entire world.

What does he mean by the power to abolish all forms of human life?

Tempered means "strengthened."

The world is very different now. For man holds in his mortal hands the power to **abolish** all forms of human poverty and all forms of human life. And yet the same revolutionary beliefs for which our **forebears** fought are still at issue around the globe—the belief that the rights of man come not from the generosity of the state but from the hand of God.

We dare not forget today that we are the **heirs** of that first revolution. Let the word go forth from this time and place, to friend and foe alike, that the torch has been passed to a new generation of Americans—born in this century, tempered by war, **disciplined** by a hard and bitter peace, proud of our

abolish put an end to
forebears ancestors
heirs people who inherit something
disciplined trained to act according to certain rules

ancient **heritage**—and unwilling to witness or permit the slow **undoing** of those human rights to which this nation has always been committed, and to which we are committed today at home and around the world.

Let every nation know, whether it wishes us well or ill, that we shall pay any price, bear any burden, meet any hardship, support any friend, oppose any foe to assure the **survival** and the success of liberty.

This much we pledge—and more.

To those old allies whose cultural and spiritual origins we share, we pledge the loyalty of faithful friends. United, there is little we cannot do in a host of new cooperative ventures.

Divided, there is little we can do—for we dare not meet a powerful challenge at odds and split **asunder**.

> A number of countries in Africa and Asia had recently become independent of colonial rule.

To those new states whom we welcome to the ranks of the free, we pledge our word that one form of colonial control shall not have passed away merely to be replaced by a far more iron **tyranny**. We shall not always expect to find them supporting our view. But we shall always hope to find them strongly supporting their own freedom—and to remember that, in the past, those who foolishly sought power by riding the back of the tiger ended up inside.

To those peoples in the huts and villages of half the globe struggling to break the bonds of mass misery, we pledge our best efforts to help them help themselves, for whatever period is required—not because the Communists may be doing it, not because we seek their votes, but because it is right. If a free society cannot help the many who are poor, it cannot save the few who are rich. . . .

> Kennedy's words paint a picture of the people living in the world's poorest countries. What image do you see in your mind as you read this?

Finally, to those nations who would make themselves our **adversary**, we offer not a pledge but a request: that both

---

heritage what is handed down from earlier generations

undoing the destruction of something already accomplished

survival the act of staying in existence

asunder into separate parts

tyranny rule by a harsh, powerful government

adversary an enemy

> What dark powers of destruction had science let loose in this period?

> Read what Kennedy says to his enemies. What words show that his tone is positive? What kind of tone could he have taken?

sides begin **anew** the quest for peace, before the dark powers of destruction **unleashed** by science **engulf** all humanity in planned or accidental self-destruction.

We dare not tempt them with weakness. For only when our arms are sufficient beyond doubt can we be certain beyond doubt that they will never be employed.

But neither can two great and powerful groups of nations take comfort from our present course—both sides **overburdened** by the cost of modern weapons, both rightly alarmed by the steady spread of the deadly atom, yet both racing to alter that uncertain balance of terror that stays the hand of mankind's final war.

anew again
unleashed let loose; released
engulf swallow up; surround completely
overburdened having too much to carry

So let us begin anew—remembering on both sides that **civility** is not a sign of weakness, and sincerity is always subject to proof. Let us never **negotiate** out of fear. But let us never fear to negotiate.

Let both sides explore what problems unite us instead of **belaboring** those problems which divide us.

Let both sides, for the first time, **formulate** serious and precise proposals for the inspection and control of arms—and bring the absolute power to destroy other nations under the absolute control of all nations.

Let both sides seek to **invoke** the wonders of science instead of its terrors. Together let us explore the stars, conquer the deserts, **eradicate** disease, tap the ocean depths and encourage the arts and commerce.

All this will not be finished in the first 100 days. Nor will it be finished in the first 1,000 days, nor in the life of this Administration, nor even perhaps in our lifetime on this planet. But let us begin.

In your hands, my fellow citizens, more than mine, will rest the final success or failure of our course. Since this country was founded, each generation of Americans has been summoned to give testimony to its national loyalty. The graves of young Americans who answered the call to service surround the globe.

Now the trumpet summons us again—not as a call to bear arms, though arms we need—not as a call to battle, though **embattled** we are—but a call to bear the burden of a long twilight struggle year in and year out, "rejoicing in hope, patient in **tribulation**"—a struggle against the common enemies of man: tyranny, poverty, disease and war itself.

> There is no real trumpet. This is an example of Kennedy's use of figurative language.

civility courtesy	**formulate** plan	**embattled** ready for battle
negotiate work to reach agreement	**invoke** call upon for help	**tribulation** suffering
belaboring going over again and again	**eradicate** get rid of	

Can we forge against these enemies a grand and **global alliance**, north and south, east and west, that can assure a more fruitful life for all mankind? Will you join in that historic effort?

In the long history of the world, only a few generations have been granted the role of defending freedom in its hour of **maximum** danger. I do not shrink from this responsibility—I welcome it. I do not believe that any of us would exchange places with any other people or any other generation. The energy, the faith, the devotion which we bring to this **endeavor** will light our country and all who serve it—and the glow from that fire can truly light the world.

> How does this statement make the speech especially effective? What was Kennedy asking people to do?

And so, my fellow Americans: ask not what your country can do for you—ask what you can do for your country.

My fellow citizens of the world: ask not what America will do for you, but what together we can do for the freedom of man.

---

global alliance an agreement among world nations

maximum the greatest possible

endeavor a sincere attempt

AFTER READING THE SELECTION

Inaugural Address by John F. Kennedy

Directions Choose the letter of the best answer or write the answer using complete sentences.

Comprehension: Identifying Facts

1. Why does Kennedy say we will help the poor countries of the world?
   A because they are our friends
   B because the Communists are helping them, too
   C because we want their vote
   D because it is the right thing to do

2. Why should the two powerful groups of nations be unhappy with the way things are?

3. What things does Kennedy name as the real enemies of all people?

Comprehension: Putting Ideas Together

4. What are the "revolutionary beliefs for which our forebears fought"?
   A that war is a thing to fight
   B that we are loyal to our friends
   C that people have certain rights from God
   D that a country needs a strong army

5. Why does Kennedy say that the country needs a strong military?

6. What does Kennedy ask of the American people?

Understanding Literature: Figurative Language

Figurative language includes idioms, metaphors, and similes. An idiom is an expression that cannot be taken exactly as it is written. For example, the expression "Don't cry over spilled milk" has nothing to do with milk at all. Metaphors and similes are ways of comparing things.

7. Kennedy described tyrants as people "who foolishly sought power by riding the back of the tiger [and] ended up inside." Use your own words to explain this metaphor.

8. Kennedy says that "the torch has been passed to a new generation of Americans." He is using figurative language. There is no real torch. What is he trying to say?

Critical Thinking

9. What were some things Kennedy wanted to do with America's enemies? Have any of his goals been reached today?

Thinking Creatively

10. Why do you think the president of the United States was talking to people of the world?

After Reading continued on next page

Persuasive Literature Unit 5

AFTER READING THE SELECTION (continued)

Inaugural Address by John F. Kennedy

 ### Grammar Check

The subject and verb in a sentence must agree. They will either both be plural or both be singular. Write this part of a sentence from Kennedy's speech.

> . . . only a few generations have been granted the role of defending freedom in its hour of maximum danger.

Circle the subject (a few generations). Underline the verb (have been granted). Rewrite the sentence using one generation as the subject. Make sure to change the verb to a singular form.

 ### Writing on Your Own

What part of this speech is most meaningful to you? Write a paragraph telling why it is meaningful to you.

 ### Speaking

Think about the four common enemies that Kennedy names (tyranny, poverty, disease, and war itself). Which one do you think is the most serious problem for people today? Give a speech about it to your class.

 ### Listening

Listen to President John F. Kennedy give his speech. You will find it at the John F. Kennedy Library and Museum Web site. Close your eyes as you listen. Pretend that you are listening to him as he gave the speech in 1961. Try to picture the images that he describes.

 ### Technology

Many speakers use computer presentations to help the audience picture the main ideas as they speak. Present part, or all, of the speech using your computer presentation. Include pictures, graphs, and graphic organizers.

Essays

A writer explaining a personal point of view is writing an essay. An essay may be about a basic issue or current event. In either case, the writer will present facts as he or she understands them. The writer's talents and limits affect what is written.

Essays have existed from the beginning of literature. Plato, a Greek philosopher of long ago, wrote dialogues that were like essays. These imaginary conversations showed his ideas about truth, beauty, and government. Around 1450, the printing press was introduced into Europe. It then became easier to publish essays. This helped many thinkers of the 1500s to the 1800s become interpreters of their societies. They include Michel de Montaigne, Thomas Paine, and Ralph Waldo Emerson.

By the 1700s and 1800s, many people could afford to buy books and newspapers. Also, more people could read. This meant many new readers. Essayists began to write opinion articles. They wrote down their ideas about many things, from gossip to opinions about the writings of others. This trend continues today. Newspaper editorials and advice columns are kinds of essays. The essay also still exists in the form of regular columns in newspapers and magazines.

What makes modern essayists popular? It may be their points of view, writing styles, or both. They are not the final authority on any subject. But their ideas are useful. They can help readers form their own opinions.

Essays

- *dialogues*
- *opinions*
- *editorials*
- *advice*

Persuasive Literature Unit 5 **453**

BEFORE READING THE SELECTION

Of Repentance   by Michel de Montaigne (trans. by J. M. Cohen)

Michel de Montaigne
(1533–1592)
French

Objectives

- To read and understand an essay
- To describe a writer's style

About the Author

Michel de Montaigne was the son of a rich French nobleman. Books and ideas were important to his family. They also became his main interest. Until he was six years old, Montaigne spoke only Latin. He came to know that language well. Montaigne practiced law for several years. Then, in 1571, his father died. He left Montaigne his share of the family money. Montaigne retired. He was only 38 years old. He spent the rest of his life happily pursuing things that interested him, especially writing. His essays' comments on society show that he was a thoughtful man and a keen observer.

Montaigne filled three books with his writings. They are lively observations on life. His early works tend to copy the thoughts of classic writers. His later works are based more on his own experiences—his travels, the unrest of the French religious wars, and the loss of a close friend. He wrote about friendship, education, and religion. Over time, he developed the habit of watching and learning from the world around him. "I stand back" was his official motto.

About the Selection

"Of Repentance" is part of Montaigne's third book of writings. It was published in 1588. It tells the story of a man who is very poor. He decides to become a thief. He is strong and quick, so he does not get caught. He also steals from people who are very far from where he lives. No one thinks a thief could carry the things so far away. They do not suspect him. By the time the man is old, he is no longer poor. Now he wants to make things right. Read to find out how the man plans to do this.

454   Unit 5   Persuasive Literature

Literary Terms An **essay** is a piece of writing that shows a writer's opinion on some basic or current issue. Sometimes, the writer does not actually tell his or her opinion. The reader has to pay attention to the words the writer uses for clues about the writer's opinion. Montaigne writes this essay without telling his opinion. This is part of his **style,** or way of writing. Writers show their styles by the kinds of sentences they use: long and complex, short, descriptive, or factual. Writers show their styles in many other ways, too. They may have certain phrases they repeat; they may use imagery; or they may state ideas in a matter-of-fact way.

essay a written work that shows a writer's opinion on some basic or current issue

style an author's way of writing

Reading on Your Own As you read the story, think about the culture of the people in the story. How is this culture different from yours?

Writing on Your Own What do you think about stealing? Write a paragraph to explain your answer.

Vocabulary Focus *Repentance* means being sorry for doing something and promising never to do it again. Read the story carefully. Decide if you think the man really repents or not.

Think Before You Read How do you think The Thief will plan to make things right?

The Robber, by Pablo Picasso.

Of Repentance

The other day, when I was on the estate of a kinsman of mine in Armagnac, I saw a peasant whom everybody called *The Thief*. He told us his story, which was like this: Born a beggar, and realizing that if he were to earn his living by the work of his hands, he would never succeed in securing himself against want, he decided to become a thief; and thanks to his physical strength, he **practised** his trade quite safely throughout his youth. He gathered his harvest and his **vintage** from other men's lands, but at such great distances and in such great stacks that no one could conceive how one man could carry away so much on his shoulders in a single night. And he took care, besides, to **equalize** and distribute the damage that he caused, so as to **minimize** the loss to each individual. Now, in his old age, he is rich for a man of his condition, thanks to his trade, which he openly confesses. And to **reconcile** God to his winnings, he has made it, he said, his daily task to **compensate** the heirs of the men he robbed by voluntary gifts. If he does not complete his task—for to do it all at once is beyond him—he will, he says, leave it as a charge to his heirs, to repay them according to the wrong he did to each, which is known to him alone. From his account, whether true or false, it seems that this man regards theft as a dishonest action, and hates it, though less than he hates poverty. He **repents** of it quite simply, but in so far as it was thus **counterbalanced** and compensated, he does not repent of it.

> As you read, think about Montaigne's style. How would you describe his writing?

> *Armagnac* is a region in southwestern France.

> *Practised* is the British spelling for *practiced*.

> *Heirs* are people who will have the right to someone's property after he or she dies.

> Look for statements in the essay that show how the writer feels. How do you think Montaigne feels about what the man has done over the years?

vintage a crop of grapes grown for wine
equalize make equal
minimize make as small as possible
reconcile bring into agreement
compensate repay
repents feels sorry for an action
counterbalanced used one act to make up for another

AFTER READING THE SELECTION

Of Repentance by Michel de Montaigne (trans. by J. M. Cohen)

Directions Choose the letter of the best answer or write the answer using complete sentences.

Comprehension: Identifying Facts

1. Why did the man become a thief?
   A His father was a thief.
   B He hated begging.
   C He did not think he could earn a living by working.
   D He thought rich people had too much stuff.

2. Why didn't anyone believe that The Thief had stolen their crops?

3. How has The Thief tried to make up for stealing?

Comprehension: Putting Ideas Together

4. Why does The Thief steal from many people, instead of just a few?
   A He wants to see what everyone has.
   B He does not want anyone to feel too much loss.
   C He thinks everyone should be robbed at least once.
   D He never feels like he has enough.

5. What will The Thief do if he dies before he pays everyone back?

6. Does The Thief regret his actions as a young man?

Understanding Literature: Essay

A writer uses an essay to comment on some idea or part of society. Sometimes, the writer will use stories to make a point. The readers have to think carefully about the details of the story.

7. What is Montaigne's personal connection with The Thief?

8. What is Montaigne's attitude toward The Thief?

Critical Thinking

9. This story is about a man who claims that stealing is wrong but steals anyway. His excuse is poverty. Below is a list of principles in which people may say they believe. The second list is examples of things people do that are against their beliefs. Match each principle with its example.

General Principle
- being on time
- being honest
- being forgiving

Example
A cheating on a test
B holding on to an angry feeling toward someone
C choosing to catch a late bus to school

Thinking Creatively

10. Do you think modern thieves are like The Thief in this essay? Explain.

Grammar Check

An infinitive is a form of a verb that begins with *to*. Since an infinitive is a verb, it can have an object. Here are some examples: to play a game, to sing a song, and to eat dinner. Find two infinitives in this essay. Write down each infinitive with its object.

 ### Writing on Your Own

Pick one of the pairs from question 9. Write a paragraph to explain how people can believe in a general principle but sometimes act in a different way.

 ### Speaking

Retell the story as if you are one of these people: a person who has been robbed, one of The Thief's heirs, or an honest beggar who lives in the area. Think about how the person feels about what happened. Use your own words to tell the story and describe how you feel.

 ### Listening and Media

Work with a small group of classmates. Decide what you think this story says about people in general. Brainstorm a list of songs that talk about these ideas, too. Write the lyrics on paper. Read the lyrics aloud. As you listen to the lyrics, think about the songwriter's ideas. Discuss with your group how songs can be like essays.

BEFORE READING THE SELECTION

from A Small Place   by Jamaica Kincaid

Jamaica Kincaid
(1949–)
Antiguan

Objectives
- To read and understand an essay
- To describe the tone of a written work
- To identify irony and sarcasm and tell the writer's purpose in using it

About the Author
Jamaica Kincaid was born in St. John's, Antigua, an island in the West Indies. She grew up in this "small place" but left for New York City when she was 16. Her original name was Elaine Potter Richardson. She changed it when she became a writer. She wanted her name to reflect her Caribbean heritage. Kincaid's first novel, *Annie John*, was published in 1985. It is based on her own childhood. She has also written short stories. She has been a staff writer for the *New Yorker* magazine. Many of Kincaid's works are about colonial governments and dishonesty. Her opinions may sting, but they certainly get her readers' attention.

About the Selection
A Small Place is a nonfiction book about Antigua. It was published in 1988. In this chapter, the writer describes how a tourist thinks about what he or she sees. She also talks about how the local people think about those same things. She writes about what tourists want and what the local people need. As you will see, these are sometimes very different things.

Literary Terms Kincaid has strong feelings about the way that people live in Antigua. She writes about the gap between the lifestyles of the local people and the tourists. Kincaid uses **irony** and **sarcasm** to make her points. Irony is using words that seem to say one thing but mean the opposite. Sarcasm is a type of irony that is much stronger and can be mean-spirited. Kincaid's tone, or attitude toward the subject, is also shown by the examples and words she uses in this essay.

> **irony** the use of words that seem to say one thing but mean the opposite
>
> **sarcasm** a grim, sometimes mean-spirited kind of irony

Reading on Your Own This essay makes generalizations about tourists. These are statements that assume all tourists are the same. As you read, look for these generalizations. Can you find one that might not be true all the time?

Writing on Your Own What is your favorite thing about going on vacation? Write a short paragraph about it.

Vocabulary Focus Antigua was a British colony until the 1970s. The writer uses British spellings throughout this essay. Some examples are *aeroplane, favour,* and *colour*. Look for other words with British spellings. Make a list of these and write the American spelling next to each word.

Think Before You Read What are some things that a tourist might see differently than the people who live in an area?

Persuasive Literature Unit 5

This is Dickinson Bay, Antigua, after Hurricane Georges, in 1998.

from A Small Place

> The writer uses many long, complex sentences. This is part of her style.

> How do you think the writer feels about tourists? As you read, look for clues.

> The island of Antigua is in the Caribbean Sea, east of Puerto Rico.

If you go to Antigua as a tourist, this is what you will see. If you come by aeroplane, you will land at the V. C. Bird International Airport. Vere Cornwall (V. C.) Bird is the Prime Minister of Antigua. You may be the sort of tourist who would wonder why a Prime Minister would want an airport named after him—why not a school, why not a hospital, why not some great public monument? You are a tourist and you have not yet seen a school in Antigua, you have not yet seen the hospital in Antigua, you have not yet seen a public monument in Antigua. As your plane descends to land, you might say, What a beautiful island Antigua is—more beautiful than any of the other islands you have seen, and they were very beautiful, in their way, but they were much too green, much too **lush** with vegetation, which indicated to you, the tourist, that they got quite a bit of rainfall, and rain is the very thing that you, just now, do not want, for you are thinking of the hard and cold and dark and long days you spent working in North America (or, worse, Europe), earning some money so that you could stay in this place (Antigua) where the sun always shines and where the climate is deliciously hot and dry for the four to ten days you are going to be staying there; and since you are on your holiday, since you are a tourist, the thought of what it might be like for someone who had to live day in, day out in a place that suffers constantly from drought, and so has to watch carefully every drop of fresh water used (while at the same time surrounded by a sea and an ocean—the Caribbean Sea on one side, the Atlantic Ocean on the other), must never cross your mind.

You **disembark** from your plane. You go through customs. Since you are a tourist, a North American or European—to be **frank,** white—and not an Antiguan black returning to Antigua from Europe or North America with cardboard boxes of much needed cheap clothes and food for relatives, you move through customs swiftly, you move through customs with ease. Your bags are not searched. You emerge from customs into the hot, clean air: immediately you feel **cleansed,** immediately you feel blessed (which is to say special); you feel free. You see a man, a taxi driver; you ask him to take you to your destination; he **quotes** you a price. You immediately think that the price is in the local **currency,** for you are a tourist and you are familiar with these things (rates of exchange) and you feel even more free, for things seem so cheap, but then your driver ends by saying, "In U.S. currency." You may say, "Hmmmm, do you have a formal sheet that lists official prices and destinations?" Your driver obeys the law and shows you

Customs is the official process for inspecting what people bring into a country.

---

lush growing thick with plants

disembark get out of (a boat) or off (a plane)

frank bluntly honest

cleansed clean; free of dirt

quotes states or offers a price

currency the form of money a country uses

Persuasive Literature Unit 5

the sheet, and he apologises for the **incredible** mistake he has made in quoting you a price off the top of his head which is so vastly different (favouring him) from the one listed. You are driven to your hotel by this taxi driver in his taxi, a brand-new Japanese-made vehicle. The road on which you are travelling is a very bad road, very much in need of repair. You are feeling wonderful, so you say, "Oh, what a marvellous change these bad roads are from the splendid highways I am used to in North America." (Or, worse, Europe.) Your driver is reckless; he is a dangerous man who drives in the middle of the road when he thinks no other cars are coming in the opposite direction, passes other cars on blind curves that run uphill, drives at sixty miles an hour on narrow, curving roads when the road sign, a rusting, beat-up thing left over from colonial days, says 40 MPH. This might frighten you (you are on your holiday; you are a tourist); this might excite you (you are on your holiday; you are a tourist), though if you are from New York and take taxis you are used to this style of driving; most of the taxi drivers in New York are from places in the world like this. You are looking out the window (because you want to get your money's worth); you notice that all the cars you see are brand-new, or almost brand-new, and that they are all Japanese-made. There are no American cars in Antigua—no new ones, at any rate; none that were manufactured in the last ten years. You continue to look at the cars and you say to yourself, Why, they look brand-new, but they have an awful sound, like an old car—a very old, **dilapidated** car. How to account for that? Well, possibly it's because they use leaded gasoline in these brand-new cars whose engines were built to use non-leaded gasoline, but you mustn't ask the person driving the car if this is so, because he or she has never heard of unleaded gasoline. You look closely at the car; you see that it's a model of a Japanese car that you might hesitate to buy; it's a model that's very expensive; it's a model that's quite impractical for a person who has to work as hard as you do

> Why would the tourist say bad roads are "a marvellous change"? What does this remark show about the tourist?

> Notice how the writer uses sarcasm here.

incredible too unlikely to be believed

dilapidated shabby from neglect

An artist displays his work in an outdoor market.

and who watches every penny you earn so that you can afford this holiday you are on. How do they afford such a car? And do they live in a **luxurious** house to match such a car? Well, no. You will be surprised, then, to see that most likely the person driving this brand-new car filled with the wrong gas lives in a house that, in comparison, is far beneath the **status** of the car; and if you were to ask why you would be told that the banks are encouraged by the government to make loans available for cars, but loans for houses not so easily available; and if you ask again why, you will be told that the two main car dealerships in Antigua are owned in part or outright by **ministers** in government. Oh, but you are on holiday and the sight of these brand-new cars driven by people who may or may not have really passed their driving test (there was once a **scandal** about driving licences for sale) would not really

luxurious quite splendid and comfortable	**status** social position relative to others **ministers** high government officials	**scandal** talk about a public disgrace or action

> What is the writer's tone here?

stir up these thoughts in you. You pass a building sitting in a sea of dust and you think, It's some **latrines** for people just passing by, but when you look again you see the building has written on it PIGOTT'S SCHOOL. You pass the hospital, the Holberton Hospital, and how wrong you are not to think about this, for though you are a tourist on your holiday, what if your heart should miss a few beats? What if a blood vessel in your neck should break? What if one of those people driving those brand-new cars filled with the wrong gas fails to pass safely while going uphill on a curve and you are in the car going in the opposite direction? Will you be comforted to know that the hospital is staffed with doctors that no actual Antiguan trusts; that Antiguans always say about the doctors, "I don't want them near me"; that Antiguans refer to them not as doctors but as "the three men" (there are three of them);

> What is the difference between medical care for officials and for ordinary people?

that when the Minister of Health himself doesn't feel well he takes the first plane to New York to see a real doctor; that if any one of the ministers in government needs medical care he flies to New York to get it?

It's a good thing that you brought your own books with you, for you couldn't just go to the library and borrow some. Antigua used to have a splendid library, but in The Earthquake (everyone talks about it that way—The Earthquake; we Antiguans, for I am one, have a great sense of things, and the more meaningful the thing, the more meaningless we make it) the library building was damaged. This was in 1974, and soon after that a sign was placed on the front of the building saying, THIS BUILDING WAS DAMAGED IN THE EARTHQUAKE OF 1974. REPAIRS ARE **PENDING**. The sign hangs there, and hangs there more than a **decade** later, with its **unfulfilled** promise of repair, and you might see this as a sort of quaintness on the part of

---

latrines small buildings used for public bathrooms

pending not yet decided; waiting for action

decade a period of 10 years

unfulfilled not finished; not completed

these islanders, these people descended from slaves—what a strange, unusual **perception** of time they have. REPAIRS ARE PENDING, and here it is many years later, but perhaps in a world that is twelve miles long and nine miles wide (the size of Antigua) twelve years and twelve minutes and twelve days are all the same. The library is one of those splendid old buildings from colonial times, and the sign telling of the repairs is a splendid old sign from colonial times. Not very long after The Earthquake Antigua got its independence from Britain, making Antigua a state in its own right, and Antiguans are so proud of this that each year, to mark the day, they go to church and thank God, a British God, for this. But you should not think of the confusion that must lie in all that and you must not think of the damaged library. You have brought your own books with you, and among them is one of those new books about economic history, one of those books explaining how the West (meaning Europe and North America after its conquest and settlement by Europeans) got rich: the West got rich not from the free (free—in this case meaning got-for-nothing) and then undervalued labour, for generations, of the people like me you see walking around you in Antigua but from the **ingenuity** of small shopkeepers in Sheffield and Yorkshire and Lancashire, or wherever; and what a great part the invention of the wristwatch played in it, for there was nothing noble-minded men could not do when they discovered they could slap time on their wrists just like that (isn't that the last straw; for not only did we have to suffer the **unspeakableness** of slavery, but the satisfaction to be had from "We made you bastards rich" is taken away, too), and so you needn't let that slightly funny feeling you have from time to time about **exploitation, oppression, domination** develop

> The writer uses irony when she describes the book the tourist is reading.

> *Sheffield, Yorkshire,* and *Lancashire* are in England. English settlers used slave labor to grow sugarcane on Antigua.

---

perception a way of seeing or observing

ingenuity cleverness; inventive skill

unspeakableness a condition too bad to be described

exploitation the use of a person or resource for selfish purposes

oppression strict rule or control through the use of force

domination control or rule of one person or group by another

into full-fledged unease, **discomfort;** you could ruin your holiday. They are not responsible for what you have; you owe them nothing; in fact, you did them a big favour, and you can provide one hundred examples. For here you are now, passing by Government House. And here you are now, passing by the Prime Minister's Office and the Parliament Building, and overlooking these, with a splendid view of St. John's Harbour, the American **Embassy**. If it were not for you, they would not have Government House, and Prime Minister's Office, and Parliament Building and embassy of powerful country. Now you are passing a mansion, an **extraordinary** house painted the colour of old cow dung, with more **aerials** and antennas attached to it than you will see even at the American Embassy. The people who live in this house are a merchant family who came to Antigua from the Middle East less than twenty years ago. When this family first came to Antigua, they sold dry goods door to door from suitcases they carried on their backs. Now they own a lot of Antigua; they regularly lend money to the government, they build enormous (for Antigua), ugly (for Antigua), concrete buildings in Antigua's capital, St. John's, which the government then rents for huge sums of money; a member of their family is the Antiguan Ambassador to Syria; Antiguans hate them. Not far from this mansion is another mansion, the home of a drug smuggler. Everybody knows he's a drug smuggler, and if just as you were driving by he stepped out of his door your driver might point him out to you as the **notorious** person that he is, for this drug smuggler is so rich people say he buys cars in tens—ten of this one, ten of that one—and that he bought a house (another mansion) near Five Islands, contents included, with cash he carried in a suitcase: three hundred and fifty thousand American dollars, and, to the surprise of the seller of the house, lots of American dollars

discomfort the feeling of being uneasy or not comfortable

embassy a building owned by a foreign government, used for diplomats from that country

extraordinary very unusual

aerials antennas for receiving radio or TV

notorious famous for bad activities

were left over. Overlooking the drug smuggler's mansion is yet another mansion, and leading up to it is the best paved road in all of Antigua—even better than the road that was paved for the Queen's visit in 1985 (when the Queen came, all the roads that she would travel on were paved anew, so that the Queen might have been left with the impression that riding in a car in Antigua was a pleasant experience). In this mansion lives a woman **sophisticated** people in Antigua call Evita. She is a notorious woman. She's young and beautiful and the girlfriend of somebody very high up in the government. Evita is notorious because her relationship with this high government official has made her the owner of **boutiques** and property and given her a say in cabinet meetings, and all sorts of other privileges such a relationship would bring a beautiful young woman.

Oh, but by now you are tired of all this looking, and you want to reach your destination—your hotel, your room. You long to **refresh** yourself; you long to eat some nice lobster, some nice local food. You take a bath, you brush your teeth. You get dressed again; as you get dressed, you look out the window. That water—have you ever seen anything like it? Far out, to the horizon, the colour of the water is navy-blue; nearer, the water is the colour of the North American sky. From there to the shore, the water is pale, silvery, clear, so clear that you can see its pinkish-white sand bottom. Oh, what beauty! Oh, what beauty! You have never seen anything like this. You are so excited. You breathe shallow. You breathe deep. You see a beautiful boy skimming the water, godlike, on a Windsurfer. You see an incredibly unattractive, fat, **pastrylike**-fleshed woman enjoying a walk on the beautiful sand, with a man, an incredibly unattractive, fat, pastrylike-fleshed man; you see the pleasure they're taking in their

> Antigua is a member of the British Commonwealth, whose head is the Queen of England.

> What do you think Kincaid is saying about wealthy people in Antigua?

> How do you know that the people on the beach are tourists? How does the writer feel about them?

sophisticated having a broad knowledge of the world

boutiques small shops that sell special, and often expensive, goods

refresh make less tired, as if by resting or eating

pastrylike looking like baked goods made of dough

Persuasive Literature Unit 5 **469**

surroundings. Still standing, looking out the window, you see yourself lying on the beach, enjoying the amazing sun (a sun so powerful and yet so beautiful, the way it is always overhead as if on permanent guard, ready to stamp out any cloud that dares to darken and so empty rain on you and ruin your holiday; a sun that is your personal friend). You see yourself taking a walk on that beach. You see yourself meeting new people (only they are new in a very limited way, for they are people just like you). You see yourself eating some delicious, locally grown food. You see yourself, you see yourself. . . . You must not wonder what exactly happened to the contents of your lavatory when you flushed it. You must not wonder where your bathwater went when you pulled out the stopper.

This is Nelson Dockyard in Antigua.

You must not wonder what happened when you brushed your teeth. Oh, it might all end up in the water you are thinking of taking a swim in; the contents of your **lavatory** might, just might, graze gently against your ankle as you wade carefree in the water, for you see, in Antigua, there is no proper sewage-disposal system. But the Caribbean Sea is very big and the Atlantic Ocean is even bigger; it would amaze even you to know the number of black slaves this ocean has swallowed up. When you sit down to eat your delicious meal, it's better that you don't know that most of what you are eating came off a plane from Miami. And before it got on a plane in Miami, who knows where it came from? A good guess is that it came from a place like Antigua first, where it was grown dirt-cheap, went to Miami, and came back. There is a world of something in this, but I can't go into it right now.

> The writer means that waste water is piped into the ocean.

The thing you have always suspected about yourself the minute you become a tourist is true: A tourist is an ugly human being. You are not an ugly person all the time; you are not an ugly person ordinarily; you are not an ugly person day to day. From day to day, you are a nice person. From day to day, all the people who are supposed to love you on the whole do. From day to day, as you walk down a busy street in the large and modern and **prosperous** city in which you work and live, dismayed, puzzled (a **cliché,** but only a cliché can explain you) at how alone you feel in this crowd, how awful it is to go unnoticed, how awful it is to go unloved, even as you are surrounded by more people than you could possibly get to know in a lifetime that lasted for **millennia,** and then out of the corner of your eye you see someone looking at you and absolute pleasure is written all over that person's face, and then you realise that you are not as revolting a presence

> How does the writer prove her claim that tourists are ugly? Does she mean ugly to look at?

lavatory a bathroom
prosperous successful; wealthy
cliché an expression or idea that has been used over and over
millennia thousands of years

as you think you are (for that look just told you so). And so, ordinarily, you are a nice person, an attractive person, a person capable of drawing to yourself the affection of other people (people just like you), a person at home in your own skin (sort of; I mean, in a way; I mean, your dismay and puzzlement are natural to you, because people like you just seem to be like that, and so many of the things people like you find **admirable** about yourselves—the things you think about, the things you think really define you—seem rooted in these feelings): a person at home in your own house (and all its nice house things), with its nice back yard (and its nice back-yard things), at home on your street, your church, in community activities, your job, at home with your family, your relatives, your friends—you are a whole person. But one day, when you are sitting somewhere, alone in that crowd, and that awful feeling of **displacedness** comes over you, and really, as an ordinary person you are not well equipped to look too far inward and set yourself aright, because being ordinary is already so **taxing,** and being ordinary takes all you have out of you, and though the words "I must get away" do not actually pass across your lips, you make a leap from being that nice blob just sitting like a boob in your **amniotic sac** of the modern experience to being a person visiting heaps of death and ruin and feeling alive and inspired at the sight of it; to being a person lying on some faraway beach, your stilled body stinking and glistening in the sand, looking like something first forgotten, then remembered, then not important enough to go back for; to being a person marvelling at the **harmony** (ordinarily, what you would say is the backwardness) and the union these other people (and they are other people) have with nature. And you look at the things they can do with a piece of ordinary cloth, the things they fashion out of cheap, **vulgarly** colored (to you) twine, the way they squat

> How does the writer describe the local people? What is the tone now?

admirable worth liking

displacedness a state of being out of place or in the wrong place

taxing tiring; difficult

amniotic sac a pouch that holds a developing baby before it is born

harmony a pleasant agreement in feeling or actions

vulgarly in bad taste; crudely

down over a hole they have made in the ground, the hole itself is something to marvel at, and since you are being an ugly person this ugly but joyful thought will swell inside you: their ancestors were not clever in the way yours were and not **ruthless** in the way yours were, for then would it not be you who would be in harmony with nature and backwards in that charming way? An ugly thing, that is what you are when you become a tourist, an ugly, empty thing, a stupid thing, a piece of rubbish pausing here and there to gaze at this and taste that, and it will never occur to you that the people who inhabit the place in which you have just paused cannot stand you, that behind their closed doors they laugh at your strangeness (you do not look the way they look); the physical sight of you does not please them; you have bad manners (it is their custom to eat their food with their hands; you try eating their way, you look silly; you try eating the way you always eat, you look silly); they do not like the way you speak (you have an accent); they collapse helpless from laughter, **mimicking** the way they imagine you must look as you carry out some everyday bodily **function**. They do not like you. *They do not like me!* That thought never actually occurs to you. Still, you feel a little uneasy. Still, you feel a little foolish.

    Still, you feel a little out of place. But the **banality** of your own life is very real to you; it drove you to this extreme, spending your days and your nights in the company of people who despise you, people you do not like really, people you would not want to have as your actual neighbour. And so you must devote yourself to puzzling out how much of what you are told is really, really true (Is ground-up bottle glass in peanut sauce really a delicacy around here, or will it do just what you think ground-up bottle glass will do? Is this rare, **multicoloured,** snout-mouthed fish really an **aphrodisiac,**

---

ruthless cruel; without mercy

mimicking copying closely

function a normal use or activity

banality the quality of having little meaning

multicoloured (American *multicolored*) having many colors

aphrodisiac a food or drug that brings about sexual desire

or will it cause you to fall asleep permanently?). Oh, the hard work all of this is, and is it any wonder, then, that on your return home you feel the need of a long rest, so that you can recover from your life as a tourist?

> Do you think the writer is sometimes a tourist herself? How does she feel about that?

That the native does not like the tourist is not hard to explain. For every native of every place is a potential tourist, and every tourist is a native of somewhere. Every native everywhere lives a life of **overwhelming** and crushing banality and boredom and desperation and **depression,** and every deed, good and bad, is an attempt to forget this. Every native would like to find a way out, every native would like a rest, every native would like a tour. But some natives—most natives in the world—cannot go anywhere. They are too poor. They are too poor to go anywhere. They are too poor to escape the **reality** of their lives; and they are too poor to live properly in the place where they live, which is the very place you, the tourist, want to go—so when the natives see you, the tourist, they envy you, they envy your ability to leave your own banality and boredom, they envy your ability to turn their own banality and boredom into a source of pleasure for yourself.

overwhelming crushing; destructive

depression a state of sadness

reality things as they actually exist

AFTER READING THE SELECTION

from A Small Place   by Jamaica Kincaid

Directions Choose the letter of the best answer or write the answer using complete sentences.

Comprehension: Identifying Facts

1. What is the weather usually like in Antigua?
   A It is rainy.
   B It is cold and damp.
   C It snows all the time.
   D It is hot and dry.

2. Why do many cars in Antigua make an awful sound?
   A They are old and need to be repaired.
   B They use the wrong type of gas.
   C They have poor sound systems.
   D They make them that way to stop people from stealing them.

3. What does Pigott's School look like?

4. Where does the Minister of Health go to see a doctor?

5. When did the library close for repairs? Why did it close?

6. According to the tourist's book, how did the West get rich?

7. What is one sign that the drug smuggler is rich?

8. Why were certain roads paved before the Queen came to Antigua?

9. From where does most of the food in Antigua come?

10. How do most native Antiguans feel about tourists?

Comprehension: Putting Ideas Together

11. How is the weather a problem for Antiguans?
    A They have to worry about floods.
    B They never have enough water.
    C They have to shovel a lot of snow.
    D They have to spend a lot of money heating their homes.

12. How is going through customs different for tourists than for the native Antiguans?
    A The tourists' bags are not searched.
    B The tourists' bags are searched carefully.
    C The local people go through customs very quickly.
    D The local people's bags are not searched.

13. What are the problems with taking a taxi in Antigua?

After Reading continued on next page

AFTER READING THE SELECTION (continued)

from A Small Place   by Jamaica Kincaid

14. Why do Antiguans have better cars than houses?

15. Why should a tourist care about the condition of the hospital in Antigua?

16. Who really helped the West get rich?

17. Why do Antiguans hate the Middle Eastern family of merchants?

18. What is wrong with the beautiful ocean water around the island?

19. Why does the writer say that tourists are ugly?

20. Few native Antiguans are able to be tourists. What is the reason for this?

Understanding Literature: Tone

Tone is the attitude the author takes toward a subject. The tone may be humorous, affectionate, or optimistic. It might be bitter, angry, or depressed. The tone may shift at certain points in the writing. One thing that affects the tone of *A Small Place* is the author's use of irony. Irony is using words that seem to say one thing but mean something else.

21. What is the tone of *A Small Place*?

22. What is ironic about tourists being pleased the island is not too lush?

23. Name another contrast between what the tourist sees and what the reality is.

24. How does Kincaid explain why people want to be tourists?

25. What do you think is the most harsh thing the author says?

Critical Thinking

26. How does reading this selection make you feel? Explain.

27. Why do you think that only the airport is named for the Prime Minister?

28. How do you think the writer wants readers to respond to this selection?

29. Kincaid is from Antigua. She now lives in New York City. Is she a good spokesperson for Antigua? Why or why not?

Thinking Creatively

30. Is the writer suggesting that people never travel? Explain.

Grammar Check

Reread the description of a tourist. The paragraph begins on page 471. List all the adjectives the writer uses to describe a tourist. Make a separate list of the adjectives the writer uses to describe this same tourist in his or her everyday life. How do these adjectives show the writer's feelings about a tourist? Were you surprised by what this showed?

 Writing on Your Own

Think of a place that you know well. How would it look to a tourist? What do you see that a tourist would not see in the same way? Write a paragraph describing what a tourist might miss.

 Speaking

Kincaid thinks of tourists as outsiders. Think about how people feel when they are treated like outsiders. This means they are made to feel they are not welcome. Do you think your community should be more welcoming? Write your own speech about this.

 Listening

In this essay, Kincaid says some very strong things. It can be hard to listen when someone says these kinds of things. However, it is important to really listen to people when they are very angry or upset. Ask a partner to read part of the essay aloud to you. As you listen, think about why Kincaid feels so strongly. Do not think about how to defend your views. Just hear what she is saying.

 Viewing

Look at some brochures or Web sites for Antigua and other Caribbean islands. Do these help prove the ideas that Kincaid wrote about? Why or why not?

Unit 5 SKILLS LESSON
Setting

The setting of a piece of writing includes time and place.

The time can be a certain year in history. It can be a season, such as winter or summer. It can even be a time in a character's life, such as the teen years.

The place might be the town or state where the action happens. It can be the haunted house in a murder mystery. Or it can be the battlefield where the speaker stands and gives his speech:

> "Now we are engaged in a great civil war. . . ." "We are met on a great battlefield of that war. . . ." ". . . a final resting place for those who here gave their lives. . . ."

The setting has a serious meaning. Without this place, there would have been no speech.

Setting is at the heart of Jamaica Kinkaid's writing on Antigua. She draws a comparison between the beauty tourists see and the poverty of the natives:

> "From there to the shore, the water is pale, silvery, clear, so clear that you can see its pinkish-white sand bottom. Oh, what beauty!"

Compare that with:

> "You must not wonder what exactly happened to the contents of your lavatory when you flushed it. Oh, it might all end up in the water you are thinking of taking a swim in . . . in Antigua, there is no proper sewage-disposal system."

Review

1. What is setting?
2. Why do time and place matter in Joan of Arc's letter?
3. Name a selection in this unit in which you think time is more important than place.
4. Think about The Thief in "Of Repentance." How does the setting in long-ago rural France make this story possible?
5. Which setting did you find most interesting? Explain.

Writing on Your Own

Think of an event at which you might make a speech. (You might choose a school event, a sports dinner, or a family gathering.) Write the beginning of a speech you would give at that event.

Unit 5 SUMMARY

In this unit, you read examples of persuasive writing. Persuasive writing is meant to affect opinion. The selections in this unit are all nonfiction. Most persuasive writing is in that form.

This unit includes speeches and essays. People give speeches for many reasons. Speeches are meant for a special audience. They are in response to some event or occasion. Even when a speech is written, it is meant to be heard. You will find it helpful to read the speeches aloud. You may find recordings of some of the speeches from this unit.

Essays give a writer's personal point of view. They may be about a basic issue or a current event. The writer presents the facts as she or he sees them. The writer's way of thinking shapes the essay. So does the writer's style, or way of writing.

Selections

- "Letter to the English" by Joan of Arc. The French heroine sends a proclamation that warns the English to leave France.

- "Nobel Lecture" by Alexander Solzhenitsyn. Upon winning the Nobel Prize, the Russian writer gives his view of the importance of world literature.

- "The Gettysburg Address" by Abraham Lincoln. The president speaks to dedicate a cemetery at the site of the Battle of Gettysburg.

- "Inaugural Address" by John F. Kennedy. After being sworn in as president of the United States, the new president addresses the country and the world.

- "Of Repentance" by Michel de Montaigne. The French essayist tells the story of a man known as The Thief.

- *A Small Place* by Jamaica Kincaid. This chapter of the book gives a sarcastic view of tourists who come to the island of Antigua.

Unit 5 REVIEW

Directions Choose the letter of the best answer or write the answer using complete sentences.

Comprehension: Identifying Facts

1. Which of these selections is from France?
   A "The Gettysburg Address"
   B "Nobel Lecture"
   C "Of Repentance"
   D *A Small Place*

2. Two selections were written during the cold war. Identify them and tell what countries their authors are from.

3. Two forms of persuasive writing are used in this unit. What are they?

4. What literary form does de Montaigne use in "Of Repentance"?

5. What was the occasion for Solzhenitsyn's speech?

Comprehension: Putting Ideas Together

6. What does Joan of Arc want to accomplish with her speech?
   A to become the queen of England
   B to get the French to control England
   C to become the queen of France
   D to get the English out of France

7. What idea is discussed in "Of Repentance"?

8. What is the main thing Solzhenitsyn asks for in "Nobel Lecture"?

9. Name one way that the speeches of Lincoln and Kennedy are alike.

10. *A Small Place* at first seems to be about travel. What is it really about?

Understanding Literature: Essays, Letters, and Speeches

Essays, letters, and speeches are nonfiction. An essay shows a writer's opinions on an issue. A letter contains thoughts and feelings written to a certain person. Most letters are personal. A speech is written for a special event. It is meant to be read aloud. Some essays and speeches are meant to persuade. Their writers try to influence the opinions of the readers.

11. What do essays, letters, and speeches have in common?

12. How is a speech different from a letter or an essay?

13. Why is Joan of Arc's speech called the "Letter to the English"? Can it be both a speech and a letter? Explain.

14. This unit has two essays. In which one is the writer more personally involved?

15. All of the selections in this unit are called persuasive writing. Which selection do you think is the most persuasive?

Critical Thinking

16. Do you think the speeches are as effective when you read them as they would be if you heard them? Explain your answer.

17. Choose one of the selections. Explain why it is still being read today.

18. Choose two of the writers in this unit. Compare their styles of writing.

19. Which selection do you think asks the most of its audience? Explain.

Thinking Creatively

20. Which selection in this unit do you like least? Why?

Speak and Listen

Choose a speech from this unit or find one in the library. You can also search the Internet. If you do not find one you like, write your own. After you choose a speech, practice reading it. Then read it aloud in class.

Writing on Your Own

Think about the beliefs and ideas you read about in this unit. Each writer had strong ideas about something that was important to him or her. Do you think their writing would have been as good if they did not have strong ideas? Write an essay about one of the writers. Tell what belief the writer had. Do you think that belief made the writing stronger? Explain why you feel the way you do.

Beyond Words

Find pictures of some of the speakers or places from this unit. You can look in textbooks or magazines, or on the Internet. Photocopy the pictures, and then cut them out. Put them on a flat surface to make a collage. (A collage is a piece of art made by pasting objects on a surface so they overlap to form a picture.) You do not have to find the exact places or people that are in the unit. But they should be things that suggest the ideas of the speeches or essays.

Test-Taking Tip

Read the test directions twice. Sometimes they will give you a helpful hint. For example, the directions may remind you to look for the best answer.

Perro (Wifredo and Helena Lam's Cat), by Wifredo Lam.

"Humor and satire are more effective techniques for expressing social statements than direct comment."
—Kristin Hunter, author

"You can pretend to be serious but you can't pretend to be funny."
—Sacha Guitry, actor, director, screenwriter

Unit 6

Humorous Literature

Some writers write in ways that make us laugh. However, not all those writers are just having fun with human nature. Some use wit as a way to get us to think about serious problems. They hope we will see that something in the world needs to be changed. Sometimes things are funny to us because we see ourselves in the writing. We may have been in the same situation or faced the same problem as someone in a story.

The selections in this unit are told in several ways. Some quickly make it clear that they are just for fun. Others are told in a serious way. At first, you might not be sure that you are reading humor. You may want to read some selections more than once. You may discover a funny spot that you missed the first time.

Unit 6 Selections	Page
SATIRE	.486
■ IRELAND "A Modest Proposal" by Jonathan Swift	.487
■ ARGENTINA "Cup Inanity and Patriotic Profanity" by Andrew Graham-Yooll, from the *Buenos Aires Herald*	.496
■ EGYPT "The Happy Man" by Naguib Mahfouz	.503
COLUMNS	.519
■ UNITED STATES "Staying at a Japanese Inn: Peace, Tranquillity, Insects" by Dave Barry	.520
■ UNITED STATES "Why Can't We Have Our Own Apartment?" by Erma Bombeck	.529
STORIES	.535
■ AUSTRIA "Lohengrin" by Leo Slezak	.536
■ UKRAINE "A Wedding Without Musicians" by Sholom Aleichem	.547

Unit 6

About Humorous Literature

Humorous literature is created to entertain readers. Some humor comes from feeling better than someone who makes a mistake. We laugh at the stern banker who slips on a banana peel. She is lying on the sidewalk, and we aren't. Other humor comes from the unexpected—a sudden reversal of events. We laugh because we expect the banker to sit on a leather chair, not on the sidewalk. Whatever our reasons, laughter is the response a humorist wants. A humorist is someone who writes funny works. The humorist may write a light piece to pass the time or poke fun at human behavior with the idea of changing it. In either case, the desire to be funny is more important than the form of expression the writer chooses.

The tone of humor depends on how angry the behavior has made the humorist. Some writers may let us sit back and enjoy someone (even the writer) slipping on a banana peel. Or the writer may inspire us to rush out and pick up the banana peel before someone else slips.

At times, humor can be carried to an extreme where it is no longer funny. For example, a piece that is written to hurt or embarrass someone is not funny. Few people find writing that stereotypes race or gender to have any value.

Humor can take almost any literary form. Neil Simon's early plays were comedies poking fun at the stress-filled lives of New Yorkers. The French writer Molière wrote many humorous plays with a serious point. Ogden Nash and Edward Lear wrote funny poems. The Unit 6 selections are grouped into three forms of humorous writing: satire, columns, and stories.

The following countries are represented in this unit: Argentina, Austria, Egypt, Ireland, Ukraine, and the United States.

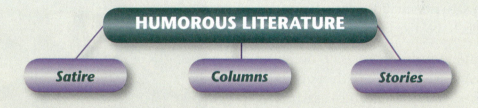

Satire

One of the oldest forms of literary humor is satire. Satire is humor that makes fun of foolishness or evil. Writers who decide to challenge others' behavior may be angry, or they may try to make people laugh at those actions. Or they can do both. Satire is a way for a writer to be angry while making people laugh at foolish or evil acts.

The talents of certain writers are well suited to satire. Geoffrey Chaucer's *Canterbury Tales* is one example. These stories and character portraits from the 1300s use satire throughout. Other well-known satirists include Mark Twain, François Rabelais, and Charles Dickens.

Some modern-day satirists do not write what we commonly think of as literature. Garry Trudeau is a satirist who created the comic *Doonesbury*. Other satirists may find their talent in writing for the television or film industry. For example, the people who write the show *The Sopranos* often satirize modern American life.

Satire requires an ability to describe human behavior accurately and vividly. A satirist sees tiny traits and behaviors. Careful word choice goes into using irony, puns, and other literary techniques. Above all, a writer using satire must have a strong sense of right and wrong. The writer must understand the difference between what society says is okay and what it knows is right. Satirists try to remind their readers of basic truths that are often ignored. One of the following selections is a reaction to social injustice. Another shows anger at foolish behavior. The third describes a man with an "illness" of being happy.

Satire
- makes fun of foolishness or evil
- uses irony, puns, sarcasm
- reacts to social injustice
- expresses anger at foolish behavior

BEFORE READING THE SELECTION

A Modest Proposal by Jonathan Swift

About the Author

Jonathan Swift
(1667–1745)
Irish

Though his parents were English, Jonathan Swift was born in Dublin, Ireland. Swift became an Anglican priest in 1695. He took his faith and his religion very seriously. Swift even left his political party because it did not support the Anglican Church of Ireland in the way he thought it should. He served in churches in England and Ireland. In 1713, he was named dean of the cathedral in Dublin. He settled there and wrote some of his greatest works.

Jonathan Swift wrote about religion and politics. He did this in both essays and stories. He felt that people could be very cruel and foolish. Swift's most famous work, *Gulliver's Travels* (1726), combines his political views and his moral views. It is about a man named Lemuel Gulliver and four trips that he takes.

About the Selection

Swift wrote "A Modest Proposal" in 1729. In this work, Swift talks about the terrible poverty of the Irish people. He is trying to show how serious the problem is. He is also showing how difficult it will be to solve. Swift suggests that the English should take the Irish babies and eat them. He says that this will help provide food for the English and help poor Irish families because they will not have to feed those children. He is not serious. He is just trying to make the point that the problem needs attention. When it was first written, many people thought he was serious. They were very angry.

Objectives

- To read and understand a satire
- To recognize the purpose of a pamphlet
- To identify an author's tone

Before Reading continued on next page

Humorous Literature Unit 6 487

BEFORE READING THE SELECTION (continued)

A Modest Proposal   by Jonathan Swift

---

satire humorous writing that makes fun of foolishness or evil

pamphlet a short printed essay about a specific topic with a paper cover

tone the attitude an author takes toward a subject

Literary Terms Jonathan Swift used **satire** to write about things that upset him. Satire is humor that makes fun of foolishness or evil. It is not usually the kind of humor that makes people laugh. It is more like a kind of ironic humor.

Swift wrote this **pamphlet** to show how angry he was about the way the English were treating the Irish people. A pamphlet is a short printed essay about a specific problem. Swift does not come out and say, "I am angry about this." Instead, he presents a ridiculous idea, that the British can just eat the Irish children. What he means is that they are acting as if they do not care at all about the Irish people and their struggles.

Swift wrote this as if he did not understand what was happening. His **tone** seems serious and simple. The tone is the attitude an author takes toward a subject.

Reading on Your Own Make a two-column chart with the headings *British* and *Irish*. As you read, use the chart to help keep track of Swift's points. In each column, list the ways this proposal will help each group of people. Based on your chart, who will benefit more, the British or the Irish?

Writing on Your Own Think about one problem in our country that really upsets you. Write two paragraphs about it. In the first, identify the problem. In the second, suggest a way to deal with it. Try using satire to describe your suggestion.

Vocabulary Focus The word *modest* means "simple" or "limited in importance." It describes something that will make only a small difference to most people. A *proposal* is an idea or suggestion. Think about the meaning of these words in the title. How does the title help Swift make his point?

Think Before You Read Swift makes a ridiculous suggestion. How do you think he expected people to respond to this work?

A Modest Proposal

A Modest Proposal FOR PREVENTING THE CHILDREN OF POOR PEOPLE IN IRELAND FROM BEING A BURDEN TO THEIR PARENTS OR COUNTRY, AND FOR MAKING THEM BENEFICIAL TO THE PUBLIC

It is a melancholy object to those who walk through this great town or travel in the country, when they see the streets, the roads, and cabin doors, crowded with beggars of the female-sex, followed by three, four, or six children, all in rags and **importuning** every passenger for an **alms**. These mothers, instead of being able to work for their honest livelihood, are forced to employ all their time in strolling to beg **sustenance** for their helpless infants, who, as they grow up, either turn thieves for want of work, or leave their dear native country to fight for the Pretender in Spain, or sell themselves to the Barbadoes.

I think it is agreed by all parties that this **prodigious** number of children in the arms or on the backs, or at the heels of their mothers, and frequently of their fathers, is in the present **deplorable** state of the kingdom a very great additional **grievance**; and therefore whoever could find out a fair, cheap, and easy method of making these children sound, useful members of the **commonwealth** would deserve so well of the public as to have his statue set up for a preserver of the nation.

As you read, keep in mind that this was printed in a pamphlet. It had no cover. There was no description of what the reader would find inside.

The *Pretender in Spain* was James Francis Edward Stuart. He was supposed to be the king of England, but the people did not accept him. He was exiled to Spain.

Barbadoes (American *Barbados*) is an island in the West Indies. Some poor people went as servants to Caribbean islands.

---

importuning begging

alms charity; a handout

sustenance something that supports life, especially food

prodigious enormous

deplorable terrible

grievance something to complain about

commonwealth the community as a whole; the nation

Potato Famine, **The Granger Collection, New York.**

But my intention is very far from being confined to provide only for the children of **professed** beggars; it is of a much greater extent, and shall take in the whole number of infants at a certain age who are born of parents in effect as little able to support them as those who demand our charity in the streets.

As to my own part, having turned my thoughts for many years upon this important subject and maturely weighed the several schemes of other projectors, I have always found them grossly mistaken in their computation. It is true, a child just dropped from its dam may be supported by her milk for a solar year, with little other nourishment; at most not above the value of two shillings, which the mother may certainly get, or the value in scraps, by her lawful occupation of begging; and it is exactly at one year old that I propose to provide for them in such a manner as instead of being a charge upon their parents or the parish, or wanting food and **raiment** for the rest of their lives, they shall on the contrary contribute to the feeding, and partly to the clothing, of many thousands. . . .

> How does the author's tone make you think you should take him seriously?

> The writer refers to the Irish as if they were animals. *Dam* is a word usually used for mother animals such as sheep. A *shilling* is an old English coin, worth only a small amount.

professed announced publicly   **raiment** clothing

I am assured by our merchants that a boy or a girl before twelve years old is no salable commodity; and even when they come to this age they will not yield above three pounds, or three pounds and half a crown at most on the Exchange; which cannot turn to account either to the parents or the kingdom, the charge of **nutriment** and rags having been at least four times that value.

I shall now humbly propose my own thoughts, which I hope will not be liable to the least objection.

I have been assured by a very knowing American of my acquaintance in London, that a young healthy child well nursed is at a year old a most delicious, nourishing, and **wholesome** food, whether stewed, roasted, baked, or boiled; and I make no doubt that it will equally serve in a **fricassee** or a **ragout**.

I do therefore humbly offer it to public consideration that of the hundred and twenty thousand children, already **computed**, twenty thousand may be reserved for breed, whereof only one-fourth part be males, which is more than we allow sheep, black cattle, or swine; and my reason is that these children are seldom the fruits of marriage, a **circumstance** not much regarded by our savages, therefore one male will be sufficient to serve four females. That the remaining hundred thousand may at a year old be offered in sale to the persons of quality and fortune through the kingdom, always advising the mother to let them suck plentifully in the last month, so as to render them plump and fat for a good table. A child will make two dishes at an entertainment for friends; and when the family dines alone, the **fore** or hind quarter will make a reasonable dish, and seasoned with a little pepper or salt will be very good boiled on the fourth day, especially in winter.

I have reckoned upon a medium that a child just born will weigh twelve pounds, and in a solar year if **tolerably** nursed increaseth to twenty-eight pounds.

How could a child be a salable commodity? *Is Swift suggesting that people don't see children as real human beings? A pound and half a crown are units of money.*

The writer uses the word humbly *the same way he offers a "modest proposal." He is actually about to propose something shocking—in a satiric way.*

Persons of quality means those in the upper classes.

---

nutriment food
wholesome healthful
fricassee a dish made with cut-up pieces of meat in gravy
ragout a stew of meat and vegetables
computed counted
circumstance an event; a situation
fore the front part
tolerably sufficiently; enough

> In what way have the landlords already devoured the parents? What is Swift's attitude toward the English landlords?

I grant this food will be somewhat dear, and therefore very proper for landlords, who, as they have already devoured most of the parents, seem to have the best title to the children....

Butchers we may be assured will not be wanting; although I rather recommend buying the children alive, and dressing them hot from the knife as we do roasting pigs.

A very worthy person, a true lover of his country, and whose virtues I highly **esteem**, was lately pleased in **discoursing** on this matter to offer a **refinement** upon my scheme. He said that many gentlemen of this kingdom, having of late destroyed their deer, he conceived that the want of venison might be well supplied by the bodies of young lads and maidens, not exceeding fourteen years of age nor under twelve, so great a number of both sexes in every county being

> This is Swift's real point: People are starving because of lack of work.

now ready to starve for want of work and service; and these to be disposed of by their parents, if alive, or otherwise by their nearest relations. But with due **deference** to so excellent a friend and so deserving a patriot, I cannot be altogether in his sentiments; for as to the males, my American acquaintance assured me from frequent experience that their flesh was generally tough and lean, like that of our schoolboys, by continual exercise, and their taste disagreeable; and to fatten them would not answer the charge....

But as to myself, having been wearied out for many years with offering vain, idle, **visionary** thoughts, and at length utterly despairing of success, I fortunately fell upon this proposal, which, as it is wholly new, so it hath something solid and real, of no expense and little trouble, full in our own power, and whereby we can **incur** no danger in *disobliging* England. For this kind of commodity will not

---

esteem think highly of

discoursing discussing

refinement a small change that will improve

deference courteous respect for another's wishes

visionary imaginary; not practical

incur bring upon oneself

disobliging going against the wishes of

bear **exportation**, the flesh being of too tender a consistence to admit a long continuance in salt, *although perhaps I could name a country which would be glad to eat up our whole nation without it.* . . .

> Swift shows special bitterness here. What is he saying about England's "appetite"?

I desire those politicians who dislike my overture, and may perhaps be so bold to attempt an answer, that they will first ask the parents of these mortals whether they would not at this day think it a great happiness to have been sold for food at a year old in the manner I prescribe, and thereby have avoided such a perpetual scene of misfortunes as they have since gone through by the oppression of landlords, the impossibility of paying rent without money or trade, the want of common sustenance, with neither house nor clothes to cover them from the **inclemencies** of the weather, and the most **inevitable** prospect of **entailing** the like or greater miseries upon their breed for ever.

> How does it help the satire to include the real facts here?

I profess, in the sincerity of my heart, that I have not the least personal interest in endeavoring to promote this necessary work, having no other motive than the *public good of my country, by advancing our trade, providing for infants, relieving the poor, and giving some pleasure to the rich.* I have no children by which I can propose to get a single penny; the youngest being nine years old, and my wife past child-bearing.

> How does the final paragraph contribute to the satire?

exportation being sent to another country for sale

inclemencies storms; discomforts

inevitable sure to happen

entailing resulting in

AFTER READING THE SELECTION

A Modest Proposal by Jonathan Swift

Directions Choose the letter of the best answer or write the answer using complete sentences.

Comprehension: Identifying Facts

1. How do the parents of most of the children in this satire make a living?
   A They are landlords.
   B They are merchants.
   C They are beggars.
   D They are doctors.

2. At what age does the satire suggest that children be sold for eating?

3. Why are older children not suitable for this use?

Comprehension: Putting Ideas Together

4. The pamphlet says that Ireland should save 20,000 children. How many of them will be boys, and how many will be girls?
   A He wants to save only boys.
   B He wants to save only girls.
   C He wants to save the same number of girls and boys.
   D He wants to save many more girls than boys.

5. Why does Swift say that this meat would be suitable for English landlords?

6. Why does Swift say that his proposal will not bother the English?

Understanding Literature: Satire

Satire is humor that pokes fun at foolishness or evil. Although it is a kind of humor, it rarely makes readers laugh. The writer is often angry about the topic. It is clear in this piece that Swift is angry and bitter. Writers use satire to show people why things need to change. They want readers to get angry about the situation, too.

7. Where does Swift reveal his strong feelings about the tragedy of Ireland's poor?

8. Swift tosses out a few specific insults in this work. What does he suggest about Americans?

Critical Thinking

9. Think about how cruel Swift's ideas sound. What kind of a point do you think he is trying to make?

Thinking Creatively

10. Reread the last paragraph of the pamphlet. What does the narrator mean when he says he has no "personal interest" in proposing this solution?

Grammar Check

When Swift wrote this pamphlet, writers used very long sentences with a lot of dependent clauses. A dependent clause cannot stand alone as a sentence. Carefully study the paragraph on page 493 that begins "I desire those politicians . . ." This entire paragraph is one sentence. Go through the paragraph and identify each dependent clause. Break up this long sentence by rewriting some of these clauses as independent clauses.

 ### Writing on Your Own

Jonathan Swift was a religious leader. He also lived in Ireland and saw for himself how poverty affected people. Which do you think prompted him to write this piece—his religious ideas or his personal experience? Write a paragraph explaining your answer.

 ### Speaking and Listening

Jonathan Swift had a special skill: He could use satire to express his anger about a situation. Many people speak out against problems in society. Some people choose to get involved in groups that help people. What do you think is the best way for people to bring attention to things that need to change? Write a speech asking people to take action. Carefully read your speech and think of anything a listener might misunderstand. Rewrite these parts, or add an explanation to help make your views clear. Give your speech to the class.

Listen to your classmates give their speeches. Take notes as you listen. Try using a different technique for each speech. You can use an outline format, or a chart or diagram listing the main ideas. Which notes were easiest to take while you listened? Which notes best help you remember what was said?

  ### Media and Technology

Pretend that Jonathan Swift is going to be on a news show. Work with a group to act out and film at least one of these scenes.

- Behind the scenes, before the show: Four writers will plan the questions they want the host to ask Mr. Swift.

- During the show: The host and Swift will talk about Swift's work.

- After the show: A reporter will ask people in the street how they feel about Swift and his "modest proposal."

BEFORE READING THE SELECTION

Cup Inanity and Patriotic Profanity   by Andrew Graham-Yooll

Buenos Aires Herald
(established 1876)
Argentinean

About the Newspaper

The Buenos Aires Herald is Argentina's only English-language daily newspaper. William Cathcart, from Scotland, founded the Herald in 1876. The Herald has survived wars, government control, terrorism, and economic crises. Over the years, it has become known for independent editorials that criticize the government. Today the Herald can be found on the Internet.

About the Selection

Argentina was a Spanish colony until 1816. Still, many Argentineans are settlers from Great Britain. In 1982, Britain and Argentina fought a short war. Argentina lost. This made relations between Argentina and Great Britain even worse than they already were.

This news editorial was written 16 years after that war. It was written during the 1998 World Cup soccer matches. Argentina had just won a match against Great Britain. Many in Argentina saw the victory as revenge for the war. The editorial describes the way that fans in both Argentina and Britain behave after the game. It also pokes fun at how seriously people take the game.

Objectives

- To read an editorial and identify the writer's opinions
- To explain how a piece of writing is an example of sarcasm
- To find the irony in sarcasm

Literary Terms Both Great Britain and Argentina are known for their "soccer hooligans"—sometimes called "yobs." These fans are rough and wild. They often start fights over games. They justify their bad behavior by calling it "patriotism." Andrew Graham-Yooll writes this **editorial** to show how much he dislikes their behavior. An editorial gives a news writer's opinion about an event.

Graham-Yooll uses **sarcasm**, a grim kind of irony, to express his opinions. He pretends that the win will make all of Argentina's problems go away. He also reminds people that more serious things than soccer are happening around them.

Reading on Your Own This editorial is about the people of Argentina and Great Britain. Identify ways that these two cultures are different from American culture. Can any of the ideas in this editorial relate to people in general? If yes, which ideas? If not, why not?

Writing on Your Own Do you think people sometimes take sports too seriously? Write a paragraph explaining your opinion.

Vocabulary Focus The ending *-ity* changes an adjective into a noun. *Inanity* is the noun form of *inane*. *Profanity* is the noun form of *profane*. Use a dictionary to find the meanings of *inane* and *profane*. Use your own words to explain the title of this editorial. (Remember that *Cup* refers to the World Cup, or soccer.)

Think Before You Read Who is the author and who published this editorial? What does this tell you about the point of view of the editorial?

> **editorial** a news writer's opinion about an event or topic
>
> **sarcasm** a grim, sometimes mean-spirited kind of irony

Cup Inanity and Patriotic Profanity

As you read this editorial, look for the writer's opinions.

What a wonderful victory for Argentina's soccer squad. **Self-congratulatory commentary** yesterday was also packed full of **plaudits** for the dozen or so millionaires who had taken such an outstanding step for the well-being of a nation.

Celebration was everywhere and the **significance** of beating England referred to patriotic **vindication** and other such inanities which filled every inch of air and available screen space. In truth, it helped Argentina to **definitively** overcome the "hand of God" incident in the 1986 World Cup involving Diego Armando Maradoña's paw, but victory was a squeak, and secured against a ten-man team. For a sense of sporting balance, it was OK. Balance requires, of course, that the Dutch thrash Argentina on Saturday.

What vindication might the Argentine team want?

Maradoña, an Argentine soccer star, scored a goal in 1986 in a game against England. He used his hands illegally.

Even if the national team wins, please, not another 1978, when people were being tortured in Sierra Chica prison while the patriotic mob were screaming their support for the **tormentors** in Government House. A few people may still be able to remember that: 1978 was also described as a sporting event.

The Dutch team did beat Argentina later.

However, Tuesday must have been really good for Argentina. The MERVAL Stock Exchange index rose four percent yesterday. And it had risen just under half a point just before the match started, against an average six months of decline.

Argentina won the World Cup in 1978. That year, the government arrested, tortured, and killed thousands of people in Argentina.

The word MERVAL is from MERcado de VALores (stock market).

self-congratulatory giving praise to oneself
commentary an explanation; a series of remarks
plaudits strong praise
significance the meaning; the importance
vindication proof that clears away blame or guilt
definitively finally; completely
tormentors those who cause great pain to others

For the **duration** of the match, three hours all told, the country froze, with a loss of GDP of 230 million pesos, according to Perfil newspaper.

That hardly matters. As a result of Tuesday's score we are all going to be so patriotic that we can assume that the foreign debt will be paid off shortly, there will be no more poor in Argentina, unemployment will be something entirely unknown (and easily forgotten), **pensioners** will have a decent retirement, cheques with the relief for the small-holders who have lost everything outside Goya will be in the post tomorrow. And the Wizard of Oz will be made President on July 31. . . .

On Tuesday patriotism meant filling the streets with litter from waste bins emptied out of office windows. The patriotic rubbish blocked drains and spread a carpet of filth over the city centre's streets. Patriotism was to wear the national **ensign** as a silly hat, scarf, Superman cape, screwed up ball of cloth. . . . Patriotism was to trail this **makeshift** dress along the street, turning it grubby not in triumph but in neglect. Patriotism was to wave bottles of beer until they had been drunk dry and then fling the empty so as to smash a store window. Patriotism involves yelling **racist** insults presented as patriotic slogans, and using the most **debased** language to describe people who are different.

The *peso* is the unit of money in Argentina. GDP stands for Gross Domestic Product, a measure of a country's economy.

Cheque is another spelling of *check*. Other British-style spellings, such as centre, are used later in the article.

duration the period of time that something lasts

pensioners people who receive pay after retiring

ensign a flag

makeshift a temporary substitute

racist referring to another race in an insulting way

debased lowered in worth

> A *horde* is a crowd.

No soccer horde has a monopoly on this behaviour and none is exempted.

Winston Churchill, or some other English worthy, once said that the British were **ungovernable**, except in war. And after the battle they were unspeakable.

This was much the case in many pubs throughout the English section of the United Kingdom yesterday.

French, Spanish, Germans and other visitors in England, who wanted to join in what they thought was sporting revelry (they obviously did not understand the natives), met with barrage after **onslaught** of drunken abuse and racist **epithets** which illustrated the many applications of a limited language education.

> *Yob* is a slang expression for a "hooligan," or street criminal.

The factors that have helped develop the yob culture, in Britain, Argentina, and wherever, are not the relaxation of rules, as some **disciplinarians** wish to have it, but the championing of **banality** in most societies that are described as advanced capitalist states—which is where the enterprising sell banality for mass consumption. (The so-called less-advanced societies are irrelevant here as they are mostly repressed by **dictatorial** rule of varying degrees of severity. However, there is always room to praise the good administration of places such as Turkey or Saudi Arabia, for example.)

> This sentence shows irony. Governments in Turkey and Saudi Arabia exert strict control.

Anyway, the magnificent Argentine victory on Tuesday provided the confirmation that the English inventors of many sports get thrashed by their pupils (by West Indians in cricket, South Africans in rugby, Argentines in soccer, and so on) with great regularity. And that confirms nothing more than that teachers and pupils descend to the pits of disgrace whether celebrating or mourning the incidents of wargames.

> Cricket, rugby, and soccer are all games that were taken to British colonies such as the West Indies.

---

ungovernable not possible to control

onslaught a violent attack or charge

epithets insulting words or phrases

disciplinarian a person who makes sure rules are carried out

banality the quality of having little meaning

dictatorial cruel

AFTER READING THE SELECTION

Cup Inanity and Patriotic Profanity   by Andrew Graham-Yooll

Directions Choose the letter of the best answer or write the answer using complete sentences.

Comprehension: Identifying Facts

1. What happened in the Argentine economy during the soccer match?
   A The GDP went up.
   B Unemployment went down.
   C Unemployment went up.
   D The MERVAL Stock Exchange went up.

2. What were some of the actions of "patriotic" Argentinean soccer fans?

3. What does the writer think causes the "yob culture"?

Comprehension: Putting Ideas Together

4. At the beginning of the editorial, the writer describes some millionaires. Who are they?
   A coaches   C soccer players
   B fans   D news reporters

5. How were the people in English pubs showing that they were "ungovernable?"

6. When the writer speaks of "wargames," what does he mean?

Understanding Literature: Sarcasm

Sarcasm is a heavy, sometimes mean-spirited kind of irony. It can be personal and meant to hurt. A writer who is using sarcasm might say exactly the opposite of what he or she feels. For example, the writer might talk about how fabulous something is when the writer really feels it is horrible.

7. The author pokes fun at the importance of the win by exaggerating its wonderful effects. What are some of the things he says will happen?

8. The writer describes foreigners in England trying to join in the "sporting revelry." (*Sporting* refers to acting with respect; *revelry* is a wild celebration.) How is this phrase sarcastic?

Critical Thinking

9. In what ways did the losers and winners act the same after the match?

Thinking Creatively

10. Do you think Americans value sports too much? Explain.

After Reading continued on next page

AFTER READING THE SELECTION (continued)

Cup Inanity and Patriotic Profanity · by Andrew Graham-Yooll

Grammar Check

A gerund is a form of a verb that ends in *–ing* and is used as a noun in a sentence. It can be the subject, direct object, or indirect object. It can also be the object of a preposition. A gerund phrase is a group of words with a gerund that is used the same way in a sentence. The gerund phrase is underlined in this sentence. It is the direct object.

> We like <u>making our own decorations</u> for the holidays.

Reread the last paragraph on page 499. Find two sentences that use gerund phrases. Write these sentences, identifying each gerund phrase and its role in the sentence.

Writing on Your Own

Think of a time when you have seen people act poorly in public. Were they acting mean or stupid? Write an editorial making fun of their behavior. Talk about groups only. Do not write about individuals.

Speaking and Listening

It is obvious that Graham-Yooll does not approve of the behavior of the soccer fans. Do you think that the way he expresses his disapproval, using sarcasm, is the best way to get his ideas across? Write a short paragraph stating your opinion, and present it to the class.

Listen carefully to the other students as they give their opinions about this selection. Have you heard anything that changes your opinion?

Research

Use the library and Internet to find out more about the history between Argentina and Great Britain. Do some research to learn about the war they fought in 1982. What caused the war? Where was it fought? How did it end?

BEFORE READING THE SELECTION

The Happy Man by Naguib Mahfouz (trans. by Akef Abadir and Roger Allen)

About the Author

Naguib Mahfouz (1911–2006) Egyptian

Naguib Mahfouz was born in Egypt. He worked for different government agencies in Egypt for most of his life. He even worked as the Director of Censorship in the Bureau of Art. Censorship has to do with preventing certain works of art or literature from being printed or produced. Amazingly, one of Mahfouz's own works was banned in Egypt. The name of the book is *Children of Gebelawi*.

Mahfouz wrote more than 30 novels. He won the Nobel Prize for Literature in 1988. A few years later, someone tried to kill him for writing *Children of Gebelawi*. Mahfouz, 82 years old at the time, survived.

About the Selection

This story comes from a collection of short stories that Mahfouz wrote, *God's World: An Anthology of Short Stories*. It is an example of satire—humor that makes fun of foolishness or evil. Mahfouz is making fun of the way many people are always unhappy, even people who are well off. This feeling is so common that it seems feeling unhappy is "normal." If we accept that as true, then feeling happy must not be normal. The man in this story tries to figure out why he is feeling this way—and what he can do about it.

Objectives

- To read and understand a narrative
- To understand how point of view affects the story
- To visualize images and identify figures of speech

Before Reading continued on next page

Humorous Literature Unit 6 503

BEFORE READING THE SELECTION (continued)

The Happy Man by Naguib Mahfouz (trans. by Akef Abadir and Roger Allen)

narrative a story or report about an event

point of view the position from which the author or storyteller tells the story

figurative language writing or speech not meant to be understood exactly as it is written; writers use figurative language to express ideas in imaginative ways

image a picture in the reader's mind created by words

figure of speech a word or phrase that means something other than what the words really say, such as idiom, metaphor, and simile

Literary Terms This story is a **narrative**, or a story or report about an event. It is told from the **point of view** of a limited narrator. The point of view is the position from which the author or storyteller tells the story. A limited third-person narrator is one who does not know everything. This narrator only knows what the main character is thinking or feeling.

This story is full of **figurative language**, or writing that is not meant to be understood exactly as it is written. Mahfouz uses this to help create **images**, or pictures in the reader's mind. Mahfouz also uses **figures of speech**, such as idioms, metaphors, and similes. These are descriptions and expressions that are not meant to be taken exactly as they are written.

Reading on Your Own Use a Main Idea Graphic (Table) to help you find the main idea of this story. Refer to Appendix A for an example of this graphic organizer. As you read the story, write the supporting details on the legs of the table. What is the main idea?

Writing on Your Own Think of a time when you were so happy that nothing could upset you. What made you feel this way? Write a paragraph about this time.

Vocabulary Focus Make a list of synonyms and antonyms for the word *happy*. After you read the story, look back at this list. Which of these synonyms express the idea of *happiness* in this story? Which of the antonyms help you better understand what the writer is trying to say *happiness* is *not*?

Think Before You Read Flip through the pages of this story. Read some of the notes in the margins. How do you think the man will solve his problem?

The Happy Man

He woke up in the morning and discovered that he was happy. "What's this?" he asked himself. He could not think of any word which described his state of mind more accurately and precisely than 'happy'. This was distinctly peculiar when compared with the state he was usually in when he woke up. He would be half-asleep from staying so late at the newspaper office. He would face life with a sense of strain and **contemplation**. Then he would get up, **whetting** his determination to face up to all inconveniences and withstand all difficulties.

Today he felt happy, full of happiness as a matter of fact. There was no arguing about it. The symptoms were quite clear and their **vigour** and obviousness were such as to impose themselves on his senses and mind all at once. Yes, indeed; he was happy. If this was not happiness, then what was? He felt that his limbs were well proportioned and functioning perfectly. They were working in superb harmony with each other and with the world around him. Inside him, he felt a boundless power, an **imperishable** energy, an ability to achieve anything with confidence, precision, and obvious success. His heart was overflowing with love for people, animals and things, and with an all-**engulfing** sense of **optimism** and joy. It was

> As you read the narrative, notice how the writer tells the story in the order that the events happened.

contemplation thoughtfulness

whetting creating an interest or a hunger

vigour (American *vigor*) a strong or intense feeling

imperishable not able to die

engulfing surrounding

optimism a hope for the best; the belief that things will turn out well

Humorous Literature Unit 6

as if he were no longer troubled or bothered by fear, anxiety, sickness, death, argument, or the question of earning a living. Even more important than that, and something he could not **analyze**, it was a feeling which penetrated to every cell of his body and soul, it played a tune full of delight, pleasure, serenity and peace, and hummed in its incredible melodies the whispering sound of the world which is denied to the unhappy.

He felt drunk with ecstasy and **savoured** it slowly with a feeling of surprise. He asked himself where it had come from and how; the past provided no explanation and the future could not justify it. Where did it come from, then, and how?! How long would it last? Would it stay with him till breakfast? Would it give him enough time to get to the newspaper office? Just a minute though, he thought . . . it won't last because it can't. If it did, man would be turned into an angel or something even higher. So he told himself that he should devote his attention to savouring it, living with it, and storing up its **nectar** before it became a **mere** memory with no way of proving it or even being sure that it had ever existed.

He ate his breakfast with a **relish**, and this time nothing **distracted** his attention while he was eating. He gave 'Uncle' Bashir who was waiting on him such a beaming smile that the poor man felt rather alarmed and taken aback. Usually he would only look in his direction to give orders or ask questions; although, on most occasions, he treated him fairly well.

"Tell me, 'Uncle' Bashir," he asked the servant, "am I a happy man?"

The poor man was startled. He realized why his servant was confused; for the first time ever he was talking to him as a **colleague** or friend. He encouraged his servant to forget about his worries and asked him with unusual insistence to answer his question.

> Notice how the narrator does not tell what the servant is thinking. This is an example of third-person point of view.

> How does the man usually treat his servant?

analyze examine; study the parts of

savoured (American *savored*) enjoyed the moment

nectar sweetness

mere not more than

relish a strong liking; great pleasure

distracted took one's attention away from something

colleague a person who works at the same level

"Through God's grace and favour, you are happy," the servant replied.

"You mean, I should be happy. Anyone with my job, living in my house, and enjoying my health, should be happy. That's what you want to say. But do you think I'm really happy?"

The servant replied, "You work too hard, Sir," after yet more insistence, "it's more than any man can stand...."

He hesitated, but his master **gestured** to him to continue with what he had to say.

"You get angry a lot," he said, "and have fierce arguments with your neighbors...."

He interrupted him by laughing loudly. "What about you," he asked, "don't you have any worries?"

"Of course, no man can be free of worry."

"You mean that complete happiness is an impossible **quest**?"

"That applies to life in general...."

How could he have dreamed up this incredible happiness? He or any other human being? It was a strange, **unique** happiness, as though it were a private secret he had been given. In the meeting hall of the newspaper building, he spotted his main **rival** in this world sitting down thumbing through a magazine. The man heard his footsteps, but did not look up from the magazine. He had undoubtedly noticed him in some way and was therefore pretending to ignore him so as to keep his own peace of mind. At some **circulation** meetings, they would argue so violently with each other that sparks began to fly and they would exchange bitter words. One stage more, and they would come to blows. A week ago, his rival had won in the union elections and he had lost. He had felt pierced by a sharp, poisoned arrow, and the world had darkened before his eyes. Now here he was approaching his rival's seat; the sight of him sitting there did not make him excited, nor did the memories of their dispute spoil his composure. He approached him with a pure and carefree heart, feeling drunk with his incredible

> Notice the figurative language that describes how the man felt when his rival won the elections. What image does this create in your mind?

---

gestured made a motion with hands

quest search

unique uncommon

rival enemy

circulation delivery of a newspaper to stores and homes

happiness; his face showed an expression full of **tolerance** and forgiveness. It was as though he were approaching some other man towards whom he had never had any feelings of **enmity**, or perhaps he might be renewing a friendship again. "Good morning!" he said without feeling any **compunction**.

> Why is the man's rival so surprised?

The man looked up in amazement. He was silent for a few moments until he recovered, and then returned the greeting **curtly**. It was as though he did not believe his eyes and ears.

He sat down alongside the man. "Marvellous weather today. . . ." he said.

"Okay. . . ." the other replied guardedly.

"Weather to fill your heart with happiness."

His rival looked at him closely and cautiously. "I'm glad that you're so happy. . . ." he muttered.

"**Inconceivably** happy. . . ." he replied with a laugh.

"I hope," the man continued in a rather hesitant tone of voice, "that I shan't spoil your happiness at the meeting of the **administrative** council. . . ."

"Not at all. My views are well known, but I don't mind if the members adopt your point of view. That won't spoil my happiness!"

"You've changed a great deal overnight," the man said with a smile.

"The fact is that I'm happy, inconceivably happy."

The man examined his face carefully. "I bet your dear son has changed his mind about staying in Canada?!" he asked.

"Never, never, my friend," he replied, laughing loudly. "He is still sticking to his decision. . . ."

"But that was the principal reason for your being so sad. . . ."

tolerance an acceptance of something, such as other people's faults or differences	**enmity** hatred **compunction** strong feelings of guilt **curtly** rudely	**inconceivably** not able to be thought about or understood **administrative** managing or decision-making

"Quite true. I've often begged him to come back out of pity for me in my loneliness and to serve his country. But he told me that he's going to open an engineering office with a Canadian partner; in fact, he's invited me to join him in it. Let him live where he'll be happy. I'm quite happy here—as you can see, inconceivably happy...."

The man still looked a little doubtful. "Quite **extraordinarily** brave!" he said.

"I don't know what it is, but I'm happy in the full meaning of the word."

Yes indeed, this was full happiness; full, firm, weighty, and vital. As deep as absolute power, widespread as the wind, fierce as fire, bewitching as scent, **transcending** nature. It could not possibly last.

The other man warmed to his display of affection. "The truth is," he said, "that I always picture you as someone with a fierce and violent temperament which causes him a good deal of trouble and leads him to trouble other people too."

"Really?"

"You don't know how to make a truce, you've no concept of **intermediate** solutions. You work with your nerves, with the marrow in your bones. You fight bitterly as though any problem is a matter of life and death!"

"Yes, that's true."

He accepted the criticism without any difficulty and with an open heart. His wave expanded into a boundless ocean of happiness. He struggled to control an innocent, happy laugh which the other man interpreted in a way far removed from its pure motives. "So then," he asked, "You think it's necessary to be able to take a balanced view of events, do you?"

"Of course. I remember, by way of example, the argument we had the day before yesterday about racism. We both had the same views on the subject; it's something worth being **zealous** about, even to the point of anger. But what kind of

---

> The phrase "serve his country" means "join the armed forces."

> How is "a matter of life and death" an example of figurative language?

---

extraordinarily remarkably; unusually

transcending going beyond

intermediate the middle

zealous very eager; strongly devoted

Humorous Literature Unit 6

anger? An intellectual anger, **abstract** to a certain extent; not the type which shatters your nerves, ruins your digestion, and gives you **palpitations**. Not so?"

"That's obvious; I quite understand...."

He struggled to control a second laugh and succeeded. His heart refused to **renounce** one drop of its joy. Racism, Vietnam, Palestine, ... no problem could **assail** that fortress of happiness which was encircling his heart. When he remembered a problem, his heart **guffawed**. He was happy. It was a **tyrannical** happiness, **despising** all misery and laughing at any hardship, it wanted to laugh, dance, sing, and distribute its spirit of laughter, dancing and singing among the various problems of the world.

He could not bear to stay in his office at the newspaper; he felt no desire to work at all. He hated the very idea of thinking about his daily business, and completely failed to bring his mind down from its stronghold in the kingdom of happiness. How could he possibly write about a trolley bus falling into the Nile when he was so intoxicated by this frightening happiness? Yes, it really was frightening. How could it be anything else, where there was no reason for it at all, when it was so strong that it made him exhausted and paralyzed his will; apart from the fact that it had been with him for half a day without letting up in the slightest degree?!

He left the pages of paper blank and started walking backwards and forwards across the room, laughing and cracking his fingers....

He felt slightly worried; it did not penetrate deep enough to spoil his happiness, but paused on the surface of his mind like an abstract idea. It occurred to him that he might recall the tragedies of his life so that he could test their effect on his happiness. Perhaps they would be able to bring back some

> A *fortress* is a wall that surrounds and protects a city. How is the man's happiness like a fortress?

> How does the man test the strength of his happiness?

abstract having to do with ideas

palpitations rapid heartbeats

renounce give up; reject

assail attack

guffawed laughed loudly

tyrannical harsh; cruel

despising looking down on

idea of balance or security, at least until his happiness began to **flag** a little. For example, he remembered his wife's death in all its various **aspects** and details. What had happened? The event appeared to him as a series of movements without any meaning or effect, as though it had happened to some other woman, the wife of another man, in some distant historical age. In fact, it had a contagious effect which prompted a smile, and then even **provoked** laughter. He could not stop himself laughing, and there he was guffawing, ha . . . ha . . . ha!

> What image is the writer creating here?

The same thing happened when he remembered the first letter his son had sent him saying that he wanted to **emigrate** to Canada. The sound of his guffaws as he paraded the bloody tragedies of the world before him would have attracted the attention of the newspaper workers and passers-by in the street, had it not been for the thickness of the walls. He could do nothing to **dislodge** his happiness. Memories of unhappy times hit him like waves being thrown on to a sandy beach under the golden rays of the sun.

> This simile compares the man's memories to waves on the beach.

He excused himself from attending the administrative council and left the newspaper office without writing a word. After lunch, he lay down on his bed as usual but could not sleep. In fact, sleep seemed an impossibility to him. Nothing gave him any **indication** that it was coming, even slowly. He was in a place alight and gleaming, **resounding** with sleeplessness and joy. He had to calm down and relax, to quieten his senses and limbs, but how could he do it? He gave up trying to sleep, and got up. He began to hum as he was walking around his house. If this keeps up, he told himself, I won't be able to sleep, just as I can't work or feel sad. It was almost time for him to go to the club, but he did not feel like meeting any friends. What was the point of exchanging views on public affairs and private worries?! What would they think if they found him laughing

---

flag lessen

aspects different ways of looking at something

provoked stirred someone to action

emigrate leave one's country

dislodge loosen; separate

indication sign, hint

resounding echoing loudly

> What is funny about the man being upset about being happy?

at every major problem? What would they say? How would they picture things? How would they explain it? No, he did not need anyone, nor did he want to spend the evening talking. He should be by himself, and go for a long walk to get rid of some of his **excess vitality** and think about his situation. What had happened to him? How was it that this incredible happiness had **overwhelmed** him? How long would he have to carry it on his shoulders? Would it keep **depriving** him of work, friends, sleep and peace of mind?! Should he **resign** himself to it? Should he abandon himself to the flood to play with him as the whim took it? Or should he look for a way out for himself through thought, action, or advice?

When he was called into the examination room in the clinic of his friend, the **specialist** in **internal medicine**, he felt a little alarmed. The doctor looked at him with a smile. "You don't look like someone who's complaining about being ill," he said.

"I haven't come to see you because I'm ill," he told the doctor in a hesitant tone of voice, "but because I'm happy!"

The doctor looked piercingly at him with a questioning air.

"Yes," he repeated to underline what he had said, "because I'm happy!"

There was a period of silence. On one side, there was anxiety, and on the other, questioning and amazement.

"It's an incredible feeling which can't be defined in any other way, but it's very serious. . . ."

The doctor laughed. "I wish your illness was contagious," he said, prodding him jokingly.

"Don't treat it as a joke. It's very serious, as I told you. I'll describe it to you. . . ."

---

excess extra

vitality energy

overwhelmed crushed; destroyed

depriving making someone do without something

resign accept

specialist a doctor who spends extra years studying one field of medicine

internal medicine a field of medicine that deals with diseases of the organs inside the body

He told him all about his happiness from the time he had woken up in the morning till he had felt compelled to visit him.

"Haven't you been taking drugs, alcohol, or **tranquillizers**?"

"Absolutely nothing like that."

"Have you had some success in an important sphere of your life; work . . . love . . . money?"

"Nothing like that either. I've twice as much to worry about as I have to make me feel glad. . . ."

"Perhaps if you were patient for a while. . . ."

"I've been patient all day. I'm afraid I'll be spending the night wandering around. . . ."

The doctor gave him a **precise**, careful, and **comprehensive** examination and then shrugged his shoulders in despair. "You're a picture of health," he said.

"And so?"

"I could advise you to take a sleeping pill, but it would be better if you consulted a nerve specialist. . . ."

The examination was repeated in the nerve specialist's clinic with the self-same precision, care, and comprehensiveness. "Your nerves are sound," the doctor told him, "they're in **enviable** condition!"

"Haven't you got a **plausible** explanation for my condition?" he asked hopefully.

"Consult a **gland** specialist!" the doctor replied, shaking his head.

> Is "a picture of health" an idiom, metaphor, or simile?

---

tranquillizers medications used to help someone relax or sleep

precise exact

comprehensive complete

enviable good; to be desired

plausible realistic; believable

gland a part of the body that helps other parts of the body work

The examination was conducted for a third time in the gland specialist's clinic with the same precision, care and comprehensiveness. "I congratulate you!" the doctor told him. "Your glands are in good condition!"

He laughed. He apologized for laughing, laughing as he did so. Laughter was his way of expressing his alarm and despair.

He left the clinic with the feeling that he was alone; alone in the hands of his tyrannical happiness with no helper, no guide and no friend. Suddenly, he remembered the doctor's sign he sometimes saw from the window of his office in the newspaper building. It was true that he had no confidence in psychiatrists even though he had read about the **significance** of **psychoanalysis**. Apart from that, he knew that their **tentacles** were very long and they kept their patients tied in a sort of long association. He laughed as he remembered the method of cure through **free association** and the problems which it eventually uncovers. He was laughing as his feet carried him towards the psychiatrist's clinic, and imagined the doctor listening to his incredible complaints about feeling happy, when he was used to hearing people complain about hysteria, **schizophrenia**, anxiety, and so on.

"The truth is, Doctor, that I've come to see you because I'm happy!"

> Why does the man feel ridiculous?

He looked at the doctor to see what effect his statement had had on him, but noticed that he was keeping his composure. He felt ridiculous. "I'm inconceivably happy...." he said in a tone of confidence.

He began to tell the doctor his story, but the latter stopped him with a gesture of his hand. "An overwhelming, incredible, **debilitating** happiness?" he asked quietly.

> How does the doctor know what the man is going to say?

He stared at him in amazement and was on the point of saying something, but the doctor spoke first. "A happiness

significance importance

psychoanalysis a method of therapy that tries to find a person's subconscious thoughts

tentacles the legs of an octopus; here it means to be controlling

free association a quick response to pictures and words

schizophrenia a very serious form of mental illness

debilitating causing someone to be unable to function in daily life

which has made you stop working," he asked, "abandon your friends, and **detest** going to sleep. . . ?"

"You're a miracle!" he shouted.

"Every time you get involved in some misfortune," the psychiatrist continued quietly, "you dissolve into laughter. . . ?"

"Sir . . . are you familiar with the invisible?"

"No!" he said with a smile, "nothing like that. But I get a similar case in my clinic at least once a week!"

> Here, the man is asking if the doctor can read his mind.

"Is it an **epidemic**?" he asked.

"I didn't say that, and I wouldn't claim that it's been possible to analyze one case into its primary elements as yet."

"But is it a disease?"

"All the cases are still under treatment."

"But are you satisfied without any doubt that they aren't natural cases. . . ?"

"That's a necessary **assumption** for the job; there's only. . . ."

"Have you noticed any of them to be **deranged** in. . . ." he asked anxiously, pointing to his head.

"Absolutely not," the doctor replied convincingly. "I assure you that they're all intelligent in every sense of the word. . . ."

> Why does the man point to his head?

The doctor thought for a moment. "We should have two sessions a week, I think?" he said.

"Very well. . . ." he replied in **resignation**.

"There's no sense in getting alarmed or feeling sad. . . ."

Alarmed, sad? He smiled, and his smile kept on getting broader. A laugh slipped out, and before long, he was dissolving into laughter. He was determined to control himself, but his resistance collapsed completely. He started guffawing loudly . . .

> Why is the statement beginning "There's no sense" funny?

> The man in the story is never identified by name. Why do you think the author did not give him a name?

---

detest hate
epidemic a widespread problem; the quick spread of disease
assumption belief; set of ideas
deranged mentally disturbed
resignation acceptance

Humorous Literature Unit 6

AFTER READING THE SELECTION

The Happy Man by Naguib Mahfouz (trans. by Akef Abadir and Roger Allen)

Directions Choose the letter of the best answer or write the answer using complete sentences.

Comprehension: Identifying Facts

1. Why is the man surprised when he wakes up feeling happy?
   A He is usually too tired to feel anything at all.
   B His best friend just died.
   C He doesn't believe in laughing.
   D He had slept in an alley.

2. What does the man think will happen to this feeling?
   A It will last a lifetime.
   B It will help him get to heaven.
   C It will not last long at all.
   D It will leave him even sadder than he was before.

3. Why is the servant confused when the man talks to him at breakfast?

4. What does the man ask his servant?

5. Where does the man work?

6. How does the man feel when he sees his main rival?

7. Where does the man's son live?

8. What happened to the man's wife?

9. How does the man feel when he thinks about sad things?

10. What does the man do instead of going to his meeting at work?

Comprehension: Putting Ideas Together

11. Why can't the man sleep when he lies down after lunch?
    A He is awakened by a phone call from work.
    B His mind is too busy.
    C He is afraid he won't be able to sleep at night.
    D He falls out of bed.

12. Why doesn't the man want to go to the club?
    A He does not think his friends will understand him.
    B He hates the club.
    C He does not like hearing about other people's problems.
    D He had a fight with his friends.

13. How does the man think that a walk will help him?

14. How is happiness "depriving" the man?

15. What does the first doctor think of the man's health?

16. Why does the man laugh at the gland specialist?

17. How does the man feel when he leaves the gland specialist's office?

516 Unit 6 *Humorous Literature*

18. What does the man think of psychiatrists before he sees one?

19. How does the man think he will be different from most of the psychiatrist's other patients?

20. What surprises the man when he talks with the psychiatrist?

Understanding Literature: Figures of Speech

A figure of speech is an expression that is not meant to be understood exactly as it is written. Some examples are idioms, metaphors, and similes. An idiom is a phrase that has a meaning beyond its exact words. Metaphors and similes are types of comparisons. A metaphor says that one think is another. A simile uses *like* or *as* to compare things.

21. Read the sentence near the top of page 506 that begins "Even more important than that . . ." To what does the writer compare the man's feeling? Is this a simile or a metaphor?

22. The narrator says that the man and his rival argued "so violently with each other that sparks began to fly." Explain the meaning of this idiom.

23. The man thinks that his happiness is "as deep as absolute power, widespread as the wind, fierce as fire, bewitching as scent." Why do you think the writer uses similes instead of adjectives to describe this?

24. The man's rival says, "You work with your nerves, with the marrow in your bones." What does he mean?

25. Why do you think the writer chose to use so much figurative language instead of using plain, matter-of-fact language? Do you think it makes the story better? Why or why not?

Critical Thinking

26. Why does the first doctor wish he had the same "problem" as the Happy Man?

27. The first doctor does not give the man medication. Why?

28. The first two doctors tell the man that he is healthy. Why does he insist that he is not well?

29. Is the psychiatrist really as amazing as the man thinks? Why or why not?

Thinking Creatively

30. Is happiness an illness? Or is it an illness to think of happiness as a problem? Explain.

After Reading **continued on next page**

AFTER READING THE SELECTION (continued)

The Happy Man   by Naguib Mahfouz (trans. by Akef Abadir and Roger Allen)

Grammar Check

A rhetorical question is a special type of question. It does not expect an answer. On page 507, the writer uses this rhetorical question: "How could he have dreamed up this incredible happiness? He or any other human being?" The narrator is not asking the reader to answer the question. Find an example of a "regular" question in the story. How is this different from the rhetorical question above?

Writing on Your Own

Pretend that you are the Happy Man. Write a paragraph as if it is the end of your first happy day. Write a second paragraph as if it is the end of the last day in this story.

Speaking

Work with a partner. Pretend that your partner is the Happy Man, and you are his friend. Give your friend advice. Tell him whether or not he should worry about his new feelings.

Listening

Dave Douglas is an American composer who plays the trumpet. He wrote a song titled "Mahfouz" and put it on his recording called *Witness*. He plays the trumpet while a singer reads from something Mahfouz wrote. Find a copy of this recording or look for it online. Listen to several minutes of it. Why do you think a musician would compose music to go with a story?

Technology

Work with a partner or small group to write a song about something from this story. It can be about the main character, one of the doctors, or even the main idea. Use a computer music program to produce music for your song.

Columns

Columns are articles that appear regularly in magazines and newspapers. Their authors receive a byline. A byline tells who wrote an article. Some columns draw attention to serious issues in the world. Others are written to entertain the readers. They are a popular form of humor. Hundreds of men and women write columns on the local level or for readers across the country. They write about a range of topics. Columnists such as Dave Barry began as local writers. They became so popular that their articles now appear all over the world. Yet their columns still retain a local flavor. This local connection appeals to many readers.

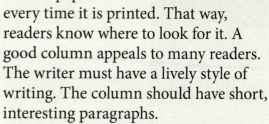

A column often appears in the same place in the magazine or newspaper every time it is printed. That way, readers know where to look for it. A good column appeals to many readers. The writer must have a lively style of writing. The column should have short, interesting paragraphs.

Following are selections by two columnists who write from the viewpoint of the average person. They struggle with parenting, work, and home repair. Readers recognize and share the stress of these activities. They enjoy relieving their tensions with a good laugh. This wide appeal has made these columns extremely popular.

COLUMNS

—appear in magazines and newspapers

—have a lively, interesting style

—inform or entertain

BEFORE READING THE SELECTION

Staying at a Japanese Inn: Peace, Tranquillity, Insects   by Dave Barry

Dave Barry
(1948–)
American

Objectives
- To read and understand a humorous selection
- To recognize exaggeration
- To identify stereotypes in humorous writing

column
an article that appears regularly in a newspaper or magazine

About the Author

Dave Barry began his career writing for a small Pennsylvania newspaper. He later took a job with the Associated Press in Philadelphia and taught classes on writing. Soon, he began writing a weekly humor **column**. Impressed, the *Miami Herald* newspaper offered him a staff position.

Subjects for Barry's column have included hopeless attempts at home repair, and battles with the hardy plants and animals of the tropics. Many of his columns are about his own family's experiences. He won the Pulitzer Prize for journalism in 1988. Barry wrote his column for the *Miami Herald* for 22 years.

Barry has also written many books. Some of them are collections of his most popular columns. He now lives in Miami, Florida.

About the Selection

Barry traveled to Japan with his wife, Beth, and their son, Robby. His book *Dave Barry Does Japan* is about his experiences. It uses cultural differences between the United States and Japan as the basis for humor. This selection is one chapter from that book.

The chapter is about the family's stay at a traditional Japanese inn. Barry describes in a funny way how the inn is different from an American hotel. For example, Barry says that he and his family tried to speak Japanese, but he is not really sure what they said. Barry uses this kind of humor throughout the selection.

Literary Terms This selection uses many techniques to make the reader laugh. He uses **exaggeration** to describe different things that he hears and sees. A writer can use exaggeration to make something seem more than it is. Barry stretches the truth to make the story funnier.

Another way that Barry makes the reader laugh is by using stereotypes, simplified ideas about other persons or cultures. Barry uses American stereotypes of Japanese culture to point out some faults in American culture. He also shows stereotypes about Americans. It is clear that Barry is not trying to criticize either people. He just shows how silly we all seem to people from other cultures. This work is a piece of **humor**, created to amuse readers.

Reading on Your Own Reread the title. Think about the connotations of the words *peace, tranquillity,* and *insects.* What images come to mind? What do you think that insects have to do with peace and tranquillity? What do you expect Barry to write about his stay at a Japanese inn?

Writing on Your Own What is something that most Americans do that you think is funny, or just silly? Write a short paragraph about it.

Vocabulary Focus Dave Barry uses words such as *traditional* and *ancient* to describe his experience at the *ryokon*. At the same time, he describes his family as typical, suburban, and hyperactive. Compare the connotations of the words describing Japan to the connotations of the words describing the American tourists.

Think Before You Read Think about some stereotypes you have heard. Make a list of the stereotypes that people have about Americans. Which of these do you think Barry will write about?

> **exaggeration** a use of words to make something seem more than it is; stretching the truth to a great extent
>
> **humor** literature created to be funny or to amuse

Staying at a Japanese Inn: Peace, Tranquillity, Insects

Kyoto is a city in Japan known for its beauty.

As you read, note how the author uses exaggeration.

When we arrived in Kyoto, we took a cab to our inn, which was a **traditional** type of Japanese inn called a *ryokan*.[1] When we pulled up in front, three women in **kimonos** came out and began bowing and saying things in Japanese and picking up our luggage. Using our Japanese skills, we said "thank you" or possibly "good night," and we bowed, and they bowed some more, which was not easy for them to do while holding our luggage, and then we started to go into the inn, at which point the women started speaking excitedly and pointing at our shoes.

Japan has a thing about shoes. You can wear them into stores and **westernized** hotels and restaurants, but you're not supposed to wear them into homes or traditional inns. You're supposed to take your shoes off at the door and put on slippers.

[1] Literally, "type of inn."

traditional referring to customs followed for many years	**kimonos** long, loose robes with wide sleeves; the robe is tied with a sash	**westernized** influenced by European or American ways

And then if you go to the bathroom, you're supposed to take off *those* slippers and put on *another* pair of slippers, which are just for the bathroom. This custom may seem silly, but there's a sound reason for it: It keeps foreigners confused. At least that's what it did for us. I was always forgetting to change **footwear**, plus the slippers were always too small for me, so to keep my feet in them, I had to kind of **mince** around.

Following the baggage-carrying ryokan ladies, I minced with Beth and Robby to our room, which was in the very simple, very beautiful Japanese style, everything in light-colored wood. There was a sliding paper screen that opened up into a little **cicada**-infested rock garden with a brook **babbling** through it. The room had no beds or bureaus or chairs, only straw floor mats and a low table. In a *ryokan*, when you want to sleep, a maid comes in and puts down some **futons** for you. In fact, the maid comes in a lot; you got the feeling she was always just outside the door, day and night, ready to come in and do something for you. Our maid, who was wearing a kimono and a beeper, came in about thirty seconds after we arrived. . . .

She said *"Hai domo!"* to us a lot. As far as I was able to determine, *"Hai domo!"* means "Yes, very!" We came to think of her as the Very Lady.

> Do you think *hai domo* really means, Yes, very!?

She gestured to indicate that we should kneel with her around the low table, then she welcomed us to the *ryokan* **via** a nice little traditional ceremony wherein she poured us some tea and served us some kind of mysterious green substance. We smiled and bowed and drank the tea, and we each ate about one **molecule** of the green substance, and we smiled some more to indicate that it was the best darned mysterious green substance we had ever eaten and we would almost surely be wolfing it down later on.

---

footwear anything worn on the feet

mince walk with very short steps

cicada a type of large insect; the males make a loud, humming noise

babbling making a low, quiet sound like water

futons thin mattresses usually used on the floor or on a frame

via by way of

molecule a tiny bit

> What stereotypes is Barry using to poke fun at himself and his family?

> What kind of humor is Barry using here?

Then the Very Lady showed us, via ancient traditional *ryokan* hand gestures, how to operate the TV remote control. She also showed us the bathroom, which was, like the rest of the inn, done in the beautiful, simple Japanese style, with lots of light–colored wood, accented by a Woody Woodpecker hand mirror.[2] The maid also showed us our *yukata,* which are lightweight **bathrobelike** garments that you're supposed to wear while you stroll (or, in my case, mince) around the *ryokan*. The idea is that you become extremely relaxed and contemplate the rock garden and listen to the brook babble and the cicadas chatter until you achieve total inner peace. Or, if you are a typical **hyperactive** American suburban mall–oriented family like us, you go stark raving mad.

Maybe the problem was that the cicadas went off at about 4:30 a.m. and apparently had gotten hold of small but powerful amplifiers. So between them and the sudden unexpected appearances of the Very Lady, we never got quite enough sleep in the *ryokan*. . . .

Another interesting thing to do in the Kyoto area is go see the **cormorant** fishing. This is a unique and traditional and weird method of catching fish using cormorants, which are a type of musical instrument similar to the trumpet.

No, just kidding. Cormorants are a type of **aquatic** bird sort of like **pelicans**. They're used in a centuries-old nighttime fishing technique still practiced in a few places, including a town near Kyoto called Uji. We took a train out there one evening, and found it to be a pleasant little river village, nice and peaceful except for a man at the train station shouting angrily over a huge truck-mounted public-address system. That's what **political activists** do in Japan: They shout angrily

---

[2] Here is another interesting *ryokan* bathroom fact: There was never any shampoo, but every day there were three new toothbrushes.

bathrobelike like a robe worn after a bath

hyperactive very active

cormorant a water bird

aquatic living in or on water

pelicans large birds whose bills have a pouch that holds fish

political activists people who take action to bring about political change

at you over powerful amplifiers turned up loud enough to **pulverize** concrete. As a persuasive technique, this leaves much to be desired. We saw quite a few of these trucks in Tokyo, and nobody paid any attention; everybody just walked briskly past.

This is smart. If you stood still and listened, you'd be deaf as a tire iron within minutes. So if the activists ever *did* attract any followers, they'd have a . . . time carrying out whatever political actions they had in mind:

"WE MUST STRENGTHEN OUR MILITARY!"

"WHAT DID HE SAY?"

"HE SAYS HE WANTS TO LENGTHEN OUR **CAPILLARIES**."

"NO, THANKS, I ALREADY ATE."

> Does the writer want readers to think he is serious?

Anyway, we walked briskly away from the angry shouting man at the Uji station, and I asked a **pedestrian** for directions, using the international symbol for cormorant fishing, which is when you have one hand pretend to be a cormorant and swoop down on the other hand, which is pretending to be a fish.

> Could the scene at the Uji station happen in the United States?

He aimed us toward the river, where we found fishermen preparing some long, narrow wooden boats. At the end of each boat was a pole sticking out over the water; suspended from this was a wire basket in which the fishermen had built a log fire. The purpose of the fire is to attract the fish, although why a creature who lives under water would be attracted to fire is beyond me. Perhaps these are unusually stupid fish.

When night had fallen and the fires were burning brightly, the fishermen brought out some baskets, three per boat, each one containing two cormorants. The men put leashes around each bird's neck, looped so that the bird could get a fish into its mouth but not swallow it. Then the men pushed off from shore and started drifting down the river, two men controlling each boat and a third man in front, near the burning basket, holding leashes attached to the six cormorants, who swam around and **squabbled** with each other.

---

pulverize pound into a powder

capillaries tiny blood vessels

pedestrian a person who travels on foot

squabbled quarreled; argued about something small

At first this approach didn't look terribly practical; my impression was that it would be a lot less trouble to try to scoop up the fish with trumpets. But it turned out that cormorants, once they stopped squabbling, did a pretty good job. They'd disappear under water, and every third or fourth time they'd come up with a fish. Whenever this happened, the leash man would haul the cormorant in, snatch the fish away, and shove the cormorant back out. You'd think eventually the cormorants would get **ticked off** about this, maybe start plotting acts of revenge.... But I guess the cormorants aren't a whole lot smarter than the fish.

Still, it made for a pleasant evening's **diversion**, a uniquely Japanese experience, and we were in a good mood as we headed back to our little Kyoto ryokan, with its peaceful babbling brook and its cheerfully chattering cicadas. Someday I will go back and kill them with a **flamethrower**.

ticked off a slang expression meaning "annoyed" or "angry"

diversion something that entertains

flamethrower a military weapon that sends out a stream of burning fuel

AFTER READING THE SELECTION

Staying at a Japanese Inn: Peace, Tranquillity, Insects — by Dave Barry

Directions Choose the letter of the best answer or write the answer using complete sentences.

Comprehension: Identifying Facts

1. What happens when Dave Barry arrives at the inn?
   - **A** He loses his luggage.
   - **B** He changes his shoes in the car.
   - **C** He carries all the luggage to the room.
   - **D** Three women come out to welcome the family.

2. What do you sleep on in a traditional inn?

3. What are cormorants, and how are they used in Japan?

Comprehension: Putting Ideas Together

4. Why does Barry think the maid is waiting outside the room?
   - **A** He saw her out there when he went for a walk.
   - **B** She came in a lot.
   - **C** The hotel manager told him she was supposed to do this.
   - **D** She told the Barry family she would be right outside.

5. Describe the Japanese custom about shoes.

6. Does the Japanese method of relaxing work for the Barrys? Explain your answer.

Understanding Literature: Exaggeration

Exaggeration stretches the truth to make something seem better or worse than it is. It describes something as bigger, stronger, smaller, or harder than it really is. Exaggeration is not meant to be understood as the truth. People sometimes use exaggeration in their speech. Here are two examples: "He eats everything in sight." "You've grown as tall as a tree." Humor is often the effect of exaggeration.

7. How does Barry exaggerate the noise the cicadas make?

8. Give one more example of exaggeration in this column.

Critical Thinking

9. Barry writes about several conflicts in this story. Describe one.

Thinking Creatively

10. Barry describes his trip to Japan in a light, funny way. Based on his writing, what kind of person do you think Barry is?

After Reading **continued on next page**

AFTER READING THE SELECTION (continued)

Staying at a Japanese Inn: Peace, Tranquillity, Insects   by Dave Barry

 Grammar Check

A semicolon is used to connect two independent clauses that are related. (You may remember that an independent clause can be written as its own sentence.) Find two sentences in this selection that use semicolons. Notice how each clause makes its own sentence. Write these clauses, and then write two of your own sentences using semicolons.

 Writing on Your Own

Think of a typical American custom. Choose something small, such as something similar to the Japanese custom with shoes. Imagine how this custom might look to someone from another country. Write a description of it from that point of view. Use exaggeration in your description.

 Speaking

Sometimes, people read a piece of humor and think the writer was serious. Find a friend or family member who has not read this story. Tell the person about the story. Explain how you knew that Barry was trying to be funny and not serious.

 Listening

Take turns telling a funny story to a partner. Listen carefully as your partner tells the story. See if your partner gives any clues about how the story will end. Did you find the story as funny as your partner did?

 Media

Watch a funny movie with a partner. Discuss the differences between humor in writing and humor in film. What can be done in a movie, to make people laugh? What can be done in a piece of writing that cannot be done in movies? Which do you think has a greater ability to be funny—movies or literature?

 Technology

Find several Internet links telling about Kyoto and places that people might like to visit. Be sure to include hotels, restaurants, common tourist places, and at least one cultural experience. Use these links to develop your own virtual tour of Kyoto. Use a word processor to format your tour and print it out.

BEFORE READING THE SELECTION

Why Can't We Have Our Own Apartment? by Erma Bombeck

Erma Bombeck
(1927–1996)
American

About the Author

Erma Bombeck grew up during the Great Depression. She went to college, married a teacher, and started a family. She found family concerns amusing, boring, and frustrating. As her family grew, she began sharing her feelings in writing. In 1964, she began to write a humor column for a weekly paper in Dayton, Ohio. The next year, her column moved to a larger newspaper. Soon, it was syndicated, or printed in newspapers all over the country. Bombeck's column, "At Wit's End," appeared several times a week in some 600 papers.

Bombeck's columns have been published in several best-selling books. Their titles are jokes themselves. Two of her most popular books are *Just Wait Till You Have Children of Your Own* and *The Grass Is Always Greener Over the Septic Tank*. Her humor has amused millions of readers.

Objectives

- To read a humorous column and identify the theme
- To identify who is speaking in written dialogue

About the Selection

The following selection is from *If Life Is a Bowl of Cherries What Am I Doing in the Pits?* It was published in 1978. Bombeck writes this story as a middle-aged parent and homemaker. It is about a family with older children, possibly teenagers or young adults. The parents decide to do something very unusual. They tell their children they are going to move out. As you read the column, think about what Bombeck might be trying to say.

Before Reading continued on next page

BEFORE READING THE SELECTION (continued)

Why Can't We Have Our Own Apartment? by Erma Bombeck

dialogue the conversation among characters in a story

theme the main idea of a literary work

Literary Terms This selection is about a funny family situation. The parents tell their children they want to move out. Bombeck uses **dialogue** to tell most of the story. Dialogue is the conversation among characters in a story. As the characters talk to each other, readers learn what is happening. Bombeck also uses the dialogue to get her **theme** across. The theme of a work is its main idea.

Reading on Your Own Faulty arguments are reasons for doing something that do not make sense. They are not logical. As you read, look for a faulty argument that the children give. What faulty argument do the parents give?

Writing on Your Own Many teenagers look forward to the day when they will move out of their parents' homes. What are some of their reasons? Write a paragraph about these.

Vocabulary Focus An idiom is an expression that cannot be understood from the meanings of the words in the expression. Erma Bombeck uses idioms in this work. Find these two idioms in the selection: "the run of the house" and "spit it out." Rewrite the sentences with these idioms using your own words. Be sure to express the same ideas without using any figurative language. Whose wording did you like better, yours or Bombeck's? Why?

Think Before You Read Brainstorm a list of things that your parents do in your home. Which of these things might the parents in this selection use as an excuse for wanting to move out?

530 Unit 6 Humorous Literature

Why Can't We Have Our Own Apartment?

We knew the kids would take it the wrong way, but we had to do it anyway.

"Children," we said, "your father and I want to get our own apartment."

One looked up from his homework and the other two even turned down the volume on the TV set. "What are you saying?"

"We are saying we'd like to move out and be on our own for a while."

"But why?" asked our daughter. "Aren't you happy here? You have your own room and the run of the house."

"I know, but a lot of parents our age are striking out on their own."

"It'll be expensive," said our son. "Have you thought about **utilities** and phone bills and newspapers and a hundred little things you take for granted around here?"

"We've thought it all through."

"Spit it out," said our daughter. "What's bothering you about living with us? Did we ask too much? What did we ask you to do? Only cook, make beds, do laundry, take care of the yard, keep the cars in running order and bring in the money. Was that so hard?"

"It's not that," I said gently. "It's just that we want to fix up our own apartment and come and go as we please."

> As you read, think about the theme of the story.

> Read the dialogue carefully. Keep track of who is saying each line.

utilities household services, such as electricity, telephone, or water

Humorous Literature Unit 6

> What family member would you expect to say what the daughter is saying?

"If it's your car you wanted, why didn't you say so? We could make arrangements."

"It's not just the car. We want to be able to play our **stereos** when we want to and come in late without someone saying, 'Where have you been?' and invite people over without other people hanging around eating our chip dip."

"What will you do for furniture?"

"We don't need all that much. We'll just take a few small **appliances**, some **linens**, our bedroom **suite**, the **typewriter**, the luggage, the card table and chairs, the old TV you never use, and some pots and pans and a few tables and chairs."

"You'll call everyday?"

We nodded.

As we headed for the car I heard one son whisper sadly, "Wait till they get their first utility bill. They'll be back."

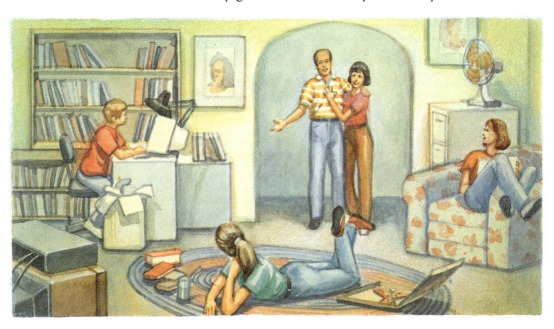

stereos sound equipment, often used to play music

appliances household equipment, such as the toaster, stove, and microwave

linens household goods made of cloth, such as sheets and towels

suite a matched set of furniture

typewriter a machine with a keyboard that produces printed words

AFTER READING THE SELECTION

Why Can't We Have Our Own Apartment? by Erma Bombeck

Directions Choose the letter of the best answer or write the answer using complete sentences.

Comprehension: Identifying Facts

1. What do the parents want to do?
   A move out of the house
   B get their children to move out
   C go on a vacation
   D buy a new car

2. What do the parents want to take with them?

3. What does one son predict will happen?

Comprehension: Putting Ideas Together

4. Why do the parents want to move out?
   A to do their own laundry
   B to be on their own
   C so they can have the TV
   D to pay their own utility bills

5. What are some of the things the children must have complained about?

6. How are roles reversed in this story?

Understanding Literature: Theme

A theme is the main idea of a literary work. It can be a broad idea, such as love or ambition. Or it can be more specific, such as how ambition can hurt people. The theme is usually not stated directly in a piece of literature. For example, a story might be about brothers and sisters who fight and argue, and then help each other during a hard time. In that case, the theme could be the importance of family.

7. What is the theme of this selection?

8. How does the writer make her treatment of the theme funny?

Critical Thinking

9. What can you conclude about the use of the car in this family?

Thinking Creatively

10. What part of this selection did you find funniest? Explain.

After Reading continued on next page

AFTER READING THE SELECTION (continued)

Why Can't We Have Our Own Apartment?   by Erma Bombeck

 Grammar Check

Quotation marks are used to show dialogue. Sometimes, the speaker is not identified. You have to figure out who is speaking from what the speaker is saying and who is speaking before and after. The speakers of dialogue in the second half of the selection are not identified. However, you can still understand that one child at a time is speaking to the parents. Write three lines of dialogue between a parent and a child. Use quotation marks correctly in the dialogue.

 Writing on Your Own

In this piece, Bombeck describes a scene that may be like something she actually thought about, but that she would never actually do. Think of something you might like to do about your family life but never have done. Write a few sentences telling what you want to do. Tell why you want to do it and whether you think you might really do it.

 Speaking and Listening

Read this selection aloud with a small group. Have each person read the lines of a different character. Then listen to another group of students as they read the selection. Did you enjoy this piece more when you read it silently or when you heard it read aloud? Why?

 Media

Pretend you are the parents in this story. Make a computer presentation showing why you want to move out. Remember that your audience is your children. Try to persuade your children to agree with your viewpoint. Use examples that you think they will understand.

Stories

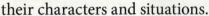

Humorous stories can be either fiction or nonfiction. In either case, their main purpose is to amuse. Many anecdotes, or short stories, are meant to be humorous. If a funny story is fairly short and ends with a punch line, it is called a joke. If someone tells a longer story in person, it is usually called a monologue or a routine. Performers on television, radio, and recordings often deliver monologues as part of their acts. Humorous stories are often short enough to be read in one sitting. But they are also long enough not to depend on a big finish. They usually have one major conflict that involves the characters and keeps the story moving. Their details and plots are often funnier than their punch lines or points. They often make us laugh at ourselves as well as their characters and situations.

Some of the world's best writers told humorous stories. Shakespeare's comedies have much humor in them. Mark Twain's stories remain beloved favorites. The following selections find humor in different situations. One story pokes fun at "high culture" when it looks at an opera. The other makes us chuckle at everyday human behavior even though the subject is very serious, not funny.

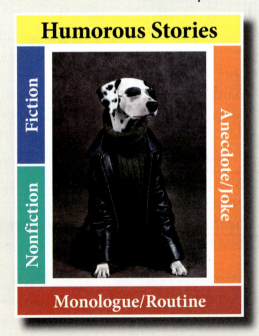

BEFORE READING THE SELECTION

Lohengrin   by Leo Slezak (trans. by Charles E. Pederson)

Leo Slezak
(1873–1946)
Austrian

Objectives

- To read and understand a parody
- To describe the plot of a story
- To identify an archetype from a story

About the Author

Leo Slezak was born in Schönberg, Moravia, in 1873. At that time, it was part of Austria. (Today, it is part of the Czech Republic.) Having a beautiful voice, he soon began to sing opera. In 1896, he sang his first leading role—as Lohengrin. He sang for many years with the Vienna Royal Opera (Hofoperntheater) and the famous conductor Gustav Mahler. In 1900, he sang the part of Lohengrin at Covent Garden in London. Slezak's singing career lasted until 1933. He was also a gifted writer and actor in films.

Leo Slezak sang many operatic roles in his long career. Still, he could see that many people had a hard time understanding opera. Slezak even joked about the opera *Il Trovatore:* "Even I don't get what's going on in this one!" He wrote a popular book that poked fun at opera guidebooks.

About the Selection

Richard Wagner wrote the opera *Lohengrin*. He based the story of Lohengrin, the "Swan Knight," on several legends from the Middle Ages. The opera was first performed in 1850. Years later, Leo Slezak sang the part of Lohengrin in this opera.

This selection is Leo Slezak's own story about the opera. He describes the action and plot in a funny way. Slezak pokes fun at the things the characters do and say. In a sense, Slezak says that he can see why some people may not enjoy the opera.

Literary Terms This is Leo Slezak's **parody** of the opera *Lohengrin*. A parody is an exaggerated look at a situation. In this story, Slezak exaggerates some of the details of the opera in order to be funny. He makes a big deal out of some of the more minor details.

At the same time, Slezak makes sure to tell the **plot**, or the series of events, in the opera. The plot of this opera has some **archetypes,** or descriptive details or themes that are found in many different cultures. One of the archetypes in *Lohengrin* is the idea of a duel, a fight to prove who is right.

Reading on Your Own Use a Story Map to help you see the problems that come up in this story. Refer to Appendix A for an example of this graphic organizer. Begin by writing the title and setting at the top. Write in the problem and different events as you read. Do you think the problem is solved?

Writing on Your Own Think of a book you read or a movie you saw that you thought was really silly. Write a paragraph or two about the story line. Name the main characters and describe the main action.

Vocabulary Focus Many words have more than one meaning. A reader can figure out which meaning the writer has in mind by reading the sentence or story and seeing which meaning fits. Look for these words in the story: *spotted, flat, nerve,* and *train*. Each of them has more than one meaning. For each word, write the sentence in which it is used in the story. Then write your own sentence using a different meaning of the word.

Think Before You Read Think about your ideas of the opera. At what feature of opera do you think Slezak will poke fun?

> **parody** an exaggerated, or extreme, look at a situation
>
> **plot** the series of events in a story
>
> **archetype** a descriptive detail, plot pattern, character type, or theme that is found in many different cultures

Lohengrin

As you read, notice how Slezak uses parody. He exaggerates the action and the story of the opera.

The Hartz (spelled Harz in German) mountains are a region of Germany famous for legends. "Hartz Mountain" is also a breed of canary.

It's a **complicated** matter, so pay careful attention, or you may never figure out what is going on.

As background you must know that long ago, magic was all the rage. In those days, people—mostly princes—were changed into all kinds of animals. It often happened that you might think you had a genuine canary from the Harz mountains, and then one day it would **reveal** itself to be a charmed **archduke**, whom some miserable, jealous fairy had changed into a bird. . . .

As the curtain rises, the stage is spotted with men. (I can hear you correcting me now. "You should say people," you say, but truly it is a bunch of men.) They are **randomly** beating their swords on their shields and singing.

King Heinrich, wearing a long false beard, sits beneath a large oak, holding court.

Telramund, an upper-class noble, has brought a **lawsuit** against Elsa von Brabant, maintaining that she killed her brother, little Gottfried.

The king does not believe Telramund, and it's not true anyway.

Elsa is called forward and questioned. She denies having done it.

Who is telling the truth? Telramund or Elsa?

I almost forgot to mention that Telramund is married. His wife is named Mrs. Ortrud. She's a truly gloomy woman, and actually she forced Telramund to bring the suit.

Think about the time and place of this opera. Is there something silly about the name Mrs. Ortrud?

complicated not easy to understand

reveal make known

archduke a royal rank equal to that of a prince

randomly without a definite pattern or plan

lawsuit a complaint brought before a court of law

In days of yore, "trial by battle" was also all the rage. If it could not be proved who was guilty or innocent, two men were allowed to fight it out. The loser was guilty. Seems like a **dubious** way to go about it.

Still, Telramund challenges anyone to strike for Elsa's honor.

Even though none of the knights thinks Elsa capable of such mean behavior, no one leaps to her defense, **despite** repeated blasts on the announcement trumpet. The king orders the trumpet to be blasted once more.

Suddenly a shining knight is seen in the distance, standing in a boat pulled by a snow-white swan.

The chorus of men shouts in confusion, pointing at the knight and looking in a sick way at the orchestra conductor. That apparently does not help, since everyone has different ideas about what's going on—what the Latin scholar calls "tohu vabohu."

Lohengrin enters, spotlights hit him from all sides, and he sings the Swan Song a quarter note flat. The swan, hearing this, swims away.

Days of yore is a phrase like "once upon a time." It means a time long past.

Tohu vabohu is actually a Hebrew term meaning "chaos."

What is the author suggesting about why the swan leaves?

dubious causing doubt as to worth or truth

despite in spite of

Humorous Literature Unit 6 539

Now comes the interesting part.

You can actually hear Telramund trembling, but he doesn't give up. He can't, since giving up is not written into the script.

First, Lohengrin goes to Elsa and asks would she like him to fight for her and would she consider marrying him, though only on condition that she never ask who he is and where he comes from.

What? Not to know with whom one has the pleasure? The nerve!

She vows never to ask, he goes over and defeats Telramund but spares his life, Mrs. Ortrud flies into a rage, Elsa flings herself on the neck of the Nameless One, the men beat their swords on their shields with joy, the king strokes his false beard, blesses the couple's **union**, and the curtain falls. That's Act I.

> Does this seem like a good spot for a happy ending?

union a marriage

Act II opens in the dark.

From a corner come **unnaturally** long **criticisms** and **mutual** accusations. Mrs. Ortrud and Telramund are arguing. He calls her "companion of his disgrace." She is also unfriendly to him.

After much back and forth, they decide to make Elsa curious and turn her against Lohengrin.

On the night before a wedding in the middle ages, the bride-to-be apparently always appeared on a balcony to talk to the moon, or if no moon was available, to the breeze.

Today such exaggerated gestures are simply not done, plus people would think you're cracked if you acted that way.

While the bride-to-be **gabs** with the breeze, Mrs. Ortrud—below the balcony—sighs so loudly that Elsa can't help but hear her. She goes down, scoops up Mrs. Ortrud from the doorway, and brings her back inside the palace.

If that isn't the dumbest thing she could do, I don't know what is.

The most experienced women in the chorus have the part of maidens in the bridal train. They scatter flowers. The men occupy themselves with marching and singing in **syncopation**. Everyone strides majestically to the church. Suddenly Mrs. Ortrud shoves her way to stand before Elsa, claiming that she should be first in line.

This causes great excitement. In the midst of it come the king and Lohengrin. Lohengrin immediately sizes up the situation, lightning bolts shooting from his eyes. Going to Elsa, he takes her aside and tells her not to get all excited and go asking him any questions, otherwise he would have to leave at once. Elsa says that of course she has no such thoughts and is so happy even to be marrying him at all. He presses her to his chest and they stride on to the church.

> *Cracked* is a slang word for "crazy."
>
> What is happening in this part of the plot?
>
> The author uses *experienced* to refer to both their acting experience and, ironically, their age.

---

unnaturally unusually; in an unexpected way

criticisms judgments that find fault

mutual shared in common

gabs slang for talks; chatters

syncopation a musical accent not on the usual beat

At the last moment, Telramund leaps from behind a pillar and scolds Lohengrin. He accuses Lohengrin of being a **sorcerer** and notes that the whole situation stinks—a lot. He goes on to question any person who rides around on swans, who sends swans away, whom no one can ask who one is, and where are his ID, his papers, his **visa**! Telramund declares the whole business of the trial by battle to be nonsense and wants a new hearing.

To be brief, Telramund is upset—with good reason, he feels.

But once a judgment has been made in someone's favor, that person can legally do anything. Telramund gets a stab in the stomach and is tossed aside.

> Does this seem like a good spot for a happy ending?

Lohengrin and Elsa resume their interrupted striding to the church, the men beat their swords on their shields with joy, and under the approving nods of the king, the curtain falls.

Act III—The Bridal Chamber

Lohengrin and Elsa are **ushered** in by the king, who—with some winks and a few practical words of advice—leaves again.

> What do you picture as the room's furnishings?

The room's furnishings alone tell the audience it's not going to be a pleasant wedding night.

Lohengrin sings for such a long time that, to get him to stop, Elsa finally asks him who he is. The fatal bomb explodes. On top of that, Telramund enters to kill Lohengrin. He misses his thrust and falls to the floor, struck dead by lightning bolts from Lohengrin's eyes.

He is cleared away.

Lohengrin says nothing to Elsa. He has to speak to the king first. Another of Lohengrin's mean tricks. As Elsa's tears fall like boric acid, the curtain falls.

> Boric acid is a salty solution used in medicine. What is the effect of comparing Elsa's tears to boric acid?

---

sorcerer a wizard

visa a paper that allows a person to enter a country

ushered showed people the way

Change of scenery. Same scene as Act I.

The king appears on horseback. The horse expresses its inner feelings, while the men beat their swords on their shields with eagerness, shouting for victory. It's off to war for them, each one panting for a hero's death.

Lohengrin is to lead a **battalion**. He enters and says he can't go with them. To his good luck, Elsa has asked him the forbidden question and he has to go home now.

The men beat their swords on their shields with despair.

Elsa is brought in. She **swoons**. In this opera, she seems only to stride or swoon.

Lohengrin strikes a **pose** and sings the tale of the Holy Grail. He has no evidence for what he's singing, only a lot of **unprovable** stuff for which no review board in the world would let him out of the army. But everyone present believes

> How is Elsa an archetype of a "maiden in distress"?

> The Holy Grail is said by legend to be the cup used by Jesus at the Last Supper. Many knights of old searched for it.

battalion a large group of soldiers
swoons faints
pose a position taken on purpose, as to have a picture taken
unprovable not possible to prove

him. Maybe they do only because it's late and no one wants to **prolong** the performance by **pressing** him for details or getting into a debate.

As Elsa gasps for breath, Lohengrin says good-bye, giving her a horn, a ring, and a sword. She is supposed to learn to play the horn, she should save the ring, and give the sword to her brother.

Talk about confusing!

Lohengrin leaves.

The men beat their swords on their shields with sadness.

Suddenly, Mrs. Ortrud appears again. She just won't go away. She cries that it was she who turned Elsa's brother into a swan, that she was guilty the entire time.

Lohengrin blasts a hole in her with the lightning from his eyes. She dies.

The swan dives, and from the water leaps an exaggeratedly attractive boy—a prince. He hugs Elsa. It's little brother Gottfried!

With no animal to pull his boat, Lohengrin can't leave. Then a handy dove comes and carries him off—although that seems just a little **unrealistic**.

Elsa swoons and screams, and the curtain falls—thank heavens, because it is late indeed. The opera is over!

> What is funny about saying the dove is unrealistic?

---

prolong make last longer   **pressing** asking in an urgent way   **unrealistic** not likely to happen in real life

AFTER READING THE SELECTION

Lohengrin by Leo Slezak (trans. by Charles E. Pederson)

Directions Choose the letter of the best answer or write the answer using complete sentences.

Comprehension: Identifying Facts

1. What does the lawsuit against Elsa accuse her of doing?
   A stealing a swan
   B killing the king
   C running away from home
   D killing her brother

2. How does Lohengrin arrive?

3. What does the swan turn into at the end?

Comprehension: Putting Ideas Together

4. Why does Lohengrin fight Telramund?
   A He and Telramund are professional fighters.
   B He wants Telramund to leave town.
   C He is fighting to prove that Elsa is innocent.
   D Telramund wants to marry Elsa.

5. Why does Elsa "gab with the breeze" on the night before her wedding?

6. Who has actually caused most of the trouble in the opera? How?

Understanding Literature: Parody

A parody pokes fun at another type of literature. A parody picks out certain features of the work. Then it exaggerates them. It is written in the same format as the piece it parodies. A parody of a song would be another song. It might make fun of the characters in the song by exaggerating their feelings or actions. It might change some of the words. Parodies take the form of plays, movies, books, and other works.

7. How does Slezak use parody to make fun of the chorus?

8. How does Slezak make fun of the hero, Lohengrin?

Critical Thinking

9. The author opens by saying the opera is complicated. Name a part of the story where he makes it sound as complicated as possible.

Thinking Creatively

10. Do you think this is a successful parody? Why or why not?

After Reading continued on next page

AFTER READING THE SELECTION (continued)

Lohengrin by Leo Slezak (trans. by Charles E. Pederson)

 ### Grammar Check

The subject and verb in a sentence must agree. They will either both be plural or both be singular. Read the paragraph below. For each sentence, write the subject and verb.

> Elsa is brought in. She swoons. In this opera, she seems only to stride or swoon.

Look back at your writing to see how the subjects and verbs agree.

 ### Writing on Your Own

Near the end of the opera, Lohengrin gives three things to Elsa—a horn, a ring, and a sword. Choose one of these objects. Write the beginning of a sequel to this opera. Make up a story about what Elsa did with that object.

 ### Speaking

Choose one of the characters from the story, such as Lohengrin, Gottfried, Elsa, or Mrs. Ortrud. Tell the story from that character's point of view.

 ### Listening

Listen to a recording of the opera *Lohengrin*. Sometimes, there is a guidebook, or explanation of the story. Listen to the singers. Why is an opera guidebook so important?

 ### Viewing

Look at several opera guidebooks. How does this story compare to those guidebooks? How is it different?

 ### Research

Do some research to find out more about Leo Slezak and his career as an opera singer. Try to find pictures of him in his various roles.

BEFORE READING THE SELECTION

A Wedding Without Musicians   by Sholom Aleichem

Shalom Aleichem
(1859–1916)
Ukrainian

About the Author

Sholom Aleichem was born Sholem (or Solomon) Rabinowitz in Pereyaslav, Ukraine. (Ukraine was then part of the Russian Empire.) He was a short-story writer, dramatist, and humorist, or someone who writes funny works. At first, he taught and wrote in Russian and Hebrew. Then he began to write in Yiddish, the traditional language of Eastern European Jews. His pen name comes from a traditional Hebrew greeting for old friends. He left Russia in 1905 and later moved to the United States.

Aleichem's works often describe the simple life of small-town Jews. He wrote more than 40 books, both novels and short stories. The play and movie of *Fiddler on the Roof* are based on Aleichem's stories in *Tevye the Dairyman*.

About the Selection

In the 1800s, Jews in Russia and Ukraine could live only in certain places. The government allowed attacks on Jews and their homes and businesses. This story tells how the Jews in one town were kept safe from such attacks. It comes from a collection called *The Railroad Stories* (1911).

Some of Aleichem's readers might not have been able to see the humor in their situation. Russian pogroms, or mass attacks, were horrible. It is important to note that the Holocaust happened years after Aleichem died. It is possible that Aleichem was trying to show that the Jewish people found strength in their ability to laugh.

Objectives

- To read and understand an anecdote
- To explain the point of view of a humorist
- To identify the irony in a work

Before Reading continued on next page

BEFORE READING THE SELECTION (continued)

A Wedding Without Musicians   by Sholom Aleichem

humorist someone who writes funny works

anecdote a short, funny story

irony the use of words that seem to say one thing but mean the opposite

Literary Terms Sholom Aleichem was a **humorist**, a person who writes funny works. He wrote about a serious topic but found something funny in the way that people act, in the things that they say, or even in the situation itself.

This story is almost like a long **anecdote**, or short, funny story. It is about Jews in the town of Heissin. Some people are on the way to Heissin, with plans to attack the Jews. Aleichem uses humor and **irony** to tell how the Jews are kept safe. Irony is the use of words that seem to say one thing but mean another.

Reading on Your Own As you read the story, pause at the end of every page to summarize what has happened so far. How does Noah Tonkonoy help the Jews of Heissin?

Writing on Your Own Are there any topics that you think a humorist should not write about? Write a paragraph to explain your answer.

Vocabulary Focus Sholom Aleichem says that this story is a miracle. Look up *miracle* in the dictionary. Do you agree that what happens in this story is an example of a miracle? Why or why not?

Think Before You Read Discuss with a partner any stories you have read about people who have been saved from disaster. How do you think the people in this story will act before they are saved?

A Wedding Without Musicians

The last time I told you about our **Straggler** Special, I described the miracle of *Hashono Rabo*. This time I shall tell you about another miracle in which the Straggler Special figured, how thanks to the Straggler Special the town of Heissin was saved from a terrible fate.

This took place during the days of the Constitution when **reprisals** against the Jews were going on everywhere. Though I must tell you that we Jews of Heissin have never been afraid of pogroms. Why? Simply because there is no one in our town who can carry out a pogrom. Of course you can imagine that if we looked very hard we could find one or two volunteers who wouldn't deny themselves the pleasure of **ventilating** us a little, that is, breaking our bones or burning down our houses. For example, when reports of pogroms began drifting in, the few squires, who are enemies of our people, wrote **confidential** letters to the proper authorities, saying it might be a good idea if "something were done" in Heissin also; but since there was no one here to do it, would they be so kind as to send help, in other words, would they **dispatch** some "people" as quickly as possible.

> As you read, note the details in this anecdote.

> The *Straggler Special* is a local train. The writer is referring to an earlier story about the same train.

> *Pogroms* were mob attacks against Jews. They happened fairly often in Russia under the tsars, especially from the 1880s to the early 1900s. The government did little to stop them.

---

straggler something that lags behind the others

reprisals acts of force in revenge for an assumed wrong

ventilating putting in motion; blowing away

confidential meant to be secret

dispatch send off quickly to a place

Humorous Literature Unit 6

And before another twenty–four hours had passed a reply came, also confidentially, that "people" were being sent. From where? From Zhmerinko, from Kazatin, Razdilno, Popelno and other such places that had distinguished themselves in beating up Jews. Do you want to know how we learned of this deep secret? We found it out through our regular source of news, Noah Tonkonoy. Noah Tonkonoy is a man whom God has **endowed** with a pair of extra-long legs and he uses them to good purpose. He never rests and he is seldom to be found at home. He is always busy with a thousand things and most of these things have to do with other people's business rather than his own. By trade he is a printer, and because he is the only printer in Heissin he knows all the squires and the police and has dealings with **officialdom** and is in on all their secrets.

Noah Tonkonoy spread the good news all over town. He told the secret to one person at a time, in strictest confidence, of course, saying, "I am telling this only to you. I wouldn't tell it to anyone else." And that was how the whole town became aware of the fact that a mob of **hooligans** was on the way, and that a plan for beating up Jews had been worked out. The plan told exactly when they would start, on which day, at which hour, and from which point, and by what means—everything to the last detail.

You can imagine what terror this struck in our hearts. Panic spread quickly. And among whom do you think it spread first? Among the poor, of course. It's a peculiar thing about poor people. When a rich man is afraid of a pogrom, you can understand why. He is afraid, poor fellow, that he will be turned into a **pauper**. But those of you who are already paupers, what are you afraid of? What have you got to lose? But you should have seen how they bundled up their children and packed up their **belongings** and began running hither and yon, looking for a place to hide. Where can a person hide? This one hides in a friendly peasant's cellar, another in the

> What is ironic about how Noah Tonkonoy tells each person the secret?

> Here is an example of how a humorist sees things differently from other writers. How would a more serious writer feel about poor people and their fear?

> Running "hither and yon" is an expression using old words for "here and there."

endowed provided with a talent or quality

officialdom an entire group of officials

hooligans troublemakers; young men who do vicious or violent acts

pauper a very poor person

belongings things a person owns

Notary's attic, a third in the **Director's** office at the factory. Everyone finds a spot for himself.

I was the only one in town who wasn't anxious to hide. I am not boasting about my bravery. But this is the way I see it: what's the sense of being afraid of a pogrom? I don't say that I am a hero. I might have been willing to hide too, when the hour of **reckoning** came. But I asked myself first, "How can I be sure that during the slaughter the friendly peasant in whose cellar I was hiding, or the Notary, or the Director of the factory himself, wouldn't...." You understand. And all that aside, how can you leave a town wide open like that? It's no trick to run away. You have to see about doing something. But, alas, what can a Jew do? He appeals to a friendly official. And that is just what we did.

> He is wondering if a Jew can trust a non-Jew in this circumstance.

In every town there is at least one friendly official you can appeal to. We had one too, the Inspector of Police, a jewel of a fellow, willing to listen to us and willing to accept a gift on occasion. We went to the Inspector with the proper gifts and asked for his protection. He reassured us at once. He told us to go home and sleep in peace. Nothing would happen. Sounds good, doesn't it? But we still had our walking newspaper, Noah, who was broadcasting another secret through the length and **breadth** of the town. The secret was that a telegram had just arrived. He swore by everything holy that he had seen it himself. What was in that telegram? Only one word—*Yediem*. An ugly word. It means simply, "We are coming." We ran back to the Inspector. "Your honor," we told him, "it looks bad." "What looks bad?" he asked, and we told him, "A telegram has just arrived." "From where?" We told him. "And what does it say?" We told him, *"Yediem."* At this he burst out laughing. "You are big fools," he said. "Only yesterday I ordered a regiment of Cossacks from Tolchin."

> What do you think it means that the Inspector would accept a gift?

notary a notary public; a person who signs or witnesses the signing of documents

director a person who directs or manages a business

reckoning paying or settling what is owed

breadth the width

> Cossacks made up special military units in the Russian army.

When we heard this we breathed more easily. When a Jew hears that a Cossack is coming, he takes courage, he can face the world again. The question remained: who would arrive first, the Cossacks from Tolchin, or the hooligans from Zhmerinko? Common sense told us that the hooligans would arrive first, because they were coming by train, while the Cossacks were coming on horseback. But we pinned all our hopes on the Straggler Special. God is merciful. He would surely perform a miracle and the Straggler would be at least a few hours late. This wasn't too much to hope for, since it happened nearly every day. But this one time it looked as though the miracle wouldn't take place. The Straggler kept going from station to station as regular as a clock. You can imagine how we felt when we learned, confidentially, of course, through Noah Tonkonoy, that a telegram had arrived from the last station, from Krishtopovka. *Yediem,* it said, and not just *yediem*—but *yediem* with a *hurrah!* in front of it.

Naturally we took this last bit of news straight to the Inspector. We begged him not to rely on the Cossacks who might or might not arrive from Tolchin sometime, but to send police to the station, at least for the sake of appearances, so that our enemies wouldn't think that we were completely at their mercy. The Inspector listened to our pleas. He did what we asked, and more. He got himself up in full uniform, with all his orders and medals, and took the whole police force, that is the **gendarme** and his assistant, to the station with him to meet the train.

> How big is the town's police force?

But our enemies weren't asleep either. They also put on their full dress uniforms, complete with ribbons and medals, took a couple of priests along, and also came to meet the train. The Inspector asked them sternly, "What are you doing here?" And they asked him the same question, "What are you doing here?" They **bandied** words back and forth, and the Inspector let them know in no uncertain terms that their trouble was for nothing. As long as he was in charge, there would be no pogrom in Heissin. They listened, smiled knowingly, and answered with **insolence**, "We shall see."

Just then a train whistle was heard from the distance. The sound struck terror to our hearts. We waited for another whistle to blow and after that for the shouts of "Hurrah!" What would happen after the Hurrah! we knew only too well from **hearsay**. We waited, but heard nothing more. What had happened? The sort of thing that could only happen to our Straggler Special.

When the Straggler Special drew into the station, the engineer stopped the locomotive, stepped out calmly and made his way toward the **buffet**. We met him halfway. "Well, my good fellow, and where are the cars?" "Which cars?" "Can't you see that you are here with the locomotive and without cars?"

> Picture the scene at the train station. What is funny about this?

gendarme a police officer
bandied exchanged
insolence rudeness
hearsay gossip
buffet a restaurant in which people serve themselves from a counter

Humorous Literature Unit 6

> What do you think of the engineer's attitude?

He stared at us. "What do I care about the cars? They are the business of the crew." "Where is the crew?" "How should I know where the crew is? The conductor blows the whistle when he is ready and I whistle back to let him know that I am starting, and off we go. I don't have an extra pair of eyes in back of my head to see what's going on behind me." That was his story and according to that he was right. But right or wrong, there stood the Straggler Special without cars and without passengers. In other words, it was a wedding without musicians.

Later we learned that a band of hooligans had been on the way to Heissin, all of them **handpicked** youths, armed to the teeth with clubs and knives and other weapons. Their spirits were high and **liquor** flowed freely. At the last station, Krishtopovka, they invited the crew to join them and treated everybody to drinks—the conductor, the fireman, the gendarmes. But in the midst of this **revelry** they forgot one little detail, to **couple** the cars back to the locomotive. And

---

handpicked chosen carefully

liquor a strong alcoholic drink

revelry a loud celebration

couple attach; link together

so the locomotive went off at the usual time to Heissin and the rest of the Straggler Special remained standing in Krishtopovka.

Neither the hooligans nor the other passengers nor the crew noticed that they were standing still. They continued to empty bottle after bottle and to make merry, until the **station master** suddenly noticed that the locomotive had gone off and left the cars behind. He spread the alarm, the crew came tumbling out. A hue and cry was raised. The hooligans blamed the crew, the crew blamed the hooligans, but what good did it do? At last they decided that the only thing to do was to set out for Heissin on foot. They took heart and began marching toward Heissin, singing and shouting as they went.

And so they arrived in their usual good form, singing and yelling and **brandishing** their clubs. But it was already too late. In the streets of Heissin the Cossacks from Tolchin were riding up and down on horseback with whips in their hands. Within half an hour not one of the hooligans remained in town. They ran off like rats in a **famine**, they melted like ice in summer.

Now, I ask you, didn't the Straggler Special deserve to be showered with gold, or at least written up?

"A hue and cry was raised" means that a great protest or a great noise was made.

What is ironic about the Straggler Special as a hero? How does this add to the anecdote?

station master the person in charge of a railroad station

brandishing waving in a threatening way

famine a severe lack of food

Humorous Literature Unit 6 555

AFTER READING THE SELECTION

A Wedding Without Musicians   by Sholom Aleichem

Directions Choose the letter of the best answer or write the answer using complete sentences.

Comprehension: Identifying Facts

1. How do the townspeople first hear about the planned pogrom?
   A The plans are printed in the newspapers.
   B They see the gangs coming with their weapons.
   C The mayor tells them.
   D A printer tells them what he read in someone's private mail.

2. What does the telegram say? What do people think it means?

3. What public official is a friend to the Jews in the town?

Comprehension: Putting Ideas Together

4. Why aren't the Jews of Heissin afraid of pogroms?
   A Pogroms are illegal in Heissin.
   B No one has ever carried out a pogrom in Heissin.
   C The Jews of Heissin have no idea what a pogrom is.
   D There are no Jews living in Heissin.

5. Why are people relieved to know the hooligans are coming by train?

6. How do the Cossacks manage to arrive before the hooligans?

Understanding Literature: Anecdote

An anecdote is a short, funny story with a single idea. It may touch on some part of a person's personality. It can give readers a good picture of a character. It can help a writer show why a certain event is important. This story includes more details and is a bit longer than a typical anecdote. It is still a short, funny story.

7. How does the story begin?

8. Why is the Straggler Special a strange hero?

Critical Thinking

9. Cruel treatment was a serious problem for Jews in Russia. Why do you think anyone would tell funny stories about it?

Thinking Creatively

10. What do you think the title of the story means?

Grammar Check

Quotation marks can be used for more than just the words a person speaks aloud. Look at the following sentence from the first paragraph:

> But I asked myself first, "How can I be sure that during the slaughter the friendly peasant in whose cellar I was hiding, or the Notary or the Director of the factory himself, wouldn't...."

How are the quotation marks used here?

 Writing on Your Own

Write a brief outline of the story. Tell what happens at the beginning of the story. Then write the events in the middle. Finally, tell how it ends.

 Speaking

What do you think the railroad company would say to the crew that was left behind in Krishtopovka? Pretend that you are the manager of the railroad. Speak to your crew, telling them how you feel about their actions.

 Listening

Take turns reading the first paragraph on page 552 (beginning "When we heard this . . .") aloud to a partner. When your partner is reading, listen for the excitement, fear, and other emotions the characters are feeling.

 Viewing and Research

Use the library and the Internet to find pictures of Russia, Russian Jews, and the Cossacks from the early 1900s. Share your findings with your classmates.

Humorous Literature **Unit 6 557**

Unit 6 SKILLS LESSON
Dialogue

Dialogue is the conversation among characters in a story. It gives their exact words. It lets readers know what characters are thinking. Dialogue also shows how characters relate to one another.

There are two ways in which dialogue is special. Quotation marks go around the speaker's words. Usually, another phrase tells who is speaking. Here is an example.

> "Stop right there!" the police officer yelled.
>
> "Not on your life," Lance whispered.

"Stop right there!" is what the officer said. "Not on your life," is what Lance said. The phrase *the police officer yelled* shows the officer is speaking. *Lance whispered* shows Lance is speaking.

Almost all of "Why Can't We Have Our Own Apartment?" is in dialogue. It's easy to tell who is speaking. The exact words of the parents and children play a large part in the humor. Each seems to say what you would expect the other to say. Here is an example.

> "But why?" asked our daughter. "Aren't you happy here? You have your own room and the run of the house."
>
> "I know, but a lot of parents our age are striking out on their own."

This example is from "A Wedding Without Musicians." The short sentences make the characters sound out of breath:

> "Your honor," we told him, "it looks bad." "What looks bad?" he asked, and we told him, "A telegram has just arrived." "From where?" We told him. "And what does it say?" We told him, "Yediem."

Review

1. What does dialogue show?
2. Why does a writer use dialogue?
3. How can you recognize dialogue?
4. How does Bombeck's dialogue add to the humor?
5. What is the effect of the dialogue in the Aleichem story?

Writing on Your Own

Write a dialogue between two characters. Include words that identify who is speaking. Put quotation marks around each character's exact words.

Unit 6 SUMMARY

In Unit 6, you read examples of different kinds of humorous writing. Some are funny because the writers describe funny situations. Some authors use humor to make serious points. Satire and irony are ways of using humor. Satire can be very serious while it is humorous.

Jonathan Swift and Andrew Graham-Yooll use humor in a serious way. They write about situations that make them angry. Their words may make us laugh. They can also make us uncomfortable. They let us see how ridiculous or awful a situation is. Sholom Aleichem makes fun of those who were mistreating the Jews. Naguib Mahfouz introduces us to a man whose "problems" we might find amusing. The other three writers intend for us to laugh in a different way. Dave Barry makes fun of himself. Leo Slezak makes fun of an opera story. Erma Bombeck turns a family story upside down.

Humor in writing can serve several purposes. You probably did not laugh out loud at the satires by Swift and Graham-Yooll. The story by Sholom Aleichem is set in a serious situation. But it might have made you smile. The Barry, Bombeck, and Slezak stories probably made you laugh. They were written to entertain. You may have found parts of Mahfouz's story funny enough to laugh out loud.

Selections

- "A Modest Proposal" by Jonathan Swift. Swift makes an outrageous suggestion for dealing with poverty in Ireland.

- "Cup Inanity and Patriotic Profanity" by Andrew Graham-Yooll. The writer views the behavior of soccer fans celebrating a victory.

- "The Happy Man" by Naguib Mahfouz. A man wakes up feeling happy and he does not know why, so he finds someone to help him with this problem.

- "Staying at a Japanese Inn: Peace, Tranquillity, Insects" by Dave Barry. Barry tells about trying to fit into a different culture.

- "Why Can't We Have Our Own Apartment?" by Erma Bombeck. Parents switch roles with children and ask to move out.

- "Lohengrin" by Leo Slezak. Slezak makes the story of an opera sound absurd.

- "A Wedding Without Musicians" by Sholom Aleichem. Part of a train doesn't arrive, and it is a good thing for Jews in a small village.

Unit 6 REVIEW

Directions Write the answers to these questions using complete sentences.

Comprehension: Identifying Facts

1. What is the term for writing that makes fun of evil or foolishness?
   A opera
   B monologue
   C anecdote
   D satire

2. What is the purpose of a pamphlet?

3. What country did Dave Barry and his family visit?

4. Which author writes about Jewish life in the early 1900s?

5. Which selection is a parody? What does it parody?

Comprehension: Putting Ideas Together

6. What does Swift *not* claim as a motive for writing his proposal?
   A providing for infants
   B relieving the poor
   C encouraging people to have larger families
   D providing pleasure to the rich

7. What danger threatens the Jews of Heissin in "A Wedding Without Musicians"?

8. Name a selection that is meant just to amuse. Explain your choice.

9. Name a selection that is meant to affect the reader's opinion. Explain your choice.

10. What is the tone of Graham-Yooll's editorial?

Understanding Literature: Irony and Exaggeration

Irony is the use of words that seem to say one thing but mean the opposite. A writer can also use irony within the plot. The ending might be the opposite of what readers expect. Exaggeration is the use of words to make something seem more than it is. It stretches the truth. In this unit, the authors use irony and exaggeration to be funny. Several of them also turn this type of humor to a serious purpose.

11. How does the writer of "Cup Inanity and Patriotic Profanity" exaggerate the effects of a soccer victory on Argentina?

12. What is ironic about the way the printer tells secrets in "A Wedding Without Musicians"?

13. How does Dave Barry use exaggeration in describing the political activist?

14. What is ironic about the title "Why Can't We Have Our Own Apartment?"

15. Give another example of exaggeration from one of the selections.

Critical Thinking

16. Do you think you would enjoy the opera *Lohengrin?* Did reading the parody make you want to see it? Why or why not?

17. Which author do you think has the gloomiest view of life? Explain.

18. What is ironic about a humorist having a gloomy view of life?

19. Erma Bombeck and Jonathan Swift have very different writing styles. Describe the differences.

Thinking Creatively

20. The authors in this unit create many images in their writing. Choose an image from one of the selections and describe it. Why did you choose this image?

Speak and Listen

Find a short humorous work of literature at your library. You may want to look for humorous poems or anecdotes. You might want to choose a monologue like those used by stand-up comics. Read the piece to yourself until you feel comfortable reading it. Then read it to the class. Or you might learn it well enough to tell it rather than reading it.

Writing on Your Own

Think of a funny TV show that you like. What is in the show that makes it funny to you? What kind of humor does it use? Write a paragraph explaining why you like the show.

Beyond Words

Work with classmates. Look for cartoons that tell a funny story without using words. Make copies of the cartoons. Then make a bulletin board display of them.

Test-Taking Tip

To answer a multiple-choice question, first read every answer choice. Cross out the choices you know are incorrect. Then choose the best answer from the remaining choices.

Appendix A: Graphic Organizers

Graphic organizers are like maps. They help guide you through literature. They can also help you plan or "map out" your own stories, research, or presentations.

1. Character Analysis Guide

This graphic organizer helps you learn more about a character in a selection.

To use: Choose a character. List four traits of that character. Write down an event from the selection that shows each character trait.

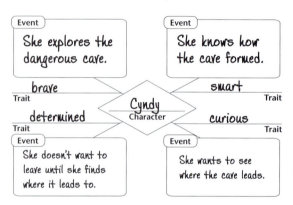

2. Story Map

This graphic organizer helps you summarize a story that you have read or plan your own story.

To use: List the title, setting, and characters. Describe the main problem of the story and the events that explain the problem. Then write how the problem is solved.

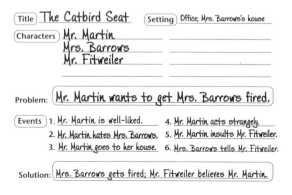

3. Main Idea Graphic (Umbrella)

This graphic organizer helps you determine the main idea of a selection or of a paragraph in the selection.

To use: List the main idea of a selection. Then, write the details that show or support the main idea of the story.

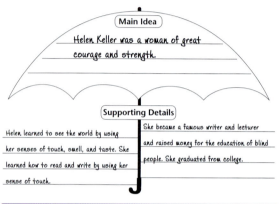

4. Main Idea Graphic (Table)

This graphic organizer is another way to determine the main idea of a selection or of a paragraph in the selection. Just like a table is held up by four strong legs, a main idea is held up or supported by many details.

To use: Write the main idea of a selection or paragraph on the tabletop. Then, write the details that show or support the main idea of the selection or paragraph on the table legs.

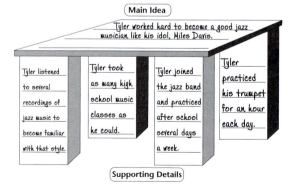

5. Main Idea Graphic (Details)

This graphic organizer is also a way to determine the main idea of a selection or of a paragraph in the selection. If the main idea of a selection or paragraph is not clear, add the details together to find it.

To use: First, list the supporting details of the selection or paragraph. Then, write one sentence that summarizes all the events. That is the main idea of the story.

7. Sequence Chain

This graphic organizer outlines a series of events in the order in which they happen. This is helpful when summarizing the plot of a story. This graphic organizer may also help you plan your own story.

To use: Fill in the box at the top with the title of the story. Then, in the boxes below, record the events in the order in which they happen in the story. Write a short sentence in each box and only include the major events of the story.

Sequence Chain for: <u>Cinderella</u>

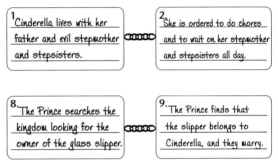

6. Venn Diagram

This graphic organizer can help you compare and contrast two stories, characters, events, or topics.

To use: List the things that are common to both stories, events, characters, and so on in the "similarities" area between the circles. List the differences on the parts that do not overlap.

What is being compared? _____

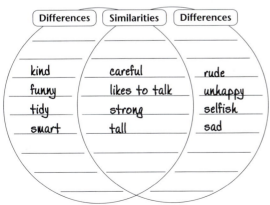

8. Concept Map

This graphic organizer helps you to organize supporting details for a story or research topic.

To use: Write the topic in the center of the graphic organizer. List ideas that support the topic on the lines. Group similar ideas and details together.

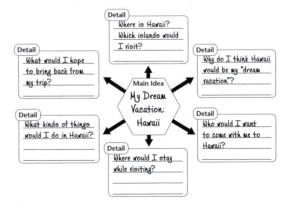

Appendix A: Graphic Organizers

9. Plot Mountain

This graphic organizer helps you organize the events of a story or plot. There are five parts in a story's plot: the exposition, the rising action, the climax, the falling action, and the resolution (or denouement). These parts represent the beginning, middle, and end of the selection.

To use:

- Write the exposition, or how the selection starts, at the left base of the mountain. What is the setting? Who are the characters?
- Then, write the rising action, or the events that lead to the climax, on the left side of the mountain. Start at the base and list the events in time order going up the left side.
- At the top of the mountain, write the climax, or the highest point of interest or suspense. All events in the rising action lead up to this one main event or turning point.
- Write the events that happen after the climax, or falling action, on the right side of the mountain. Start at the top of the mountain, or climax, and put the events in time order going down the right-hand side.
- Finally, write the resolution, or denouement, at the right base of the mountain. The resolution explains how the problem, or conflict, in the story is solved or how the story ends.

10. Structured Overview

This graphic organizer shows you how a main idea branches out in a selection.

To use: Write the main idea of a selection in the top box. Then, branch out and list events and details that support the main idea. Continue to branch off more boxes as needed to fill in the details of the story.

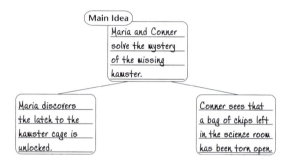

11. Semantic Table

This graphic organizer can help you understand the differences among words that have similar meanings.

To use: Choose a topic. List nouns for that topic in the top row. Put adjectives that describe your topic in the first column. Then, fill in the rest of the grid by checking those adjectives that are appropriate for the nouns. That way, in your writing, you can use words that make sense for your story.

Topic: __Homes__

Adjectives \ Nouns →	apartment	4-bedroom home	cabin
large	—	✓	—
expensive	—	✓	—
quiet	—	✓	✓

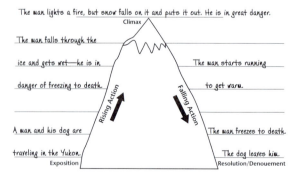

12. Prediction Guide

This graphic organizer can be used to predict, or try to figure out, how a selection might end. Before finishing a selection, fill in this guide.

To use: List the time, place, and characters in the selection. Write what the problem, or conflict, is in the story. Then, try to predict possible endings or solutions. Compare your predictions with others.

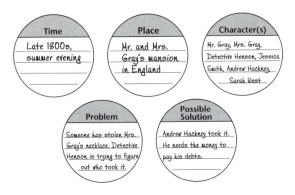

13. Semantic Line

This graphic organizer can help you think of synonyms for words that are used too often in writing.

To use: At the end of each line, write two overused words that mean the opposite. Then, fill in the lines with words of similar meaning. In the example below, the opposite words are *beautiful* and *ugly*. Words that are closer in meaning to beautiful are at the top. Words that are closer in meaning to ugly are at the bottom. The word *plain* falls in the middle.

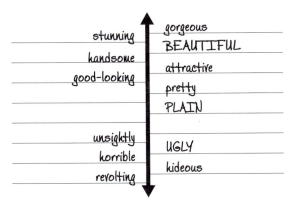

14. KWL Chart

This graphic organizer can help you learn about a topic before you start reading a selection or conducting research.

To use: Before you start reading a selection or conducting research, fill in the organizer. Write the topic on the line. In the first column, write what you already *know (K)* about your topic. Next, list what you *want (W)* to know about your topic in the next column. Then, as you start reading a selection or conducting research, write down what you *learn (L)* in the last column.

Topic: __Mount Everest__

K What I Know	W What I Want to Know	L What I Have Learned
It's a tall mountain in Asia. People may have tried to climb it. It's part of a larger mountain chain. It's one of the most famous mountains in the world.	How tall is it? Is it the tallest? What mountain chain is it part of?	It is 29,035 ft. It is the tallest in the world. It is part of the Himalayas. People have climbed it before. Some people have died trying.

Appendix A: Graphic Organizers **565**

Appendix B: Grammar

Parts of Speech

Adjectives
- Adjectives describe nouns and pronouns. They answer *What kind? Which one? How many?* or *How much?* Example: The *new* book costs *five* dollars.
- Comparative adjectives compare two nouns and usually end in *–er.* Example: *newer*
- Superlative adjectives compare three or more nouns and usually end in *–est.* Example: *newest*

Adverbs
- Adverbs modify verbs, adjectives, and other adverbs. They answer *When? How? How often?* and *How long?* Many adverbs end in *–ly.* Example: She laughed *loudly.*

Conjunctions
- Conjunctions connect parts of a sentence.
- Coordinating conjunctions connect two equal parts of a sentence using words like *and, but, nor, or, for, yet, so,* and *as well as.* Example: Do you want milk *or* water?
- Correlative conjunctions are used in pairs and connect equal parts of a sentence. Correlative conjunctions are *both/and, neither/nor, either/or, but/also.* Example: The teenagers had *neither* the time *nor* the money.
- Subordinating conjunctions connect two unequal parts of a sentence using words like *after, although, before, because, since, if, unless, while.* Example: *Since* you are arriving late, we will eat dinner at 7 p.m.

Interjections
- Interjections are words or phrases that show strong feeling, often followed by exclamation points. Examples: Wow! Ouch! Oops!

Nouns
- A noun names a person, place, thing, or idea.
- Proper nouns are names that are capitalized. Examples: Susan, New York

Prepositions
- Prepositions relate nouns and pronouns to other words in a sentence. Examples: above, from, with

Pronouns
- Pronouns replace nouns. Antecedents are the nouns that the pronouns replace. Example: Jorge takes karate lessons, and *he* practices every week.
- Demonstrative pronouns identify particular nouns: *this* hat, *those* shoes
- Indefinite pronouns do not refer to particular nouns. Examples: all, everyone, none
- Interrogative pronouns begin questions. Examples: who, which, what
- Personal pronouns refer to people or things. Examples: I, me, you, it, he, she, we, us, they, him, her, them
- Possessive pronouns show ownership. Examples: my, mine, his, hers, its, our, yours, their, ours, theirs
- Reflexive pronouns follow a verb or preposition and refer to the noun or pronoun that comes before. Examples: myself, themselves, himself, herself
- Relative pronouns introduce a subordinate clause. Examples: who, whom, whose, which, that, what

Verbs

- Verbs show action or express states of being.
- If the verbs are *transitive*, they link the action to something or someone. Example: John *hit* the ball. Action verbs that are *intransitive* do not link the action to something or someone. Example: The ball *flew*.
- Linking verbs connect a subject with a word or words that describe it. Some linking verbs are *am, are, was, were, is,* and *be*. Example: Susan *is* student council president.

Grammar Glossary

Active and Passive Voice

- Active voice is when the subject is *doing* the action. A sentence written in active voice is often shorter and easier to understand. Example: Jane drove the car to school.
- Passive voice is when the subject *receives* the action. A sentence written in passive voice can be awkward. Use a passive sentence only when the doer is unknown or unnecessary. Example: The car was driven by Jane.

Antecedent

- An antecedent is the noun or pronoun that a pronoun refers to in a sentence. Example: Kevin ran for Student Council so that he could help improve the school. *Kevin* is the antecedent for the pronoun *he*.

Appositives

- An appositive is a noun or pronoun that follows another noun or pronoun. An appositive renames or adds detail about the word. Example: Mr. Smith, *our principal,* is a great leader.

Clauses

- A clause is a group of words that contains a subject and a verb. There are independent and dependent clauses.
- An independent clause can stand alone because it expresses a complete thought. Example: Our dog eats twice a day. She also walks two miles a day. Two independent clauses can also be joined to form one sentence by using a comma and a coordinating conjunction, such as *and, but, nor, or, for, yet, so,* and *as well as*. Example: Our dog eats twice a day, *and* she walks two miles a day.
- A dependent clause cannot stand alone because it does not express a complete thought. Example: Because exercise is good for pets. This is a fragment or incomplete sentence. To fix this, combine a dependent clause with an independent clause. Example: Our dog walks two miles a day because exercise is good for pets.

Complements

- A complement completes the meaning of a verb. There are three types of complements: direct objects, indirect objects, and subject complements.
- A direct object is a word or group of words that receives the action of the verb. Example: Jane set the table. (*The table* is the complement or direct object of the verb *set*.)
- An indirect object is a word or group of words that follow the verb and tell for whom or what the action is done. An indirect object always comes before a direct object in a sentence. Example: Setting the table saved her mother some time. (*Her mother* is the complement or indirect object of the verb *saved*.)
- A subject complement is a word or group of words that further identify the subject of a sentence. A subject complement always follows a linking verb. Example: Buddy is the best dog. (The word *dog* is the complement of the subject *Buddy*.)

Contractions

- A contraction is two words made into one by replacing one or more letters with an apostrophe. Examples: *didn't* (did not), *you're* (you are)

Double Negatives

- A double negative is the use of two negative words, such as *no* or *not*, in a sentence. To fix a double negative, make one word positive. Incorrect: She *did not* get *no* dessert after dinner. Correct: She did not get *any* dessert after dinner.

Fragments

- A fragment is not a complete sentence. It may have a subject and verb, but it does not express a complete thought. Incorrect: The leaves that fell in the yard. Correct: The leaves that fell in the yard needed to be raked.

Gerunds

- A gerund is a verb with an *–ing* ending. It is used as a noun. Example: Golfing is fun! Here, *golfing* is a noun and the subject of the sentence.

Infinitives

- An infinitive is the word *to* plus the present tense of a verb. An infinitive can be a noun, adjective, or adverb in a sentence. Example: To write was her dream job. Here, *To write* is the infinitive, and it serves as a noun.

Modifiers

- A modifier is a word or group of words that change the meanings of other words in the sentence. Adjectives and adverbs are modifiers.

- A dangling or misplaced modifier is a group of descriptive words that is not near the word it modifies. This confuses the reader. Incorrect: Tucked up in the closet, Sarah found her grandma's photographs. *Tucked up in the closet* modifies Sarah. However, the photographs, not Sarah, are tucked up in the closet! Correct: Sarah found her grandma's photographs tucked up in the closet.

Parallel Structure

- Parallel structure is the use of words to balance ideas that are equally important. Incorrect: In the winter, I love to skate, snowmen, and to ski. Correct: In the winter, I love *to skate*, *to make snowmen*, and *to ski*.

Phrases

- A phrase is a group of words that does not have both a subject and a verb. Types of phrases include gerund phrases, infinitive phrases, and participial phrases.

- A gerund phrase has a gerund plus any modifiers and complements. The entire phrase serves as a noun. Example: Playing basketball with his friends was Trevor's favorite pastime. *Playing basketball with his friends* is the gerund phrase.

- An infinitive phrase has an infinitive plus any modifiers and complements. The entire phrase serves as a noun, adjective, or adverb in a sentence. Example: My mother liked to bake cookies on the weekend. *To bake cookies on the weekend* is the infinitive phrase.

- A participial phrase has a participle (a verb in its present form *[–ing]* or past form *[–ed or –en]*) plus all of its modifiers and complements. The entire phrase serves as an adjective in a sentence. Example: Wearing the robes of a king, Luis read his lines perfectly during play tryouts. *Wearing the robes of a king* is the participial phrase, and it modifies or describes the subject, Luis.

Plural Nouns

- A plural shows more than one of a particular noun. Use the following rules to create the plural form. Remember that there are exceptions to many spelling rules that you must simply memorize.
- Add *–s* to most singular nouns. Example: table/tables
- Add *–es* to a noun if it ends in *–ch*, *–sh*, *–s*, *–x*, and *–z*. Example: chur*ch*/chur*ch*es
- If a noun ends with a vowel and a *–y*, add an *–s* to make the plural. Example: donk*ey*/donk*ey*s
- If a noun ends with a consonant and a *–y*, drop the *–y* and add an *–ies* to make the plural. Example: pup*py*/pup*pies*
- If a noun ends in an *–f* or *–fe*, change the *–f* or *–fe* to a *v* and add *–es*. Example: kni*fe*/kni*ves*
- If a noun ends in an *–o*, sometimes you add *–es* and sometimes you add *–s*. Look in a dictionary to find out. Examples: potat*o*/potatoes, radi*o*/radios

Possessives

- A possessive noun shows ownership of an object, action, or idea. A possessive noun ends in *'s*. Example: Susan's book
- A possessive pronoun also shows ownership of an object, action, or idea. Example: his glove

Pronoun–Antecedent Agreement

- Pronoun-antecedent agreement occurs when the pronoun matches the antecedent (the word it refers to) in gender and number.
- To agree in gender:
  – Replace the name of a male person with a masculine pronoun. Example: *Jake* ran down the field, and *he* scored.
  – Replace the name of a female person with a feminine pronoun. Example: *Ana* read "The Most Dangerous Game," and *she* loved it.
  – Replace singular names with *it* or *its*. Example: The *kitten* ran through the room, and *it* pounced on the ball.
  – Replace plural names with *they*, *them*, or *their*. Example: The *tenth graders* came into the gym, and *they* played volleyball.
- To agree in number:
  – Make the pronoun singular if its antecedent is singular. Example: *Michael* told *himself* that he did the right thing.
  – Make the pronoun plural if its antecedent is plural. Example: The hungry *teenagers* ordered sandwiches for *themselves*.

Run-on Sentences

- A run-on sentence is the combination of two or more sentences without proper punctuation.
- To correct a run-on sentence, you can break it into two or more sentences by using capital letters and periods. Incorrect: The house was built in 1960 it needs new windows. Correct: The house was built in 1960. It needs new windows.
- You can also correct a run-on sentence by adding a comma and a coordinating conjunction to separate the sentences. Correct: The house was built in 1960, *so* it needs new windows.
- Another way to correct a run-on sentence is by adding a semicolon between the sentences. A semicolon should stand alone and should not have a coordinating conjunction after it. Correct: The house was built in 1960; it needs new windows.

Sentence Construction

- A simple sentence has one independent clause that includes a subject and a predicate. Example: The afternoon was warm and sunny.

- A compound sentence has two or more independent clauses joined by a comma and a coordinating conjunction or joined by a semicolon. Example: The afternoon was warm and sunny, so we decided to drive to the beach.

- A complex sentence has one independent clause and one or more dependent clauses. Example: We are going to the beach if you want to come along.

- A compound–complex sentence has two or more independent clauses joined by a comma and a coordinating conjunction. It has at least one dependent clause. Example: Although the morning was cold and damp, the afternoon was warm and sunny, so we decided to drive to the beach.

Sentence Types

- You can use a declarative sentence, an exclamatory sentence, an imperative sentence, or an interrogative sentence in writing.

- A declarative sentence tells us something about a person, place, or thing. This type of sentence ends with a period. Example: Martin Luther King Jr. fought for civil rights.

- An exclamatory sentence shows strong feeling or surprise. This type of sentence ends with an exclamation point. Example: I can't believe the price of gasoline!

- An imperative sentence gives commands. This type of sentence ends with a period. (Note: The subject of an imperative sentence is the implied "you.") Example: Please read chapter two by next Monday.

- An interrogative sentence asks a question. This type of sentence ends with a question mark. Example: Will you join us for dinner?

Subjects and Predicates

- The subject of a sentence names the person or thing doing the action. The subject contains a noun or a pronoun. Example: The students created posters and brochures. The subject of this sentence is *The students*. The predicate of this sentence (see definition below) is *created posters and brochures*.

- The predicate of a sentence tells what the person or thing is doing. The predicate contains a verb. Example: The fans waited for the hockey game to begin. The predicate of this sentence is *waited for the hockey game to begin*. The subject of this sentence is *The fans*.

Punctuation Guidelines

Apostrophe

- Shows ownership (possessive nouns): Kelly's backpack

- Shows plural possessive nouns: The five students' success was due to hard work.

- Shows missing letters in contractions: that's (that is)

Colon

- Introduces a list after a complete sentence: We learned about planets: Mars, Venus, and Jupiter.

- Adds or explains more about a complete sentence: Lunch was one option: pizza.

- Follows the salutation in a formal letter or in a business letter: Dear Mr. Jackson:
- Separates the hour and the minute: 2:15
- Introduces a long quotation: Lincoln wrote: "Four score and seven years ago . . ."

Comma

- Separates three or more items in a series: We planted corn, squash, and tomatoes.
- Joins two independent clauses when used with a coordinating conjunction: Sam and Raul did their homework, and then they left.
- Separates a city and state: Los Angeles, California
- Separates a day and year: October 15, 2006
- Follows the salutation and closing in a friendly letter: Dear Shanice, Love always,
- Follows the closing in a business letter: Sincerely,
- Sets off a restrictive phrase clause: Angela, the youngest runner, won the race.
- Sets off an introductory phrase or clause: Before he started the experiment, Jason put on safety glasses.

Dash

- Sets off an explanation in a sentence: The three poets—Langston Hughes, Robert Frost, and William Carlos Williams—are modernist poets.
- Shows a pause or break in thought: After years away, I returned—and found lots had changed.

Ellipses

- Show that words have been left out of a text: Our dog dove into the lake . . . and swam to shore.

Exclamation Point

- Shows emotion: Our team won!

Hyphen

- Divides a word at the end of a line: We en-joyed the beaches.
- Separates a compound adjective before a noun to make its meaning clearer: much-loved book
- Separates a compound number: thirty-three.
- Separates a fraction when used as an adjective: two-thirds full

Period

- Marks the end of a statement or command: July is the warmest month.
- Follows most abbreviations: Mrs., Dr., Inc., Jr.

Question Mark

- Marks the end of a question: How many eggs are left?

Quotation Marks

- Enclose the exact words of a speaker: He said, "I'll buy that book."
- Enclose the titles of short works: "Dover Beach," "America the Beautiful"

Semicolon

- Separates items in a series when commas are within the items: We went to Sioux Falls, South Dakota; Des Moines, Iowa; and Kansas City, Kansas.
- Joins two independent clauses that are closely related: We went to the movie; they came with us.

Capitalization Guidelines

Capitalize:

- the first word of a sentence: The teacher asked her students to read.
- the first word and any important words in a title: To Kill a Mockingbird
- all proper nouns: Marlon Smith, Atlanta, March
- the pronoun *I*
- languages: English, French
- abbreviations: Mrs., Sgt., FDR, EST

Commonly Confused Words

accept, except

- *Accept* (verb) means "to receive." Example: The children will *accept* ice cream.
- *Except* (preposition) means "leaving out." Example: The children enjoyed all flavors *except* strawberry.

affect, effect

- *Affect* (verb) means "to have an effect on." Example: This storm will *affect* our town.
- *Effect* (noun) means "a result or an outcome." Example: The *effect* was a struggling local economy.

its, it's

- *Its* (adjective) is the possessive form of "it." Example: Our hamster liked to run on the wheel inside *its* cage.
- *It's* is a contraction for "it is." Example: *It's* a long time before lunch.

lie, lay

- *Lie* (verb) means "to rest." Example: Jenny had a headache, so she needed to *lie* down.
- *Lay* (verb) means "to place." Example: Jamal went to *lay* his baseball glove on the bench.

lose, loose

- *Lose* (verb) means "to misplace or not find something." Example: I always *lose* my sunglasses when I go to the beach.
- *Loose* (adjective) means "free or without limits." Example: Someone let Sparky *loose* from his leash.

than, then

- *Than* (conjunction) shows a comparison. Example: You are older *than* I am.
- *Then* (adverb) means "at that time." Example: Will turned the doorknob and *then* slowly opened the door.

their, there, they're

- *Their* (pronoun) shows possession. Example: This is *their* house.
- *There* (adverb) means "place." Example: Sit over *there*.
- *They're* is a contraction for "they are." Example: *They're* coming over for dinner.

to, too, two

- *To* (preposition) shows purpose, movement, or connection. Example: We drove *to* the store.
- *Too* (adverb) means "also or more than wanted." Example: I, *too*, felt it was *too* hot to go outside.
- *Two* is a number. Example: Ava has *two* more years of high school.

your, you're

- *Your* (adjective) shows possession and means "belonging to you." Example: Take off *your* hat, please.
- *You're* is a contraction for "you are." Example: *You're* the best artist in the school.

Appendix C: Writing

Types of Writing

Before you can begin the writing process, you need to understand the types, purposes, and formats of different types of writing.

Descriptive Writing

Descriptive writing covers all writing genres. Description can be used to tell a story, to analyze and explain research, or to persuade. Descriptive writing uses images and colorful details to "paint a picture" for the reader.

Five Senses in Descriptive Writing

Consider the five senses in your descriptive writing: sight, smell, touch, sound, and taste. Using your senses to help describe an object, place, or person makes your writing more interesting. Before you begin, ask yourself the following:

- How does something look? Describe the color, size, and/or shape. What is it like?

- What smell or smells are present? Describe any pleasant or unpleasant smells. Compare the smells to other smells you know.

- How does something feel? Think about textures. Also think about emotions or feelings that result from the touching.

- What sounds do you hear? Describe the volume and the pitch. Are the sounds loud and shrill, or quiet and peaceful? What do the sounds remind you of?

- What does something taste like? Compare it to a taste you know, good or bad.

Expository Writing

Expository writing explains and informs through essays, articles, reports, and instructions. Like descriptive writing, it covers all writing genres. The purpose of this type of writing is to give more information about a subject. This can be done in many ways. The two most common formats in the study of literature are the compare and contrast paper and the cause and effect paper.

- Compare and Contrast Paper—This paper shows the similarities and differences of two or more characters, objects, settings, situations, writing styles, problems, or ideas.

- Cause and Effect Paper—This paper explains why certain things happen or how specific actions led to a result. A cause and effect paper can be set up by writing about the result (effect) first, followed by the events that led up to it (causes). Or, the paper can trace the events (causes), in order, that lead up to the result (effect).

Narrative Writing

Narrative writing tells a story. The story can be true (nonfiction) or made up (fiction). Narratives entertain or inform readers about a series of events. Poetry, stories, diaries, letters, biographies, and autobiographies are all types of narrative writing.

Key Elements in Narrative Writing

Think about the type of narrative you want to write and these key elements of your story:

- Characters: Who are the major and minor characters in the story? What do they look like? How do they act?

- Dialogue: What conversations take place among the characters? How does the dialogue show the reader something about the personalities of the characters?
- Setting: Where and when do the events take place? How does the setting affect the plot?
- Plot: What events happen in the story? In what order do the events occur? What is the problem that the main character is struggling with? How is the problem solved?

There are two common ways to set up your narrative paper. You can start at the beginning and tell your story in chronological order, or in the order in which the events happened. Or, you can start at the ending of your story and, through a flashback, tell what events led up to the present time.

Persuasive Writing

Persuasive writing is used when you want to convince your reader that your opinion on a topic is the right one. The goal of this paper is to have your reader agree with what you say. To do this, you need to know your topic well, and you need to give lots of reasons and supporting details. Editorials (opinion writing) in the newspaper, advertisements, and book reviews are all types of persuasive writing.

Key Elements of Persuasive Writing

Choosing a topic that you know well and that you feel strongly about is important for persuasive writing. The feelings or emotions that you have about the topic will come through in your paper and make a stronger argument. Also, be sure that you have a good balance between appealing to the reader's mind (using facts, statistics, experts, and so on) and appealing to the reader's heart (using words that make them feel angry, sad, and so on). Think about these key elements:

- Topic: Is your topic a good one for your audience? Do you know a lot about your topic? Is your topic narrow enough so that you can cover it in a paper?
- Opinion: Is your opinion clear? Do you know enough about the opposite side of your opinion to get rid of those arguments in your paper?
- Reasons: Do you have at least three reasons that explain why you feel the way you do? Are these reasons logical?
- Supporting details or evidence: Do you have facts, statistics, experts, or personal experience that can support each reason?
- Opposing arguments: Can you address the opposite side and get rid of their arguments?
- Conclusion: Can you offer a solution or recommendation to the reader?
- Word choice: Can you find words that set the tone for your opinion? Will these words affect your readers emotionally?

There are two common ways to set up this paper. The first format is a six-paragraph paper: one paragraph for your introduction, three paragraphs for each of your three reasons, one paragraph for the opposing arguments and your responses to them, and one paragraph for your conclusion. Or you can write a five-paragraph paper where you place the opposing arguments and responses to each of your three reasons within the same paragraphs.

Research Report

A research report is an in-depth study of a topic. This type of writing has many uses in all subjects. It involves digging for information in many sources, including books, magazines, newspapers, the Internet, almanacs, encyclopedias, and other places of data. There are many key elements in writing a research report. Choosing a thesis statement, finding support or evidence for that thesis, and citing where you found your information are all important.

There are several uses of a research report in literature. You can explore a writer's life, a particular writing movement, or a certain writer's style. You could also write about a selection.

Business Writing

Business writing has many forms: memos, meeting minutes, brochures, manuals, reports, job applications, contracts, college essays. No matter what the format, the goal of business writing is clear communication. Keep the following key elements in mind when you are doing business writing:

- Format: What type of writing are you doing?
- Purpose: What is the purpose of your writing? Is the purpose clear in your introduction?
- Audience: Are your words and ideas appropriate for your audience?
- Organization: Are your ideas well-organized and easy to follow?
- Style: Are your ideas clearly written and to the point?

The Writing Process

The writing process is a little different for each writer and for each writing assignment. However, the goals of writing never change: Writers want to:

- have a purpose for their writing
- get their readers' attention and keep it
- present their ideas clearly
- choose their words carefully

To meet these goals, writers need to move through a writing process. This process allows them to explore, organize, write, revise, and share their ideas. There are five steps to this writing process: prewriting; drafting; revising; editing and proofreading; and publishing and evaluating.

Use the following steps for any writing assignment:

Step 1: Prewriting

Prewriting is where you explore ideas and decide what to write about. Here are some approaches.

Brainstorming

Brainstorming is fast, fun, and full of ideas. Start by stating a topic. Then write down everything you can think of about that topic. Ask questions about the topic. If you are in a group, have one person write everything down. Think of as many words and ideas as you can in a short time. Don't worry about neatness, spelling, or grammar. When you are finished, group words that are similar. These groups may become your supporting ideas.

Graphic Organizers

Graphic organizers are maps that can lead you through your prewriting. They provide pictures or charts that you fill in. Read the descriptions of these organizers in Appendix A, and choose the ones that will help you organize your ideas.

Outline

An outline can help you organize your information. Write your main ideas next to each Roman numeral. Write your supporting details next to the letters under each Roman numeral. Keep your ideas brief and to the point. Here's an example to follow:

> Topic for persuasive paper: Lincoln High School should have a swimming pool.
>
> I. Health benefits for students
>   A. Weight control
>   B. Good exercise
> II. Water safety benefits for students
>   A. Learn-to-swim programs
>   B. Water safety measures to help others
> III. School benefits
>   A. Swim team
>   B. Added rotation for gym class
> IV. Community benefits
>   A. More physically fit community members
>   B. More jobs for community members

Narrowing Your Topic

Narrowing your topic means to focus your ideas on a specific area. You may be interested in writing about Edgar Allan Poe, but that is a broad topic. What about Poe interests you? Think about your purpose for writing. Is your goal to persuade, to explain, or to compare? Narrowing your scope and knowing your purpose will keep you focused.

Note-Taking and Research

Refer to the "How to Use This Book" section at the beginning of this textbook and Appendix D for help with note-taking and research skills.

Planning Your Voice

Your voice is your special way of using language in your writing. Readers can get to know your personality and thoughts by your sentence structure, word choice, and tone. How will your writing tell what you want to say in your own way? How will it be different from the way others write?

Step 2: Drafting

In the drafting step, you will write your paper. Use your brainstorming notes, outline, and graphic organizers from your prewriting stage as your guide. Your paper will need to include an introduction, a body, and a conclusion.

Introduction

The introduction states your topic and purpose. It includes a *thesis statement*, which is a sentence that tells the main idea of your entire paper. The last line of your introduction is a good place for your thesis statement. That way, your reader has a clear idea of the purpose of your paper before starting to read your points.

Your introduction should make people want to read more. Think about what your audience might like. Try one of these methods:

- asking a question
- sharing a brief story
- describing something
- giving a surprising fact
- using an important quotation

When you begin drafting, just write your introduction. Do not try to make it perfect the first time. You can always change it later.

Body

The body of your paper is made up of several paragraphs. Each paragraph also has a topic sentence, supporting details, and a concluding statement or summary. Remember, too, that each paragraph needs to support your thesis statement in your introduction.

- The topic sentence is usually the first sentence of a paragraph. It lets the reader know what your paragraph is going to be about.
- The supporting details of a paragraph are the sentences that support or tell more about your topic sentence. They can include facts, explanations, examples, statistics, and/or experts' ideas.
- The last sentence of your paragraph is a concluding statement or summary. A concluding statement is a judgment. It is based on the facts that you presented in your paragraph. A summary briefly repeats the main ideas of your paragraph. It repeats your idea or ideas in slightly different words. It does not add new information.

Conclusion

The conclusion ties together the main ideas of the paper. If you asked a question in your introduction, the conclusion answers it. If you outlined a problem, your conclusion offers solutions. The conclusion should not simply restate your thesis and supporting points.

Title of the Paper

Make sure to title your paper. Use a title that is interesting, but relates well to your topic.

Step 3: Revising

Now that you've explored ideas and put them into a draft, it's time to revise. During this step, you will rewrite parts or sections of your paper. All good writing goes through many drafts. To help you make the necessary changes, use the checklists below to review your paper.

Overall Paper

- ☑ Do I have an interesting title that draws readers in?
- ☑ Does the title tell my audience what my paper is about?
- ☑ Do I have an introduction, body, and conclusion?
- ☑ Is my paper the correct length?

Introduction

- ☑ Have I used a method to interest my readers?
- ☑ Do I have a thesis statement that tells the main idea of my paper?
- ☑ Is my thesis statement clearly stated?

Body

- ☑ Do I start every paragraph on a new line?
- ☑ Is the first line of every paragraph indented?
- ☑ Does the first sentence (topic sentence) in every paragraph explain the main idea of the paragraph? Does it attract my readers' attention?
- ☑ Do I include facts, explanations, examples, statistics, and/or experts' ideas that support the topic sentence?
- ☑ Do I need to take out any sentences that do not relate to the topic sentence?
- ☑ Do the paragraphs flow in a logical order? Does each point build on the last one?
- ☑ Do good transition words lead readers from one paragraph to the next?

Conclusion

- ☑ Does the conclusion tie together the main ideas of my paper?
- ☑ Does it offer a solution, make a suggestion, or answer any questions that the readers might have?

Writing Style

- ☑ Do I use words and concepts that my audience understands?
- ☑ Is the tone too formal or informal for my audience?
- ☑ Are my sentences the right length for my audience?
- ☑ Do I have good sentence variety and word choice?

Step 4: Editing and Proofreading

During the editing and proofreading step, check your paper or another student's paper for errors in grammar, punctuation, capitalization, and spelling. Use the following checklists to help guide you. Read and focus on one sentence at a time. Cover up everything but the sentence you are reading. Reading from the end of the paper backward also works for some students. Note changes using the proofreader marks shown on the following page. Check a dictionary or style manual when you're not sure about something.

Grammar

- ☑ Is there a subject and a verb in every sentence?
- ☑ Do the subject and verb agree in every sentence?
- ☑ Is the verb tense logical in every sentence?
- ☑ Is the verb tense consistent in every sentence?
- ☑ Have you used interesting, lively verbs?
- ☑ Do all pronouns have clear antecedents?
- ☑ Can repeated or unnecessary words be left out?
- ☑ Are there any run-on sentences that need to be corrected?
- ☑ Does sentence length vary with long and short sentences?

Punctuation

- ☑ Does every sentence end with the correct punctuation mark?
- ☑ Are all direct quotations punctuated correctly?
- ☑ Do commas separate words in a series?
- ☑ Is there a comma and a coordinating conjunction separating each compound sentence?
- ☑ Is there a comma after an introductory phrase or clause?
- ☑ Are apostrophes used correctly in contractions and possessive nouns?

Capitalization

- ☑ Is the first word of every sentence capitalized?
- ☑ Are all proper nouns and adjectives capitalized?
- ☑ Are the important words in the title of the paper capitalized?

Spelling

- ☑ Are words that sound alike spelled correctly (such as *to*, *too*, and *two*)?
- ☑ Is every plural noun spelled correctly?
- ☑ Are words with *ie* or *ei* spelled correctly?
- ☑ Is the silent *e* dropped before adding an ending that starts with a vowel?
- ☑ Is the consonant doubling rule used correctly?

If the paper was typed, make any necessary changes and run the spell-check and grammar-check programs one more time.

Proofreading Marks

Below are some common proofreading marks. Print out your paper and use these marks to correct errors.

Symbol	Meaning
¶	Start new paragraph
◯	Close up
#	Add a space
⁀	Switch words or letters
≡	Capitalize this letter
/	Lowercase this letter
℮	Omit space, letter, mark, or word
∧	Insert space, mark, or word
⊙	Insert a period
⌃,	Insert a comma
◯sp	Spell out
. . . stet	Leave as is (write dots under words)

Step 5: Publishing and Evaluating

Once you have made the final text changes, make sure that the overall format of your paper is correct. Follow the guidelines that were set up by your teacher. Here are some general guidelines that are commonly used.

Readability

- Double space all text.
- Use an easy-to-read font such as Times Roman, Comic Sans, Ariel, or New York.
- Use a 12-point type size.
- Make sure that you have met any word, paragraph, or page count guidelines.

Format

- Make at least a one-inch margin around each page.
- Place the title of the paper, your name, your class period, and the date according to your teacher's guidelines. If you need a title page, make sure that you have a separate page with this information. If you do not need a title page, place your name, class period, and date in the upper right-hand corner of the first page. Center the title below that.
- Check to see if your pages need to be numbered. If so, number them in the upper right-hand corner or according to your teacher's guidelines.
- Label any charts and graphics as needed.
- Check that your title and any subheads are in boldface print.
- Check that your paragraphs are indented.

Citations

- Cite direct quotations, paraphrases, and summaries properly. Refer to the Modern Language Association (MLA) or American Psychological Association (APA) rules.
- Punctuate all citations properly. Refer to MLA or APA rules.

Bibliographies

- Include a list of books and other materials you reviewed during your research. This is a reference list only. Below are examples of how you would list a book, magazine article, and Web site using MLA style:

Book:
Author's Last Name, Author's First Name. *Book Title*. Publisher's City: Publisher's Name, Year.

London, Jack. *The Call of the Wild*. New York: Scholastic, 2001.

Magazine:
Author's Last Name, Author's First Name. "Article Title." *Magazine Title*. Volume Date: Page numbers.

Young, Diane. "At the High End of the River." *Southern Living*. June 2000: 126–131.

Web Site:
Article Title. Date accessed. URL

Circle of Stories. 25 Jan. 2006. <http://www.pbs.org/circleofstories/>

Appendix D: Research

Planning and Writing a Research Report

⬇ *Use the following steps to guide you in writing a research report.*

Step 1: Planning the Report

Choose a subject. Then narrow your topic. You may be interested in the poetry of Robert Frost, but that subject is too broad. Narrow your focus. The graphic organizers in Appendix A may help you narrow your topic and identify supporting details.

Step 2: Finding Useful Information

Go to the library and browse the card catalog for books. Check almanacs, encyclopedias, atlases, and other sources in the reference section. Also review *The Reader's Guide to Periodical Literature* for magazines.

Draw from primary sources. Primary sources are first-hand accounts of information, such as speeches, observations, research results, and interviews. Secondary sources interpret and analyze primary sources.

Use the Internet to further explore your topic. Be careful; some Internet sources are not reliable. Avoid chat rooms, news groups, and personal Web sites. Check the credibility of sites by reviewing the site name and sponsor. Web sites whose URL ends with .org, .gov, and .edu are typically good sources.

Step 3: Logging Information

Use index cards to take notes. Include this information for each source:

- name of author or editor
- title of book or title of article and magazine
- page numbers
- volume numbers
- date of publication
- name of publishing company
- Web site information for Internet sources
- relevant information or direct quotations

Step 4: Getting Organized

Group your cards by similar details and organize them into categories. Find a system that works for you in organizing your cards. You can color-code them, use different-colored index cards for different sections, label them, and so on. Do not use any note cards that do not fit the categories that you have set up. Make conclusions about your research. Write a final topic outline.

Step 5: Writing Your Report

Follow the writing process in Appendix C to write your report. Use your own words to write the ideas you found in your sources (paraphrase). Do not plagiarize—steal and pass off another's words as your own. Write an author's exact words for direct quotations, and name the author or source.

Step 6: Preparing a Bibliography or Works Cited Page

Use the information on your note cards to write a bibliography or works cited page. If you are writing a bibliography, put your note cards in alphabetical order by *title*. If you are writing a works cited page, put your note cards in alphabetical order by *author*.

See *Bibliographies* in Appendix C.

Research Tools

Almanac
An annual publication containing data and tables on politics, religion, education, sports, and more

American Psychological Association (APA) Style
A guide to proper citation to avoid plagiarism in research papers for the social sciences

Atlas
A bound collection of maps of cities, states, regions, and countries including statistics and illustrations

Audio Recording
Recordings of speeches, debates, public proceedings, interviews, etc.

The Chicago Manual of Style
Writing, editing, proofreading, and revising guidelines for the publishing industry

Database
A large collection of data stored electronically and able to be searched

Dictionary
A reference book of words, spellings, pronunciations, meanings, parts of speech, and word origins

Experiment
A series of tests to prove or disprove something

Field Study
Observation, data collection, and interpretation done outside of a laboratory

Glossary
A collection of terms and their meanings

Government Publications
A report of a government action, bill, handbook, or census data usually provided by the Government Printing Office

Grammar Reference
Explanation and examples of parts of speech, sentence structure, and word usage

History
A chronological record that explains past events

Information Services
A stored collection of information organized for easy searching

Internet/World Wide Web
A worldwide network of connected computers that share information

Interview
A dialogue between a subject and a reporter or investigator to gather information

Journal
A type of magazine offering current information on certain subjects such as medicine, the economy, and current events

Microfiche
Historical, printed materials saved to small, thin sheets of film for organization, storage, and use

Modern Language Association (MLA) Handbook
A guide to proper citation to avoid plagiarism in research papers for the humanities

News Source
A newspaper or a radio, television, satellite, or World Wide Web sending of current events and issues presented in a timely manner

Periodical
A magazine, newspaper, or journal

The Reader's Guide to Periodical Literature
A searchable, organized database of magazines, newspapers, and journals used for research

Speech
A public address to inform and to explain

Technical Document
A proposal, instruction manual, training manual, report, chart, table, or other document that provides information

Thesaurus
A book of words and their synonyms, or words that have almost the same meanings

Vertical File
A storage file of original documents or copies of original documents

Appendix E: Speaking

Types of Public Speaking

Public speaking offers a way to inform, to explain, and to entertain. Here are some common types of public speaking:

Debate

A debate is a formal event where two or more people share opposing arguments in response to questions. Often, someone wins by answering questions with solid information.

Descriptive Speech

A descriptive speech uses the five senses of sight, smell, touch, taste, and sound to give vivid details.

Entertaining Speech

An entertaining speech relies on humor through jokes, stories, wit, or making fun of oneself. The humor must be appropriate for the audience and purpose of the speech.

Expository Speech

An expository speech provides more detailed information about a subject. This can be done through classification, analysis, definition, cause and effect, or compare and contrast.

Group Discussion

A group discussion allows the sharing of ideas among three or more people. A group discussion may be impromptu (without being planned) or may include a set topic and list of questions.

Impromptu Speech

An impromptu speech happens at a moment's notice without being planned. The speaker is given a random topic to discuss within a given time period.

Interview

An interview is a dialogue between a subject and a reporter or investigator. An interview draws out information using a question-and-answer format.

Literature Recitation

A literature recitation is the act of presenting a memorized speech, poem, story, or scene in its entire form or with chosen excerpts.

Literature Response

A literature response can serve many purposes. A speaker can compare and contrast plots or characters. An analysis of the work of one author can be presented. Writing style, genre, or period can also be shared.

Narrative

A narrative is a fiction or nonfiction story told with descriptive detail. The speaker also must use voice variation if acting out character dialogue.

Reflective Speech

A reflective speech provides thoughtful analysis of ideas, current events, and processes.

Role Playing

Role playing is when two or more people act out roles to show an idea or practice a character in a story. Role playing can be an effective tool for learning.

Preparing Your Speech

Use the following steps to prepare your speech:

Step 1: Defining Your Purpose

Ask yourself:

- Do I want to inform?
- Do I want to explain something?
- Do I want to entertain?
- Do I want to involve the audience through group discussion, role playing, or debate?
- Do I want to get the audience to act on a subject or an issue?

Step 2: Knowing Your Audience

Ask yourself:

- What information does my audience already know about the topic?
- What questions, concerns, or opinions do they have about the topic?
- How formal or informal does my presentation need to be?
- What words are familiar to my audience? What needs explanation?
- How does my audience prefer to get information? Do they like visuals, audience participation, or lecture?

Step 3: Knowing Your Setting

Ask yourself:

- Who is my audience?
- Is the room large enough to need a microphone and a projector?
- How is the room set up? Am I on stage with a podium or can I interact with the audience?
- Will other noises or activity distract the audience?

Step 4: Narrowing Your Topic

Ask yourself:

- What topic is right for the event? Is it timely? Will it match the mood of the event?
- Is there enough time to share it?
- What topic is right for me to present? Is it something I know and enjoy? Is it something people want to hear from me?

Step 5: Prewriting

Ask yourself:

- What examples, statistics, stories, or descriptions will help me get across my point?
- If telling a story, do I have a sequence of events that includes a beginning, middle, and end?

Step 6: Drafting Your Speech

Your speech will include an introduction, a body, and a conclusion.

The introduction states your topic and purpose. It includes a thesis statement that tells your position. Your introduction should also establish your credibility. Share why you are the right person to give that speech based on your experiences. Lastly, your introduction needs to get people's attention so they want to listen. At the top of the next page are some possible ways to start your speech.

- Ask a question.
- Share a story.
- Describe something.
- Give a surprising fact.
- Share a meaningful quotation.
- Make a memorable, purposeful entrance.

The body of your speech tells more about your main idea and tries to prevent listener misunderstandings. It should include any of the following supporting evidence:

- facts
- details
- explanations
- reasons
- examples
- personal stories or experiences
- experts
- literary devices and images

The conclusion of your speech ties your speech together. If you asked a question in your introduction, the conclusion answers it. If you outlined a problem, your conclusion offers solutions. If you told a story, revisit that story. You may even want to ask your audience to get involved, take action, or become more informed on your topic.

Step 7: Selecting Visuals

Ask yourself:

- Is a visual aid needed for the audience to better understand my topic?
- What visual aids work best for my topic?
- Do I have access to the right technology?

The size of your audience and the setting for your speech will also impact what you select. Remember that a projection screen and overhead speakers are necessary for large groups. If you plan on giving handouts to audience members, have handouts ready for pickup by the entrance of the room. A slide show or a video presentation will need a darkened room. Be sure that you have someone available to help you with the lights.

Practicing and Delivering Your Speech

Giving a speech is about more than simply talking. You want to look comfortable and confident.

Practice how you move, how you sound, and how you work with visuals and the audience.

Know Your Script

Every speaker is afraid of forgetting his or her speech. Each handles this fear in a different way. Choose the device that works for you.

- **Memorization:** Know your speech by heart. Say it often so you sound natural.
- **Word-for-word scripts:** Highlight key phrases to keep you on track. Keep the script on a podium, so you are not waving sheets of paper around as you talk. Be careful not to read from your script. The audience wants to see your eyes.
- **Outlines:** Write a sentence outline of your main points and supporting details that you want to say in a specific way. Transitions and other words can be spoken impromptu (without being planned).

- Key words: Write down key words that will remind you what to say, like "Tell story about the dog."
- Put your entire speech, outline, or key words on note cards to stay on track. They are small and not as obvious as paper. Number them in case they get out of order.

Know Yourself

Your voice and appearance are the two most powerful things you bring to a speech. Practice the following, so you are comfortable, confident, and convincing:

- Body language: Stand tall. Keep your feet shoulder-width apart. Don't cross your arms or bury your hands in your pockets. Use gestures to make a point. For example, hold up two fingers when you say, "My second point is . . ." Try to relax; that way, you will be in better control of your body.
- Eye contact: Look at your audience. Spend a minute or two looking at every side of the room and not just the front row. The audience will feel as if you are talking to them.
- Voice strategies: Clearly pronounce your words. Speak at a comfortable rate and loud enough for everyone to hear you. Vary your volume, rate, and pitch when you are trying to emphasize something. For example, you could say, "I have a secret. . . ." Then, you could lean toward the audience and speak in a loud, clear whisper as if you are telling them a secret. This adds dramatic effect and engages the audience.
- Repetition of key phrases or words: Repetition is one way to help people remember your point. If something is important, say it twice. Use transitions such as, "This is so important it is worth repeating" or "As I said before, we must act now."

Appendix F: Listening

Listening Strategy Checklist

Here are some ways you can ensure that you are a good listener.

Be an Active Listener
- ☑ Complete reading assignments that are due prior to the presentation.
- ☑ Focus on what is being said.
- ☑ Ask for definitions of unfamiliar terms.
- ☑ Ask questions to clarify what you heard.
- ☑ Ask the speaker to recommend other readings or resources.

Be a Critical Listener
- ☑ Identify the thesis or main idea of the speech.
- ☑ Try to predict what the speaker is going to say based on what you already know.
- ☑ Determine the speaker's purpose of the speech.
- ☑ Note supporting facts, statistics, examples, and other details.
- ☑ Determine if supporting detail is relevant, factual, and appropriate.
- ☑ Form your conclusions about the presentation.

Be an Appreciative Listener
- ☑ Relax.
- ☑ Enjoy the listening experience.
- ☑ Welcome the opportunity to laugh and learn.

Be a Thoughtful and Feeling Listener
- ☑ Understand the experiences of the speaker.
- ☑ Value the emotion he or she brings to the subject.
- ☑ Summarize or paraphrase what you believe the speaker just said.
- ☑ Tell the speaker that you understand his or her feelings.

Be an Alert Listener
- ☑ Sit up straight.
- ☑ Sit near the speaker and face the speaker directly.
- ☑ Make eye contact and nod to show you are listening.
- ☑ Open your arms so you are open to receiving information.

Analyze the Speaker
- ☑ Does the speaker have the experiences and knowledge to speak on the topic?
- ☑ Is the speaker prepared?
- ☑ Does the speaker appear confident?
- ☑ Is the speaker's body language appropriate?
- ☑ What do the speaker's tone, volume, and word choices show?

Identify the Details
- ☑ Listen for the tendency of the speaker to favor or oppose something without real cause.
- ☑ Be aware of propaganda—someone forcing an opinion on you.
- ☑ Don't be swayed by the clever way the speaker presents something.
- ☑ After the speech ask about words that you don't know.

Identify Fallacies of Logic

A fallacy is a false idea intended to trick someone. Here are some common fallacies:

- *Ad hominem*: This type of fallacy attacks a person's character, lifestyle, or beliefs. Example: Joe should not be on the school board because he skipped classes in college.
- False causality: This type of fallacy gives a cause–effect relationship that is not logical. This fallacy assumes that something caused something else only because it came before the consequence. Example: Ever since that new family moved into the neighborhood, our kids are getting into trouble.
- Red herring: This type of fallacy uses distractions to take attention away from the main issue. Example: Since more than half of our nation's people are overweight, we should not open a fast-food restaurant in our town.
- Overgeneralization: This type of fallacy uses words such as *every, always*, or *never*. Claims do not allow for exceptions to be made. Example: People who make more than a million dollars a year never pay their fair share of taxes.
- Bandwagon effect: This type of fallacy appeals to one's desire to be a part of the crowd. It is based on popular opinion and not on evidence. Example: Anyone who believes that our town is a great place to live should vote for the local tax increase.

Take Notes

- Write down key messages and phrases, not everything that is said.
- Abbreviate words.
- Listen for cues that identify important details, like "Here's an example" or "To illustrate what I mean."
- Draw graphs, charts, and diagrams for future reference.
- Draw arrows, stars, and circles to highlight information or group information.
- Highlight or circle anything that needs to be clarified or explained.
- Use the note-taking strategies explained in "How to Use This Book" at the beginning of this textbook.

Appendix G: Viewing

Visual aids can help communicate information and ideas. The following checklist gives pointers for viewing and interpreting visual aids.

Design Elements

Colors
- ☑ What colors stand out?
- ☑ What feelings do they make you think of?
- ☑ What do they symbolize or represent?
- ☑ Are colors used realistically or for emphasis?

Shapes
- ☑ What shapes are created by space or enclosed in lines?
- ☑ What is important about the shapes? What are they meant to symbolize or represent?

Lines
- ☑ What direction do the lines lead you?
- ☑ Which objects are you meant to focus on?
- ☑ What is the importance of the lines?
- ☑ Do lines divide or segment areas? Why do you think this is?

Textures
- ☑ What textures are used?
- ☑ What emotions or moods are they meant to affect?

Point of View
Point of view shows the artist's feelings toward the subject. Analyze this point of view:
- ☑ What point of view is the artist taking?
- ☑ Do you agree with this point of view?
- ☑ Is the artist successful in communicating this point of view?

Graphics

Line Graphs
Line graphs show changes in numbers over time.
- ☑ What numbers and time frame are represented?
- ☑ Does the information represent appropriate changes?

Pie Graphs
Pie graphs represent parts of a whole.
- ☑ What total number does the pie represent?
- ☑ Do the numbers represent an appropriate-sized sample?

Bar Graphs
Bar graphs compare amounts.
- ☑ What amounts are represented?
- ☑ Are the amounts appropriate?

Charts and Tables
Charts and tables organize information for easy comparison.
- ☑ What is being presented?
- ☑ Do columns and rows give equal data to compare and contrast?

Maps
- ☑ What land formations are shown?
- ☑ What boundaries are shown?
- ☑ Are there any keys or symbols on the map? What do they mean?

Appendix H: Media and Technology

Forms of Media

Television, movies, and music are some common forms of media that you know a lot about. Here are some others.

Advertisement

An advertisement selling a product or a service can be placed in a newspaper or magazine, on the Internet, or on television or radio.

Broadcast News

Broadcast news is offered on a 24-hour cycle through nightly newscasts, all-day news channels, and the Internet.

Documentary

A documentary shares information about people's lives, historic events, objects, or places. It is based on facts and evidence.

Internet and World Wide Web

This worldwide computer network offers audio and video clips, news, reference materials, research, and graphics.

Journal

A journal records experiences, current research, or ideas about a topic for a target audience.

Magazine

A magazine includes articles, stories, photos, and graphics of general interest.

Newspaper

A newspaper most often is printed daily or weekly.

Photography

Traditionally, photography has been the art or process of producing images on a film surface using light. Today, digital images are often used.

The Media and You

The media's role is to entertain, to inform, and to advertise. Media can help raise people's awareness about current issues. Media also can give clues about the needs and beliefs of the people.

Use a critical eye and ear to sort through the thousands of messages presented to you daily. Be aware of the media's use of oversimplified ideas about people, decent and acceptable language, and appropriate messages. Consider these questions:

- Who is being shown and why?
- What is being said? Is it based on fact?
- How do I feel about what and how it is said?

Technology and You

Technology can improve communication. Consider the following when selecting technology for research or presentations:

Audio/Sound

Speeches, music, sound effects, and other elements can set a mood or reinforce an idea.

Computers

- Desktop publishing programs offer tools for making newsletters and posters.
- Software programs are available for designing publications, Web sites, databases, and more.
- Word processing programs feature dictionaries, grammar-check and spell-check programs, and templates for memos, reports, letters, and more.

Multimedia

Slide shows, movies, and other electronic media can help the learning process.

Visual Aids

Charts, tables, maps, props, drawings, and graphs provide visual representation of information.

Appendix I: World Atlas

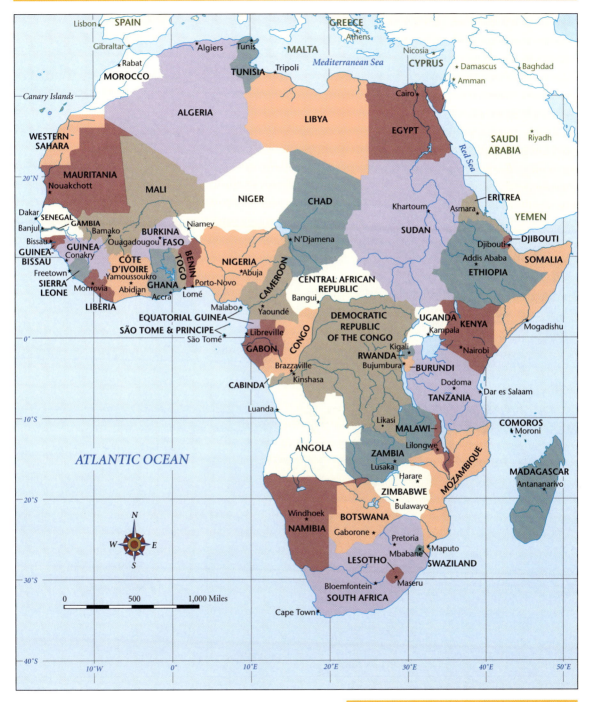

Africa

Appendix I: World Atlas 591

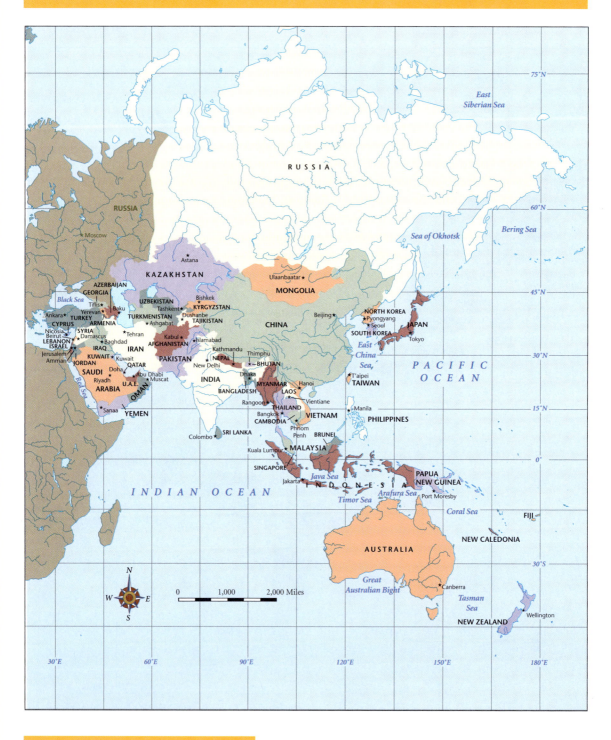

Asia and Australia

Europe

Appendix I: World Atlas 593

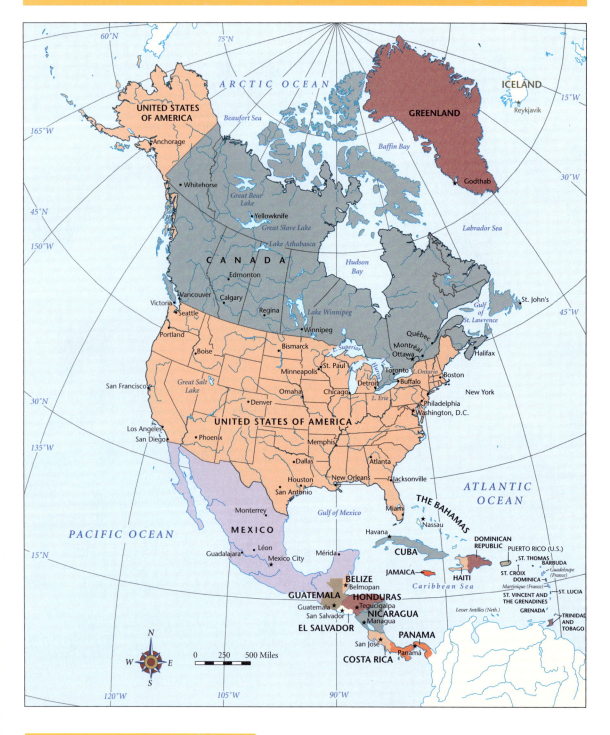

North America

South America

Appendix I: World Atlas 595

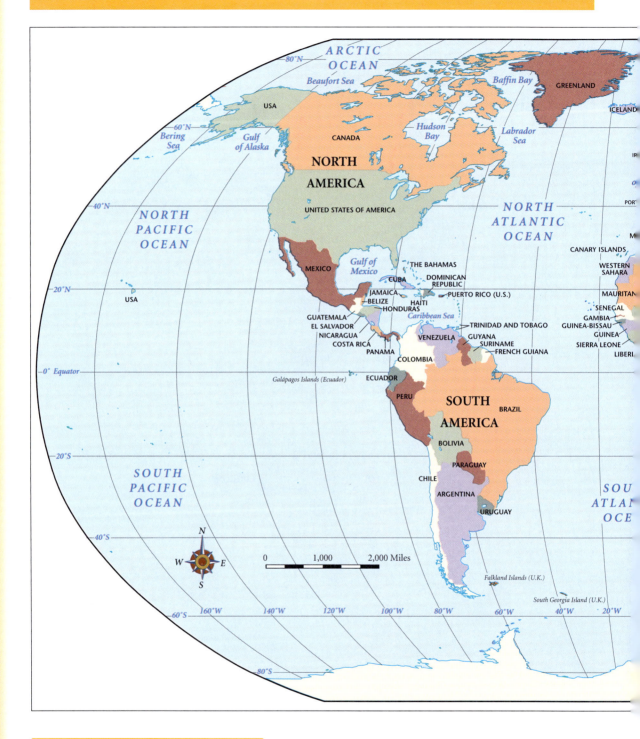

World

World

Appendix I: World Atlas

Appendix J: Student Passport to World Cultures

Antigua and Barbuda

Population: 68,320.

Nationality: noun: Antiguan(s); adjective: Antiguan.

Ethnic groups: Black, British, Portuguese, Lebanese, Syrian.

Languages: English (official), local dialects.

Religions: mostly Protestant, some Roman Catholic.

Area: 171 sq mi (443 sq km); about 2.5 times larger than Washington, D.C.

Location: Caribbean Sea.

Profile: Columbus claimed Antigua for Spain in 1493. The British settled there in 1632, growing tobacco and sugar. African slaves worked on the sugar plantations in Antigua until slavery was outlawed in 1834. Today, tourism is the main industry. On November 1, 1981, the British-owned state of Antigua became independent as Antigua and Barbuda.

Argentina (Argentine Republic)

Population: 39,144,753.

Nationality: noun: Argentine(s); adjective: Argentine.

Ethnic groups: 97% European; 3% Amerindian.

Languages: Spanish (official), English, Italian, German, French.

Religion: 92% Roman Catholic.

Area: 1,068,302 sq mi (2,766,890 sq km); about three-tenths the size of the United States.

Location: southernmost country in South America.

Profile: Argentina is the second largest country in South America. It has a mild climate generally, but there are varying altitudes with different climates. Among its many natural resources are petroleum products, uranium, timber, beef, pork, fish, cotton, fruits, wool, and cereals. Argentina ships much grain worldwide. Argentina is also known for its musical and dance style, the tango, and for its frequent world championships in polo. Its literacy rate is one of the highest in the world.

Austria (Republic of Austria)

Population: 8,174,726.

Nationality: noun: Austrian(s); adjective: Austrian.

Ethnic group: 88% German.

Languages: German (official). Also, Serbo-Croatian, Slovenian.

Religions: 78% Roman Catholic, 5% Protestant.

Area: 32,377 sq mi (83,855 sq km); between South Carolina and Maine in size.

Location: south central Europe.

Profile: In 1914, the killing of Archduke Franz Ferdinand triggered World War I. After the war, the Austrian empire disappeared, replaced by a republic. Hitler annexed the country before World War II. From 1945 to 1955, the United States, the USSR, Great Britain, and France occupied the country. Then it became a neutral democracy. Austria is proud of its mountains and natural beauty. Its people enjoy outdoor sports such as skiing. Its rich history has brought together many cultures of eastern and western Europe. The result is a distinctive culture unlike those of other German-speaking countries. Today, Austria is a neutral country, allowing it to act as an international center of government and politics. Yet, despite its international flavor, Austria holds its rural heritage dear.

Canada

Population: 32,507,874.

Nationality: noun: Canadian(s); adjective: Canadian.

Ethnic groups: 28% British, 23% French, 2% Amerindian, 15% other European.

Languages: English, French (both official).

Religions: 46% Roman Catholic, 36% Protestant, 18% other.

Area: 3,855,101 sq mi (9,984,670 sq km); largest country in land size in the Western Hemisphere.

Location: northern half of North America.

Profile: Canada is the second largest nation in the world. The Bay of Fundy, an inlet of the Atlantic Ocean off the coasts of Nova Scotia and New Brunswick in eastern Canada, has the highest tides in the world. In 1534, explorer Jacques Cartier traveled up the St. Lawrence River. Iroquois who helped guide Cartier used the word *kanata*, which is the Huron-Iroquois word for *village*. Canada got its name when Cartier used the word *Canada* to refer to the area.

July 1, 1867, is known as Dominion Day. That was the day when the original Dominion of Canada came into being. Canada's most important national holiday is now Canada Day, celebrated on July 1 of each year in remembrance of Dominion Day. Canada is divided into 10 provinces and 3 territories. Nearly one-fourth of all the fresh water in the world is in Canada, and forests cover nearly half of Canada. Hockey is the national sport.

Chile (Republic of Chile)

Population: 15,823,957.

Nationality: noun: Chilean(s); adjective: Chilean.

Ethnic groups: 95% European and Mestizo, 3% Amerindian.

Language: Spanish (official).

Religions: 89% Roman Catholic, 11% Protestant.

Area: 292,260 sq mi (756,950 sq km); slightly larger than Texas.

Location: western coast of South America.

Profile: Chile is sometimes called the "Shoestring Nation" because it is 10 times as long as it is wide. In the north, it is warm; in the south, cold. The Andes Mountains are a tourist attraction for those who fish, ski, and enjoy other sports such as mountain climbing. Although Chile's farmlands are fertile, it cannot produce enough food to feed its people. Mineral deposits are the country's main source of income.

China (People's Republic of China)

Population: 1,298,847,624.

Nationality: noun: Chinese (singular and plural); adjective: Chinese.

Ethnic groups: 92% Han Chinese; Zhuang, Uygur, Hui, Yi, Tibetan, Miao, Manchu, Mongol, Buyi, Korean, and numerous others.

Languages: Standard Chinese or Mandarin (official); Yue (Cantonese), Wu (Shanghaiese), Minbei (Fuzhou), Minnan (Hokkien-Taiwanese), Xiang, Gan, Hakka dialects, and minority languages.

Religions: officially atheist; Taoism, Buddhism, some Muslims, Christians.

Appendix J: Student Passport to World Cultures **599**

Area: 3,705,405 sq mi (9,596,960 sq km); between the United States and Canada in size.

Location: eastern Asia.

Profile: China has one of the world's oldest civilizations. With more than a billion citizens, it has the largest population in the world. Until the early 1900s, China was ruled by dynasties. During this time, the Chinese people made many important contributions to civilization. When the last dynasty failed, China became a republic. However, since 1949, the government has been ruled by the Communist Party. The arts have always been important in China. Evidence appears in beautiful porcelain and landscape painting, for example, as well as in the writings of Confucius.

Colombia (Republic of Colombia)

Population: 42,310,775.

Nationality: noun: Colombian(s); adjective: Colombian.

Ethnic groups: 58% mestizo, 20% European, 14% Creole, 8% Black, Amerindian.

Language: Spanish (official).

Religion: 90% Roman Catholic.

Area: 439,735 sq mi (1,138,910 sq km); between Texas and Alaska in size.

Location: northwest corner of South America.

Profile: In the early 1800s, Colombia was part of Gran Colombia, which included the modern-day countries of Ecuador, Panama, Venezuela, and Colombia. Its climate varies from the swampy Pacific coast—the rainiest in South America—to the cold, high mountain ranges in the west. Colombia holds first place for the production of mild coffee beans. Although the government has remained fairly stable, illegal trafficking in drugs has caused many problems.

Dominican Republic

Population: 8,833,634.

Nationality: noun: Dominican(s); adjective: Dominican.

Ethnic groups: 73% Creole, 16% white, 11% Black.

Language: Spanish (official).

Religion: 95% Roman Catholic.

Area: 18,815 sq mi (48,730 sq km); about twice the size of Vermont.

Location: West Indies.

Profile: The Dominican Republic shares the island of Hispaniola with Haiti. It is made up of 31 provinces. The largest city in the Dominican Republic, Santo Domingo, was founded in 1496. Supposedly, this city as the ashes of explorer Christopher Columbus buried in a cathedral. It is the largest settlement of Europeans in the Western Hemisphere. At different times in history, the country has been ruled by Spain, France, Haiti, and the United States Most of the country's income is from tourism. However, agriculture—in particular, sugar, coffee, and tobacco—is a large part of the economy. In fact, the Dominican Republic has had one of the fastest economic growth rates in the world in the last 10 years.

Egypt (Arab Republic of Egypt)

Population: 76,117,421.

Nationality: noun: Egyptians(s); adjective: Egyptian.

Ethnic group: 99% Egyptian Arab.

Languages: Arabic (official); English, French.

Religions: 94% Muslim (mostly Sunni), 6% Coptic Christian and other.

Area: 386,662 sq mi (1,001,450 sq km); about two-thirds the size of Alaska.

600 Appendix J: Student Passport to World Cultures

Location: northeast Africa.

Profile: Egypt's capital is the city of Cairo. The Country developed in the Nile River valley, where most people live today. The Nile River, at 4,000 miles, is the longest river in the world. It floods its bands every year, providing irrigation and minerals for crops, such as rice, corn, wheat, beans, fruit, and vegetables. As early as 30,000 B.C., the Egyptians learned how to use a reed from the Nile River—papyrus—to make paper. The country is rich in natural resources as well: petroleum, natural gas, iron ore, limestone, and manganese, to name a few. Hosni Mubarak has been president of Egypt since 1981.

England. See United Kingdom.

France (French Republic)

Population: 60,424,213.

Nationality: noun: Frenchman (men), Frenchwoman (women), French (collective plural); adjective: French.

Ethnic groups: French, Teutonic, Slavic, North African, Indochinese, and Basque minorities.

Languages: French (official; 100% of population); rapidly declining regional dialects (Provençal, Breton, Alsatian, Corsican, Catalan, Basque, Flemish).

Religions: 83–88% Roman Catholic, 2% Protestant, 5%–10% Muslim (North African workers), 1% Jewish, 6% unaffiliated.

Area: 211,209 sq mi (547,030 sq km); between California and Texas in size.

Location: western Europe.

Profile: France, the largest country in Western Europe, has a varied geography and climate. Its culture stretches back thousands of years. Contributors include the Celts, Romans, and Germanic peoples who once invaded this land. Strong leaders such as Charlemagne, Louis XIV, and Napoleon brought France to a position of world importance. The French today have maintained their appreciation of the arts. They delight in preparing and cooking food. A high standard of living gives them time to enjoy family life, another important part of their culture. Sports, such as soccer and bicycling, are popular.

Germany
(Federal Republic of Germany)

Population: 82,424,609.

Nationality: noun: German(s); adjective: German.

Ethnic groups: 92% German, 2% Turkish, other.

Language: German (official).

Religions: 34% Protestant, 34% Roman Catholic, 28% unaffiliated or other, 4% Muslim.

Area: 137,847 sq mi (357,021 sq km); about the size of Virginia and North and South Carolina combined.

Location: central Europe.

Profile: Germany has historically been a strong military power in Europe. As part of the Holy Roman Empire and Prussia, it controlled the cultures of the lands it invaded. Germany and Adolf Hitler's Third Reich were defeated in World War II, and the country was divided into East Germany and West Germany. Even divided, the people spoke the same language and many practiced the same Christian faith. They formally agreed to reunite in 1990. Since then, Germany has had to deal with many problems brought on by the complex process of reunifying, including finding ways to finance industrial improvements in the former East Germany. A reunified Germany draws from the country's past. It includes a love of outdoor sports, regional costumes worn on special occasions, and foods that were first prepared before modern-day refrigeration.

Appendix J: Student Passport to World Cultures

Ghana

Population: 20,757,032.

Nationality: noun: Ghanaian(s); adjective: Ghanaian.

Ethnic groups: 44% Akan, 16% Moshi-Dagomba, 13% Ewe, 8% Ga, 3% Gurma, 1% Yoruba.

Languages: English (official); about 75 African languages including Akan, Moshi-Dagomba, Ewe, and Ga are spoken as well.

Religions: 63% Christian, 21% indigenous beliefs, 16% Muslim.

Area: 92,456 sq mi (239,460 sq km); about twice the size of Mississippi.

Location: southern coast of West Africa.

Profile: Ghana is thought to be the earliest kingdom in sub-Saharan Africa. It was formerly called the Gold Coast. It became an independent nation in 1957, the first British colony south of the Sahara to gain independence. About one-third of the population of Ghana lives in cities. Ghana's natural resources, mainly gold, timber, and cocoa, are chief sources of income. The world largest artificial lake, Lake Volta, is in Ghana. Kofi Annan, the secretary general of the United Nations, is from Ghana.

Great Britain.

See United Kingdom.

Haiti (Republic of Haiti)

Population: 7,656,166.

Nationality: noun: Haitian(s); adjective: Haitian.

Ethnic groups: 95% Black, 5% Creole and other.

Languages: French, Creole (both official).

Religions: 80% Roman Catholic, 16% Protestant, voodoo widely practiced.

Area: 10,714 sq mi (27,750 sq km); between Hawaii and Massachusetts in size.

Location: West Indies.

Profile: Haiti shares the island of Hispaniola with the Dominican Republic. It was a successful and wealthy French colony, due to the import of African slaves to clear the land and harvest the sugar cane. In 1791, the former slave Toussaint L'Ouverture led a rebellion of slaves against the French. On January 1, 1804, it became the independent Black nation of Haiti. As of 1804, the United States and Haiti were the only two independent nations in the Western world. Haiti is currently the poorest country in the Western Hemisphere, with 80% of the population living in poverty. Deforestation—the cutting of trees for fuel—has affected much of Haiti. Without these trees, the land is subject to erosion. Haiti often suffers from natural disasters, such as hurricanes.

India (Republic of India)

Population: 1,065,070,607.

Nationality: noun: Indian(s); adjective: Indian.

Ethnic groups: 72% Indo-Aryan, 27% Dravidian, Mongoloid, and others.

Languages: Hindi, English, and 14 other official languages; 24 languages spoken by a million or more persons each; numerous other languages and dialects; Hindi is the national language and primary tongue of 30% of the people; English enjoys associate status but is the most important language for national, political, and commercial communication; Hindustani, a variant of Hindi/Urdu, is spoken throughout northern India.

Religions: 82% Hindu, 12% Muslim, 2% Christian, 2% Sikh.

Area: 1,269,345 sq mi (3,287,590 sq km); slightly more than one-third the size of the United States.

Location: southern Asia.

Profile: The Indus River valley was home to the first Indians. They had a well-developed civilization; it was one of the oldest in the world. As invaders conquered India, the civilization weakened. Europeans came to India around 1600. Among them were the British, who formed the British East India Trading Company. The company grew until it gave the British almost complete control of India for centuries. After many years of struggle, India finally became an independent nation in 1947. Today, India is a democratic republic. Most of its people are Hindus. This means that its customs and traditions are based on the Hindu religion. The most famous of India's beautiful temples and mosques is the Taj Mahal.

Iran (Islamic Republic of Iran)

Population: 67,503,205.

Nationality: noun: Iranian(s); adjective: Iranian.

Ethnic groups: 51% Persian, 24% Zeria, 8% Giloaki/Mazandarani, 7% Kurd, 3% Arab, 2% Lur, 2% Balochi, 2% Turkmen.

Languages: Farsi/Persian (official), Kurdish, Pashto, Luri, Balochi, Gilaki, Mazandarami, Azeri and Turkic languages; Arabic; Turkish.

Religion: Muslim (official; 89% Shi'a, 10% Sunni).

Area: 636,296 sq mi (1,648,000 sq km); the size of Alaska and Washington combined.

Location: Middle East, bordering the Gulf of Oman, the Persian Gulf, and the Caspian Sea, between Iraq and Pakistan.

Profile: Formerly known as Persia, Iran's history goes back thousands of years, when it was a mighty empire of artistic, cultural, and scientific learning. Today, Iran's natural resources, especially crude oil, have contributed to the growth of the country's economy. Unfortunately, Iran's unstable government and border conflicts with its neighbor Iraq have led to hardship and war for its citizens. The United States and Iran have also clashed over Iran's use of terrorism for economic gain. This dispute started when Iranian militants seized the U.S. embassy and took hostages (many of them Americans) in order to release frozen Iranian assets. Currently, the United States has placed controls or sanctions on Iran's trade because of Iran's support of international terrorism and its high budget cost for the development of nuclear weapons.

Iraq (Republic of Iraq)

Population: 25,374,691.

Nationality: noun: Iraqi(s); adjective: Iraqi.

Ethnic groups: 75%–80% Arab, 15–20% Kurdish.

Languages: Arabic (official); Kurdish (official in Kurdish regions), Assyrian, Armenian.

Religions: Muslim (official; 60–65% Shi'a, 32–37% Sunni).

Area: 168,754 sq mi (437,071 sq km); about three times the size of Iowa.

Location: Middle East, bordering the Persian Gulf, between Iran and Kuwait.

Profile: An area of Iraq between the Tigris and Euphrates Rivers was the site of one of the oldest civilizations in the world, Mesopotamia. This mostly desert region is rich in oil reserves, a mainstay of Iraq's economy. Oil has been and continues to be a bargaining chip for trade in order to improve the lives of Iraq's citizens.

This resource has also led to much conflict in the Middle East. Border disputes with Iran and Kuwait have resulted in longstanding warfare and loss of life. Iraq's unstable government, known for its terrorist tactics, has oppressed its economy and its people. Because of Iraq's refusal to allow the United Nations to inspect their nuclear weapons arsenal, U.S. troops, backed by other nations, invaded Iraq in 2003. While the troops were successful at toppling the government and removing Iraq's leader, Saddam Hussein, Hussein's supporters have continued the fighting. The United States plans to remain in Iraq until a stable government is established.

Ireland

Population: 3,969,558.

Nationality: noun: Irishman (men), Irishwoman (women), Irish (collective plural); adjective: Irish.

Ethnic groups: Celtic with English minority.

Languages: Irish (Gaelic) and English (official); English widely spoken.

Religions: 92% Roman Catholic, 3% Anglican, 4% other.

Area: 27,135 sq mi (70,280 sq km); slightly larger than West Virginia.

Location: Atlantic Ocean, west of Great Britain.

Profile: In the 400s, St. Patrick converted Ireland, at first a collection of warring Celtic chieftainships, to Christianity. It was first invaded by the Vikings in the 800s. Although joined with England in 1800 by the Act of Union, Ireland was not well represented in the British parliament. In 1949, Ireland severed all ties to the British crown and became a fully independent republic. Since then, its history has been dominated by economic problems and "The Troubles." In this anti-British violence, the Irish Republican Army, a guerrilla group, has attempted to drive the British troops from Northern Ireland. Ireland's cultural contributions are strongest in literature. Consider the writings of George Bernard Shaw, William Butler Yeats, and James Joyce. The most important national holiday in Ireland is Saint Patrick's Day, March 17.

Israel (State of Israel)

Population: 6,199,008.

Nationality: noun: Israeli(s); adjective: Israeli.

Ethnic groups: 80% Jewish, 20% Arab and other.

Languages: Hebrew (official), Arab (official for Arab minority); English most widely spoken foreign language.

Religions: 80% Judaism, 15% Islam (mostly Sunni Muslim), 2% Christian, 3% Druze or other.

Area: 8,019 sq mi (20,770 sq km); slightly larger than Massachusetts.

Location: Middle East, eastern end of Mediterranean Sea.

Profile: The Jewish people, led by Moses, escaped slavery in Egypt and set up a kingdom along the Mediterranean Sea. Through the years, the numbers of Jews living in Palestine (as the area was called) decreased as the Arab population increased. After World War I, the Jews began resettling in Palestine. During World War II, millions of Jews fled to Palestine to avoid the Holocaust. In 1948, the United Nations divided Palestine into two states, one for the Jews and one for the Arabs. The Israeli people, who come from all parts of the world, are bound together by the Jewish religion. They are set apart from their neighbors by language, religion, and customs. They tend to be literate, skilled, and hardworking. Border fights continue between Israel and its Arab neighbors.

Many people on both sides have been killed. Israel is short of water and fertile land. Its farms are typically on the coast, where the climate is pleasant and there is enough rainfall for farming. The main crops are olives, grapes, and citrus fruits, especially lemons and oranges.

Japan

Population: 127,333,002.

Nationality: noun: Japanese (singular, plural); adjective: Japanese.

Ethnic groups: 99% Japanese, 1% Korean, Chinese, and other.

Language: Japanese (official).

Religions: Most Japanese (84%) observe both Shinto and Buddhist rites; about 16% belong to other faiths, including 0.8% Christian.

Area: 145,883 sq mi (377,835 sq km); slightly larger than Montana.

Location: off east coast of Asia.

Profile: Japan is a mountainous country made up of four main islands. In its early years, powerful families or military leaders ruled. Under the leadership of Emperor Mutsuhitos, many advancements were made. A constitution was written and a two-house Parliament established. Japan was destroyed during World War II. But with the help of the United States and others, it rebuilt its industries and government. Today, Japan is a high-technology, industrial country. Though Western influence is strong, the Japanese maintain their own culture. Education is especially important to them; Japan's literacy rate is 100%.

Netherlands
(Kingdom of the Netherlands)

Population: 16,318,199.

Nationality: noun: Dutchman (men), Dutchwoman (women); adjective: Dutch.

Ethnic groups: 83% Dutch, Moroccans, Turks, and other.

Language: Dutch (official).

Religions: 31% Roman Catholic, 21% Protestant, 36% unaffiliated, 4% Muslim.

Area: 16,033 sq mi (41,526 sq km); about 1.3 times the size of Maryland.

Location: northwestern Europe.

Profile: During the Holy Roman Empire, the Netherlands was originally the low-lying area near the mouths of the Rhine, Meuse, and Schelde Rivers. Despite its small size, the Netherlands became a world power in the 1600s. It maintained extraordinary influence and prestige in European affairs into the 1900s. While devastated by World War II, political stability allowed a dramatic postwar recovery. Today, its main crops are grains, potatoes, sugar beets, livestock; its natural resources include natural gas, crude oil, and fertile soil. The Netherlands is famous for flower farming, especially tulips.

Appendix J: Student Passport to World Cultures

Nigeria
(Federal Republic of Nigeria)

Population: 137,253,133.

Nationality: noun: Nigerian(s); adjective: Nigerian.

Ethnic groups: 250 tribal groups; Hausa and Fulani in north, Yoruba in southwest, and Ibos in southeast make up 68% of population.

Languages: English (official); Hausa, Yoruba, Ibo, Fulani, and several other languages also widely spoken.

Religions: 50% Muslim, 40% Christian, 10% indigenous beliefs.

Area: 356,669 sq mi (923,768 sq km); about 1.3 times the size of Texas.

Location: south coast of West Africa.

Profile: Nigeria's history goes back around 2,000 years. It is the most populated country in Africa. It is also one of the richest countries in Africa, with mineral resources and large oil deposits on the Niger River. There is also coal in the river's delta. But most Nigerians are farmers. Since Nigerians tend to speak English and love movies, most movies are in English. Its four ethnic groups distrust one another. In 1967, a civil war broke out when one group tried to set up an independent country, Biafra. The war ended in 1970 with the defeat of the Biafrans.

Pakistan
(Islamic Republic of Pakistan)

Population: 159,196,336.

Nationality: noun: Pakistani(s); adjective: Pakistani.

Ethnic groups: Punjabi, Sindhi, Pashtun (Pathun), Balochi, Juhajir (immigrants from India and their descendants).

Languages: Urdu and English (both official); Punjabi, Sindhi, Pashtu, Balochi.

Religions: 97% Muslim (77% Sunni, 20% Shi'a); 3% Christian, Hindu, and other.

Area: 310,403 sq mi (803,940 sq km); about twice the size of California.

Location: western part of South Asia.

Profile: Around 350 B.C., Alexander the Great made the middle of the Indus River valley—what is now Pakistan—part of his empire. Arab invaders brought the religion of Islam at the start of the 700s. Ever since, the region has been deeply committed to Islam. Pakistan remains a strong Islamic country. Wheat, rice, cotton, and tobacco—its main crops—are grown in the Indus River valley; livestock is farmed in the drier areas of the north and west. Pakistan's natural resources include land, extensive natural gas reserves, some crude oil, coal, and iron ore. Its industry is limited to textiles and food processing. Seeking a balance of power with India, Pakistan tested nuclear weapons in 1998.

Philippines
(Republic of the Philippines)

Population: 86,241,697.

Nationality: noun, adjective: Filipino(s).

Ethnic groups: 91.5% Christian Malay, 4% Muslim Malay, 1.5% Chinese, other.

Languages: Filipino (based on Tagalog) and English (both official).

Religions: 83% Roman Catholic, 9% Protestant, 5% Muslim, 3% Buddhist and other.

Area: 115,830 sq mi (300,000 sq km); slightly larger than Arizona.

Location: Off the southeast coast of Asia.

Profile: The Philippine Islands were controlled by the Spanish from around 1500 to 1898. As a result, Christianity became the main religion, in particular, Roman Catholicism. Control passed to the United States after the Spanish-American War in 1898. Of the 7,100 islands in the Philippines, only about 700 are inhabited. Many have rich soil and natural resources. The islands' tropical climate is good for farming and lumbering. The people are mostly Filipinos, a mixture of Malaysian, Spanish, Chinese, Indian, and Arabian heritage. Many Filipinos work for the wealthy farmers who own most of the land.

Poland (Republic of Poland)

Population: 38,626,349.

Nationality: noun: Pole(s); adjective: Polish.

Ethnic groups: 98% Polish, 7% German, Ukranian, Byelorussian.

Language: Polish (official).

Religions: 95% Roman Catholic (about 75% practicing); 5% Eastern Orthodox, Protestant, and other.

Area: 120,728 sq mi (312,685 sq km); about the size of Virginia and North and South Carolina combined.

Location: east central Europe.

Profile: Poland's strong culture has developed over many centuries. One influence is its early Slavic culture. Another is its varied geography and climate, and a long history of conflict. Both still color Polish life today. Early on, Poland had much power. Then it ceased to exist as a nation. But culture has kept the Poles unified over the years. Today, this cultural unity is bringing Poland a renewed sense of independence. Once a Communist nation, today it is a democratic republic. Poles enjoy a common language and a rich history of contributions to the arts and sciences.

Russia (Russian Federation)

Population: 143,782,338.

Nationality: noun: Russian(s); adjective: Russian.

Ethnic groups: 82% Russian, 4% Tatar, 3% Ukranian, Chuvash, Bashkir, Belarusian, Moldavian.

Languages: Russian (official); local dialects.

Religions: Russian Orthodox, Muslim.

Area: 6,592,769 sq mi (17,075,200 sq km); almost twice the size of the United States.

Location: eastern Europe, across northern Asia to Pacific Ocean.

Profile: In the 800s, the Russian state began in the city of Kiev. In the 1200s, Mongol invaders destroyed Kiev. The tsars ruled Russia from Moscow until 1917 when the Communists took over. Mikhail Gorbachev tried to reform Communist society in 1985. But the democratic movement took control with Boris Yeltsin as its leader. In December 1991, the Soviet Union broke into separate republics, and the Commonwealth of Independent States came into being. They comprise 15 separate, independent countries. The largest is Russia, or "Great Russia." It has more than half the population and about three-quarters of the land of the old Soviet Union. The Commonwealth's chief crops are grain, potatoes, sugar beets, vegetables, and sunflowers. Its natural resources include coal, petroleum, natural gas, gold, and iron; its major industries are the extraction and processing of raw materials, and machine-building, from rolling mills to high-performance aircraft. Russia measures about 6,000 miles from western to eastern border. Within these borders is a great variety of climate, from frozen Siberia to the arid southwest. Much of the country is in the northern latitudes. More than half the Commonwealth is flat with rolling hills. Russia also has a great diversity of people. More than 100 distinct languages are spoken, and many religious faiths are followed. The culture of Russia is old and deep. It has excelled in classical music, literature, ballet, and art. Russia has also produced many great scientists.

South Africa
(Republic of South Africa)

Population: 42,718,530.

Nationality: noun: South African(s); adjective: South African.

Ethnic groups: 75% Black, 14% white, 8% mixed, 3% Indian.

Languages: Afrikaans, English, Zulu, Xhosa, Sotho, Ndebele, Pedi, Swazi, Tsonga, Venda, Tswana (all official).

Religions: 68% Christian; 29% indigenous beliefs and animist.

Area: 471,010 sq mi (1,219,912 sq km); between Texas and Alaska in size.

Location: southern end of Africa.

Profile: The Dutch settled the Republic of South Africa in the 1600s. Except for a narrow coastal plain, the country is mostly a great plateau, including grasslands, savanna, and desert. South Africa's well-developed economy produces 40% of the manufactured goods of Africa, 50% of its minerals, and 20% of its farm products. It is the wealthiest nation in Africa. In 1948, apartheid (or "separate development") became official government policy. However, in May 1996, South Africa did away with apartheid and became a democracy. It is now under the leadership of Thabo Mbeki.

South Korea
(Republic of Korea)

Population: 48,598,175.

Nationality: noun: Korean(s); adjective: Korean.

Ethnic group: Korean.

Languages: Korean; English widely taught in high school.

Religions: 49% Christian, 47% Buddhist, 3% Confucianist.

Area: 38,023 sq mi (98,480 sq km); between Indiana and Kentucky in size.

Location: peninsula between China and Japan.

Profile: Korea was invaded many times by both China and Japan. Japan ruled it from 1910 to 1945. Today, Korea is no longer one country. It is divided into North Korea, ruled by Communists, and South Korea, a republic. The Korean alphabet is considered highly scientific. The Korean lifestyle reflects the teachings of Confucius. South Korea, which has twice as many people as North Korea, is a modern, industrial, democratic nation. South Korea's chief crops are rice, barley, vegetables, legumes, chickens, pigs, and cattle. Its natural resources include coal, tungsten, and graphite. Major industries include electronics, automobiles, chemicals, and shipbuilding.

Sweden
(Kingdom of Sweden)

Population: 8,986,400.

Nationality: noun: Swede(s), adjective: Swedish.

Ethnic groups: 89% Swedish; 2% Finnish, 9% Sami and others.

Languages: Swedish (official); Sami- and Finnish-speaking minorities.

Religion: 87% Lutheran.

Area: 173,731 sq mi (449,964 sq km); slightly larger than California.

Location: Scandinavian peninsula in northern Europe.

Profile: The earliest Swedes were the Svear. They dominated a trading empire in the 900s. Sweden is long and narrow. Its terrain is mostly flat or gently rolling lowlands; there are mountains in the north and west. Nature is special to the Swedes. While Sweden has different climates, it tends to be cool in the summer and cold in the winter. The country's chief crops are grain, sugar beets, potatoes, meat, and milk; its natural resources include iron ore, zinc, lead, copper, silver, timber, uranium, and hydropower. Swedes are industrious and work hard to improve their society.

Turkey (Republic of Turkey)

Population: 68,893,918.

Nationality: noun: Turk(s); adjective: Turkish.

Ethnic groups: 80% Turkish, 20% Kurdish.

Languages: Turkish (official); Kurdish, Arabic, Armenian, Greek.

Religion: Muslim (mostly Sunni).

Area: 301,383 sq mi (780,578 sq km); about the size of Texas and Virginia combined.

Location: Between the Mediterranean and Black Seas in southeastern Europe.

Profile: Turkey's coastal plains made it a center of agricultural growth many centuries ago. Olives, tobacco, citrus fruits, and sugar beets are important crops in this country's economy. Turkey is also a large producer of textiles and clothing, with one-third of its citizens working in these industries. Turkey joined the United Nations in 1945 and NATO in 1952. In recent years, Turkey's unstable government has led to warfare and border disputes. This country has also been the epicenter of severe earthquakes, especially in the northern region.

Ukraine (Republic of Ukraine)

Population: 47,732,079.

Nationality: noun: Ukranian(s); adjective: Ukranian.

Ethnic groups: 78% Ukranian, 17% Russian, Jewish.

Languages: Ukranian (official); Russian, Romanian, Polish, Hungarian.

Religions: Christian: Ukranian Orthodox, Ukranian Autocephalous Orthodox, Ukranian Greek Catholic.

Area: 233,090 sq mi (603,700 sq km); about twice the size of Arizona.

Location: eastern Europe.

Profile: Ukraine is the third largest country in the Commonwealth of Independent States (Russia) and the most densely populated of the former Soviet republics. Established in the 800s, Ukraine is the heartland of ancient Russia and the center for Ukranian Orthodox religion. Its people are called East Slavs or "Little Russians." Kiev, the capital and cultural center of Ukraine, is considered the Mother of Russian cities. It is an ancient Christian city with many cathedrals and monuments that date back to the 11th and 12th centuries. Ukraine contributes beets, grain, coal, and iron to the Commonwealth.

United Kingdom
(United Kingdom of Great Britain and Northern Ireland)

Population: 60,270,708.

Nationality: noun: Briton(s), British (collective plural); adjective: British.

Ethnic groups: 81.5% English, 9.6% Scottish, 2.4% Irish, 1.9% Welsh, 1.9% Ulster, 2.8% West Indian, Indo-Pakistani, other.

Languages: English, Welsh, Scottish form of Gaelic.

Religions: 72% Christian, 3% Muslim, many others.

Area: 94,525 sq mi (244,820 sq km); slightly smaller than Oregon.

Location: off northwest coast of Europe.

Profile: Many factors have shaped British culture. Its four countries (England, Scotland, Wales, and Northern Ireland) share a varied geography and a mild, wet climate. The rich British culture has roots in invaders' cultures. These include Celts, Romans, Vikings, and French. Britain has shared its culture with many other countries. This includes the United States and other former colonies. Many countries use the principles of law and government developed in Britain. The Industrial Revolution begun in Great Britain changed most world cultures. Many British writers are loved all over the world. Today, Britain has emerged from two world wars as a modern industrial power. The British enjoy a high level of social support from the government. Everyday life in Britain includes typically British sports like rugby and cricket, unique customs, and excellent schools.

United States of America

Population: 293,027,571.

Nationality: noun: American(s); adjective: American.

Ethnic groups: 75.1% white, 12.5% Hispanic of any race or group, 12.3% Black, 3.6% Asian, 0.9% Amerindian and Alaska Native.

Languages: English (official); large Spanish-speaking minority.

Religions: 56% Protestant, 28% Roman Catholic, 10% none, 2% Jewish, 4% other.

Area: 3,718,709 sq mi (9,631,418 sq km); fourth-largest country in the world.

Location: southern half of North America.

Profile: The United States is one of the largest and strongest countries in the world. Its geography changes greatly from the Pacific Ocean on the West Coast to the Atlantic Ocean on the East Coast. Deserts, forests, mountains, and plains are all included. The United States is an international economic leader. It is the world's second-largest producer, and number-one exporter, of grain. Other natural resources include coal, copper, lead, uranium, gold, iron, nickel, silver, crude oil, natural gas, and timber. Major industries in the United States include petroleum, steel, motor vehicles, aerospace, telecommunications, chemicals, electronics, food processing, consumer goods, fishing, lumber, and mining.

Vietnam
(Socialist Republic of Vietnam)

Population: 82,689,518.

Nationality: noun: Vietnamese (singular, plural); adjective: Vietnamese.

Ethnic groups: 85–90% Vietnamese, Chinese; ethnic minorities include Hmong, Thai, Meo, Khmer, Man, Cham, other mountain groups.

Languages: Vietnamese (official); French, Chinese, English, Khmer, ethnic languages (Mon-Khmer and Malayo-Polynesian).

Religions: Buddhist, Confucian, Taoist, Roman Catholic.

Area: 127,244 sq mi (329,560 sq km); about the size of Virginia and North and South Carolina combined.

Location: Southeast Asia.

Profile: The Chinese first ruled the Vietnamese by the year 111. In the 1800s, the French ruled them. With the French withdrawal in 1954, Vietnam was divided into North Vietnam and South Vietnam. The two countries fought for over a decade. The United States and the Soviet Union were also involved. In 1975, North Vietnam and South Vietnam were reunited under Communist rule. The Vietnamese people have borrowed traditions from China, France, and India. They tend to be shy. They greet people with a slight bow and with the palms of their hands open. The teachings of Confucius have influenced the rural people, and they live simply. Vietnam's chief crops are rice, corn, potatoes, rubber, soybeans, and coffee. Its major industries are food processing, textiles, and machine-building.

Wales (Constituent Principality of the United Kingdom of Great Britain and Northern Ireland)

Profile: The history of Wales involves many struggles. Some invaders came from inside Britain and some from outside. The land has been controlled by Romans, Saxons, Picts, Vikings, and Norman French. Finally, in 1536, the Act of Union made it a principality within Britain. The climate of Wales is temperate. Its terrain includes high plateaus with mountain ranges cut through by river valleys. It is a land of small farms. In the mountains and moors, sheep farming is a major occupation. Along the coast, dairy and mixed farming are the rule. Among the old heavy industries, even coal mining has almost ceased in Wales. *See also* United Kingdom.

Handbook of Literary Terms

A

Abstract image (ab′ strakt im′ ij) a word or idea that refers to something general, a state of being, or a quality that cannot be reached by the five senses (p. 399)

Action (ak′ shən) what goes on in a story (p. 75)

Allusion (ə lü′ zhən) a reference to a historical event, a person, a place, or a work of literature (pp. 197, 279)

Ambiguity (am bə gyü′ ə tē) being difficult to understand; able to be understood in more than one way (p. 54)

Anecdote (an′ ik dōt) a short, funny story (p. 548)

Archetype (är′ kə tīp) a descriptive detail, plot pattern, character type, or theme that is found in many different cultures. (p. 537)

Author's purpose (o′ thərs pėr′ pəs) the reason the author writes: to entertain, to inform, to express opinions, or to persuade (p. 179)

Autobiography (o tə bī og′ rə fē) a person's life story written by that person (p. 197)

B

Biography (bī og′ rə fē) a person's life story told by someone else (p. 240)

Blank verse (blangk vėrs) unrhymed iambic pentameter (p. 294)

Byline (bī′ līn) a line in a news article that tells who wrote it (p. 279)

C

Character (kar′ ik tər) a person or animal in a story, poem, or play (p. 6)

Character development (kar′ ik tər di vel′ əp mənt) the way a writer develops characters by revealing personality traits (p. 313)

Classical drama (klas′ ə kəl drä′ mə) plays, often about wealthy or important people, that follow the style of ancient Greek and Latin drama; Shakespeare wrote plays in this style (p. 294)

Climax (klī′ maks) the high point of interest or suspense in a story or play (pp. 6, 93)

Column (kol′ əm) an article that appears regularly in a newspaper or magazine (p. 520)

Comedy (kom′ ə dē) a play with a happy ending, intended to amuse its audience (p. 294)

Coming-of-age-story (kum′ ing ov āj stôr′ ē) a story that tells how a young person matures (p. 104)

Concrete image (kon′ krēt im′ ij) opposite of abstract; it refers to people and things that can be reached by the five senses (p. 399)

Conflict (kon′ flikt) the struggle of the main character against himself or herself, another person, or nature (pp. 54, 313)

D

Denouement (dā nü män′) the final outcome of the main event in a story (pp. 6, 54, 93)

Description (di skrip′ shən) a written picture of the characters, events, and settings in a story (p. 232)

Detective story (di tek′ tiv stôr′ ē) a story in which the main character usually solves a crime (p. 22)

Dialogue (dī′ ə log) the conversation among characters in a story; the words that characters in a play speak (pp. 135, 240, 294, 530)

Diary (dī′ ə rē) a daily record of personal events, thoughts, or private feelings (p. 158)

Dramatic monologue (drə mat′ ik mon′ l og) a poem in which a character talks to the reader (p. 399)

E

Editorial (ed ə tôr′ ē əl) a news writer's personal opinion about an event or topic (pp. 279, 497)

Elegy (el′ ə jē) a poem that mourns someone's death (p. 361)

Essay (es′ ā) a written work that shows a writer's opinion on some basic or current issue (pp. 179, 455)

Exaggeration (eg zaj ə rā′ shən) a use of words to make something seem more than it is; stretching the truth to a great extent (p. 521)

Excerpt (ek′ sėrpt) a short passage from a longer piece of writing (pp. 158, 246)

Exposition (ek spə zish′ ən) the beginning of the story, or introduction (pp. 6, 93)

Expressionistic drama (ek spresh′ ən is tik drä′ mə) a form of drama that is not realistic; the characters' inner feelings are more important than their actions (p. 330)

F

Falling action (fȯl′ ing ak′ shən) the action in a story or play during which the excitement dies down (pp. 6, 93)

Feature story (fē′ cher stôr′ ē) a news story that examines the effect and importance of an event (p. 273)

Fiction (fik′ shən) writing that is imaginative and designed to entertain; the author creates the events and characters (p. 5)

Figurative language (fig′ yər ə tiv lang′ gwij) writing or speech not meant to be understood exactly as it is written; writers use figurative language to express ideas in imaginative ways (pp. 371, 445, 504)

Figure of speech (fig′ yər ov spēch) a word or phrase that means something other than what the words really say, such as idiom, metaphor, and simile (p. 504)

First person (fėrst pėr′ sən) written as if the author is telling the story from his or her point of view; uses *I* or *we* (pp. 6, 197)

Flashback (flash′ bak) a look into the past at some point in a story (p. 116)

Folktale (fōk′ tāl) a story that has been handed down from one generation to another (p. 135)

Free verse (frē vėrs) poetry that does not have a set rhyming pattern or line length; it uses actual speech patterns for the rhythms of sound (p. 351)

H

Haiku (hī′ kü) a form of Japanese poetry having three lines with five syllables in the first, seven in the second, and five in the third (p. 376)

Historical fiction (hi stôr′ ə kəl fik′ shən) fictional writing that draws on factual events of history (p. 126)

Humor (hyü′ mər) literature created to be funny or to amuse (p. 521)

Humorist (hyü′ mər ist) someone who writes funny works (p. 548)

I

Iambic pentameter (ī am′ bik pen tam′ ə tər) five two-beat sounds in a line of poetry where the second syllable is stressed in each pattern (pp. 294, 302, 382)

Idiom (id′ ē əm) an expression that cannot be understood from the literal meaning of its words (Example: Tom is barking up the wrong tree.) (p. 126)

Image (im′ ij) a picture in the reader's mind created by words (pp. 445, 504)

Imagery (im′ ij rē) the use of word pictures that appeal to the five senses (p. 365)

Irony (ī′ rə nē) the use of words or situations that seem to suggest one thing but mean the opposite (pp. 37, 461, 548)

J

Journalism (jėr′ nl iz əm) the gathering and presenting of news to the public (p. 264)

L

Legend (lej′ ənd) a story handed down from one generation to the next, usually about real people, places, or events in history (p. 187)

Letter (let′ ər) a document of impressions and feelings written to a particular person (p. 167)

Lyric poem (lir′ ik pō′ əm) a poem that has rhythm and expresses one strong emotion (p. 361)

a	hat	e	let	ī	ice	ȯ	order	u̇	put	sh	she	ə	a in about
ā	age	ē	equal	o	hot	oi	oil	ü	rule	th	thin		e in taken
ä	far	ėr	term	ō	open	ou	out	ch	child	ᴛʜ	then		i in pencil
â	care	i	it	ȯ	saw	u	cup	ng	long	zh	measure		o in lemon
													u in circus

Handbook of Literary Terms

M

Memoir (mem′ wär) writing based on personal experience (p. 232)

Metaphor (met′ ə fôr) a figure of speech that says one thing is another; it makes a comparison, but no words of comparison (*like* or *as*) are used (p. 388)

Monologue (mon′ l òg) a longer story or speech told by one person (p. 330)

Mood (müd) the feeling created by a piece of writing (pp. 75, 414)

Moral (môr′ əl) a lesson or message told in a story (p. 135)

Mystery (mis′ tər ē) a story about a crime that is solved (p. 6)

Myth (mith) a story that explains how some things in the natural world came to be (p. 394)

N

Narrator (nar′ ā tər) the teller of a story (pp. 6, 210, 361)

Narrative (nar′ ə tiv) a story or report about an event; usually told in chronological order (p. 504)

Naturalism (nach ə rə li′ zəm) writing that represents the world in a natural, or realistic, way; often shows characters and their environment in conflict (p. 84)

News cycle (nüz sī′ kəl) the length of time between the publishing of a news item and an update or reaction to the item (p. 273)

News story (nüz stôr′ ē) the first report of an event; mainly covers the basic facts (p. 257)

Nonfiction (non fik′ shən) writing about real people and events (p. 158)

Novel (nov′ əl) fiction that is book-length and has more plot and character details than a short story (p. 22)

O

Ode (ōd) a poem written in praise of someone or something (p. 371)

Onomatopoeia (on ə mat ə pē′ ə) the use of words that sound like their meaning (Example: *buzz, crackle, hiss, sizzle, zoom*.) (p. 377)

P

Pamphlet (pam′ flit) a short printed essay about a specific topic; it has a paper cover (p. 488)

Paradox (par′ ə doks) a statement that seems to mean two opposite things (Example: She loved and hated him at the same time.) (p. 126)

Parody (par′ ə dē) an exaggerated look at a situation (pp. 37, 537)

Pen name (pen nām) a false name used for writing (p. 173)

Personification (pər son ə fə kā′ shən) giving human characteristics to a nonhuman object (pp. 167, 388)

Persuasive (pər swā′ siv) meant to influence (p. 420)

Playwright (plā′ rīt) the author of a play (p. 294)

Plot (plot) the series of events in a story; also how it includes exposition, rising action, climax, falling action, resolution/denouement (pp. 6, 93, 537)

Poem/poetry (pō′ əm/pō′ i trē) a short piece of literature that often has a pattern of rhythm and rhyme; a poet paints powerful or beautiful ideas with words (p. 350)

Point of view (point ov vyü) the position from which the author or storyteller tells the story (pp. 197, 264, 504)

Proclamation (prok lə mā′ shən) a letter about important events that is meant to be read aloud (p. 414)

Protagonist (prō tag′ ə nist) the main character of the story (p. 22)

Pun (pun) humorous use of words or phrases (p. 173)

R

Realism (rē′ ə liz əm) a writing style that looks at ordinary people and objects (p. 371)

Realistic drama (rē ə lis′ tik drä′ ma) a play that tells a story just as it might happen in real life (p. 313)

Regionalism (rē′ jə nə liz əm) a word or phrase that comes from a particular area (p. 75)

Repetition (rep ə tish´ ən) using a word, phrase, or image more than once to show that it is important (p. 439)

Resolution (rez ə lü´ shən) the final outcome of the main event in a story (pp. 6, 54, 93)

Rhyme (rīm) words with the same vowel and ending sounds (p. 351)

Rhyme scheme (rīm skēm) a pattern of end rhymes in a poem (p. 382)

Rhythm (riTH´ əm) a pattern created by the stressed and unstressed syllables in a line of poetry (p. 351)

Rising action (rīz´ ing ak´ shən) the buildup of excitement in a story (pp. 6, 93)

S

Sarcasm (sär´ kaz əm) a grim, sometimes mean-spirited kind of irony (pp. 461, 497)

Satire (sat´ īr) humorous writing that makes fun of foolishness or evil (pp. 173, 488)

Science fiction (sī´ əns fik´ shən) a blend of fact and fantasy that imagines the effects of science and technology on life in the future (p. 36)

Sequence (sē´ kwəns) the order of events in a literary work (p. 187)

Setting (set´ ing) the time and place in a story (pp. 75, 210, 365, 439)

Simile (sim´ ə lē) a figure of speech that makes a comparison between two unlike objects using the word *like* or *as* (pp. 330, 356)

Sketch (sketch) a brief writing that often runs from subject to subject and is often humorous (p. 197)

Speech (spēch) a written work meant to be read aloud (p. 420)

Stanza (stan´ zə) a group of lines that form a unit in a poem and often have the same rhythm and rhyme (p. 382)

Style (stīl) an author's way of writing (pp. 116, 232, 455)

Surrealism (sə rē´ ə liz əm) a writing style that has a dreamlike quality and odd, unexpected images (p. 371)

Suspense (sə spens´) a feeling of uncertainty about what will happen next (p. 93)

Symbol (sim´ bəl) something that stands for something else (pp. 116, 351)

Symbolism (sim´ bə liz əm) the use of a person, place, or thing to represent something larger than itself (pp. 141, 388)

T

Theme (thēm) the main idea of a literary work (pp. 356, 420, 530)

Third person (thėrd pėr´ sən) a point of view that refers to characters as "he" or "she" and expresses some characters' thoughts (p. 104)

Tone (tōn) the attitude an author takes toward a subject (pp. 179, 445, 488)

Tragedy (traj´ ə dē) a play that ends with the suffering or death of one or more of the main characters (p. 294)

Turning point (tėrn´ ing point) a story about an experience that changes the life of a literary character (pp. 104, 210)

V

Verbal irony (vər bəl ī´ re nē) the use of words that seem to say one thing but mean the opposite (p. 330)

Villanelle (vi le nel´) a 19-line poem with several repeating rhymes (p. 382)

a	hat	e	let	ī	ice	ô	order	ů	put	sh	she		a	in about
ā	age	ē	equal	o	hot	oi	oil	ü	rule	th	thin	ə	e	in taken
ä	far	ėr	term	ō	open	ou	out	ch	child	TH	then		i	in pencil
â	care	i	it	ȯ	saw	u	cup	ng	long	zh	measure		o	in lemon
													u	in circus

Handbook of Literary Terms

Glossary

A

abandoned (ə ban´ dend) no longer lived in (p. 117)

abhor (ab hôr´) to dislike intensely; to find disgusting (p. 333)

abject (ab´ jekt) humble; without self-respect, miserable (p. 260)

abolish (ə bol´ ish) put an end to (p. 446)

abreast (ə brest´) side by side; in an even line (p. 216)

abruptly (ə brupt´ lē) suddenly (pp. 79, 122, 203)

absolute (ab´ sə lüt) complete (p. 25)

abstinence (ab´ stə nəns) stopping oneself from doing something; self-denial (p. 88)

abstract (ab strakt´) having to do with ideas (p. 510)

acclaimed (ə klāmd´) stated strongly (p. 433)

accordance (ə kôrd´ ns) agreement (pp. 202, 423)

accosted (ə kȯst´ ed) approached and spoke to in a challenging way (p. 221)

addicted (ə dik´ tid) controlled by a bad habit (p. 318)

addictions (ə dik´ shənz) harmful habits (p. 336)

adequately (ad´ ə kwit lē) well enough (p. 193)

administering (ad min´ ə stə ring) managing (p. 56)

administrative (ad min ə strā´ tiv) managing or decision-making (p. 508)

admirable (ad´ mər ə bəl) worth liking (p. 472)

admonished (ad mon´ ishd) warned; scolded with a warning (p. 215)

adolescent (ad l es´ nt) a teenager or young person (p. 161)

adroit (ə droit´) skillful (p. 162)

adversary (ad´ vər ser ē) an enemy (p. 447)

aerials (er´ ē əlz) antennas for receiving radio or TV (p. 468)

affected (ə fek´ tid) false; used to impress others (p. 160)

affectionate (ə fek´ shə nit) showing loving, fond feelings for someone (p. 159)

affectionately (ə fek´ shə nit lē) with love and tenderness (p. 301)

afflicted (ə flik´ tid) troubled or harmed (p. 137)

affections (ə fek´ shənz) emotions or feelings (p. 338)

aficionado (ə fis yə nä´ dō) a fan; someone who knows about and admires someone or something, following it closely (p. 181)

agenda (ə jen´ də) a list of things to be done (p. 258)

aggression (ə gresh´ ən) a move to attack (p. 260)

aggressive (ə gres´ iv) ready to do combat (p. 23)

aggressors (ə gres´ ərz) aggressive people (p. 23)

agitation (aj ə tā´ shən) strong emotion; disturbance (p. 8)

ailment (āl´ mənt) sickness (p. 305)

aired (ârd) openly discussed (p. 267)

alarming (a lär´ ming) frightening (p. 268)

alms (äms) charity; a handout (p. 489)

ambling (am´ bling) slow-moving (p. 85)

amiable (ā´ mē ə bəl) friendly (p. 38)

amniotic sac (am nē ot´ ik sak) a pouch that holds a developing baby before it is born (p. 472)

ample (am´ pəl) enough to satisfy (p. 221)

amusement (ə myüz´ mənt) entertainment (p. 49)

analysis (ə nal´ ə sis) a study of how parts fit together (p. 431)

analyze (an´ ə līz) examine; study the parts of (p. 506)

anew (ə nü´) again (p. 448)

anonymity (an ə nim´ ə tē) being unknown (p. 269)

antedated (an´ ti dāt ed) came before (p. 46)

anthology (an thol´ ə jē) a collection of writings (p. 430)

anticipated (an tis´ ə pāt id) expected (p. 258)

anxieties (ang zī´ ə tēz) fears (p. 130)

aphrodisiac (af rə dē´ zē ak) a food or drug that brings about sexual desire (p. 473)

apologetically (ə pol ə jet´ ik lē) in a way that shows regret (p. 223)

apology (ə pol´ ə je) an expression of regret for something one has done (p. 323)

appalled (ə pȯld´) filled with horror or dismay (p. 318)

apparent (ə par´ ənt) easily understood (p. 203)

appliances (ə plī´ əns ez) household equipment, such as the toaster, stove, and microwave (p. 532)

application (ap lə kā´ shən) use of something (p. 265)

appropriations (ə prō prē ā′ shənz) public money to be spent on certain things (p. 42)

aptitude (ap′ tə tüd) natural ability or talent (p. 60)

aquatic (ə kwat′ ik) living in or on water (p. 524)

archduke (ärch dük′) a royal rank equal to that of a prince (p. 538)

aright (ə rīt′) correctly (p. 89)

aristocratic (ə ris tə krat′ ik) of high social class (p. 10); noble or superior in appearance (p. 250)

armaments (är′ mə mənts) weapons (p. 281)

arms (ärmz) weapons (p. 275)

arsenals (är′ sə nəlz) storehouses for weapons (p. 268)

artillery (är til′ ər ē) branch of the military armed with large guns (p. 10)

ascertain (as ər tān′) find out (p. 31)

askew (ə skyü′) to one side (p. 87)

aspects (as′ pektz) different ways of looking at something (p. 511)

assail (ə sāl′) attack (p. 510)

assimilated (ə sim′ ə lāt ed) took in (p. 423)

assumption (ə sump′ shən) belief; set of ideas (p. 515)

asunder (ə sun′ dər) into separate parts (p. 447)

audacity (ȯ das′ ə tē) boldness (p. 315)

austere (ȯ stir′) stern and serious (p. 217)

avenger (ə venj′ ər) someone who does harm in return for a wrong (p. 99)

averted (ə vėrt′ ed) looking away (p. 9); turned away (p. 121)

B

babbling (bab′ ə ling) making a low, quiet sound like water (p. 523)

backbreaking (bak′ brā king) very difficult (p. 267)

backtracked (bak′ trakd) went back the way one came (p. 223)

balked (bȯkd) stopped and refused to go (p. 212)

banality (ba nal′ ə tē) the quality of having little meaning (pp. 473, 500)

bandied (ban′ dēd) exchanged (p. 553)

bantam (ban′ təm) a small barnyard fowl (p. 378)

barrier (bār′ ē ər) something that blocks (p. 24)

bathrobelike (bath′ rōb′ līk) like a robe worn after a bath (p. 524)

battalion (bə tal′ yən) a large group of soldiers (p. 543)

bawling (bȯl′ ing) crying loudly (p. 215)

beckoning (bek′ ən ing) signalling with a motion of the hand (p. 213)

begone (bi gȯn′) a command meaning "go away" (p. 305)

behalf (bi haf′) interest (p. 297)

belaboring (bi lā′ bər ing) going over again and again (p. 449)

belligerent (bə lij′ ər ənt) hostile; warlike (p. 224)

belongings (bi lȯng′ ingz) things a person owns (p. 550)

beneficial (ben ə fish′ əl) doing good; helpful (p. 109)

benzene (ben′ zēn) a colorless, flammable liquid (p. 211)

bequeathed (bi kwēᵺd′) gave to, as in a will (p. 10)

bestowed (bi stōd′) given (p. 137)

betel (bē′ tl) an Asian plant whose leaves are chewed (p. 363)

bewitching (bi wich′ ing) fascinating (p. 336)

biases (bī′ ə səz) ideas that have already been formed and are not based on new experiences; prejudices (p. 182)

bigoted (big′ ə tid) stubbornly holding a belief and disliking those who disagree (p. 426)

billiards (bil′ yərdz) a game similar to pool, played with a cue and solid balls on a large oblong table with raised edges (p. 331)

binding (bīn′ ding) sewing the edges together (p. 128)

blanched (blanchd) turned pale (p. 14)

blurted (blėrt′ ed) said suddenly and without thinking (p. 214)

boarding house (bôr′ ding hous) a place to live where one pays for a room and meals (p. 315)

bosom (bu̇z′ əm) the breast of a human (p. 227)

boutiques (bü tēks′) small shops that sell special, often expensive, goods (p. 469)

brandishing (bran′ dish ing) waving in a threatening way (pp. 433, 555)

a	hat	e	let	ī	ice	ȯ	order	u̇	put	sh	she	ə	a in about
ā	age	ē	equal	o	hot	oi	oil	ü	rule	th	thin		e in taken
ä	far	ėr	term	ō	open	ou	out	ch	child	ᵺ	then		i in pencil
â	care	i	it	ȯ	saw	u	cup	ng	long	zh	measure		o in lemon
													u in circus

Glossary **617**

breach (brēch) failure (p. 301); a break (p. 434)

breadth (bredth) width; extent (pp. 120, 551)

breakthrough (brāk′ thrü) a major accomplishment (p. 47)

breeching (brēch′ ing) strap of harness behind a horse's rear legs (p. 87)

brood (brüd) think about something in a moody way (p. 303)

buffet (bu fā′) a restaurant in which people serve themselves from a counter (p. 553)

bungalow (bung′ gə lō) a low, one-story house (p. 23)

burrs (bėrz) rough or prickly coverings around nuts (p. 118)

C

cadences (kād′ ns əz) rhythms of speech (p. 43)

calculating (kal′ kyə lāt ing) deciding; figuring out (p. 337)

calculation (kəl′ kyə lā′ shən) a mathematical process or answer (p. 55)

calligraphy (kə lig′ rə fē) artistic handwriting (p. 58)

capillaries (kap′ ə ler ē) tiny blood vessels (p. 525)

capricious (kə prish′ əs) acting on impulse; hard to predict (p. 45)

captivated (kap′ tə vāt ed) fascinated, deeply interested (p. 211)

caress (kə res′) a gentle touch (p. 95)

castes (kasts) social classes (p. 432)

catastrophic (kat ə strof′ ik) terrible (p. 43)

censored (sen′ sərd) kept away from people's view (p. 235)

certified (sėr′ tə fīd) confirmed that standards have been met (p. 59)

challenged (chal′ ənjd) dared; invited to do something difficult (p. 144)

cherished (cher′ isht) kept fondly in mind (p. 162)

chestnut (ches′ nut) a type of tree that has nuts enclosed in a prickly casing (p. 117)

Christendom (kris′ n dəm) all Christians (p. 416)

Christening (kris′ n ing) a ceremony for naming and baptizing a child (p. 335)

chronic (kron′ ik) continuing for a long time (p. 305)

cicada (sə kā′ də) a type of large insect; the males make a loud, humming noise (p. 523)

cipher (sī′ fər) a zero (p. 38)

circulation (sėr kyə lā′ shən) delivery of a newspaper to stores and homes (p. 507)

circumstance (sėr′ kəm stans) an event; a situation (p. 491)

circumstances (sėr′ kəm stans es) conditions (p. 49); the way someone lives (p. 160)

civil service (siv′ əl sėr′ vis) jobs that nongovernment workers do for the government, such as post office workers (p. 199)

civility (sə vil′ ə tē) courtesy (p. 449)

classed (klast) grouped (p. 145)

cleansed (klenzd) clean; free of dirt (p. 463)

cliché (klē shā′) an expression or idea that has been used over and over (p. 471)

client (klī′ ənt) a customer; a person for whom one does a professional service (p. 7)

colleague (kol′ eg) a person who works at the same level (p. 506)

collective (kə lek′ tiv) grouped together (p. 427)

commentary (kom′ ən ter ē) an explanation; a series of remarks (p. 498)

commiserate (kə miz′ ə rāt) to express sorrow and sympathy (p. 108)

committed (kə mit′ ed) done or performed (p. 303)

commonwealth (kom′ ən welth′) the community as a whole; the nation (p. 489)

communion (kə myü′ nyən) a sharing of feelings (p. 193)

compartment (kəm pärt′ mənt) an enclosed space (p. 27)

compass (kum′ pəs) limited area (p. 86)

compatriots (kəm pā′ trē əts) people from the same country (p. 428)

compel (kəm pel′) force (p. 48)

compelling (kəm pel′ ing) forceful (p. 221)

compensate (kom′ pən sāt) repay (p. 457)

competitive (kəm pet′ ə tiv) involving the effort to win (p. 202)

compiled (kəm pīld′) put together information into a record (p. 63)

compliance (kəm plī′ əns) agreeing to a demand (p. 219)

complicated (kom′ plə kā tid) difficult; hard (p. 41); not easy to understand (pp. 66, 538)

complicity (kəm plis′ ə tē) state of being involved in a wrong action (p. 434)

comprehensive (kom pri hen′ siv) knowing (p. 8); complete (p. 513)

compulsions (kəm pul′ shənz) the forces or reasons behind an action (p. 260)

compunction (kəm pungk′ shən) strong feelings of guilt (p. 508)

computes (kəm pyütz′) finds a number; works mathematical problems (p. 39)

computed (kəm pyüt′ id) counted (p. 491)

conceived (kən sēvd′) formed in the mind (p. 441)

conception (kən sep′ shən) an idea; a mental picture (p. 430)

concisely (kən sīs′ lē) briefly (p. 432)

concussions (kən kush′ ənz) shocks; injuries (p. 422)

confidential (kon fə den′ shəl) meant to be secret (p. 549)

confirmed (kən fėrmd′) made sure by having someone else agree (p. 249)

conflict (kon′ flikt) a battle; the fighting (p. 117)

confounded (kən foun′ did) confused; puzzled (p. 216)

congregate (kong′ grə gāt) collect or gather (p. 223)

conscientious (kon shē en′ shəs) careful to do things right (p. 96)

consecrate (kon′ sə krāt) dedicate to a serious purpose (p. 441)

consequence (kon′ sə kwens) importance (p. 13)

consequently (kon′ sə kwent lē) as a result (p. 38)

conservative (kən sėr′ və tiv) not liking change (p. 45)

consolatory (kən sol′ ə tôr ē) comforting (p. 216)

constituted (kon′ stə tüt ed) made up (p. 432)

constraint (kən strānt′) force that limits freedom of thought or action (p. 424)

constructively (kən struk′ tiv lē) helpfully (p. 274)

consumption (kən sump′ shən) the process of eating or drinking (p. 58)

contemplated (kän′ təm plā tid) looked at thoughtfully (p. 215)

contemplation (kon təm plā′ shən) thoughtfulness (p. 505)

contemporary (kən tem′ pə rer ē) current; modern (p. 427)

contemptuous (kən temp′ chü əs) showing dislike (p. 332)

context (kon′ tekst) the setting or situation (p. 266)

contorted (kən tôrt′ id) twisted; hard to follow (p. 169)

contradiction (kon trə dik′ shən) something that means its opposite (p. 42)

contrivances (kən trī′ vəns əz) mechanical devices (p. 46)

conveyed (kən vād′) brought from one place to another; carried (p. 190)

convulsed (kən vulst′) shaken or pulled jerkily (p. 14)

convulsively (kən vul′ siv lē) shaking violently (p. 422)

coolies (kü′ lēz) unskilled workers who do odd jobs (p. 205)

cope (kōp) manage successfully (p. 198)

coppice (kop′ is) a dense growth of bushes; a small wood (p. 87)

cormorant (kôr′ mər ənt) a water bird (p. 524)

coroner (kôr′ ə nər) the official who decides the cause of death (p. 16)

correlate (kôr′ ə lāt) show a relationship (p. 433)

corrugated (kôr′ ə gāt ed) wrinkled (p. 39)

corrupt (kə rupt′) dishonest (p. 259)

cosmopolitan (koz mə pol′ ə tən) including people from many places (p. 105)

coteries (kō′ tər ēz) groups of people who meet often (p. 215)

counterbalanced (koun tər bal′ ənsd) used one act to make up for another (p. 457)

counterpart (koun′ tər pärt) equal (p. 274)

couple (kup′ əl) attach; link together (p. 554)

courtesy (kėr′ tə sē) an act of politeness (p. 202)

coverage (kuv′ ər ij) the way something is reported in newspapers or on television (p. 56)

cowed (koud) frightened by threats (p. 119)

credence (krēd′ ns) belief; proof (p. 221)

a	hat	e	let	ī	ice	ô	order	ù	put	sh	she		ə	a	in about
ā	age	ē	equal	o	hot	oi	oil	ü	rule	th	thin			e	in taken
ä	far	ėr	term	ō	open	ou	out	ch	child	ᵀH	then			i	in pencil
â	care	i	it	ȯ	saw	u	cup	ng	long	zh	measure			o	in lemon
														u	in circus

Glossary **619**

criticisms (krit´ ə siz əmz) judgments that find fault (p. 541)

crucial (krü´ shel) very important (p. 268)

cruelty (krü´ əl tē) something that causes pain or suffering (p. 163)

crusty (krus´ tē) gruff; stern in manner (p. 372)

cubicle (kyü´ bə kəl) a small room (p. 217)

cul-de-sac (kul də sak´) a dead-end street with houses all around it (p. 234)

curdled (ker´ dlid) spoiled (p. 128)

currency (kėr´ ən sē) the form of money a country uses (p. 463)

curry (kėr´ ē) a food dish seasoned with a spicy powder (p. 201)

curt (kėrt) short (p. 30)

curtailing (kėr tāl´ ing) cutting short (p. 427)

curtly (kėrt´ lē) rudely (p. 508)

D

dashed (dashd) ran quickly (p. 118)

data (dā´ tə) information (pp. 42, 56)

deadening (ded´ n ing) making less intense or lively, (p. 169)

debarked (di bärkt´) got off, as from a ship (p. 68)

debased (di bāst´) lowered in worth (p. 499)

debilitating (di bil´ ə tāt ing) causing someone to be unable to function in daily life (p. 514)

decade (dek´ ād) a period of 10 years (p. 466)

deceit (di sēt´) a trick (p. 422)

decrepit (di krep´ it) worn out (p. 434)

deductions (di duk´ shənz) answers found by reasoning (p. 7)

defensive (di fen´ siv) done to defend oneself (p. 259)

deference (def´ ər əns) respect; courteous respect for another's wishes (pp. 110, 492)

definitively (di fin´ ə tiv lē) finally; completely (p. 498)

defray (di frā´) pay the costs (p. 9)

degenerated (di jen´ ə rā ted) became much worse (p. 429)

deliberately (di lib´ ər it lē) carefully considered; on purpose (pp. 265, 314)

delicacy (del´ ə kə sē) a special, enjoyable food (p. 223)

delicious (di lish´ əs) delightful (p. 174)

delusions (di lü´ zhənz) false or imaginary visions; things a person hears or sees that are not real (p. 307)

departing (di pärt´ ing) leaving; going away (p. 357)

deplorable (di plôr´ ə bəl) terrible (p. 489)

deployment (di ploi´ mənt) the spreading of troops or weapons in a larger area (p. 268)

deposition (dep ə zish´ ən) a statement (p. 30)

depravity (di prav´ ə tē) a wicked act (p. 430)

depression (di presh´ ən) a state of sadness (p. 474)

depriving (di prīv´ ing) making someone do without something (p. 512)

deranged (di rānjd´) mentally disturbed (p. 515)

deserted (di zėr´ tid) empty (p. 205)

designated (dez´ ig nāt id) selected for a role or purpose (p. 58)

despair (di spâr´) a heavy feeling of hopelessness (p. 144)

despised (di spizd´) looked down upon (p. 323)

despising (di spiz´ ing) looking down on (p. 510)

despite (di spīt´) in spite of (p. 539)

destiny (des´ tə nē) fate (p. 99); a person's fate or future (p. 227)

detached (di tacht´) not connected (p. 429)

detachment (di tach´ mənt) a small military unit of soldiers (p. 118)

deterrent (di tėr´ ənt) something that prevents or discourages an action (p. 267)

detest (di test´) hate (p. 515)

detonations (de tə nā´ shənz) explosions (p. 275)

detract (di trakt´) take away (p. 441)

detrimental (det rə men´ tl) harmful (p. 426)

development (di vel´ əp mənt) an area prepared for commercial use (p. 25); growth, progress (p. 265)

dictator (dik´ tā tər) the ruler in a government with only one person in charge (p. 130)

dictatorial (dik tə tôr´ ē əl) cruel (p. 500)

differentiated (dif ə ren´ shē āt id) shown to be different (p. 426)

dilapidated (də lap´ ə dā tid) shabby from neglect (p. 464)

dilemma (də lem´ ə) a situation that requires a difficult choice (p. 428)

director (də rek´ tər) a person who directs or manages a business (p. 551)

disability (dis ə bil′ ə tē) a weakened physical or mental condition (p. 303)

disarmament (dis är′ mə mənt) the decrease of weapons (p. 281)

disbelief (dis bi lēf′) a refusal to believe (p. 315)

disbursed (dis bėrsd′) paid out or handed out (p. 60)

disciplinarian (dis ə plə ner′ ē ən) a person who makes sure rules are carried out (p. 500)

discipline (dis′ ə plin) punishment given as a correction (p. 220)

disciplined (dis′ ə plind) trained to act according to certain rules (p. 446)

discomfort (dis kum′ fərt) the feeling of being uneasy or not comfortable (p. 468)

disconcertingly (dis kən sėrt′ ing lē) in an upsetting way (p. 107)

disconsolate (dis kon′ sə lit) very sad (p. 331)

discord (dis′ kôrd) arguments; disagreements (p. 251)

discordance (dis kôrd′ ns) a harsh, confused sound (p. 424)

discordant (dis kôrd′ nt) unpleasant; disturbing (p. 335)

discoursing (dis kôrs′ ing) discussing (p. 492)

discrepancies (dis krep′ ən sēz) differences; conflicts (p. 422)

disembark (dis em bärk′) to get out of (a boat) or off (a plane) (p. 463)

disembodied (dis em bod′ ēd) existing apart from a body (p. 235)

disfigured (dis fig′ yərd) damaged or spoiled (p. 223)

disinfection (dis in fek′ shən) getting rid of germs that can cause disease (p. 66)

dislodge (dis loj′) loosen; separate (p. 511)

dismissive (dis mis′ iv) in a manner that discards or sends away (p. 425)

disobliging (dis ə blīj′ ing) going against the wishes of (p. 492)

disparity (dis par′ ə tē) difference (p. 425)

dispatch (dis pach′) send off quickly to a place (p. 549)

dispatched (dis pacht′) sent out (p. 65)

dispel (dis pel′) make disappear (p. 17)

dispensable (dis pen′ sə bəl) not necessary (p. 49)

dispersed (dis pėrsd′) scattered in different directions (p. 434)

dispirited (dis pər′ ə tid) discouraged; depressed (p. 180)

displacedness (dis plās′ id nis) a state of being out of place or in the wrong place (p. 472)

disputation (dis pyə tā′ shən) a discussion or debate (p. 169)

dissolute (dis′ ə lüt) wicked; of bad character (p. 10)

dissuaded (di swād′ ed) persuaded someone not to take a certain action (p. 260)

dissuasion (di swā′ zhən) discouraging someone from an action (p. 108)

distinguished (dis ting′ gwisht) appearing important or famous (p. 249)

distracted (dis trak′ tid) took one's attention away from something (p. 506)

divergent (də vėr′ jənt) drawing apart; differing (p. 424)

diversion (də vėr′ zhən) something that entertains (p. 526)

divert (də vėrt′) turn aside (p. 44)

divine (də vīn′) coming from a god (p. 193)

domination (dom ə nā′ shən) control or rule of one person or group by another (p. 467)

draught (draft) (American *draft*) a current of air (p. 333)

dubious (dü′ bē əs) causing doubt as to worth or truth (p. 539)

dumbfounded (dum found′ id) stunned into silence (p. 425)

dunce (duns) a stupid person (p. 106)

duration (du rā′ shən) the period of time that something lasts (p. 499)

dwells (dwelz) lives; makes a home (p. 299)

dwindling (dwin′ dling) getting smaller (p. 128)

dynamic (dī nam′ ik) full of energy; changing (p. 429)

dystrophy (dis′ trə fē) illness caused by poor nutrition (p. 59)

a	hat	e	let	ī	ice	ô	order	ù	put	sh	she	ə {	a	in about
ā	age	ē	equal	o	hot	oi	oil	ü	rule	th	thin		e	in taken
ä	far	ėr	term	ō	open	ou	out	ch	child	ᴛʜ	then		i	in pencil
â	care	i	it	ò	saw	u	cup	ng	long	zh	measure		o	in lemon
													u	in circus

Glossary **621**

E

ebbing (eb´ bing) fading away; becoming less (p. 322)

eccentrically (ek sen´ trik al lē) oddly, in an unexpected way (p. 59)

eclectic (e klek´ tik) made up of things from all different places (p. 233)

ecliptic (i klip´ tik) circle formed where the plane of Earth's orbit and another object cross (p. 59)

effective (ə fek´ tiv) true; actual (p. 352)

elderly (el´ dər lē) old (p. 27)

electric eels (i lek´ trik ēlz) long, thin fish that can produce an electric current (p. 242)

elevated (el´ ə vā tid) raised up (p. 130)

eliminate (i lim´ ə nāt) get rid of (p. 48)

emanating (em ə nat´ ing) coming out (p. 235)

embalming (em bäm´ ing) preserving; making something smell good (p. 214)

embassy (em´ bə sē) a building owned by a foreign government, used for diplomats from that country (p. 468)

embattled (em bat´ ld) locked in a struggle (p. 38); ready for battle (p. 449)

embrace (em brās´) adopt; welcome (p. 226)

emigrate (em ə grāt´) leaving one's country (p. 511)

emitted (i mit´ ed) sent out (p. 96)

emotionally (i mō´ shə nəl lē) with strong feelings (p. 250)

encamp (en kamp´) set up camp (p. 11)

encroached (en krōcht´) gradually entered or occupied (p. 422)

endeavor (en dev´ ər) a sincere attempt (p. 450)

endowed (en dou´ əd) provided with a talent or quality (p. 550)

engulf (en gulf´) swallow up; surround completely (p. 448)

enlarges (en lärj´ əz) makes bigger (p. 352)

enmity (en´ mə tē) hatred (p. 508)

ensign (en´ sīn) a flag (p. 499)

entailing (en tāl´ ing) resulting in (p. 493)

entice (en tīs´) tempt (p. 429)

entrusted (en trust´ ed) to hand over for care (p. 188)

enviable (en´ vē ə bəl) good; to be desired (p. 513)

epidemic (ep ə dem´ ik) a widespread problem; the quick spread of disease (p. 515)

epithets (ep´ ə thets) insulting words or phrases (p. 500)

epochs (ep´ əks) long periods of history (p. 422)

equality (i kwol´ ə tē) state of being equal (p. 48)

equalize (ē´ kwə līz) make equal (p. 457)

equivalent (i kwiv´ ə lənt) something that is equal (p. 43)

eradicate (i rad´ ə kāt) get rid of (p. 449)

erected (i rek´ tid) put upright; built (p. 144)

escalation (es kə lā´ shən) an increase; rapid growth (p. 281)

essence (es´ ns) the basic quality of something (p. 432)

esteem (e stēm´) think highly of (p. 492)

etherealization (i thir ē ə liz ā´ shən) making things lighter (p. 46)

eucalyptus (yü kə lip´ təs) a tall tree with strong-smelling leaves (p. 204)

evaders (i vād´ ėrz) people who avoid doing something (p. 259)

evaluate (i val´ yü āt) judge the worth of (p. 423)

evenly (ē´ vən lē) without a change in tone (p. 317)

exaggerate (eg zaj´ ə rāt) make something greater or more serious than it really is (p. 162)

exasperating (eg zas´ pə rāt ing) annoying (p. 425)

excess (ek ses´) more than is needed; too much (p. 180)

excessive (ek ses´ iv) too much (p. 110)

exclusive (ek sklü´ siv) having a lot of style; in fashion (p. 23); keeping most people out; reserved for a small, select group (p. 234)

excursion (ek skėr´ zhən) a trip; an expedition (pp. 62, 97)

executive (eg zek´ yə tiv) relating to the branch of government that carries out the laws (p. 267)

exigencies (ek´ sə jən sēz) things that demand immediate attention (p. 48)

existential (eg zi sten´ shəl) based on real experience (p. 251)

expansionism (ek span´ shə niz əm) a country's practice of spreading out to gain land (p. 259)

expectantly (ek spek´ tənt lē) eagerly waiting to hear or see something (p. 321)

expenditures (ek spen´ də chərz) spending (p. 259)

expletives (ek´ splə tivz) curse words (p. 175)

exploitation (ek sploi tā′ shən) the unfair use of something for selfish reasons (p. 425); the use of a person or resource for selfish purposes (p. 467)

exportation (ek spôr tā′ shən) being sent to another country for sale (p. 493)

extinguished (ek sting′ gwisht) put out (p. 169)

extraneous (ek strā′ nē əs) not necessary (p. 61)

extraordinarily (ek strôr də ner′ i lē) remarkably; unusually (p. 509)

extraordinary (ek strôr də ner′ ē) remarkable (p. 199); very unusual (p. 468)

F

facet (fas′ it) one part or angle (p. 427)

faction (fak′ shən) a group; often one that disagrees with others (p. 96)

famine (fam′ ən) a severe lack of food (p. 555)

fancy (fan′ sē) imagination (p. 86)

fatigue (fə tēg′) a tired feeling (p. 95)

favorable (fā′ vər ə bəl) promoting success (p. 25)

feigned (fānd) pretended (p. 96)

fiancé (fē än sā′) the man a woman is engaged to marry (p. 332)

fiasco (fē as′ kō) a complete failure (p. 316)

fickle (fik′ əl) not faithful; not reliable (p. 188)

filial piety (fil′ eəl pī′ ə tē) respect for family members (p. 137)

filth (filth) foul matter; dirt (p. 322)

financial broker (fə nan′ shəl brō′ kər) one who helps others invest money (p. 24)

finery (fī′ nər ē) elegant, dressy clothing (p. 241)

finite (fī′ nīt) limited (p. 44)

fit (fit) sudden outburst (p. 301)

flag (flag) lessen (p. 511)

flamethrower (flām′ thrō′ ər) a military weapon that sends out a stream of burning fuel (p. 526)

flawless (flô′ lis) perfect; without any marks (p. 299)

fluently (flü′ ənt lē) using language easily (p. 106)

flurry (flėr′ ē) burst of activity (p. 400)

fodder (fod′ ər) dry food for farm animals (p. 119)

footwear (fút′ wâr) anything worn on the feet (p. 523)

foppishly (fop′ ish lē) vainly; overly proud of one's looks (p. 217)

fore (fôr) the front part (p. 491)

forebears (fôr′ bârz) ancestors (p. 446)

foresee (fôr sē′) know in advance (p. 24)

formalise (fôr′ mə līz) (American *formalize*) to make official; to sign an agreement (p. 274)

formalities (fôr mal′ ə tēz) official rules; customs (p. 68)

formulate (fôr′ myə lāt) plan (p. 449)

forsaken (fôr sā′ kən) abandoned; left alone (p. 111)

forthwith (fôrth with′) immediately (p. 259)

fortnight (fôrt′ nīt) a period of two weeks (p. 12)

fragrance (frā′ grəns) sweetness of smell (p. 204)

frank (frangk) bluntly honest (p. 463)

free association (frē ə sō sē ā′ shən) a quick response to pictures and words (p. 514)

frenetic (frə net′ ik) very excited; active (p. 181)

frenzy (fren′ zē) a wild excitement (p. 77)

fricassee (frik ə sē′) a dish made with cut-up pieces of meat in gravy (p. 491)

frivolously (friv′ ə ləs lē) not seriously; playfully (p. 428)

function (fungk′ shən) a normal use or activity (p. 473)

functioning (fungk′ shən ing) working properly (p. 60)

fundamentals (fun də men′ tlz) the basics (p. 48)

futons (fü′ tonz) thin mattresses usually used on the floor or on a frame (p. 523)

G

gabs (gabz) slang word for *talks*; chatters (p. 541)

gangly (gang′ glē) tall, thin, and ungraceful (p. 372)

gashes (gash′ əz) long, deep cuts (p. 299)

gemstone (jem′ stōn) a jewel (p. 193)

gendarme (zhän′ därm) a police officer (p. 553)

gender (jen′ dər) sex; male or female (p. 58)

gestured (jes′ chərd) made a motion with hands (p. 507)

a	hat	e	let	ī	ice	ô	order	ú	put	sh	she		ə	a	in about
ā	age	ē	equal	o	hot	oi	oil	ü	rule	th	thin			e	in taken
ä	far	ėr	term	ō	open	ou	out	ch	child	ᴛʜ	then			i	in pencil
â	care	i	it	ò	saw	u	cup	ng	long	zh	measure			o	in lemon
														u	in circus

Glossary

gland (gland) a part of the body that helps other parts of the body work (p. 513)

glimmered (glim´ ėrd) gave off a dim light (p. 39)

global alliance (glō´ bəl ə lī´ əns) an agreement among world nations (p. 450)

global (glō´ bəl) worldwide (p. 267)

gory (gôr´ ē) stained with blood (p. 301)

gourd (gôrd) a kind of vegetable that grows on a vine (p. 117)

grave (grāv) serious (p. 383)

graveyard (grāv´ yärd) a place where people are buried (p. 352)

gravity (grav´ ə tē) seriousness (p. 280)

graybeards (grā´ birdz) old men (p. 363)

grievance (grē´ vəns) something to complain about (p. 489)

grieved (grēvd) caused harm or sadness (p. 383)

grossly (grōs´ lē) totally (p. 211)

grudgingly (gruj´ ing lē) unwillingly (p. 110)

guarantor (gar´ ən tôr) a person or thing that promises a certain result (p. 281)

guavas (gwä´ vəz) a kind of tropical fruit (p. 128)

guffawed (gu fȯd´) laughed loudly (p. 510)

H

haggard (hag´ ərd) looking worn because of worry (p. 8); looking thin and tired (p. 42)

hale (hāl) full of life (p. 25)

hallow (hal´ ō) set apart as holy (p. 441)

handpicked (hand´ pikt´) chosen carefully (p. 554)

harmony (här´ mə nē) agreement (p. 161); a pleasant agreement in feeling or actions (p. 472)

hastened (hā´ snd) hurried (p. 137)

hastily (hās´ tə lē) quickly (p. 80)

hazard (haz´ ərd) something dangerous (p. 60)

headmistress (hed mis´ tris) female principal of a school (p. 198)

hearsay (hir´ sā) gossip (p. 553)

heartfelt (härt´ felt) deeply felt; sincere (p. 321)

heartily (här´ tl ē) with enthusiasm (pp. 267, 331); completely; with excitement; with all one's heart (p. 401)

hearty (här´ tē) sincere (p. 297)

hectic (hek´ tik) confused; full of fast activity (p. 212)

hegemonic (hi jem´ ən ik) having influence over others (p. 260)

heightened (hīt´ nd) made stronger (p. 190)

heirs (ârz) people who inherit something (p. 446)

hence (hens) from this time (p. 220); from here (p. 416)

herbalist (hėr´ bə list) a person who makes medicines from herbs (p. 109)

heritage (her´ ə tij) what is handed down from earlier generations (p. 447)

hesitated (hez´ ə tā ted) stopped (p. 121)

Hindi (hin´ dē) a language widely spoken in India (p. 199)

hoard (hôrd) save for the future (p. 373)

holster (hōl´ stər) a case for a pistol (p. 94)

holy writ (hō´ lē rit) a piece of religious writing such as the Bible (p. 373)

homily (hom´ ə lē) a sermon (p. 107)

hooligans (hü´ lə gənz) troublemakers; young men who do vicious or violent acts (p. 550)

hornswoggling (hȯ(r)n´ swägəl ing) tricking someone (p. 41)

hospitality (hos pə tal´ ə tē) the friendly treatment of guests (p. 11); the practice of going out of one's way to treat guests well (p. 137)

hostile (hos´ tl) angrily opposed to (p. 110)

hubbub (hub´ ub) noise; sound of people all talking at once (p. 142)

humidity (hyü mid´ ə tē) the amount of moisture in the air (p. 57)

humiliating (hyü mil´ ē āt ing) causing shame or loss of dignity (p. 425)

humiliation (hyü mil ē ā´ shən) the state of being disgraced or shamed (p. 221)

hydroponics (hī drə pon´ iks) a method of growing plants in water (p. 46)

hyperactive (hī pər ak´ tiv) very active (p. 524)

I

idiosyncrasy (id ē ō sing´ krə sē) a habit or odd response that a person has (p. 135)

ignition (ig nish´ ən) a car's starter (p. 25)

ignorance (ig´ nər əns) lack of knowledge or understanding (p. 227)

illiterate (i lit´ ər it) not knowing how to read or write (p. 227)

illusionist (i lü´ zhən ist) a magician (p. 39)

immemorial (im ə môr´ ē əl) beyond the limits of memory (p. 422)

imminent (im´ ə nənt) about to happen (p. 425)

immortal (i môr´ tl) one who lives forever (p. 243)

impaled (im pāld´) speared; stuck on a sharp stick (p. 372)

impending (im pen´ ding) about to happen (p. 14)

impenetrable (im pen´ ə trə bəl) not able to be pierced or broken (p. 43)

imperative (im per´ ə tiv) commanding (p. 39)

imperishable (im per´ i shə bəl) not able to die (p. 505)

impingement (im pinj´ mənt) the act of intruding or disturbing (p. 45)

implore (im plôr´) beg (p. 111)

importuning (im pôr tün´ ing) begging (p. 489)

impressed (im presd´) affected deeply (p. 14)

improvised (im´ prə vīzd) invented or put together on the spur of the moment (p. 67)

in earnest (in ėr´ nist) sincere; honest (p. 174)

inability (in ə bil´ ə tē) lack of ability (p. 198)

inattentive (in ə ten´ tiv) not paying attention (p. 203)

incalculable (in kal´ kyə lə bəl) not possible to measure in advance (p. 43)

incandescent (in kən des´ nt) glowing; very bright (p. 372)

incapable (in kā´ pə bəl) without the ability (p. 109)

incessantly (in ses´ nt lē) without stopping (p. 159)

incision (in sizh´ ən) a thin cut (p. 99)

inclemencies (in klem´ ən sēz) storms; discomforts (p. 493)

inclination (in klə nā´ shən) a way of thinking (p. 23); a liking (p. 212); a leaning toward something (p. 428)

incomprehensible (in kom pri hen´ sə bəl) not capable of being understood (p. 201)

incomprehension (in kom pri hen´ shən) lack of understanding (p. 425)

inconceivably (in kən sēv´ ə blē) not able to be thought about or understood (p. 508)

incongruous (in kong´ grü əs) not in agreement with each other; not belonging together (p. 233)

inconvenience (in kən vē´ nyəns) trouble or annoyance (p. 26)

incredible (in kred´ ə bəl) too unlikely to be believed (p. 464)

incur (in kėr´) bring upon oneself (p. 492)

indication (in də kā´ shən) sign, hint (p. 511)

indications (in də kā´ shənz) signs (p. 337)

indifferent (in dif´ ər ənt) not caring (p. 56)

indistinct (in dis tingkt´) not clear (p. 86)

indivisibility (in də viz ə bil´ ə tē) state of not being able to be divided (p. 429)

indoctrination (in dok trə nā´ shən) teachings from a certain point of view (p. 432)

ineligible (in el´ ə jə bəl) not qualified (p. 219)

ineradicable (in i rad´ ə kə bəl) impossible to erase or remove (p. 98)

inertias (in ėr´ shəz) desires not to move or change; stillness (p. 182)

inevitable (in ev´ ə tə bəl) sure to happen (pp. 88, 493)

inexorably (in ek´ sər ə blē) in a way that will not be stopped (p. 433)

inexplicable (in ik splik´ ə bəl) not possible to explain (p. 119)

infamy (in´ fə mē) disgrace (p. 334)

infected (in fek´ tid) sick; diseased (p. 128)

infectious (in fek´ shəs) easily spread from person to person (p. 251)

infer (in fėr´) conclude (p. 251)

infinitely (in´ fə nit lē) without any limits (p. 108)

inflexible (in flek´ sə bəl) stiff; rigid (p. 96)

infuriating (in fyur´ ē āt ing) causing great anger (p. 315)

ingenious (in jē´ nyəs) clever (p. 45)

a	hat	e	let	ī	ice	ô	order	ù	put	sh	she	ə	a in about
ā	age	ē	equal	o	hot	oi	oil	ü	rule	th	thin		e in taken
ä	far	ėr	term	ō	open	ou	out	ch	child	ᵺ	then		i in pencil
â	care			i	it	ò	saw	u	cup	ng	long	zh	measure		o in lemon
													u in circus

Glossary **625**

ingenuity (in jə nü´ ə tē) cleverness; inventive skill (p. 467)

inkling (ing´ kling) a hint or idea (p. 218)

innermost (in´ ər mōst) most personal; deepest (p. 162)

inscrutable (in skrü´ tə bəl) not easily understood (p. 217)

insignificant (in sig nif´ ə kənt) small; not important (p. 168)

insolence (in´ sə ləns) rudeness (p. 553)

insufficiencies (in sə fish´ ən sēz) lack of enough of something (p. 182)

insular (in´ sə lər) limited in outlook and experience (p. 199)

integers (in´ tə jərz) whole numbers such as 1, 2, 3 (p. 47)

integrity (in teg´ rə tē) honesty (p. 258)

intellectual (in tə lek´ chü əl) having to do with the mind (p. 46)

intensified (in ten´ sə fīd) became stronger or deeper (pp. 11, 235)

intensity (in ten´ sə tē) strength (pp. 200, 258)

intention (in ten´ shən) aim; plan to do something (pp. 89, 275)

intermediate (in tėr mē´ dē it) the middle (p. 509)

interminable (in tėr´ mə nə bəl) endless (p. 174)

internal medicine (in tėr´ nl med´ ə sən) a field of medicine that deals with diseases of the organs inside the body (p. 512)

internship (in´ tėrn ship) a time of supervised training (p. 59)

interred (in tėrd´) buried (p. 428)

intervene (in tər vēn´) come in between (p. 221)

intimate (in´ tə mit) very close (p. 433)

intimidated (in tim´ ə dāt id) frightened (p. 199)

intricate (in´ trə kit) complex; difficult to arrange (p. 213)

intrigues (in trēgz´) secrets or underhanded plans (p. 332)

introspections (in trə spek´ shənz) personal thoughts or ideas (p. 429)

intuition (in tü ish´ ən) way of knowing without proof (pp. 7, 47)

invaluable (in val´ yü ə bəl) beyond price (p. 427)

invasion (in vā´ zhən) an entering by force (p. 120)

inventory (in´ vən tôr ē) the stock of supplies (p. 56)

invest (in vest´) use money for later profit (p. 24)

invoke (in vōk´) call upon for help (p. 449)

ironic (ī ron´ ik) mocking (p. 425)

irrefutable (i ref´ yə tə bəl) impossible to prove wrong (p. 427)

irritated (ir´ ə tāt əd) annoyed (p. 28)

isolated (ī´ sə lāt id) kept apart from others (p. 251)

jalousies (jal´ ə sez) window shutters or blinds (p. 128)

jasmine (jaz´ mən) a vine or bush with sweet-smelling flowers (p. 203)

jubilant (jü´ bə lənt) happily excited (p. 363)

jurisdiction (jür is dik´ shən) the area where one has authority (p. 432)

K

karma (kär´ mə) fate; destiny (p. 189)

kilometers (kə lom´ ə tərz) distances of 1,000 meters; each equals about .62 mile (p. 352)

kimonos (kə mō´ nəz) long, loose robes with wide sleeves; the robe is tied with a sash (p. 522)

kohl (kōl) dark powder used as eye makeup (p. 200)

laborious (lə bôr´ ē əs) requiring long, hard work (pp. 182, 193)

lacerated (las´ ə rāt id) torn (p. 432)

laden (lād´ n) loaded with; heavy (p. 48)

lament (lə ment´) regret; express concern about (p. 234)

lamentations (lam en tā´ shənz) cries of grief or sorrow (p. 221)

landscape (land´ skāp) a stretch of land forming a single scene (p. 79)

latrines (lə trēnz´) toilets (191); small buildings used for public bathrooms (p. 466)

latter (lat´ ər) the second of two things mentioned (p. 159)

lavatory (lav´ ə tôr ē) a bathroom (p. 471)

lavishly (lav´ ish lē) generously; using more than is necessary (p. 214)

lawsuit (lo´ süt) a complaint brought before a court of law (p. 538)

leasehold (lēs´ hōld) property held by lease (p. 87)

leave (lēv) a vacation; permission to be away from work (p. 105)

liberated (lib′ ə rāt id) free from outside control (p. 299)

linens (lin′ ənz) household goods made of cloth, such as sheets and towels (p. 532)

lingering (ling′ gər ing) lasting a long time; staying on (p. 80)

liquor (lik′ ər) a strong alcoholic drink (p. 554)

loathing (lō′ ᴛHing) intense dislike (p. 15)

loathsome (lōᴛH′ səm) disgusting (p. 16)

locks (loks) the hair of the head (p. 301)

lofty (lȯf′ tē) high (p. 117)

logical (loj′ ə kəl) reasonable (p. 7)

longed (lȯngd) greatly wished for (p. 332)

lot (lot) fate; state in life (p. 226)

lugubrious (lə gü′ brē əs) extremely sad; mournful (p. 180)

lush (lush) having lots of plants (p. 362); growing thick with plants (p. 463)

luster (lus′ tər) shine (p. 401)

luxurious (lug zhu̇r′ ē əs) quite splendid and comfortable (p. 465)

M

magnitude (mag′ nə tüd) greatness; importance (p. 227)

maintaining (mān tān′ ing) insisting (p. 266)

makeshift (māk′ shift) a temporary substitute (p. 499)

malice (mal′ is) ill will (p. 337)

mallets (mal′ itz) short-handled, heavy hammers (p. 190)

maneuvers (mə nü′ vərz) changes in course or position (p. 61)

manhood (man′ hu̇d) courage (p. 303)

mania (mā′ nē ə) an intense, almost insane, excitement (p. 11)

manifested (man′ ə fest ed) showed (p. 428)

manifold (man′ ə fōld) of many kinds (p. 9)

manipulates (mə nip′ yə lāts) handles or manages (p. 45)

manipulations (mə nip yə lā′ shənz) actions of control or operation (p. 64)

manner (man′ ər) kinds (p. 242)

manor (man′ ər) the main house on an estate (p. 12)

manure (mə nu̇r′) animal waste used as fertilizer (p. 191)

matriarchs (mā′ trē ärks) women who rule their families (p. 214)

maximum (mak′ sə məm) the greatest possible (p. 450)

mayflies (mā′ flīz) insects that hatch in the water and live only a few days (p. 367)

meanderings (mē an′ dər ingz) winding paths (p. 427)

measure (mezh′ ər) an amount (p. 441)

meddle (med′ l) interfere (p. 319)

mediate (mē′ dē āt) to help settle a disagreement (p. 260)

melancholy (mel′ ən kol ē) sadness (p. 42)

membrane (mem′ brān) a thin layer of material (p. 431)

mercenary (mėr′ sə ner ē) concerned only with making money (p. 429)

merciless (mėr′ si lis) cruel; without mercy (p. 85)

mere (mir) not more than (p. 506)

merit (mer′ it) a positive quality (p. 23)

metropolis (mə trop′ ə lis) a city (p. 7)

militarisation (mil ə tu̇ rī zā′ shən) (American *militarization*) the process of being taken over or used by the military (p. 266)

millennia (mə len′ ē ə) thousands of years (p. 471)

millet (mil′ it) a cereal grain whose small seeds are used for food (p. 223)

mimicking (mim′ ik ing) copying closely (p. 473)

mince (mins) walk with very short steps (p. 523)

mingle (ming′ gəl) mix (p. 297)

minimize (min′ ə mīz) make as small as possible (p. 457)

ministers (min′ ə stərz) high government officials (p. 465)

minutely (mī nüt′ lē) paying attention to small details (p. 219)

mirage (mə räzh′) an optical illusion; something you see that is not really there (p. 169)

mischance (mis chans′) bad luck (p. 301)

a	hat	e	let	ī	ice	ȯ	order	u̇	put	sh	she
ā	age	ē	equal	o	hot	oi	oil	ü	rule	th	thin
ä	far	ėr	term	ō	open	ou	out	ch	child	ᴛH	then
â	care	i	it	ȯ	saw	u	cup	ng	long	zh	measure

ə { a in about, e in taken, i in pencil, o in lemon, u in circus }

misery (miz´ ər ē) great pain (p. 163)

mission (mish´ ən) a task; an assignment (p. 119)

misunderstand (mis un dər stand´) take in a wrong way (p. 160)

mock (mok) make fun of (p. 318)

mocking (mok´ ing) laughing in disgust and anger (p. 169)

molecule (mol´ ə kyül) a tiny bit (p. 523)

monitored (mon´ ə tərd) measured with an instrument or a device (p. 268)

monotonous (mə not´ n əs) dull; boring (p. 64)

monotony (mə not´ n ē) sameness (p. 190)

monsoons (mon sünz´) seasonal winds that bring rain to southern Asia (p. 188)

moratorium (môr ə tôr´ ē əm) a temporary pause or delay in an action (p. 274)

mores (môr´ āz) traditional customs (p. 224)

morons (môr´ onz) very stupid people (p. 333)

morose (mə rōs´) gloomy (p. 10)

morsels (môr´ səlz) small bits of food (p. 373)

multicoloured (mul´ ti kul ərd) (American *multicolored*) having many colors (p. 473)

murderer (mėr´ dər ər) someone who kills another person (p. 98)

murderess (mėr´ dər es) a woman who kills someone (p. 109)

mutes (myütz) people who cannot talk (p. 367)

mutilated (myü´ tl lā id) cut up; badly damaged (p. 95)

mutual (myü´ chü əl) shared (pp. 252, 423, 541)

N

nectar (nek´ tər) sweetness (p. 506)

needled (nē´ dld) made angry (p. 319)

negligence (neg´ lə jəns) carelessness (p. 60)

negotiate (ni gō´ shē āt) work to reach agreement (p. 449)

negotiations (ni gō shē ā´ shənz) discussions leading to an agreement (p. 106)

neigh (nā) the cry of a horse (p. 357)

nevertheless (nev ər ᴛʜə les´) all the same (p. 109); however (p. 372)

nomadic (nō mad´ ik) marked by traveling and having no home (p. 233)

norm (nôrm) the usual pattern (p. 274)

not inconsiderable (not in kən sid´ ər ə bəl) important enough to demand attention (p. 434)

notary (nō´ tər ē) a notary public; a person who signs or witnesses the signing of documents (p. 551)

notoriety (nō´ tə rī´ ə tē) bad name; reputation (p. 217)

notorious (nō tôr´ ē əs) famous for bad activities (p. 468)

nurtured (nėr´ chərd) cared for (p. 189)

nutrients (nü´ trē əntz) food needed for growth (p. 193)

nutriment (nü´ trə mənt) food (p. 491)

O

oarsman (ôrz´ mən) the one rowing a boat (p. 366)

obscenities (əb sen´ ə tēz) curses (p. 222)

obsesses (əb ses´ əz) takes up all of one's thoughts (p. 182)

obsolete (ob´ sə lēt) out of date (p. 363)

obstinate (ob´ stə nit) stubborn (p. 234)

obstinately (ob´ stə nit lē) stubbornly (p. 109)

obtained (əb tānd´) got (p. 144)

occupant (ok´ yə pənt) a person who lives or stays in a certain place (p. 16)

officialdom (ə fish´ el dəm) an entire group of officials (p. 550)

onslaught (on´ slȯt) an attack (p. 433); a violent attack or charge (p. 500)

openly (ō´ pən lē) publicly; in front of others (p. 250)

opponents (ə pō´ nəntz) those on the other side of a fight or discussion (p. 225)

oppression (ə presh´ ən) strict rule or control through the use of force (p. 467)

optimism (op´ tə miz əm) a hope for the best; a belief that things will turn out well (p. 505)

option (op´ shən) a choice (p. 265)

oracle (ôr´ ə kəl) a person who gives wise advice (p. 211)

ordeal (ôr dēl´) a severe test (p. 218)

originated (ə rij´ ə nāt ed) started (p. 27); began (p. 38)

outrageous (out rā´ jəs) extreme (p. 372)

outset (out´ set) the beginning (p. 7)

overburdened (ō vər bėrd´ nd) having too much to carry (p. 448)

overdue (ō vər dü´) past due; late (p. 321)

overjoyed (ō vər joid´) delighted; very happy (p. 86)

overload (ō´ vər lōd) constant activity (p. 127)

overwhelmed (ō vər hwelmd´) crushed; destroyed (p. 512)

overwhelming (ō vər hwel´ ming) crushing; destructive (p. 474)

overwhelmingly (ō vər hwel´ ming lē) with strength impossible to resist (p. 49)

P

painstaking (pānz´ tā king) very careful (p. 39)

palatial (pə lā´ shəl) elaborate; like a palace (p. 259)

palpitating (pal´ pə tāt ing) rapidly beating (p. 201)

palpitations (pal pə tā´ shənz) rapid heartbeats (p. 510)

paradoxically (par ə dok´ sə kəl lē) in a way that seems to mean two opposite things (p. 219)

parapet (par´ ə pet) a railing along the edge of a roof or wall (p. 11)

parcel (pär´ səl) an area of land (p. 191)

parching (pärch´ ing) causing to become dry (p. 107)

parsonage (pär´ sə nij) a house where a church minister lives (p. 15)

partake (pär tāk´) share; take part (p. 434)

participants (pär tis´ ə pənts) people who take part in something (p. 55)

passion (pash´ ən) an object of deep interest (p. 24)

passions (pash´ ənz) strong feelings for or about something (p. 336)

pastor (pas´ tər) a Christian minister (p. 106)

pastrylike (pā´ strē līk) looking like baked goods made of dough (p. 469)

pauper (pȯ pər) a very poor person (p. 550)

pedestrian (pə des´ trē ən) a person who travels on foot (p. 525)

peevishness (pē´ vish nəs) annoyance; bad temper (p. 205)

pelicans (pel´ ə kən) large birds whose bills have a pouch that holds fish (p. 524)

pending (pen´ ding) not yet decided; waiting for action (p. 466)

pensioners (pen´ shə nərz) people who receive pay after retiring (p. 499)

pensively (pen´ sive lē) in a sadly thoughtful way (p. 334)

perceived (pər sēvd´) seen; known through the senses (p. 430)

perception (pər sep´ shən) a way of seeing or observing (p. 467)

perfunctorily (pər fungk´ trə lē) without thought or care (p. 110)

perilous (per´ ə ləs) dangerous (p. 235)

perilously (per´ ə ləs lē) dangerously (p. 280)

perish (per´ ish) be destroyed; die (p. 441)

perpetrated (pėr´ pə trāt əd) carried out (p. 10)

persevered (pėr sə vird´) carried on in spite of difficulties (p. 110)

perseveringly (pėr sə vir´ ing lē) keeping at something in spite of difficulties (p. 226)

persistent (pər sis´ tənt) not giving up (p. 235)

perusing (pə rüz´ ing) reading carefully (p. 219)

petitioner (pə tish´ ən ər) one who asks for help (p. 174)

petty (pet´ ē) mean (p. 338)

philosophy (fə los´ ə fē) a basic theory; a viewpoint (p. 211)

pitch (pich) complete (p. 174)

pitiable (pit´ ē ə bəl) causing a feeling of pity (p. 8)

placative (plā´ kə tiv) calming; ready to ease another person's mind (p. 46)

placidly (plas´ id lē) calmly (p. 38)

plagues (plāgz) destructive things that come suddenly; nuisances (p. 188)

plaudits (plȯ´ dits) strong praise (p. 498)

plausible (plȯ´ zə bəl) realistic; believable (p. 513)

plight (plīt) a serious problem or condition (p. 89)

pneumonia (nü mō´ nyə) an infection in the lungs (p. 128)

poised (poizd) held up; balanced (p. 97)

political activists (pə lit´ ə kəl ak´ tə vists) people who take action to bring about political change (p. 524)

pollination (pol ə nā´ shən) transfer of pollen to make plants fertile (p. 58)

a	hat	e	let	ī	ice	ȯ	order	u̇	put	sh	she	ə	a	in about
ā	age	ē	equal	o	hot	oi	oil	ü	rule	th	thin		e	in taken
ä	far	ėr	term	ō	open	ou	out	ch	child	ᴛʜ	then		i	in pencil
â	care	i	it	ȯ	saw	u	cup	ng	long	zh	measure		o	in lemon
													u	in circus

Glossary **629**

pool (pül) combine one's money with others in a group project (p. 241)

pose (pōz) a position taken on purpose, as to have a picture taken (p. 543)

postmonsoon (pōst mon sün´) after the rainy season (p. 199)

potential (pə ten´ shəl) the ability for action or growth in the future (p. 281)

precarious (pri kâr´ ē əs) dangerous (p. 43); not secure (p. 198)

precise (pri sīs´) exact (pp. 162, 513)

precisely (pri sis´ lē) exactly (p. 65)

precision (pri sizh´ ən) exactness (p. 96)

precursors (pri kėr´ sərz) things that announce something else is coming (p. 181)

predetermination (prē di tėr mən ā´ shən) arranging in advance (p. 58)

prejudiced (prej´ ə dist) having an unfair opinion (p. 162)

premature (prē mə chùr´) earlier than expected (p. 8)

pressing (pres´ ing) asking in an urgent way (p. 544)

pretext (prē´ tekst) an excuse for not doing something (p. 225)

prig (prig) a person who is easily offended (p. 120)

primitive (prim´ ə tiv) simple or crude (pp. 66, 241)

priority (prī ôr´ ə tē) order of importance (p. 211)

privacy (prī və sē) state of being alone, away from others (p. 49)

privies (priv´ ēz) outhouses (p. 217)

procedures (prə sē´ jərz) ways of doing something (p. 61)

proceedings (prə sē´ dingz) series of events (p. 200)

prodigious (prə dij´ əs) enormous (p. 489)

profane (prə fān´) not holy or sacred (p. 175)

professed (prə fest´) announced publicly (p. 490)

prolong (prə lȯng´) make last longer (p. 544)

proposition (prop ə zish´ ən) an idea or statement (p. 441)

proprietor (prə prī´ ə tər) the owner of a business (p. 76)

prosperous (pros´ pər əs) successful; wealthy (p. 471)

protestations (prot ə stā´ shən) strong objections (p. 214)

protruding (prō trüd´ ing) sticking out (p. 15)

provincial (prə vin´ shəl) small; limited in attitude (p. 199)

provoked (prə vōkd´) stirred someone to action (p. 511)

psychic (sī´ kik) having to do with mind and spirit (p. 60)

psychoanalysis (sī kō ə nal´ ə sis) a method of therapy that tries to find a person's subconscious thoughts (p. 514)

psychoneurotic (sī kō nu rot´ ik) having mental problems (p. 61)

pulsating (pul´ sāt ing) moving in a regular rhythm (p. 422)

pulverize (pul´ və rīz´) pound into a powder (p. 525)

pumice (pum´ is) a light rock from a volcano (p. 62)

punctures (pungk´ chərz) small holes caused by a sharp object (p. 16)

purged (pėrjd) cleaned; washed away (p. 212)

pyramids (pir´ ə midz) figures with four triangles for sides (p. 62)

Q

qualification (kwäl ə fə kā´ shən) suitable ability (p. 107)

quavered (kwā´ vərd) spoke in a trembling voice (p. 41)

quench (kwench) to satisfy; to put out (p. 76)

quest (kwest) search (p. 507)

quit (kwit) leave (p. 305)

quotes (kwōtz) states or offers a price (p. 463)

R

racist (rā´ sist) referring to another race in an insulting way (p. 499)

rage (rāj) speak furiously (p. 383)

ragout (ra gü´) a stew of meat and vegetables (p. 491)

raiment (rā´ mənt) clothing (p. 490)

random (ran´ dəm) by chance; without purpose (p. 41)

randomly (ran´ dəm lē) without a definite pattern or plan (p. 538)

ranks (rangks) official positions (p. 297)

rapidity (rə pid´ ə tē) speed (p. 16)

rarefaction (rer ə fak´ shən) the state of being thin or less dense (p. 434)

rash (rash) bold; hasty (p. 108)

rasped (raspd) scraped with a harsh sound (p. 96)

rational (rash´ ə nəl) based on reason (p. 44)

rave (rāv) speak wildly (p. 383)

razor (rā′ zər) an instrument used for shaving (p. 79)

reacts (rē aktz′) acts in response to something (p. 320)

reap (rēp) get a reward; gather something in (p. 395)

reality (rē al′ ə tē) things as they actually exist (p. 474)

rebelled (ri beld′) went against rules or authority (p. 252)

recalcitrant (ri kal′ sə trənt) stubborn; resisting authority (p. 47)

recall (ri kȯl′) call back; remember (p. 17)

recalled (ri kȯld′) remembered (p. 118)

recalling (ri kȯl′ ing) remembering (p. 129)

receptive (ri sep′ tiv) ready to accept (p. 190)

reciprocate (ri sip′ rə kāt) to give something in return (p. 258)

reciprocity (res ə pros′ ə tē) an equal exchange (p. 431)

reckoning (rek′ ə ning) paying or settling what is owed (p. 551)

reconcile (rek′ ən sīl) bring into agreement (p. 457)

reconstruction (rē kən struk′ shən) the rebuilding of something (p. 59)

recourse (rē′ kôrs) something to turn to for help (p. 328)

re-enactment (rē en akt′ mənt) acting out something that happened once before (p. 111)

refinement (ri fīn′ mənt) a small change that will improve (p. 492)

refresh (ri fresh′) to make less tired, as if by resting or eating (p. 469)

regally (rē′ gəl lē) in a royal way (p. 23)

regent (re′ jent) one who rules in place of a king (p. 415)

registration (rej ə strā′ shən) an official document (p. 31)

regretful (ri gret′ fəl) remembering with sorrow or grief (p. 216)

reigns (rānz) rules or controls (p. 159)

rejuvenated (ri jü′ və nāt id) restored to youthfulness (p. 98)

relentlessly (ri lent′ lis lē) without stopping (p. 85)

reliable (ri lī′ ə bəl) trusted (p. 59)

relinquishing (ri ling′ kwish ing) releasing or letting go (p. 415)

relish (rel′ ish) a strong liking; great pleasure (p. 506)

reliving (rē liv′ ing) living over again; remembering (p. 363)

reluctant (ri luk′ tənt) not willing (p. 64)

reluctantly (ri luk′ tənt lē) unwillingly (p. 212)

remorse (ri môrs′) regret for having done something harmful (p. 111)

renounce (ri nouns′) give up; reject (p. 510)

rental (ren′ tl) available to be rented (p. 26)

repents (ri pentz′) feels sorry for an action (p. 457)

reprisals (ri prī′ zəlz) acts of force in revenge for an assumed wrong (p. 549)

reproaching (ri prōch′ ing) scolding; blaming (p. 305)

requisitioned (rek wə zish′ ənd) demanded, taken (p. 252)

resign (ri zīn′) accept (p. 512)

resignation (rez ig nā′ shən) acceptance (p. 515)

resounding (ri zoun′ ding) echoing loudly (p. 511)

resourceful (ri sôrs′ fəl) able to find ways to get things done (p. 243)

restive (res′ tiv) hard to handle (p. 79)

restless (rest′ lis) never still or quiet (p. 159)

restraint (ri strānt′) control over actions or feelings (p. 275)

retorted (ri tôrt′ ed) replied with anger (p. 7)

retrieve (ri trēv′) pick up (p. 29)

revealed (ri vēld′) showed (pp. 17, 32, 318); to make known (p. 416)

revelry (rev′ əl rē) a loud celebration (p. 554)

revered (ri vird′) honored and respected (p. 211)

rigid (rij′ id) stiff (pp. 204, 318, 336)

rigmarole (rig′ mə rōl) nonsense (p. 41)

ritual (rich′ ü əl) routine; something done regularly (p. 234)

rituals (rich′ ü əlz) series of acts done in a traditional order (p. 191)

a	hat	e	let	ī	ice	ȯ	order	u̇	put	sh	she	ə	a in about
ā	age	ē	equal	o	hot	oi	oil	ü	rule	th	thin		e in taken
ä	far	ėr	term	ō	open	ou	out	ch	child	ᴛʜ	then		i in pencil
â	care	i	it	ȯ	saw	u	cup	ng	long	zh	measure		o in lemon
													u in circus

rival (rī´ vəl) enemy (p. 507)

rotation (rō tā´ shən) the motion of a planet spinning on its axis (p. 55)

rouge (rüzh) reddish powder used to add color to the face (p. 241)

rounds (roundz) a pattern of assigned duties (p. 57)

ruckus (ruk´ əs) a noisy disturbance (p. 121)

ruddy (rud´ ē) having a healthy, reddish color (p. 362)

rude (rüd) rough; crudely made (p. 76)

ruefully (rü´ fəl lē) expressing regret or pity (p. 216)

ruff (ruf) a collar that stands out from the neck (p. 378)

ruthless (rüth´ lis) cruel; without mercy (pp. 16, 473)

S

sackcloth (sak´ klȯth) rough, coarse cloth (p. 87)

sage (sāj) a wise person (p. 243)

salvation (sal vā´ shən) rescue from evil or problems (p. 432)

sanctions (sank´ shənz) actions to stop or cut down aid or trade (p. 258)

sane (sān) healthy; well (p. 129)

sanity (san´ ə tē) soundness of mind (p. 224)

sari (sär´ ē) a draped outer garment of lightweight cloth traditionally worn by Indian women (p. 202)

savoured (sā´ vərd) (American *savored*) enjoyed the moment (p. 506)

say-so (sā´ sō) the right to decide (p. 251)

scandal (skan´ dl) talk about a public disgrace or action (p. 465)

schizophrenia (skit sə frē´ nē ə) a very serious form of mental illness (p. 514)

scoff (skȯf) show disrespect (p. 225)

scropbrush (skrop´ brush) a brush to scrub with (p. 212)

scrupulously (skrü´ pyə ləs lē) with great care and in good conscience (p. 137)

seared (sird) burned (p. 12)

secrecy (sē´ krə sē) the conditional of being hidden (p. 25)

security (si kyur´ ə tē) safety (p. 14, 258)

sedately (si dāt´ lē) calmly; with dignity (p. 202)

seemly (sēm´ lē) in good taste; proper (p. 130)

seismologist (sīz mol´ ə jist) a person who studies earthquakes (p. 267)

self-congratulatory (self kən grach´ ə lə tôr ē) giving praise to oneself (p. 498)

self-regulating (self reg´ yə lā ting) making adjustments without outside help (p. 57)

sensual (sen´ shü əl) pleasing to the senses (p. 190)

separation (sep ə rā´ shən) the act of leaving one another (p. 357); the state of being apart (p. 291)

serum (sīr´ əm) a liquid containing medicine (p. 64)

servitude (sėr´ və tüd) lack of freedom; slavery (p. 182)

shame (shām) a painful feeling caused by having done something wrong (p. 318)

shan't (shant) a short form of *shall not* (p. 338)

sheer (shir) pure; not mixed with anything (p. 315)

shielded (shēld´ ed) protected (p. 281)

shun (shun) avoid (p. 226)

siesta (sē es´ tə) a nap, usually taken after the noonday meal (p. 201)

significance (sig nif´ ə kəns) meaning; importance (pp. 226, 252, 498)

sisal (sī´ səl) a long, strong white fiber used to make ropes and twine (p. 214)

skeptically (skep´ tə kəl lē) with doubt (p. 46)

skirmish (skėr´ mish) a conflict; dispute (p. 222)

slithered (sliŦH´ ərd) to move along by gliding, as a snake (p. 336)

slogan (slō´ gən) a saying or motto used by a group (p. 281)

smoke out (smōk out) find; make known (p. 38)

snare (snâr) a trap (p. 121)

solemn (sol´ əm) serious; important in a religious way (p. 400)

solitary (sol´ ə ter ē) alone (p. 352)

sophisticated (sə fis´ tə kā tid) having a broad knowledge of the world (p. 469)

sorcerer (sôr´ sər ər) a wizard (p. 542)

sordid (sôr´ did) dirty; selfish (p. 42)

sorghum (sôr´ gəm) cereal grain ground into fine meal or made into a sweet syrup (p. 223)

sound (sound) healthy (p. 299)

sparsely (spärs´ lē) thinly scattered; very spread out (p. 234)

spattered (spat´ ərd) splashed (p. 8)

specialist (spesh´ ə list) a doctor who spends extra years studying one field of medicine (p. 512)

specific (spi sif´ ik) particular (p. 48)

specimens (spes´ ə mənz) examples of different groups of things (p. 122)

speedily (spēd´ ə lē) quickly (p. 16)

spines (spīnz) thorns (p. 119)

spit (spit) a narrow rod that holds meat to be cooked over a fire (p. 373)

spite (spīt) to show ill will (p. 400)

splendid (splen´ did) glorious; excellent (p. 316)

sporadically (spə rad´ ik al lē) now and then (p. 366)

sprinted (sprint´ ed) ran a short distance at top speed (p. 203)

spurning (spėrn´ ning) refusing (p. 260)

sputum (spyü´ təm) spit (p. 66)

squabbled (skwäb´ əld) quarreled; argued about something small (p. 525)

squeegee (skwē´ jē) a tool used to scrape water from a flat surface (p. 241)

stabilised (stā´ bə līzd) (American *stabilized*) stopped making changes; made steady (p. 275)

starts (stärts) quick, jerking movements (p. 303)

station master (stā´ shən mas´ tər) the person in charge of a railroad station (p. 555)

status (stā´ təs) standing or position (p. 234); social position relative to others (p. 465)

stealthiness (stel´ thē nəs) quietness (p. 175)

stereo (ster´ ē ō) sound equipment, often used to play music (p. 532)

sterile (ster´ əl) free from germs (p. 56)

stifle (stī´ fəl) to hold back (p. 120)

stifled (stī´ fəld) choked or smothered (p. 160)

straggler (strag´ lər) something that lags behind the others (p. 549)

strategic (stra tē´ jik) related to military planning (p. 265)

stricken (strik´ ən) struck; strongly affected (p. 14)

strop (strop) a strip of leather used for sharpening razors (p. 94)

stubble (stub´ əl) short, stiff growth (p. 119)

stylus (stī´ ləs) a sharp, pointed tool (p. 39)

subsided (səb sīd´ id) became quiet (p. 41)

successive (sək ses´ iv) following (p. 10)

succumb (sə kum´) give in (p. 130)

suffocation (suf ə kā´ shən) suffering from not having enough air (p. 60)

suicidal (sü ə sī´ dl) deeply unhappy; wanting to kill oneself (p. 317)

suitable (sü´ tə bəl) fitting; proper for the purpose (p. 144)

suite (swēt) a matched set of furniture (p. 532)

sullenly (sul´ ən lē) in a gloomy way (p. 64)

summon (sum´ ən) call; tell to come (p. 307)

superb (sù pėrb´) of unusually high quality (p. 159)

superfluous (sù pėr´ flü əs) extra; unnecessary (p. 66)

surge (sėrj) rise up from the group (p. 395)

survival (sər vī´ vəl) the act of staying in existence (p. 447)

survived (sər vīvd´) made it out alive (p. 249)

suspicious (sə spish´ əs) causing distrust (p. 120)

sustenance (sus´ tə nəns) something that supports life, especially food (p. 489)

swathed (swäᵮHd) wrapped with a band of material (p. 216)

sway (swā) influence (p. 227)

swoons (swünz) faints (p. 543)

symmetry (sim´ ə trē) balanced; even; being the same on both sides (p. 234)

syncopation (sing kə pā´ shən) a musical accent not on the usual beat (p. 541)

T

taboo (tə bü´) forbidden by social customs (p. 224)

taken aback (tā´ kən ə bak´) startled (p. 118)

tangential (tan jen´ shəl) change of course (p. 61)

a hat	e let	ī ice	ô order	ù put	sh she		a in about
ā age	ē equal	o hot	oi oil	ü rule	th thin	ə {	e in taken
ä far	ėr term	ō open	ou out	ch child	ᵮH then		i in pencil
â care	i it	ó saw	u cup	ng long	zh measure		o in lemon
							u in circus

Glossary **633**

taro (tär´ ō) a plant grown for its edible, starchy root (p. 188)

taxing (taks´ ing) tiring; difficult (p. 472)

tedious (tē´ dē əs) boring (p. 180)

temerity (tə mer´ ə tē) foolish boldness (p. 430)

tendency (ten´ dən sē) a pattern of doing things a certain way (p. 64)

tension (ten´ shən) uneasy or angry relationship (p. 274); the condition of being stretched (p. 431)

tentacles (ten´ te kəlz) the legs of an octopus; here it means to be controlling (p. 514)

tepid (tep´ id) slightly warm (p. 203)

terminal (tėr´ mə nəl) station (p. 26)

theological (thē ə loj´ ə kəl) related to the study of religion (p. 109)

thrash (thrash) beat or strike (p. 243)

threshold (thresh´ ōld) beginning point (p. 268)

tiara (tē âr´ ə) a small crown (p. 9)

ticked off (tikt ȯf) a slang expression meaning "annoyed" or "angry" (p. 526)

tidbits (tid´ bitz) small bits of knowledge (p. 25)

tilling (til´ ing) making land ready for growing crops (p. 120)

tirade (tī´ rād) a long, violent, scolding speech (p. 222)

to wit (tü wit) an expression meaning "that is to say" (p. 174)

toasts (tōsts) speeches made along with drinks to honor someone (p. 299)

togs (togs) clothes (p. 213)

tolerable (tol´ ər ə bəl) able to be endured (p. 424)

tolerably (tol´ ər ə blē) sufficiently; enough (p. 491)

tolerance (tol´ ər əns) an acceptance of something, such as other people's faults or differences (p. 508)

tormentors (tôr´ ment ərs) those who cause great pain to others (p. 498)

touched (tucht) affected (p. 250)

traditional (trə dish´ ə nəl) referring to customs followed for many years (p. 522)

trait (trāt) a quality of character (p. 212)

tranquillity (trang kwil´ ə tē) calmness; peace (p. 163)

tranquillizers (trang´ kwə lī zərs) medications used to help someone relax or sleep (p. 513)

transcending (tran send´ ing) going beyond (p. 509)

transcribed (tran skrībd´) made a copy of (p. 65)

transformed (tran sfōrmd´) changed (pp. 235, 395)

transgression (trans gresh´ ən) act of disobeying the law; sin (p. 235)

treading (tred´ ing) walking (p. 318)

tribulation (trib yə lā´ shən) suffering (p. 449)

tribune (trib´ yün) a platform from which to speak to a group (p. 427)

trivial (triv´ ē əl) not important (p. 9)

tussled (tus´ əld) struggled; wrestled (p. 214)

typewriter (tip´ rī tər) a machine with a keyboard, that produces printed words (p. 532)

tyrannical (tə ran´ ə kəl) harsh; cruel (p. 510)

tyrannous (tir´ ə nəs) unfairly cruel (p. 220)

tyranny (tir´ ə nē) rule by a harsh, powerful government (p. 447)

U

unaccountably (un ə koun´ tə blē) mysteriously; without explanation (p. 86)

unbearable (un bâr´ ə bəl) painful; hard to endure (p. 249)

uncluttered (un klut´ ərd) empty; not filled with things (p. 242)

undoing (un dü´ ing) the destruction of something already accomplished (p. 447)

unfulfilled (un fu̇l fild´) not finished; not completed, (p. 466)

ungodly (un god´ lē) wicked; awful (p. 213)

ungovernable (un guv´ ər nə bəl) not possible to control (p. 500)

unhindered (un hin´ dərd) not prevented or stopped (p. 251)

unilateral (yü nə lat´ ər əl) involving only one side in an issue (p. 274)

union (yü´ nyən) a marriage (p. 540)

unique (yü nēk´) uncommon (p. 507)

unleashed (un lēsht´) let loose; released (p. 448)

unlovable (un luv´ ə bəl) difficult to love (p. 372)

unnaturally (un nach´ ər əl lē) unusually; in an unexpected way (p. 541)

unprovable (un prüv´ ə bəl) not possible to prove (p. 399)

unrealistic (un rē ə lis´ tik) not likely to happen in real life (p. 399)

unsolicited (un sə lis′ it ed) not requested (p. 216)

unspeakable (un spē′ kə bəl) too bad to be described (p. 333)

unspeakableness (un spē′ kə bəl nes) a condition too bad to be described (p. 467)

unsuspecting (un sə spek′ ting) trusting; not suspicious (p. 77)

unworthy (un wėr′ ᴛHē) not deserving (p. 372)

uphold (up hōld′) maintain; keep (p. 163)

ushered (ush′ ərd) conducted; escorted (p. 217); showed people the way (p. 542)

utilitiesy (yü til′ ə tēz) household services, such as electricity, telephone, or water (p. 531)

V

vagabonds (vag′ ə bondz) homeless people who wander from place to place (p. 11)

vagrant (vā′ grənt) random; wandering from place to place (p. 233)

valid (val′ id) completely acceptable (p. 199); genuine (p. 167); reliable (p. 324)

vehemently (vē′ ə mənt lē) with strong emotion (p. 107); forcefully; violently (p. 224)

veld (velt) the South African grassland (p. 215)

ventilating (ven′ tl āt ing) putting in motion; blowing away (p. 549)

ventilator (ven′ tl ā tər) a passage in a house that air is blown through (p. 15)

ventured (ven′ chərd) dared to say (p. 97)

veranda (və ran′ də) a roofed porch extending along the outside of a building (p. 200)

via (vī′ ə) by way of (p. 523)

viands (vī′ əndz) food or drinks (p. 137)

vigour (vig′ ər) (American *vigor*) a strong or intense feeling (p. 505)

vindication (vin də kā′ shən) proof that clears away blame or guilt (p. 498)

vintage (vin′ tij) a crop of grapes grown for wine (p. 457)

violated (vī′ ə lāt ed) ruined by force (p. 415)

violent (vī′ ə lənt) hard; with great physical force (p. 39); caused by a strong feeling (p. 335)

violently (vī′ ə lənt lē) with strong physical force or rough action (p. 322)

visa (vē′ zə) a paper that allows a person to enter a country (p. 542)

visionary (vizh′ ə ner ē) imaginary; not practical (p. 492)

vistas (vis′ təs) large areas of land (p. 130)

vital (vī′ tl) very important; necessary (63)

vitality (vī tal′ ə tē) energy (p.512)

void (void) a feeling of emptiness (p. 226); empty space (p. 233)

vulgarly (vul′ gər lē) in bad taste; crudely (p. 472)

W

waning (wān′ ing) growing smaller, as the visible part of the moon (p. 57)

warheads (wôr′ hedz) the front parts of missiles or bombs that contain the explosive (p. 268)

waver (wā′ vər) be unsure (p. 162)

weaponry (wep′ ən rē) different types of weapons seen as a group (p. 266)

westernized (wes′ tər nīzd) influenced by European or American ways (p. 522)

wethers (weᴛH′ ərz) male sheep or goats (p. 87)

whetting (wet′ ing) creating an interest or a hunger (p. 505)

wholesome (hōl′ səm) healthful (p. 491)

widower (wid′ ō ər) a man whose wife has died (p. 120)

withheld (with held′) kept (p. 415)

wizened (wiz′ nd) dried up; wrinkled (pp. 202, 215)

woe (wō) misfortune; great sorrow (p. 77)

wolf (wu̇lf) eat hungrily, like an animal (p. 373)

wretched (rech′ id) worthless; seen with scorn (pp. 13, 29); miserable; very unhappy (p. 337)

writhed (riᴛHd) twisted as in pain (p. 14)

Y

yearn (yėrn) wish for deeply (p. 362)

Z

zealous (zel′ əs) very eager; strongly devoted (p. 509)

a	hat	e	let	ī	ice	ô	order	u̇	put	sh	she	ə	a in about
ā	age	ē	equal	o	hot	oi	oil	ü	rule	th	thin		e in taken
ä	far	ėr	term	ō	open	ou	out	ch	child	ᴛH	then		i in pencil
â	care	i	it	ȯ	saw	u	cup	ng	long	zh	measure		o in lemon
													u in circus

Glossary 635

Index of Authors and Titles

A

Account Evened With India, Says PM, 256
Achebe, Chinua, 103
Adventure of the Speckled Band, The, 5
Aleichem, Sholom, 547
Alvarez, Julia, 125
Amichai, Yehuda, 350
Anne Frank: The Diary of a Young Girl, 157
Asimov, Isaac, 36
Atwood, Margaret, 178

B

Barry, Dave, 520
Basho, 376
Basoalto, Neftali Ricardo Reyes y. *See* Neruda, Pablo
BBC Online Network (Internet news network), 272
Bird's Last Flight, The, 387
Bombeck, Erma, 529
Buenos Aires Herald (newspaper), 496
Building Atomic Security, 281
Busia, Abena, 393
By Any Other Name, 196
Bye-bye, 140

C

Cegua, The, 76
China Men, 239
Clemens, Samuel L. *See* Twain, Mark
Cranes, 115
Cup Inanity and Patriotic Profanity, 496

D

Dawn (newspaper), 256
Death Arrives on Schedule, 21
de Montaigne, Michel, 454
de Volkskrant (newspaper), 278
Diameter of the Bomb, The, 350
Diary of a Young Girl, The, 157
Do Not Go Gentle Into That Good Night, 381

Doyle, Sir Arthur Conan, 5

E

Expedition, The, 53

F

Feeling of Power, The, 36
Frank, Anne, 157
Frightening Joy, The, 278
Fugard, Athol, 312

G

Gettysburg Address, The, 438
Graham-Yooll, Andrew. *See Buenos Aires Herald*

H

Happy Man, The, 503
Hayslip, Le Ly, 186
Hikmet, Nazim, 398
Hwang Sun-won, 115

I

Inaugural Address, 444
In the Time of the Butterflies, 125

J

Jeanne d'Arc. *See* Joan of Arc
Joan of Arc, 413
Just Lather, That's All, 92

K

Kaffir Boy, 209
Kennedy, John F., 444
Kikaku, 376
Kincaid, Jamaica, 460
Kingston, Maxine Hong, 239

L

Last Seven Months of Anne Frank, The, 246
Letter to the English, 413

Letter to Indira Tagore, 166
Letter to the Reverend J. H. Twichell, 172
Li Po, 355
Lincoln, Abraham, 438
Lindwer, Willy, 246
Lohengrin, 536
Lorenzen, Rudolf, 53

M

Macbeth, 293
Hahfouz, Naguib, 503
Marriage Is a Private Affair, 103
Martin, Hansjörg, 21
Master and Man, 83
"Master Harold"... and the Boys, 312
Mathabane, Mark, 209
Mawu of the Waters, 393
Mindoro, 364
Modest Proposal, A, 487

N

Nafisi, Azar, 231
Neruda, Pablo, 370
Nguyen Th Vinh, 360
Nobel Lecture, 419

O

Ode to a Pair of Socks, 370
Of Repentance, 454

P

Pakistan Nuclear Moratorium Welcomed, 272
Polite Idiosyncrasy, A, 136

R

Rabinowitz, Solomon. *See* Aleichem, Sholom
Rau, Santha Rama, 196
Reading Lolita in Tehran, 231
Reyes y Basoalto, Neftali Ricardo. *See* Neruda, Pablo
Richardson, Elaine Potter. *See* Kincaid, Jamaica

S

San Souci, Robert D., 76
Shakespeare, William, 293
Slezak, Leo, 536
Small Place, A, 460
Solzhenitsyn, Alexander, 419
Some Advice to Those Who Will Serve Time in Prison, 398
Speckled Band, The Adventure of the, 5
Staying at a Japanese Inn: Peace, Tranquillity, Insects, 520
Story of the Bat, The, 140
Strindberg, August, 329
Stronger, The, 329
Sunico, Ramón, 364
Swift, Jonathan, 487

T

Tagore, Rabindranath, 150
Taking Leave of a Friend, 355
Téllez, Hernando, 92
Tests Are Nowhere Near India's: Fernandes, 263
Three Haiku, 376
Thomas, Dylan, 381
Thoughts of Hanoi, 360
Times of India, The (newspaper), 263
Tolstoy, Leo, 83
Twain, Mark, 172

W

Wedding Without Musicians, A, 547
When Heaven and Earth Changed Places, 186
Why Can't We Have Our Own Apartment? 529
Writing with Intent, 178
Wroblewski, Tomasz. *See* Zycie Warszawy

Y

Youssef, Saadi, 387

Z

Ziauddin, M. *See* Dawn
Zycie Warszawy (newspaper), 281

Index of Selections by Country

AFRICA

Ghana
Abena Busia *Mawu of the Waters,* 393

Egypt
Naguib Mahfouz *The Happy Man,* 503

Nigeria
Chinua Achebe *Marriage Is a Private Affair,* 103

South Africa
Athol Fugard *"Master Harold" . . . and the Boys,* 312
Mark Mathabane *Kaffir Boy,* 209

CANADA
Margaret Atwood *Writing with Intent,* 178

EASTERN EUROPE AND RUSSIA

Poland
Tomasz Wroblewski, from *Zycie Warszawy* (newspaper) *Building Atomic Security,* 281

Russia
Alexander Solzhenitsyn *Nobel Lecture,* 419
Leo Tolstoy *Master and Man,* 83

Ukraine
Sholom Aleichem *A Wedding Without Musicians,* 549

THE FAR EAST

China
Li Po *Taking Leave of a Friend,* 355
A Polite Idiosyncrasy, 136

Japan
Basho, Kikaku *Three Haiku,* 376

Korea
Hwang Sun-won *Cranes,* 115

Philippines
Ramón Sunico *Mindoro,* 364

Vietnam
Le Ly Hayslip *When Heaven and Earth Changed Places,* 186
Nguyen Thi Vinh *Thoughts of Hanoi,* 360

LATIN AMERICA AND THE CARIBBEAN

Antigua
Jamaica Kincaid *A Small Place,* 460

Argentina
Andrew Graham-Yooll, from the *Buenos Aires Herald* (newspaper) *Cup Inanity and Patriotic Profanity,* 496

Chile
Pablo Neruda *Ode to a Pair of Socks,* 370

Colombia
Hernando Téllez *Just Lather, That's All,* 92

Dominican Republic
Julia Alvarez *In the Time of the Butterflies,* 125

Haiti
Bye-bye, 140

MIDDLE EAST AND INDIA

India
Santha Rama Rau *By Any Other Name,* 196
Rabindranath Tagore *Letter to Indira Tagore,* 166
From the *Times of India* (newspaper) *Tests Are Nowhere Near India's: Fernandes,* 263

Iran
Azar Nafisi *Reading Lolita in Tehran*, 231

Iraq
Saadi Youssef *The Bird's Last Flight*, 387

Israel
Yehuda Amichai *The Diameter of the Bomb*, 350

Pakistan
M. Ziauddin, from *Dawn* (newspaper) *Account Evened With India, Says PM*, 256

Turkey
Nazim Hikmet *Some Advice to Those Who Will Serve Time in Prison*, 398

UNITED STATES

Isaac Asimov *The Feeling of Power*, 36
Dave Barry *Staying at a Japanese Inn: Peace, Tranquillity, Insects*, 520
Erma Bombeck *Why Can't We Have Our Own Apartment?*, 529
John F. Kennedy *Inaugural Address*, 444
Maxine Hong Kingston *China Men*, 239
Abraham Lincoln *the Gettysburg Address*, 438
Robert D. San Souci *The Cegua*, 76
Mark Twain *Letter to the Rev. J. H. Twichell*, 172
The Story of the Bat, 140

WESTERN EUROPE

Austria
Leo Slezak *Lohengrin*, 536

England
William Shakespeare *Macbeth*, 293

France
Joan of Arc *Letter to the English*, 413
Michel de Montaigne *Of Repentance*, 454

Germany
Rudolf Lorenzen *The Expedition*, 53
Hansjörg Martin *Death Arrives on Schedule*, 21

Great Britain
BBC Online Network (Internet news network) *Pakistan Nuclear Moratorium Welcomed*, 272
Sir Arthur Conan Doyle *The Adventure of the Speckled Band*, 5

Ireland
Jonathan Swift *A Modest Proposal*, 487

Netherlands
Anne Frank *The Diary of a Young Girl*, 157
Willy Lindwer *The Last Seven Months of Anne Frank*, 246
de Volkskrant (newspaper) *The Frightening Joy*, 278

Sweden
August Strindberg *The Stronger*, 329

Wales
Dylan Thomas *Do Not Go Gentle Into That Good Night*, 381

Index of Fine Art

xx	*Face With Snake.* Stéphan Daigle	378	*Bird and Magnolia.* Nakabayashi Chikuto
88	*Woodland Trail in Winter.* Boris Walentinowitsch Scherkow	401	*Prisoner of the State.* Eastman Johnson
95	*In the Barbershop.* Ilya Bolotowsky	413	*Joan of Arc.* Robert Alexander Hillingford
98	*Rural Landscape (Paisaje Campestre).* Susana Gonzalez-Pagliere	415	*Joan of Arc in Armor.* Albert Lynch
117	*Cranes and Pine Tree.* Japanese art	438	*Abraham Lincoln.* Artist Unknown
288	*Performers.* Freshman Brown	441	*Painting of the Battle of Gettysburg.* Edwin Forbes
293	*William Shakespeare.* Artist Unknown	456	*The Robber.* Pablo Picasso
298	*Macbeth Sees the Ghost of the Murdered Banquo.* Artist Unknown	454	*Michel de Montaigne.* Artist Unknown
337	*Girls Seated at the Table.* Jules Pascin	483	*Perro (Wifredo and Helena Lam's Cat).* Wifredo Lam
346	*Illustration with Moon and Birds.* Ron Rovtar	487	*Jonathan Swift.* Artist Unknown
355	*Portrait of Li Po.* Liang Kai	490	*Potato Famine.* The Granger Collection

Index

A

Abadir, Akef, 503
Abstract image, 400, 402
    defined, 399
Account Evened With India, Says PM, 256–62
Accuracy, 365
Achebe, Chinua, 103
Action, 78, 93, 99, 290, 292, 297, 313, 314, 328, 536, 537, 538
    defined, 75
Acts, 292, 293, 535
    one-, 314
Adjectives, 158, 197, 445, 497
"Adventure of the Speckled Band, The" (from), 5–20
Adventure stories, 3, 73–101
    "Cegua, The," 74–82
    "Just Lather, That's All," 92–101
    Master and Man (from), 83–91
    types of, 73
Advertisements, 409
Aleichem, Sholom, 547
Allen, Roger, 503
Allusions, 106, 107, 198, 199, 232, 235, 243, 280, 428
    defined, 197, 279
Alvarez, Julia, 125
Ambiguity
    defined, 54
Amichai, Yehuda, 350
Analysis, 255, 273
Anecdotes, 238, 535, 549, 555, 556
    defined, 548
Anne Frank: The Diary of a Young Girl (from), 157–65
Antagonists, 290
Anthology, reading, x
Antonyms, 504
Archetype, 543
    defined, 537
Articles, 519. *See also* News stories
    travel, 196
Asimov, Isaac, 36
Atwood, Margaret, 178

Audience, 167, 297, 301, 305, 311, 381, 412, 434, 440, 446
Author's point of view, 185, 197
Author's purpose, 116, 182, 361, 371, 399
    defined, 179
Autobiographies, 154–55, 178, 185–237, 203, 207, 232
    "By Any Other Name," 196–208
    defined, 197
    Kaffir Boy (from), 209–30
    Reading Lolita in Tehran, A Memoir in Books (from), 231–37
    "When Heaven and Earth Changed Places" (from), 186–95
    Writing with Intent: Essays, Reviews, Personal Prose 1983-2005 (from), 178–84

B

Barry, Dave, 520
Basho, 376
BBC Online Network (12 June 1998), 272
Behn, Harry, 377
Bias, 257
Bich, Nguyen Ngoc, 361
Biographies, 102, 154–55, 238–54
    China Men (from), 239–45
    defined, 240
    Last Seven Months of Anne Frank, The (from), 246–54
"Bird's Last Flight, The," 387–92
Blank verse, 292, 296, 298, 348
    defined, 294
Blasing, Randy, 399
Bloch, Chana, 350
Bombeck, Erma, 529
Brackets, 318
Building Atomic Security, 278–79, 281–83
Busia, Abena, 393
"By Any Other Name," 196–208
"Bye-bye," 140–43, 146–47

Byline, 153, 519
    defined, 279

C

Capital letters, 424
"*Cegua*, The," 74–82
Character Analysis Guide, 562
Character development, 313, 316
    defined, 313
Characterization, 95, 120, 342
Characters, 2, 9, 22, 23, 35, 36, 54, 69, 73, 84, 103, 104, 105, 116, 126, 135, 210, 240, 298, 311, 316, 328, 330, 331, 334, 530, 535, 536, 537. *See also* Antagonists; Heroes; Protagonists
    animals as, 2, 140, 141
    defined, 6
    experiences of, 102
    main, 4, 22, 54, 61, 73, 104, 290, 294, 313, 328, 329, 504
    objects as, 2
    portraits, 486
Character traits, 313, 486
China Men (from), 239–45
Chinese people, 134
Chorus, 291
Classical drama, 289, 292, 311
    defined, 294
    Macbeth (from), 293–310
Clemens, Samuel L. *See* Twain, Mark
Climax, 6, 22, 31, 99
    defined, 93
Cohen, J.M., 454
Columns, 485, 519–34, 529
    defined, 520
    "Staying at a Japanese Inn: Peace, Tranquillity, Insects," 520–28
    "Why Can't We Have Our Own Apartment?", 529–34
Comedy, 290, 292, 535
    defined, 294
Coming-of-age story, 102
    defined, 104
Commercials, 409

Index **641**

Compare/contrast, 220–21, 279, 296–307, 364, 371, 377, 388, 425, 441, 466
Compound words, 54, 365
Comprehension, 80, 322, 332, 365, 400, 446, 523, 541, 551
Concept Map, 386, 563
Concrete image, 399, 401, 402
Conflict, 55, 64, 69, 71, 134, 290, 292, 319, 328, 334, 535
    defined, 54, 313
    against him/herself, 54, 319, 328
    against nature, 54, 84, 85
    against others, 54, 55, 59
Connotation, 93, 179, 313, 382, 439, 521
Context clues, 174, 187, 257, 363, 419, 455, 462, 537
"Cranes," 115–24
Creation myth, 394
Creek people, 140
Critical essays, 169
Cultural differences, 75, 126, 420, 455, 497, 520, 521, 525, 537
"Cup Inanity and Patriotic Profanity," 496–502

D

Dawn (29 May 1998), 256–62
"Death Arrives on Schedule," 21–34
Debates, 438, 444
Denotation, 93, 179, 382, 439
Denouement/resolution, 22, 31, 69, 99, 292, 305
    defined, 6, 54, 93
Description, 84, 126, 172, 197, 210, 234, 240, 295, 350, 351, 367, 376, 377, 388, 455, 472, 489, 504, 507, 537
    defined, 232
Details, analyzing, 5, 365
Details, supporting, 22, 232, 311, 351, 504, 535, 537, 549
Detective stories, 2–3, 4, 24, 33
    "Adventure of the Speckled Band, The," 5–20
    "Death Arrives on Schedule," 21–34
    defined, 22
De Volkskrant (29 May 1998), 278

Dialogue, 137, 241, 244, 291, 292, 296, 298, 313, 316, 453, 531, 558
    defined, 135, 294, 530
    punctuation of, 232
"Diameter of the Bomb, The," 350–54
Diaries, 154–55, 156, 164, 178
    Anne Frank: The Diary of a Young Girl (from), 157–65
    defined, 158
    Writing with Intent: Essays, Reviews, Personal Prose 1983–2005 (from), 178–84
Dictionary, 37, 93, 167, 179, 257, 361, 371, 382, 439, 497, 548
Documentaries, 53
"Do Not Go Gentle Into That Good Night," 381–86
Doyle, Sir Arthur Conan, 5
Drama, 288–345, 309
    classical, 289, 292, 293–311, 294, 311
    expressionistic, 289, 328–41, 330, 331, 340
    forms of, 290, 292, 294, 305, 535
    neoclassical, 292
    realistic, 289, 311, 312–27, 313, 314, 326, 328, 330
Dramatic monologue, 400
    defined, 399
Drawing conclusions, 12, 273
Dutta, Krishna, 166

E

Editorials, 255, 280, 282, 409, 453, 496, 498
    defined, 279, 497
Elegy, 348, 363
    defined, 361
Ellipses, 158, 162
Entertainment, 2, 35, 43, 257, 412, 484, 519, 535
Epics, 348
Essays, 92, 166, 180, 182, 387, 409, 453–77, 454, 457, 458, 461, 480, 487, 488
    critical, 169
    defined, 179, 455
    "Of Repentance," 454–59

    Small Place, A (from), 460–77
Exaggeration, 37, 522, 527, 537, 538, 560
    defined, 521
Excerpts, 128, 253, 295, 318
    Anne Frank: The Diary of a Young Girl (from), 157–65
    "By Any Other Name," 196–208
    defined, 158, 247
    Last Seven Months of Anne Frank, The (from), 246–54
    "Master Harold" ...and the Boys (from), 312–27
    Small Place, A (from), 460–77
    In the Time of the Butterflies (from), 125–32
"Expedition, The," 53–72
Exposition, 22, 23, 94, 257
    defined, 6, 93
Expressionistic drama, 289, 328, 331, 340
    defined, 330
    Stronger, The, 329–41
Eyewitness accounts, 247

F

Facts, 37, 238, 255, 258, 263, 264, 350, 453, 455, 493
Falling action, 22, 31, 99
    defined, 6, 93
Fantasy, 35, 37
Feature stories, 154, 255, 274
    defined, 273
    "Pakistan Nuclear Moratorium Welcomed," 272–77
"Feeling of Power, The," 36–52
Fiction, 1–151, 73, 151, 172, 196, 364, 410, 535
    defined, 5
    adventure stories, 73–101
    detective stories, 4–34
    folktales, 133–47
    historical, 126
    Latin American, 2
    science fiction, 35–72
    turning points, 102–32

Figurative language, 372, 374, 449, 451, 507, 509, 530
    defined, 371, 445, 504
Figures of speech, 330, 356, 388, 410, 517
    defined, 504
Films/movies, 5, 6, 53, 73, 92, 102, 157, 486, 536, 537, 547
    documentary, 246
First person, 7, 19, 93, 94, 102, 104, 126, 185, 199, 207
    defined, 6, 197
Flashback, 121
    defined, 116
Folktales, 2–3, 133–47, 138
    "Bye-bye," 140–43, 146–47
    defined, 135
    "Polite Idiosyncrasy, A," 134–39
    "Story of the Bat, The," 140–41, 144–47
Foote, Paul, 83
Foreshadowing, 295, 307
Frank, Anne, 157
Free verse, 352, 353
    defined, 351
Frightening Joy, The, 278–80, 282–83
Fugard, Athol, 312

G

Genre, 2, 102, 154, 410
Genre Definitions, xi
"Gettysburg Address, The," 438–43
Ghost writer, 185
Graham-Yooll, Andrew, 496
Grammar, 566–72
    abbreviations, British v. American, 271
    adjectives, 124, 477, 566
    adverbs, 171, 386, 566
    antecedents, 567
    apostrophes, 570
    appositives, 418, 567
    brackets/parentheses for stage directions, 310
    British English, 262
    British spelling, 277
    capitalization, 572
    capitalization rules, 208
    character paragraph, 327
    clauses, 567
    clauses, dependent/independent, 392, 495
    clauses, subordinate/independent, 82, 91
    colons, 34, 570–71
    colons/phrases, 369
    commas, 571
    commonly confused words, 572
    complements, 567
    conjunctions, 566
    contractions, 568
    dashes, 571
    dashes/ellipses, 341
    dialogue with punctuation, 52
    double negatives, 568
    ellipses, 114, 571
    em dashes, 443
    fragments, 20, 568
    fragments in poetry, 375
    gerund phrases, 502
    gerunds, 72, 568
    in haiku, 380
    hyphens, 571
    infinitives, 254, 403, 459, 568
    interjections, 566
    modifiers, 568
    nouns, 566
    nouns, plural, 569
    parallel structure, 101, 283, 568
    participles, 359
    past tense, 177
    periods, 571
    phrases, 568
    possessives, 569
    prepositions, 566
    pronoun-antecedent agreement, 569
    pronouns, 566
    pronouns, possessive, 230
    punctuation marks, 397
    question marks, 571
    quotation marks, 534, 557, 571
    rhetorical questions, 518
    semicolons, 571
    semicolons/independent clauses, 528
    sentence construction, 570
    sentences, declarative/interrogative, 195
    sentences, long with semicolons, 132
    sentences, run-on, 354, 569
    sentences, with noun phrases, 437
    sentence types, 570
    subjects/predicates, 570
    subject/verb agreement, 452, 546
    verbs, 567
    verb tenses/changing, 184
    voice, active/passive, 139, 567
    which/that, use of, 237
    who/whom, use of, 147, 245
    word order, 165
Graphic Organizers, 158, 295, 445, 504, 537, 562–65
    Character Analysis Guide, 562
    Concept Map, 386, 563
    K-W-L Chart, 187, 565
    Main Idea Graphic (Details), 563
    Main Idea Graphic (Table), 504, 562
    Main Idea Graphic (Umbrella), 562
    Plot Mountain, 101, 564
    Prediction Guide, 565
    Semantic Line, 158, 295, 565
    Semantic Table, 564
    Sequence Chain, 20, 563
    Story Map, 537, 562
    Structured Overview, 445, 564
    using, xv
    Venn Diagram, 147, 232, 369, 563
Gray, Olivia, 376

H

Haiku, 348, 377, 378, 379
    defined, 376
Haitian people, 140
"Happy Man, The," 503–18
Hayslip, Le Ly, 186
Heroes, 141, 311
Hikmet, Nazim, 398
Historical fiction, 128

defined, 126
In the Time of the Butterflies (from), 125–32
Holman, J. Martin, 115
Homophones, 116
"How to Use This Book," x–xix
Human interest stories, 255
Humor, 37, 172, 173, 187, 196, 197, 373, 483, 484, 488, 503, 515, 519, 520, 524, 529, 530, 537, 544, 547, 548. *See also* Comedy; Stories, humorous
    defined, 521
    ironic, 488
    satire, 486
    techniques of, 521
Humorist, 484, 547, 550
    defined, 548
Humorous literature, 483–561
    columns, 519–34
    satire, 486–518
    stories, 535–57
Hyphens, 279

I

Iambic pentameter, 292, 383
    defined, 294, 382
Idioms, 128, 131, 504, 513, 530
    defined, 126
Illustrations, 84
    in comic strips, 486
Imagery, 167, 179, 347, 357, 361, 366, 368, 394, 410, 439, 447, 455, 507, 511, 521, 542, 553
    abstract, 399, 400, 402
    concrete, 399, 401, 402
    defined, 365, 445, 504
    realistic, 372
    surrealistic, 372
"Inaugural Address," 444–52
Informative, 257, 260, 268, 272, 412
Internet, 154, 156–57, 255, 496
Interpretation, 255
Interviews, 246, 247, 251, 263
In the Time of the Butterflies (from), 125–32
Irony, 38, 43, 49, 51, 410, 467, 486, 488, 497, 500, 550, 555, 560
    defined, 37, 461, 548
    situational, 37
    verbal, 37, 135

J

Joan of Arc, 413
Joke, 535
Journalism, 154–55, 255–83, 270, 387
    Account Evened With India, Says PM, 256–62
    Building Atomic Security, 278–79, 281–83
    defined, 264
    Frightening Joy, The, 278, 282–83
    Pakistan Nuclear Moratorium Welcomed, 272–77
    Test Are Nowhere Near India's: Fernandes, 263–71
Journals, 154–55, 156, 247, 388, 394
"Just Lather, That's All," 92–101

K

Kaffir Boy (from), 209–30
Kennedy, John F., 444
Kikaku, Takarai, 376–77
Kincaid, Jamaica, 460
Kingston, Maxine Hong, 239
Konuk, Mutlu, 399
Krabbenhoft, Ken, 370
K-W-L Chart, 187, 565

L

Language, 410
    British, 7, 296
    classical, 292
    everyday, 21, 311
    musical, 381
    old-fashioned, 6, 550
Last Seven Months of Anne Frank, The (from), 246–54
Legend, 76, 189, 191, 194, 536, 543
    defined, 187
Letters, 135, 154–55, 156, 174, 176, 356, 361, 399, 412, 414, 480
    defined, 167
"Letter to Indira Tagore," 166–71
"Letter to the English," 413–18
"Letter to the Reverend J.H. Twichell," 172–77
Lincoln, Abraham, 438
Lindwer, Willy, 246
Listening, 441, 587–88

active, 587
alert, 587
analyzing speakers, 587
analyzing with checklist, 262
appreciative, 587
to articles read aloud, 271
to audio speech, 452
to audio v. reading, 184
to class debate, 52
to classmates/notes, 132
critical, 587
to debate/notes, 283
to description, 230
to diary entry, 165
to drama read aloud, 327
evaluating as, 502
evaluating skills of, 369
to family memories, 245
for feedback on reading aloud, 397
for forms of speech, 341
to funny stories, 528
to group presentations, 359
to haiku aloud, 380
to humorous stories, 177
identifying details, 587
identify logic fallacies, 588
to interviews, 254
to jargon/slang, 147
to letters, 171
to music compositions, 518
to mystery resolution, 20
note-taking as, 495, 588
to opera recording, 546
to opinions/notes, 386
paraphrasing and, 208
to persuasive speech, 82
to poetry read aloud, 354, 403
to poetry read aloud/review, 375
to political speeches, 443
to proclamations/notes, 418
to radio announcements, 277
to reading aloud, 101, 557
to reading aloud v. silently, 437, 534
role-playing characters, 124
to scene read aloud, 310
skills form, 392
to song lyrics, 459
speeches, analyzing as, 237

to speeches, use notes/
    outline, 91
  to stories retold, 195
  to story endings, 139
  to strong opinions, 477
  to summaries, 72
  to tradition skit, 114
Literary techniques, 410, 486
Literary terms, xv
Literature, 133, 290, 387, 412, 426,
    430, 431, 453, 503
  about Drama, 288–91
  about Fiction, 1–3
  about Humorous, 482–85
  about Nonfiction, 152–55
  about Persuasive, 408–11
  about Poetry, 346–49
  children's, 364
  Korean, 115
  oral, 133
  reading, xiv
"Lohengrin," 536–46
Lorenzen, Rudolf, 53
Lyric poem, 362
  defined, 361
  "Thoughts of Hanoi,"
      360–63, 368–69

M

Macbeth (from), 293–310
  Modern English, 293–310
  Shakespeare's Original,
      293–310
Magazines, 92, 350, 453, 460, 519
  eyewitness accounts in, 247
  human interest stories in, 255
Mahfouz, Naguib, 503
Main Idea Graphic (Details), 563
Main Idea Graphic (Table), 504,
    562
Main Idea Graphic (Umbrella), 562
"Marriage Is a Private Affair,"
    103–14
Martin, Hansjörg, 21
Master and Man (from), 83–91
"Master Harold" . . . *and the Boys*
    (from), 312–27
Mathabane, Mark, 209
Mattawa, Khaled, 387
"Mawu of the Waters," 393–97

Meanings, 6, 37, 46, 382, 419
  multiple, 22, 173, 174, 351,
      356, 537
  of poems, 347
  of titles, 125, 257, 382, 488,
      497, 521, 529
  of word parts, 240, 273
Media, 590
  Bill of Rights, using, 341
  computer presentation, 534
  film v. reading, 20
  forms of, 590
  funny movies/literature, 528
  on Holocaust, 165
  information from, 230
  magazine articles, 72
  music for poetry reading, 380
  newspaper article, 34
  news reporters, 354
  role-playing, 418, 495
  songs v. essays, 459
  song writing, 195
  television speeches, 443
  video v. reading, 310
  writing script for different,
      271
  you and, 590
Memoirs, 233
  defined, 232
  Reading Lolita in Tehran,
  A Memoir in Books (from),
      231–37
Merwin, W.S., 361
Metaphors, 371, 389, 410, 504, 510,
    513
  defined, 388
"Mindoro," 364–69
"Modest Proposal, A," 487–95
Monologue, 535
  defined, 330
  dramatic, 332, 348
Montaigne, Michel de, 454
Mood, 172, 295, 378, 406, 416
  change of, 78
  defined, 75, 414
Mooyaart, B.M., 158
Morals, 83, 135
  defined, 135
Motivation, 23
Muskogee people. See Creek
    people

Mysteries, 24. See also Detective
    stories
  defined, 6
Myths, 140, 393, 395, 396
  creation, 394
  defined, 394

N

Nafisi, Azar, 231
Narrative, 505
  defined, 504
Narrator, 7, 93, 102, 126, 137, 213,
    313, 328, 363, 388, 506. See
    also Point of view
  all-knowing, 104, 105, 108,
      135, 137
  defined, 6, 210, 361
  limited, 504
Naturalism, 87, 90
  defined, 84
Neruda, Pablo, 370
News
  broadcast, 414
  immediate, 255, 263
  papers, 2, 53, 92, 154, 255,
      256, 264, 278, 279, 381, 453,
      496, 519, 529
News cycle, 275, 276
  defined, 273
News stories, 154, 258, 261, 263,
    264, 272, 273, 350. See also
    Feature stories; Journalism;
    Sidebars
  defined, 257
  eyewitness accounts in, 247
  human interest in, 255
  purpose of, 260
"Nobel Lecture," 419–37
Nonfiction, 152–287, 172, 410, 535
  Autobiographies, 185–237
  Biographies, 238–54
  defined, 158
  Diaries, Journals, and
      Letters, 153–84
  genres of, 154
  Journalism, 255–83
Note-taking, xvi, 54, 420
Nouns, 104, 394, 445, 497

Index **645**

Novels, 2, 21, 30, 36, 53, 83, 115, 125, 126, 166, 172, 350, 351, 387, 410, 419, 460, 503, 547
   defined, 22

O

Objectives, 5, 21, 36, 53, 74, 83, 92, 103, 115, 125, 134, 157, 166, 172, 178, 186, 209, 231, 239, 246, 256, 263, 272, 278, 293, 312, 329, 350, 355, 360, 364, 370, 376, 381, 387, 393, 398, 413, 419, 438, 444, 454, 460, 487, 496, 503, 520, 529, 536, 547
Ode, 373
   defined, 371
"Ode to a Pair of Socks," 370–75
"Of Repentance," 454–59
Onomatopoeia, 378
   defined, 377
Opinions, 169, 179, 180, 238, 255, 257, 264, 278, 279, 410, 453, 455, 460, 497
Oral literature, 133, 393
Oras, Ants, 329
Oxymoron, 235

P

Pakistan Nuclear Moratorium Welcomed, 272–77
Pamphlet, 489
   defined, 488
Paradox, 130
   defined, 126
Parody, 41, 538, 545
   defined, 37, 537
Patterns, 361, 382
   as rhyme schemes, 348
   rhythmic, 348
   of verse, 290
Pederson, Charles E., 21, 53, 536
Pen name, 175, 376, 547
   defined, 173
Personification, 169, 170, 389
   defined, 167, 388
Persuasive, 257, 412, 422, 434, 436
   defined, 420
Persuasive literature, 408–81
   essays, 453–77

   purpose of, 410
   speeches, 412–52
Phrases, 297, 371, 377, 439, 455, 539
Plays, 6, 157, 198, 272, 289, 290, 291, 292, 294, 303, 311, 312, 329, 350, 381, 410, 438, 484, 547
   television, 53
Playwright, 289, 300
   defined, 294
Plot Mountain, 101, 564
Plots, 2, 4, 23, 25, 73, 94, 148, 535, 536, 538, 541
   defined, 6, 93, 537
   main event of, 54
   stages of, 22, 93
Poetry, 6, 103, 115, 166, 347–407, 360, 364, 376, 377, 381, 387, 393, 398, 410
   defined, 350
   forms of, 376, 377
   humorous, 484
   literary approach of, 348
   lyrical, 360–63, 361, 362, 368–69
   purpose of, 348
   realism, 371, 372
   subgenres of, 348
   surrealism, 372
Poets, 348, 351, 355, 361, 376, 377, 399
   classical, 348
   surrealist, 371
   symbolist, 371
Point of view, 94, 255, 265, 280, 284, 351, 497
   defined, 197, 264, 504
   first person, 6, 7, 19, 93, 94, 102, 104, 126, 185, 197, 199, 207
   of narrator, 102
   personal, 453
   third person, 94, 102, 103, 104, 108, 113, 238, 504, 506
Po, Li, 355
"Polite Idiosyncrasy, A," 134–39
Pound, Ezra, 355
Predict, 75, 93, 104, 307, 351, 399, 455, 504
Prediction Guide, 565
Prefixes, 37

Problem, 96, 537
Proclamation, 412, 416, 417
   defined, 414
Prose, 178
Protagonists, 23, 54, 56, 68, 73, 102, 104, 290, 328. *See also* Heroes
   change in, 84
   change of main, 54, 61
   defined, 22
Punctuation, 371
   of dialogue, 232
Puns, 174, 486
   defined, 173

Q

Questions, 247, 251, 299, 426, 445
Quotation marks, 135, 137
Quotations, 238, 412

R

Rabinowitz, Sholem (Solomon). *See* Aleichem, Sholom
Radio, 103, 264, 272, 535
   play, 381
Raffel, Burton, 361
Rau, Santha Rama, 196
Reading aloud, 294, 297, 347, 348, 361, 362, 381, 382, 412, 413, 414, 416, 439
Reading Lolita in Tehran, A Memoir in Books (from), 231–37
Reading, purpose of, 313
Realism, 372
   defined, 371
Realistic drama, 289, 311, 314, 326, 328, 330
   defined, 313
   "Master Harold" . . . *and the Boys,* (from), 312–27
Recordings, 535
Regionalism, 76, 81
   defined, 75
Repetition, 290, 382, 426, 441, 442, 455
   defined, 439
Rereading, 173, 371
Research, 581–82
   Argentina/Great Britain, 502

author/apartheid question, 230
on Center for African Studies, 397
on Chinese folktales, 139
civil rights organizations, 327
on death poetry, 392
finding useful information, 581
on fingerprinting, 34
getting organized, 581
Holocaust memorials, 165
on immigrants, 245
Korean war, 124
Leo Slezak/pictures, 546
logging information, 581
Main Idea Graphic (Details), using, 254
on M. Atwood, 184
on Neruda's odes, 375
Nobel Prize Foundation, 437
nuclear testing summary, 277
planets, 52
planning reports, 581
preparing Bibliography/Works Cited Page, 581
primary/secondary sources for, 132
proclamation, 418
on *Romeo and Juliet* allusion, 208
Russian Jews/Cossacks, 557
tools, 582
Twain's puns/satire, 177
writing reports, 581
Resolution/denouement, 22, 31, 54, 69, 99, 292, 305
  defined, 6, 93
Rhyme, 290, 294, 347, 348, 352, 382
  defined, 351
Rhyme schemes, 348, 383, 385
  defined, 382
Rhythm, 290, 294, 347, 348, 361, 362, 381, 382
  defined, 350
Rising action, 22, 25, 96, 100
  defined, 6, 93
Robinson, Andrew, 166
Roots, of words, 37, 46
Routine, 535

S

San Souci, Robert D., 74
Sarcasm, 464, 501
  defined, 461, 497
Satire, 175, 484–85, 486, 491, 493, 494, 503
  "Cup Inanity and Patriotic Profanity," 496–502
  defined, 173, 488
  "Happy Man, The," 503–18
  "Modest Proposal, A," 487–95
Scene, 293, 294, 296, 314
Science fiction, 2–3, 35–72, 37
  defined, 36
  "Expedition, The," 53–72
  "Feeling of Power, The," 36–52
Screenplays, 53
Scripts, 21, 53
Semantic Line, 158, 295, 565
Semantic Table, 564
Sentences, 462. *See also* Grammar
  kinds of, 455
Sequence, 189, 505
  defined, 187
  of events, 84
Sequence Chain, 20, 563
Settings, 2, 35, 38, 73, 74, 76, 77, 93, 137, 180, 188, 226, 241, 286, 292, 296, 311, 367, 440, 478, 537, 538
  defined, 75, 210, 365, 439
Shakespeare, William, 293, 311
Short stories, 2, 21, 22, 53, 92, 103, 115, 166, 350, 351, 360, 381, 387, 460, 503, 535, 547
  ending of, 54
Sidebars, 255
Similes, 337, 357, 358, 371, 504, 511, 513
  defined, 330, 356
Situational irony, 135
Sketch, 205
  "By Any Other Name," 196–208
  defined, 197
Skills Lesson
  on characterization, 342
  on dialogue, 558
  on plot, 148
  on point of view, 284

on setting, 478
on style, 404
Slezak, Leo, 536
Small Place, A (from), 460–77
Solzhenitsyn, Alexander, 419
"Some Advice to Those Who Will Serve Time in Prison," 398–403
Songs, 190, 347, 348, 393
Sonnet, 348
Sources, 238
Speaking, 583–86
  advice, 518
  on Atwood's purpose, 184
  as character, 91, 546
  as characters describing, 245
  in class debate, 52, 283
  on conclusions, 254
  debates, 583
  define purpose of, 584
  descriptive, 583
  drafting, 584–85
  enemies speech, 452
  entertaining, 583
  on excerpt, 132
  expository, 583
  on expression, 208
  family stories, 147
  with figurative language, 171
  group discussion, 72, 101, 583
  group report, 359
  on haiku writing, 380
  on hospitality, 477
  humorous stories, 177
  on humor/serious writing, 528
  impromptu, 583
  interview, 583
  on kindness, 354
  knowing audience, 584
  knowing script, 585–86
  knowing setting, 584
  knowing yourself, 586
  literature recitation, 369, 583
  literature response, 165, 583
  monologue aloud, 341
  narrative, 583
  narrowing topic, 584
  on opinions, 386, 392
  oral presentation, retelling, 82
  persuasive, 34, 237

preparing speech, 230
prewriting, 584
as prime minister, 262
on public action, 495
radio announcement, 277
reading aloud, 271, 310, 403, 437
reading aloud as characters, 534
reading aloud practice, 375
reading as storytelling, 397
reading proclamation aloud, 418
reflective, 583
retelling story, 459
rhetorical questions in, 195
role-playing, 20, 124, 327, 557, 583
on sarcasm opinion, 502
selecting visuals, 585
speech writing, 443
on story endings, 139
tradition skit, 114
Speaking skills, 438
Speeches, 409, 439, 440, 480
    defined, 420
    "Gettysburg Address, The," 438–43
    "Inaugural Address," 444–52
    kinds of, 412
    "Letter to the English," 413–18
    "Nobel Lecture," 419–37
Spelling
    alternate, 362
    British, 6, 11, 214, 265, 268, 420, 433, 457, 461, 499
Stage directions, 296, 297, 317, 320, 334
Stanza, 383
    defined, 382
"Staying at a Japanese Inn: Peace, Tranquillity, Insects," 520–28
Stereotypes, 521, 524
Stories, humorous, 484–85, 486, 487, 535–57
    "Lohengrin," 536–46
    purpose of, 535
    "Wedding Without Musicians, A," 547–57

Story Map, 537, 562
"Story of the Bat, The," 140–41, 144–47
Strindberg, August, 329
Stronger, The, 329–41
Structured Overview, 445, 564
"Study Guide, A," x–xix
Style, 117, 123, 236, 404, 453, 457, 462
    defined, 116, 232, 455
    formal, 84
    realism, 371
    surrealism, 371
    symbolism, 371
Suffixes, 37, 104, 264, 445
Summarizing, 264, 318, 548
Sunico, Ramón, 364
Sun-won, Hwang, 115
Surrealism, 372
    defined, 371
Suspense, 75, 92, 96
    defined, 93
Swift, Jonathan, 487
Syllables, 294, 298, 348, 377, 378
Symbolism, 142, 146, 233, 371, 389, 391, 395
    defined, 141, 388
Symbols, 111, 122, 348, 352, 394, 425, 430
    defined, 116, 350
Synonym, 93, 126, 295, 351, 371, 382, 414, 504

T

Tagore, Rabindranath, 166
"Taking Leave of a Friend," 355–59
Technology, 590
    computer music program for song writing, 518
    computer presentations, 452
    create editorial page with, 283
    desktop publishing brochure, 397
    filming scenes, 495
    Internet search on Tolstoy, 91
    poem videos, 369
    recording role-playing, 310
    recording song, 195

    story illustrations with, 114
    theater equipment, 341
    TV interview, 82
    video of Twain/Livy, 177
    virtual tours, 528
    you and, 590
Television shows, 5, 6, 21, 73, 102, 246, 255, 263, 264, 272, 444, 486, 535
    dramas, 311
    plays, 53
Téllez, Hernando, 92
Tests Are Nowhere Near India's: Fernandes, 263–71
Test-Taking Tips, xix, 151, 287, 345, 407, 481, 561
Theme, 104, 179, 211, 274, 330, 357, 364, 365, 376, 387, 432, 439, 531, 533, 537
    defined, 356, 420, 530
Third person, 94, 102, 103, 108, 113, 238, 506
    defined, 104
    limited, 504
Thomas, Dylan, 381
"Thoughts of Hanoi," 360–63, 368–69
Three-Column Chart, using, xvi
Three Haiku, 376–80
Times of India (1 June 1998), 263
Tolstoy, Leo, 83
Tone, 180, 182, 183, 274, 448, 461, 466, 472, 476, 484, 490
    defined; 179, 445, 488
Topics, 178, 196, 279, 548
Tragedy, 290, 292, 305
    defined, 294
Trask, Willard, 413
Travel articles, 196
Turning points, 3, 103, 111, 209, 227, 229
    coming-of-age stories, 102, 104
    "Cranes," 115–24
    defined, 104, 210
    "Marriage Is a Private Affair," 103–14
    In the Time of the Butterflies (from), 125–32
Twain, Mark, 172, 173, 175
Two-column chart, 488

U

Unit Reviews, 150–51, 286–87, 344–45, 406–7, 480–81
Unit Summaries, 149, 285, 343, 405, 479, 559

V

Venn Diagram, 147, 232, 369, 563
Verbal irony, 135, 338
    defined, 330
Verbs, 104, 394
    past/past perfect tenses, 141
Verses, 290, 311, 348, 376
    dramatic, 292
Viewing, 589
    bats using Venn Diagram, 147
    brochures/web sites, 477
    Character Analysis Guides, 327
    comparing with Venn Diagram, 369
    Concept Map, 386
    drawing from description, 237
    Main Idea Graphic (Details), 403
    maps, 262
    opera guidebooks, 546
    painting of poem imagery, 359
    Plot Mountain organizer, 101
    Prediction Guide, 418
    Russian Jews/Cossacks, 557
    with Sequence Chain, 20
    Tagore's paintings, 171
Villanelle, 348, 383
    defined, 382
Vinh, Nguyen Thi, 360
Vocabulary words, xviii

W

"Wedding Without Musicians, A," 547–57
"When Heaven and Earth Changed Places" (from), 186–95
"Why Can't We Have Our Own Apartment?", 529–34
Word choices, 84, 93, 126, 348, 351, 414, 439, 461, 486, 530
Word origins, 167
World Wide Web, 5, 256, 272
Writing, 573–80
    on Anne Frank, 254
    on author's motivation, 495
    autobiography, 287
    on banning books, 237
    on being afraid, 82
    bibliographies/indexes, 580
    as characters, 518
    on character's reasons, 52
    compare poem/short story, 407
    description, 573
    description, exaggerated, 528
    description, from notes, 195
    description, places, 477
    dialogue for ghost, 310
    editorials, 502
    essay with facts, 20
    expository, 573
    expository paragraph, 277
    on family life, 534
    in first person, 284
    haiku on nature, 380
    on journalistic sources, 271
    letters, 177
    letter to advice columnist, 341
    letter to editor, 132, 283
    on Lincoln's speech, 443
    literature response, 147, 165, 452
    narrative, 573–74
    on natural disasters, 91
    new resolution/denouement, 72
    news stories, 262
    opera sequel, 546
    on opinions, 386
    on ordinary things, 375
    outlines, 437, 557
    paragraph, 459
    on people, 397
    personal narratives, 34
    personification, using, 171
    persuasive, 574
    play ending, 327
    poems, 359
    on poetry images, 392
    process of, 575–80
        drafting, 576–77
        editing/proofreading, 578–79
        prewriting, 575–76
        publishing/evaluating, 579–80
        revising, 577–78
    proclamation, 418
    on public events, 354
    with regionalisms, 75
    research report, 575
    rewriting with topic sentence/details, 101
    sense imagery in, 369
    sketches, 208
    on sounds, 403
    story beginning, third person, 114
    story ending, 124, 151
    subject/verb agreement in, 139
    summarizing, 245
    theater reviews, 345
    on theme, 230
    ways to start, 184
Writing with Intent: Essays, Reviews, Personal Prose 1983-2005 (from), 178–84
Wroblewski, Tomasz, 153

Y

Yates, Donald A., 92
Youssef, Saadi, 387

Z

Ziauddin, M., 256
Zycie Warszawy (2 June 1998), 278

Acknowledgments

Every effort has been made to locate the copyright owners of material used in this textbook. Omissions brought to our attention will be corrected in subsequent editions.

Page 1: Quotation from *The Writer* by Margaret Culkin Banning. From the *Beacon Book of Quotations by Women,* © 1992 by Rosalie Maggio.

Pages 23–31: "Death Arrives on Schedule" by Hansjörg Martin from *Blut an Der Manschette,* translated by Chuck E. Pederson.

Pages 38–49: "The Feeling of Power," copyright © 1957 by Quinn Publishing Company, Inc., from *Isaac Asimov: The Complete Stories of Vol. I* by Isaac Asimov. Used by permission of Doubleday, a division of Random House, Inc.

Pages 55–69: From *"The Expedition" (Die Expedition)* by Rudolf Lorenzen, trans. by Charles E. Pederson. Reprinted by permission of Herbach & Haase Literarische Agentur.

Pages 76–80: "The Cegua," from *Short and Shivery: 30 Chilling Tales* by Robert D. San Souci, Illus. by Katherine Coville, copyright © 1987 by Robert D. San Souci. Illustrations © 1987 by Doubleday, a division of Bantam Doubleday Dell Publishing Group, Inc. Used by permission of Random House Children's Books, a division of Random House, Inc.

Pages 85–89: From "Master and Man" by Leo Tolstoy from *Master and Man and Other Stories* translated with an introduction by Paul Foote, Penguin Classics, 1977, pp. 115-119. Copyright © Paul Foote, 1977. Reproduced by permission of Penguin Books Ltd.

Pages 94–99: "Just Lather, That's All" by Hernando Téllez, trans. by Donald A. Yates as appeared in *Contemporary Latin American Short Stories* edited by Pat McNees. Reprinted by permission of Donald A. Yates.

Pages 105–111: "Marriage is a Private Affair" from *Girls at War and Other Stories* by Chinua Achebe, copyright © 1972, 1973 by Chinua Achebe. Used by permission of Doubleday, a division of Random House, Inc.

Pages 117–122: "Cranes" from *Shadows of a Sound* © 1990 by Hwang Sun-wŏn, translated by J. Martin Holman. Published by Mercury House, San Francisco, CA, and reprinted by permission. Please visit: www.mercuryhouse.org.

Pages 127–130: From *In the Time of the Butterflies.* Copyright © 1994 by Julia Alvarez. Published by Plume, an imprint of Penguin Books (USA) and originally in hardcover by Algonquin Group of Chapel Hill. Reprinted by permission of Susan Bergholz Literary Services, New York. All rights reserved.

Pages 144–145: "The Story of the Bat" and background information from *Dee Brown's Folktales of the Native American Retold for Our Times* by Dee Brown, copyright 1979, 1993 by Dee Brown. Reprinted by permission of Henry Holt and Company, LLC.

Pages 159–163: From *The Diary of a Young Girl: The Definitive Edition* by Anne Frank. Otto H. Frank & Mirjam Pressler, Editors, translated by Susan Massotty, copyright © 1995 by Doubleday, a division of Random House, Inc. Used by permission of Doubleday, a division of Random House, Inc.

Pages 168–169: "Letter to Indira Tagore" by Rabindranath Tagore from *Rabindranath Tagore: An Anthology,* Krishna Dutta and Andrew Robinson eds./trans. (New York, 1997, St. Martin's Press). Copyright Krishna Dutta and Andrew Robinson. Reprinted by permission of Andrew Robinson.

Pages 180–182: From "Nine Beginnings" from the book *Writing with Intent: Essays, Reviews, Personal Prose—1983–2005* by Margaret Atwood. Copyright © 2004, 2005 by O.W. Toad, Ltd. Appears by permission of the publisher, Carroll & Graf Publishers, A division of Avalon Publishing Group. Also from *Moving Targets* copyright © by O. W. Toad Ltd. Reprinted by permission of House of Anansi Press, Toronto.

Pages 188–193: From *When Heaven and Earth Changed Places* by Le Ly Hayslip, copyright © 1989 by Le Ly Hayslip and Charles Jay Wurts. Used by permission of Doubleday, a division of Random House, Inc.

Pages 198–205: "By Any Other Name" from *Gifts of Passage* by Santha Rama Rau. Copyright 1951 by Santha Rama Rau. Copyright renewed © 1979 by Santha Rama Rau. Reprinted by permission of HarperCollins Publishers. "By Any Other Name" originally appeared in *The New Yorker.*

Pages 211–227: Reprinted with the permission of Scribner, an imprint of Simon & Schuster Adult Publishing Group from *Kaffir Boy* by Mark Mathabane. Copyright © 1986 by Mark Mathabane.

Pages 233–235: From *Reading Lolita in Tehran* by Azar Nafisi, copyright © 2002 by Azar Nafisi. Used by permission of Random House, Inc.

Pages 241–243: "The Father of China" from *China Men* by Maxine Hong Kingston, copyright © 1977, 1978, 1979, 1980 by Maxine Hong Kingston. Used by permission of Alfred A. Knopf, a division of Random House, Inc.

Pages 248–252: From *The Last Seven Months of Anne Frank* by Willy Lindwer, English translation copyright © 1991 by Random House, Inc. Used by permission of Pantheon Books, a division of Random House, Inc.

Pages 258–260: "Account Evened With India, Says PM, Pakistan Opts to Go Nuclear" by M. Ziauddin from *The Dawn,* 29 May 1998. Reprinted by permission.

Pages 265–269: "Tests Are Nowhere Near India's: Fernandes" from *The Times of India,* Monday, 1 June 1998.

Pages 274–275: "Pakistan Nuclear Moratorium Welcomed" from *BBC Online Network,* Friday, June 12, 1998. Reprinted by permission of BBC News Interactive.

Page 280: "The Frightening Joy" from *De Volkskrant,* Amsterdam, Friday, 29 May 1998.

Page 281: From "Building Atomic Security" by Tomasz Wroblewski as appeared in World Press Review, Vol. 45, Issue 8, August 1998.

Page 288: Quotation from *The Roman Way,* by Edith Hamilton, © 1960 by Edith Hamilton.

Pages 296–307: From "Macbeth" Act 3, Scene 4 from *The Complete Works of William Shakespeare* by William Shakespeare, the Cambridge text established by John Dover Wilson.

Pages 296–307: "Macbeth" Act 3, Scene 4 from *Shakespeare Made Easy: Macbeth* by William Shakespeare, edited and translated by Alan Durband. Copyright © 1985. Reprinted with permission from Hutchinson and Co. Ltd. and Barrons Educational Series, Inc.

Pages 314–324: From *"Master Harold". . . and the Boys* by Athol Fugard, copyright © 1982 by Athol Fugard. Used by permission of Alfred A. Knopf, a division of Random House, Inc.

Pages 331–338: *The Stronger* by August Strindberg, translated by Ants Oras. Reprinted by permission of Hele Lüüs.

Page 347: Quotation from *All the Women Caught in Flaring Light, Crime Against Nature,* by Minnie Bruce Pratt. From the *Beacon Book of Quotations by Women,* © 1992 by Rosalie Maggio.

Page 352: "The Diameter of the Bomb" from *The Selected Poetry of Yehuda Amichai* by Yehuda Amichai edited and translated by Chana Bloch and Stephen Mitchell, pp.18. Reprinted by permission of University of California Press.

Page 357: "Taking Leave of a Friend" by Rihaku, Translated by Ezra Pound, from *Personae,* copyright © 1926 by Ezra Pound. Reprinted by permission of New Directions Publishing Corp.

Pages 362–363: "Thoughts of Hanoi" from *A Thousand Years of Vietnamese Poetry* by Nguyen Thi Vinh, translated by Nguyen Ngoc Bich with Burton Raffel and W. S. Mervin, 1974.

Pages 366–367: "Mindoro" by Ramón C. Sunico. Reprinted by permission of Ramón C. Sunico.

Pages 372–373: "Ode to a Pair of Socks" from *Odes to Common Things* by Pablo Neruda. Copyright © 1994 by Pablo Neruda and Fundacion Pablo Neruda (Odes in Spanish); Copyright © 1994 by Ken Krabbenhoft (Odes in English); Copyright © 1994 by Ferris Cook (Illustrations and Compilation). By permission of Little, Brown and Co., Inc.

Page 378: From *More Cricket Songs* translated by Harry Behn. Copyright © 1971 Harry Behn. Copyright Renewed 1999 Prescott Behn, Pamela Behn Adam, and Peter Behn. Used by permission of Marian Reiner.

Pages 383–384: "Do Not Go Gentle Into That Good Night" by Dylan Thomas, from *The Poems of Dylan Thomas,* copyright © 1952 by Dylan Thomas. Reprinted by permission of New Directions Publishing Corp.

Pages 389–390: "The Bird's Last Flight" by Saadi Youssef, translated from the Arabic by Khaled Mattawa.

Page 395: "Mawu of the Waters" by Abena Busia from *Testimonies of Exile.* Africa World Press: Trenton NJ, 1990, copyright Abena P.A. Busia. Reprinted by permission.

Pages 400–401: "Some Advice to Those Who Will Serve Time in Prison" by Nazim Hikmet from *Poems of Nazim Hikmet,* translated by Randy Blasing and Mutlu Konuk. Translation copyright © 1994, 2002 by Randy Blasing and Mutlu Konuk. Reprinted by permission of Persea Books, Inc. (New York)

Pages 415–416: "Letter to the English," from *Joan of Arc In Her Own Words* translated by Willard Trask, Copyright 1996 by Books & Co./Turtle Point Press. Reprinted by permission.

Pages 421–434: "Nobel Lecture" by Alexander Solzhenitsyn. © The Nobel Foundation 1970. Reprinted by permission of The Nobel Foundation.

Page 457: From "Of Repentance" from *Essays* by Michel de Montaigne translated with an introduction by J. M. Cohen, Penguin Classics, 1958, pp. 243-244. Copyright © J.M. Cohen, 1958. Reproduced by permission of Penguin Books Ltd.

Pages 462–474: Excerpt from *A Small Place* by Jamaica Kincaid. Copyright © 1988 by Jamica Kincaid. Reprinted by permission of Farrar, Straus and Giroux, LLC.

Page 482: Quotations (top) from *Black Women Writers at Work,* Kristin Hunter, Claudia Tate, ed., 1983. From the *Beacon Book of Quotations by Women,* Rosalie Maggio, 1992. (bottom) from: Workshop on World Humor Nov. 1984, Sacha Guitry; *New York Times* March 17, 1985; *The New International Dictionary of Quotations,* Miner & Rawson, © 1986, 1993, 2000.

Pages 498–500: "Cup Inanity and Patriotic Profanity" by Andrew Graham-Yooll from *the Buenos Aires Herald Weekly On Line,* Thursday, July 2, 1998. Reprinted by permission.

Pages 505–515: "The Happy Man", by Nagib Mahfuz from *God's World: An Anthology of Short Stories,* trans. by Akef Abadir and Roger Allen. Reprinted by permission of Roger Allen.

Pages 522–526: From *Dave Barry Does Japan* by Dave Barry, copyright © 1992 by Dave Barry. Used by permission of Random House, Inc.

Pages 531–532: "Why Can't We Have Our Own Apartment?" from *If Life Is a Bowl of Cherries What Am I Doing In the Pits?* by Erma Bombeck. Reprinted with permission from The Aaron M. Priest Literary Agency, Inc.

Pages 538–544: "Lohengrin" by Leo Slezak, trans. by Charles E. Pederson, from *Der Wortbruch* by Leo Slezak.

Pages 549–555: "A Wedding Without Musicians" from *Tevye's Daughters* by Sholom Aleichem, copyright 1949 by the Children of Scholom Aleichem and Crown Publishers, a division of Random House, Inc. Used by permission of Crown Publishers, a division of Random House, Inc.

Pages 598–611: Statistics from *The World Almanac and Book of Facts 2005,* © 2005 World Almanac Education Group, a WRC Media Inc. company.

Acknowledgments

Photo Credits

Cover, © Royalty Free/Punchstock; page x middle, © Andres Rodriguez/Shutterstock; bottom, © Anna Chelnokova/Shutterstock; page xviii top, © PhotoDisc Volumes Education 2 41307; © Copyright 1999 PhotoDisc, Inc.; bottom, © Blend Images, LLC, AR052605400; page xx, © Stéphan Daigle/Corbis; page 4, © germán ariel berra/ShutterStock; page 4, © ChipPix/ShutterStock; page 5, © Brown Brothers, Sterling, PA; page 11, © Rachel Taylor; page 12, © Rachel Taylor; page 16, © Judy King; page 21, © Scott Sanders/Shutterstock; page 26, © Duck/zefa/Corbis; page 29, © Sándor Kárpisz/ShutterStock; page 30, PhotoDisc © 2007; page 35, © cre8tive studios/ShutterStock; page 35, Andy Attiliis/Images.com; page 36, © Alex Gotfryd/Corbis; page 43, © Royalty-Free/Getty Images; page 53, © L. Haslam, reprinted by permission of Schöffling & Company.; page 62, © Stasys Eidiejus/Shutterstock; page 69, © Dariush M./Shutterstock; page 73, © Angela Davis/Shutterstock; page 73, © Bill McKelvie/Shutterstock; page 74, Photo courtesy Robert D. San Souci.; page 77, © Jeff Spackman; page 79, © Jeff Spackman; page 83, The Granger Collection, New York; page 88, © Bridgeman Art Library, London/SuperStock; page 92, Photo by B. Téllez. Used by permission.; page 95, © Estate of Ilya Bolotowsky/Licensed by VAGA, New York, NY; page 98, © Kactus Foto/SuperStock; page 102, © Junji Takemoto/ShutterStock; page 102, © cyro pintos/ShutterStock; page 103, © Frank May/epa/Corbis; page 105, © Richard Gerstner/ShutterStock; page 108, © Tiburon Studios/ShutterStock; page 111, © Cecilia Lim H M/Shutterstock; page 115, Courtesy of the Korean Cultural Center, NY; page 117, © Christie's Images/SuperStock; page 120–121, © Horace Bristol/Corbis; page 125, Photo copyright © by Bill Eichner. Reprinted by permission of Susan Bergholz Literary Services, New York. All rights reserved.; page 127, © Royalty-Free/Corbis; page 130, © Sri Sadono/Shutterstock; page 133, © Dhoxax/ShutterStock; page 133, © Alexis Puentes/ShutterStock; page 134, © ijansempoi/Shutterstock; page 136, © Winson Trang; page 140 © J C Hix/ShutterStock; page 143 © Julie Nicholls/Corbis; page 145 © Kevin Schafer/Corbis; page 152 © Bob Krist/Corbis; page 156 © Scott Rothstein/ShutterStock; page 156 © Scott Rothstein/ShutterStock; page 157 © SuperStock, Inc./SuperStock; page 161 © AP/Wide World Photos; 163 © AP/Wide World Photos; page 166 The Granger Collection, New York; page 168 © Ben Edwards/Tony Stone Worldwide/Getty Images; page 172 © Brown Brothers, Sterling, PA; page 175 © Joel Iskowitz; page 178 © Colin McPherson/Colin McPherson/Corbis; page 181 © Norman Pogson/Shutterstock; page 182 © Royalty-Free/Corbis; page 185 © Ulrike Hammerich/ShutterStock; page 185 © Scott Rothstein/ShutterStock; page 186 © Alain Buu/Liaison/Getty Images; page 189 © AP/Wide World Photos; page 192 © Bettmann/Corbis; page 196 © Archive Photos/Getty Images; page 198 © Sandy Rabinowitz; page 204 © Sandy Rabinowitz; page 209 © Gail Mathabane; page 212 © Mark Mathabane; page 215 © Mark Mathabane; page 218 © Mark Mathabane; page 222 © Bettmann/Corbis; page 227 © David Turnley/Corbis; page 231 © Lili Iravani; page 233 © Kurt Stier/Corbis; page 238 © Cindy Hughes/ShutterStock; page 238 © Scott Rothstein/ShutterStock; page 239 © Christopher Felver/Corbis; page 243 © Bettmann/Corbis; page 246 © H. Pick-Goslar Foundation; page 248 © H. Pick-Goslar Foundation; page 251 © H. Pick-Goslar Foundation; page 252 © H. Pick-Goslar Foundation; page 255 © Jim Jurica/ShutterStock; page 255 © J. Helgason/ShutterStock; page 256 © Rachel Taylor; page 258 © Saeed Ahmed/AP/Wide World Photos; page 263 © Rachel Taylor; page 269 © Ajit Kumar/AP/Wide World Photos; page 272 © Paul Cowan/Shutterstock; page 275 © Agence France Presse/Getty Images; page 278 © Rachel Taylor; page 278 © Rachel Taylor; page 280 © Ajit Kumar/AP/Wide World Photos; page 288 © Freshman Brown/SuperStock; page 292 © Lance Bellers/Shutterstock; page 292 © Royalty-Free/Corbis; page 293 © National Portrait Gallery/SuperStock; page 295 © Robbie Jack/Corbis; page 296, 298, 300, 302, 304, 306 © Najin/Shutterstock; page 298 © Superstock, Inc./SuperStock; page 311 © Ernesto Lopez Albert/ShutterStock; 311 © Billy Lobo H./ShutterStock; page 312 © Archive Photos/Getty Images; page 317 © Gerry Goodstein; page 323 Archive Photos/Getty Images; page 328 © A.S. Zain/ShutterStock; page 328 © Neven Mendrila/ShutterStock; page 329 © Brown Brothers, Sterling, PA; page 333 National Museum of American Art, Washington, DC/Art Resource, NY; page 337 © Christie's Images/SuperStock; page 346 © Ron Rovtar/Stock Asylum; page 350 © Nancy Crampton; page 352 © Ian O'Leary/Tony Stone/Getty Images; page 355 © Liang Kai, by permission of China Span; page 357 © Bill Mitchell/Archive/Getty Images; page 360 © Gabriel Openshaw/Shutterstock; page 363 © Alison Wright/Corbis; page 364 © Photo by Lita Puyat; page 366 © Roger Ressmeyer/Corbis; page 370 © UPI/Bettmann/Corbis; page 372, 373 © Judy King; page 376 © The Image Works; page 378(all) © From "A Haiku Garden" by Stephen Addiss with Fumiko and Akira Yamamoto, 1996, Weatherhill; page 381 The Granger Collection, New York; page 384 © Terry Vine/Tony Stone/Getty Images; page 387 Courtesy, Graywolf Press.; page 390 © Images.com/Corbis; page 393 © Stefan Ekernas/Shutterstock; page 395 © Images.com/Corbis; page 398 © Hashim Pudiyapura/Shutterstock; page 401 © David David Gallery/SuperStock; page 408 The Granger Collection, New York; page 412 © Jim Jurica/Shutterstock; page 412 © Wendy Kaveney Photography/Shutterstock; page 413 © Christie's Images/SuperStock; page 415 © Bettmann/Corbis; page 419 © Pascal Le Segretain/Sygma/Corbis; page 421 © Images.com/Corbis; page 423 © Images.com/Corbis; page 426 © Diana Ong/SuperStock; page 430 © Susanne Schuenke/SuperStock; page 432–433 © Antonio Petrone/Shutterstock; page 438 © Brown Brothers, Sterling, PA; page 440–441 © Corbis; page 444 The Granger Collection, New York; page 446 © AP/Wide World Photos; page 448 © Corbis; page 453 © Judy Marie Stepanian/Shutterstock; page 453 © Vicki Wehrman/Images.com; page 454 The Granger Collection, New York; page 456 © 2007 Estate of Pablo Picasso / Artists Rights Society (ARS), New York; page 460 © Bembaron Jeremy/Sygma/Corbis; page 462 © Cosmo Condina/Tony Stone/Getty Images; page 465 © Allan Aflack, Courtesy of the Antigua Tourism Board; page 470 © Allan Aflack, Courtesy of the Antigua Tourism Board; page 482 © 2007 Artists Rights Society (ARS), New York/ADAGP, Paris, Photo: Lowe Art Museum/SuperStock; page 486 © Orlando Diaz/Shutterstock; page 486 Royalty-Free/Images.com; page 487 © Stock Montage, Inc.; page 490 The Granger Collection, New York; page 493 © Sean Sexton Collection/Corbis; page 496 © Rachel Taylor; page 499 © Diego Silvestre/Shutterstock; page 503 © Barry Iverson/Getty Images; page 505 © Royalty-Free/Corbis; page 508 © Images.com/Corbis; page 513 © Images.com/Corbis; page 519 © Fred S/Shutterstock; page 519 © Nikolay Misharev/Shutterstock; page 520 © Bob Daemmrich/Corbis; page 522 © Images.com/Corbis; page 526 © Dennis Cox/ChinaStock; page 529 © Frank Capri/Archive Photos/Getty Images; page 532 © Guy Porfirio; page 535 © Clara Natoli/Shutterstock; page 535 © ingret/Shutterstock; page 536 © Brown Brothers, Sterling, PA; 539 © Karen Lafoya; page 540 © Karen Lafoya; page 543 © Karen Lafoya; page 547 © Archive Photos/Getty Images; page 552 © Carole Katchen; page 554 © Carole Katchen; page 555 © Carole Katchen;